Handbook of American Popular Culture

Handbook of

ALMANACS
DEBATE AND
PUBLIC ADDRESS
ILLUSTRATION
JAZZ
LEISURE VEHICLES,
PLEASURE BOATS,
AND AIRCRAFT
MAGAZINES
MAGIC AND MAGICIANS
MEDICINE AND
THE PHYSICIAN
IN POPULAR CULTURE
MINORITIES
IN POPULAR CULTURE
NEWSPAPERS
PHYSICAL FITNESS
PORNOGRAPHY
PROPAGANDA
RECORDS AND
THE RECORDING INDUSTRY
REGIONALISM
IN POPULAR CULTURE
SCIENCE
IN POPULAR CULTURE
STAMP AND
COIN COLLECTING
TRAINS AND
RAILROADING

American Popular Culture

edited by
M. THOMAS INGE

VOLUME 3

GREENWOOD PRESS
WESTPORT, CONNECTICUT • LONDON, ENGLAND

Library of Congress Cataloging in Publication Data

Main entry under title:

Handbook of American popular culture.

Includes bibliographies and indexes.
1. United States—Popular culture.
2. United States—Popular culture—Sources.
3. United States—Popular culture—Bibliography.
I. Inge, M. Thomas.
E169.1.H2643 973 77-95357

ISBN 0-313-22025-5 (v. 3) (lib. bdg.)

Library of Congress Catalog Card Number: 77-95357
ISBN: 0-313-22025-5

First published in 1981

Greenwood Press
A division of Congressional Information Service, Inc.
88 Post Road West
Westport, Connecticut 06881

Printed in the United States of America

10 9 8 7 6 5 4 3 2 1

Finally, this one is for Tonette

Contents

Preface

The serious, scholarly study of mass or popular culture is a fairly recent phenomenon, although some early investigations were first initiated within the established disciplines. For example, sociologists have long found that the materials with which Americans amuse themselves are fascinating for what they reflect about the people and their attitudes, morals, and mores. Popular culture, in other words, is a mirror wherein society can see itself and better understand its own character and needs. One unresolved circular question this approach poses is whether the mass media merely reflect what society wants or whether they influence it to want what the media provide. Is the violence commonly found on television there because we prefer to watch those shows which use it, or do we prefer to watch it because our baser instincts have been stimulated by its frequent use? Thus, the sociological study of popular culture has often been initiated in the name of other causes: to deal with social problems, to attempt to understand society and human nature, or to engage in moral reform.

Some of the early film studies took place in English departments, where literary critics realized that some of the same techniques applied to the appreciation of fiction, poetry, and drama could be applied with great profit to the appreciation of motion pictures. In order to justify offering a course in film, however, all too often it was necessary to make a literary attachment explicit in the description, hence the now almost obligatory "Fiction and Film" course found in most English curricula. Such courses usually examine adaptations of novels and stories into film. If the instructor reaches the simple conclusion that the novel is always better than the film version (and I know a few who do), little has been accomplished. If, on the other hand, the instructor uses the separate art forms to elucidate each other through an examination of the necessarily different artistic techniques and creative strategies as applied to similar subject matter, the result can be an increased respect for both forms of expression. Such an approach has encouraged the development of some perceptive film criticism.

It is no longer necessary to justify the study of the popular arts by an alliance with some other social or cultural purpose. We have come to recognize that each form or medium of expression has its own aesthetic principles, techniques, and ways of conveying ideas. Each has been subject to misuse and ineptitude, but each has also witnessed levels of artistic accomplishment remarkable by any standards, although finally each form must be evaluated within and by its own self-generated set of standards and objectives. There are hundreds of courses being taught in film, television, radio, science fiction, popular music, the detective novel, or comic art in American colleges and universities, sometimes with uneasy homes in departments of English, history, sociology, art history, mass communications, or American studies. The next decade will see the development of popular culture programs organized, as they should be, on an inter-disciplinary basis. Already one degree-granting program has been established at Bowling Green State University in Ohio, which is also the seat of the Popular Culture Association and its publication, *Journal of Popular Culture,* established by Ray B. Browne in 1968. Scholars who have previously distinguished themselves in traditional fields are more frequently turning their attention to this new area of inquiry, as did Russel B. Nye in *The Unembarrassed Muse: The Popular Arts in America* (1970) and John Cawelti in *The Six-Gun Mystique* (1971).

This three-volume handbook is the first organized effort to assemble in one place the basic bibliographic data needed to begin the study of several of the major areas of popular culture. Each chapter, prepared by an authority on the subject, provides a brief chronological survey of the development of the medium; a critical guide in essay form to the standard or most useful bibliographies, reference works, histories, critical studies, and journals; a description of the existing research centers and collections of primary and secondary materials; and a checklist of works cited in the text. With this handbook, the student, scholar, librarian, or general reader can easily locate the kind of information needed to complete a research paper or project, answer a question, build a basic library, or read about a topic or personality as a matter of interest.

Undoubtedly the essays contain oversights in terms of research collections and published materials. In future editions, however, we hope to remedy oversights and make the essays more comprehensive and accurate. To that end, corrections and suggestions should be directed to the editor in care of the Department of English, Clemson University, Clemson, South Carolina 29631.

M. Thomas Inge

Handbook of American Popular Culture

CHAPTER 1 Almanacs

Robert K. Dodge

Americans today are only vaguely aware of the importance of almanacs during the first two hundred fifty years of American history. Most of us can quote a few of Poor Richard's sayings and associate them with an almanac; most of us probably remember the story of Abraham Lincoln and his use of an almanac to prove the innocence of a client; and many of us may remember reading in our history books that a Bible and an almanac constituted the only reading matter for most of our pioneers.

Anything else we remember about early American almanacs is probably associated with a sense of the quaint, of people who spelled with a final "k" and who attempted to predict the weather a year in advance.

Almanacs were much more than quaint. They were the forerunners of modern magazines and city directories. They served as calendars and road maps. They helped to publicize the U.S. Constitution. They served as vehicles for advertising and for politics and religion, and they spread humor throughout the country. They provide us an important source of information about American life and attitudes in the seventeenth, eighteenth, and nineteenth centuries.

HISTORIC OUTLINE

In 1639 Stephen Daye printed America's first almanac in Cambridge, Massachusetts. For the next two and a half centuries and longer, almanacs constituted an important part of American life.

Most seventeenth-century almanacs appear quite modest. Almost all of them are sixteen-page pamphlets. A few extended to twenty-four or even thirty-two pages, beginning the gradual but steady tendency of American almanacs to lengthen. The sixteen-page almanacs devoted a separate page to each month. (Some of today's "factual" almanacs of a thousand or more pages devote fewer pages to the calendar.) Another page was often used to introduce the calendar and to give information concerning the dates of eclipses. Two of the three additional pages consisted of the front and back covers. The remaining page, usually the inside of the back cover, was sometimes used for advertisements, sometimes to provide information on events of the coming year, and sometimes to present an essay on the science of astronomy.

The calendar, considered the heart of the almanac, contained such information as the time of sunrise and sunset, the beginning date of each season (under the old-style calendar more variable than today), the phases of the moon, and usually some astrological information as well. If the intended readership included commercial fishermen or shippers, the calendar would include information on tides. The longer almanacs often allotted two pages to each month, although at least one twenty-four-page almanac included a nine-page explanation of its twelve-page calendar.

In the eighteenth century the almanac industry became more competitive. After all, the printing of an almanac had become a very profitable sideline for many American printers. They had a guaranteed market among farmers, commercial fishermen, and sailors. Naturally each almanac maker wanted to capture as large a share of the market as possible. It was perhaps competition more than any other influence that led to the changes in the eighteenth-century almanac, changes that make them more interesting to the student of American popular culture than are the majority of the almanacs from the seventeenth century.

Early competition concentrated on the accuracy of the calendar. Almanac makers extolled the virtues of their own calendars and often pointed out real or imagined inaccuracies in their competitors'. Sometimes a free errata sheet for the calendar of a major competitor was offered with the purchase of an almanac.

Another form of competition involved piracy. One of the reasons that bibliographies list so many editions of such popular titles as Thomas Greenleaf's and Abraham Weatherwise's almanacs appears to be that some of the editions were piracies. In at least one case the piracy had more involved motives, at least if Nathaniel Ames, publisher of one of America's first best-selling almanacs, was correct in his assessment of the competition. Ames complained that his competitors had banded together to produce a fraudulent and inaccurate almanac under his name in order to discredit him and his calendars.[1]

Ames and James Franklin can be credited with beginning to change the rules of almanac competition. They realized that the accuracy of a calendar as a sales inducement could be pushed only to a certain point, and they began the process of including other material to sell their almanacs. Ames often included short paragraphs on current events and on morality in general. James Franklin invented the character of Poor Robin, who gave his readers the sayings of Poor Robin.

While Ames and James Franklin began the process of changing the rules of competition, it was Benjamin Franklin who carried the process to its completion. Benjamin Franklin's first almanac burst upon the Philadelphia scene with the creation of Poor Richard and the prediction of the death of Titan Leeds, at the time the most popular almanac maker in the city.

Both the sayings of Poor Richard and the prediction, to which Leeds foolishly responded, helped Franklin's almanac to capture the attention of Philadelphia, and as Franklin saw the popularity of Poor Richard's sayings grow, he increased their number. The idea for the prediction, like the idea for the sayings, was borrowed: the prediction from Jonathan Swift, a well-known British almanac maker who later developed a reputation for satire; the sayings from his brother. But, while Franklin treated the prediction almost exactly as Swift had, he developed the sayings far beyond what his brother had done.

Other almanac makers soon accepted the idea that material other than the calendar could make their almanacs sell. In the decades following the introduction of Poor Richard, almanacs grew longer and longer as publishers competed to include more and more material that the public would buy. It is such material that makes eighteenth- and nineteenth-century almanacs so interesting to the student of American popular culture.

For example, historians of farming in early America will find hundreds of "valuable receipts" for improving soil, increasing crop yields, and curing diseases in livestock. Many of the receipts appear to be based on superstition, and a few appear to be based on even less than that, but many more seem to represent a real interest in the establishment of an empirical science of farming. Two of the better suggestions include the use of lime as a fertilizer (useful only when the soil is acidic) and the addition of green organic material to the soil.

Other receipts offered cures for various human ailments. The gout, bloody flux, toothache, and nosebleed are provided with "sure and certain" cures. The science of medicine appears even less advanced than that of agriculture, but a trial-and-error methodology was beginning here as well.

Some almanacs included recipes for the preparation and preservation of food. Such recipes impress the modern reader with their emphasis on preservation and with the large quantities they were intended to serve. Measurements tended to be imprecise.

Many of the almanacs contained descriptions of American customs. One almanac printed an essay in favor of the New England custom of bundling. According to the essay, bundlers were almost always pure, and that new fangled innovation, the sofa, was far more dangerous to a woman's chastity. A long poem against bundling appeared in one of the Andrew Beers almanacs for 1793. Unlike the essay, the moralistic poem includes much detail about what its author thought took place in the bundling bed. One quatrain describes a man and a woman who had bundled together, each wearing a full set of clothing and wrapped in a separate sheet. The man, however, caught the itch from the woman, and she caught a bastard from him.[2]

Other described customs included bees and peddling. A few publishers, most notably Robert Thomas of *The (Old) Farmer's Almanack,* opposed the custom of social gatherings known as bees as wasteful of time and property. Thomas believed that a family had plenty of time during the long winter to husk its corn as it became necessary without the expense of entertaining all of the neighbors. Most almanac makers, however, considered bees of all kinds to be either harmless entertainment or positive ways for neighbors to help each other.

Peddlers constituted an important method of distribution for the almanac industry. Other media might criticize the peddler and, perhaps, deservedly so, but, as many of today's newspapers romanticize the newsboy, so did almanacs tend to romanticize the peddler.

Judging from what was printed in almanacs, early Americans must have liked to read about the exotic and the horrible. Indian captivity narratives and other stories of Indian cruelty abound, as do stories of Indian stoicism. Stories of cannibalism in America and Africa are common. Some almanacs described exotic animals, such as the giraffe and the elephant. The myth of the elephant's memory was demonstrated. Sentimental stories were popular as well. Some of the sentimental stories appear grotesque, at best, to the modern reader, but they do represent one form of popular story for the time.

By the last half of the eighteenth century, many of the almanacs had begun to provide pure information in the style of the present *World Almanac and Book of Facts* or the other large present-day almanacs familiar to most of us. The information was usually local, but a selection of almanacs would provide such information for most of the United States. What clubs existed in a particular city? What were the roads and their condition? Who were the political officers? What were the churches and who were the clergymen? Most localities had one or more almanacs that attempted to answer such questions. A few even attempted to name every family in the locality.

Other kinds of information dealt with current events, including politics. The first balloon ascension was noted in many almanacs and even inspired the publication of the *Balloon Almanac.* The settlement of the frontier was a popular topic, as was the American Revolution and later the adoption of the Constitution. Laws and tariffs were reprinted. George Washington's "Farewell Address" was widely reprinted, as were many of the writings of Benjamin Franklin.

Another topic that must interest the student of popular culture is humor. Comic almanacs flourished in the nineteenth century. The David Crockett almanacs are probably the best known, but Josh Billings (Henry Wheeler Shaw), Commodore Rollingpin (John Henton Carter), and others produced comic almanacs. *All-My-Nack, Allminax,* and *Allmaniac* were among the comic misspellings. In addition, many of the serious almanacs contained comic material, much as *Reader's Digest* and other magazines do today. Such comic material constitutes one of the few sources of early popular humor still available to us. Between 1776 and 1800, for example, more than 1,500 comic items were published in serious American almanacs. Certainly much of the comedy was literary rather than popular, and much of it was not even very comic. In some cases the comic items seem to have been copied directly from British sources. Nevertheless, this body of humor is worthy of study simply because it does constitute almost the only source of written popular humor before the *Spirit of the Times* and its competing journals, and the almanac remained an important source even after that.

The nineteenth century saw the development of advertising almanacs, especially those advertising patent medicines. Milton Drake says that about fifty patent medicine almanacs were published in the century, many of them in continuous publication for several years.[3] Many other groups used almanacs for advertising in the nineteenth century. Drake lists religious groups, uplift groups, political groups, labor and professional groups, fraternal groups, and pressure groups, as well as straightforward sales-related advertisers such as those printing and distributing almanacs in this century. The *Christian Almanac,* one of the religious almanacs, grew to have a circulation of 300,000 in 1850.[4]

The twentieth century has brought about additional changes in U.S. almanacs. The almanac of pure information has certainly become the dominant form. For some publishers, the word *almanac* has come to mean any yearly compilation of information and statistics, whether in a particular field (for example, the *Nurse's Almanac* and the *Standard Educational Almanac*) or more general (the *World Almanac and Book of Facts*). The calendar, if it exists at all, has been relegated to a very minor role. In the case of a few publications, such as *The People's Almanac* by David Wallechinsky and Irving Wallace, even the characteristic of yearly publication has been dropped. A few old-time or family almanacs are still published. Most prominent among them is the *Old Farmer's Almanac,* a direct descendant of Robert B. Thomas' *Farmer's Almanac.* Its appeal to a sense of nostalgia and quaintness had gained it a circulation of 2 million in 1970.

Scholars interested in American ethnic groups will find that U.S. almanacs have been published in at least twenty languages including twelve European languages and six American Indian languages.

REFERENCE WORKS

Two bibliographies are essential to the study of American almanacs. The first, *American Bibliography* by Charles Evans, is a fourteen-volume work which claims to be a dictionary of all "books, pamphlets and periodical publications" printed in America before 1821. Before his death, however, Evans had carried the bibliography only through part of 1799. The American Antiquarian Society (AAS) finished 1799, 1800, and the index, which has a separate heading for almanacs. The Evans-American Antiquarian Society publication lists more than five thousand almanacs as having been printed in America before the end of 1800. It is somewhat confusing that these listings include almanacs published *for* 1801. With few exceptions almanacs were published in the fall or winter of the year preceding the year of their calendar.

Evans's entries, some of which were taken from advertisements and other sources, contain some ghosts. In at least one case an almanac appears to be listed under two different titles. Nevertheless, Evans's bibliography is important for at least two reasons. Evans and the American Antiquarian Society were among the first to consider the almanacs an important scholarly resource. Besides, this bibliography and its supplement provides access to *Early American Imprints,* a Readex Microprint Edition edited by Clifford K. Shipton and published by the American Antiquarian Society.

Any library with a set of these microcards and the later supplement, also edited by Shipton, holds a representative collection of seventeenth- and eighteenth-century American almanacs. It may appear that the collection is biased toward almanacs published in the Northeast, but it must be remembered that by far the majority of almanac publishers, especially in these two centuries, were located in the Northeast.

Access to the supplement to *Early American Imprints* is provided by the two-volume *Supplement to Charles Evans' American Bibliography* by Roger P. Bristol, which has a separate heading for almanacs in the index. The index lists nearly a thousand almanacs not included in *American Bibliography.*

From 1958 to 1966, Ralph Shaw and Richard Shoemaker published twenty-two additional volumes of *American Bibliography* on a less comprehensive plan than that of Evans. Their work is subtitled *A Preliminary Checklist for 1801-1819,* and they call it "a preliminary step in filling the gap in American bibliography."[5] Like the Evans-AAS volumes, the Shaw-Shoemaker volumes locate entries whose locations are known, but, because there is no separate listing for almanacs in the index, it is necessary to search each volume in order to find all of the almanacs.

In 1967, Richard Shoemaker again began expanding *American Bibliography* by publishing *A Checklist of American Imprints.* Beginning with 1820, that series now extends through 1833. In addition to Shoemaker, Gayle and M. Frances Cooper and Scott and Carol Bruntjen have worked as compilers. There are comprehensive title and author indexes for 1820 to 1829, but, as with the Shaw-Shoemaker volumes of *American Bibliography,* the student of almanacs must search each volume or read through the entire title index. These volumes provide locations. Most useful for the almanac researcher, then, are the Evans-AAS volumes and the supplement, which have a more usable index and provide access to the AAS microcard collection.

The second indispensable bibliography is Milton Drake's two-volume *Almanacs of the United States,* which attempts to list and locate all American almanacs published before 1850. In addition, for some states, notably those in the Confederacy and some of the Western states, Drake carries the list into the 1870s. Drake's work contains 14,385 entries and locates nearly 75,000 copies. Drake canvassed 558 libraries and read about "four hundred bibliographical works in search of defunct issues."[6] Drake believes that he has, in fact, listed 85 percent or more of the almanacs published before 1850. As a bibliography of almanacs, Drake obviously supersedes Evans. Evans, however, is still essential to most almanac researchers for the access it gives to the AAS microcard collection.

In addition to his list, Drake provides an interesting and informative introduction. We learn, for example, that the old story of Lincoln saving a client with an almanac is supported by Illinois court records of an account of a British lawyer who had earlier used a fraudulent almanac to save his client in the same way. Drake also includes a list of American towns and cities where almanacs were published and the date of the earliest listed almanac for each town. He lists about 350 such cities and towns. Finally, Drake includes a bibliography of secondary source material, most of which his work has superseded.

To seek out almanacs published after 1850 is much more difficult because there is no specialized almanac bibliography such as Drake's, and many of the compilers of general bibliographies did not consider almanacs worthy of inclusion. Those general bibliographies that do include almanacs often seem to include too few. The *American Catalogue* is one of only a few general bibliographies that list almanacs. For the period from 1895 to 1900 it lists only forty almanacs and forty-seven calendars and yearbooks. *The American Catalogue,* founded by F. Leypoldt and continued by Lynds E. Jones and R. R. Bowker, lists books in print from 1876 to 1910. Its subject index has a heading for almanacs and another for calendars and yearbooks. *The Catalogue of Public Documents* put out by the Superintendent of Documents lists calendars and nautical almanacs published by agencies of the U.S. government.

RESEARCH COLLECTIONS

The first library to collect almanacs aggressively was that of the American Antiquarian Society under the direction of Clarence Brigham. Consequently, the AAS has perhaps the largest collection of early American almanacs of any library. It is this collection that formed the basis for the almanac representation in their microcard edition of *Early American Imprints.*

The holdings of the AAS are so great that when Milton Drake began work on his *Almanacs of the United States* he believed that a canvass of the AAS holdings together with those of the Library of Congress, the New York Public Library, Rutgers University, the New York Historical Society, "and a scattering of others" would serve to find "everything that matters."[7] That search did net Drake ten thousand entries and located twenty thousand copies, but his expansion of the search to more than five hundred libraries netted an additional four thousand entries and fifty-five thousand located copies.

Most of the almanacs of early America were produced for a specific locality. It may be expected that state and local libraries will provide good sources for almanacs originally published within the locality or state that they serve and that they will, perhaps, hold copies not found in such giant collections as the AAS and the Library of Congress.

It is no surprise, then, that researchers interested in almanacs published in early Virginia will find copies, often unique, in the College of William and Mary, the Colonial Williamsburg Library, and the Virginia Historical Society Library, as well as in the Library of Congress. It is somewhat surprising that for very early Virginia almanacs the Huntington Library in San Marino, California, is an important source, as is the Washington State Historical Library and the William L. Clements Library in Ann Arbor, Michigan. The Huntington Library has collected many of the earliest almanacs from several of the states that have a colonial history. It owns the only extant copy of *An Almanack* for 1646, published in Cambridge, Massachusetts, by Stephen Daye. According to Drake, it is the earliest almanac still extant.

For almanacs published in Alabama, the important local libraries include the University of Alabama and the Alabama Department of Archives and History in Montgomery; for those published in California, the important local libraries are the Bancroft Library and the University of California Library in Berkeley, the California State Library in Sacramento, the California Historical Society in San Francisco, and, somewhat less important, the University of California at Los Angeles.

For Connecticut, the following local libraries have important holdings: the Connecticut Historical Society and the Connecticut State Library in Hartford, Yale University in New Haven, and local historical societies in New Haven, Litchfield, and New London. The Western Reserve Historical Society in Cleveland, Ohio, also has several Connecticut almanacs.

For Delaware, the Henry Francis DuPont Winterthur Museum in Winterthur has an important collection of early almanacs. The University of Delaware in Newark has a collection of nineteenth-century almanacs. The

Pennsylvania Historical Society Library in Philadelphia appears to have a larger collection than either of the in-state libraries.

For the District of Columbia, the best local resources are, of course, the Library of Congress and the Public Library of the District of Columbia.

The De Renne Georgia Library in Athens is the best in-state source for almanacs published in Georgia. Emory University in Atlanta and the Georgia Historical Society in Savannah as well as the Atlanta Public Library have some holdings.

For Illinois, the Newberry Library and the Chicago Historical Society in Chicago and the Illinois Historical Library in Springfield provide the best local sources for almanac research.

For Indiana, consult the Indiana Historical Society and the Indiana State Library in Indianapolis, as well as Earlham College in Richmond and Indiana University in Bloomington. The Ohio State Historical Society in Columbus, Ohio, also has several Indiana almanacs.

The Kentucky Historical Society in Frankfort, the Louisville Free Public Library, the Lexington Public Library, and the University of Kentucky Library in Lexington have holdings of almanacs published in Kentucky, as do the Indiana Historical Society and the Washington State Historical Society.

Of the almanacs published in Louisiana, only a few are listed by Drake as being held in Louisiana libraries. The Howard-Tilton Memorial Library at Tulane University in New Orleans has all of them.

For Maine, the important in-state sources include the Maine Historical Society and Longfellow House in Portland as well as the Bowdoin College Library in Brunswick and the Bangor Public Library.

For Maryland there are two important local libraries: the Enoch Pratt Library and the Maryland Historical Society, both in Baltimore.

Massachusetts, along with Pennsylvania and New York, was one of the top three almanac-producing states. There are many libraries with important holdings of almanacs published in Massachusetts. Probably the most important in-state library for Massachusetts is the American Antiquarian Society Library in Worcester, but the Massachusetts Historical Society and the Boston Public Library in Boston and Harvard University in Cambridge rival it as far as in-state almanacs are concerned. In addition, both the New York and Pennsylvania historical societies have significant holdings of Massachusetts almanacs, and many libraries throughout the state have some almanacs. The *(Old) Farmer's Almanack* was originally published in Massachusetts and appears to be the most widely collected of all American almanacs. Drake lists eighty libraries in twenty-four states holding copies of the 1850 edition of this Boston almanac.

Few almanacs were published in Michigan. Consult the Burton Historical Collection and the Detroit Public Library in Detroit as well as the Michigan

State Library in Lansing. Even fewer were published in Minnesota, and there are no significant in-state holdings of Minnesota almanacs. The only significant in-state holdings of Mississippi almanacs are at the State Department of Archives and History in Jackson. For Missouri, the most significant holdings are at the Missouri Historical Society in St. Louis, but the Missouri State Historical Society in Columbia and the Mercantile Library Association in St. Louis are worth consulting.

For New Hampshire, whose presses produced about five hundred almanacs, the most important in-state library is that of the New Hampshire Historical Society in Concord. The State Library in Concord and the Dartmouth College Library are also important.

New Jersey has two important libraries of almanac holdings: Rutgers University in New Brunswick and the New Jersey Historical Society in Newark.

New York produced far more almanacs than any other state. Several libraries hold significant numbers of New York almanacs, including the New York Public Library, the New York Historical Society, the Long Island Historical Society, and the Pierpont Morgan Library, all of New York City, and the New York State Library in Buffalo. In addition to the national collections, such out-of-state libraries as the John Carter Brown Library in Providence, Rhode Island, the Pennsylvania Historical Society, the American Philosophical Society, and the Rosenbach Foundation of Philadelphia, and the Huntington Library have collections that are significant.

In North Carolina, the University of North Carolina at Chapel Hill and Duke University at Durham have the two largest collections. The North Carolina Historical Commission and the State Library in Raleigh have smaller collections.

Several Ohio libraries have significant holdings of Ohio almanacs. They are: the Ohio State Library in Columbus, the Public Library of Cincinnati and Hamilton County, the Historical and Philosophical Society of Ohio, which is also in Cincinnati, the Western Reserve Historical Society in Cleveland, the Dayton Public Library, and Marietta College.

Few almanacs were published in Oregon. The Oregon Historical Society in Portland has most of them. The Library Association of Portland and the University of Oregon in Eugene also have holdings.

Pennsylvania is the third largest almanac-producing state. The Historical Society of Pennsylvania and the American Philosophical Society, both in Philadelphia, have large holdings of Pennsylvania almanacs. Each has some unique copies, as does the Library Company of Philadelphia. The Rosenbach Foundation of Philadelphia has several almanacs, at least one of which is unique, as do the New York Historical Society and the John Carter Brown Library.

The Rhode Island Historical Society has large holdings of Rhode Island almanacs as does the John Carter Brown Library. Both are in Providence. For South Carolina, the most significant in-state holdings are in the Charleston Library and the South Carolina Historical Society. Both are located in Charleston. The South Carolina State Library in Columbia also has some almanacs.

The Tennessee State Library in Nashville has succeeded in collecting most of the almanacs published in that state. All but one of the few almanacs published in Utah are held by the Library of the Church of Jesus Christ of Latter Day Saints in Salt Lake City. In-state libraries that have collected Vermont almanacs include the Vermont State Library and the Vermont Historical Society in Montpelier and the University of Vermont in Burlington.

Apart from the five national collections already listed and the in-state collections, some libraries have significant national or regional holdings, although they are not comparable to those of the AAS or the Library of Congress. Such historical societies as the Western Reserve, the Washington State, the Massachusetts, and the Pennsylvania have collected actively both inside and outside their states. The Harvard, Yale, Indiana, Brown, and Texas university libraries have also accumulated large holdings of out-of-state almanacs, as have the American Philosophical Society and the Huntington Library.

Any scholar interested in examining American almanacs should realize how very spread out they are. To be sure, they are concentrated in the Northeast, from Washington, D.C., to Boston, but many unique copies can be found in California and throughout the state libraries. A scholar should probably begin by consulting a copy of Drake's bibliography, from which much of the above information has been taken, deciding which almanacs he or she needs to examine and planning a reasonable travel schedule. He or she should also bear in mind that many U.S. libraries have several thousand copies of almanacs published before 1801 available on microcard.

HISTORY AND CRITICISM

Like many other articles of popular culture, almanacs have too often been considered beneath the efforts of scholarship. Aside from biographers of Franklin, few scholars gave much attention to American almanacs until George Lyman Kittredge wrote *The Old Farmer and His Almanack* and Clarence Brigham began his efforts to build up the AAS collection of almanacs.

The Old Farmer and His Almanack deals with the almanacs of Robert B. Thomas. Kittredge brilliantly discusses the divisions of Thomas' almanac, including The Farmer's Calendar, the letters to the editor, the sayings, and the anecdotes. Kittredge's best chapters deal with Thomas' folk wisdom, the characters he created for The Farmer's Calendar, and the letters. Perhaps the most significant aspect of Kittredge's book, however, was that it gave a certain respectability to the study of almanacs. If the great scholar of Shakespeare and early British literature considered almanacs important enough to devote an entire book to one almanac, then perhaps other almanacs deserved a closer look.

Samuel Briggs's *The Essays, Humor and Poems of Nathaniel Ames, Father and Son, of Dedham, Massachusetts from Their Almanacks, 1726-1775* reprints much of the Ames almanacs, omitting the calendars. It also contains several essays by Briggs: "Almanacks," "The Rise of the Almanack in America," "The Ames Family, and the Town of Dedham," "The Old Tavern," "Notes on Each Almanack." Of the essays "The Rise of the Almanack in America" is one of the most interesting.

Richard M. Dorson edited *Davy Crockett: American Comic Legend,* which contains material on the Crockett almanacs. Joseph Leach's *The Typical Texan: Biography of an American Myth* is important as a scholarly book on a subject other than almanacs that uses almanacs as an important source of material.

Milton Drake's *Almanacs of the United States* has already been fully discussed under the Reference Works section. It is an essential book for anyone who wants to study American almanacs.

Robb Sagendorph's *America and Her Almanacs: Wit, Wisdom and Weather* is less a scholarly book than an exercise in nostalgia. At the time he wrote *America and Her Almanacs,* Sagendorph had been editor of the *Old Farmer's Almanac* for thirty-one years. He claims, with some accuracy, that "reading the early almanacs is the only way to see into the heart of Colonial America." It may not be the only way, but it is an excellent way, and Sagendorph's book provides a great deal of almanac material to read and more than two hundred woodcuts reproduced from the almanacs. One chapter is devoted to *Poor Richard.*

In 1970 Henry Wheeler Shaw's *Josh Billings' Farmers' Allminax* was reprinted in a volume called *Old Probability: Perhaps Rain-Perhaps Not. Old Probability* is nothing more than a reprint of the Josh Billings' almanacs.

Marion Barber Stowell's *Early American Almanacs: The Colonial Weekday Bible* may be the most important almanac book since Drake's bibliography. *Early American Almanacs* is one of only a few books that attempts to deal with the entire spectrum of American almanacs for a specific period. Stowell studied some 450 almanacs of the seventeenth and eighteenth century. She described many of the almanac makers and provided many examples from the almanacs. It is possible that she could have been more successful in her immense task if there had been a larger body of competent scholarship preceding her. She does succeed in showing the importance of almanacs to early America and in creating the first systematic, broadly based study of early American almanacs that is not primarily bibliographical.

Clarence Brigham wrote two articles for the *Proceedings of the American Antiquarian Society,* "An Account of American Almanacs and Their Value for Historical Study" and "Report of the Librarian," which contains a summary of the AAS collection of American almanacs. Both articles helped encourage the use of almanacs as documentary sources. The AAS had already begun using its *Proceedings* to encourage almanac study. As early as 1907 Victor Hugo Paltsits had published "The Almanacs of Roger Sherman, 1750-1761," and in 1914 George Emery Littlefield published "Notes on the Calendar and the Almanac" in the *Proceedings.*

A number of articles have dealt with the almanacs of one publisher or of one author. Alfred B. Page covered the almanacs of John Tulley from 1687 to 1702, and Frank H. Severance published "The Story of Phinney's Western Almanack, with Notes on Other Calendars and Weather Forecasters of Buffalo." Jasper Marsh wrote "Amos Pope and His Almanacs," and Arthur D. Graeff published a series of articles in volumes 5 and 6 (1938 and 1939) of the *American-German Review.* The articles, seldom more than two pages long, are entitled "Pennsylvania German Almanacs." F. G. Woodward published "An Early Tennessee Almanac and Its Maker: Hill's Almanac 1825-1862," and Robert Sidwell wrote "An Odd Fish: Samuel Keimer and a Footnote to American Educational History." Keimer was a publisher of an almanac in Philadelphia, but Sidwell deals with him primarily as an educator.

In 1968 two articles were published dealing with John Henton Carter, the author of *Commodore Rollingpin's Almanac.* John T. Flanagan's "John Henton Carter, Alias 'Commodore Rollingpin'" and James T. Swift's "From Pantry to Pen: The Saga of Commodore Rollingpin" both concentrate on the man as well as his work.

Another article that deals with comic almanacs is David Kesterson's "Josh Billings 'Defolks' Rural America," in which Kesterson compares Billing's parody with the farmer's almanac tradition which inspired it.

Also of interest are articles that use almanacs as source material. Chester E. Eisinger's "The Farmer in the Eighteenth Century Almanac" uses almanacs to determine the strength of the agrarian view of life in eighteenth-century America. Elsie H. and Curtis Booker's "Patent Medicines Before the Wiley Act of 1906" uses almanac advertising as a source. Robert Dodge's "Didactic Humor in the Almanacs of Early America" uses almanacs as a source of early American humor. Giles E. Gobetz's "Slovenian Ethnic Studies" and Jon Stanley Wenrick's "Indians in Almanacs, 1783-1815" use almanacs as sources for ethnic study.

Two dissertations have dealt with American almanacs: Jon Stanley Wenrick's "For Education and Entertainment—Almanacs in the Early American

Republic, 1783-1815" and Marion Barber McDowell's (now Marion Barber Stowell) "Early American Almanacs: The History of a Neglected Literary Genre."

NOTES

1. Samuel Briggs, *The Essays, Humor and Poems of Nathaniel Ames, Father and Son, of Dedham, Massachusetts from Their Almanacks, 1726-1775* (Detroit: Singing Tree Press, 1969), p. 372.
2. "A Song Upon Bundling," *Beers's Almanac for 1793* (Hartford, Conn.: Hudson and Goodwin, 1792), pp. 26-27.
3. Milton Drake, *Almanacs of the United States* (New York: Scarecrow Press, 1962) 1; xiii.
4. Drake, p. x.
5. Ralph R. Shaw and Richard H. Shoemaker, *American Bibliography: A Preliminary Checklist for 1801* (New York: Scarecrow Press, 1958), p. iii.
6. Drake, 1; xv.
7. Drake, 1; xv.

BIBLIOGRAPHY

Booker, Elsie H., and Curtis. "Patent Medicines Before the Wiley Act of 1906." *North Carolina Folklore,* 18 (November 1970), 130-42.

Briggs, Samuel. *The Essays, Humor and Poems of Nathaniel Ames, Father and Son, of Dedham, Massachusetts from their Almanacks, 1726-1775.* Cleveland: Western Reserve Press, 1891. Reprint. Detroit: Singing Tree Press, 1969.

Brigham, Clarence. "An Account of American Almanacs and Their Value for Historical Study." *Proceedings* of the American Antiquarian Society, n.s. 34 (October 1925), 3-28.

———"Report of the Librarian." *Proceedings* of the American Antiquarian Society, n.s. 35 (October 1926), 190-218.

Bristol, Roger P. *Supplement to Charles Evans' American Bibliography.* Charlottesville: University Press of Virginia, 1970.

Danforth, Samuel. *An Almanack for the Year of Our Lord 1646....* Cambridge: Printed by Stephen Day, 1646.

Dodge, Robert. "Didactic Humor in the Almanacs of Early America." *Journal of Popular Culture,* 5 (Winter 1971), 592-605.

Dorson, Richard M. *Davy Crockett: American Comic Legend.* New York: Spiral Editions, 1939.

Drake, Milton. *Almanacs of the United States.* 2 vols. New York: Scarecrow Press, 1962.

Eisinger, Chester E. "The Farmer in the Eighteenth Century Almanac." *Agricultural History,* 28 (July 1954), 107-12.

Evans, Charles. *American Bibliography.* 14 vols. Worcester, Mass: American Antiquarian Society, 1903-55. Reprint. New York: Peter Smith, 1941-67.

Flanagan, John T. "John Henton Carter, Alias 'Commodore Rollingpin.' *Missouri Historical Review,* 63 (October 1968), 38-64.

Gobetz, Giles E. "Slovenian Ethnic Studies." *Journal of Ethnic Studies,* 2 (Winter 1975), 99-103.

Graeff, Arthur D. "Pennsylvania German Almanacs." *American-German Review,* 5 (April-May 1939), 4-7, 36; 5 (June-July 1939), 30-33, 37-38; 5 (August-September 1939), 24-29; 6 (October-November 1939), 10-12, 40; 6 (December 1939-January 1940), 12-19; 6 (April-May 1940), 10-13, 37; 6 (June-July 1940), 9-12; 6 (August-September 1940), 10-14.

Kesterson, David. "Josh Billings 'Defolks' Rural America." *Tennessee Folklore Society Bulletin,* 41 (1975), 57-64.

Kittredge, George Lyman. *The Old Farmer and His Almanack.* Cambridge: Harvard University Press, 1920. Reprint. New York: B. Blom, 1967.

Leach, Joseph. *The Typical Texan: Biography of an American Myth.* Dallas: Southern Methodist University Press, 1952.

Leypoldt, F., Lynds E. Jones, and R.R. Bowker. *The American Catalogue.* New York: Bowker, 1880-1911. Reprint. New York: Peter Smith, 1941.

Littlefield, George Emery. "Notes on the Calendar and the Almanac." *Proeedings* of the American Antiquarian Society, n.s. 24 (October 1914), 11-64.

McDowell, Marion Barber (now Marion Barber Stowell). "Early American Almanacs: The History of a Neglected Literary Genre." Ph. D. dissertation, Florida State University, 1974.

Marsh, Jasper. "Amos Pope and His Almanacs." *Danvers Historical Society, Historical Collections,* 10 (1922), 93-114.

Page, Alfred B. "The Almanacs of John Tulley: 1687-1702." *Publications of the Colonial Society of Massachusetts,* 13 (July 1912), 207-23.

Paltsits, Victor Hugo. "The Almanacs of Roger Sherman, 1750-1761." *Proceedings* of the American Antiquarian Society, n.s. 18 (April 1907), 213-58.

Rowland, Howard S., and Beatrice Rowland. *The Nurses' Almanac.* Germantown, Md.: Aspen Systems, 1978.

Sagendorph, Robb. *America and Her Almanacs: Wit, Wisdom and Weather.* Boston: Yankee-Little Brown, 1970.

Severance, Frank H. "The Story of Phinney's Western Almanack, with Notes on other Calendars and Weather Forecasters of Buffalo." Buffalo Historical Society *Publications,* 24 (December 1920), 343-58.

Shaw, Henry Wheeler. *Old Probability: Perhaps Rain—Perhaps Not.* New York: G. W. Carleton, 1876. Reprint. Upper Saddle River, N.J.: Literature House/Gregg Press, 1970.

Shaw, Ralph R., and Richard H. Shoemaker. *American Bibliography: A Preliminary Checklist for 1801-1819.* 20 vols. New York: Scarecrow Press 1958-64.

Shipton, Clifford K. *Early American Imprints, 1639-1800.* Worcester, Mass.: the American Antiquarian Society 1956-1964.

———. *Early American Imprints, 1639-1800. Supplement.* Worcester, Mass.: The American Antiquarian Society, 1966-1968.

Shoemaker, Richard, et al. *A Checklist of American Imprints, 1820-1833,* yearly. Metuchen, N.J.: Scarecrow Press, 1964-.

Sidwell, Robert T. "An Odd Fish: Samuel Keimer and a Footnote to American Educational History." *History of Education Quarterly,* 6 (Spring 1966), 16-30.

The Standard Education Almanac. Los Angeles: Academic Media, 1968-.

Stowell, Marion Barber. *Early American Almanacs: The Colonial Weekday Bible.* New York: Burt Franklin, 1977.

Superintendent of Documents. *The Catalogue of Public Documents.* Washington, D.C.: Government Printing Office, 1896-1941. Reprint. New York: Johnson Reprint/Kraus Reprint, 1963.

Swift, James T. "From Pantry to Pen: The Saga of Commodore Rollingpin." *Missouri Historical Bulletin,* 24 (January 1968), 113-21.

Wallechinsky, David, and Irving Wallace. *The People's Almanac.* Garden City, N.Y.: Doubleday, 1975.

Wenrick, Jon Stanley. "For Education and Entertainment—Almanacs in the Early American Republic, 1783-1815." Ph. D. dissertation, Claremont Graduate School, 1974.

———. "Indians in Almanacs, 1783-1815." *Indian Historian,* 8 (Winter 1977), 36-42.

Woodward, F. G. "An Early Tennessee Almanac and Its Maker: Hill's Almanac 1825-1862." *Tennessee Folklore Society Bulletin,* 18 (March 1952), 9-14.

The World Almanac and Book of Facts. New York: Press Publishing (1868-1923), New York World (1924-31), New York World-Telegram (1932-66), and Newspaper Enterprise Association (1967-).

CHAPTER 2 Debate and Public Address

Robert H. Janke

Debate and public address in the United States are two distinct but related areas within the academic discipline of speech communication. The study of debate is frequently grouped with argumentation or included as a component of forensics, whereas the study of public address is often coupled with rhetoric. In this essay, however, debate and public address are generally considered as a single area of inquiry, although the section dealing with reference works also treats educational debate and public speaking as separate skills in communication.

Culture in the United States is perceived as a matter of taste, with many factors, primarily economics and education, influencing each individual's preferences. It is pluralistic, ranging from the high to the low, with boundaries loose and ever changing. A treatment of debate and public address as an element of American popular culture could appropriately begin with a frequently quoted statement by William Norwood Brigance from the preface to his celebrated work, *A History and Criticism of American Public Address:* "Most of the mighty movements affecting the destiny of the American nation have gathered strength in obscure places from the talk of nameless men, and gained final momentum from leaders who could state in common words the needs and hopes of common people." [1] This momentum might come from the sophisticated inaugural address of a patrician president or from the outspoken words of an uneducated civil rights worker. Great speakers through the centuries have shared the ability to move their listeners to action, whether at a political meeting, a religious assembly, or an outdoor rally or through broadcasts on radio and television. In the democratic American process, the people, responding either directly or indirectly to these speakers, take action that determines the course of historical events.

This essay deals with such speakers and their words. Its scope is necessarily wide; however, it does not include such related areas as mass communication, interpersonal communication, group discussion, parliamentary procedure, or the issues of freedom of speech or the right to communicate. Since space is limited, this essay is selective and the descriptions brief, the intent being to serve as a guide to important and practical source material.

HISTORIC OUTLINE

The history of debate and public address in the United States is, in essence, the religious, political, and social history of the nation. Therefore, an outline of value to the student should include, in chronological order, a selection of the most significant speakers, popular issues, and contemporary events that have contributed to this history.

The most significant speakers of early New England were the preachers, who exerted considerable influence, for they were also teachers and leaders whose sermons adapted the established theology to everyday application. John Winthrop was the first governor of Massachusetts Bay Colony. Defeated in his bid for re-election, he was tried and found innocent of charges of illegal arbitrariness. In what many consider to be the first notable speech delivered in America, Winthrop, in 1635, argued in his speech on liberty that man was not free to do simply as he wished but must submit to civil and lawful authority, an authority which encompassed a moral covenant between God and man, an authority which was looked upon as the "ecclesiastical elect."

This theological approach, known as theocracy, was upheld by four generations of the Mather family, who, as America's first dynasty, were influential in shaping the lives of the colonists during the later seventeenth and early eighteenth centuries. Increase Mather, son of Richard Mather, was highly educated but known for the plain language of his sermons and his positive stand toward the Salem witchcraft trials. However, it was Increase's son, Cotton Mather, who became New England's leading preacher, taking part in the vital issues of the day, including his support for the inoculation against smallpox. Cotton's son, Samuel Mather, the fourth generation of the dynasty, succeeded his father and grandfather as pastor of North Church but was less influential than his distinguished predecessors.

In 1727, Jonathan Edwards assumed the pastorate in Northampton, Massachusetts, from his grandfather, Solomon Stoddard, a liberal preacher who some years prior had broken tradition with the Mathers by opening the sacrament to all who would partake. From among Edwards's hundreds of sermons, the best known is "Sinners in the Hands of an Angry God," preached in 1741, which epitomized his theme that all men were sinners facing damnation and could be saved only through God's arbitrary, predestined choice.

New concepts in religion, however, spread up and down the colonies, specifically through the traveling evangelism of George Whitefield, who preached more than 18,000 sermons, primarily on New Calvinism, which offered personal salvation through the acceptance of Christ and sanctioned a sense of freedom previously unknown to the Colonists.

During this same period the seeds of freedom were also developing in the political sphere. The concept of the town meeting, which took many forms throughout the Colonies from Charleston to Boston, gave the Colonists the opportunity to air grievances and discuss issues in a democratic manner. Increasingly these issues centered on British rule and the union of the Colonies. As early as 1754, addressing the representatives to the congress at Albany, Benjamin Franklin of Philadelphia advocated a confederation. In Boston, Samuel Adams, a highly effective orator, aroused the citizens to the cause with his fiery speeches, one in particular delivered in Faneuil Hall in 1770 following the massacre of five colonists by British soldiers; at a meeting three years later his heated oratory triggered the dumping of the tea into Boston harbor.

While such men as Samuel Adams and his compatriot James Otis were addressing assemblies for the revolutionary cause in Boston, Patrick Henry was arguing for American independence in Virginia. His speech in that state's House of Burgesses in opposition to King George III's Stamp Act of 1765, delivered to shouts of "Treason!" is recognized as a triumph in American oratory. Henry's statement delivered on March 23, 1775, at St. John's Church in Richmond, is now part of American folklore: "I know not what course others may take; but as for me, give me liberty, or give me death!"[2]

Some of the most intense and significant debates of this period in American history took place in 1787 and 1788 as the various states deliberated the proposed Federal Constitution. In Virginia, the opponents were evenly matched. The Antifederalists, led by Patrick Henry who thought that Virginia should refrain from immediate ratification, lost by a narrow margin to the Federalists, led by James Madison who cogently refuted the points made by Henry. In a similar dispute in New York, Alexander Hamilton's oratory in favor of the Federalist cause defeated the Antifederalists under the leadership of Governor Clinton. Eventually the Constitution was ratified, and the fledgling government was launched as George Washington assumed the presidency in 1789. Washington's statement from his "Farewell Address" of 1797 is frequently quoted in political debate: "'Tis our true policy to steer clear of permanent alliances with any portion of the foreign world."[3]

The popular issues treated in the debates and public addresses during the first half of the nineteenth century included such matters as tariffs, New England manufacturing, foreign interests, centralization of government, expansion, internal improvements, sectionalism, slavery, nullification, and secession. These issues were debated at thousands of rallies, platforms, and "stumps" across the country, as well as in the famed halls of the nation's capitol.

Three of America's most distinguished orators emerged during this early national period referred to as America's Golden Age of Oratory: Henry Clay from the West, the North's Daniel Webster, and the Southerner John C. Calhoun, known as the Great Triumvirate. Clay's eloquent speech on the New Army Bill, delivered before the House in 1813, rallied the forces necessary to bring the War of 1812 to a successful conclusion. In 1824 his speech to the House on the Greek Revolution, supporting the Greeks in their conflict with the Turks, was received abroad with great interest. Clay, popularly called the Great Pacificator during the Missouri controversy in 1820, continued to play this role throughout his long career. Daniel Webster, considered America's foremost public speaker, was known equally for his political, legal, and platform or special occasion speaking. He is best remembered for his debate in the Senate in 1830 with Robert Y. Hayne of South Carolina, who argued for the states' right of nullification, the right to put liberty first and union afterward. Webster's famous reply, concluding with the statement, "Liberty *and* Union, now and forever, one and inseparable!"[4] has ever since been identified with popular American oratory. Calhoun was the most effective orator from the South, a leading spokesman for states' rights and slavery. But in the final speech of his career, on the Clay Compromise Measures of 1850, he could not persuade his fellow senators to support his stand against Clay and Webster in their combined efforts to preserve the Union.

Other prominent public speakers of the early nineteenth century included John Quincy Adams, known for his compromises on the Treaty of Ghent and arguments for the Monroe Doctrine; Thomas Hart Benton, long-time senator from Missouri whose oratorical skills were directed at western expansion; and Thomas Corwin, political leader from Ohio whose speech, "Against War with Mexico," delivered to the Senate, caused him to be burned in effigy as a traitor in 1847.

Some twenty years earlier had begun an era of what was called platform speaking, reflected in the emergence and development of professional orators who addressed themselves, either voluntarily or for a fee, to specific issues, usually concerned with some demand for social reform, such as abolition, women's rights, or prohibition.

Antislavery spokesmen included William Lloyd Garrison of Massachusetts, who agitated against slavery through the New England Antislavery Society, the American Antislavery Society, and numerous other abolitionist societies which he helped to establish; Wendell Phillips, public orator noted for his speech delivered in 1837 to an overflowing crowd in Boston's Faneuil Hall on the murder of abolitionist Elijah Lovejoy; and Charles Sumner, who is best known for his offensive "Crime against Kansas" speech, delivered to the Senate in 1856 in opposition to the Kansas-Nebraska bill. (This speech resulted in Sumner's being severely assaulted by his opponents and left unconscious on the floor of the Senate.) Edward Everett was a well-known and highly skilled orator who, as circumstances evolved, was the principal speaker at the ceremony dedicating the cemetery on the battlefield at Gettysburg in 1863, an occasion made famous by the brief address of Abraham Lincoln.

Numerous blacks also spoke in public on the slavery question, chief among these being Frederick Douglass, an exslave whose greatest speeches included "The Meaning of July Fourth for the Negro," delivered in Corinthian Hall, Rochester, New York, on July 5, 1852, and the "West India Emancipation" speech delivered at Canandaigua, New York, on August 4, 1857. Other black speakers prominent during this period were Charles Lennox Remond, Henry Highland Garnet, Samuel Ringgold Ward, James McCune Smith, and Robert Purvis. Some decades later, Booker T. Washington, founder of Tuskegee Institute, became the major voice of the Negro. His most celebrated speech, delivered in Atlanta, Georgia, at the Cotton States and International Exposition in 1895, while conceding that progress would be a struggle, sought the "blotting-out of sectional differences and racial animosities and suspicions."[5]

Abraham Lincoln was among the most effective popular orators of the midcentury period. Upon accepting the Republican nomination in Illinois for the U.S. Senate in 1858, he declared: "'A house divided against itself cannot stand.' I believe this government cannot endure, permanently half *slave* and half *free*."[6] His opponent, Stephen A. Douglas, the Little Giant, refuted Lincoln's statement several weeks later by arguing that the people should have the right to decide for themselves. The stage was thus set for a series of seven debates which attracted audiences numbering into the thousands across the prairies of Illinois. These debates are still the best known in American history. Although Douglas won the Senate seat, the debates provided the path to the presidency for Lincoln only two years later. Lincoln's masterpiece, the Gettysburg Address, delivered on November 19, 1863, and since memorized by millions of schoolchildren, ranks among the world's great speeches. Also considered a special work of oratorical literature is his "Second Inaugural Address," delivered March 4, 1865, famed for the words: "With malice toward none, with charity for all, with firmness in the right as God gives us to see the right, let us strive on to finish the work we are in."[7]

Following the Civil War the issues facing the nation were new and varied, but no popular debate topic was more crucial than that dealing with the reconstruction of the Southern states. Robert G. Ingersoll was known for his verbal brilliance while defending the cause of the Northern Republicans. Georgia's Henry Grady became known as the spokesman for the new South.

A distinctive feature of this era of platform speaking, a period when the role of women in American society was universally acknowledged as being inferior to that of men, was that women, despite resistance and sometimes ridicule, emerged as public speakers on popular issues. With an address on July 4, 1828, in New Harmony, Indiana, Frances Wright became the first woman orator, appealing for reforms in education. Other women orators followed, such as Angelina Grimké, a Southerner who moved Northern audiences to the antislavery cause, and Abbey Kelley Foster, who spoke out fiercely on the issues of woman's rights and temperance, often denouncing her audiences and frequently meeting with public disapproval. The speaking career of Ernestine L. Rose was largely concerned with human rights, particularly the rights of women; and Lucy Stone traveled and spoke extensively for women's rights. Pioneer black women orators, concerned mainly with antislavery and women's rights, were Sojourner Truth, Frances Ellen Watkins Harper, and Sarah P. Remond. In 1848 in Seneca Falls, New York, Elizabeth Cady Stanton addressed the first Woman's Rights Convention, which she and Lucretia Mott had promoted. A leading advocate for the cause of prohibition was Frances E. Willard, who crusaded widely for temperance, presiding over the National Women's Christian Temperance Union and eventually broadening her advocacy to include labor reform and women's liberation.

Susan B. Anthony was foremost in the woman's movement as a speaker and organizer. She lectured for more than forty-five years, and her influence on popular culture was reflected in 1979 when her likeness was sculptured for the obverse of the one dollar coin.

During the nineteenth century two uniquely American media concerned with public address were the "lyceums" and the "Chautauquas." Thousands of lyceums, organized and staffed by civic-minded volunteers, flourished in cities across the nation at this time, operating mainly in auditoriums during the winter months. Originally intended to provide a platform for series of educational lectures by local specialists, the lyceums soon attracted the nation's leading statesmen and scholars touring as professional lecturers, drawing large crowds, and earning large fees. The long list of traveling speakers included such prominent personalities as Henry Ward Beecher, Ralph Waldo Emerson, Horace Greeley, Oliver Wendell Holmes, James Russell Lowell, Theodore Parker, and Daniel Webster. Wendell Phillips's "The Lost Arts," delivered some two thousand times over a period of forty years, was a major attraction.

The Chautauquas originated and operated in a different manner. At Lake Chautauqua, New York, during the summer of 1874, John H. Vincent offered a program of lecture courses. Based on the success and growth of his project, he acquired a partner, Keith Vawter, and in 1904 organized what became known as "traveling Chautauquas." The Chautauquas, traveling with tents mostly through the rural areas during the summer months, were particularly popular with the masses, and their programs featuring distinguished speakers on appealing topics catered to mass tastes. William Jennings Bryan and Russell H. Conwell were audience favorites. Conwell presented his lecture, "Acres of Diamonds," to over six thousand audiences during a period of more than fifty years and with his huge profits founded Temple University. It is estimated that during a single year Chautauqua programs were offered in some ten thousand communities, with a total audience of four million.

As the various lyceums either disappeared or merged to form literary societies during the period after the Civil War, newly formed lecture bureaus supplied speakers who gave audiences what they wanted to hear, utilizing local facilities for public address and providing eminent speakers for substantial fees. James B. Pond became a major entrepreneur whose contracted speakers included the best that money could attract: Henry Ward Beecher, Chauncey M. Depew, John B. Gough, Robert G. Ingersoll, and Wendell Phillips, to name only a few. Mark Twain was extremely successful on the lecture circuit, earning more money from public address than from publication. With the coming of the economic depression of 1929, the traveling Chautauqua phenomenon waned, but through the 1930s and 1940s lecture bureaus continued to supply large and enthusiastic audiences with such speakers as Richard Halliburton, Eleanor Roosevelt, and Lowell Thomas.

From the early days of Colonial "theocracy" through the expansion into the many different denominations existing today, the clergy wielded considerable persuasive power. Some of these individuals made significant contributions to American popular culture. Theodore Parker's noteworthy sermon, "The Transient and the Permanent in Christianity," delivered in a South Boston church in 1841, established him as an advocate of modernist doctrines and aroused wide criticism. He became known for his sermons against slavery, the most noted being his denunciation of Webster for his speech of March 7, 1850. Henry Ward Beecher, like his father, Lyman Beecher, was a powerful orator for many causes, including the antislavery movement, and is recognized as the greatest American preacher of the nineteenth century. His "Memorial Sermon on Abraham Lincoln," delivered April 23, 1865, is a sublime example of oratorical tribute.

Skillfully organized revivalism became big business during the latter half of the nineteenth century, and the best-known revivalist was Dwight L. Moody. Not ordained, Moody preached in convention halls, warehouses, and theaters to audiences numbering well into the thousands. Following Moody by a generation and addressing audiences into the early decades of the twentieth century, Billy (William A.) Sunday, a former baseball player with the Chicago White Sox, also not ordained, continued in the tradition of Moody in "saving souls." Sunday was an energetic preacher who put sawdust on the floor so that sinners would not make a noise as they walked down the aisle to the foot of his speaking platform, a ritual known as "hitting the sawdust trail." Archbishop Fulton J. Sheen, a Roman Catholic traditionalist with a commanding presence and a sharp intellect, brought his evangelism to a radio and television audience estimated at thirty million at its peak. His television program, "Life Is Worth Living," won an Emmy Award in 1952. Presently, Billy (William F.) Graham, the foremost Protestant evangelist, attracts large audiences with a quiet yet forceful and sincere manner. A recurrent theme of Graham's sermons calls for humility before God.

As the nineteenth century drew to a close, the Populists were advocating free coinage of silver, agrarian reform, and a graduated federal income tax. Involved in these issues was the most prominent speaker of the period, William Jennings Bryan, a Nebraskan Democrat with Jeffersonian principles. His address to the Democratic convention in Chicago in 1896, "The Cross of Gold," advocating the cause of labor and the farmer, is considered a highpoint in convention oratory. Bryan had a long and popular career as a proponent for humanity, democracy, and religious orthodoxy, which culminated in 1924 in the world-famous Scopes "Monkey Trial" in Dayton, Tennessee, where he argued eloquently for the cause of the divine creation of man. He was resoundingly defeated by Clarence S. Darrow, the lawyer for the defense of the theory of evolution.

The popular hero of the Spanish-American War, Theodore Roosevelt, New York Republican, assuming the presidency in 1901, spoke extensively and successfully to break up the trusts of big business and the railroads and to promote conservation. Roosevelt's well-known speech calling for decency in government, "The Man with the Muck-Rake," delivered in Washington, D.C., in 1906, reflected the tenor of the time. Other progressives noted for public address were also campaigning for reform, including Albert J. Beveridge, Robert M. LaFollette, and William E. Borah.

In the early years of the twentieth century, issues of war and peace, as well as reform, engulfed Democratic President Woodrow Wilson, a crusading, intellectual speaker. Wilson's famous "Peace Without Victory" speech delivered to the Senate on January 21, 1917, intended to convince the warring European powers to resolve their conflict, was to no avail: three months later, on April 2, Wilson had to appear before a joint session of Congress to ask for a declaration of war. This momentous "War Message" was enthusiastically endorsed, and the nation embarked on its first world war. Following the conclusion of this war, against strong opposition from the Senate led by Henry Cabot Lodge, Wilson traveled to Versailles, and on January 25, 1919, appealed to the international delegates for the formation of a League of Nations as a means to render justice and maintain peace. Although the world was not then ready for Wilson's idealistic dream, his concepts would find realistic expression a generation later in the formation of the United Nations.

Faced with the darkest depression known in this country, Democrat Franklin D. Roosevelt assumed the presidency on March 4, 1933, and the era of the New Deal was launched. His inaugural address, transmitted by radio, was heard by more people than any previous public address, and his words brought a renewal of hope and confidence:

> This great Nation will endure as it has endured, will revive and prosper. So, first of all, let me assert my firm belief that the only thing we have to fear is fear itself—nameless, unreasoning, unjustified terror which paralyzes needed efforts to convert retreat into advance.[8]

A week later, on March 12, Roosevelt gave his first radio "fireside chat," in which he personalized the workings of government. The fireside chat's success was immediate. Roosevelt continued to bring the problems and solutions of government directly to the people, who responded by backing him in his programs for recovery and reform. Roosevelt used a fireside chat as a means of addressing the nation on December 9, 1941, after the Japanese had attacked Pearl Harbor: "Together with other free peoples, we are now fighting to maintain our right to live among our world neighbors in freedom and in common decency, without fear of assault....We are going to win the war and we are going to win the peace that follows."[9]

The "peace that followed" ushered in an era known as the Cold War. An "iron curtain," a term employed by Winston Churchill in a speech delivered at Westminster College in Fulton, Missouri, on March 5, 1946, was drawn between the forces of communism and the free peoples of the Western world. Democratic President Harry Truman, faced with a major crisis when the communist army of North Korea invaded South Korea in June 1950, used a radio address to declare a national emergency. Less than a year later, in an historic controversy over military policy, Truman relieved General of the Army Douglas MacArthur of his command of the United Nations Forces in the Far East, and MacArthur was honored with an invitation to address a joint session of Congress. On April 19, 1951, the respected World War II hero, receiving a tremendous ovation, stated his position and said goodby:

> But I still remember the refrain of one of the most popular barrack ballads of that day which proclaimed most proudly that 'Old soldiers never die; they just fade away.' And like the old soldier of that ballad, I now close my military career and just fade away—an old soldier who tried to do his duty as God gave him the light to see that duty.[10]

A new type of participatory government, made possible by electronics, was introduced with the debates and public addresses of the two national political conventions and the succeeding presidential campaigns in 1952, when for the first time these proceedings were brought directly to the people coast-to-coast via television. Never before had so many people witnessed history in the making. The Republicans nominated General of the Army

Dwight D. Eisenhower; the Democrats nominated the articulate governor of Illinois, Adlai E. Stevenson. Eisenhower was elected by the largest popular vote ever cast for a presidential candidate, and his Inaugural Address, televised on January 20, 1953, was the first to be seen and heard by millions of people throughout the country.[11]

The power of television as an element in determining the course of political events was dramatically emphasized during the fall of 1960, when the Republican candidate for the presidency, Vice President Richard M. Nixon, faced the Democratic nominee, Senator John F. Kennedy. Although the original impression of the electorate was that the candidates were equally qualified, Kennedy's fluency and charisma, transmitted to millions of viewers through the medium of television, carried the debates and, ultimately, the election. Kennedy's concise, eloquent Inaugural Address, telecast on January 20, 1961, noted for its epigram, "Ask not what your country can do for you—ask what you can do for your country,"[12] sought to inspire a new beginning, a New Frontier, in attempts to solve problems both at home and abroad.

The major domestic problem facing the nation during this period was civil rights. In the forefront of black protest was Martin Luther King, Jr., who delivered hundreds of speeches and organized marches, boycotts, and sit-ins to achieve his vision of nonviolent integration. King's "I Have a Dream" speech, delivered on August 28, 1963, from the steps of the Lincoln Memorial to a crowd of more than 200,000 blacks and whites who had marched on Washington, is the most renowned public address of the civil rights movement. Advocating an opposing point of view was Malcolm X (Malcolm Little), whose address, "The Ballot or the Bullet," delivered on April 3, 1964, in Cleveland, pressed for black nationalism. Black rhetoric became more militant with Stokely Carmichael, who coined the slogan, "Black Power," and H. Rap Brown, who threatened armed confrontation. The revolutionary public statements of Black Panthers Huey P. Newton, Eldridge Cleaver, and Bobby Seale expressed the ideology of Marx and Lenin. As the struggle continued into the 1970s, the debate and public address of black revolution became less inflammatory.

Concurrent with black agitation as a vital oratorical issue was the complex problem of the war in Vietnam. The question of how to achieve a permanent peace divided the nation. President Kennedy's commencement address at American University, delivered June 10, 1963, calling for peaceful solutions to international problems, led to the Nuclear Test Ban Treaty and detente with the Soviet Union. Outspoken against appeasement with the Soviet Union was conservative Republican Senator Barry M. Goldwater, whose speech delivered at a rally sponsored by the Detroit Economic Club on March 25, 1964, exhorted: "Let our arms match our cause! Let our men match the times! This is the way to peace through strength."[13] As the Vietnam War continued, prominent vocal advocates of peace included Senators J. William

Fulbright, George McGovern, Eugene McCarthy, and Robert F. Kennedy. The administration's Vietnam policy was openly probed on television by the Senate Foreign Relations Committee. Amid great dissension within the leadership of his own party, Democratic President Lyndon B. Johnson in an historic nationally televised address on March 31, 1968, announced both the cessation of bombing in Vietnam and his decision to resign at the end of his term. Unrest in the country was strong. Educators, clergymen, and other groups addressed themselves to the war issue, but young people across the nation became the most potent voice for peace. Hundreds of student demonstrations and protests on college and university campuses, some peaceful, others violent, emphatically expressed opposition to the war. Such public expression undoubtedly contributed greatly to the ceasefire agreement, effective January 28, 1973, with which the Nixon administration brought U.S. involvement in Vietnam to a close.

During this same period, the Space Age became a popular issue of debate and public address. Astronaut John H. Glenn, Jr., following his orbital flight around the earth, an exploit witnessed by an estimated 135 million television viewers, declared before a joint session of Congress on February 26, 1962, that "what we have done so far are but small building blocks in a huge pyramid to come."[14] Seven years later, on July 20, 1969, Neil Armstrong became the first human being to set foot on the moon, the first person to address the planet Earth from a planetary body. Millions of people all over the world watched and listened as Armstrong proclaimed: "That's one small step for a man, one giant leap for mankind."[15]

During the 1970s, one of the popular issues debated endlessly was women's rights, including the passage of the Equal Rights Amendment. This issue was exemplified by the public addresses and activities of Representative Shirley Chisholm, the first black woman elected to Congress, who in 1972 actively sought the Democratic presidential nomination. Other prominent issues of the decade included the energy crisis, culminating in an antinuclear rally in Washington, D.C., in 1979; and homosexual or "gay" rights, whose activists also marched on Washington during that year.

Earlier, the 1976 presidential campaign had been distinguished by three nationally televised debates between candidates President Gerald R. Ford and Governor Jimmy Carter, marking the first such encounter since the Kennedy-Nixon debates. Although the Ford-Carter debates were considered inconclusive, they afforded maximum mass involvement in debate and public address.

The debate and public address, however, having the greatest impact on popular culture during the past decade focused on two historic events. First, as part of the aftermath of the Watergate incident, the American public witnessed the televised debate by the Committee on the Judiciary of the House of Representatives in 1974, as members considered the possible impeachment of President Nixon. Less than two weeks later, in an address unprecedented in American history, speaking to the nation via television from the White House, Nixon announced his resignation.

The other historic event of major oratorical importance during the decade was the celebration of the United States' Bicentennial during 1976. Speech activities across the nation involved many thousands, including students from more than 8,500 high schools, colleges, and universities, who argued pertinent topics as part of the Bicentennial Youth Debate program. At one Bicentennial ceremony, President Ford, in a brief address delivered at the National Archives in Washington, D.C., on July 2, 1976, praised the far-sighted Americans who framed the Bill of Rights, "which protects us day and night in the exercise of our fundamental freedoms—to pray, to publish, to speak as we please."[16]

From the town meeting to the march on Washington, debate and public address, stimulated and magnified in modern times by radio and television, has been an integral part of American popular culture. Through the power of public speaking the American people have reached the crucial decisions that have governed the country as well as the personal choices by which they have lived. Essentially, the debate and public address of America's past not only has served the immediacy of particular occasions but also has provided a rich heritage of permanent and popular literature.

REFERENCE WORKS

The following reference works in debate and public address include not only resources for scholarly inquiry but also means through which communication skills can be learned. There is as yet no monumental reference work specifically designated as an encyclopedia of American debate and public address. For information pertaining to a particular orator, a great debate, a controversial issue, or an historical movement, a library's conventional card index system is a good first reference. The standard encyclopedias frequently offer a concise overview.

The federal government is a major source of reference material. The U.S. Congress's *Congressional Record* is of inestimable value because it routinely prints more debates and speeches than any other U.S. publication. From the First Congress to the present, the proceedings have been reported in four series of publications: *Annals of Congress* (1789-1824); *Register of Debates* (1824-37); *Congressional Globe* (1833-73); and *Congressional Record* (1873 to date), issued daily and biweekly, and also permanently bound and indexed. Although not a verbatim or complete account of daily Congressional proceedings, the *Record* is the official and most authoritative publication of the words spoken on the floor of the two houses. The presidential papers, including messages to Congress, speeches, and transcripts of news conferences, can be found in the U.S. General Services Administration's *Weekly Compilation of Presidential Documents* and annual *Public Papers of the Presidents of the United States.* Volumes have been published for each year of office for Presidents Hoover, Truman, Eisenhower, Kennedy, Johnson, Nixon, Ford, and Carter. The *Department of State Bulletin,* issued monthly by the U.S. Department of State's Bureau of Public Affairs, is the official record of this country's foreign policy and includes major addresses and news conferences of the president and the secretary of state as well as statements made before Congressional committees by the secretary and other senior Department of State officials. In addition, the government produces many thousands of publications annually. These publications cover almost every conceivable subject and can be especially useful as a source for factual data in the preparation of a speech. Since 1895, the U.S. Superintendent of Documents has issued a monthly catalog under various titles, and periodically indexed, listing current publications. There is also bibliographic access, through a number of sources, to publications dating back to 1774. Joe Morehead's *Introduction to United States Public Documents* is an up-to-date guide to both the governmental depository library system and nondepository publications, as well as to publications, reports, and materials of the legislative branch, the presidency, departments and agencies, the judiciary, independent and regulatory agencies, and advisory committees and commissions. Although the materials cited are not exhaustive, this work reflects the technology of the computer and micropublications and is an excellent starting point for gaining information from federal publications. *Government Publications and Their Use,* by Laurence F. Schmeckebier and Roy B. Eastin, although dated, offers a comprehensive description of materials available, including information on Congressional debates and presidential speeches. Walter L. Newsome's *New Guide to Popular Government Publications* is an annotated listing of approximately 2,500 titles, selected for their popular interest and use. Other specialized guides, directories, abstracts, bibliographies, indexes, catalogs, and textbooks are described below.

The student who is embarking on a research project in speech communication can find much rudimentary information, including an annotated listing of basic references, in Gerilyn Tandberg's practical handbook, *Research Guide in Speech.* Two charts are of special interest: one relating the approaches to rhetorical criticism and the other highlighting the history of oratory. An earlier effort, now somewhat dated, *A Bibliographic Guide to Research in Speech and Dramatic Art,* by Oscar G. Brockett, Samuel L. Becker, and Donald C. Bryant, also offers a list of bibliographic aids and reference works in the field of speech and attempts to place these guides in the context of relevant materials both in related fields and in the category of general reference works. Ernest G. Bormann's *Theory and Research in the*

Communicative Arts is intended for the student interested in exploring the nature of theorizing in speech and examining the various methods of research in speech.

Much information can be found in the *Speech Communication Directory*, published annually by the Speech Communication Association, Annandale, Virginia, in cooperation with its four regional organizations: Central States Speech Association, Eastern Communication Association, Southern Speech Communication Association, and Western Speech Communication Association. This directory lists the names and addresses of the officers of the divisions, boards, commissions, and committees of the national organization as well as those heading the regional, state, and various affiliated and related speech organizations. Alphabetical and geographical listings of the total membership are a virtual Who's Who in the field of speech communication. Also included is a roster of institutions of higher education that offer programs in speech and the names of appropriate administrative officers. The Speech Communication Association publishes a separate directory of graduate programs in the speech communication arts and sciences.

Abstracts provide a convenient form for surveying contemporary information and allow the researcher to determine if further pursuit is warranted. *Abstracts of Popular Culture: A Quarterly Publication of International Popular Phenomena*, edited by Ray B. Browne, contains entries gleaned from more than 600 domestic and foreign periodicals, including abstracts from primary speech communication journals. *Communication Abstracts*, edited by Thomas F. Gordon, a new quarterly international information service, provides abstracts of recent books, journal articles, research reports, and other communications-related literature. More than sixty journals are used to provide entries in the various subfields of communication, including speech communication and popular culture as it relates to the mass media. A short-lived publication, *Speech Abstracts*, edited successively by Earl R. Cain and David H. Krueger, offers abstracts of articles from the major speech journals for the years 1968 through 1970. Despite some omissions, this work is of value for the period. In addition, *Speech Communication Abstracts*, edited by Paul T. Adalian, Jr., abstracts and indexes over fifty journals, including international, national, and state publications, within the broad field of speech communication. This work supersedes *Speech Communication Index* and is published tri-annually with an annual cumulation in conjunction with *Theatre/Drama Abstracts*. More than seven thousand doctoral dissertations offering insight into contemporary research and thought in communication and theater are listed in *A Guide to Doctoral Dissertations in Communication Studies and Theater*, edited by Richard Leo Enos and Jeanne L. McClaran. This guide includes dissertations filed through 1977, and among its divisions are forensics, public address and rhetorical criticism, and rhetoric. Abstracts of dissertations in debate and public address are compiled monthly under the subheading "Speech" in the "Communications and the Arts" section of *Dissertation Abstracts International: The Humanities and Social Sciences.*

The major bibliographies and indexes in the area of debate and public address include the following: *Bibliography of Speech Education,* compiled by Lester Thonssen and Elizabeth Fatherson in 1939, and its *Supplement: 1939-1948,* compiled by Thonssen, Mary Margaret Robb, and Dorothea Thonssen, is an authoritative listing of articles, books, and advanced degree theses from the nineteenth century through 1948, indexed by the various areas of speech and dramatic art, including public speaking, debate, radio speaking, after-dinner speaking, and pulpit speaking. *Rhetoric and Public Address: A Bibliography, 1947-1961,* compiled and edited by James W. Cleary and Frederick W. Haberman, is a comprehensive and clearly organized listing of articles, books, monographs, and doctoral dissertations that appeared during the period. *Bibliography of Speech and Allied Areas, 1950-1960,* by Dorothy I. Mulgrave, Clark S. Marlor, and Elmer E. Baker, Jr., is a selective compilation of doctoral dissertations and books. A major division of the work on public address includes subheadings for debate, history, orators, public speaking, and rhetoric. From 1948 through 1969, "A Bibliography of Rhetoric and Public Address for the Year [1947-]," compiled by Frederick W. Haberman and others, which appeared initially in *Quarterly Journal of Speech* and subsequently in *Speech Monographs* (now *Communication Monographs*), offers a comprehensive bibliography of contemporary studies in the history, theory, and criticism of public address. From 1970 through 1975, this bibliography was published, together with other selective bibliographies and listings of graduate theses and dissertations in the various areas of speech communication, in *Bibliographic Annual in Speech Communication,* edited successively by Ned A. Shearer and Patrick C. Kennicott. Unfortunately this bibliography was discontinued with the 1975 edition. "A Bibliography of Speech and Theatre in the South for the Year [1954-]," compiled by Ralph T. Eubanks and others over the years, appears annually in *Southern Speech Communication Journal.* This bibliography lists the more significant titles relevant to speech literature of the South as well as material pertaining to black studies, even though they may not be directly related to the South. *Index to Journals in Communication Studies through 1974,* by Ronald J. Matlon and Irene R. Matlon, lists the contents, volume by volume, of the major journals in speech communication from their inception through 1974. Subjects of the articles are indexed, with some cross-indexing, under the nine main divisions of the Speech Communication Association, including forensics and public address. *Speech Index: An Index to 259 Collections of World Famous Orations and Speeches for Various Occasions,* composed by Roberta Briggs Sutton in 1966, a 1966-70 supplement composed by Roberta Briggs Sutton and Charity Mitchell, and a succeeding 1971-75 supplement composed by Charity Mitchell, provide a guide to speeches of famous orators from the earliest times to the present. Entries are arranged and cross-referenced by speaker, subject, and type of speech.

Recordings of speeches are an excellent original source for research, and currently available recorded speeches can be found in the catalogs of various recording companies. Among the leading producers are Caedmon Records (1995 Broadway, New York, N.Y. 10023), which produces the series, "Great American Speeches" and "The Great Debates"; CBS Records (51 West 52nd Street, New York, N.Y. 10019), producer of the "I Can Hear It Now" series; and Spoken Arts (310 North Avenue, New Rochelle, N.Y. 10801), which features history-making speeches, including those concerned with civil rights. In addition, the catalog of Listening Library, Inc. (1 Park Avenue, Old Greenwich, Conn. 06870) lists long-playing and cassette recordings dealing with the how-to aspects of debate and public speaking, recordings which can be valuable for self-instruction. ABC-Schwann (137 Newbury Street, Boston, Mass. 02116) publishes a monthly guide to records and tapes with a semi-annual supplement listing spoken word recordings. This guide is available at retail record dealers.

A specialized dealer of particular interest is an organization known as Arnold's Archives (1106 Eastwood, S.E., East Grand Rapids, Mich. 49506), which offers spoken word recordings by hundreds of figures in popular culture from all walks of life. Available are the recorded voices of such diverse personalities as P. T. Barnum, Roberto Clemente, Jack Dempsey, John Foster Dulles, Amelia Earhart, Helen Keller, Fiorello LaGuardia, Joe Louis, Joseph R. McCarthy, Jacqueline Kennedy Onassis, Babe Ruth, Norman Thomas, and Walter Winchell.

Helen Roach's *Spoken Records* is a lively anecdotal reference. In a chapter entitled "Documentaries, Lectures, Interviews, and Speeches," the author describes recordings of addresses delivered by well-known persons, largely political leaders, including John F. Kennedy, Martin Luther King, Jr., Malcolm X, Will Rogers, Franklin D. Roosevelt, and Adlai E. Stevenson.

Professional speakers who are stimulating or entertaining are always in demand, and prospective audiences sometimes have difficulty in locating them. The International Platform Association, with executive offices in Cleveland Heights, Ohio, is an organization of approximately six thousand members who are professional lecturers and others who appear before live audiences to inform and entertain, as well as program chairmen, booking agents, and men and women of various fields who are interested in oratory and the power of the spoken word. The organization was founded in 1903 as the International Lyceum Association and traces its origins to Daniel Webster and the American Lyceum Association. Contemporary speakers and lecturers are also indexed in two new references. Paul Wasserman's

Speakers and Lecturers: How to Find Them. A Directory of Booking Agents, Lecture Bureaus, Companies, Professional and Trade Associations, Universities, and Other Groups Which Organize and Schedule Engagements for Lecturers and Public Speakers on All Subjects, with Details about Speakers, Subjects, and Arrangements can be of use in bringing together speakers and audiences, although the listings in some areas fall short of being complete. Howard J. Langer's *Directory of Speakers* contains an alphabetical listing of more than 1,500 available speakers. This work is indexed by both geographical area and subject and includes a short biographical sketch of each speaker.

Debating and public speaking is not only an area of interest to the critic or historian but also a skill which can be acquired. Skill in debating and public speaking is probably best learned in the classroom under the guidance of an instructor with the aid of a suitable textbook selected from the over-abundant supply on the market. Several of the more widely recognized books and sources that offer instruction in speaking in public are presented first; then publications that treat educational debate are considered. Many texts, of course, are written so that a person of average intelligence and discipline can use them as references for self-study. *Principles and Types of Speech Communication,* by Douglas Ehninger, Alan H. Monroe, and Bruce E. Gronbeck, used on college campuses for more than four decades and now in its eighth edition, is a reputable reference. The authors are known for the development of a step-by-step motivated sequence to be used in the preparation of a speech. Included are chapters detailing the adapting of a speech to an audience, outlining a speech, and the use of visual aids, as well as sample speeches for study and analysis. *Public Speaking as a Liberal Art,* by John F. Wilson and Carroll C. Arnold, is a solid presentation combining the classical and the contemporary approaches to the art of public speaking. The work emphasizes the traditional processes of invention and disposition and offers interesting chapters on the judging of public speaking and the heritage of rhetorical theory. Raymond S. Ross's *Speech Communication: Fundamentals and Practice* is a basic, authoritative text which focuses on the arts and skills of speech communication within the context of social behavior. Examples and illustrations are plentiful. In addition to traditional textbooks, there are numerous how-to books designed for the popular trade. Included among these, Dale Carnegie's *The Quick and Easy Way to Effective Speaking,* which uses an informal anecdotal format, gives useful advice on preparing and delivering a talk. Dorothy Sarnoff's *Speech Can Change Your Life: Tips on Speech, Conversation and Speechmaking* is an entertaining and practical presentation on how to prepare and deliver a speech as well as a handbook on voice and articulation. Jacob M. Braude has authored several books on various aspects of speaking, including *The Complete Art of Public Speaking.* Braude offers here a brief guide to speaking in public and a compilation of over 1,600 ideas or quotations, arranged by categories, which can be used as source material in preparing a talk. *Speaking Up: A Book for Every Woman Who Wants to Speak Effectively,* by Janet Stone and Jane Bachner, considers speaking in public from a feminist point of view. Their "you can do it!" approach is of special value for the novice female speaker. Dorothy Uris's *A Woman's Voice: A Handbook to Successful Private and Public Speaking* is also especially written for the woman who seeks self-improvement in speaking skills. Uris presents pertinent advice on "freeing your voice" as well as on creating and delivering a speech. A number of books written or compiled by Herbert V. Prochnow, including several in conjunction with Herbert V. Prochnow, Jr., offer collections of humorous stories, epigrams, quotations, and unusual facts and illustrations for the speaker or toastmaster. Among them are *The Public Speaker's Treasure Chest: A Compendium of Source Material to Make Your Speech Sparkle* and a companion volume, *The Toastmaster's Treasure Chest.*

Instruction in public speaking is also offered by both commercial and noncommercial organizations in communities throughout the country. Listings of such organizations can be obtained by consulting the Yellow Pages of the local telephone directory under a heading such as "public speaking instructions." Possibly the best-known commercial organization engaged in the teaching of public speaking is Dale Carnegie, which is international in scope. The Carnegie method has proven successful for hundreds of thousands of students since 1912. Other commercial programs may be equally effective.

Among the noncommercial organizations that provide opportunities to develop skills in public speaking is Toastmasters International, with its world headquarters in Santa Ana, California. Since the founding of its first club in 1924, over a million men and women have participated in the clubs' oral communication projects. Toastmasters clubs, now numbering more than 3,500 with a membership of about 75,000 in over forty countries, each consist of twenty to forty persons who meet regularly to learn and practice techniques of public speaking and constructive evaluation. An annual directory provides a geographical listing of the clubs, and a monthly publication is devoted to relevant news and articles. Included in the organization's activities is the annual sponsorship of the World Championship of Public Speaking. International Toastmistress Clubs, founded in 1938 and now numbering 1,300 local groups with a membership of approximately 27,000 adults, is another organization devoted to speech improvement and communication skills. Headquartered in Downey, California, this organization publishes a bimonthly magazine and an annual roster of clubs.

Educational debate is formally organized in this country on two levels, secondary and collegiate, both of which are primarily extracurricular and contest-oriented. The nationwide high school debate proposition (topic) is selected and framed annually by the Committee on Discussion and Debate Materials and Interstate Cooperation of the National University Extension Association, with offices in Eugene, Oregon. Each year the Committee on Intercollegiate Discussion and Debate of the Speech Communication Association supervises the selecting and framing of a proposititon which is debated on the college level at tournaments across the nation. The U.S. Superintendent of Documents annually publishes and offers free of charge a bibliography pertinent to each of the two topics: *Subject Bibliography 043*, which includes publications relating to the national high school debate topic; and *Subject Bibliography 176*, which includes publications relating to the college debate topic. Each of these bibliographies lists a guide to the topic in addition to related government publications. These guides, compiled in accordance with Public Law 88-246 by the Congressional Research Service of the Library of Congress, are authoritative references which include information reprinted from a variety of sources as well as comprehensive bibliographies. These guides may be purchased from the Superintendent of Documents for a reasonable fee. Pertinent resources for the annual debate topics are also available from various publishers. Among the leading sources that specialize in the high school topic are the Speech Communication Association, Annandale, Virginia; the National Forensic League, Ripon, Wisconsin; and the National Textbook Company, Skokie, Illinois. The Study Group of the Alan Company, Clayton, Missouri, and Springboards, Inc., St. Louis, Missouri, offer handbooks and other materials relating to the college topic.

Numerous textbooks present the theory and principles of educational debate and their application. Austin J. Freeley's *Argumentation and Debate: Rational Decision Making* is a substantial text designed for the traditional undergraduate course in argumentation and debate. Chapters dealing with evidence, reasoning, case construction, evaluation, and tournament procedures are clear and authoritative. Appendixes include the first Kennedy-Nixon debate, a transcript of an intercollegiate debate, and a listing of the national intercollegiate debate propositions from the academic year 1920-21 through 1975-76. *Decision by Debate*, by Douglas Ehninger and Wayne Brockriede, considers debate as both an academic exercise and a social force extending beyond the classroom. In presenting a person-centered perspective on argument and debate, the authors provide a foundation for practical application: analyzing a question, developing a proof, and defending a position. Although this book contains no transcripts of debates or detailed treatment of tournaments, it is a solid and current study. *Academic Debate: Practicing Argumentative Theory*, by Donald W. Klopf and Ronald E. Cambra, is a brief, plainly written guide to the fundamentals of educational debate and includes chapters on analyzing the proposition, argument, the affirmative case, the negative case, refutation and rebuttal, the cross-questioning process, and debate behavior. *Modern Debate Case Techniques,* edited by Donald R. Terry, providing an analysis of the various types of debate cases and an explanation of argumentative structure, is a useful supplementary aid for the debater. *Directing Forensics: Contest & Debate Speaking,* by Don F. Faules, Richard D. Rieke, and Jack Rhodes, is an up-to-date handbook for the teacher or coach, inexperienced or experienced. Topics include administering a forensic program, coaching individual events, judging a forensic contest, and administering a tournament. A narrower focus is found in *Managing Forensic Tournaments,* by Paul Hunsinger, Donald R. Terry, and Roy V. Wood, a manual which deals specifically with tournament preparation and direction.

Excellent as a first reference in researching the area of educational debate is Arthur N. Kruger's *Argumentation and Debate: A Classified Bibliography.* This work contains approximately six thousand entries, of which about 650 are listings of doctoral dissertations and master's theses. With an emphasis on studies published in the United States during the twentieth century, the bibliography is subdivided according to all areas of debate, including history, ethics, debate organizations, forms of debate, high school forensics, collections, and bibliographies, and is indexed by both author and subject.

Compilations of intercollegiate debates provide useful reference tools for many aspects of debating. Among these compilations are the following two series: *Intercollegiate Debates: Being Briefs and Reports of Many Intercollegiate Debates,* a work of twenty-two volumes, edited successively by Paul M. Pearson and Egbert Ray Nichols, presents selective affirmative and negative debates on important topics of the day as argued by various college debate teams from 1909 to 1941. A compilation of thirty-seven volumes, *University Debaters' Annual: Constructive and Rebuttal Speeches Delivered in Debates of American Colleges and Universities during the College Year,* edited successively by Edward Charles Mabie, Edith M. Phelps, and Ruth Ulman, offers representative intercollegiate debates and other forensic activities presented on American campuses from the academic year 1914-15 through 1950-51. Selected bibliography and briefs accompany each debate. Debates from these two series as well as numerous other debates, arguments, and briefs are listed by subject in *Debate Index,* compiled by Edith M. Phelps; *Debate Index Supplement,* compiled by Julia E. Johnsen; and *Debate Index Second Supplement,* compiled by Joseph R. Dunlap and Martin A. Kuhn. *Championship Debating—West Point National Debate Tournament Final-Round Debates and Critiques, 1949-60,* together with a second volume published six years later, both edited by Russel R. Windes and Arthur N. Kruger, provides a record of the annual National Debate Tournament from its inception at the U.S. Military Academy in 1947 through 1966, when the American Forensics Association assumed responsibility for conducting the tournament. *Fifty Years of International Debate, 1922-1972,* by Robert N. Hall and Jack L. Rhodes, is a brief documentation beginning with the visit of the Oxford University debating team to Bates College, Lewiston, Maine, in 1922, and concluding with the visit on American campuses of a team from the Soviet Union in the spring of 1972.

RESEARCH COLLECTIONS

The researcher in debate and public address will find it difficult to locate specific collections so designated. Collections are more easily located by the name of the speaker, subject, issue, or area of inquiry.

For example, Lee Ash's computerized compilation, *Subject Collections: A Guide to Special Book Collections and Subject Emphases as Reported by University, College, Public, and Special Libraries and Museums in the United States and Canada* is a comprehensive alphabetical listing of subjects and persons for whom collections have been established. But, contrary to expectations, this work provides no pertinent listings for debate, public address, oratory, or rhetoric. The only listing under "Public Speaking and Speakers" is that of the Chauncey Mitchell Depew Collection in the library of George Washington University. Entries are included for presidential collections from George Washington through Richard Milhous Nixon.

A second guide of considerable scope is *Directory of Special Libraries and Information Centers: A Guide to Special Libraries, Information Centers, Archives, and Data Centers Maintained by Government Agencies, Business, Industry, Newspapers, Educational Institutions, Nonprofit Organizations, and Societies in the Fields of Science, Technology, Medicine, Law, Art, Religion, History, Social Sciences, and Humanistic Studies,* edited by Margaret L. Young and Harold C. Young. Again, there are no listings for debate, public address, oratory, or rhetoric in the subject index, and the listings under "Speech" are a combination of speech communication and speech pathology. Among the research collections in speech communication described by Young and Young are those at the following centers: Haskins Laboratories Library, New Haven, Connecticut; Abbot Memorial Library, Emerson College, Boston; and English, Communication, and Theatre Graduate Library, Ohio State University, Columbus. This directory also describes numerous collections of sound recordings.

A third major source of information for aspects of debate and public address is the *American Library Directory,* edited annually by Jaques Cattell Press. The collections of more than 32,000 libraries are listed by geographical communities within each state, the regions administered by the United States, and the provinces of Canada. Among the listings are the following collections of interest: the Issues-Research Library of the Democratic

National Committee in Washington, D.C., which houses the proceedings of the Democratic National Conventions; the Republican National Committee Library, also in Washington, D.C., which holds records of political interest; the libraries and archives of ABC, CBS, and NBC in New York, where each of the three major commercial radio and television networks maintains collections dealing, in part, with current issues and events; and the Channel 13 Library of the Educational Broadcasting Corporation in New York, which holds audiovisual materials and videotapes of public affairs.

Special Collections in Libraries of the Southeast, edited by J. B. Howell, smaller in scope than the above three guides, includes relevant collections in all types of libraries in the ten states comprising the southeastern part of the country. These collections are listed by person or subject under geographical communities for each state. This guide is especially useful for researching prominent local citizens and regional history.

Complementing these four directories for researchers in debate and public address is the *National Union Catalogue of Manuscript Collections,* compiled by the U.S. Library of Congress. The first sixteen volumes in this on-going series, which cover the years 1959 through 1978, describe approximately 42,200 collections located in 1,076 different repositories in the United States. The cumulative index is a separate publication and categorizes approximately 440,000 references to topical subjects and personal, family, corporate, and geographical names. Obviously this is a most valuable source for researchers.

The Educational Resources Information Center (ERIC), operated by the National Institute of Education (NIE), U.S. Department of Education, offers access to tens of thousands of unpublished, noncopyrighted documents as well as education-related journal articles. ERIC consists of a network of sixteen clearinghouses, each specializing in a particular educational area, integrated through a central computerized facility. The Speech Communication Module of the ERIC Clearinghouse on Reading and Communications Skills processes materials related to debate and public address into the data bank. (ERIC/RCS Speech Communication Module, Speech Communication Association, 5105 Backlick Road, Annandale, Va. 22003). Three guides, readily available at many college and university libraries, are necessary to institute a customized computer search for information on a given topic. *Thesaurus of ERIC Descriptors* is the source of subject headings and vocabulary for information retrieval from the ERIC collections. The U.S. Department of Education's *Resources in Education* (originated in November, 1966, as *Research in Education*), a monthly publication issued by the NIE, indexes and abstracts such "fugitive literature" as speeches, position papers, and research reports. Microfiche and hard copies of most of the listed documents are available from ERIC Document Reproduction Service, Arlington, Virginia, for a reasonable fee. *Current Index to Journals in Education,* a monthly publication inaugurated in January 1969, and cumulated semi-annually, cites articles from over seven hundred publications in the field of education and peripherally related areas, including the major speech journals. Reprints of many of the journal articles can be ordered from University Microfilms International, Ann Arbor, Michigan.

Collections of audio and video recordings have reflected the growth of the recording and broadcasting industries. The Association for Recorded Sound Collections, founded in 1967, serves the interests of the collector or individual concerned with research and publication in historical-discographic information, including spoken word recordings. The *Association for Recorded Sound Collections Journal,* published three times a year, offers pertinent articles and reviews.

A substantial collection of spoken word recordings is housed by the Audiovisual Archives Division of the National Archives in Washington, D.C. Recordings of speeches, panel discussions, press conferences, court and conference proceedings, interviews, entertainment programs, and news broadcasts, numbering more than ninety thousand, have been gathered largely from the various federal agencies but include as well many from private, commercial, and foreign sources. The sound archives date from 1896 and include the voices of Presidents Theodore Roosevelt, William Howard Taft, Woodrow Wilson, Warren G. Harding, and Calvin Coolidge. Charles A. Lindbergh's address to the Press Club in 1927 and John F. Kennedy's address in 1961 concerning Alan Shepard's flight into outer space are only two examples of the treasures in this collection. A discography, *Sound Recordings in the Audiovisual Archives Division of the National Archives: Preliminary Draft Prepared for the National Archives Conference on the Use of Audiovisual Archives as Original Source Materials,* by the U.S. National Archives and Records Service, describes the holdings and includes indexes to program series and persons whose voices are known to be recorded in the holdings. Selected holdings are annotated in brochures issued by the National Archives Trust Fund Board, National Archives and Records Service, General Services Administration, Washington, D.C. 20408.

The Motion Picture, Broadcasting, and Recorded Sound Division of the Library of Congress holds some 900,000 sound recordings on disc, tape, wire, and cylinder. Included are radio programs from 1924 to the present and television programs on tape and film from 1948 to the present. Read Greyer's "An Index to Commercial Spoken Word Recordings in the Library of Congress," published in the *Association for Recorded Sound Collections Journal,* although hardly a complete listing of spoken word recordings, indexes seventy-one recordings by album title, specific speaker or event, and manufacturer's name.

A list of significant collections of recordings throughout the country must include the following: Yale Collection of Historical Sound Recordings,

Sterling Memorial Library, Yale University, New Haven, Connecticut, which contains recordings of historical interest in the fields of art, music, jazz, drama, politics, literature, and documentary from the end of the nineteenth century to the present, with an emphasis on the history of performance practice in the arts; G. Robert Vincent Voice Library, Michigan State University, East Lansing, which houses historical sound recordings of voices and events in all fields of human endeavor; Library Reserve/Audio Visual Room, University of Minnesota, Minneapolis, which includes the U.S. government radio transcriptions of World War II among its special collections; Record Library of the Donnell Library Center, New York Public Library, New York City, which includes recordings of speeches and documentaries; Audio Archives of the George Arents Research Library for Special Collections, E. S. Bird Library, Syracuse University, Syracuse, New York, which includes among its 250,000 items sound recordings of political leaders, poets, theatrical personalities, singers, and transcriptions of audio broadcastings dating from the earliest of the Thomas Edison cylinder recordings to the present. Substantial collections of recordings are also found at Pacifica Tape Library, Los Angeles, California; Stanford Archive of Recorded Sound, Music Library, Stanford University, Stanford, California; Educational Media Center, National Center for Audio Tapes, University of Colorado, Boulder; Broadcast Pioneers Library, Washington, D.C.; Library Listening Rooms, Louisiana State University, Baton Rouge; and Reynolds Audio-Visual Division, Rochester Public Library, Rochester, New York.

The Vanderbilt Television News Archive, Nashville, Tennessee, contains videotapes which are made daily of the evening news telecasts of the three major networks as seen in Nashville. While the major holdings are of news broadcasts, the collection includes presidential speeches and accompanying comments; complete coverage of the Democratic and Republican National Conventions of 1968, 1972, and 1976; the Watergate hearings of 1973; the Nixon impeachment debates of 1974; the Rockefeller and Ford confirmation hearings; and the Bert Lance hearings of 1977. These tapes are indexed by subject and date in *Television News Index and Abstracts: A Guide to the Videotape Collection of the Network Evening News Programs in the Vanderbilt Television News Archive.*

HISTORY AND CRITICISM

Any contemporary approach to the history and criticism of American debate and public address has its roots in the rhetorical theory of philosophers and scholars dating back to the ancient Greeks. Among the preeminent classical works that modern critics embrace are: Plato's *Gorgias* and *Phaedrus;* Aristotle's *The Rhetoric,* considered to this day the single most thorough and influential philosophical analysis of the art of speaking; Cicero's *De Oratore*

(55 BC); Quintilian's *Institutio Oratoria (Education of an Orator,* ca. AD 93); Longinus's *On the Sublime* (ca. AD first half of the first century); Francis Bacon's *The Advancement of Learning* (1605); George Campbell's *The Philosophy of Rhetoric* (1776); Hugh Blair's *Lectures on Rhetoric and Belles Lettres* (1783); and Richard Whately's *Elements of Rhetoric* (1828). Complete translations and reprints of these works are readily available. Pertinent excerpts from the writings named above of Plato, Aristotle, Cicero, Quintilian, and Longinus may be found in translation in *Readings in Classical Rhetoric,* edited by Thomas W. Benson and Michael H. Prosser; and *The Rhetoric of Blair, Campbell, and Whately,* by James L. Golden and Edward P. J. Corbett, offers substantial selections from the works of these three theorists.

The emergence of public address as a specific area of scholarly study in U.S. higher education is a phenomenon of the twentieth century, beginning about 1915. An overview recounting the study and practice of rhetorical criticism from this period through its development into the 1970s can be found in Charles J. Stewart's "Historical Survey: Rhetorical Criticism in Twentieth Century America," the lead essay in *Explorations in Rhetorical Criticism,* edited by G. P. Mohrmann, Charles J. Stewart, and Donovan J. Ochs.

Major contemporary theorists of rhetoric include Kenneth Burke, Marshall McLuhan, I. A. Richards, Chaim Perelman, Stephen Toulmin, and Richard M. Weaver. Selections by each of these scholars as well as relevant essays are included in *Contemporary Theories of Rhetoric: Selected Readings,* edited by Richard L. Johannesen. *Historical Studies of Rhetoric and Rhetoricians,* edited by Raymond F. Howes, offers twenty-two essays by distinguished scholars, including Carroll C. Arnold, Hoyt H. Hudson, Everett Lee Hunt, Wayland Maxfield Parrish, Karl R. Wallace, Herbert A. Wichelns, and James A. Winans. In a work sponsored by the Speech Communication Association and edited by Lloyd F. Bitzer and Edwin Black, *The Prospect of Rhetoric: Report of the National Developmental Project,* leading rhetoricians attempt to answer the question, What is the essential outline of a conception of rhetoric useful in the second half of the twentieth century? This report concludes in part that, because modern technology has created new channels and techniques of communication, the scope of rhetorical studies should be broadened to explore such contemporary phenomena as popular music, news reporting and interpretation, and film, which have become increasingly influential in American culture. A collection of essays, *Form and Genre: Shaping Rhetorical Action,* edited by Karlyn Kohrs Campbell and Kathleen Hall Jamieson, was published as a result of the 1976 conference on "'Significant Form' in Rhetorical Criticism," under the auspices of the Speech Communication Association. The contributors, who included Herbert Simons, Edwin Black, Michael Halloran, Ronald

Carpenter, Bruce E. Gronbeck, Ernest G. Bormann, and the editors, explore theoretical perspectives and their possible application to new rhetorical understanding.

Among the many significant essays published during this century of interest to the modern student of critical and historical theory, three are paramount. "The Literary Criticism of Oratory" (1925) by Herbert A. Wichelns sets forth the neo-Aristotelian approach, which established the standard for much of the criticism that followed in the 1930s and 1940s. "Public Address: A Study in Social and Intellectual History" (1947) by Ernest J. Wrage urges an idea-centered critical orientation as an alternative to the traditional speaker-centered approach. Both of these essays have been reprinted in *Methods of Rhetorical Criticism: A Twentieth-Century Perspective,* by Robert L. Scott and Bernard L. Brock. The third essay, "Rhetoric: Its Function and Its Scope" (1953) by Donald C. Bryant, discusses aspects of rhetoric as instrumental, critical, philosophical, and social disciplines. Bryant's essay is frequently anthologized and has been reexamined in his more recent *Rhetorical Dimensions in Criticism.*

Several distinguished collections of essays published in honor of an esteemed colleague have contributed greatly to the whole of speech history and criticism. *Studies in Rhetoric and Public Speaking in Honor of James Albert Winans,* edited by A. M. Drummond, is a volume of eleven scholarly papers including the aforementioned "The Literary Criticism of Oratory." The seventeen studies offered in *The Rhetorical Idiom: Essays in Rhetoric, Oratory, Language, and Drama Presented to Herbert August Wichelns with a Reprinting of His "Literary Criticism of Oratory" (1925),* edited by Donald C. Bryant, includes Karl R. Wallace's "Rhetoric, Politics, and Education of the Ready Man," of political interest, and Bryant's "'A Peece of a Logician': The Critical Essayist as Rhetorician," of literary interest. *American Public Address: Studies in Honor of Albert Craig Baird,* edited by Loren Reid, presents fifteen critical essays on such speakers as Oliver Wendell Holmes, Clarence Darrow, Ralph J. Bunche, and Edward R. Murrow.

A number of academic texts have been published during the last several decades on the theory and practice of rhetorical criticism. The various theoretical definitions and critical methodologies expounded in these works are not mutually exclusive. In the critical evaluation of debate and public address, it is wise not to rely solely on the work of one critic or one system. For a comprehensive introductory treatise that is grounded in the classics there is none better than *Speech Criticism,* by Lester Thonssen, A. Craig Baird, and Waldo W. Braden. The authors deal with the nature of rhetorical criticism, development of theory, methods of the critics, and standards of judgment and provide extensive bibliographies for further study. Carroll C. Arnold's introductory textbook, *Criticism of Oral Rhetoric,* clearly written and practical, uses a traditionalist approach to analysis. The beginning student may also wish to peruse an earlier work, Anthony Hillbruner's *Critical Dimensions: The Art of Public Address Criticism,* in which the author cogently and concisely treats the standard extrinsic and intrinsic factors of public address. Also intended for the beginning student is a slim paperback which approaches the criticism and evaluation of public address from a traditional rhetorical point of view, Robert S. Cathcart's *Post-Communication: Critical Analysis and Evaluation.* Edwin Black's provocative and controversial work, *Rhetorical Criticism: A Study in Method,* is written for the advanced or graduate student and the professional audience. Black attacks the shortcomings of the various approaches to rhetorical criticism, particularly the neo-Aristotelian, as he considers the entire genre of the argumentative process.

Other works deal forthrightly with the process and practice of critical analysis by providing applicable examples of important speeches and illuminating a particular means by which "to do criticism." Lionel Crocker's *Rhetorical Analysis of Speeches* offers a paragraph-by-paragraph rhetorical analysis of eleven speeches by such orators as Franklin D. Roosevelt, Harry Emerson Fosdick, Wendell L. Willkie, and Lyndon B. Johnson, as well as the famous persuasive speeches of Brutus and Antony in Shakespeare's *Julius Caesar* (III, ii). L. Patrick Devlin's *Contemporary Political Speaking,* in analyzing the nature of oral politics, presents thirteen topics and speakers of political significance in the 1960s and 1970s, including verbatim transcripts of their speeches. *Critiques of Contemporary Rhetoric,* by Karlyn Kohrs Campbell, discusses the rhetorical process and the traditional, psychological, and dramatistic systems of criticism and includes nine speeches by such leaders as Richard M. Nixon, George Wald, Spiro T. Agnew, Eldridge Cleaver, Jo Freeman, and Emmet John Hughes. In *A Choice of Worlds: The Practice and Criticism of Public Discourse,* assuming that the student of public address is both a producer and a consumer, James R. Andrews presents six basic principles of rhetoric as guides for both the speaker and the critic and for illustration selects twelve speeches on historical and contemporary issues.

History of American Oratory, by Warren Choate Shaw, published in 1928, is recognized as the first comprehensive history of American oratory. Shaw presents descriptive studies of twenty-one representative orators from Patrick Henry to Woodrow Wilson and includes a pertinent bibliography for each. More influential, however, is *A History and Criticism of American Public Address,* a seminal study published in two volumes in 1943, edited by William Norwood Brigance, and followed twelve years later by a third volume, edited by Marie Kathryn Hochmuth. Brigance's work is divided into two parts: Part 1 presents an historical background of public address from the Colonial period through 1930; Part 2 offers twenty-nine analytical studies of leaders from the fields of religion, reform, law, general culture, education, labor, and statecraft, ranging chronologically from Jonathan Edwards to Woodrow Wilson. The analyses vary in style and scope but are uniformly sound. Hochmuth introduces the third volume with a significant essay, "The Criticism of Rhetoric," and presents critical studies of such orators as Alexander Hamilton, Susan B. Anthony, Clarence Darrow, Theodore Roosevelt, William E. Borah, Harry Emerson Fosdick, and Franklin D. Roosevelt. The extensive footnotes, bibliographies, and indexes contribute to the usefulness of these three volumes.

Highly recommended is Robert T. Oliver's *History of Public Speaking in America,* an evaluative work of broad scope which illuminates the influence of public address on the flow of history from the earliest period through the era of Woodrow Wilson. Oliver's style is anecdotal, and the history is interesting to read. The study is thoroughly researched and includes extensive bibliographies. A volume as insightful and utilitarian as Oliver's, but more current in coverage, is *America in Controversy: History of American Public Address,* edited by DeWitte Holland. While Oliver concentrates largely on individual orators and their contributions, Holland presents an idea- and issue-centered study, an analytic work which traces twenty-four significant debates beginning with evangelism among the Indians in the Massachusetts Bay Colony through the peace movement and the Vietnam War. The rhetoric of the polarity of views is developed and supported for such major controversies as the separation of church and state, the Constitution, slavery, imperialism, the agrarian issue, socialism, suffrage and prohibition, the New Deal, internal communism, the black revolution, freedom of speech in the 1960s, and youth protests.

More than 200 debates beginning with those pertaining to the Stamp Act and concluding with those dealing with the repeal of the Silver Purchase Act are presented chronologically in the fourteen volumes of *Great Debates in American History: From the Debates in the British Parliament on the Colonial Stamp Act (1764-1765) to the Debates in Congress at the Close of the Taft Administration (1912-1913),* edited by Marion Mills Miller. This is an estimable source containing explanations, the debates themselves, and summaries of how decisions and compromises were reached by the leaders who forged the country. Miller's work discusses the relevant debates leading up to the Revolutionary War as well as the popular Lincoln-Douglas debates of 1858, which prefigured the outbreak of the Civil War. Both of these periods of American history have been treated by contemporary rhetorical scholars. Three monographs sponsored on the occasion of the nation's Bicentennial by the Speech Communication Association as part of its series entitled "The Continuing American Revolution" offer scholarly research and thought treating the American Revolution as an ongoing process of communication symbolizing the American experience. Barbara A. Larson's

Prologue to Revolution: The War Sermons of the Reverend Samuel Davies, A Rhetorical Study provides critical insights into the religious and secular events and issues of the late 1750s, which formed a frame of reference for the revolution that followed. Ronald F. Reid's *The American Revolution and the Rhetoric of History* presents a study of the relationships between rhetoric and history, arguing that the past must be seen as it actually was. *The American Ideology: Reflections of the Revolution in American Rhetoric,* by Kurt W. Ritter and James R. Andrews, critically illuminates the rhetorical process that shaped and reflected American ideology through ceremonial discourse from the period of the American Revolution and continuing to the contemporary civil rights struggle. Strong documentation contributes to the value of all three works. In addition, Richard Allen Heckman's *Lincoln vs. Douglas: The Great Debates Campaign* assesses the role of the Lincoln-Douglas debates in the history of American oratory. The reader is also referred to Lionel Crocker's *An Analysis of Lincoln and Douglas as Public Speakers and Debaters,* which offers the texts of the debates as well as a number of studies reflecting on the speaking effectiveness of the two political leaders. *Anti-Slavery and Disunion, 1858-1861: Studies in the Rhetoric of Compromise and Conflict,* edited by J. Jeffery Auer, presents a solid integration of historical analysis and rhetorical criticism in twenty-three essays relating to the central issues preceding the Civil War.

No series of debates since the Lincoln-Douglas debates has captured the imagination of the American public and the attention of scholars of debate and public address as completely as that between John F. Kennedy and Richard M. Nixon during the presidential campaign of 1960. The foremost book dealing with this clash is *The Great Debates: Background—Perspective—Effects,* edited by Sidney Kraus, later reissued as *The Great Debates: Kennedy vs. Nixon, 1960.* This work is an overview which presents the texts of the four debates as well as insights of various communications experts. Interesting to read, also, is Nixon's account of these debates in his book, *Six Crises.* (He writes here, too, about his "Checkers" speech and his debate with Khrushchev.) The debates in the fall of 1976 between Jimmy Carter and President Gerald R. Ford mark the second such series of face-to-face exchanges between presidential candidates. A three-volume work, *The Presidential Campaign 1976,* compiled under the direction of the Committee on House Administration, U.S. House of Representatives, sets forth the significant issues of the campaign as the candidates themselves saw them and gives the texts of speeches, interviews, and statements, as well as the full transcripts of the debates, including the formal exchange between the vice presidential running mates, Senators Walter F. Mondale and Robert Dole.

Two works of so-called regional oratory offer rich evaluative studies of representative oratory and orators. Waldo W. Braden's *Oratory in the*

Old South: 1828-1860 presents nine essays ranging from "The Rhetoric of the Nullifiers" to "The Southern Unionist, 1850-1860" and concludes that there is no genre of Southern oratory, thereby destroying the myth of the Southern orator. Included is a bibliography selected to illuminate the concept of Southern oratory. *Landmarks in Western Oratory,* edited by David H. Grover, brings together criticism of the oration of the Plains Indians, the Mormons, Henry Spalding, Thomas Starr King, and Upton Sinclair, among others, and suggests that Western oratory has an indigenous quality of its own.

Preaching in American History: Selected Issues in the American Pulpit, 1630-1967, edited by DeWitte Holland, is a collection of twenty essays which describe and analyze significant issues debated by America's religious leaders, mostly Protestant but including some Roman Catholic and Jewish, over a span of more than three centuries. Much of this important work is devoted to modern preaching and issues that are vital today. A companion volume, *Sermons in American History: Selected Issues in the American Pulpit 1630-1967,* also edited by Holland, presents representative sermons on the major issues covered in the former work. (This collection is annotated under "Anthologies and Reprints" below.) Henry H. Mitchell's *Black Preaching* provides a history of black preaching and insights into the black sermon and the role of the black preacher. Two aspects of contemporary preaching are discussed in the following articles: "Television Evangelism: Milking the Flock," by John Mariani, which describes the awesome scope and power of modern preaching via the media, and "Preaching in a Pop Culture," by Lycurgus M. Starkey, Jr., who suggests that today's preachers use the current idiom of popular culture to reach the masses.

The first history of black oratory in the United States during the twentieth century is Marcus H. Boulware's *The Oratory of Negro Leaders: 1900-1968.* Boulware presents a survey, largely biographical, of prominent black speakers from Booker T. Washington to Martin Luther King, Jr., and includes chapters on public addresses of black women, fraternal oratory, and church and pulpit oratory, as well as radio and television speaking. Although the work is not critical, it offers a vital description of black oratory during the period. The critical study *The Rhetoric of Black Americans,* written by James L. Golden and Richard D. Rieke, explores the role of persuasive black rhetoric in the use of the competing strategies of assimilation, separation, and revolution in achieving the goal of the "good life." Interweaving more than fifty complete texts of addresses, debates, sermons, interviews, essays, and letters from the early period of the struggle to 1970, the work offers a rhetorical analysis by theme. The history and criticism of black oratory is supplemented by two books that offer perspectives and source materials on debate and public address of the 1960s: *The Rhetoric of Black Power,* by Robert L. Scott and Wayne Brockriede, presents public speeches and critical essays on the issues of black power. Included are two different interpretations by Stokely Carmichael, "Stokely Carmichael Explains Black Power to a Black Audience in Detroit" and "Stokely Carmichael Explains Black Power to a White Audience in Whitewater, Wisconsin," in addition to a description of black power by Charles V. Hamilton. *The Black Panthers Speak,* edited by Philip S. Foner, sets forth primary source materials, including official documents of the Panthers and selected essays and speeches of Huey P. Newton, Bobby Seale, Eldridge Cleaver, David Hilliard, Fred Hampton, and some of the Panther women. Foner's work does not offer a critical analysis but serves as an excellent basis for further research in Black Panther rhetoric. A readable study in social and intellectual history that provides background material for an exploration of the contemporary black movement can be found in *Forerunners of Black Power: The Rhetoric of Abolition,* edited by Ernest G. Bormann. The work includes essays in speech criticism and a diverse collection of abolition speeches.

A vast majority of the published work in the history and criticism of debate and public address pertains to famous persons of the past or present, their orations, and the issues they debated, whereas comparatively little has been published in readily accessible form about "unknown" or lesser known speakers and their addresses. *Rhetoric of the People: Is There Any Better or Equal Hope in the World?* edited by Harold Barrett, contains fourteen essays concerning the oral discourse of the ordinary citizen's involvement in public life. These clearly written, analytical essays range from "Every Man His Own Orator: The Impact of the Frontier on American Public Address" to "Student Campaign Speaking for Eugene McCarthy in the Presidential Primary Contest of 1968." J. Jeffery Auer's *The Rhetoric of Our Times* presents forty-two articles, speeches, and analyses dealing with the "gut issues" of the 1960s. Included among the socially relevant topics are: "Student Protests: From Dissent to Defiance?", "The Rhetoric of the Streets: Some Legal and Ethical Considerations," "American Public Address and the Mass Media," and "The Ku Klux Klan Presents Its Case to the Public, 1960." A book also dealing with contemporary rhetorical issues, including chapters on popular arts, music, film, and graffiti, but with an off-beat format and colloquial style, is Irving J. Rein's *Rudy's Red Wagon: Communication Strategies in Contemporary Society.* Rein uses a variety of typographic forms, cartoons, and quotations to produce a highly readable, though loose, strategy to counter the techniques of manipulation in today's communication systems.

Several specialized topical studies contribute to the understanding of American debate and public address and are of general interest. *A History of Speech Education in America: Background Studies,* edited by Karl R. Wallace, is an authoritative examination of the development of rhetoric and speech education in this country, covering a span from Colonial times to the mid-1920s. Included are chapters dealing with the elocutionary movement, the Delsartian tradition, intercollegiate debating, private schools of speech, and the national speech organizations. Lillian O'Connor's *Pioneer Women Orators: Rhetoric in the Ante-Bellum Reform Movement* is a critical study of the women orators of the mid-nineteenth century who crusaded on the issues of slavery, temperance, and women's rights. Although the critical merits of this work are limited, it does provide an historical setting and biographical data for the first women to be recognized from a public platform. *Aboriginal American Oratory: The Tradition of Eloquence among the Indians of the United States,* by Louis Thomas Jones, records fond descriptive appreciation of the inherent eloquence of Indian oratory. The work is interesting, illustrated, and although not a definitive study includes notes and references. *American Demagogues: Twentieth Century,* by Reinhard H. Luthin, discusses the public career of ten "masters of the masses" who lusted for power during the first half of this century. Easily readable essays with extensive bibliographic notes are devoted to such popular leaders as James M. Curley, Frank Hague, Eugene Talmadge, Huey P. Long, and Joseph R. McCarthy, all highly skilled in the art of political oratory.

Finally, the various professional journals offer an excellent source of contemporary scholarship. Two of the most prestigious publications are *Quarterly Journal of Speech* and *Communication Monographs,* both published by the Speech Communication Association. *Quarterly Journal of Speech* offers historical, critical, empirical, and theoretical investigations into all areas of human communication. In addition to the six to eight essays appearing in each issue are critical reviews of books that have been recently published in the various areas of speech. *Communication Monographs* is devoted to all modes of inquiry into communication theory, broadly defined. Periodicals of a similar nature are also published quarterly by each of the four regional divisions of the Speech Communication Association: *Communication Quarterly* (Eastern Communication Association), *Southern Speech Communication Journal* (Southern Speech Communication Association), *Central States Speech Journal* (Central States Speech Association), and *Western Journal of Speech Communication* (Western Speech Communication Association). *Journal of the American Forensic Association,* published quarterly, presents scholarly studies in argumentation, persuasion, discussion, debate, parliamentary speaking, and other types of forensic activities. Annually, the spring issue features a "Bibliography of Argumentation and Debate," and the summer issue includes the final debate of the National Debate Tournament. Other useful publications include *Speaker and Gavel,* a quarterly publication of Delta Sigma Rho-Tau Kappa Alpha, a national honorary forensic society for college students; *Forensic,* a quarterly publication of Pi Kappa Delta, a national honorary fraternal organization also for those involved in collegiate forensic speaking; and *Rostrum,* published monthly by the National Forensic League, an honorary society for high school students. These offer essays, tournament notes, and other articles relating to forensics.

ANTHOLOGIES AND REPRINTS

Anthologies of speeches are numerous and are infinitely organized and categorized. In addition to pure anthologies, some volumes dealing with the history or criticism of public address and some designated primarily as speech textbooks contain noteworthy speeches. Many collections have been published, moreover, of the addresses of an individual well-known speaker, for example, Mark Twain, W. E. B. Du Bois, Robert G. Ingersoll, Adlai E. Stevenson, Robert F. Kennedy, Norman Vincent Peale, Billy Graham, Malcolm X, and Spiro T. Agnew, to name only a few. These are best located by checking the card catalog of any good-sized library, particularly college and university libraries, under the name of the speaker. Some anthologies attempt to give complete and authoritative texts of speeches; others for quite legitimate reasons present edited or abridged versions.

The turn of the century brought several multi-volume anthologies that became standard references and are still highly regarded by scholars and students of oratory. Among them are: David J. Brewer's ten-volume compilation, *The World's Best Orations from the Earliest Period to the Present Time,* which gives prominence to English and American orators. More than 620 speeches delivered by 383 speakers from the time of Pericles to the late nineteenth century are included. The series is arranged alphabetically by orator, for whom a short biographical sketch is given, and is scrupulously indexed in Volume 10. Guy Carleton Lee's ten-volume work, *The World's Orators: Comprising the Great Orations of the World's History with Introductory Essays, Biographical Sketches and Critical Notes,* is exactly what its title implies, the final three volumes dealing exclusively with orators of America. Volume 8 covers the secular oratory of the eighteenth century; Volume 9 presents the classical oratory of the first half of the nineteenth century; and Volume 10 is concerned largely with the period of the Civil War and includes a general index. William Jennings Bryan's *The World's Famous Orations* is also a ten-volume work whose last three volumes are devoted to American oratory. These volumes cover public speaking in America for the years 1774 to 1905; Volume 10 also contains an index to the series.

Ashley H. Thorndike's work of fifteen volumes, *Modern Eloquence: A Library of the World's Best Spoken Thought,* published in 1928, is, indeed, almost a library in itself. The various volumes are devoted to specialized areas: after-dinner speeches, of which more than three hundred are presented; speeches dealing with such commercial and professional interests as banking, economics, railroads, law, medicine, engineering, labor, journalism, theater, ministry, and science; public affairs including citizenship, government, and education; the standard historical masterpieces, one volume being devoted to American history; speeches concerning World War I; plus humorous, inspirational, and scientific lectures. A general index in Volume 15 guides by speaker, speech, occasion, subject, or quotation. A diversified collection of speeches delivered by prominent Americans from the Colonial period to the outbreak of World War II is included in *The World's Great Speeches,* a comprehensive single-volume anthology edited by Lewis Copeland. A section devoted to American industry and government contains speeches by William Green, Fiorello H. LaGuardia, David Sarnoff, and Thomas E. Dewey; a section dealing with national defense presents addresses by Wendell L. Willkie, Cordell Hull, Harold L. Ickes, Norman Thomas, Fulton J. Sheen, Dorothy Thompson, and Henry A. Wallace; and a section of informal speeches includes those of Henry Ward Beecher, Edward Everett Hale, Mark Twain, Irwin S. Cobb, Will Rogers, and John D. Rockefeller, Jr.

Among those sources which are particularly concerned with contemporary oration, the most respected anthology is *Representative American Speeches,* an annual series compiled since 1938 successively by A. Craig Baird and Lester Thonssen, and presently by Waldo W. Braden. Each volume contains about twenty speeches, not necessarily the "best" speeches of each year but rather those most representative. More than eight hundred speeches have been printed to date, as delivered by about five hundred different speakers, many from the political arena, with Franklin D. Roosevelt and Dwight D. Eisenhower being the most frequently represented. A cumulative author index for the years 1937-38 through 1959-60 appears in the 1959-60 volume and for the years 1960-61 through 1969-70 in the 1969-70 volume. The 1978-79 volume contains a cumulative author index for 1970-71. A second highly regarded source of contemporary speeches delivered by leaders from all fields of endeavor on current national questions is the journal *Vital Speeches of the Day.* The texts of eight to ten speeches are impartially selected and presented semimonthly, and the publication is indexed annually in November. A third source of contemporary speeches is the *New York Times*; its *Index* is complete from September 1851 to the present.

Companion anthologies edited by Ernest J. Wrage and Barnet Baskerville, *American Forum: Speeches on Historic Issues, 1788-1900* and *Contemporary Forum: American Speeches on Twentieth-Century Issues*, present an issue-centered history of significantly relevant oration. Each issue is illuminated with speeches representing competing points of view, an historical context, and biographical sketches of the speakers. The first compilation contains twenty-six speeches arranged chronologically in relation to basic historic issues beginning with the speeches of Patrick Henry and James Madison on the ratification of the federal constitution and concluding with the speeches of Albert J. Beveridge and William Jennings Bryan on U.S. imperialism. The thirty-two speeches of the second anthology deal with issues of the twentieth century: the Progressive era, the League of Nations debate, the question of modernism vs. fundamentalism in religion, the polemics of the New Deal, issues in higher education and social change, isolationism, the Cold War, and desegregation. Especially useful are the bibliographical notes indicating supplementary information and other speeches on the topic. Also issue-centered is *Selected American Speeches on Basic Issues (1850-1950)*, edited by Carl G. Brandt and Edward M. Shafter, Jr. Complete texts of nineteen noteworthy public addresses with appropriate background information are presented in three parts: "Time of Civil Strife: Slavery and States' Rights," "The Dawn of the Twentieth Century: American Nationalism and Expansion," and "World Wars I and II: Crises and Controversies."

Several works which have been compiled primarily for use as textbooks also have value as research tools. Glenn R. Capp's *Famous Speeches in American History* contains the eighteen speeches that professors of public address voted the most significant. The speeches range chronologically from Patrick Henry's "Liberty or Death" to John F. Kennedy's "Inaugural Address" and include orations by George Washington, Daniel Webster, Ralph Waldo Emerson, Abraham Lincoln, Henry W. Grady, Booker T. Washington, William Jennings Bryan, Theodore Roosevelt, Woodrow Wilson, Franklin D. Roosevelt, Douglas MacArthur, and Adlai E. Stevenson. *American Speeches*, by Wayland Maxfield Parrish and Marie Hochmuth, presents twenty-eight classic speeches beginning chronologically with Jonathan Edwards's "Sinners in the Hands of an Angry God" and concluding with Franklin D. Roosevelt's "America Has Not Been Disappointed," in addition to an introductory essay on rhetorical criticism and a thorough analysis of Abraham Lincoln's "First Inaugural Address." *Selected Speeches from American History*, edited by Robert T. Oliver and Eugene E. White, presents twenty-two distinguished speeches as case studies in persuasion, ranging form George Whitefield's "Abraham's Offering up His Son Isaac" to Pope Paul VI's "Address at the United Nations." *Contemporary American Speeches: A Sourcebook of Speech Forms and Principles*, edited by Wil A. Linkugel, R. R. Allen, and Richard L. Johannesen, offers forty-one speeches delivered during the 1960s and 1970s. They are an uncommon mixture of the well-known and the little-known, selected to illustrate speech forms and principles and to guide the student in speech analysis. Included are Louis Hausman's "Older Americans: A National Resource," Jimmy Carter's "Fireside Chat: United on U.S. Goals," and Gerald R. Ford's "Republican National Convention Acceptance Speech," as well as nine speeches delivered by college students on such topics as the Chicano movement, mental retardation, and Soviet military superiority over the United States.

John Graham's *Great American Speeches, 1898-1963: Texts and Studies,* presents twenty-four significant speeches beginning with William Jennings Bryan's "Naboth's Vineyard" and concluding with Adlai E. Stevenson's "Eulogy: John Fitzgerald Kennedy." The volume includes headnotes and offers critical studies centering on Franklin D. Roosevelt, Douglas MacArthur, and John F. Kennedy. This anthology is singular in that the complete texts of the speeches are available on Caedmon Records as part of their series of Great American Speeches, with the more recent addresses being the voices of the actual speakers. A thematic collection of interest to the history and criticism of public address is Charles W. Lomas's *The Agitator in American Society,* which presents thirteen representative speeches illustrating the rhetoric of violence, socialism and social reform, civil rights, and anti-communism. Two anthologies dealing with the public address of the 1960s exemplify the rhetoric and illuminate the issues of the period: *The Great Society: A Sourcebook of Speeches,* edited by Glenn R. Capp, traces the evolution and analyzes the basic concept of the Great Society in addition to the specific issues of civil rights, education, and poverty. Twenty speeches are included by such leaders as John F. Kennedy, Lyndon B. Johnson, Hubert H. Humphrey, Dwight D. Eisenhower, George W. Romney, Ronald Reagan, Ralph J. Bunche, Richard M. Nixon, and Sargent Shriver. *In Pursuit of Peace: Speeches of the Sixties,* edited by Donald W. Zacharias, offers an informative introduction and ten key speeches, each with headnotes, paired so as to present opposing points of view in five areas: "Scientists and Politics," "Peace and Security," "Religion and War," "Soldiers and Peace," and "Dissent and Vietnam."

Three paperbound anthologies designed for popular reference and enjoyment are Houston Peterson's *A Treasury of the World's Great Speeches,* George W. Hibbitt's *The Dolphin Book of Speeches,* and Stewart H. Benedict's *Famous American Speeches.* Peterson's collection dates from Biblical times to the mid-1960s and includes for each speech a foreword and an afterword which give details of the speaker, the setting, and the effect of the speech on the audience. Among the speeches are Elizabeth Cady Stanton's keynote address in 1848 to the first women's rights convention as well as the Sacco and Vanzetti claims of innocence in 1927. Hibbitt's collection is also comprehensive in scope, dating from the Greeks to the mid-1960s. Included are Clare Boothe Luce's "American Morality and Nuclear Diplomacy," John H. Glenn, Jr.'s "A New Era," and several eulogies rendered upon the assassination of John F. Kennedy. Benedict's collection, a slim volume of twenty-three classic speeches, includes William Faulkner's "Nobel Prize Speech" and Douglas MacArthur's "Old Soldiers Never Die." Charles Hurd's *A Treasury of Great American Speeches* is also styled for popular taste. A palatable newspaper format presents the "who, what, when, where, and why" as an introduction to each speech. Running a gamut from John Winthrop's "'Liberty is the proper end and object of authority'" to Richard M. Nixon's "'We cannot learn from one another until we stop shouting at one another,'" the anthology contains addresses delivered by almost one hundred speakers, including Alfred E. Smith, Robert C. Benchley, John L. Lewis, George S. Patton, Cornelia Otis Skinner, and Carl Sandburg.

A survey of presidential rhetoric is compiled in two specialized anthologies significant for debaters, speakers, and others interested in a panorama of the American way of life: *The State of the Union Messages of the Presidents, 1790-1966,* edited by Fred L. Israel, and *The President Speaks: The Inaugural Addresses of the American Presidents from Washington to Nixon,* edited by Davis Newton Lott. The individual addresses in Israel's three-volume work are not annotated, but the usefulness of the anthology is enhanced by the inclusion of a comprehensive index of significant events and policy in U.S. history. Similarly, Lott does not attempt to analyze or evaluate the inaugural addresses but does offer for each speech a capsule description of "The President," "The Nation," and "The World," as well as a perspective on the speaking occasion. Lott's work is thus more informative than the anthology published by the U.S. Superintendent of Documents, *Inaugural Addresses of the Presidents of the United States from George Washington 1789 to Richard Milhous Nixon 1973,* which presents the speeches without comment.

Public address from the pulpit has played a significant role in the evolution of American history and culture and has been duly anthologized. A comprehensive anthology encompassing Christian preaching in America from the early period of Jonathan Edwards to the modern era of Billy Graham and Martin Luther King, Jr., can be found in the thirteen volumes of *20 Centuries of Great Preaching: An Encyclopedia of Preaching,* edited by Clyde E. Fant, Jr., and William M. Pinson, Jr. Among other American preachers whose sermons the editors considered relevant to the issues and needs of their day are Lyman Beecher, John Jasper, Henry Ward Beecher, Dwight L. Moody, Sam Jones, Billy Sunday, Rufus Jones, Henry Sloane Coffin, Harry Emerson Fosdick, Fulton J. Sheen, Walter Maier, Norman Vincent Peale, and Peter Marshall. The work includes biographies of the preachers and is thoroughly indexed in Volume 13. *Sermons in American History: Selected Issues in the American Pulpit 1630-1967,* edited by DeWitte Holland, presents brief analyses of twenty selected issues and sermons representing various points of view on these issues. Included are the sermons of noted preachers as well as those not well known, speaking on such topics as "The Ecumenical Movement," "The Thrust of the Radical Right," and "The Pulpit and Race Relations, 1954-1966." (This work is a companion volume to Holland's *Preaching in Amer-*

ican History: Selected Issues in the American Pulpit, 1630-1967, annotated under "History and Criticism" above.) *Outstanding Black Sermons,* edited by J. Alfred Smith, Sr., presents thirteen contemporary sermons relating to the black experience as interpreted by as many preachers. A bimonthly periodical devoted to religious issues, *New Pulpit Digest,* publishes some of the best sermons currently being preached across the United States.

Greater public awareness of minority oratory came with the civil rights issues and the arousing of black consciousness during the past two decades. The most comprehensive of the anthologies devoted exclusively to the black speaker is Philip S. Foner's *The Voice of Black America: Major Speeches by Negroes in the United States, 1797-1971.* Divided into six chronological sections beginning with "The Antebellum Period, 1797-1860" and concluding with "Civil Rights to Black Power, September 1963-1971," Foner presents scores of important speeches, many of which have never appeared in book form, each with a brief historical setting. Among the more contemporary speeches are "The Third World and the Ghetto" by H. Rap Brown, "It's Time for a Change" by Shirley Chisholm, and "The Legacy of George Jackson" by Angela Davis. Other voices include those of Paul Robeson, Langston Hughes, Martin Luther King, Jr., Lorraine Hansberry, Dick Gregory, Malcolm X, Ossie Davis, Adam Clayton Powell, Jr., Kenneth B. Clark, Eldridge Cleaver, Julian Bond, and Huey P. Newton. Not as broad in scope as Foner's work are three anthologies worth noting: *Rhetoric of Racial Revolt,* by Roy L. Hill; *The Negro Speaks: The Rhetoric of Contemporary Black Leaders,* edited by Jamye Coleman Williams and McDonald Williams; and *The Voice of Black Rhetoric: Selections,* edited by Arthur L. Smith and Stephen Robb. Hill's work is a collection of almost fifty speeches dealing with racial relations, the speeches ranging from those of Booker T. Washington to Malcolm X and including those of Elijah Muhammad, Marian Anderson, James Baldwin, Martin Luther King, Jr., Thurgood Marshall, and A. Philip Randolph. The study provides biographical sketches, introductions, commentaries, and some analyses, but these are brief and at random. The Williams's book reprints a cross-section of twenty-three speeches, many of them abridged, beginning with William L. Dawson's "Race Is Not a Limitation" in 1945, and extending chronologically to Edward W. Brooke's "Address to the National Convention of the NAACP" in 1967. Other speakers include Patricia Roberts Harris, Ralph J. Bunche, Carl T. Rowan, Roy Wilkins, Sadie T. M. Alexander, Whitney M. Young, Jr., Constance Baker Motley, Edith S. Sampson, and Howard Thurman. A portrait of each speaker brightens the text. Smith and Robb present an anthology of significant speeches of twenty orators spanning in time from David Walker (1828) to H. Rap Brown (1967). The work includes a well-written introduction, headnotes, and a pertinent bibliography. Two vintage anthologies, historically significant and readily available, are Alice Moore Dunbar's *Masterpieces of Negro Eloquence: The Best Speeches Delivered by the Negro from the Days of Slavery to the Present Time,* published in 1914 on the occasion of the fiftieth anniversary of the Proclamation of Emancipation and reissued in 1970 as part of the Basic Afro-American Reprint Library, and Carter G. Woodson's *Negro Orators and Their Orations,* published in 1925 and reprinted in 1969. Dunbar presents without introduction or commentary the public addresses of forty-nine speakers ranging from Prince Saunders to W. E. B. Du Bois. Woodson's work is wider in scope and includes early protest speeches by such pseudonymous orators as "Othello" and "A Free Negro," as well as "The Negro's First Speech in Congress" by John Willis Menard and orations by Frederick Douglass and Booker T. Washington. A short sketch of each orator is presented and an effort is made to publish the complete unaltered text.

Popular interest in minority oration encompasses a sympathetic understanding of the American Indian. W. C. Vanderwerth's *Indian Oratory: Famous Speeches by Noted Indian Chieftains* offers an interesting, illustrated collection with authoritative headnotes. The speeches range from Teedyuscung's "I Gave the Halloo" in 1758 to Quanah Parker's "Some White People Do That, Too" in 1910. Chief Joseph's "An Indian's Views of Indian Affairs," one of the most widely quoted speeches delivered by an American Indian, is reprinted in full. Four centuries of Indian oratory, arranged chronologically, can be found in *I Have Spoken: American History Through the Voices of the Indians,* compiled by Virginia Irving Armstrong. A total of 251 speeches, parts of speeches, and statements, each with a very brief introduction, together with notes on the original sources of the speeches, are presented in a simple, highly readable format. Both collections include sizable bibliographies of works pertaining to the Indian. These two anthologies offer valuable insight into the events of American history and into the contribution of Indian oratory to the whole of American public address.

NOTES

1. William Norwood Brigance, ed., *A History and Criticism of American Public Address,* 2 vols. (New York: McGraw-Hill, 1943; reprint ed. New York: Russell & Russell, 1960), 1; vii.

2. Patrick Henry, "Liberty or Death," in *American Speeches,* ed. Wayland Maxfield Parrish and Marie Hochmuth (New York: Longmans, Green, 1954), p. 94. Many of the popular speeches from which brief passages are quoted in this essay can be found in more than one of the sources cited below.

3. George Washington, "Farewell Address," in *Famous Speeches in American History,* ed. Glenn R. Capp (Indianapolis: Bobbs-Merrill, 1963), p. 40.

4. Daniel Webster, "Second Speech on Foote's Resolution—Reply to Hayne," in *American Speeches,* ed. Wayland Maxfield Parrish and Marie Hochmuth (New York: Longmans, Green, 1954), p. 229.

5. Booker T. Washington, "Atlanta Exposition Address," in *The Voice of Black America: Major Speeches by Negroes in the United States, 1797-1971,* ed. Philip S. Foner (New York: Simon & Schuster, 1972), p. 582.

6. Abraham Lincoln, "A House Divided," in *American Forum: Speeches on Historic Issues, 1788-1900,* ed. Ernest J. Wrage and Barnet Baskerville (New York: Harper & Brothers, 1960; reprint ed. Seattle: University of Washington Press, 1967), p.180.

7. Abraham Lincoln, "Second Inaugural Address," in *Famous Speeches in American History,* ed. Glenn R. Capp (Indianapolis: Bobbs-Merrill, 1963), p. 94.

8. Franklin D. Roosevelt, "First Inaugural Address," in *Contemporary Forum: American Speeches on Twentieth-Century Issues,* ed. Ernest J. Wrage and Barnet Baskerville (New York: Harper & Brothers, 1962; reprint ed. Seattle: University of Washington Press, 1969), p. 157.

9. Franklin D. Roosevelt, "America's Answer to Japan's Challenge," in *Selected American Speeches on Basic Issues (1850-1950),* ed. Carl G. Brandt and Edward M. Shafter, Jr. (Boston: Houghton Mifflin Riverside Press, 1960), pp. 413, 420.

10. Douglas MacArthur, "American Policy in the Pacific," in *Representative American Speeches: 1951-1952,* Vol. 24, No. 3 of *The Reference Shelf,* ed. A. Craig Baird (New York: H. W. Wilson, 1952), p. 30.

11. There had been a limited television coverage for Harry Truman's inaugural address on January 20, 1949.

12. John F. Kennedy, "Inaugural Address," in *Representative American Speeches: 1960-1961,* Vol. 33, No. 3 of *The Reference Shelf,* ed. Lester Thonssen (New York: H. W. Wilson, 1961), p. 39.

13. Barry M. Goldwater, "Peace Through Strength," in *In Pursuit of Peace: Speeches of the Sixties,* ed. Donald W. Zacharias (New York: Random House, 1970), pp. 82-83.

14. John H. Glenn, Jr., "Address before the Joint Meeting of Congress," in *Representative American Speeches: 1961-1962,* Vol. 34, No. 4 of *The Reference Shelf,* ed. Lester Thonssen (New York: H. W. Wilson, 1962), p. 206.

15. Neil Armstrong, quoted by John Noble Wilford, "Astronauts Land on Plain; Collect Rocks, Plant Flag," *New York Times,* July 21, 1969, p. 1. See also Wernher Von Braun, "The First Men on the Moon," *Encyclopedia Americana,* International Ed., Vol. 25, New York: Americana Corp., 1976, p, 360.

16. Gerald R. Ford, "Bicentennial of American Independence," in *Representative American Speeches: 1976-1977,* Vol. 49, No. 4 of *The Reference Shelf,* ed. Waldo W. Braden (New York: H. W. Wilson, 1977), p. 196.

BIBLIOGRAPHY

BOOKS AND ARTICLES

Adalian, Paul T., Jr., ed. *Speech Communication Abstracts.* Pleasant Hill, Cal.: Theatre/Drama & Speech Communication Information Center, 1974-.

Andrews, James R. *A Choice of Worlds: The Practice and Criticism of Public Discourse.* New York: Harper & Row, 1973.

Arnold, Carroll C. *Criticism of Oral Rhetoric.* Columbus, Ohio: Charles E. Merrill, 1974.

Ash, Lee, comp. *Subject Collections: A Guide to Special Book Collections and Subject Emphases as Reported by University, College, Public, and Special Libraries and Museums in the United States and Canada.* 5th ed. rev. and enl. New York: R. R. Bowker, 1978.

Auer, J. Jeffery, ed. *Anti-Slavery and Disunion, 1858-1861: Studies in the Rhetoric of Compromise and Conflict.* New York: Harper & Row, 1963.

______. *The Rhetoric of Our Times.* New York: Appleton-Century-Crofts, 1969.

Barrett, Harold, ed. *Rhetoric of the People: Is There Any Better or Equal Hope in the World.* Amsterdam: Rodopi N.V., 1974.

Benson, Thomas W., and Michael H. Prosser, eds. *Readings in Classical Rhetoric.* Boston: Allyn and Bacon, 1969.

Bitzer, Lloyd F., and Edwin Black, eds. *The Prospect of Rhetoric: Report of the National Developmental Project.* Englewood Cliffs, N.J.: Prentice-Hall, 1971.

Black, Edwin. *Rhetorical Criticism: A Study in Method.* New York: Macmillan, 1965. Reprint. Madison: University of Wisconsin Press, 1978.

Bormann, Ernest G. *Theory and Research in the Communicative Arts.* New York: Holt, Rinehart and Winston, 1965.

______, ed. *Forerunners of Black Power: The Rhetoric of Abolition.* Englewood Cliffs, N.J.: Prentice-Hall, 1971.

Boulware, Marcus H. *The Oratory of Negro Leaders: 1900-1968.* Foreword by Alex Haley. Westport, Conn.: Negro Universities Press, 1969.

Braden, Waldo W., ed. *Oratory in the Old South: 1828-1860.* Baton Rouge: Louisiana State University Press, 1970.

Braude, Jacob M. *The Complete Art of Public Speaking.* New York: Bantam, 1970.

Brigance, William Norwood, ed. *A History and Criticism of American Public Address.* 2 vols. New York: McGraw-Hill, 1943. Reprint. New York: Russell & Russell, 1960.

Brockett, Oscar G., Samuel L. Becker, and Donald C. Bryant. *A Bibliographical Guide to Research in Speech and Dramatic Art.* Glenview, Ill.: Scott, Foresman, 1963.

Browne, Ray B., ed. *Abstracts of Popular Culture: A Quarterly Publication of International Popular Phenomena.* Bowling Green, Ohio: Bowling Green University Popular Press, 1976-.

Bryant, Donald C. "Rhetoric: Its Function and Its Scope." *Quarterly Journal of Speech,* 39 (December 1953), 401-24.

______. *Rhetorical Dimensions in Criticism.* Baton Rouge: Louisiana State University Press, 1973.

______, ed. *The Rhetorical Idiom: Essays in Rhetoric, Oratory, Language, and Drama Presented to Herbert August Wichelns with a Reprinting of His "Literary Criticism of Oratory" (1925).* Ithaca, N.Y.: Cornell University Press, 1958. Reprint. New York: Russell & Russell, 1966.

Cain, Earl R., ed. *Speech Abstracts.* Vol. 1. Long Beach, Cal.: Department of Speech Communication, California State College-Long Beach, 1970. See Krueger, David H., ed., below.

Campbell, Karlyn Kohrs. *Critiques of Contemporary Rhetoric.* Belmont, Calif.: Wadsworth, 1972.

———, and Kathleen Hall Jamieson, eds. *Form and Genre: Shaping Rhetorical Action.* Falls Church, Va.: Speech Communication Association, 1978.

Carnegie, Dale. *The Quick and Easy Way to Effective Speaking.* Revision by Dorothy Carnegie of *Public Speaking and Influencing Men in Business,* by Dale Carnegie (1962). New York: Pocket Books-Simon & Schuster, 1977.

Cathcart, Robert S. *Post-Communication: Critical Analysis and Evaluation.* Indianapolis: Bobbs-Merrill, 1966.

Cattell, Jaques, Press, ed. *American Library Directory.* 32nd ed. New York: R. R. Bowker, 1979.

Cleary, James W., and Frederick W. Haberman, comps. and eds. *Rhetoric and Public Address: A Bibliography, 1947-1961.* Madison: University of Wisconsin Press, 1964.

Crocker, Lionel. *An Analysis of Lincoln and Douglas as Public Speakers and Debaters.* Springfield, Ill.: Charles C. Thomas, 1968.

———. *Rhetorical Analysis of Speeches.* Boston: Allyn and Bacon, 1967.

Current Index to Journals in Education. Vols. 1-11, No. 2. New York: Macmillan Information, January 1969-February 1979; Vol. 11, No.3-. Phoenix, Ariz.: Oryx Press, March 1979-.

Devlin, L. Patrick. *Contemporary Political Speaking.* Belmont, Calif.: Wadsworth, 1971.

Dissertation Abstracts International: The Humanities and Social Sciences. Ann Arbor, Mich.: University Microfilms International, 1938-.

Drummond, A. M., ed. *Studies in Rhetoric and Public Speaking in Honor of James Albert Winans.* By pupils and colleagues. New York: Century, 1925. Reprint. New York: Russell & Russell, 1962.

Dunlap, Joseph R., and Martin A. Kuhn, comps. *Debate Index Second Supplement.* Vol. 36, No. 3 of *The Reference Shelf.* New York: H. W. Wilson, 1964. See Johnsen, Julia E., comp.; and Phelps, Edith M.,comp., below.

Ehninger, Douglas, and Wayne Brockriede. *Decision by Debate.* 2nd ed. New York: Harper & Row, 1978.

Ehninger, Douglas, Alan H. Monroe, and Bruce E. Gronbeck. *Principles and Types of Speech Communication.* 8th ed. Glenview, Ill.: Scott, Foresman, 1978.

Enos, Richard Leo, and Jeanne L. McClaran, eds. *A Guide to Doctoral Dissertations in Communication Studies and Theater.* Ann Arbor, Mich.: University Microfilms International, 1978.

Eubanks, Ralph T., et al. "A Bibliography of Speech and Theatre in the South for the Year [1954-]." Title varies. *Southern Speech Communication Journal* (formerly *Southern Speech Journal),* Vols. 20- (1955-).

Faules, Don F., Richard D. Rieke, and Jack Rhodes. *Directing Forensics: Contest & Debate Speaking.* 2nd ed. Denver: Morton, 1978.

Foner, Philip S., ed. *The Black Panthers Speak.* Preface by Julian Bond. Philadelphia: Lippincott, 1970.

Freeley, Austin J. *Argumentation and Debate: Rational Decision Making.* 4th ed. Belmont, Calif.: Wadsworth, 1976.

Golden, James L., and Edward P. J. Corbett. *The Rhetoric of Blair, Campbell, and Whately.* New York: Holt, Rinehart and Winston, 1968.

Golden, James L., and Richard D. Rieke. *The Rhetoric of Black Americans.* Columbus, Ohio: Charles E. Merrill, 1971.

Gordon, Thomas F., ed. *Communication Abstracts.* Beverly Hills, Cal.: Sage, 1978-.

Greyer, Read. "An Index to Commercial Spoken Word Recordings in the Library of Congress." *Association for Recorded Sound Collections Journal,* No. 2/3 (1973), 34-73.

Grover, David H., ed. *Landmarks in Western Oratory.* Laramie: University of Wyoming and Western Speech Association, 1968.

Haberman, Frederick W., et al. "A Bibliography of Rhetoric and Public Address for the Year [1947-]." *Quarterly Journal of Speech.* Vols. 34-36 (1948-50); *Communication Monographs* (formerly *Speech Monographs).* Vols. 18-36 (1951-69). Falls Church, Va.: Speech Communication Association, 1948-69.

Hall, Robert N., and Jack L. Rhodes. *Fifty Years of International Debate, 1922-1972.* New York: Speech Communication Association, n.d.

Heckman, Richard Allen. *Lincoln vs. Douglas: The Great Debates Campaign.* Washington, D.C.: Public Affairs Press, 1967.

Hillbruner, Anthony. *Critical Dimensions: The Art of Public Address Criticism.* New York: Random House, 1966.

Hochmuth, Marie Kathryn, ed. *A History and Criticism of American Public Address.* Vol. 3. New York: Longmans, Green, 1955. Reprint. New York: Russell & Russell, 1965.

Holland, DeWitte, ed. *America in Controversy: History of American Public Address.* Dubuque, Iowa: Wm. C. Brown, 1973.

______. *Preaching in American History: Selected Issues in the American Pulpit, 1630-1967.* Nashville, Tenn.: Abingdon Press, 1969.

Howell, J. B., ed. *Special Collections in Libraries of the Southeast.* Introduction by Frances Neel Cheney. Jackson, Miss.: Howick House, 1978.

Howes, Raymond F., ed. *Historical Studies of Rhetoric and Rhetoricians.* Ithaca, N.Y.: Cornell University Press, 1961.

Hunsinger, Paul, Donald R. Terry, and Roy V. Wood. *Managing Forensic Tournaments.* Skokie, Ill.: National Textbook, 1970.

Johannesen, Richard L., ed. *Contemporary Theories of Rhetoric: Selected Readings.* New York: Harper & Row, 1971.

Johnsen, Julia E., comp. *Debate Index Supplement.* Vol. 14, No. 9 of *The Reference Shelf.* New York: H. W. Wilson, 1941. See Dunlap, Joseph R., and Martin A. Kuhn, comps., above; and Phelps, Edith M., comp., below.

Jones, Louis Thomas. *Aboriginal American Oratory: The Tradition of Eloquence Among the Indians of the United States.* Los Angeles: Southwest Museum, 1965.

Kennicott, Patrick C., ed. *Bibliographic Annual in Speech Communication.* Falls Church, Va.: Speech Communication Association, 1973-75.

Klopf, Donald W., and Ronald E. Cambra. *Academic Debate: Practicing Argumentative Theory.* 2nd ed. Denver: Morton, 1979.

Kraus, Sidney, ed. *The Great Debates: Background—Perspective—Effects.* Introduction by Harold D. Lasswell. Bloomington: Indiana University Press, 1962.

Reprint. Gloucester, Mass.: Peter Smith, 1968. Revised ed. *The Great Debates: Kennedy vs. Nixon, 1960.* Bloomington: Indiana University Press, 1977.

Krueger, David H., ed. *Speech Abstracts.* Vols. 2-3. Long Beach, Cal.: Department of Speech Communication, California State College-Long Beach, 1971-72. See Cain, Earl R., ed., above.

Kruger, Arthur N. *Argumentation and Debate: A Classified Bibliography.* 2nd ed. Metuchen, N.J.: Scarecrow Press, 1975.

Langer, Howard J., ed. *Directory of Speakers.* Phoenix, Ariz.: Oryx Press, 1980.

Larson, Barbara A. *Prologue to Revolution: The War Sermons of the Reverend Samuel Davies, A Rhetorical Study.* Bicentennial Monographs. Edited by Robert S. Cathcart. Falls Church, Va.: Speech Communication Association, 1978.

Luthin, Reinhard H. *American Demagogues: Twentieth Century.* Introduction by Allan Nevins. Boston: Beacon Press, 1954. Reprint. Gloucester, Mass.: Peter Smith, 1959.

Mabie, Edward Charles, ed. *University Debaters' Annual: Constructive and Rebuttal Speeches Delivered in Debates of American Colleges and Universities during the College Year.* Vols. 1-2 (1914/15-1915/16). New York: H.W. Wilson, 1915-16. See Phelps, Edith M., ed.; and Ulman, Ruth, ed., below.

Mariani, John. "Television Evangelism: Milking the Flock." *Saturday Review,* February 3, 1979, pp. 22-25.

Matlon, Ronald J., and Irene R. Matlon. *Index to Journals in Communication Studies through 1974.* Falls Church, Va.: Speech Communication Association, 1975.

Miller, Marion Mills, ed. *Great Debates in American History: From the Debates in the British Parliament on the Colonial Stamp Act (1764-1765) to the Debates in Congress at the Close of the Taft Administration (1912-1913).* 14 vols. New York: Current Literature, 1913. Reprint. (3 vols.) Metuchen, N.J.: Mini-Print, 1970.

Mitchell, Charity. *Speech Index: An Index to Collections of World Famous Orations and Speeches for Various Occasions.* 4th ed. supp., 1971-75. Metuchen, N.J.: Scarecrow Press, 1977. See Sutton, Roberta Briggs; and Sutton, Roberta Briggs, and Charity Mitchell, below.

Mitchell, Henry H. *Black Preaching.* Philadelphia: Lippincott, 1970.

Mohrmann, G. P., Charles J. Stewart, and Donovan J. Ochs, eds. *Explorations in Rhetorical Criticism.* University Park: Pennsylvania State University Press, 1973.

Morehead, Joe. *Introduction to United States Public Documents.* 2nd ed. Littleton, Colo.: Libraries Unlimited, 1978.

Mulgrave, Dorothy I., Clark S. Marlor, and Elmer E. Baker, Jr. *Bibliography of Speech and Allied Areas, 1950-1960.* Philadelphia: Chilton, 1962. Reprint. Westport, Conn.: Greenwood Press, 1972.

New York Times Index. New York: New York Times, 1851-.

Newsome, Walter L. *New Guide to Popular Government Publications.* Littleton, Colo.: Libraries Unlimited, 1978.

Nichols, Egbert Ray, ed. *Intercollegiate Debates.* Subtitle varies. Vols. 2-22. New York: Noble and Noble, 1910-41. See Pearson, Paul M., ed., below.

Nixon, Richard M. *Six Crises.* New York: Doubleday, 1962.

O'Connor, Lillian. *Pioneer Women Orators: Rhetoric in the Ante-Bellum Reform Movement.* New York: Columbia University Press, 1954.

Oliver, Robert T. *History of Public Speaking in America.* Boston: Allyn and Bacon, 1965. Reprint. Westport, Conn.: Greenwood Press, 1978.

Pearson, Paul M., ed. *Intercollegiate Debates: Being Briefs and Reports of Many Intercollegiate Debates.* Vol. 1. New York: Hinds, Hayden & Eldredge, 1909. See Nichols, Egbert Ray, ed., above.

Phelps, Edith M., comp. *Debate Index.* Rev. ed. Vol 12, No. 9 of *The Reference Shelf.* New York: H. W. Wilson, 1939. See Dunlap, Joseph R., and Martin A. Kuhn, comps.; and Johnsen, Julia E., comp., above.

______, ed. *University Debaters' Annual: Constructive and Rebuttal Speeches Delivered in Debates of American Colleges and Universities during the College Year.* Vols. 3-33 (1916/17-1946-47). New York: H. W. Wilson, 1917-47. See Mabie, Edward Charles, ed., above; and Ulman, Ruth, ed., below.

Prochnow, Herbert V., and Herbert V. Prochnow, Jr. *The Public Speaker's Treasure Chest: A Compendium of Source Material to Make Your Speech Sparkle.* 3rd ed. rev. and enl. New York: Harper & Row, 1977.

______. *The Toastmaster's Treasure Chest.* New York: Harper & Row, 1979.

Reid, Loren, ed. *American Public Address: Studies in Honor of Albert Craig Baird.* Columbia: University of Missouri Press, 1961.

Reid, Ronald F. *The American Revolution and the Rhetoric of History.* Bicentennial Monographs. Edited by Robert S. Cathcart. Falls Church, Va.: Speech Communication Association, 1978.

Rein, Irving J. *Rudy's Red Wagon: Communication Strategies in Contemporary Society.* Glenview, Ill.: Scott, Foresman, 1972.

Ritter, Kurt W., and James R. Andrews. *The American Ideology: Reflections of the Revolution in American Rhetoric.* Bicentennial Monographs. Edited by Robert S. Cathcart. Falls Church, Va.: Speech Communication Association, 1978.

Roach, Helen. *Spoken Records.* 3rd ed. Metuchen, N.J.: Scarecrow Press, 1970.

Ross, Raymond S. *Speech Communication: Fundamentals and Practice.* 5th ed. Englewood Cliffs, N.J.: Prentice-Hall, 1980.

Sarnoff, Dorothy. *Speech Can Change Your Life: Tips on Speech, Conversation and Speechmaking.* New York: Dell-Doubleday, 1972.

Schmeckebier, Laurence F., and Roy B. Eastin. *Government Publications and Their Use.* 2nd rev. ed. Washington, D.C.: Brookings Institution, 1969.

Scott, Robert L., and Bernard L. Brock. *Methods of Rhetorical Criticism: A Twentieth-Century Perspective.* New York: Harper & Row, 1972.

Scott, Robert L., and Wayne Brockriede. *The Rhetoric of Black Power.* New York: Harper & Row, 1969.

Shaw, Warren Choate. *History of American Oratory.* Indianapolis: Bobbs-Merrill, 1928.

Shearer, Ned A., ed. *Bibliographic Annual in Speech Communication.* Falls Church, Va: Speech Communication Association, 1970-72.

Speech Communication Directory, [1935-] (formerly *Speech Communication Association Directory* and *Speech Association of America Directory).* Annandale, Va.: Speech Communication Association, 1935-.

Starkey, Lycurgus M., Jr. "Preaching in a Pop Culture." *Religion in Life,* 41 (Summer 1972), 196-204.

Stone, Janet, and Jane Bachner. *Speaking Up: A Book for Every Woman Who Wants to Speak Effectively.* New York: McGraw-Hill, 1978.

Sutton, Roberta Briggs. *Speech Index: An Index to 259 Collections of World Famous Orations and Speeches for Various Occasions.* 4th ed. rev. and enl. New York: Scarecrow Press, 1966. See Mitchell, Charity, above; and Sutton, Roberta Briggs, and Charity Mitchell, below.

———, and Charity Mitchell. *Speech Index: An Index to Collections of World Famous Orations and Speeches for Various Occasions.* 4th ed. supp., 1966-70. Metuchen, N.J.: Scarecrow Press, 1972. See Mitchell, Charity and Sutton, Roberta Briggs, above.

Tandberg, Gerilyn. *Research Guide in Speech.* Morristown, N.J.: General Learning Press, 1974.

Television News Index and Abstracts: A Guide to the Videotape Collection of the Network Evening News Programs in the Vanderbilt Television News Archive. Nashville, Tenn.: Joint Universities Libraries, 1974-.

Terry, Donald R., ed. *Modern Debate Case Techniques.* Skokie, Ill.: National Textbook, 1970.

Thesaurus of ERIC Descriptors. 7th ed. New York: Macmillan, 1977.

Thonssen, Lester, A. Craig Baird, and Waldo W. Braden. *Speech Criticism.* 2nd ed. New York: Ronald Press, 1970.

Thonssen, Lester, and Elizabeth Fatherson, comps. *Bibliography of Speech Education.* New York: H. W. Wilson, 1939.

Thonssen, Lester, Mary Margaret Robb, and Dorothea Thonssen, comps. *Bibliography of Speech Education. Supplement: 1939-1948.* New York: H. W. Wilson, 1950.

Ulman, Ruth, ed. *University Debaters' Annual: Reports of Debates and Other Forensic Activities of American Colleges and Universities during the Academic Year.* Vols. 34-37 (1947/48-1950/51). New York: H. W. Wilson, 1948-51. See Mabie, Edward Charles, ed.; and Phelps, Edith M., ed., above.

U.S. Congress. *Annals of Congress.* 1st-18th Cong., lst sess.,1789-1824. Washington, D.C.: Gales and Seaton, 1834-56.

———. *Congressional Globe.* 23rd-42nd Cong., 1833-1873. Washington, D.C.: Globe Office, 1834-73.

———. *Congressional Record: Containing the Proceedings and Debates of the 43rd- Congress 1873-.* Washington, D.C.: Government Printing Office, 1874, and subsequent years.

———. *Register of Debates.* 18th Cong., 2nd sess. 25th Cong., 1st sess., 1824-1837. Washington, D.C.: Gales and Seaton, 1825-37.

———. House. Committee on House Administration. *The Presidential Campaign 1976.* 3 vols. Washington, D.C.: Government Printing Office, 1978.

U.S. Department of Education. National Institute of Education. *Resources in Education.* Washington, D.C.: Government Printing Office, 1966-.

U.S. Department of State. Bureau of Public Affairs. *Department of State Bulletin.* Washington, D.C.: Government Printing Office, 1939-.

U.S. General Services Administration. *Public Papers of the Presidents of the United States.* Washington, D.C.: Government Printing Office, 1945-.

______. *Weekly Compilation of Presidential Documents.* Washington, D.C.: Government Printing Office, 1965-.

U.S. Library of Congress. *National Union Catalogue of Manuscript Collections.* Washington, D.C.: Library of Congress, 1962-.

U.S. National Archives and Records Service. *Sound Recordings in the Audiovisual Archives Division of the National Archives: Preliminary Draft Prepared for the National Archives Conference on the Use of Audiovisual Archives as Original Source Materials.* Ed. Mayfield S. Bray and Leslie C. Waffen. GSA DC 76-11829. Washington, D.C., 1972.

U.S. Superintendent of Documents. *Publications Relating to the 1975-76 College Debate Topic.* Subject Bibliography 176. Washington, D.C.: Government Printing Office, 1975, and subsequent years.

______. *Publications Relating to the 1975-76 National High School Debate Topic.* Subject Bibliography 043. Washington, D.C.: Government Printing Office, 1975, and subsequent years.

Uris, Dorothy. *A Woman's Voice: A Handbook to Successful Private and Public Speaking.* New York: Stein and Day, 1975.

Wallace, Karl R., ed. *History of Speech Education in America: Background Studies.* New York: Appleton-Century-Crofts, 1954.

Wasserman, Paul, ed. *Speakers and Lecturers: How to Find Them. A Directory of Booking Agents, Lecture Bureaus, Companies, Professional and Trade Associations, Universities, and Other Groups Which Organize and Schedule Engagements for Lecturers and Public Speakers on All Subjects, with Details about Speakers, Subjects, and Arrangements.* Detroit: Gale Research, 1979.

Wichelns, Herbert A. "The Literary Criticism of Oratory." In *Studies in Rhetoric and Public Speaking in Honor of James Albert Winans.* By pupils and colleagues. Ed. A. M. Drummond. New York: Century, 1925, pp. 181-216. Reprint. New York: Russell & Russell, 1962. In *The Rhetorical Idiom: Essays in Rhetoric, Oratory, Language, and Drama Presented to Herbert August Wichelns with a Reprinting of His "Literary Criticism of Oratory" (1925).* Edited by Donald C. Bryant. Ithaca, N.Y.: Cornell University Press, 1958, pp. 5-42. Reprint. New York: Russell & Russell, 1966. Also in *Methods of Rhetorical Criticism: A Twentieth-Century Perspective.* By Robert L. Scott and Bernard L. Brock. New York: Harper & Row, 1972, pp. 27-60.

Wilson, John F., and Caroll C. Arnold. *Public Speaking as a Liberal Art.* 4th ed. Boston: Allyn and Bacon, 1978.

Windes, Russel R., and Arthur N. Kruger, eds. *Championship Debating—West Point National Debate Tournament Final-Round Debates and Critiques, 1949-60.* Portland, Me.: J. Weston Walch, 1961.

______. *Championship Debating.* Vol. 2 (1961-66). Portland, Me.: J. Weston Walch, 1967.

Wrage, Ernest J. "Public Address: A Study in Social and Intellectual History." *Quarterly Journal of Speech,* 33 (December 1947), 451-57. Reprinted in Robert L. Scott and Bernard L. Brock, *Methods of Rhetorical Criticism: A Twentieth-Century Perspective.* New York: Harper & Row, 1972, pp. 103-11.

Young, Margaret L., and Harold C. Young, eds. *Directory of Special Libraries and Information Centers: A Guide to Special Libraries, Information Centers, Archives, and Data Centers Maintained by Government Agencies, Business, Industry, Newspapers, Educational Institutions, Nonprofit Organizations, and Societies in the Fields of Science, Technology, Medicine, Law, Art, Religion, History, Social Sciences, and Humanistic Studies.* 5th ed. 3 vols. Detroit: Gale Research, 1979.

ANTHOLOGIES AND REPRINTS

Armstrong, Virginia Irving, comp. *I Have Spoken: American History Through the Voices of the Indians.* Introduction by Frederick W. Turner, III. Chicago: Sage Books/Swallow Press, 1971.

Baird, A. Craig, ed. *Representative American Speeches.* Vols. 11-31 (1937/38-1958/59) of *The Reference Shelf.* New York: H. W. Wilson, 1938-59. See Braden, Waldo W., ed; and Thonssen, Lester, ed., below.

Benedict, Stewart, H., ed. *Famous American Speeches.* New York: Laurel-Dell, 1967.

Braden, Waldo W., ed. *Representative American Speeches.* Vols. 43- (1970/71-) of *The Reference Shelf.* New York: H. W. Wilson, 1971-. See Baird, A. Craig, ed., above; and Thonssen, Lester, ed., below.

Brandt, Carl G., and Edward M. Shafter, Jr., eds. *Selected American Speeches on Basic Issues (1850-1950).* Boston: Houghton Mifflin/Riverside Press, 1960.

Brewer, David J., ed. *The World's Best Orations from the Earliest Period to the Present Time.* 10 vols. St. Louis: Ferd. P. Kaiser, 1900; reprint ed. (2 vols.) Metuchen, N.J.: Scarecrow Press, 1970.

Bryan, William Jennings, ed. *The World's Famous Orations.* Vols. 8-10. New York: Funk and Wagnalls, 1906.

Capp, Glenn R. *Famous Speeches in American History.* Indianapolis: Bobbs-Merrill, 1963.

———,ed. *The Great Society: A Sourcebook of Speeches.* Belmont, Calif.: Dickenson, 1967.

Copeland, Lewis, ed. *The World's Great Speeches.* Garden City, N.Y.: Garden City Publishing, 1942.

Dunbar, Alice Moore, ed. *Masterpieces of Negro Eloquence: The Best Speeches Delivered by the Negro from the Days of Slavery to the Present Time.* New York: Bookery, 1914; reprint ed. New York: Johnson Reprint, 1970.

Fant, Clyde E., Jr., and William M. Pinson, Jr., eds. *20 Centuries of Great Preaching: An Encyclopedia of Preaching.* 13 vols. Waco, Tex.: Word Books, 1971.

Foner, Philip S., ed. *The Voice of Black America: Major Speeches by Negroes in the United States, 1797-1971.* New York: Simon & Schuster, 1972. Reprint (2 vols.) New York: Capricorn Books, 1975.

Graham, John, ed. *Great American Speeches, 1898-1963: Texts and Studies.* New York: Appleton-Century-Crofts, 1970.

Hibbitt, George W., ed. *The Dolphin Book of Speeches.* Garden City, N.Y.: Dolphin-Doubleday, 1965.

Hill, Roy L. *Rhetoric of Racial Revolt.* Denver: Golden Bell Press, 1964.

Holland, DeWitte, ed. *Sermons in American History: Selected Issues in the American Pulpit 1630-1967.* Nashville, Tenn.: Abingdon Press, 1971.

Hurd, Charles, comp. *A Treasury of Great American Speeches.* New and revised edition by Andrew Bauer. New York: Hawthorn Books, 1970.

Israel, Fred L., ed. *The State of the Union Messages of the Presidents, 1790-1966.* Introduction by Arthur M. Schlesinger. 3 vols. New York: Bowker and Chelsea House, 1967.

Lee, Guy Carleton, ed. *The World's Orators: Comprising the Great Orations of the World's History with Introductory Essays, Biographical Sketches and Critical Notes.* Vols. 8-10. New York: Putnam's/Knickerbocker Press, 1900-1901.

Linkugel, Wil A., R. R. Allen, and Richard L. Johannesen. *Contemporary American Speeches: A Sourcebook of Speech Forms and Principles.* 4th ed. Dubuque, Iowa: Kendall/Hunt, 1978.

Lomas, Charles W. *The Agitator in American Society.* Englewood Cliffs, N.J.: Prentice-Hall, 1968.

Lott, Davis Newton, ed. *The President Speaks: The Inaugural Addresses of the American Presidents from Washington to Nixon.* 3rd ed. New York: Holt, Rinehart and Winston, 1969.

Oliver, Robert T., and Eugene E. White, eds. *Selected Speeches from American History.* Boston: Allyn and Bacon, 1966.

Parrish, Wayland Maxfield, and Marie Hochmuth, eds. *American Speeches.* New York: Longmans, Green, 1954.

Peterson, Houston, ed. *A Treasury of the World's Great Speeches.* Rev. and enl. ed. New York: Fireside-Simon & Schuster, 1965.

Smith, Arthur L., and Stephen Robb, eds. *The Voice of Black Rhetoric: Selections.* Boston: Allyn and Bacon, 1971.

Smith, J. Alfred, Sr., ed. *Outstanding Black Sermons.* Valley Forge, Pa.: Judson Press, 1976.

Thonssen, Lester, ed. *Representative American Speeches.* Vols. 32-42 (1959/60-1969/70) of *The Reference Shelf.* New York: H. W. Wilson, 1960-70. See Baird, A. Craig, ed.; and Braden, Waldo W., ed., above.

Thorndike, Ashley H., ed. *Modern Eloquence: A Library of the World's Best Spoken Thought.* 15 vols. New York: Modern Eloquence, 1928.

U.S. Superintendent of Documents. *Inaugural Addresses of the Presidents of the United States from George Washington 1789 to Richard Milhous Nixon 1973.* Washington, D.C.: Government Printing Office, 1974.

Vanderwerth, W. C. *Indian Oratory: Famous Speeches by Noted Indian Chieftains.* Foreword by William R. Carmack. Norman: University of Oklahoma Press, 1971.

Williams, Jamye Coleman, and McDonald Williams, eds. *The Negro Speaks: The Rhetoric of Contemporary Black Leaders.* New York: Noble and Noble, 1970.

Woodson, Carter G., ed. *Negro Orators and Their Orations.* Washington, D.C.: Associated, 1925. Reprint. New York: Russell & Russell, 1969.

Wrage, Ernest J., and Barnet Baskerville, eds. *American Forum: Speeches on Historic Issues, 1788-1900.* New York: Harper & Brothers, 1960. Reprint. Seattle: University of Washington Press, 1967.

———. *Contemporary Forum: American Speeches on Twentieth-Century Issues.*

New York: Harper & Brothers, 1962. Reprint. Seattle: University of Washington Press, 1969.

Zacharias, Donald W., ed. *In Pursuit of Peace: Speeches of the Sixties.* New York: Random House, 1970.

PERIODICALS

Association for Recorded Sound Collections Journal. Manassas, Va., 1968-.

Central States Speech Journal. Kent, Ohio, 1949-.

Communication Monographs (formerly *Speech Monographs*). Annandale, Va., 1934-

Communication Quarterly (formerly *Today's Speech*). Philadelphia, Penn., 1953-.

Forensic. Tacoma, Wash., 1915-.

Journal of the American Forensic Association (formerly *The Register*). Evanston, Ill., 1964-.

New Pulpit Digest (merger of *Pulpit Digest* and *Pulpit Preaching*). Jackson, Miss., 1972-.

Quarterly Journal of Speech (formerly *Quarterly Journal of Speech Education* and *Quarterly Journal of Public Speaking*). Annandale, Va., 1915-.

Rostrum (formerly *Bulletin*). Ripon, Wisc., 1934.-

Southern Speech Communication Journal (formerly *Southern Speech Journal*). Pensacola, Fla., 1935-.

Speaker and Gavel (merger of *Speaker* and *Gavel*). Lawrence, Kans., 1963-.

Vital Speeches of the Day. Southold, N.Y., 1934-.

Western Journal of Speech Communication (formerly *Western Speech Journal*). Albuquerque, N.M.,1937.

CHAPTER 3 Illustration

James J. Best

Popular illustration refers to artwork intentionally designed for mass consumption by means of reproduction on paper, that is, magazine and book illustrations and posters. The job of the illustrator is to create images that can be used in whole or in part to tell stories and recreate events in ways that are intelligible to a mass audience. Unlike the easel artist, who has few constraints on how, what, when, or why he or she paints, the illustrator is constrained by the subject matter he is illustrating, the way the illustration will be reproduced, the audience for the illustration, the art editor for whom he is working, and the publication deadlines.

To the extent that illustrators have been successful in their task, the vehicles for their illustrations—illustrated magazines, books, and posters—become art galleries for the mass public. In the days before television, before radio, even before photography, illustrations had an enormous impact on society and culture in America. During the Golden Age of American illustration (1890-1915) U.S. illustrators were far better known to the public than their contemporaries in the fine arts; far more people saw Howard Pyle illustrations on the pages of *Harper's* than saw the Armory exhibit in New York City, and Charles Dana Gibson's "Gibson Girls" had a profound impact on beauty and styling at the turn of the century.

Popular illustration requires a literate public, the technology for inexpensive reproduction of artwork, and the means for inexpensive distribution to the public. Because of these constraints, the content, techniques, and vehicles for public illustration have varied through time. As popular tastes have changed so have the popularity of various illustrators and sources of illustrations. The historical outline which follows will chart many of those changes.

Unfortunately, popular illustration has not been the subject of extensive or intensive scholarly research. A resurgence of interest in illustration—signalled by an increasing number of museum exhibits, new books dealing with various American illustrators, and the republication of a number of illustrated "classics"—may give legitimacy and interest to the study of popular illustration, past and present. To the extent that popular illustration is artwork for a mass public, it is important that we understand its content and style. Several of the sections that follow contain discussions of the major written works, scholarly research reports, and various research sites for the study of popular illustration.

It should be noted that several topics are not covered in this review. There is very little discussion of etchings and chromolithographs from the last century or of movie posters and other genre posters.

HISTORICAL OUTLINE

The history of popular illustration in the United States dates from the eighteenth century, but illustrations were not widely used until the Civil War, when technological developments and popular demand resulted in an enormous growth in their use. As with many American cultural phenomena, the roots of popular illustration can be traced to England, where illustrations by Thomas Rowlandson, William Blake, and Thomas Bewick were popular and were soon "copied" (frequently without attribution) by American engravers. Alexander Anderson was the first American to achieve stature as a "native" American illustrator, but F. O. C. Darley was the first illustrator of importance whose work was widely recognized—to the extent that he received credit on the title page and covers of books which he illustrated. During the period 1840-60 Darley dominated the field of American illustration, illustrating works by Washington Irving, *The Sketch Book of Geoffrey Crayon, Esq.* (1848), *A History of New York* (1850), *The Alhambra* (1851), and *The Life of George Washington* (1855-59); Francis Parkman, *The California and Oregon Trail* (1849); James Fenimore Cooper (thirty-two volumes published between 1859 and 1861); as well as a number of volumes of *The Library of Humorous American Works* (1846-69). His illustrations were distinctly "American," unpretentious, frontier-oriented, and humorous in an earthy way; they appealed to readers who recognized themselves and their fellow men in the pictures Darley created, pictures which were both familiar and "real."

The Civil War and an increasingly literate public created a demand for comprehensive coverage of Civil War battle action, in both words and pictures. *Harper's Weekly* and *Leslie's Illustrated Weekly* dispatched reporters and artists to cover major battles, and readers saw pictures of battles within weeks of their occurrence. Battlefield illustrators did rough sketches which were dispatched to New York, where engravers, frequently using their imaginations to fill in the voids, translated the rough sketches into front-page visual images. So successful was *Harper's Weekly* that its press run at the peak of the Civil War reached 250,000 copies, and its Civil War issues represent a vivid pictorial history of the period. The best of the war illustrations can be seen in commemorative volumes published by the two weeklies, *Harper's Illustrated History of the Civil War* (1895) and *Frank Leslie's Illustrated History of the Civil War* (1895), which feature illustrations by the leading war illustrators William and Alfred Waud, Thomas Nast, and Winslow Homer.

The success of *Harper's Weekly* led the House of Harper to expand its use of illustrations in its monthly magazine, *Harper's Monthly,* its children's magazine, *Harper's Young People,* and in its books. Under the direction of art editor Charles Parsons, *Harper's Monthly* recruited a staff of illustrators—most notably Edwin Abbey, A. B. Frost, Alfred Kemble, and Howard Pyle—who became leading figures in the Golden Age of American illustration. As the circulation of *Harper's* increased, two other monthlies, *Century* and *Scribner's,* entered the field of high-quality illustrated magazines. These three magazines dominated the field of magazine illustration from 1890 to 1915, and an illustrator whose work was published in any of these three was a "recognized" illustrator.

Although magazine illustration provided the most fruitful field for illustrators, book illustration was also attractive. Book illustration frequently paid more, meant more work on a particular topic, and allowed greater artistic freedom as to which scenes to illustrate. Not all of the leading magazine illustrators were also successful as book illustrators; only a handful achieved recognition in both fields. Most notable among this select group were Howard Pyle, N. C. Wyeth, Howard Chandler Christy, Charles Dana Gibson, Elizabeth Shippen Green, Jessie Wilcox Smith, and Maxfield Parrish.

Preeminent among this group of illustrators was Howard Pyle. Pyle received recognition for his early book illustrations in *Robin Hood* (1883), *Pepper and Salt* (1886), *The Wonder Clock* (1888) and *Otto of the Silver Hand* (1888), as well as his black-and-white line drawings, half-tones, and color illustrations for *Harper's Monthly.* More important, Pyle established the first school for the training of illustrators, and his success as a teacher was reflected in the work of his students. N. C. Wyeth, Frank Schoonover, Maxfield Parrish, Elizabeth Shippen Green, and Thornton Oakley were among his students at Chadds Ford, Pennsylvania, and in Wilmington, Delaware, and their artwork appeared in all the major illustrated magazines of the day. Pyle's emphasis on capturing the essence of the action in a story, on involving the reading in the illustration, and on historical accuracy, resulted in illustrations that were stylistically and substantively different from those of their contemporaries. One has only to contrast the women portrayed by Elizabeth Shippen Green and Jessie Wilcox Smith with the Gibson and Christy "American beauties."

At the same time a tradition of Western or "cowboy" illustration was developing, led by Frederic Remington and Charles Russell, a tradition continued by Will James and Harold Von Schmidt. Quite frequently it was part of an illustrator's training to get into the "real" world: N. C. Wyeth went to the still-Wild West of 1904, and Frank Schoonover spent almost two years in the back country of Canada. These experiences provided both illustrators with enough material for a continuing series of commissions for illustrations.

The Golden Age of American illustration was far more reflective of American society than it was of European illustration. Pyle and his students, with their emphasis on romantic realism, and Christy, Gibson, and James Montgomery Flagg, with their idealization of the American woman, are quite different in content and style from the leading English illustrators of the period, who were illustrating fantasy worlds of fairies and elves (Arthur Rackham, Edmund Dulac, and W. Heath Robinson) or introducing Art Nouveau to the world (Aubrey Beardsley and Kay Nielsen). Rackhams's illustrations for *Alice's Adventures in Wonderland* (1907), *Poe's Tales of Mystery and Imagination* (1935), and *Peter Pan in Kensington Garden* (1906); Dulac's illustrations for *Tanglewood Tales* (1918) and *Stories From the Arabian Nights* (1907); W. Heath Robinson's black-and-white illustrations from *Shakespeare's Comedy of a Midsummer Night's Dream* (1914); Beardsley's line drawings for *The Rape of the Lock* (1896); and Kay Nielsen's color work for *East of the Sun and West of the Moon* (1922) are decidedly different from those of their American contemporaries. The most popular American illustrators at the turn of the century were the romantic realists, primarily concerned with accurately depicting the historical past, which their readers had never seen, or idealizing the present, to which their readers could aspire. Even the fantasy illustrations of W. W. Denslow in the most popular children's book of the period, *The Wonderful Wizard of Oz* (1900), placed a very real girl from Kansas in the company of a scarecrow, a lion, and a tin woodsman. And Dorothy is certainly different from the children who decorate the pages of Kate Greenaway's *Under the Willows* (1879) and *The Pied Piper of Hamlin* (1888), the most popular English children's books of the time.

In one area of popular illustration—poster art—American illustrators copied the styles and techniques of their European counterparts. The modern poster dates to France in the 1870s and 1880s, where Chéret and Toulouse-Lautrec created a new form of popular illustration. British poster art developed differently from the French. French posters were gay and colorful, but the poster artists sought to make their figures three-dimensional, whereas British poster artists, influenced by Japanese block prints, made extensive use of large masses and solid colors. As a result Chéret's posters are quite different from those of John Hassall, Dudley Hardy, and the Beggarstaffs. Aubrey Beardsley combined elements of both styles into the development of Art Nouveau, and he was instrumental in introducing it to the United States. The most prominent American poster artists prior to World War I were Will Bradley, Edward Penfield, and Maxfield Parrish. Penfield and

Parrish moved easily between magazine and book illustration and poster art; Penfield's posters for *Harper's* are strikingly similar to his magazine illustrations, whereas Parrish used the same asexual adolescent in his prize-winning *Century* poster and the frontispiece for *Poems of Childhood* (1904). Will Bradley, on the other hand, worked mainly in poster art and magazine covers, and it is in Bradley's work that one can see most clearly the impact of the European Art Nouveau tradition.

World War I had a major impact on American illustration. A number of illustrators, under the auspices of the Society of Illustrators (founded in 1901), devoted their very considerable energies to creating war posters for the government. Howard Chandler Christy, C. B. Falls, James Montgomery Flagg, J. C. Leyendecker, Joseph Pennell, Coles Phillips, and Harrison Fisher (to name but a few) lent their talents to promoting war bond drives, raising money for the Red Cross, recruiting volunteers for the armed services, and publicizing German atrocities. James Montgomery Flagg's poster of himself in a top hat and cutaway jacket in red, white, and blue, "Uncle Sam Wants You," created an image which persists to the present.

But World War I marked the end of the Golden Age of American illustration, signalling a change in the demand for and use of illustrations. Never again were posters as popular as an advertising medium. The nature of magazine illustration also changed. Whereas the first decade of the century saw *Century, Harper's,* and *Scribner's* as the leading illustrated magazines, by the 1930s these three had been replaced by the *Saturday Evening Post, Collier's, Cosmopolitan, Woman's Home Companion, Redbook, Ladies' Home Journal,* and *American,* general mass market or women's magazines, which published the greatest number of illustrations. Color illustrations appeared only as covers, so that doing a cover for the *Saturday Evening Post* was not only lucrative but also a sign of recognition. Because of the shift in the market for illustrations, very few magazine illustrators who were popular before World War I retained their popularity into the 1930s. Charles Dana Gibson's "Gibson Girl" looked out of place on the pages of *Life* in the early 1930s. Two of the most prominent illustrators who made the transition were Norman Rockwell, whose covers for the *Saturday Evening Post* over forty years display an amazing ability to change content and style to keep pace with a changing society, and J. C. Leyendecker, whose idealized men were the 1930s equivalents of the Gibson Girls, which made them outmoded by the 1940s, when Leyendecker's popularity waned. During their careers Leyendecker and Rockwell each completed more than three hundred *Post* covers.

With the decline in the number and quality of illustrated magazines, many illustrators shifted their energies to new markets. The "pulps" were one. In the twenty years following World War I, cheap specialized magazines proliferated, offering escapist reading at low cost, and this market created an increasing demand for illustrators who could work quickly and whose covers would attract newsstand readers. Although this was not as prestigious as doing covers for the *Post,* it did provide a livelihood for many illustrators.

The nature of book illustration also changed after World War I. The economics of publishing dictated that book illustrations be done in black and white and, ideally, on the same paper stock as the text. As a result, line drawings and black-and-white illustrations returned, and full-page color plates printed on slick paper virtually disappeared. Several new illustrators handled this genre well, notably Rockwell Kent and Lynd Ward. Kent's *Salamina* (1934) and *N by E* (1930), as well as Ward's *Mad Man's Drum* (1930) and *Song Without Words* (1936) are striking in their use of black-and-white figures against stark contrasting backgrounds. Lynd Ward's work represents a major breakthrough in book illustration; borrowing from the Belgian, Frans Masereel, Ward created "books without words," where illustrations carried the entire burden of conveying the textual message to the reader.

With the changing market for illustrations, many illustrators moved into other areas of illustration. Two of the most popular were advertising art and children's books. A number of illustrators who had achieved success prior to World War I found themselves doing more advertising work after the war; Frank Schoonover adapted some of his Western illustrations for Colt Firearms, Maxfield Parrish did advertisements for Jello, N. C. Wyeth did calendar art for Mazda-Edison, and Coles Phillips used his "fadeaway" illustrations to sell silverware and lingerie. Perhaps the most successful advertising illustrator in the 1930s was J. C. Leyendecker, whose Arrow Shirt advertisements were instantly recognizable.

Children's books became an even larger market for illustration than before, and a new generation of illustrators emerged in which no one figure or "school" dominated, as Howard Pyle and his students had at the beginning of the century. They were replaced in the 1920s and 1930s by Johnny Gruelle and his Raggedy Ann and Andy books, Jean de Brunhoff's Babar the Elephant series, Ernest Sheppard and his illustrations for the Winnie-the-Pooh series, the Dr. Seuss series, and illustrated books based on Disney movies, as well as books illustrated by Ludwig Bemelmans, Wanda Gag, Willy Pogany, Helen Sewell, and Morris Artzybasheff.

During World War II poster art re-emerged as a major form of popular illustration, although it never achieved the importance and status—nor the artistic impact—of its earlier counterparts. During World War II the government had other, more efficient media for mobilizing the citizenry, namely, movies and radio. As a consequence the number of posters printed by the government was comparatively low, and the quality of poster art was not particularly high. In a somewhat crude but probably effective way, posters warned Americans that "Loose Lips Sink Ships."

The period since World War II has seen some fundamental changes in the content and form of popular illustration. Children's books have retained their importance as sources of illustrations, and much of the most creative illustrations are to be found there, illustrations of increasing beauty, sophistication, and subtlety. Although illustrated books for adults have not experienced a renaissance (surprising, considering the popularity of art and "coffee table" books), there has been a growth in magazine illustration. The *Saturday Evening Post* died in the 1960s, but the demand for artwork has increased, due to the astonishing growth in the number of specialty magazines. *Sports Illustrated,* for example, is a major publisher of high-quality illustrations—on a weekly basis. Science fiction and rock music magazines are also major consumers of contemporary illustrations. Poster art has also made a resurgence, sparked no doubt by the development of posters protesting the Vietnam War, racism, and environmental degradation. In addition, the demand for paperback book covers, record album jackets, and advertising art has created an expanding market for popular illustrations.

Although the number of illustrators has increased with the growth of the market, there are very few illustrators whose illustrations are as widely recognized as the work of illustrators at the turn of the century. The death of Norman Rockwell marked the end of an era. The age of "romantic realism" in American illustration has passed; contemporary illustrators now use a variety of styles and techniques to convey their messages. As society has become more artistically sophisticated and more visually oriented, the nature of American popular illustration has changed. Nonetheless, its basic function remains the same.

REFERENCE WORKS

To date there is no single comprehensive bibliographical source that lists the major illustrators and all their published works. Compiling such a bibliography would be a valuable but monumental task; my research on magazine illustrators in *Century, Harper's* and *Scribner's* found that 252 illustrators contributed almost 5,000 illustrations during the five year period 1906-10. Two basic types of bibliographies do exist: reasonably complete bibliographies of books illustrated by a selected set of illustrators and complete bibliographies of illustrations by a single illustrator.

In the first group are three major bibliographies of selected illustrators. Theodore Bolton's *American Book Illustration* is a bibliographical checklist of 123 American illustrators and the books they illustrated; it lists each illustrator alphabetically along with the major illustrated books, including the number and type of illustrations as well as where the illustrations had been published previously. The work is time-bound, however, with its coverage ending in the mid-1930s, and there is no listing on non-book illustrations except when book illustrations had first appeared in magazines. Also several illustrators are included who are not major illustrators, and several obvious choices for inclusion are missing. Nonetheless, it is still the most complete bibliography of general book illustrators and their work. Bertha E. Mahoney's, Louise P. Latimer's, and Beulah Folmsbee's *Illustrator's of Children's Books, 1744-1945* and its 1958 and 1968 supplements constitute the best bibliographic sources on children's illustrated books. These works contain brief bibliographies of more than five hundred illustrators as well as bibliographies organized by author and illustrator. In addition, there are several excellent bibliographic essays analyzing trends in children's book illustration. As with the Bolton book, however, there is no coverage of magazine illustrations, particularly important since a number of illustrators at the turn of the century published much of their work in children's magazines. This defect is remedied, in part, by John M. Shaw's *The Poems, Poets, and Illustrators of St. Nicholas Magazine, 1873-1943,* which lists the illustrators and their contributions to this important children's magazine. Jeff Dykes' *Fifty Great Western Illustrators* is a long awaited and welcome bibliography of Western book illustration, covering the major Western illustrators of the past one hundred years. There are some interesting inclusions, N. C. Wyeth, whose Western illustrations encompass only a comparatively small proportion of his total production, for example. This bibliography is exceptional since it lists not only books illustrated but also exhibits in which the artwork appeared and articles written by and about the illustrator. But, like most other bibliographies, there is very little attention given to magazine illustrations. Harold McCracken's *Frederic Remington: Artist of the Old West* adds to the Dykes bibliography by listing Remington's many magazine illustrations.

There are a number of more or less complete bibliographies for selected individual illustrators. One of the most useful (because of Darley's influential role in the early development of American illustration) is Theodore Bolton's *The Book Illustrations of Felix Octavius Carr Darley,* which lists all his major illustrated books and includes an excellent bibliographic essay detailing his development as an illustrator as well as his role in American illustration. An excellent addition to Bolton's work is Christine Anne Hahler's exhibit catalog, *. . . illustrated by Darley,* which provides a more extended bibliographic essay and 152 examples of Darley's illustrations. A third work on Darley by Ethel King, *Darley, The Most Popular Illustrator of His Time,* is poorly written, rambling, frequently incorrect, and often irrelevant.

The work of Howard Pyle and some of his students is well documented. The basic reference work for Pyle's published material is Willard S. Morse's and Gertrude Brinckle's *Howard Pyle, A Record of His Illustrations and Writings,* one of the most comprehensive bibliographies on any one illustrator ever compiled. It lists almost all magazines and books written and/or illustrated by Pyle, describing them in terms of the titles of illustrations, size, and color. Together with Henry C. Pitz's *Howard Pyle,* Charles D. Abbott's *Howard Pyle: A Chronicle,* and the Delaware Art Museum exhibition catalog, *Howard Pyle: Diversity in Depth,* edited by Rowland Elzea, there is now a comprehensive listing and analysis of his life and works. The Pitz volume is probably the best general purpose reference book on Pyle, including a list (incomplete) of his students and a bibliography of his magazine and book illustrations (also incomplete). John P. Apgar's *Frank Schoonover, Painter-Illustrator: A Bibliography* lists the number and type of illustrations for each book illustrated by Schoonover but does not include his many magazine illustrations. Cortland Schoonover's *Frank Schoonover, Illustrator of the North American Frontier* provides an excellent cross-section of his artwork, as well as a biography and numerous statements of his illustration philosophy. The Allens' book, *N. C. Wyeth,* contains the best organized bibliography of an American illustrator and is a model of what could be done. In addition to listing the books which he illustrated, by title and type of illustration—with cross references when illustrations were later published as part of another collection—the book lists magazine illustrations, advertising materials, murals, calendar art, and even the one plate for which he did the illustration. In addition, Betsy James Wyeth's sensitive editing of her father-in-law's letters, *The Wyeths,* gives us a uniquely personal perspective on Wyeth's forty-year career as an illustrator, particularly his relationship with his mentor, Howard Pyle, and the continual struggle between his desire to do "fine art" and the demand for his work as an illustrator. Coy Ludwig's *Maxfield Parrish* contains a comprehensive bibliography of Parrish's published artwork, including his very substantial calendar and advertising output, while Paul W. Skeeters' *Maxfield Parrish, The Early Years* reproduces in folio size many of Parrish's book illustrations as they appeared in many of his early books. Pyle's women students and their work are discussed in detail in Catherine Connell Stryker's exhibition catalog, *The Studio at Cogslea,* which contains a reasonably complete bibliography for Jessie Wilcox Smith, Elizabeth Shippen Green, and Violet Oakley, and *Jessie Wilcox Smith* by S. Michael Schnessel, is the definitive work on that illustrator and her work and also describes in passing the work of many of Pyle's other students.

A number of other illustrators have had books written about them and their work. Among the best of these are Fairfax Downey, *Portrait of an Era as Drawn by C. D. Gibson;* Michael Schau, *All American Girl: The Art of Coles Phillips* and *J. C. Leyendecker;* Henry Reed, *The A. B. Frost Book;* Carl J. Weinhardt, *The Most of John Held, Jr.;* Walt Reed, *Harold Von Schmidt;* and Susan Meyers, *James Montgomery Flagg.* Each of these works gives the reader a reasonably good picture of the scope of the illustrator's life and work, if not specific information about it. Norman Rockwell's lengthy and prolific career has produced a spate of books dealing with one or more aspects of his career. Three of the best are Christopher Finch, *Norman Rockwell's America* and Thomas Buechner's two books, *Norman Rockwell: Artist and Illustrator* and *Norman Rockwell: A Sixty Year Perspective.*

There are comparatively few published works dealing in depth with various poster artists. Probably the best is Clarence Hornung's *Will Bradley: His Graphic Art,* which deals with Bradley's posters, magazine covers, and book illustrations but does not provide a detailed bibliography of his work. Dover Publications has put out a series of poster books that provide examples of major categories of poster art, including Joseph Darracott, *The First World War in Posters,* and Haywood and Blanche Cirker, *The Golden Age of the Poster.* Avon Books is publishing a series of "theme" poster books, showing circus posters, dance posters, bicycle posters, and so on.

Surprisingly, there is very little written on advertising art. The seminal work is *The Mechanical Bride,* by Herbert Marshall McLuhan. Perhaps the most useful single volume on advertising art and popular culture is Robert Atwar, Donald McQuade, and John W. Wright, *Edsels, Luckies, and Frigidaires,* which reviews one hundred years of advertising art through the medium of 250 commercial ads.

RESEARCH COLLECTIONS

It is difficult to do research on American illustrators and their artwork because much of the original artwork no longer exists. Until the early 1900s, illustrations were the property of the publisher rather than the artist, and many publishing houses had vast and fast-growing collections, which were periodically weeded out, art editors keeping choice pieces and disposing of the remainder with friends or the trash heap. As a result, comparatively few illustrations are still available for study, and in many instances, particularly for lesser-known illustrators, there is little knowledge as to whether the original artwork is still available and, if so, where. Even when the artwork was returned to the illustrator, the illustrator frequently did not keep it; Cortland Schoonover found that his father Frank Schoonover kept only eight hundred of the approximately six thousand illustrations he had published during his lifetime.

Researchers who wish to study the original artwork for illustrations must focus on those large-scale collections which are accessible to the public. Very few collections are either complete or comprehensive, however. The Delaware Art Museum, which contains over seven hundred sketches and almost five hundred illustrations by Howard Pyle, does not have several of the most important Pyle illustrations, which reside in the Brandywine River museum, the Philadelphia Free Library, or in private collections.

The Brandywine River Museum, frequently thought of by the public as the "Wyeth Museum," contains 348 paintings, of which less than twenty are by N. C. Wyeth. Other important Wyeth artwork is housed in the Delaware Art Museum, the Children's Room of the Philadelphia Free Library, and private collections.

Clearly, anyone wishing to study the artwork of Howard Pyle or N. C. Wyeth must explore a number of sources. The problems associated with studying other, less visible, illustrators are multiplied. In recent exhibitions mounted by the Delaware Art Museum, fifty-four of fifty-five illustrations by Douglas Duer came from private collections, thirty-nine of forty illustrations by W. H. D. Koerner were donated by private collectors, and in a major exhibition of one of Pyle's leading students, Stanley Arthurs, only nine of the seventy-two illustrations came from the museum's holdings.

Several museums and universities have extensive collections of illustrations by various illustrators. The Print Division of the Library of Congress, one of the largest collections, contains forty thousand lithographs, engravings, woodcuts, and original prints from the eighteenth and nineteenth century, as well as sixty thousand American and foreign posters dating from 1850 to the present. The poster collection is one of the most complete and comprehensive in the nation. In addition, the Brooklyn Museum, the Thornton Oakley collection of the Philadelphia Free Library, the Philadelphia Art Museum, the New York Public Library, the Grunwald Center for Graphic Arts at UCLA, the F. R. Gruger Collection at the University of Oregon, and the Museum of American Art in New Britain, Connecticut, contain major and important collections of illustrations. The collection of the New York Public Library ranks second only to the Library of Congress in size and importance. The Amon Carter Museum of Art in Fort Worth, Texas, and the Buffalo Bill Cody Museum in Cody, Wyoming, are two important research centers for Western art. Lastly, The Society of Illustrators Museum contains over 360 paintings, drawings, and sketches by twentieth-century illustrators, including a wide cross-section of artwork from editorial, advertising, and book illustrators.

The best source of illustrations is the books and magazines in which they originally appeared. The best single collection of such material is the Library of Congress, which contains copies of all copyrighted materials. In addition, the library has several specialized collections of interest to students of popular illustration. The Juvenile Collection, for example, contains approximately fifteen thousand volumes, catalogued chronologically by the author. The library is also acquiring the Lessing J. Rosenwald collection of incunabula, illustrated books, and fine printed and bound books, one of the largest and best collections of fine illustrated books in private hands.

Most other libraries lack the comprehensive breadth or depth of the

Library of Congress collection, but some of the best holdings of published illustrated materials are in the Spencer Collection of the New York Public Library, the Philadelphia Free Library, the Newberry Library in Chicago, the Detroit Public Library, and the Metropolitan Museum of Art in New York. In addition there are good holdings at the university libraries at UCLA, Princeton, Johns Hopkins, and the Anne E. Moore Collection at Columbia Teachers College. One frequently overlooked source are the specialized holdings in the possession of individual collectors or dealers. Many book collectors will have better collections of illustrated materials than nearby libraries and will frequently allow researchers limited access to their holdings. Antiquarian book dealers who specialize in illustrated and children's books are knowledgeable and usually possess bibliographies and other materials of interest to researchers. For example, Milton Riessman of the Victoria Bookshop in New York City has a collection of over three hundred illustrated books in which black Americans are depicted, most of these books dating from the nineteenth and early twentieth centuries.

The scholar who seeks to go beyond the artwork and published materials will find the task very difficult indeed. Records, correspondence, diaries, and day books of individual illustrators and publishers have been fragmented or destroyed; much of Howard Pyle's correspondence was destroyed after his death. The records that are available are more the result of luck and the initiative of research scholars than anything else. Thornton Oakley willed his collection of Howard Pyle's artwork and memorabilia to the Philadelphia Free Library, but much of the material has not yet been catalogued. Some of Frank Schoonover's papers are at the Delaware Art Museum, some at the Philadelphia Free Library, and still others in the possession of his son, Cortland. F. R. Gruger's materials are currently housed at the University of Oregon, and Norman Rockwell's correspondence and documents are currently being gathered for placement in an appropriate museum or library. The Society of Illustrators has an archive of material from Arthur William Brown, Wallace Morgan, Rene Clarke, William Meade Prince, Charles Dana Gibson, and James Montgomery Flagg, who were founders, members, or benefactors of the society. The materials on Gibson and Flagg are particularly important since they were founders and early presidents of the society as well as major illustrators. Access to these materials is on written request. The Archives of American Art, with depositories in a number of major cities, are another major source of information.

Another source of information, the records of publishing companies, particularly those which were major consumers of illustrated work, are frequently missing or incomplete. The early records of *Scribner's* are now on deposit at the Princeton University Library, but the collection has not been catalogued completely and is therefore of limited use to researchers. But what has happened to the records of the *Saturday Evening Post*, the pre-pictorial *Life, McClure's*, and *Century*—magazines no longer in publication? These records, which could provide important information on how and why certain illustrators were more likely to be published in certain magazines, how much illustrators were paid for their work, and why their illustrations were selected, are crucial for those who want to understand the role of illustration in American popular culture.

HISTORY AND CRITICISM

Because of the large number of illustrators and illustrations and the lack of comprehensive bibliographies, even for the most prolific of popular illustrators, there have been few attempts to write the definitive history of popular illustration. The several attempts merit discussion.

Walter Reed has edited *The Illustrator in America: 1900-1960,* which provides a decade-by-decade capsule description of the major illustrators and their work. At the beginning of each decade chapter an illustrator provides an historical and artistic overview of the decade. The very brief biographies, which tell where each illustrator published much of his work, detail changes in magazine illustration; the decade-by-decade presentation of illustration examples does more to demonstrate the continuities and changes in illustration during the sixty-year period than do the historical overviews written by the practitioners. One major weakness of the book is that it focuses largely on magazine illustrators, thus overlooking a few illustrators who work primarily in books or poster art.

Another mode of analysis is to focus on the "great" illustrators in American history. Susan Meyers' *America's Great Illustrators* is the leading example of this genre. She analyzes in some depth ten "great" illustrators—Howard Pyle, N. C. Wyeth, Frederic Remington, Maxfield Parrish, J. C. Leyendecker, Norman Rockwell, Charles Dana Gibson, Howard Chandler Christy, James Montgomery Flagg, and John Held, Jr.—and also provides examples of their work and a comparative chronology. Perhaps the most useful part of the book, since much of the information and artwork is available elsewhere, is the introduction, in which Meyers compares and contrasts the artwork and approaches to illustration of the ten men. Obviously, one can always argue with her choice of "great" illustrators. As an overview of American illustration, particularly during the first forty years of this century, this volume performs an important service.

A major source of information about the history and criticism of American illustration is found in museum exhibition catalogs or books derived from them. The best of these is Henry C. Pitz, *200 Years of American Illustration,* which celebrates the seventy-fifth anniversary of the Society of Illustrators with the publication of 850 illustrations by 530 American illustrators. The

325 pages of illustrations—line drawings, half-tones, and color—represent the most comprehensive display of the breadth and depth of American illustration yet published. Arranged by decade, one can use the book to compare David McCauley's pen and ink drawings of the details of medieval cathedral construction, Robert Handville's semi-abstract depiction of the 1971 Muhammad Ali-Joe Frazier fight for *Sports Illustrated,* James Bama's pensive portrait of Robert Kennedy for Bantam Books, Steven Dohanos' "photo-realism" tempera of a policeman taking an ice cream break for the *Saturday Evening Post,* James Thurber's simple crayon drawing of "Spot" for the *New Yorker,* the seascapes of Anton Otto Fisher, and the historic realism of N. C. Wyeth and Howard Pyle. In addition, Pitz has written a series of essays giving brief historial descriptions of major developments in the field, analyzing major illustrators, and looking at alternative uses of illustrations as magazine covers, posters, advertisements, and humor. Aside from the brevity of the review essays and Pitz's emphasis on Pyle, the book also suffers from some factual errors and mislabeling of some of the illustrations.

Somewhat more restricted in scope and time period is the 1972 catalog, *A Century of American Illustration,* an exhibit held at the Brooklyn Museum of Arts and Sciences. One hundred nineteen illustrations are used to show the scope of American illustration between 1850 and 1972. The period is divided into two eras—1850-1920 and 1920-72—and each period merits a very brief analysis in the catalog. The analysis is cursory, although the illustrations used in the catalog show much of the diversity in illustration during the period.

Several other exhibit catalogs are worthy of note. The 1976 catalog of the Grunwald Center for the Graphic Arts at UCLA, *The American Personality: The Artist-Illustrator of Life in the United States, 1860-1930,* contains a fine collection of illustrations in black and white and a series of ten topical essays dealing with various facets of illustration as a way of depicting American life. The first essay, "Literature and Art for the Masses: The Dime Novel," is an excellent supplement to Bill Blackbeard's bibliographic essay on the pulps in Volume 1 of *The Handbook of American Popular Culture.* Two essays, "American Women and the Woman Illustrator" and "The American Frontier" suffer in comparison with the Delaware Art Museum monograph on Howard Pyle's women students and several analyses of Western illustration. "The 'Special Artist' of the American Wars" is a useful essay on a much neglected topic, but it focuses very little attention on military artists of World War II. One essay, "The Afro-American Artist-Illustrator," could have been very useful, since very little has been written on the topic, but the essay is unfortunately superficial. The unevenness of the essays notwithstanding, this catalog is a very useful survey of the quality of illustration during the seventy-year period and provides some insights into selected illustration topics.

Rowland Elzea's catalog for a 1972 exhibition at the Delaware Art Museum, *The Golden Age of American Illustration, 1880-1914,* is a good survey of leading illustrators as well as an analysis of the development of illustration during the thirty-four-year period, particularly the important role played by magazines in that development. As with many exhibition catalogs, there are a multitude of illustrations, the heaviest emphasis on those illustrators whose works hang in the Delaware Art Museum or whose works are pivotal for the period, for example, Howard Pyle and his students. As such, this catalog is one of the best collections of illustrations by Howard Pyle and his students.

Another Delaware Art Museum exhibition catalog, edited by Dorie Schmidt in 1979, *The American Magazine, 1890-1940,* uses the slick paper magazine format to introduce the reader to the exhibit and a very solid collection of articles on magazines and their role in American culture. Michael Barson's article adds to our growing analysis of pulp fiction magazines, and Peter C. Rollins and George H. Straley write about the impact of magazine editors on their magazines. There are several articles relating to magazine illustration: Margaret Cohen discusses the importance of cover art for magazine sales, Rowland Elzea analyzes the contributors to the early *Life,* and Elizabeth Hawkes writes an analysis of magazines and their illustrations, raising a number of interesting questions.

The Brandywine River Museum has also issued several exhibition catalogs highlighting its collections of illustrator's artwork, particularly that of Howard Pyle and N. C. Wyeth. One of the most useful is a 1976 catalog, *The Art of American Illustration,* edited by Joan H. Gorman, which includes a brief history of American illustration and brief biographical sketches of ninety-one illustrators, some of whom are rarely covered in other sources.

There has been very little systematic empirical research on American illustration. One of the few such studies is James J.Best's "The Brandywine School and Magazine Illustration: Harper's, Scribner's, and Century, 1906-1910" which counts the number, type, and source of 5,000 magazine illustrations that appeared in the three major monthly illustrated magazines over the five-year period. The research indicates that the illustration content of the three magazines was decidedly different, with *Harper's* carrying a substantially greater proportion of illustrations by Howard Pyle and his students than the other two magazines. Rowland Elzea's piece in Dorey Schmidt's *The American Magazine, 1890-1940* notes a similar specialization in *Life* magazine, with one-third of the illustrators doing two-thirds of the illustrations. Both of these studies raise questions about the relationship between magazine art editors and professional illustrators, the two people who determined what appeared in magazines.

Most of the biographies mentioned earlier are uncritical in their evaluation of their subject's illustrations. Henry C. Pitz's two books on Howard Pyle and his students, *Howard Pyle* and *The Brandywine Tradition,* do a good job of analyzing the relationship between Pyle and his students, particularly Pyle's unique teaching style and philosophy of illustration. The book on Pyle contains one chapter devoted to the mysticism in Pyle's illustrations. N. C. Wyeth's letters in *The Wyeths,* edited by Betsy James Wyeth, offer an interesting and increasingly critical insight into Wyeth's relationship with Pyle. The two books dealing with Pyle's women students, *Jessie Wilcox Smith* by S. Michael Schnessel and *The Studios at Cogslea,* a catalog by Catherine Connell Stryker, deal sensitively and critically with the relationship between Pyle and his women students and also analyze illustration as a professional career field for women at the turn of the century. Christopher Finch's *Norman Rockwell's America* discusses how Rockwell's illustrations have changed through time in terms of theme and style and makes well-considered judgements on which of Rockwell's many illustrations are his best.

Historically, various magazines have published articles dealing with American illustration. The *Quarterly Illustrator* and *Monthly Illustrator* were both short-lived efforts to provide information about and analysis of contemporary illustrators during the 1890s. The *Studio* and *International Studio* periodically published critiques of American illustrators and their work during the Golden Age of American illustration. Since the 1930s, the *American Artist* has periodically reviewed the illustrations of various illustrators, with many of these reviews being written by Henry C. Pitz. The February 1975 issue of the *American Artist* is devoted to tracing the familial ties and artistic heritage of the Wyeth family. More contemporary illustration is reviewed in *Illustrators,* an annual of American illustration.

The history of poster art is examined in detail in a number of books. Bevis Hillier's *Posters* examines the development of poster art in France and England during the pre-World War I, interwar, and post-World War II periods. Victor Margolin's book, *American Poster Renaissance,* focuses more narrowly on the development of poster art in America in the 1890s. Margolin identifies three different styles of poster art—decorative, descriptive, and illustrative—and shows examples of each style by their leading exponents—Will Bradley, Edward Penfield, and Maxfield Parrish, respectively. In addition to delineating the major styles of the period, Margolin analyzes the roles poster art played in American life at the turn of the century. Ervine Metzl's *The Poster: Its History and Art* goes one step further to develop an aesthetic for judging poster art, namely, the poster should not be overburdened with detail, should not be too literal, must enlist the viewer as participant, must imply a world of continuing action, and must sell a product or idea. This last criterion is crucial; it is possible to have posters that are good art but bad advertising, just as it is possible to have bad art that nonetheless sells a product. The ideal poster is both good art and good advertising. From this aesthetic perspective Metzl can evaluate the leading poster artists of the turn of the century, and he concludes that some, notably the Beggarstaffs (John Pryde and William Nicholson) in Britain, did posters that were good art but bad advertising. Gary Yanker's *Prop Art* seeks to develop a similar analysis of the role and function of contemporary propaganda posters, examining what propaganda posters are designed to do, how they seek to achieve their effects, and how well they do.

Unfortunately, no one has developed a similar framework for analyzing and evaluating the quality of magazine and book illustrations. For many years illustrators debated whether they were "artists" whose illustrations were not limited by the text or "illustrators" whose artwork was tied to and reflective of the printed word. This question, whether illustration could be or was "high" rather than "popular" art, was bothersome for many illustrators. This concern was reflected in the professional careers of Charles Dana Gibson, James Montgomery Flagg, N. C. Wyeth, and F. R. Gruger, who periodically took leave of their illustration work to do "fine art," traveling to Paris to paint or to study with leading easel artists of their day. Their comparatively high salaries and the disdain with which they were frequently held by poorer but higher status artists compounded their discomfort. Some artists—William Glackens, Winslow Homer, and John Sloan—began their careers as illustrators and then made the transition to easel art. Very few easel artists were interested in becoming illustrators, although Edward Hopper tried to be an easel artist, was unsuccessful, became a successful illustrator, and then returned to easel art.

Because illustrations serve to visualize a print media, Rowland Elzea in *The Golden Age of American Illustration* catalog suggests that the illustrator, as opposed to the easel painter, must satisfy himself, the text, and the public in order to be successful. Doing so requires a knowledge of the dramatic points in the text and the ability to convey that drama pictorially to the reader and to involve the reader in a visual image of the story in a way that the reader understands and enjoys. At the same time the illustrator must have the artistic freedom to illustrate what he wants in his own style—to remain true to himself. According to Charles D. Abbott, *Howard Pyle: A Chronicle,* Pyle sensed that which is central to both the artist and the illustrator:

> For after all, a man is not an artist by virtue of clever technique or brilliant methods; he is fundamentally an artist in the degree that he is able to sense and appreciate the significance of life that surrounds himself, and to express that significance to the minds of others. (p. 226)

The major difference between the artist and the illustrator in their fulfillment of this central task is that the illustrator is constrained in his or her task by the text to be illustrated, whereas the artist is constrained only by his or her imagination.

The idea that the illustrator must deal with a text and can be judged on the basis of how well his work conveys the author's intent has not been used very often as the basis for evaluating the artwork of various illustrators. This is surprising since many of the illustrators have worked on more than one topic and many of the literary classics have been illustrated by more than one illustrator over time. Few comparisons have been made, however. Frederick Joseph Harvey Darton, in *Modern Book-Illustration in Great Britain and America,* has done a critical review of four illustrated versions of Chaucer; and John Lewis, in *The Twentieth Century Book,* compares ten different illustrated editions of *Treasure Island,* showing how illustrative styles have changed between 1884 and 1963.

Perhaps the best test of the success of an illustrator (but not an artist) is whether the illustrations were popular with the public and whether they remain popular today. If we use the test of longevity as the measure of illustration success, the honor roll of American illustrators would be comparatively short. But perhaps the best measure of success is how popular the illustrator was in his or her own time. We run the risk of arguing that the most popular and successful illustrators were those whose work was published, and only those whose works were published were popular and successful—a tautology. Nonetheless, those illustrators whose work appeared most frequently in their time must be accounted as successes in their day, if not ours.

BIBLIOGRAPHY

BOOKS AND ARTICLES

Abbott, Charles D. *Howard Pyle: A Chronicle.* New York: Harper & Brothers, 1925.

Allen, Douglas, and Douglas Allen, Jr. *N. C. Wyeth.* New York: Bonanza Books, 1972.

Apgar, John P. *Frank Schoonover, Painter-Illustrator: A Bibliography.* Morristown, N.J.: published by author, 1969.

Atwar, Robert, Donald McQuade, and John W. Wright. *Edsels, Luckies and Frigidaires.* New York: Delacorte Press, 1979.

Bader, Barbara. *American Picture Books: From Noah's Ark to the Beast Within.* New York: Macmillan, 1976.

Best, James J. "The Brandywine School and Magazine Illustration: *Harper's, Scribner's,* and *Century,* 1906-1910." *Journal of American Culture,* 3 (Spring 1980), 128-44.

Blackbeard, Bill. "The Pulps." In *Handbook of Popular Culture, Vol. 1.* Edited by M. Thomas Inge. Westport, Conn.: Greenwood Press, 1978, pp. 195-223.

Blanck, Jacob. *Peter Parley to Penrod.* New York: Bowker, 1939.

Bland, David. *The Illustration of Books.* London: Faber and Faber, n.d.

Bolton, Theodore. *American Book Illustration: Bibliographical Checklist of 123 Artists.* New York: Bowker, 1938.

———. *The Book Illustrations of Felix Octavius Carr Darley.* Worcester, Mass.: American Antiquarian Society, 1952.

Broder, Patricia James. *Dean Cornwell, Dean of Illustrators.* New York: Watson-Guptill, 1978.

Brown, Arthur W. "Howard Chandler Christy." *American Artist*, 16 (January 1952), 50-51, 68.

Buechner, Thomas. *Norman Rockwell: Artist and Illustrator.* New York: Henry Abrams, 1970.

———. *Norman Rockwell: A Sixty Year Perspective.* New York: Henry Abrams, 1972.

Cirker, Haywood, and Blanche Cirker. *The Golden Age of the Poster.* New York: Dover, 1971.

Darracott, Joseph, ed. *The First World War in Posters.* New York: Dover, 1974.

Darton, Frederick Joseph Harvey. *Modern Book Illustration in Great Britain and America.* London: The Studio, 1931.

Downey, Fairfax. *Portrait of an Era as Drawn by C. D. Gibson.* New York: Scribner's, 1936.

Dykes, Jeff. *Fifty Great Western Illustrators: A Bibliographical Checklist.* Flagstaff, Arizona: Northland Press, 1975.

Ellis, Richard W. *Book Illustration.* Kingsport, Tenn.: Kingsport Press, 1952.

Finch, Christopher. *Norman Rockwell's America.* New York: Henry Abrams, 1975.

Frank Leslie's Illustrated History of the Civil War. New York: Mrs. F. Leslie, 1895.

Gallo, Max. *The Poster in History.* New York: American Heritage, 1972.

Gowan, Alan. *The Unchanging Arts.* New York: J. B. Lippincott, 1971.

Guptill, Arthur. *Norman Rockwell: Illustrator.* New York: Watson-Guptill, 1946.

Halsey, Jr., Ashley. *Illustrating for the Saturday Evening Post.* Boston: Arlington House, 1951.

Harper's Illustrated History of the Civil War. New York: Harper and Bros., 1895.

Hillier, Bevis. *Posters.* New York: Stein and Day, 1969.

Hornung, Clarence. *Will Bradley: His Graphic Art.* New York: Dover, 1974.

King, Ethel. *Darley, The Most Popular Illustrator of His Time.* Brooklyn, N.Y.: T. Gaus' Sons, 1964.

Kingman, Lee. "The High Art of Illustration." *Horn Book Magazine*, 50 (October 1974), 94-103.

Kingman, Lee, Joanna Foster, and Ruth Giles Lontoft. *Illustration of Children's Books, 1956-66.* Boston: Horn Book, 1968.

Klemin, Diana. *The Illustrated Book.* New York: Charles Potter, 1970.

Lewis, John. *The Twentieth Century Book.* London: Studio Vista, 1967.

Ludwig, Coy. *Maxfield Parrish.* New York: Watson-Guptill, 1973.

McCracken, Harold. *Frederic Remington: Artist of the Old West.* New York: Lippincott, 1947.

McLuhan, Herbert Marshall. *The Mechanical Bride.* New York: Vanguard Press, 1951.

Mahoney, Bertha E., Louise P. Latimer, and Beulah Folmsbee. *Illustrators of Children's Books, 1744-1945.* Boston: Horn Books, 1947.

Margolin Victor. *American Poster Renaissance.* New York: Watson-Guptill, 1975.

Metzl, Ervine. *The Poster: Its History and Art.* New York: Watson-Guptill, 1963.

Meyers, Susan. *America's Great Illustrators.* New York: Henry N. Abrams, 1978.

———. "Howard Chandler Christy." *American Artist*, 42 (May 1978), 42-47, 98-101.

———. *James Montgomery Flagg.* New York: Watson-Guptill, 1974.

———. "Three Generations of the Wyeth Family." *American Artist,* 39 (February 1975).

Morse, Willard S., and Gertrude Brinckle. *Howard Pyle: A Record of His Illustrations and Writings.* Wilmington, Del.: privately printed, 1921. Reprint. Detroit: Singing Tree Press, 1969.

Mott, Frank Luther. *A History of American Magazines: Vol. V, 1905-1930.* Cambridge: Harvard University Press, 1968.

Peppin, Brigid. *Fantasy: The Golden Age of Fantastic Illustration.* New York: New American Library, 1976.

Perlman, Bernard. *The Golden Age of American Illustration: F. R. Gruger and His Circle.* Westport, Conn.: Northern Lights, 1978.

Pitz, Henry C. "Book Illustration Since 1937." *American Artist,* 31 (April 1967), 64-71, 101.

———. *The Brandywine Tradition.* New York: Weathervane Books, 1968.

———. "George Harding." *American Artist,* 21 (December 1957), 29-35.

———. *Howard Pyle.* New York: Clarkson and Potter, 1975.

———. "Millions of Pictures, Part I." *American Artist,* 15 (November 1961), 35-39, 76-77.

———. "Millions of Pictures, Part II." *American Artist,* 15 (December 1961), 52-57, 85-88.

———. "N. C. Wyeth." *American Heritage,* 17 (October 1965), 36-55, 82-84.

———. *The Practice of Illustration.* New York: Watson-Guptill, 1947.

———. *200 Years of American Illustration.* New York: Random House, 1977.

Reed, Henry. *The A. B. Frost Book.* Rutland, Vt.: Charles E. Tuttle, 1972.

———, ed. *The Illustrator in America: 1900-1960.* New York: Reinhold, 1966.

Reed, Walt. *Harold Von Schmidt.* Flagstaff, Ariz.: Northland Press, 1972.

Schau, Michael. *All American Girl: The Art of Coles Phillips.* New York: Watson-Guptill, 1975.

———. *J. C. Leyendecker.* New York: Watson-Guptill, 1976.

Schnessel, S. Michael. *Jessie Wilcox Smith.* New York: Crowell, 1977.

Schoonover, Cortland. *Frank Schoonover, Illustrator of the North American Frontier.* New York: Watson-Guptill, 1976.

Shaw, John M. *The Poems, Poets, and Illustrators of St. Nicholas Magazine, 1873-1943.* Tallahassee: Florida State University Press, n.d.

Shinn, Everett. "William Glackens as an Illustrator." *American Artist,* 9 (November 1945), 22-27, 37.

Skeeters, Paul. *Maxfield Parrish: The Early Years.* Secaucus, N.J.: Chartwell Books, 1973.

Smith, F. Hopkinson. *American Illustrators.* New York: Scribner's, 1893.

Viguers, Ruth Hill, Marcia Dalphin, and Bertha Mahoney Miller. *Illustrators of Children's Books, 1946-56.* Boston: Horn Book, 1958.

Watson, Ernest W. "Harvey Dunn: Milestone in the Tradition of American Illustration." *American Artist,* 6 (June 1942), 16-20, 31.

Weinhardt, Carl J. *The Most of John Held, Jr.* Brattleboro, Vt.: Stephen Greene Press, 1972.

Weitenkampf, Frank. *The Illustrated Book.* Cambridge: Harvard University Press, 1938.

______. *American Graphic Art.* New York: Scribner's, 1912.

Wyeth, Betsy James, ed. *The Wyeths.* Boston: Gambit Press, 1971.

Yanker, Gary. *Prop Art.* New York: Darien House, 1972.

MUSEUM CATALOGS

The American Personality: The Artist-Illustrator of Life in the United States, 1860-1930. Los Angeles: Grunwald Center for the Graphic Arts, 1976.

The Artist and the Book: 1860-1960. Boston: Museum of Fine Arts and Harvard University Library, 1961.

A Century of American Illustration. Brooklyn, N.Y.: Brooklyn Museum of Arts and Sciences, 1972.

Elzea, Rowland, ed. *Howard Pyle: Diversity in Depth.* Wilmington: Delaware Art Museum, 1973.

______. *The Golden Age of American Illustration.* Wilmington: Delaware Art Museum, 1972.

Gorman, Joan H., ed. *The Art of American Illustration.* Chadds Ford, Penn.: Brandywine River Museum, 1976.

Hahler, Christine Anne, ed. *...illustrated by Darley.* Wilmington: Delaware Art Museum, 1979.

Schmidt, Dorey, ed. *The American Magazine: 1890-1940.* Wilmington: Delaware Art Museum, 1979.

Stryker, Catherine Connell, ed. *The Studios at Cogslea.* Wilmington: Delaware Art Museum, 1976.

PERIODICALS

American Artist. New York, 1937-.

Graphis Annual, International Advertising Art. New York, 1952/53-.

Illustrators, The Annual of American Illustration. New York, 1959-.

International Studio. New York, 1897-1931.

Monthly Illustrator. New York, 1895-97.

Quarterly Illustrator. New York, 1893-95.

Studio. London, 1893-.

CHAPTER 4 Jazz

Bill Bennett

Despite the growth of critical esteem for the genre of American music known as jazz, the last three years have seen this vital and innovative music continue to suffer from the application of adjectives like *ephemeral* and from the denigration of popular music in support of so-called classical or serious music. Still the bibliography of jazz keeps growing, and the critical foundation of jazz—including the thoughtful observations of the likes of Ernest Ansermet ("classical" approbation in the year 1918! His essay is reprinted in Martin Williams, *The Art of Jazz*), Hugues Panassié, Martin Williams, Marshall Stearns, Gunther Schuller, Andre Hodeir, and others—grows in analytical depth with each passing year. In the same manner, the influence of jazz on the world's music in this century can be heard as more and more pervasive.

HISTORIC OUTLINE

The jazz tradition springs from the American cultural experiment; it is the precise musical analogy to the melting pot. Jazz was spawned in an evolutionary stream whose headwaters mark the point where African culture became Afro-American. True enough, jazz is "black music," but, more importantly, jazz is a music of black Americans. In the absence of either its African or American components, one can only suppose that jazz would not exist.

The most influential—and, not coincidentally, most African—root strain in jazz is the blues. Speaking strictly musically, the blues is a culturally rich and homogeneous musical genre, formally and harmonically quite unlike any other musical development in this world. Its antecedents, which are primarily melodic, are certainly African, but there is similar certainty that the formalization and harmonization of that melodic seed have taken place in the American South. The simple I-IV-V harmonic essence of the blues and the settling of the song form into an even twelve measures are as momentous a development in terms of world music as one could seek in the music of America.

Form and harmony aside, to this day the most striking aspect of the blues remains the so-called blue notes, the celebrated deviations from the tempered scale that shade the emotional spectrum of these powerful, compact songs. The ambiguity, in terms of Western harmony, of these notes, which take the third and seventh degrees of the scale from major to minor and back again, reflects the ambiguous circumstances that the blues have come to symbolize: in a narrow sense, the place of the black man in a white society; in a larger sense, the plight of humanity in a random universe. The blues, which idiomatically trigger the perception and sensation of sadness, are at the same time a celebration, the means of naming the bogey men of modern life and thus making them less fearful. As such, the blues invite the exorcism of individual troubles; and this aspect, along with the basic simplicity of the form, seems to invite improvisation.

The next important melding of African and European elements into an American music came with the advent of ragtime, which developed as a sort of danceable parlor music with the piano at center stage. The syncopations that characterize ragtime are as African as can be, while the melody, harmony, and basic 4/4 meter harken to Europe, specifically to the march and polka. The classic rag might consist of three sixteen-bar strains, which might be arranged A-A-B-A-C-B-C, or very nearly a rondo. Scott Joplin, the best-known of the ragtime composers, eventually went so far as to attempt a ragtime opera, *Treemonisha,* but there were many other musicians at work in the field, including James Scott, James Reese Europe, Luckey Roberts, Joseph Lamb, and Eubie Blake, whose compositions still prove rewarding to student and listener alike.

A third important strain in the development of jazz is the brass band, in all likelihood the legacy of the American martial tradition. Such bands were the cornerstone of the nation's entertainment in the nineteenth century, and nowhere more so than in New Orleans, where French, African, Caribbean, and English cultures met at the mouth of the Mississippi. There is reason, as well as romantic inclination, to believe that the funeral traditions of the New Orleans black community were instrumental in the gestation of jazz. As ragtime rhythms grew popular, it makes sense to imagine the vibrant and possibly blues-tinged marches played on the way back from the cemetery taking on at the urging of some visionary cornetist—perhaps the legendary Buddy Bolden—a sudden wildness, a rhythmic freedom that demanded attention. This, we may believe, was the birth of swing.

Swing is a different, and larger, rhythmic concept than syncopation. Ragtime syncopation is a device, albeit essential to the ragtime style, which generally takes the form of an offbeat anticipation to sustain interest and inspire a sense of melodic momentum. Swing is a more complete homage to the Afro-American's cultural ancestry, allowing variation all around the beat according to the dictates of constantly implied polyrhythmic foundations, the integrity of the phrase, or sheer instinctual bravado.

The swing factor developed gradually from an aberration among the established brass bands of New Orleans into the guiding principle of a number of smaller ensembles playing a rough-hewn, energetic music that came to be called "jass." The word itself apparently derives from a euphemism for sexual activity. In addition to their rhythmic proclivities, these bands relied on improvisation to realize their ensemble playing; what emerged was a kind of spontaneous counterpoint, a collective improvisation unique in musical history. The lead voice belonged to a trumpet or, more often, a cornet; the clarinet took the treble obbligato role, and a trombone filled the baritone void. A banjo established the chord patterns of the chosen melody, while a tuba—later a bass fiddle—followed the oom-pah contours of the march-time polka. The drummer played a fairly limited role in the early ensemble, occasionally dropping into stop-time to highlight the intertwining lines of his compeers.

If we do accept New Orleans as the "birthplace" of jazz, we can at least debunk the role of prostitution as "mother" to the music. New Orleans's fabled red-light district, Storyville, unquestionably afforded many musicians work in the early years of this century, and many of these players were undoubtedly jazz musicians. However, as Duke Ellington has so bluntly put it, "They didn't learn it there."

The finest of the early bands, at least insofar as recorded evidence is concerned, was that of Joe "King" Oliver. His Creole Jazz Band made its recorded debut in 1923, featuring, in support of Oliver's then-nonpareil horn, a young second cornetist named Louis Armstrong.

Armstrong, who would become a worldwide symbol of American talent and opportunity, was far more than just a mugging entertainer: he emerged from under Oliver's stylistic wing to become the first great, and in many ways quintessential, jazz soloist. That Armstrong was building on an established tradition—the contributions of Buddy Bolden, Mutt Carey, Freddie Keppard, and others—cannot be questioned. At the same time, however, there can be little doubt as to the magnitude of Armstrong's contribution. As is so often the case in jazz, there is little point in trying to separate Armstrong's stylistic innovations from his sheer instrumental virtuosity; they are too closely bound to permit such academic dissections. Still, we can point to aspects of the Armstrong sound and document their influence in the larger plane of world music. We know, for instance, that the soulful vibrato with which Armstrong could worry a single note was absent from the vocabulary of nineteenth-century brassmen and that, today, any well-trained trumpet player includes this device among his expressive techniques. But all of Armstrong's trade tricks, even his seamless glissandos and unheard of high notes, cannot account for the compelling personality of his playing. For it was Louis Armstrong who at last brought the swing factor into focus, who refined Afro-American polyrhythmic urges into an improvisational medium that played freely around the established dictates of melody, harmony, and meter. Armstrong at his best is a fine blend of restraint and expansive gesture, ranging from the subtlest rhythmic reinterpretations of a melodic line, through simple embellishments, to full-fledged improvisation.

Armstrong was not alone in blazing this trail into solo territory. Soprano saxophonist Sidney Bechet, with whom Armstrong recorded as early as 1924, brought his instrument out of its traditional obbligato role with his startlingly effective, arpeggio-based style. And cornetist Bix Beiderbecke's delicately crystalline solo structures were, in their way, just as daring as Armstrong's strokes of genius.

From the early, collectively improvised polyphony of jazz to the advent of the soloist was a major step. Sure to follow were ensemble arrangements that drew on the developing jazz tradition in order to frame those solos structurally. Ferdinand "Jelly Roll" Morton's claim to the invention of jazz is suspect, though he probably should be credited with having done the groundwork for the jazz orchestra. Morton's ensemble arrangements (hear his Red Hot Peppers recordings), essentially an extension of his ragtime-derived piano style, reflect a consciousness of form and texture that would blossom in the work of other bandleaders, notably Fletcher Henderson. Henderson, working initially with saxophonist-arranger Don Redman, began the expansion of the five-to-ten piece jazz band into the thirteen to seventeen pieces characteristic of the "big band" sound.

While Henderson was honing his arranging skills, which would later make such a contribution to the success of Benny Goodman's band in New York, similar trails were being cleared in other parts of the country. Kansas City was the center of one such area of activity, the essence of which came to be represented by the Count Basie Orchestra of the 1930s and 1940s. Basie's band brought together the classic rhythm section (the continuo of jazz) with a number of excellent soloists, including the great tenor saxophonist Lester Young. The sophistication they brought to the riff tune, with its bluesy exuberance and potent call-and-response patterns, helped launch the so-called Swing Era.

Meanwhile, in the New York of the 1920s, Edward Kennedy "Duke" Ellington was beginning the long career that would establish him as one of America's great composers. With Ellington, individualistic if not always virtuosic players were essential to the complex and innovative arrangements that would necessarily change with the band's personnel. While it is generally agreed that the Ellington band reached its peak in the early 1940s, the whole of his fifty years as composer and bandleader will repay intensive study, bringing to light Ellington's brilliant employment of such musical forces as altoist Johnny Hodges, tenor man Ben Webster, bassist Jimmy Blanton, trombonist Joe "Tricky Sam" Nanton, and so many others.

With the establishment of the solo-ensemble format, which may be considered a sophisticated extension of the call-and-response legacy of African music, and the development of the jazz orchestra, the stage was set for the popular success and excesses of the Swing Era. The mainstream standards of jazz had been formed and were soon to be challenged by a new generation of jazz musicians coming of age in the war-torn 1940s. Leaping off from the harmonic achievements of Coleman Hawkins and Art Tatum, young men such as Charlie Parker, Dizzy Gillespie, and Thelonious Monk were responsible for the musical revolution that carried the onomatopoeic monicker be-bop. Armstrong's basic melodic unit, the swung quarter note, suddenly became an eighth note; the range of harmonic extensions available to the improviser similarly opened up. Smaller (four or five piece) soloistic bands were the medium for this complex new music, in which the balance between composition and improvisation shifted once more toward the spontaneous edge.

The harmonic frontiers probed by be-bop prompted some rather more restrained forays in the early 1950s. Led by Miles Davis, a former Charlie Parker sideman, and arranger Gil Evans, this "Cool School" added occasional new voices to the jazz band—the French horn, for instance—and moved at a more introspective pace than had bop; like bop, however, cool jazz was effectively a listener's music, to be danced to at one's own risk. Conversely, the music was played at the musician's own risk, for financial success (read "popularity") visited dance-oriented jazzmen more often than their esoteric counterparts. What is important is that, like so much jazz, dance-oriented or not, the music that came out of the be-bop revolution (including cool, a vertically oriented reduction of be-bop) demands consideration as art music.

Be-bop also produced a linear reduction of itself, which came to be known as "funky" jazz, or hard bop. Hard bop used the small band format of its forebear to carry arrangements blending the harmonic progress of bop with rhythm-and-blues-flavored structures. The bands of Art Blakey and Horace Silver are archtypical hard bop units, though the movement also nurtured more individualistic talents, such as Wayne Shorter, who would reach prominence with later Miles Davis bands, and Sonny Rollins, who in many ways remains to this day the quintessential tenor saxophonist.

An often interesting, just as often pretentious offshoot of cool jazz came to be known as third stream jazz, a conscious effort to meld the jazz tradition with European concert music. Its major proponents included composer Gunther Schuller and pianist John Lewis, who, as music director of the Modern Jazz Quartet, would create a refined and often Baroque-tinged chamber jazz.

The 1950s also spawned a number of great compositions, many of them from the prolific pens of Charles Mingus and Thelonious Monk. Monk, like Jelly Roll Morton a composer whose themes sprang directly from his instrumental style, enjoyed a popular vogue in the 1960s more attributable to the simultaneous "weirdness" and simplicity of his melodies than to the sophistication of their harmonies, both stated and implied. Mingus enriched the mainstream conception of the jazz ensemble with shades of the collectively improvised polyphony of the music's earliest manifestations; in so doing, he presaged and paved the way for the free jazz movement.

Along with the work of Mingus, Monk, the Modern Jazz Quartet, and Sonny Rollins, the contributions of Miles Davis's groups were among the most significant of the 1950s. The forced near-virtuosity of his be-bop days had given way to a more relaxed, more musical approach in his cool phase; his trumpet musings had become an unmistakable voice by the middle of the decade, owing more perhaps to Louis Armstrong than anyone since. Late in the decade, the Davis band, which included John Coltrane, recorded the first, or at least most influential, exploration of modal jazz to date. Coltrane, in his vertically oriented style, would later take these ideas to the extremes of virtuosity, as in "Impressions," and sheer soulful expression, as in "Spiritual."

Meanwhile, innovation blossomed on the West Coast: the quartet of Ornette Coleman and the concept of free jazz. Coleman's scheme depended on relatively simple thematic material fleshed out through collective improvisation and harmonized by implication, often by microtonal degrees. Coltrane would pick up the free spirit, as would Miles Davis, whose mid-1960s quintet remains one of the most successful examples of a collectively improvising band. The avant garde of jazz continues in relatively good health into the 1980s, where the benefits of perspective have introduced often startling allusions to the past glories of jazz.

A footnote that becomes the thesis: The preceding has been a thumbnail tracing of the roots and milestones of jazz, its history considered only in terms of the tradition. The fact remains that the greater significance of jazz may well be defined by future music historians as the scope of its influences on the popular music of the world. The blues is far and away America's most significant formal contribution to world music; similarly, "jazz" is our most important stylistic contribution. Given the musical influences of jazz on America—from Paul Whiteman, through George Gershwin, Cole Porter, Harold Arlen, and other great writers in the American popular song form, to rock bands like Little Feat—we can yet detail much broader cultural influences through which we can better understand the place of jazz in American culture.

Prime examples of such influences would have to include *The Jazz Singer*, which has to rank as one of the world's foremost cinematic malapropisms (recently re-miscast with Neil Diamond in the role "created" by Al Jolson). Indeed, film has contributed greatly to the propagation of jazz *and* its misperception by the public, helping for instance, Louis Armstrong to be christened an Uncle Tom by a later, media-reared generation of black

Americans. Films are, after all, a mass entertainment medium, which a purist's jazz has never been; consequently, we are given *The Benny Goodman Story* and *The Gene Krupa Story* rather than film biographies of Duke Ellington or Big Sid Catlett. Beyond this, however, we find Hollywood's cruelty to the music from which it has borrowed so much extending to the propagation of sinister sterotypes, which for all their collective grains of truth have served to maintain jazz's bad name. If a film romanticizes the moody atmosphere of the jazz club, it is sustaining the jazz club, not jazz; the music is left standing at the box office of the concert stage.

The point is that drug addiction, alcoholism, and venereal disease are tragic sociological side issues to the history of jazz. True, Charlie Parker was a heroin addict; but, more importantly, he was a brilliant musician, an improvising artist of the highest order. What jazz musicians have accomplished they have accomplished in spite of the tremendous socioeconomic obstacles in their path. At the same time, however, we must recognize the role of these obstacles in shaping the feelings that, in their turn, have helped to shape the jazz tradition.

REFERENCE WORKS

Reference books on jazz fall rather neatly into three categories: the encyclopedia and occasional "dictionary," the discography, and the bibliography. For the most part, the encyclopedias will prove initially most useful, providing as they do background information on the musicians who make and have made jazz. Discographies are the vital link between these histories and the creative sounds that make these men and women worthy of study; and bibliographies map the route to the opinions and research of others.

ENCYLOPEDIAS

There are three essential resources with which the jazz researcher must be familiar. The three volumes of Leonard Feather's *Encyclopedia of Jazz—The New Edition of the Encyclopedia of Jazz* (1960), *The Encyclopedia of Jazz in the Sixties* (1967), and, co-authored by Ira Gitler, *The Encyclopedia of Jazz in the Seventies* (1977)—provide brief biographies and critical evaluations of most significant jazz musicians through the years, along with introductory essays of some interest and appendixes which tend toward trivia. John Chilton's *Who's Who of Jazz: Storyville to Swing Street,* recently revised for Time-Life Records and their Giants of Jazz Series, fills in several of the lacunae in Feather's research, focusing on musicians born prior to 1920. The Chilton book is less critically oriented and tends to be somewhat more specific in terms of its biographical sketches.

The third invaluable source is Roger D. Kinkle's *The Complete Encyclo-*

pedia of Popular Music and Jazz, 1900-1950. Kinkle's four volumes include alphabetical entries for artists and composers as well as a guide to this "Music Year by Year," all cross-indexed for the researcher's convenience.

There are, of course, many other reference sources, though their merits must be qualified. *Blues Who's Who: A Biograpical Dictionary of Blues Singers,* by Sheldon Harris is a commendable, if occasionally spotty, effort to make bluesmen accessible; it is probably the best existing starting point for blues research. *New Orleans Jazz: A Family Album,* by Al Rose and Edmond Souchon, is notable for its photographs, but its information should be crosschecked. A better overall photo reference book is *A Pictorial History of Jazz,* by Orrin Keepnews and Bill Grauer, Jr.

DISCOGRAPHIES

Discographies are a much simpler matter, thanks to the exhaustive work that has gone into this vital area of jazz research. Jazz has often been described as the product of an oral tradition; the stylistic and inflectional nuances of the jazz sound essentially defy the capabilities of standard musical notation to record them. The rapid development of jazz in the last eighty years would very likely have been impossible without the benefit of phonography, which has made the triumphs and innovations of the genre immediately available to others in the field. In the same sense, jazz records are the foundation of any serious scholarship in the field. Ever since the publication of Hugues Panassié's *Le Jazz Hot* in 1934, discography has been a science of passion and importance to the followers of jazz.

Two standard works dominate the field. Brian Rust's *Jazz Records, 1897-1942* is the authoritative source on early jazz recordings; also worthy of mention are Rust's efforts in peripherally related areas: *The American Dance Band Discography, 1917-1942* and *The Complete Entertainment Discography, from the Mid-1890s to 1942.* The post-1942 era is the domain of Jorgen Grunnett Jepsen's *Jazz Records: A Discography, 1942-1965.* Jepsen has so far extended his work through 1965, but a new edition covering the years from 1942 to 1978 is currently in preparation. From Belgium comes the six-volume *60 Years of Recorded Jazz, 1917-1977,* compiled by Walter Bruyninckx, with four volumes currently available and the remainder due out shortly. Though far from readily available, this set would appear to be in the same league with the works of Rust and Jepsen.

Blues discographies are as yet in the sole-source situation that marked the jazz field until recently. That is, the bare essentials are as comprehensive as they come. *Blues and Gospel Records, 1902-1942,* by R. M. W. Dixon and J. Godrich, is the fundamental work, followed (as Jepsen follows Rust) by Mike Leadbitter and Neil Slaven on *Blues Records 1943-1966.*

Beyond these standard references, there are many more focused discographical studies available, although many of them contain no more information than can be found in the general works cited above. One exemplary exception is *Duke Ellington's Story on Records,* compiled in Italy by Massagli, Volonte, and Pusateri. Where most discographies provide such information as recording session dates, locations, personnel, matrix numbers, and reissues, this work goes on to detail the formal structure of each piece and identifies soloists, their instruments, and the number of bars played. It is hard to imagine a better and more thorough discographical effort.

Also worth noting at this juncture is the exhaustive bio-discography, *Hendersonia: The Music of Fletcher Henderson,* a comprehensive study of the career of Fletcher Henderson assembled by Walter C. Allen. It is a most distinguished achievement in jazz scholarship.

BIBLIOGRAPHIES

The sheer volume of jazz literature has long since passed the point of manageability for the individual researcher; there are enough discographies alone to require bibliographical assistance. For help in this area, consult David G. Cooper's 1975 *International Bibliography of Discographies;* jazz and blues listings comprise about one-third of the work's total.

Of the more general listings and surveys of jazz literature, the most useful must be Donald Kennington's *The Literature of Jazz: A Critical Guide,* a highly intelligent survey of the field. A somewhat more comprehensive guide to jazz literature can be found in the *International Jazz Bibliography: Jazz Books from 1919 to 1968*, by Herzog zu Mecklenberg. Carl-Gregor, with its supplements, which bring it up to date through 1973. Another slightly obscure but potentially useful work is *The New Expanded Bibliography of Jazz Compositions Based on the Chord Progressions of Standard Tunes*, compiled by Reese Markewich and published in 1974; this genealogy of popular song in the twentieth-century United States can save many steps and remove much of the guesswork from jazz research—though it is always wise and often instructive to confirm any such reports with one's own ears.

A final addendum to this brief look at jazz discographies would fall under the heading of filmography. *Jazz in the Movies: A Guide to Jazz Musicians 1917-1977,* by David Meeker, is everything its title suggests and as valuable in its way as a discography. As documentary film and video presentations become more and more important to the educational mainstream, so will this book and its successors.

RESEARCH COLLECTIONS

The jazz archive may well find its musical analogy in the jazz repertory concept: both stem from the notion that the future of jazz is intrinsically involved in its past, and both are relatively youthful ideas. Jazz archives are comparatively few in number and too often short on conceptual maturity. In fact, there are only two collections that can truly be said to have weathered the storms of adolescence. The single most comprehensive concentration of jazz material is without doubt The Institute of Jazz Studies at Rutgers University, Newark, New Jersey—a short ride from Manhattan. These extensive collections, currently under the direction of Dan Morgenstern, include books, records, magazines, photographs, clipping files, and memorabilia and are soon to house the Jazz Oral History Program of the National Endowment for the Arts. The second mature entity would be the William Ransom Hogan Jazz Archives, housed at Tulane University in New Orleans; the location gives sufficient notice of the collection's emphasis but not of the thoroughly professional approach taken by the Tulane archivists under the direction of Dick Allen.

Other collections may be of significant service to the researcher as well. Of these, two of the most notable are in New York City, and one is in Washington, D.C.: the Schomburg Collection of Negro Literature and History, and the Rodgers and Hammerstein Archive of Recorded Sound (housed, respectively, at the Harlem and Lincoln Center Branches of the New York Public Library), and the Recorded Sound and Music Divisions of the Library of Congress in Washington, D.C. West Coast researchers may wish to address queries to the John Edwards Memorial Foundation at the University of California at Los Angeles; those in the Midwest to the Archives of Traditional Music at Indiana University, Bloomington; and those in the Southwest to North Texas State University in Denton.

These listings comprise the main body of jazz reference works and collections. Though far from comprehensive, they make note of the basic research tools that can help any diligent researcher toward his goal. In many ways, these resources are the second step in the promulgation of a jazz scholar. The first will ever be the cultivation of a mature critical sense capable of discrimination based on an operative, sensitive aesthetic and of putting any given sound in perspective with regard to the jazz tradition.

HISTORY AND CRITICISM

Any music as spontaneous as jazz invites subjective appraisal; not surprisingly, that same subjectivity permeates many of the published histories of jazz. Sometimes the subjective element is yet rational and sometimes even eloquent; at others it can be as embarrassing as a teen fan letter. The above, then, by way of objective recognition of this writer's prejudices, which permeate the following survey.

There may be no finer introduction to the origins of jazz than that provided by Gunther Schuller in his *Early Jazz: Its Roots and Musical Development,* the first volume in an ongoing history of jazz. His discussion of African musical forms and their relationship to the blues tradition is superb, as are his analyses of examples from the recordings of the era and carrying through the early 1930s. The care and scholarship that went into this book are obvious; subsequent volumes in this history should be the object of eager anticipation.

Lacking those succeeding volumes, however, one must look elsewhere for a "complete" history of this music, that is, one that will bring us into the recent past without extreme embarrassment. Marshall W. Stearns's *The Story of Jazz* is a scrupulous, solid account with particular strength and fascination in its root theories and a worthwhile concentration on the music of the Caribbean; Stearns continues through the early 1950s with little depreciation. *Shining Trumpets: A History of Jazz,* by Rudi Blesh, makes it through the mid-1940s and is a thoroughgoing work, if somehow unbalanced in favor of older styles. Andre Hodeir's *Jazz: Its Evolution and Essence* is the best of the French critic's published studies, providing plenty of background interspersed with in-depth critiques, in their turn full of insight and imagination. In this book, Hodeir manages to stay away from the somewhat groundless abstractions that mark his later publications, including the by any standards far-out *The Worlds of Jazz.*

It may be a sign of the increasing complexities of this music called jazz, but the fact is that recent attempts at comprehensive histories have produced nothing definitive. The most satisfying, for several reasons, is Albert Murray's *Stomping the Blues.* Aside from the extremely attractive design with which this volume has been favored, Murray effectively paints the jazz aesthetic in tracing the development of the music through its major standard-bearers. His prose, itself redolent of the quality of a thoughtful trumpet solo, speaks in the same tones used by Duke Ellington and makes the blues a very real, palpable aesthetic entity. If Murray feels somehow cheated as jazz moves away from its functional, dance-inspired heritage, we yet know what Murray knows—that it still swings.

Three other recent histories and/or textbooks bear mention here. *The Making of Jazz: A Comprehensive History,* by James Lincoln Collier, is the best of the three, very nearly earning its titular claim. Much original thought pervades the book, which is weakest when Collier ventures into the speculative waters of psychomusicology. The second and third books, Charles Nanry's *The Jazz Text* and Frank Tirro's *Jazz: A History*, have this much in common: they are both keyed to The Smithsonian Collection of Classic Jazz, six LPs' worth of gems selected and annotated by Martin Williams; the classroom merits of this anthology have been widely recognized since its introduction in 1973. Unfortunately, neither of the texts in question lives up to the promise of such a text-cum-recording combination. Charles

Nanry's *The Jazz Text,* written in collaboration with Edward Berger, presents jazz history with a decidedly sociological cast. In and of itself this is no sin, and such a study should prove useful to certain researchers; as a basic text, however, it has some serious flaws, including a rather digressive organizational scheme which tends to play down the importance of individual innovations and contributions to the music. In terms of history, flaws are one thing, errors quite another; unfortunately, Frank Tirro's *Jazz: A History* is plagued by the latter. Errors of fact are compounded for this reader by what appear to me errors of interpretation and misplaced emphasis. If students enjoy finding fault with their textbooks, then it may be that this work is a useful curricular center; if not, or if sound pedagogical judgment prevails, this is one to avoid.

For the beginner seeking the essence of jazz, there exists a noteworthy primer: *Where's the Melody?,* by Martin Williams, tells the story of jazz in layman's language. Advanced beginners may graduate to Williams's *The Jazz Tradition,* a musical orientation course in one volume; taken with Murray's *Stomping the Blues,* it provides all the foundation a listener could ask for through essays on sixteen of the music's major figures.

Williams also served as editor of the Macmillan Jazz Masters series and contributed to it *Jazz Masters of New Orleans* and *Jazz Masters in Transition, 1957-1969.* The former is perhaps the best critical summation of New Orleans jazz ever produced; the latter, a collection of incidental essays of more than occasional interest. The rest of the series includes Richard Hadlock on *Jazz Masters of the Twenties;* Rex William Stewart, the great Ellington cornetist, on *Jazz Masters of the Thirties;* Ira Gitler on *Jazz Masters of the Forties;* and Joe Goldberg on *Jazz Masters of the Fifties.* Of these, Gitler's is the most important, detailing clearly the events leading up to the be-bop revolution; it is certainly the magnum opus in Gitler's lengthy career as an observer and critic of the jazz scene. A volume on the 1960s has been planned for some time, though it is not as yet near publication.

Three more veterans of the jazz wars come with a critical warning. Leonard Feather's *The Book of Jazz: A Guide to the Entire Field* is marred by oversights, and such oddities as an unaccountable animosity toward the music and style of Jelly Roll Morton. These same tendencies seem to infect Feather's other works, though his commendable encyclopedias have by and large managed to escape with a well-balanced perspective. Joachim Berendt's *The Jazz Book: From New Orleans to Rock and Free Jazz* may well be, as a cover boasts, "The most widely read book on Jazz *ever* written"; by the same token, I suppose, Benny Goodman *is* the King of Swing. Berendt's book is not bad, merely shallow. More wrongheaded is *The Jazz Story: From the '90s to the '60s,* by Dave Dexter, Jr.; the less said about this opinionated and often vituperative tome, the better.

There are, of course, many more specifically focused studies in jazz, including several subgeneric works of value to students of the music. Ragtime, despite the recent revival in its popularity, will be hard pressed to inspire better critical studies than *They All Played Ragtime* by Rudi Blesh and Harriet Janis, and *The Art of Ragtime* by William J. Schafer and Johannes Reidel. The fifteen years (1958-73) that separate the publication of these two books produced a change not so much in the level of perception as in approach, with the later book taking a more academic route; both are reliable sources. On the other hand, Samuel B. Charters's *Jazz: New Orleans, 1885-1963* proves unreliable, being full of unattributed oral history.

Blues criticism is too often the realm of writers with a larger store of zeal than scholarship. Still, there are useful published resources available to the blues researcher.

The history of jazz is inextricably entwined with the history of the blues, though the blues as such have always had a life of their own within the broader field of African-influenced American music. If one cared to make such distinctions, the blues might be considered the "folk" side and jazz the "art" side of the same coin.

While an in-depth, front-to-back history of the blues has yet to be written, Paul Oliver's *The Story of the Blues* provides a good, readable popular history of the blues from one of the idiom's most prolific scholars. Samuel B. Charters's *The Country Blues* is an attempt to chronicle the tradition that titles the book, but its smooth style stumbles over substance too often; its credibility cannot be said to emerge unscathed.

More useful to the blues researcher will be Charters's two volumes covering pre-World War II country blues singers. *The Bluesmen* surveys Mississippi, Texas, and Alabama, and its companion study, *Sweet as the Showers of Rain,* focuses on Tennessee, Georgia, and the Carolinas. Another survey, more critical in nature, is Derrick Stewart-Baxter's *Ma Rainey and the Classic Blues Singers,* which centers on the women who first carried the blues into the recording studios during the 1920s.

Musicology meets the blues in two books of great value: Jeff Todd Titon's *Early Downhome Blues: A Musical and Cultural Analysis,* and John Fahey's *Charley Patton.* Titon's book is an exemplary analysis of recorded country blues from the period 1926-30; Fahey follows a brief biography of Patton with an in-depth analysis of his music.

Blacks, Whites and Blues, by Tony Russell, traces the development of the black and white folk music traditions and the relationships between the two; throughout, Russell emphasizes the importance of the blues to both traditions. Paul Oliver follows a different set of relationships in *Savannah Syncopators: African Retentions in the Blues.* Oliver's thesis, implicit in his title, may seem obvious, but his approach to the subject repays study. Oliver's respectful attitude is also the key to the success of his *The Meaning of the Blues,* a seminal examination of 350 blues lyrics; the same subject concerns Samuel B. Charters in his *The Poetry of the Blues.*

Two volumes are of special interest, one of narrow focus, the other much broader: Ekkehard Jost's *Free Jazz* is a fascinating and often successful attempt to come to musicological grips with the innovations of the avant garde; Jost's is a very timely effort, inasmuch as the avant garde now dates back more than twenty years. On a much broader plane, Wilfrid Mellers's *Music in a New Found Land* is a wonderful treatment of American music in general, with an appropriately deep and surprisingly perceptive coverage of jazz.

AUTOBIOGRAPHIES AND BIOGRAPHIES

Jazz has often been called a player's art. Not surprisingly, then, many valuable components of jazz literature take the form of life stories of jazzmen. To begin almost at the beginning, two of the many works devoted to Louis Armstrong should suffice, one being Armstrong's own *Satchmo: My Life in New Orleans;* the other, *Louis: The Louis Armstrong Story 1900-1971,* by Max Jones and John Chilton, will do very well as a central authoritative source.

There is more on New Orleans in George M. "Pops" Foster's *Pops Foster: The Autobiography of a New Orleans Jazzman,* and in Sidney Bechet's self-history, *Treat it Gentle: An Autobiography;* the latter is certainly one of the most engaging books of its kind.

Alan Lomax's *Mr. Jelly Roll: The Fortunes of Jelly Roll Morton, New Orleans Creole and "Inventor of Jazz"* remains the most thorough biographical record of the first great jazz composer. The book's major flaw is its narrative framework, which tends to get in the way of Morton's chronology. And, although Lomax has dutifully tried to peel off the layers of fiction in which Morton habitually dressed, it is inevitable that a few minor apocrypha slipped through.

Chris Albertson's *Bessie* is a finely wrought portrait of Bessie Smith, the classic singer of classic blues; taken with the Stewart-Baxter volume mentioned above, it provides a wonderfully proportioned view of a vanishing subgenre of jazz.

Bumper stickers in Davenport, Iowa, and around the nation, still proudly proclaim, "Bix lives!" And it often seems that the tragic implications of Beiderbecke's early demise threaten to swallow his very real contribution to jazz music. Fortunately, Richard M. Sudhalter keeps things in perspective, nimbly sidestepping the melodramatic potential of his subject in *Bix: Man and Legend.*

No jazzman is surrounded by more legend than Charlie Parker, the quintessential be-bopper and alto saxophonist extraordinaire. Too often, however, Parker's career as a musical genius takes on the lurid pall of his life as an addict. There is, unfortunately, no thorough biography of Parker. In its absence, Max Harrison's *Charlie Parker* will have to do. Ross Russell's *Bird Lives: The High Life and Hard Times of Charlie (Yardbird) Parker* will not. The latter is too sensationalist to be a reliable reference, although it does grant the reader some sense of the be-bop era—and of the "intimacy" Parker shared with the author.

Dizzy Gillespie, to whom Parker was "the other side of my heartbeat," has done himself proud in his recent autobiography, *To Be or Not to Bop: Memoirs.* Here, again, is a great deal of be-bop flavor, but in this case the framework and treatment are considerably more substantial.

Fats Waller, stride piano master and toast of the town, has recently spawned two lesser biographies to stand next to Ed Kirkeby's admirable *Ain't Misbehavin': The Story of Fats Waller;* neither compares very well. Joel Vance's *Fats Waller: His Life and Times* is very simply a slight effort; Fats's son, Maurice Waller's collaboration with Anthony Calabrese, titled simply *Fats Waller,* is somewhat more substantial but still leaves a great deal to be desired. Like so many filial efforts, this biography goes from cloying to coy in its efforts to maintain interest—often at the expense of those achievements which make the subject parent interesting.

One would expect more from Mercer Ellington, a musician in his own right, if not of his father's magnitude. Mercer's *Duke Ellington in Person: An Intimate Memoir,* written with Stanley Dance, proves disappointing, however, for many of the same reasons that the Waller book fails. There is, though, a more intense bitterness present in the Ellington book that the psychomusicologists in our midst may find interesting.

Duke's history is much better served by the one-two punch of his autobiography, *Music Is My Mistress,* and Barry Ulanov's *Duke Ellington.* Duke's own words ring true in his book, even if the occasional fact is reharmonized to suit the composition at hand. Ulanov's book, published in 1946, covers only the first half of Ellington's career but does so with care and great perception.

If Ellington himself speaks in *Music Is My Mistress,* his peers have their say in *The World of Duke Ellington* by Stanley Dance. As in Dance's other recent books *(The World of Swing* and *The World of Earl Hines,* and his collaborative effort on the autobiography of trombonist Dickie Wells, *The Night People: Reminiscences of a Jazzman),* oral history plays a major role; these books thus provide a great deal of primary source material as well as Dance's own decidedly mainstream perceptions.

It is worth noting that Dance is currently engaged with "The World of

Count Basie," following the same basic plan. Other biographies of promise still in the works include a study of Benny Carter's life by Monroe and Edward Berger, and a biography of Count Basie by Albert Murray.

JOURNALS AND PERIODICALS

There is but one American scholarly journal devoted to jazz: *The Journal of Jazz Studies*, published by the Institute of Jazz Studies of Rutgers University. The Austrian journal *Jazzforschung* is another source of scholarly jazz research and analysis.

This lack of scholarly journals is not necessarily a setback for the jazz researcher, however, for popular music and scholarship have not always been on the most cordial terms. Indeed, research in American popular music of the eighteenth and nineteenth centuries is quite often aided and abetted by, if not in fact strictly limited to, accounts of performances in the popular press. There are, of course, certain compromises one must make: whereas academics had a tendency in those good old days to sneer and patronize the popular music of their times, journalists go only as deep as the spirit may move them—and rarely beyond simple description.

Jazz journalism is a variegated beast, to be sure, and often deceptive. Too often enthusiasm passes for expertise; too often articles are no more than formulaic interviews ("Was your family musical? When did you start playing? Who were your influences?"). The fact is that in many instances those magazines which explicitly declare themselves for jazz will prove of little or no use to the researcher, save perhaps as some gauge of contemporary attitudes.

This is not to say that there have not been jazz magazines that stand as valuable documents to this day. *Metronome*, for example, began its published life in 1885 as a high-toned music magazine, narrowing its focus to jazz in the 1930s; the magazine and its editorial standards survived until 1961. A sadder story yet concerns the fate of *The Jazz Review*, quite possibly the finest jazz magazine ever; despite its nonpareil editorial quality, *The Jazz Review* could hold on for only twenty-one issues (1958-60.)

Meanwhile, there were certain blossomings of jazz culture in magazines appealing to a broader public. *Esquire*, that protean men's magazine, took up the jazz standard and carried it high during the 1940s. The 1950s brought serious appreciation of jazz to the *Saturday Review* and the *New Yorker*.

As one jazz magazine dies, there always seems to be another ready to fill the void; on the other hand, there are some whose survival instinct seems always to find a way. *Downbeat* is now into its fifth decade of publication, its peaks and valleys of editorial vicissitude now having settled into a rather monotonous pop-oriented posture. Magazine publishing is, after all, a business, and today more than ever a business that must aggressively seek out the largest possible circulation—which necessarily prescribes the lowest common editorial denominator, the "havin' a swingin' time" school of jazz journalism. Thus it is that newcomers to the field, such as *Musician, Player & Listener* and the seriously intentioned *Jazz Magazine*, are forced to make concessions to current trends in order to meet next month's advertising and circulation quotas.

Still, some periodicals do manage to take their jazz more or less seriously and still survive—a feat which *Jazz Magazine* is struggling to accomplish. There is also *Coda,* the Canadian journal and longtime proselytizer on behalf of the avant garde, which seems to be showing signs of an editorial thaw that may allow for a wider range of articles.

If jazz found a home in some general interest magazines of the 1940s and 1950s, some of today's better critics find at least a partial home in consumer-oriented magazines, especially those catering to the audiophile market, such as *Stereo Review, High Fidelity,* and *Audio.* Trade papers, particularly *Billboard,* occasionally have business-oriented articles on jazz, some of them of considerable interest. Even *Rolling Stone,* house organ of the Now generation, occasionally curtseys to Madame Jazz.

ANTHOLOGIES AND REISSUES

Perhaps the most encouraging development in jazz over the last five years has been the return to circulation of many of the greatest recordings in the genre. Record companies have answered the escalation of interest in jazz by reviving such long-dormant labels as Riverside, Verve, EmArcy, Bluebird, and Blue Note. Moreover, these reissues often carry extensive annotative liner essays, which combine with the impressive quality of remastering techniques to create a product vastly superior to the bootleg issues and collector's items that had previously been *the* vinyl link to the recorded past.

Where does one start to listen to almost sixty years' worth of recorded jazz? One solid starting point, as good as any and better than most, is the *Smithsonian Collection of Classic Jazz.*. From there, the path widens; the catalog of New World Records, available for the most part only through libraries, serves to document many of the major developments in American musical history, mostly in terms of anthological surveys; the Smithsonian Collection includes numerous other, tightly focused jazz collections; and, taken with several grains of salt, the Time-Life Giants of Jazz series may prove helpful.

These, in combination with various reissues covering the careers—or recording contracts—of the music's major innovators, including Armstrong,

Morton, Basie (and Young), Ellington, Parker, Monk, Davis, Rollins, Coltrane, and Coleman, provide the basic repertoire on which the critic/scholar must draw in order to keep his or her observations in perspective.

What these records, in their full-throated vitality, affirm is that the history of this music is best read in the music itself. Biographies, facts, and particulars can serve to confirm the suspicions of the critical ear, but little more; in the long run it is the ear that must make the decisions. True enough, critical guides can help to perceive subtleties of form and style, but they cannot instill an appreciation of the great undefinable: "soul," some have called it, "swing" is another common alias. But whatever it is called, the experience of three generations of jazzmen suggests that it cannot be taught; it must be "got." The popularity of jazz, then, within the realm of American popular music depends on its availability to developing ears, not "accessibility," for that factor is often merely a misnomer for trivialities. What jazz requires is exposure: broadcast exposure, curricular exposure, institutional exposure in a variety of settings. In the four score years of its history, jazz and the world have taken each other to heart—while Americans have by and large taken the music and the artists behind it for granted. We have a great deal yet to learn from this at once visceral and delicate, expressive, indomitable... *swinging* music.

BIBLIOGRAPHY

REFERENCE WORKS

Allen, Walter C. *Hendersonia: The Music of Fletcher Henderson.* Highland Park, N.J.: published privately, 1973.

Bruyninckx, Walter. *60 Years of Recorded Jazz, 1917-1977.* Mechelen, Belgium: Bruyninckx, 1968-

Carl-Gregor, Herzog zu Mecklenburg. *International Jazz Bibliography: Jazz Books from 1919 to 1968.* Sammlung musikwissenschaftlicher Abhändlungen, no. 49. Strasbourg: Heitz, 1969.

______. *1970 Supplement to International Jazz Bibliography and International Drum and Percussion Bibliography.* Beitrage zur Jazzforschung, no. 3. Graz: Universal Edition, 1971.

______. *1971/72/73 Supplement to International Jazz Bibliography and Selective Bibliography of Some Jazz Background Literature and Bibliographies of Two Subjects Previously Excluded.* Beitrage zur Jazzforschung, no. 6. Graz: Universal Edition, 1975.

Chilton, John. *Who's Who of Jazz: Storyville to Swing Street.* London: Bloomsbury Book Shop, 1970.

Cooper, David E. *International Bibliography of Discographies.* Littleton, Colo.: Libraries Unlimited, 1975.

Dixon, R. M. W., and J. Godrich. *Blues and Gospel Records, 1902-1942.* 2nd ed. London: Storyville, 1969.

Feather, Leonard. *The Encyclopedia of Jazz in the Sixties.* New York: Horizon Press, 1967.

———. *The New Edition of the Encyclopedia of Jazz.* New York: Horizon Press, 1960.

———, and Ira Gitler. *The Encyclopedia of Jazz in the Seventies.* New York: Horizon Press, 1977.

Harris, Sheldon. *Blues Who's Who: A Biographical Dictionary of Blues Singers.* New Rochelle, N.Y.: Arlington House, 1979.

Jepsen, Jorgen Grunnett. *Jazz Records: A Discography, 1942-1965.* Holte, Denmark: Knudsen, 1963-1965.

Keepnews, Orrin, and Bill Grauer, Jr. *A Pictorial History of Jazz.* 2nd rev. ed. New York: Crown, 1966.

Kennington, Donald. *The Literature of Jazz: A Critical Guide.* Chicago: American Library Association, 1971.

Kinkle, Roger D. *The Complete Encyclopedia of Popular Music and Jazz, 1900-1950.* New Rochelle, N.Y.: Arlington House, 1974.

Leadbitter, Mike, and Neil Slaven. *Blues Records 1943-1966.* New York: Oak, 1968.

Markewich, Reese. *The New Expanded Bibliography of Jazz Compositions Based on the Chord Progressions of Standard Tunes.* Riverdale, N.Y.: Markewich, 1974.

Massagli, Volonte, and Pusateri. *Duke Ellington's Story on Records.* Milan: Raretone, 1972-

Meeker, David. *Jazz in the Movies: A Guide to Jazz Musicians 1917-1977.* New Rochelle, N.Y.: Arlington House, 1977.

Panassié, Hugues. *Le Jazz Hot.* Paris: Correa, 1934.

Rose, Al, and Edmond Souchon. *New Orleans Jazz: A Family Album.* Baton Rouge: Louisiana State University Press, 1967.

Rust, Brian. *The American Dance Band Discography, 1917-1942.* New Rochelle, N.Y.: Arlington House, 1976.

———, and Allen Debus. *The Complete Entertainment Discography, from the Mid-1890s to 1942.* New Rochelle, N.Y.: Arlington House, 1973.

———. *Jazz Records, 1897-1942.* London: Storyville, 1970.

HISTORY AND CRITICISM

Albertson, Chris. *Bessie.* New York: Stein and Day, 1972.

Armstrong, Louis. *Satchmo: My Life in New Orleans.* Englewood Cliffs, N.J.: Prentice-Hall, 1954.

Bechet, Sidney. *Treat It Gentle: An Autobiography.* New York: Hill and Wang, 1960.

Berendt, Joachim. *The Jazz Book: From New Orleans to Rock and Free Jazz.* New York: Lawrence Hill, 1975.

Blesh, Rudi. *Shining Trumpets: A History of Jazz.* 2nd ed. New York: Knopf, 1958.

———, and Harriet Janis. *They All Played Ragtime.* 4th ed. New York: Oak, 1971.

Charters, Samuel B. *The Bluesmen.* New York: Oak, 1967.

———. *The Country Blues.* New York: Holt, Rinehart and Winston, 1959. Reprint. New York: Da Capo Press, 1975.

———. *Jazz: New Orleans, 1885-1963*. Rev. ed. New York: Oak, 1963.
———. *The Poetry of the Blues*. New York: Oak, 1963.
———. *Sweet as the Showers of Rain*. New York: Oak, 1977.
Collier, James Lincoln. *The Making of Jazz: A Comprehensive History*. Boston: Houghton Mifflin, 1978.
Dance, Stanley. *The World of Duke Ellington*. New York: Scribner's, 1970.
———. *The World of Earl Hines*. New York: Scribner's, 1977.
———. *The World of Swing*. New York: Scribner's, 1974.
Dexter, Dave, Jr. *The Jazz Story: From the '90s to the '60s*. Englewood Cliffs, N.J.: Prentice-Hall, 1964.
Ellington, Duke. *Music Is My Mistress*. Garden City, N.Y.: Doubleday, 1973.
Ellington, Mercer, with Stanley Dance. *Duke Ellington in Person: An Intimate Memoir*. Boston: Houghton Mifflin, 1978.
Fahey, John. *Charley Patton*. London: Studio Vista, 1970.
Feather, Leonard. *The Book of Jazz: A Guide to the Entire Field*. New York: Horizon Press, 1965.
Foster, George M. "Pops." As told to Tom Stoddard. *Pops Foster: The Autobiography of a New Orleans Jazzman*. Berkeley: University of California Press, 1971.
Gillespie, John Birks "Dizzy," with Al Fraser. *To Be or Not to Bop: Memoirs*. Garden City, N.Y.: Doubleday, 1979.
Gitler, Ira. *Jazz Masters of the Forties*. New York: Macmillan, 1966.
Goldberg, Joe. *Jazz Masters of the Fifties*. New York: Macmillan, 1965.
Hadlock, Richard. *Jazz Masters of the Twenties*. New York: Macmillan, 1965.
Harrison, Max. *Charlie Parker*. London: Cassell, 1960.
Hodeir, Andre. *Jazz: Its Evolution and Essence*. New York: Grove Press, 1956.
———. *The Worlds of Jazz*. New York: Grove Press, 1972.
Jones, Max, and John Chilton. *Louis: The Louis Armstong Story 1900-1971*. Boston: Little, Brown, 1971.
Jost, Ekkehard. *Free Jazz*. Graz: Universal Edition, 1974.
Kirkeby, Ed. *Ain't Misbehavin': The Story of Fats Waller*. New York: Dodd, Mead, 1966.
Lomax, Alan. *Mr. Jelly Roll: The Fortunes of Jelly Roll Morton, New Orleans Creole and "Inventor of Jazz."* New York: Grove Press, 1950.
Mellers, Wilfrid. *Music in a New Found Land*. New York: Knopf, 1967.
Murray, Albert. *Stomping the Blues*. New York: McGraw-Hill, 1976.
Nanry, Charles, with Edward Berger. *The Jazz Text*. New York: Van Nostrand Reinhold, 1979.
Oliver, Paul. *Blues Fell This Morning*. London: Cassell, 1960. Reprinted as *The Meaning of the Blues*. New York: Collier Books, 1963.
———. *Savannah Syncopators: African Retentions of the Blues*. New York: Stein and Day, 1970.
———. *The Story of the Blues*. New York: Chilton Book, 1969.
Russell, Ross. *Bird Lives! The High Life and Hard Times of Charlie (Yardbird) Parker*. New York: Charterhouse, 1973.
Russell, Tony. *Blacks, Whites and Blues*. London: Studio Vista, 1970.
Schafer, William J., and Johannes Reidel. *The Art of Ragtime*. Baton Rouge: Louisiana State University Press, 1973.

Schuller, Gunther. *Early Jazz: Its Roots and Musical Development.* New York: Oxford University Press, 1968.
Stearns, Marshall W. *The Story of Jazz.* New York: Oxford University Press, 1956.
Stewart, Rex William. *Jazz Masters of the Thirties.* New York: Macmillan, 1972.
Stewart-Baxter, Derrick. *Ma Rainey and the Classic Blues Singers.* London: Studio Vista, 1970.
Sudhalter, Richard M. *Bix: Man and Legend.* New Rochelle, N.Y.: Arlington House, 1974.
Tirro, Frank. *Jazz: A History.* New York: Norton, 1977.
Titon, Jeff Todd. *Early Downhome Blues: A Musical and Cultural Analysis.* Urbana: University of Illinois Press, 1977.
Ulanov, Barry. *Duke Ellington.* New York: Creative Age Press, 1946.
Vance, Joel. *Fats Waller: His Life and Times.* Chicago: Contemporary Books, 1977.
Waller, Maurice, and Anthony Calabrese. *Fats Waller.* New York: Schirmer Books, 1977.
Wells, Dicky, and Stanley Dance. *The Night People: Reminiscences of a Jazzman.* Boston: Crescendo, 1971.
Williams, Martin. *Jazz Masters in Transition, 1957-1969.* New York: Macmillan, 1970.
______. *Jazz Masters of New Orleans.* New York: Macmillan, 1967.
______. *The Jazz Tradition.* New York: Oxford University Press, 1970.
______. *Where's the Melody?* New York: Funk and Wagnalls, 1967.
______, ed. *The Art of Jazz.* New York: Oxford University Press, 1959; reprint ed. New York: Da Capo Press, 1979.

JOURNALS AND PERIODICALS

Audio. Philadelphia, 1947-.
Billboard. Los Angeles, 1894-.
Coda. Toronto, 1962-.
Downbeat. Chicago, 1934-.
Esquire. New York, 1933-.
High Fidelity/Musical America. Great Barrington, Mass., 1951-.
Jazz Magazine. Northport, N.Y., 1976-.
Jazz Review. New York, 1958-60.
Jazzforschung. Graz, 1969-.
Journal of Jazz Studies. Newark, N.J., 1973.
Metronome. New York, 1885-1961.
Musician, Player & Listener. Boston, 1977.
New Yorker. New York, 1925-.
Rolling Stone. New York, 1967-.
Saturday Review. New York, 1924-.
Stereo Review. New York, 1958-.

CHAPTER 5 Leisure Vehicles, Pleasure Boats, and Aircraft

Bernard Mergen

The subject of recreational travel is large and complex; it is also a matter of considerable economic and social importance.[1] Despite the high rate of inflation and gasoline shortages, the manufacture and sales of pickup trucks, motor homes, vans, off-road vehicles, snowmobiles, trail bikes, motorcycles, motorboats, and airplanes have increased enormously. Bicycles, sailboats, canoes, gliders, and balloons have also proliferated. Statistics showing the number of participants in cycling, boating, flying, vanning, and "truckin'," while impressive, tell only part of the story. For the student of American popular culture, the study of recreational travel, pleasure boating, and flying offers ways of combining some of the major issues of our time in research that has public policy as well as academic usefulness.

The issue of leisure, what it is and what it means in our society, is the most obvious area of investigation. How do people conceive of and use their nonwork time? What are the relationships between such variables as class, race, age, sex, and region and the use of recreational vehicles, pleasure boats, and aircraft? What are the appeals of speed, fantasy, and competition in the kind of play associated with the use of these artifacts of modern technology? A second issue, commercialism, raises the question: to what extent is our leisure time manipulated by businessmen interested in selling machines without regard to safety or environmental damage? The leisure vehicle industry—manufacturing, marketing, and servicing—is inextricably linked to both national and international economics. What role should the government play in the regulation of these industries? What control is necessary of individual owners of planes, boats, and vehicles? The third major issue, that of conservation of natural resources, raises the question of the future. How will those subcultures which support each of the recreational vehicle, boat, and aircraft types respond to shortages of fuel and restrictions on land and water use? As recently as 1974, a group of recreation and natural resource experts developed a set of future leisure environments for the U.S. Forest Service that included restriction of off-road vehicles in public recreation areas and the banning of private aircraft from metropolitan airports by 1980. At the same time, they predicted air strips and helicopter ports at most popular recreation areas and small private submarines as common as snowmobiles today by the year 2000. By 2050, their report concluded, only foot travel would be allowed in major public parks, but hover craft would be widely used, as would jet-powered back packs and one-man low-speed helicopters.[2]

Recreational vehicles are a product of our economy, technology, and value system. They must be studied in the context of many related activities, especially when we see that a person's choice of a leisure activity is often closely related to his work, social class, educational level, age, and family status. The use of a camper, van, boat, or plane is obviously related to such ancillary activities as hunting, fishing, scuba diving, photography, amateur radio operating, and camping. As the history of boating, flying, cycling, and recreational driving reveals, each activity has unique origins. Unlike less mechanized and less expensive pastimes, their present is a product of past decisions made deliberately and consciously by individuals who had much to gain and often much to lose.

HISTORIC OUTLINE

Of the forms of transportation considered in this essay, boating was clearly the earliest. The pleasure yacht was introduced into England in the seventeenth century by the Dutch, and by 1713 American shipbuilders had developed the schooner, a small, fast ship which could be used for fishing and coastal freight. Impromptu races between fishermen inspired wealthier colonists to invest in "well-fitted pleasure boats" through the eighteenth century. In Ireland and England the aristocracy organized yachting clubs to regulate the growth of pleasure boating and to supervise races among members. Many historians point to George Crowninshield's brigantine, *Cleopatra's Barge,* built in 1816, as the first American yacht, but Thomas Doubleday was sailing his twenty-foot sloop in Cape Cod Bay in the same year. The two basic types of pleasure boating, the day sailor and the ocean cruiser, seem to have appeared simultaneously.

By the 1830s, the first generation of American yachtsmen were testing their ships in competition and making technical improvements based on their experience. Robert L. Stevens, Edwin A. Stevens, and John C. Stevens, sons of the great inventor, turned their talents to sailing and their boat, *Gimcrack,* designed by George Steers, became the first ship of the fleet of the New York Yacht Club when it was organized in 1844. Seven years later, Steers's yacht, *America,* astounded the British by winning the Queen's Cup at Cowes.

The end of the Civil War signaled the beginning of ostentatious yachting by American millionaires. The transatlantic race among *Vesta,* owned by

Pierre Lorillard, Jr., *Fleetwing,* owned by George and Franklin Osgood, and *Henrietta,* which belonged to James Gordon Bennett, Jr., drew national attention in 1866. The 1870s witnessed the diffusion of yachting across the nation and the founding of clubs on both coasts, the Gulf of Mexico, and the Great Lakes. One of the first journals devoted to water sports, *Aquatic Monthly and Nautical Review,* appeared in 1872, with news of rowing contests and yacht club regattas. By 1884, when the National Watercraft Collection of ship models was begun, yachting was firmly in the hands of professional marine architects such as Edward Burgess and Nathaniel Greene Herreshoff and devoted amateur sailors such as George I. Tyson and Malcolm Forbes. Burgess's *Puritan,* which successfully defended the America's Cup in 1885, broke with the tradition of broad beam, shallow draft sloops by adding a lead keel and reducing the waterline length. Five years later, Herreshoff continued this trend toward narrow, deeper-hulled craft in his *Gloriana.* Like most changes in yacht design, these were made solely to increase speed and to circumvent the rules regarding size, weight, and sail area.

The 1880s were also a decade of steam yachts and naphtha-powered motor launches, heralding the age of motorboating in the twentieth century. In the 1890s, journals such as *American Yachtsman* and *Rudder* helped to popularize small boat racing as well as cruising. Joshua Slocum's solo voyage around the world in 1895-1898, the poetry of John Masefield, and the popular spy novel, *The Riddle of the Sands* (1903) by Erskine Childers all helped to create a romantic image of the sea and encouraged thousands of young men and women to take up sailing. Professional marine photographers such as N. L. Stebbins and Henry Greenwood Peabody published their work in books and magazines for thousands more who would never walk a deck or hoist a sail but who participated vicariously in every America's Cup challenge and Bermuda Race. Although the automobile caused a brief decline in yachting, the work of L. Herreshoff, William Gardner, who developed the "Star" class sailboat in 1911, and John Alden, whose designs led to the construction of more than five thousand boats, contributed to the democratization of yachting. Sailing dinghies led the revival of yachting in the 1920s and 1930s. Collegiate racing, junior racing, and ladies racing all became an accepted part of yacht club activities. The gasoline engine brought new kinds of boating activity, as exemplified by Gar Wood's *Miss America* speed boats, which were approaching 100 miles per hour by 1928. Flying and yachting were pursued by many both in the United States and abroad as the journals *Flugzeug und Yacht* and *Aviation and Yachting* suggest.

Although the Depression and World War II disrupted yachting, the postwar years were a bonanza for the boating industry. New technology produced safer, less expensive boats of all types. In the late 1970s almost 50 million Americans participated in some kind of boating. *Boating* has a circulation over 200,000, and *Sail* about 170,000. *Canoe,* the publication of the American Canoe

Association which celebrates its centennial in 1980, has 30,000 subscribers. Although the variety of boating activities makes it difficult to generalize about the people who own and operate the "Snipes," "Sunfish," "Lightnings," "Tempests," and various motorboats, it is clear that the old masculine world of yachting is being replaced by a familial one. The past decade has seen the publication of innumerable books with titles like *Family Under Sail: A Handbook for First Mates* by Jane Kirstein, *The Woman's Guide to Boating and Cooking* by Lael Morgan, and *How to Be a First-Rate Mate: A Sailing Guide for Women* by Gloria Sloane. This trend affects the other forms of recreational travel as well.

Cycling also began as a male activity but eventually became a vehicle (literally) of women's liberation. Today bicycling is generally considered a family activity, and even motorcycling is promoted as a way to meet "the nicest people." Cycling, like ballooning, was French in origin, and the two remained linked until late in the nineteenth century. Neither developed very rapidly. In 1817, Baron Karl von Drais de Sauerbrun developed a bicycle with a fork over the front wheel to allow steering by handlebars; still later, in 1839, Kirkpatrick Macmillan, a Scottish blacksmith, added cranks attached to a system of rods and levers.

Almost a generation later, in the 1860s, Pierre Lallement and Pierre Michoux placed the cranks and pedals on the front wheel to create the highly successful velocipede. The next cycle, the ordinary or penny-farthing, with its large front wheel, required skill and practice to operate. Acrobats were quick to incorporate it into their acts, and French cycling instructors helped to give bicycling a continental, high-status image. Bicycles were promoted at the Philadelphia Centennial Exhibition, and in 1877 Colonel Albert A. Pope began his campaign for the bicycle and better roads. Two years later, *Bicycling World* began publishing news and technical information, becoming the official journal of the League of American Wheelmen (LAW) in 1880.

The perfection of the safety bicycle in 1884 led to the cycling boom of the 1890s. The LAW had over 100,000 members by the end of the century, many of them women whom reformers encouraged to discard their corsets and confining garments and take up cycling as healthful exercise. Almost as suddenly as it had begun, the cycling mania ceased, as bicyclists left their wheels to younger brothers and sisters and took up motoring. It was not until 1972 that bicycles again outsold automobiles. Almost the same fate was suffered by the motorcycle. Although inventors had tried to attach steam engines to bicycles and tricycles since the late 1860s, it was not until 1885 that Gottlieb Daimler successfully attached a gasoline engine to a frame similar to a velocipede. Further improvements made cheap, reliable motorcycles widely available by 1906, when *Motorcycle Illustrated* began publication.

From the beginning, motorcycles were associated with a violent, libidinous, antisocial male subculture. As Sam Kent Brooks points out in his excellent study of the motorcycle in American culture, the association of the motorcyclist with the lone horseman of Western mythology was strong, despite the fact that motorcyclists tended from the beginning to form clubs and ride in groups. By 1912, Andrew Carey Lincoln and Lieutenant Howard Payson had created a fictional world of "motorcycle chums" for boys to read and emulate. Perhaps, as Brooks suggests, the appeal of the motorcycle was even deeper than the image of the cowboy. "To the practiced and regular rider," Brooks quotes the authors of an 1898 book on cycling, "the motorcycle becomes so far like the lower part of the centaur that steering is almost unconscious and the balancing a matter of instinctive bodily sway."[3]

Curiously, motorcycling made a comeback in the 1960s under the stimulus of economic prosperity and an aggressive advertising campaign by Japanese manufacturers. Today the image of the motorcyclist is paradoxically split between the outlaw "Hell's Angels" and "Easy Rider" type and the weekend touring cyclist. The problems posed by the current popularity of cycling is neatly summarized in a recent publication of the Bureau of Outdoor Recreation (now the Heritage Conservation and Recreation Service). Noting that different users consume trails "psychologically" in different ways, the report argues that bicyclists, like hunters, are goal-oriented, needing point-to-point trails in which the trail is more important than the scenery. Motorcyclists and snowmobilers are more concerned with the stimulus from their machines, so their trails should emphasize difficulty of terrain.[4]

Snowmobiles are second only to minibikes in popularity among off-road or all-terrain recreational vehicles. The A. C. Nielsen Company calls it the third fastest growing sport in the United States, just behind tennis and skiing, with more than 7 million participants driving almost a million machines. Yet snowmobiles are only a small part of the leisure vehicle industry. Since the perfection of the Model A, the automobile industry has encouraged the development of pleasure driving. In 1914, the *Ford Times* claimed "campers received motor-morphic medicine because of the laws of motion. Babies were put in cradles, children rode rocking horses, savages swayed to sinuous dances, and grandmother rocked ceaselessly in a rocking chair."[5] As auto camping caught on, car owners began to modify and customize their machines. Trailers were made by cutting an old car in half and hitching the rear seat and wheels to another automobile. Home-built vans were made to look like Pullman cars, clapboard cottages, and prairie schooners. By 1930, the Covered Wagon Company of Mt. Clemens, Michigan, was mass producing trailers, and a new industry was born.

Although trailer owners had organized as early as 1919, as the Tin Can Tourists, the 1930s was the decade of rapid expansion and public awareness. *Trailer Travel Magazine* began publication in 1936, and popular periodicals such as *Fortune*, *Harper's*, *Nation*, and *Time*, discovered "The Trailer Epidemic." Wally Byam's Airstream trailer made its appearance in 1935, a product of new technology and styles. Until the 1950s, recreational vehicles were limited to trailers and converted automobiles and trucks. Developments of the past thirty years have redefined the term. Today the recreational vehicle (RV) may be defined as "a permanent compartment carried by a motorist to cook and/or sleep in."[6] This includes pickup campers, motor homes, camping trailers, travel trailers, and fifth-wheel trailers. It excludes the off-road and all-terrain vehicles such as jeeps, dune buggies, snowmobiles, and trail bikes. Vans, too, should be considered another category. The reasons for these distinctions are partly technical and partly sociological. RV owners tend to be older, married with children, and in the middle-income group. The image the RV industry seeks to project is solidly "middle American." "In their own small way," writes a spokesman in 1979, "RVs have strongly contributed to the rejuvenation of family life. Children find out how much fun parents can really be and that regular TV is not a necessity. At the same time RVs are an aid in bringing families together in a wholesome outdoor setting. Children are also learning the fundamentals of conservation and ecology."[7]

Off-road vehicle owners, on the other hand, tend to be younger, less affluent, and a good deal noisier. They seek action, adventure, and speed. Although the Jeep appeared in 1940, the greatest diffusion of four-wheel drive vehicles has been in the past ten years. *Off Road* magazine, which claims a circulation of 125,000, began publishing in 1969 and was quickly followed by *4 w d*, published by *Road and Track;* and *Pickup, Van & 4-Wheel Drive.* The impact of off-road vehicles tends to be localized and seasonal, but in some parts of the country the organizations and subcultures associated with them are highly visible and politically powerful. Perhaps most visible on city streets are the vanners in their customized, elaborately painted and decorated vehicles. According to one observer, vanners are often former hot rodders who have turned to vanning after getting married and having children and because the results of their customizing are more satisfying. The pleasure of customizing a van is "glancing over your shoulder and seeing you're surrounded by an environment of your own making. . . . Whether for families or for single people, the van is a playground for personality, a space to shape fantasy."[8]

Of all the fantasies man has indulged in, perhaps the greatest is flight. Flying for pleasure may date from Icarus and Daedalus or the twelfth-century Chinese, but for Americans the connection is again French. Following Jacque and Joseph Montgolfier's balloon ascent in 1783, French balloonists gave frequent demonstrations in the United States. The first American balloonist is said to have been thirteen-year-old Edward Warren, who volunteered to ride in a balloon constructed by Peter Carnes. His ascent, made at Bladensburg, Maryland, on June 24, 1784, preceded Josiah Meggs's in New Haven, Connecticut, by a year. For the next forty-seven years only Frenchmen attempted flights in the United States. In 1835, however, John Wise began to generate interest in ballooning by selling rides in his hot air balloon, *The Meteor.* Within a few years Wise had a rival in the person of Thaddeus Sabieski Constantine Lowe, known as Professor Carlincourt, whose balloon, *Enterprise,* became the model for several that Lowe built for the Union Army. After the Civil War, Wise continued his career as showman and scientific experimenter until his disappearance in a balloon over Lake Michigan in 1879.

Experiments in gliding and parachuting were also being conducted by Americans and Europeans. In the 1890s Octave Chanute made over 7,000 glider flights in Dune Park, Indiana, and in 1894, Charles Proteus Steinmetz of General Electric organized the first club, the Mohawk Aerial Navigation and Exploration Company. Although Germans and Russians were far ahead of Americans in developing the technology of gliders, the fact that the Wright Brothers succeeded in attaching a motor to one of their gliders overshadows the other achievements. Most of the energy of American inventors and engineers went into perfecting the airplane, yet gliders continued to play a role in the general development of aviation. In 1928, Charles Lindbergh lent his enormous prestige to Hawley Bowlus, who designed sailplanes that were competitive with European models. Anne Morrow Lindbergh was the first American woman to obtain a glider pilot license, while Richard Du Pont used his family connections to bring the best German ideas on soaring to the attention of Americans. When World War II broke out, however, there were only 165 glider pilots in the United States, compared to 186,000 in Germany. In the past twenty years, soaring as a pastime and for competition has become increasingly popular, and American pilots have set altitude and distance records. *Soaring and Motorgliding* magazine claims a circulation of 16,000. Moreover, the development of flexible-wing kite-like gliders by Francis M. Rogallo and others in the late 1940s has led to the boom in hang gliding, a less expensive and more accessible recreation than monoplane gliding.

Like soaring, parachuting is not yet a mass sport, but it has two popular journals, *Parachutist* and *Sky Diver Magazine,* the former with a circulation of 16,000. Experiments with parachutes began with ballooning, but parachute jumps remained a novelty until the development of powered aircraft. Although a barnstormer named Tiny Broadwick is said to have made the first intentional free fall from a plane in 1914, it was not until after World War II that American parachutists began to develop the skills that have led to maneuvers involving as many as fifty skydivers in elaborate patterns. The passing of objects between men and women falling at several hundred miles an hour through thousands of feet of space has become seemingly routine in television commercials, but it is a development of the past twenty-five years. Technological improvements in the parachutes themselves have made jumps of great accuracy possible and have attracted thousands of new participants. Even though only one-quarter of those who try jumping repeat the experience, sky diving is a growing recreational activity.

Flying private airplanes for pleasure, however, remains the most popular of all forms of airborne recreational travel. From 1911, when John and Alfred Moisant opened the first flying school in the United States, to the present, millions of Americans have received pilot's licenses. Today it is estimated that there are 750,000 weekend flyers in the United States flying 150,000 planes. Although owning a plane is expensive—a new two-seater costs at least $20,000—a number of manufacturers have provided small planes suitable for pleasure flying since 1907, when Alberto Santos Dumont, the Brazilian flyer and aeronautical engineer, introduced his *Demoiselle.* In 1937, Piper Aircraft Corporation, which absorbed the Taylor Aircraft Company, began to manufacture the small planes which have become synonymous with private flying. Cessna, Beechcraft, Grumman, and, in the 1950s, Lear Jet, joined Piper in providing a wide range of models for business and pleasure flying.

This brief survey of leisure transportation underscores the need for research and writing that will place leisure activities in the context of history. While we know that the use of recreational vehicles, pleasure boats, and aircraft is correlated with income and, to a degree, with region and social status, we need to know more about the men and women who make and use these objects. Studies of companies, clubs, and individuals should be undertaken by scholars who can evaluate the place of leisure travel in American culture. Because recreational travel occurs in every place in the country, it should be relatively easy to begin compiling information. Students should be encouraged to read and analyze trade journals and club newsletters for clues to cultural beliefs and values. Oral histories can be gathered and archives begun. Only then can we answer the question posed recently on a church billboard: "Will recreation wreck creation?"

REFERENCE WORKS

Good bibliographies on the history of leisure vehicles, pleasure boats, and aircraft are hard to come by. There are many reference works, guides, and abstracts for these subjects, but they usually cover only the most technical matters. The cultural and social dimensions of recreational travel, topics of interest to students of American popular culture, have generally been ignored. Standard references such as *Readers Guide,* the *Social Science Index,* and the *Humanities Index* will yield some useful materials, as will some of the computer-based bibliographic search services such as DIALOG from Lockheed Information Systems. Since leisure vehicles, boats, and planes are used outdoors, bibliographies on the environmental impact of outdoor recreation come closest to covering the subject.

Rural Recreation and Tourism Abstracts, an English publication, covers a wide range of activities and is especially useful for comparative studies. Geoffrey Wall's "Impacts of Outdoor Recreation on the Environment," Council of Planning Librarians Exchange Bibliography no. 1363, is a good, brief survey of books and articles published in the 1970s. There is no general bibliography on pleasure boating, but the Gale Research Company has recently published *Bicycling: A Guide to Information Sources* edited by Mark and Barbara Schultz, and a *Recreation and Outdoor Life Directory* edited by Paul and Steven R. Wasserman is scheduled for publication. Flying is better provided with research tools. William B. Gamble's *History of Aeronautics: A Selected List of References to Material in the New York Public Library*, and N. H. Randers-Pehrson and A. G. Renstrom's *Aeronautic Americana: A Bibliography of Books and Pamphlets on Aeronautics Published in America Before 1900* provide exhaustive guides to the early days of flight. Michael Horan, *Index to Parachuting, 1900-1975: An Annotated Bibliography* has provided a valuable reference work for his subject, a model for researchers in related fields.

The Pocket Encyclopedia of World Aircraft in Color: Private Aircraft, Business and General Purpose Since 1946, by Kenneth Munson, provides brief historical sketches of each of the several hundred airplanes described. It is a literate, well-illustrated guide. This is true, too, of Michael J. H. Taylor's editing of *Jane's Pocket Book of Home Built Aircraft*. Less encyclopedic and more personal is Jules Bergman's *Anyone Can Fly*, which explains why airplanes fly and how to fly a small plane and describes several types of aircraft. The Editors of Flying Magazine have published a similar book, *Sport Flying*, which explains aerobatics, racing, competitive soaring, and ballooning, as well as how to build a plane. *Fly: The Complete Book of Sky Sailing* by Rick Carrier, *The Encyclopedia of Hot Air Balloons* by Paul Gamson, and *The Balloon Book*, by Paul Fillingham, are also "how-to" books with chapters on the history of their respective types of flying. Carrier also lists the names of several manufacturers, organizations, and publications concerned with soaring and hang gliding.

The Illustrated Encyclopedia of Boating is really more of a nautical dictionary, but its author, Alan Lucas, provides good clear explanations of highly technical subjects and terms. For information on marketing and business trends in boating, the market research firms of Frost and Sullivan, and Predicasts, Inc., publish occasional reports. More accessible are the many catalogs and resource books published for every conceivable recreational activity. One of the most comprehensive is *The Explorers Ltd. Source Book*, which contains information on periodicals, associations, books, and products for off-road touring, river touring, offshore sailing, hang gliding, ballooning, parachuting, and bicycle touring, among other activities. Of the many organizations that can supply scholars with information on boating, the Boat Owners Association of the United States, 880 Pickett Street,

Alexandria, Virginia 22304; the U.S. Coast Guard Auxiliary, Washington, D.C. 20590; and the American Canoe Association, Denver, Colorado 80222, are the most important.

Associations for other forms of leisure travel include Antique Bicycle Club of America in New York City 10471; the League of American Wheelmen, P.O. Box 988, Baltimore, Maryland 21203; the Motorcycle Industry Council, 4100 Birch Street, Suite 101, Newport Beach, California 92660; the American Motorcyclist Association, P.O. Box 141, Westerville, Ohio 43081; the Recreational Vehicle Industry Association, P.O. Box 204, 14650 Lee Road, Chantilly, Virginia 22021; the Recreational Vehicle Dealers Association, Suite 412, 3251 Old Lee Highway, Fairfax, Virginia 22030; the International Snowmobile Industry Association, Suite 850 South, 1800 M Street, N.W., Washington, D.C. 20036; the Aircraft Owners and Pilots Association, 7315 Wisconsin Avenue, Bethesda, Maryland 20014; the United States Parachute Association, 806 15th Street, N.W., Washington, D.C. 20005; and the Balloon Federation of America, 821 15th Street, N.W., Washington, D.C. 20005. This list is merely suggestive; there are many other national, regional, and local groups representing manufacturers, retailers, and consumers.

There are four encyclopedic collections of outdoor pastimes from the second half of the nineteenth century that contain material on leisure travel. The earliest, John Henry Walsh's *Enclyclopedia of Rural Sports* has sections on yachting, riding, driving, and pedestrianism. *The Book of American Pastimes*, published by Charles A. Peverelly in 1866, describes the uniforms of various yacht clubs and gives details of several early races. *The Tribune Book of Open Air Sports*, edited by Henry Hall in 1887, begins with a chapter entitled "Why We Want to Be Strong" by William Blaikie, and contains sections on canoeing, cycling, and ice yachting. The chapter on yachting was written by Hall, who is identified as a special agent for the U.S. Census on Shipbuilding. The prolific John D. Champlin teamed with Arthur E. Bostwick to produce *The Young Folks' Cyclopaedia of Games and Sports* in 1890. Cycling and sailing are well covered.

RESEARCH COLLECTIONS

There are major research collections in several museums and libraries. Within the Smithsonian Institution, the Museum of American History has research materials on cycling and sailing. Especially important are the drawings made during the late 1930s by members of the Historic American Merchant Marine Survey, a project designed to record all types of American sailing craft. The museum also has the models of the aforementioned National Watercraft Collection and material on cycling. The National Air and Space Museum has extensive collections of primary material, including a large number of photographs of early aircraft. John Allen's *Aviation and Space Museums of America* provides details on several other collections of aeronautical materials. The Mariners Museum in Newport News, Virginia, has some good material on pleasure boats, and the Maritime Museum Association of San Diego, California, has the luxury motor yacht, *Medea*, on display. For English museums, see Jill Sutcliffe's *Boating and Boats*, a simple but useful guide.

HISTORY AND CRITICISM

A handful of general histories of sport provide a useful introduction to leisure travel in the context of American social history. John Krout's *Annals of American Sport*, a volume in the superb Pageant of America series, is an illustrated historical survey of recreation from Colonial times to 1929. Krout is especially good on yachting and cycling, but he also mentions the invention of roller skates in 1863, and the skating mania that swept the United States in the 1880s when "Professor" A. F. Smith performed at the Casino Rink in Chicago. Foster Rhea Dulles's *America Learns to Play* is the standard work on the history of leisure, but it is badly out of date. John R. Betts's *America's Sporting Heritage, 1850-1950*, helps update Dulles, but his book is also a superficial survey. Betts is best when discussing the growth of sports journalism. *The Final Report of the President's Commission on Olympic Sports 1975-1977* provides useful sketches of yachting, cycling, canoeing, and kayaking as Olympic sports. Finally, one general periodical stands out as indispensible for the study of leisure vehicles and boating, *Popular Mechanics.* Since 1902 *Popular Mechanics* has been providing craftsmen with ideas and plans and small boys (and girls, too) with hours of pleasant dreaming. Its present circulation of 1,736,000 is too large to ignore, and its influence on American popular culture has yet to be explored.

There is no comprehensive history of pleasure boating, but Douglas H. C. Phillips-Birt's *The History of Yachting* is a good beginning. Written from a British point of view it is more than fair to American boating. The best American studies are Arthur Hamilton Clark's *The History of Yachting, 1600-1815* and Howard I. Chapelle's *American Sailing Craft.* The former is as literary as the latter is technological, but both are classics. From Clark we learn that *yacht* comes from the Dutch *jaght*, which in turn comes from *jagen* and refers to the swift horses used in hunting. Pepys's diary for 1660 contains the word. Chapelle describes all the types of fishing and commercial ships—New Haven sharpies, skipjacks, friendship sloops, Cape Cod cat boats, and Gloucester schooners—many of which became prototypes for pleasure boats. Additional technical details on yachts of the nineteenth century are provided by William Stephens in two essential books, *American Yachting* and *Traditions and Memories of American Yachting.*

More limited aspects of yachting are treated in Reginald Crabtree's *The Luxury Yachts from Steam to Diesel* and Alfred F. Loomis's *Ocean Racing: The Great Blue-Water Yacht Races, 1866-1935*. More important are studies of the men who designed and promoted yachting. The best of these is Bill Robinson's *The Great American Yacht Designers,* which describes the work of Nathaniel Herreshoff, Clinton Crane, John Alden, Philip Rhodes, Bill Tripp, Ray Hunt, Bill Lapworth, and Olin Stephens. Each of the men deserves a full-length biography, as do Edward Burgess, William Gardner, Sherman Hoyt, and many others. Samuel Carter's *The Boatbuilders of Bristol: The Story of the Amazing Herreshoff Family of Rhode Island* is a bit too uncritical, but his subjects were indeed amazing. Karl Friederich Herreschoff (sic), adopted by Frederick the Great, immigrated to Rhode Island in 1786, and married the daughter of the wealthy merchant John Brown. For over fifty years, his sons and grandsons dominated yachting as no family has ever dominated a sport. *An L. Francis Herreshoff Reader* and other books by L. Francis Herreshoff help complete the portrait of this arrogant and talented family. A biography of John Rushton and a history of canoeing in the nineteenth century is provided by Atwood Manley in *Rushton and His Times in American Canoeing.*

Histories of yacht clubs begin with Benjamin Adams, *Amateur Yachting,* an account of the Quaker City Yacht Club in 1886, which encourages Americans to take up yachting as preparation for war. The following year, Frederick S. Cozzens's *Yachts and Yachting* told the story of the New York Yacht Club, illustrated with nice sketches by Cozzens. In 1894, Henry A. Mott's *The Yachts and Yachtsmen of America* contained the histories of forty-five clubs. Two recent histories, Anthony Anable's *The History of the Riverside Yacht Club, 1888-1972,* and the Royal Vancouver Yacht Club's *Annals of the Royal Vancouver Yacht Club, 1903-1965,* suggest the possibilities for research in this area. *Sherman Hoyt's Memoirs* is an excellent autobiography of a man who began sailing with the Seawanhaka Yacht Club in 1894, and went on to compete in several America's Cup races in the 1920s and 1930s.

Maritime photography is a subject worthy of study by itself. Edward Burgess's *American and English Yachts* is beautifully illustrated with the work of N. L. Stebbins, "Marine and Landscape Photographer." *Representative American Yachts,* by Henry Greenwood Peabody of Boston, is a collection of one hundred magnificent photographs. Frances Benjamin Johnston was invited to photograph the Kaiser's Cup race of 1905, and her excellent photos are in the Prints and Photographs Division of the Library of Congress, as is the collection of Charles E. Bolles of Brooklyn, and additional work by Peabody and Stebbins.

Recent research on the economic and social significance of boating includes Elwell B. Thomas's *This Business of Boating,* which provides details on getting into the boat and marina business, and I. Ashkenazy's article in *Oceans* on the 47 percent increase in boating since 1960. Ashkenazy attributes most of this growth to improved technology. Donald Field and Joseph O'Leary provide some interesting information on the social context of boating in their essay in the *Journal of Leisure Research.* Field and O'Leary found that family groups were more important in visiting the beach and swimming, whereas friendship groups were disproportionately represented in fishing. In power boating, family-friendship groups were overrepresented.

Among the many journals published for yachting and power boating, *American Yachtsman, Rudder,* and *Yachting* stand out in the early years. All contain club news, technical information, and occasional essays and verse. In 1888, young Hamlin Garland published "My Cabin" in *American Yachtsman,* one stanza of which reads:

> My cabin cowers in the onward sweep
> Of the terrible northern blast;
> Above its roof wild clouds leap
> And shriek as they hurry past;
> The snow-waves hiss along the plain;
> Like hungry wolves they stretch and strain;
> They race and ramp with rushing beat;
> Like stealthy tread of myriad feet

In the 1970s, Bernard Goldhirsh challenged the established publishers with *Sail* and *Motorboat.* With a circulation of 170,000, *Sail* is the largest sailing magazine in the world. *Yachting* survives, but *Rudder* merged with *Sea. Motorboat* is second to the Ziff-Davis Company's *Boating.* All these magazines offer well-illustrated feature stories on cruising and racing, how-to articles, and equipment evaluations. Comparisons with England, France, and Germany may be made by perusing *Yachting World, La Revue Nautique,* and *Die Yacht. The American Neptune* is a scholarly quarterly devoted chiefly to commercial maritime history.

The history of the bicycle is told in Robert A. Smith's *A Social History of the Bicycle: Its Early Life and Times in America,* Frederick Alderson's *Bicycling: A History,* and Seamus McGonagle's *The Bicycle in Life, Love, War and Literature.* A more analytical view of the bicycle and its social impact is taken by Sally Ruth Simms in her study of "The Bicycle, the Bloomer, and the 'New Women': Images of the American Woman Awheel, 1890-1899," and by Gary Allan Tobin in "The Bicycle Boom of the 1890's: The Development of Private Transportation and the Birth of the Modern Tourist." Both authors reveal some of the unintended consequences of cycling. Industry journals such as *American Bicyclist and Motorcyclist* and participants magazines such as *Outing* (which incorporated *Wheelman* in

1884) and *Bicycling* provide a good overview of technological and social changes.

The motorcycle has received less judicious treatment, although Sam Brooks's dissertation, "The Motorcycle in American Culture: From Conception to 1935," is a good beginning. Brooks's thesis, that motorcycle riders were from the beginning likely to defy accepted social conventions, needs further testing, but the image of the motorcycle rider as a rebel has been sustained by writers such as Tom Wolfe and Hunter S. Thompson. Thierry Sagnier tries to counter that image in *Bike! Motorcycles and the People Who Ride Them*, but even he admits that the motorcycle is part of the youth cult in the 1970s. Magazines like *Chopper* and its mildly pornographic cousin, *Easy Riders*, with combined circulations of almost 100,000, easily offset the more restrained image of motorcycle touring contained in *Rider* and *Road Rider*. The British have always taken a more serious view of motorcycling, as the books of Richard Hough and L.J. Setright, Eric Walford, James Sheldon, David Wise, and C. F. Caunter illustrate.

Homes on Wheels is a sympathetic study of the contemporary RV subculture by Michael Aaron Rockland, chairman of the American Studies Department of Rutgers University. Rockland interviewed some of the ten million Americans who travel and live in recreational vehicles, as well as some of the eight hundred entrepreneurs who build them. The book is illustrated with photographs by Amy Stromsten. The recreational vehicle industry has also been surveyed by Carlton Edwards, a professor at Michigan State University, and Al Griffin, a popular writer. Edwards's *Homes for Travel and Living* is a compendium of history, commercial and technological information, and legal matters. His bibliography is very useful, and he raises many important points, such as the potential for mobile homes to provide low-cost housing. The shift from vacationing to year-round living, satirized by Lucille Ball and Desi Arnaz in the film *The Long, Long Trailer* in 1954, continues, and its consequences need to be studied. Ted J. Born's "Elderly RV Campers Along the Lower Colorado River: A Preliminary Typology," suggest that public campgrounds have become a kind of ghetto for the retired poor, and Sheila Johnson's *Idle Haven: Community Building Among the Working Class Retired* also emphasizes the economic problems of mobile home dwellers.

In contrast, Arnold Wolfe's breezy *Vans and Vanners* is a participant observer's sanguine report on the semi-nomadic life of customized van owners. The nation's estimated 300,000 vanners are sociable, belonging to more than 400 clubs which sponsor "fox hunts," a kind of hide-and-go-seek played by the van drivers with the aid of CB radios; "road rallies," which include various kinds of competition; "truck-ins," bacchanals which sometimes tarnish the family image of vanning; and "caravans," migrations of vanners across hundreds of miles of highway for the sheer joy of driving and camping together. Caravanning is like having your neighborhood on wheels, according to Wolfe, who described the typical vanner:

> Only 5 percent of the more than 2,500 vanners at the Third National Truck-in at Bowling Green listed their occupation as "professional." Only 7.5 percent of these vanners have college degrees, though nearly eight out of ten are under thirty years old. More than three out of ten indicated their work was connected with automobiles or automobile products, while more than 56 percent said they were "craftsmen, foremen or kindred workers; operatives or production workers; laborers" and "service workers."[9]

The elaborate painting of vans, or "trickin'," is the most public feature of vanning. Wolfe's book is well illustrated with color photographs that indicate a preference for Western landscapes and tropical beaches in the murals that adorn the sides of many vans. The iconography of the van needs to be studied, but it may be that there is less than meets the eye. Customized vans have been around for more than sixty years, and, if the photographs in T. H. Watkins' essay in *American West* are any indication, they have always looked like picture postcards on wheels. "The American Courtship of House and Car" is an important topic, as David Neuman has pointed out in the *Journal of Popular Culture,* and the ability to combine comfort with adventure makes the appeal of van and trailer living very strong. The desire to individualize and decorate machines is not unique to vanners and hot rodders, of course, as anyone who has seen the cabs of diesel trucks in Mexico can testify. S. I. Hallet has described the phenomenon in another country in "Wandering Art: Decorated Trucks of Afghanistan," in *Natural History.*

The desire to live their adventure fantasies motivates the owners of four-wheel drive and off-road vehicles. Studies of snowmobile and four-wheel drive vehicles repeatedly emphasize their desire to escape the ordinary, to live the American dream of exploring the unknown, and to identify with a rugged, military image. These were the conclusions of Bruce Firestone and Clifton Egan of the English Department at Clemson University, of Gregory Hill in an article in *Journal of Leisure Research,* and of the Task Force on Off-Road Recreational Vehicles sponsored by the Secretary of the Interior. Hill discovered that snowmobilers in central New York State drove as much at night as in the day. Other studies have shown that snowmobilers spend more time in their activity than other recreational vehicle owners and more money on their equipment than bicyclists, campers, or tennis players. Not surprisingly, Timothy B. Knopp and John D. Tyger found significant differences in attitudes toward the environment between snowmobilers and cross-country skiers, but a startling statistic was that although over 50 percent of the ski tourers had graduated from college, only 10.2 percent of the snowmobilers had completed sixteen years of school.

Further research needs to be done on what appears to be enormous social class differences among recreation subcultures.

When Joseph-Armand Bombardier of Valcourt, Quebec, first put a Model T engine and a propeller on a sleigh in 1922, he began the snowmobile industry. Although, as Clarke Wallace points out in his *The Complete Snowmobiler,* the basic design was not perfected until 1958, the impact since then has been swift and widespread. *Snowsports* magazine claims to reach a million readers, and a recent article on names for snowmobiles suggests that homemade versions probably preceded the mass-produced models of the past two decades. What is called the "snowsled" in New England is the "auto-neige" in French Canada, while "snowbug" and "snowbuggy" are popular in Michigan. "Power toboggan" is used in Manitoba, "iron dog" in Alaska, and "snow machine" in the Mid-west. In Minnesota "snowcats" and "skidogs" fight it out, but some old-timers prefer "power sled."[10] Other topics of interest to folklorists, anthropologists, and students of popular culture are raised in Pertti J. Pelto's *The Snowmobile Revolution: Technology and Social Change in the Arctic,* a study of the effect of the snowmobile on Finnish Lapps in the 1960s. Pelto found that the machines had produced great changes in the economy and social structure, leading to greater class stratification. John McPhee mentions similar changes in the lives of Alaskans in *Coming into the Country.*

Snowmobiles and other recreational vehicles may be studied through their organizations and publications which are countless. The trailer magazines are the earliest, while *Off Road, 4 w d, Pickup, Van and 4-wheel Drive, Van World,* and *Truckin'* are products of the late 1960s and 1970s. With circulations between 100 and 200,000, these publications have established equal footing with the older yachting and flying magazines.

Although flying is a popular subject for books and articles, there are many gaps in the historical record. Jeremiah Milbank's *First Century of Flight in America* is the best work on early ballooning, and Will Hayes's *The Complete Ballooning Book* brings the story down to the present. For important personal accounts, see John Wise, *Through the Air: A Narrative of Forty Years Experience as an Aeronaut,* and Charles McCarry, *Double Eagle.* Some of the adventures of the pioneering Wise have been mentioned earlier. His book is well illustrated with engravings. *Double Eagle* is the story of the first successful transatlantic balloon flight by Ben Abruzzo, Maxie Anderson, and Larry Newman. Magazines such as *Ballooning* and *Buoyant Flight* contain information on significant flights, races, clubs, and equipment. A model for scholars interested in the social significance of activities such as ballooning is Claudia Kidwell's "Apparel for Ballooning with Speculations on More Commonplace Garb," in *Costume: The Journal of the Costume Society.*

Soaring and hang gliding are described in six books. Derek Piggott's

Gliding: A Handbook on Soaring Flight appeared first in 1958, and remains a useful introduction. *On Silent Wings* by Don Dwiggins is the best general history, and D. S. Halacy, *With Wings as Eagles: The Story of Soaring,* and James E. Mrazek, *Hang Gliding and Soaring: A Complete Introduction to the Newest Way to Fly,* are useful supplements. Mrazek, a World War II glider infantry battalion commander, brings considerable experience to his subject. The most recent accounts are *Hang Gliding,* by Martin Hunt and David Hunn, and *A Hole in the Wind: Hang Gliding and the Quest for Flight,* by Hank Harrison. Parachuting is fairly well covered by Dwiggins in *Bailout: The Story of Parachuting and Skydiving* and Bud Sellick in *Parachutes and Parachuting.* Recent developments can be followed in the specialized journals and in popular articles such as Tony Gonzales and Judi Tobias, "Joys of Free Fall," in *Adventure Travel.* Serious analysis of the sport is just beginning, as in the paper presented by Michael Salter of the University of Windsor, Ontario, at the Fifth Annual Meeting of the Association for the Anthropological Study of Play on "Parachuting to Sky Diving: Process Shifts in an Adult Sport."

There is no American equivalent of Terence Boughton's *The Story of the British Light Aeroplane,* and there is great need for biographies and histories of manufacturers and pilots. Devon E. Francis's *Mr. Piper and His Cubs* is only a modest beginning. *American Aviation Historical Society Journal* contains some good essays on private flying, but most of the history of recreational air travel is still locked in the memories and personal papers of the pioneers. *Flying,* with a circulation of 380,000 is the most important trade journal, with *Air Progress, AOPA Pilot, Sport Aviation,* and *Homebuilt Aircraft* providing equally valuable information.

NOTES

1. I would like to thank the following individuals for their help in preparing this essay: Julia Herron, Administrator, Member Communications and Publications, Recreational Vehicle Industry Association; Judy Hinds, Editor, Recreational Vehicle Dealers Association; John Haifley, Tempest sailor; Robert Humphrey, Department of Anthropology, George Washington University; Dom Pisano, Reference Librarian, National Air and Space Museum; Tom Narbeth, Assistant Reference Librarian, George Washington University; Donald Berkebile, Curator, American Division of Transportation, Museum of American History; and Andrew Mergen, expert.

2. Elwood L. Shafer, George H. Moeller, and Russell E. Getty, "Future Leisure Environments," U.S. Department of Agriculture, Forest Service Research Paper, NE-301, Upper Darby, Penn., 1974, p. 7.

3. Sammy Kent Brooks, "The Motorcycle in American Culture: From Conception to 1935" (Ph.D. diss. George Washington University, 1975), p. 38.

4. Bureau of Outdoor Recreation, "America's Trails," *Outdoor Recreation Action,* 42 (Winter 1976), 39.

5. Reynold M. Wik, *Henry Ford and Grass Roots America* (Ann Arbor: University of Michigan Press, 1972), p. 27.

6. Al Griffin, *Recreational Vehicles* (Chicago: Regnery, 1973), p. 7.

7. James B. Summers, "The RV Industry and Its Future," *RVDA News*, 12 (June 1979), 4.

8. Arnold Wolfe, *Vans and Vanners* (Matteson, Ill.: Greatlakes Living Press, 1976), pp. 2, 4.

9. Wolfe, *Vans and Vanners*, p. 47.

10. *Snowsports* (October 1972), 19.

BIBLIOGRAPHY

BOOKS AND ARTICLES

Adams, Benjamin. *Amateur Yachting*. Philadelphia: B. F. Adams, 1886.

Alderson, Frederick. *Bicycling: A History*. New York: Praeger, 1972.

Allen, John. *Aviation and Space Museums of America*. New York: Arco, 1975.

Anable, Anthony. *The History of the Riverside Yacht Club, 1888-1972*. Riverside, Conn.: Riverside Yacht Club, 1974.

Ashkenazy, I. "Boating Explosion." *Oceans*, 11 (March 1978), 25-27.

Badaracco, R. J. "ORV's: Often Rough on Visitors." *Parks and Recreation*, 11 (September 1976), 32-35, 68-75.

Baldwin, Malcolm F. *The Off-Road Vehicle and Environmental Quality: A Report on the Social and Environmental Effects of Off-Road Vehicles, Particularly Snowmobiles*. Washington, D.C.: Conservation Foundation, 1970.

Bergman, Jules, *Anyone Can Fly*. Garden City, N.Y.: Doubleday, 1976.

Betts, John R. *America's Sporting Heritage, 1850-1950*. Reading, Mass.: Addison-Wesley, 1974.

Born, Ted J. "Elderly RV Campers Along the Lower Colorado River: A Preliminary Typology." *Journal of Leisure Research*, 8 (Fall 1976), 256-62.

Boughton, Terence. *The Story of the British Light Aeroplane*. London: John Murray, 1963.

Brooks, Sammy Kent. "The Motorcycle in American Culture: From Conception to 1935." Ph.D. dissertation, George Washington University, 1975.

Burdge, Rabel J. "Levels of Occupational Prestige and Leisure Activity." *Journal of Leisure Research*, 1 (Summer 1969), 262-74.

Bureau of Outdoor Recreation. "America's Trails." *Outdoor Recreation Action*, 42 (Winter 1976), 38-39.

Burgess, Edward. *American and English Yachts*. New York: Scribner's, 1887.

Butler, R. W. "The Impact of Off-Road Vehicles on Travel." *Journal of Travel Research*, 13 (Spring 1975), 13-16.

Byam, Wally. *Trailer Travel Here and Abroad: The New Way to Adventurous Living*. New York: McKay, 1960.

Carrier, Rick. *Fly: The Complete Book of Sky Sailing*. New York: McGraw-Hill, 1974.

Carter, Samuel. *The Boatbuilders of Bristol: The Story of the Amazing Herreshoff Family of Rhode Island*. Garden City, N.Y.: Doubleday, 1970.

Caunter, C. F. *The History and Development of Cycles as Illustrated by the Collection of Cycles in the Science Museum.* London: Her Majesty's Stationery Office, 1972.

Chadwick, Henry. *Beadle's Dime Hand-Book of Yachting and Rowing.* New York: Beadle, 1867.

Champlin, John D., and Arthur E. Bostwick. *The Young Folks' Cyclopaedia of Games and Sports.* New York: Holt, 1890.

Chapelle, Howard I. *American Sailing Craft.* New York: Kennedy, 1936. Reprint ed. Camden, Me.: International Marine, 1975.

______. *The History of American Sailing Ships.* New York: Norton, 1935. Reprint ed. New York: Bonanza Books, n.d.

______. *The National Watercraft Collection.* Washington, D.C.: Smithsonian Institution Press 1976.

Clark, Arthur Hamilton. *The History of Yachting, 1600-1815.* New York: Putnam's, 1904.

Clemens, Samuel. *Mark Twain Able Yachtsman Interviews Himself on Why Lipton Failed to Lift the Cup.* New York: private printing, 1920.

Cozzens, Frederick S. *American Yachts: A Series of Watercolor Sketches.* Text by J. D. Jerrold Kelly. New York:,Scribner's 1884.

______. *Yachts and Yachting.* New York: Cassell, 1887.

Crabtree, Reginald. *The Luxury Yacht from Steam to Diesel.* New York: Drake, 1974.

Drury, Margaret J. *Mobile Homes: The Unrecognized Revolution in American Housing.* Ithaca, N.Y.: Cornell University Press, 1967.

Dukes, Anne K. "Thrill of Four Wheel Drive." *Mademoiselle*, 84 (April 1978), 50.

Dulles, Foster Rhea. *America Learns to Play.* New York: Appleton-Century, 1940.

Dwiggins, Don. *Bailout: The Story of Parachuting and Skydiving.* New York: Macmillan, 1969.

______. *On Silent Wings.* New York: Grosset & Dunlop, 1970.

Editors of Flying Magazine. *Best of Flying.* New York: Van Nostrand Reinhold, 1977.

______. *Sport Flying.* New York: Scribner's 1976.

Editors of Yacht Racing-Cruising Magazine. *Encyclopedia of Sailing.* New York: Harper & Row, 1978.

Edwards, Carlton. *Homes for Travel and Living.* East Lansing, Mich.: Carl Edwards, 1977.

Explorers, Ltd. *The Explorers Ltd. Source Book.* New York: Harper & Row, 1977.

Field, Donald, and Joseph O'Leary. "Social Groups as a Basis for Assessing Participation in Selected Water Activities." *Journal of Leisure Research*, 5 (Spring, 1973), 16-25.

Fillingham, Paul. *The Balloon Book.* New York: McKay, 1977.

Final Report of the President's Commission on Olympic Sports 1975-1977: Volume II, Findings of Fact and Supporting Material. Washington, D.C.: Government Printing Office, 1977.

Firestone, Bruce, and Clifton Egan. "The Four Wheel Drive Vehicle: A Southern Rural Institution." Unpublished introduction to the documentary film, "A Thrill You Hadn't Ever Saw," Southeastern American Studies Association Meeting, Tampa, Florida, April 5-7, 1979.

Francis, Devon E. *Mr. Piper and His Cubs.* Ames: Iowa State University Press, 1973.

Frost and Sullivan. *Recreational Boating and Associated Equipment Markets.* New York: Frost & Sullivan, 1976.

Gamble, William B., ed. *History of Aeronautics: A Selected List of References to Material in the New York Public Library.* New York: Arno Reprint, 1971.

Gamson, Paul. *The Encyclopedia of Hot Air Balloons.* New York: Drake, 1978.

Griffin, Al. *Recreational Vehicles.* Chicago: Regnery, 1973.

Gonzales, Tony, and Judi Tobias. "Joys of Free Fall." *Adventure Travel,* 2 (October 1979), 48-53.

Halacy, D. S. *With Wings as Eagles: The Story of Soaring.* Bobbs-Merrill, 1975.

Hall, Henry. *The Tribune Book of Open Air Sports.* New York: Tribune, 1887.

Hallet, S. I. "Wandering Art: Decorated Trucks of Afghanistan." *Natural History,* 85 (February 1976), 66-71.

Harrison, Hank. *A Hole in the Wind: Hang Gliding and the Quest for Flight.* Indianapolis: Bobbs-Merrill, 1979.

Hayes, Will. *The Complete Ballooning Book.* Mountain View, Calif.: World, 1977.

Herreshoff, L. Francis. *An L. Francis Herreshoff Reader.* Camden, Me: International Marine, 1978.

Hill, Gregory. "Central New York Snowmobilers and Patterns of Vehicle Use." *Journal of Leisure Research,* 6 (Fall 1974), 280-92.

Horan, Michael. *Index to Parachuting, 1900-1975: An Annotated Bibliography.* New York: Garland, 1977

Hough, Richard, and L. J. Setright. *History of the World's Motorcycles.* New York: Harper & Row, 1973.

Hoyt, Charles Sherman. *Sherman Hoyt's Memoirs.* New York: Van Nostrand, 1950.

Hunt, Martin, and David Hunn. *Hang Gliding.* New York: Arco, 1977.

Johnson, Sheila. *Idle Haven: Community Building Among the Working Class Retired.* Berkeley: University of California Press, 1971.

Jones, Tristan. *Saga of a Wayward Sailor.* Mission, Kans.: Andrews and McMeel, 1979.

Keith, J. E. "Snowmobiling—A Look at Participants." *Journal of Travel Research,* 17 (Fall 1978), 30.

Kemp, Peter. *History of Ships.* New York: Two Continents, 1978.

Kidwell, Claudia. "Apparel for Ballooning with Sepculations on More Commonplace Garb." *Costume: The Journal of the Costume Society,* 11(1977), 73-87.

Kirstein, Jane. *Family Under Sail: A Handbook for First Mates.* New York: Macmillan, 1970.

Knopp, Timothy B., and John D. Tyger. "A Study of Conflict in Recreational Land Use: Snowmobiling vs. Ski-Touring." *Journal of Leisure Research* 5 (Summer 1973), 6-17.

Krout, John. *Annals of American Sport.* New Haven: Yale University Press, 1929.

Lincoln, Andrew Carey. *The Motorcycle Chums in the Land of the Sky.* Chicago: M. A. Donohue, 1912.

Loomis, Alfred F. *Ocean Racing: The Great Blue-Water Yacht Races, 1866-1935.* New York: Morrow 1936. Reprint. New York: Arno, 1967.

Lucas, Alan. *The Illustrated Encyclopedia of Boating.* Hong Kong: Horwitz, 1977.

McCarry, Charles, with Ben Ambruzzo, Maxie Anderson, and Larry Newman. *Double Eagle.* Boston: Little, Brown, 1979.

McGonagle, Seamus. *The Bicycle in Life, Love, War and Literature.* New York: Barnes, 1968.

McPhee, John. *Coming into the Country.* New York: Farrar, Straus & Giroux, 1977.

Manley, Atwood. *Rushton and His Times in American Canoeing.* Syracuse, N.Y.: Syracuse University Press, 1968.

Milbank, Jeremiah. *First Century of Flight in America.* Princeton: Princeton University Press, 1943.

Morgan, Lael. *The Woman's Guide to Boating and Cooking.* Freeport, Me.: B. Wheelwright, 1968. Rev. ed. Garden City, N.Y.: 1974

Mott, Henry A., ed. *The Yachts and Yachtsmen of America.* New York: International Yacht, 1894.

Mrazek, James E. *Hang Gliding and Soaring: A Complete Introduction to the Newest Way to Fly.* New York: St. Martin's Press, 1976.

Munson, Kenneth. *The Pocket Encyclopedia of World Aircraft in Color: Private Aircraft, Business and General Purpose Since 1946.* New York: Macmillan, 1969.

National Transportation Safety Board. Bureau of Surface Transporation Safety. *Safety Aspects of Recreational Vehicles.* Washington, D.C.: Government Printing Office, 1972.

Neuman, David. "The American Courtship of House and Car." *Journal of Popular Culture,* 7 (Fall 1973), 434-45.

Oliver, Smith Hempstone, and Donald H. Berkebile. *The Smithsonian Collection of Automobiles and Motorcycles.* Washington, D.C.: Smithsonian Institution, 1968.

______. *Wheels and Wheeling: The Smithsonian Cycle Collection.* Washington, D.C.: Smithsonian Institution, 1974.

Olyslager Organization. *The Jeep.* London: F. Warne, 1971.

Partridge, Michael. *Motorcycle Pioneers: The Men, the Machines, the Events, 1860-1930.* New York: Arco, 1977.

Payson, Lt. Howard. *The Motorcycle Chums Around the World.* New York: Hurst, 1912.

Peabody, Henry Greenwood. *Representative American Yachts.* Boston: Henry G. Peabody, 1893.

Pelto, Pertti J. *The Snowmobile Revolution: Technology and Social Change in the Arctic.* Menlo Park, Calif.: Cummings, 1973.

Peverelly, Charles A. *The Book of American Pastimes.* New York: the author, 1866.

Phillips-Birt, Douglas H. C. *The History of Yachting.* London: Elm Tree Books, 1974.

Piggott, Derek. *Gliding: A Handbook on Soaring Flight.* New York: Macmillan, 1958.

Pirsig, Robert. *Zen and the Art of Motorcycle Maintenance.* New York: Morrow, 1974.

Porter, Luther Henry. *Wheels and Wheeling.* Boston: Wheelman, 1892.

Predicasts, Inc. *Recreational Boating.* Cleveland: Ross, 1976.

Randers-Pehrson, N. H., and A. G. Renstrom. *Aeronautic Americana: A Bibliography of Books and Pamphlets on Aeronautics Published in America Before 1900.* New York: Aeronautic America, 1943.

Robinson, Bill. *The Great American Yacht Designers.* New York: Knopf, 1974.

Rockland, Michael Aaron. *Homes on Wheels.* New Brunswick, N.J.: Rutgers University Press, 1980.

Royal Vancouver Yacht Club. *Annals of the Royal Vancouver Yacht Club, 1903-1965.* Vancouver: The Club, 1966.

Sagnier, Thierry. *Bike! Motorcycles and the People Who Ride Them.* New York: Harper & Row, 1974.

Salter, Michael. "Parachuting to Sky Diving: Process Shifts in an Adult Sport." Paper presented at the Fifth Annual Meeting of the Association for the Anthropological Study of Play, Henniker, N.H.: March 30, 1979.

Santos-Dumont, Alberto. *My Airships.* New York: Century, 1904. Reprint ed. New York: Dover, 1973.

Schultz, Mark, and Barbara Schultz, eds. *Bicycling: A Guide to Information Sources.* Detroit: Gale Research, 1979.

Sellick, Bud. *Parachutes and Parachuting.* Englewood Cliffs, N.J.: Prentice-Hall, 1971.

Shafer, Elwood L., George H. Moeller, and Russell E. Getty. "Future Leisure Environments." U.S. Department of Agriculture, Forest Service Research Paper, NE-301. Upper Darby, Penn., 1974.

Sheldon, James. *Veteran and Vintage Motorcycles.* London: Batsford, 1961.

Sheridan, David. "Dirt Motorbikes and Dune Buggies Threaten Deserts." *Smithsonian,* 9 (September 1978), 67-75.

Simms, Sally Ruth. "The Bicycle, the Bloomer, and the 'New Woman': Images of the American Woman Awheel, 1890-1899." Master's thesis, George Washington University, 1975.

Sloane, Gloria. *How to Be a First-Rate Mate: A Sailing Guide for Women.* New York: Quadrangle, 1974.

Smith, Robert A. *A Social History of the Bicycle: Its Early Life and Times in America.* New York: American Heritage Press, 1972.

Snowmobile and Off-the-Road Vehicle Research Symposium. Sponsored by the Department of Park and Recreation Resources and the Agricultural Experiment Station, Michigan State University, and the Bureau of Outdoor Recreation, Department of the Interior. East Lansing, Mich., 1971.

Stephens, William. *American Yachting.* New York: Macmillan, 1904.

———. *Traditions and Memories of American Yachting.* New York: Hearst Magazines, 1942.

Stubelius, Svante. *Airship, Aeroplane, Aircraft: Studies in the History of Terms for Aircraft in English.* Göteborg, Sweden: Elanders Boktryckeri Aktiebolag, 1958.

———. *Balloon Flying-Machine, Helicopter: Further Studies in the History of Terms for Aircraft in English.* Göteborg, Sweden: Elanders Boktryckeri, Aktiebolag, 1960.

Sutcliffe, Jill. *Boating and Boats.* London: Routledge & Kegan Paul, 1976.

Task Force on Off-Road Recreation Vehicles. Washington, D.C.: Government Printing Office, 1971.

Taylor, Marshall W. *The Fastest Bicycle Rider in the World.* Worcester, Mass.: Wormley, 1928.

Taylor, Michael J. H., ed. *Jane's Pocket Book of Home Built Aircraft.* New York: Collier Books, 1977.

Thomas, Elwell B. *This Business of Boating.* Cambridge, Md.: Cornell Maritime Press, 1949.

Thompson, Hunter S. *Hell's Angels.* New York: Random House, 1967.

Thrasher, W. E. *Ballooning: A Pictorial Guide and World Directory.* Homestead, Fla.: Thrasher Balloons, 1978.

Tobin, Gary Allan. "The Bicycle Boom of the 1890's: The Development of Private Transporation and the Birth of the Modern Tourist." *Journal of Popular Culture,* 7 (Spring 1974), 838-49.

Vaughan, Rodger. *Ted Turner: The Man Behind the Mouth.* Marion, Ohio: Sail Books, 1979.

Wagenvoord, James, *Bikes and Riders.* New York: Avon, 1972.

Walford, Eric. *Early Days in the British Motorcycle Industry.* Coventry; British Motorcycle and Motorcycle Manufacturers and Trade Union, 1932.

Wall, Geoffrey. "Impacts of Outdoor Recreation on the Environment." Council of Planning Librarians Exchange Bibliography, no. 1363. Monticello, Ill.: n.p., October 1977.

Wallace, Clarke. *The Complete Snowmobiler.* New York: Scribner's, 1971.

Walsh, John Henry. *Encyclopedia of Rural Sports.* Philadelphia: Porter and Coates, [ca. 1867].

Wasserman, Paul, and Steven R. Wasserman, eds. *Recreation and Outdoor Life Directory.* Detroit: Gale Research, forthcoming.

Watkins, T. H. "Home on the Road." *American West,* 13 (September-October 1976), 36-49.

Wik, Reynold M. *Henry Ford and Grass Roots America.* Ann Arbor: University of Michigan Press, 1972.

Wise, David. *Historic Motorcycles.* London: Hamlyn, 1973.

Wise, John. *Through the Air: A Narrative of Forty Years Experience as an Aeronaut.* Philadelphia: To-day, 1873.

Wolfe, Arnold. *Vans and Vanners.* Matteson, Ill.: Greatlakes Living Press, 1976. Baby." *Esquire,* 60 (November 1963), 114-18.

Zonker, Patricia. *Murdercycles.* Chicage: Nelson-Hall, 1978.

PERIODICALS

Air Progress. Canoga Park, Calif., 1942-.

American Aviation Historical Society Journal. Santa Ana, Calif., 1956-.

American Bicyclist and Motorcyclist. New York, 1906-. (Began as *Motorcycle Illustrated;* Title varies.)

American Neptune. Salem, Mass., 1941-.

American Yachtsman. New York, 1887-1908.

AOPA Pilot. Washington, D.C., 1958-.

Aquatic Monthly and Nautical Review. New York, 1872-76.

Aviation and Yachting. Detroit, 1933-48. (Title varies.)

Aviation Collector's News. Harrisburg, Penn., 1965-.

Ballooning. Washington, D.C., 1968-.

Bicycling. Emmaus, Penn., 1960-.
Boating. Chicago, 1956-.
Buoyant Flight. Akron, Ohio, 1953-.
Canoe. Denver, Colo., 1973-.
Choppers and Big Bike Magazine. Encino, Calif., 1968-. (Title varies.)
Cruising World. Newport, R.I., 1975-.
Cycle World. Newport Beach, Calif., 1962-.
Easy Riders. Seal Beach, Calif., 1971-. (Title and place vary.)
Flugzeug und Yacht. Vienna, 1923-26.
Flying. New York, 1927-.
Ford Times. Detroit, 1908-17.
4 w d. Newport Beach, Calif., 1971-.
Homebuilt Aircraft. Santa Monica, Calif., 1951?-.
Motorboat. Boston, 1973-.
Motorcycle Illustrated. See *American Bicyclist and Motorcyclist.*
Off Road. Los Angeles, 1969-.
Outing. New York, 1882-1923.
Parachutist. Washington, D.C., 1960-.
Pickup, Van and 4-Wheel Drive. Newport Beach, Calif., 1972-.
Popular Mechanics. New York, 1902-.
RVDA News. Fairfax, Va. 1968-.
La Revue Nautique. Paris, 1926-39, 1944-.
Rider. Calabasas, Calif., 1974-.
Road Rider. South Laguna, Calif., 1970-.
Rudder. See *Sea.*
Rural Recreation and Tourism Abstracts. Farnham Royal, England, 1976-.
Sail. Boston, 1970-.
Sailing. Port Washington, Wisc., 1966-.
Sea (Combined with *Rudder*) New York, 1890-.
Sky Diver Magazine. Buena Park, Calif., 1959-.
Snowsports. Minneapolis, 1965-.
Soaring and Motorgliding. Santa Monica, Calif., 1937-.
Sport Aviation. Hales Corner, Wisc., 1951-.
Trailer Life. Calabasas, Calif., 1941-.
Trailer Topics Magazine. Chicago, 1937-.
Trailer Travel Magazine. Chicago, 1936-. (Continued as *Woodall's Trailer Travel,* Highland Park, Ill., 1976-.)
Truckin'. Anaheim, Calif., 1975-.
Van World Magazine. Encino, Calif. 1975-.
Woodall's Trailer Travel. See *Trailer Travel Magazine.*
Die Yacht. Berlin, 1904-.
Yachting. New York, 1907-.
Yachting World. London, 1894-.

CHAPTER 6 Magazines

Dorothy Schmidt

More than any other medium, the magazine represents America. Other nations produce periodicals, but nowhere else is there the multicolored, multivoiced flood of print that inundates Americans weekly, monthly, and quarterly. With a readership of more than 80 percent of the population, American magazines are not only dazzling in their design and diversity but complex in content and purpose. As consumer products, magazines develop and satisfy the tastes of contemporary Americans; as primary advertising tools of business and industry, magazines help provide the market that supplies the demand for products; and as instruments of entertainment and enlightenment, magazines both create and respond to current social values and the panorama of American culture.

The idea of such periodicals apparently arose almost concurrently in France, England, Germany, and other European countries, but the term *magazine* was first used in English in the early eighteenth century. The *New English Dictionary* cites the *Gentlemen's Magazine*, founded in 1731, as its first example of the word used to describe a collection of articles, fiction, poetry, and "miscellany" gathered into one place, as a storehouse, or treasure chest. The descriptive term caught on so well that by mid-century several publications included the word *magazine* either in their titles or subtitles. Today, two and a half centuries later, *magazine* is still the preferred and most commonly used designation for thousands of miscellaneous collections for the general public. Other terms such as *bulletin, journal, quarterly,* and *review* are used for more specialized publications, including business, professional, trade, and scholarly periodicals, but even many of these are actually consumer or mass magazines.

Not only content but form and frequency of publication have been used as criteria for differentiating between magazines and other periodicals, especially newspapers. While no entirely satisfactory or mutually exclusive categories for periodicals have been established, magazines are usually produced in pamphlet form with a stitched, stapled, or glued cover, rather than as broadsheets or tabloids. As for frequency of publication, magazines traditionally have appeared monthly; but, again, exceptions can be noted, especially in the modern weekly newsmagazines which offer analysis and commentary on current events to augment the news coverage of radio, televison, and newspapers.

A recent expansion of the use of the *magazine* label based largely on content occurred with the initiation of televison magazine programs, for example, "Sixty Minutes" and "20/20," which provide viewers with a variety of features, including human interest stories, personality profiles, news analyses, and interpretations of various aspects of American life in a cross-media adaptation of the usual contents of the printed periodical.

Difficult to define though they may be, magazines hold a unique place in U.S. print media. In form and periodicity, magazines are more durable than newsprint, less formidable than hardbound books, less precipitate than newspapers, yet more timely than books; and magazine content must be designed to attract and hold reader allegiance to ensure either repeated purchases or continuing subscriptions.

Although no single magazine has ever claimed the allegiance of the total U.S. reading public, over 180 million persons read magazines regularly, and most read five or six different publications. The perennial world circulation leader has been *Reader's Digest,* but currently the most widely distributed magazine in the United States is *TV Guide,* with a circulation approaching the 50 million mark. *TV Guide* contains not only televison programming schedules and criticism but lucid articles on current personalities and events as well. Its popularity is an ironic refutation of the predicted doom of print media with the advent of electronic media. Instead, not only have magazines survived, they have thrived; indeed, many have achieved record circulations in the tens of millions. Other publishers have successfully and profitably identified a more limited market and produced periodicals specifically for that segment of the mass market. Thus magazines on the American scene have changed, and are still changing, but there seems to be no stemming of the flood. Each calendar year brings some new magazine addressed to some as yet untapped topic or market.

Today thousands of titles, ranging from *Analog* to *Sesame Street Magazine,* from *Scientific American* to *Rolling Stone,* from the *New Yorker* to *Handyman,* tempt readers to exercise private interests and hobbies, while general magazines such as *Reader's Digest, Ladies' Home Journal, Atlantic,* and *Time* have broad circulations. Increasingly, historians, sociologists, and cultural anthropologists have begun to acknowledge the importance of magazines as material artifacts and historical sources far more revealing of the culture of their times than any other single source, thus recognizing, in truth, the magazine's initial and continuing function as a very "storehouse" of information and diversion.

HISTORIC OUTLINE

For obvious reason, the development of magazines had to await the invention of printing in 1450. Most examples of the new process were either single flat sheets, appropriately called broadsides, or bound volumes such as Bibles and other treatises. A subsequent development was the printing of several flat sheets folded together without binding as tabloids. Eventually, though, someone decided to put a stitch through the fold to keep the pages from sliding around, and the magazine began its distinctive existence. In large degree, however, form followed content in magazine development so that the early English magazines were single-sheet issues, looking almost exactly like their contemporary newspapers but containing comment rather than news.

Magazine content was varied almost from the beginning. Daniel Defoe, credited with starting one of the first magazines in England, in 1710 used the *Review* as a kind of privileged communication among members of his immediate society. A little later Joseph Addison and Richard Steele, first in the *Tatler* and then the *Spectator,* commented on a wide variety of issues then current in London. Essays and short stories originated in the pages of early magazines.

Although printing presses were among the first cargoes to the American colonies, it was not until 1741 that an American magazine, somewhat imitative of its English cousins, was printed and identified as such. If asked, most Americans would probably name the *Saturday Evening Post,* founded by Benjamin Franklin, as the oldest American magazine—a misconception on both counts fostered by the cover claims of that widely known publication. Although purporting to have been established in 1728, the magazine was actually started in 1821, using the offices and press of the defunct *Pennsylvania Gazette,* which, though owned by Franklin, had been founded by someone else and was actually a newspaper, not a magazine. Franklin *almost* printed the first magazine in the colonies, but his *General Magazine, and Historical Chronicle for All the British Plantations in America* lost that premier position to the *American Magazine, or A Monthly View of the Political State of the British Colonies* issued three days earlier by rival publisher Andrew Bradford. Such are the near misses in historical firsts.

Although neither magazine survived even a full year of publication, other magazines were soon launched. Rogers' and Fowle's *American Magazine and Historical Chronicle,* founded in Boston in 1743, lasted three years, thus earning the laurel of magazine historian Frank Luther Mott as the "first really important American magazine." Several other magazines, including another *American Magazine and Monthly Chronicle* by Bradford, the *New American Magazine,* the *Royal American Magazine,* and other variations on the same theme, enjoyed brief lives, but the political foment of the colonies during the next quarter-century did not offer a favorable environment for sustained publication. According to Mott, only two American magazines, the *Pennsylvania Magazine,* which employed Thomas Paine, and the *United State Magazine,* were printed during the course of the Revolution.

The post-Revolutionary period was characterized by a number of other firsts: the first acknowledgement of women's interest in magazines, with the *Gentleman's and Lady's Town and Country Magazine;* the first children's periodical; the first magazine for music lovers, which contained music scores; and the first sectarian magazine, briefly edited by Methodist Bishops Coke and Asbury.

Magazine content included political news, essays on various aspects of society, short fiction and sketches, poems, and, not infrequently, polemics. Little advertising, beyond a few classifieds, was sold, and revenue consisted mainly of subscription fees from a limited circulation. Even the distribution of the periodicals was somewhat haphazard and sporadic by modern standards. With early postal regulations seldom clear about the status of periodicals, some earnest postmasters making their own interpretations barred magazines from the mails entirely. But even in adverse environments American magazines flourished because Americans wanted to read them.

The emergence of periodicals dominated by strong editorial figures was one characteristic of the early nineteenth century. James Playsted Wood, in *Magazines in the United States,* writes, "A strong editor, even a strongly wrong-headed editor, has usually meant a strong and influential magazine; whereas intelligent editors of moderate means and no firm opinions have often produced colorless and comparatively ineffective magazines."[1] One early example of a strong editor was Joseph Dennie, whose magazine *Port Folio* ran from 1807 to 1821 and served as a model for subsequent literate and urbane publications. Dennie's strength is indicated by the survival of his periodical even while it espoused the unpopular Tory cause. Another editor and publication worthy of note was Charles Brockden Brown and his *Monthly Magazine and American Review,* the first of a series called by Mott, "second only to *Port Folio* in importance."[2] Under various titles, Brockden Brown edited the *Literary Magazine* for almost a decade.

The proliferation of magazines during this period included an expansion of magazine content and purpose beyond literature and public opinion. New magazines were directed toward religious groups, the medical profession, women, farmers, and other groups, thus beginning the trend toward specialization which was somewhat deflected by the mushrooming of the great mass magazines in the first half of the twentieth century but which by the present day has become the mainstream of magazine publishing: the specialized magazine for the special interest group.

One of the most influential women's periodicals of the nineteenth century, indeed, of all time, was *Godey's Lady's Book.* Under the leadership of Sara Josepha Hale, *Godey's* achieved wide circulation during its sixty-eight years of publication. Gowns and other apparel were assiduously copied and sewn from the color fashion plates by dressmakers both amateur and professional. *Godey's,* however, was not merely a fashion book; its contents provided enlightenment for the female mind, and Hale crusaded within its pages for women's right to education in an age which predated women's suffrage in the United States. Within its pages, Edgar Allan Poe described "The Literati of New York," sometimes astutely and sometimes with rather saccharine sanctimony; writers like William Cullen Bryant, Walt Whitman, and Nathaniel Hawthorne were also contributors to this popular magazine.

And there were others. Caroline Kirkland spent six years trying to inject a little frontier freshness and literary quality into the *Union* magazine, which publisher John Sartain viewed primarily as a showcase for his own outstanding engraving talents. The period from 1820 to 1850 saw the births of the *Saturday Evening Post, Graham's Magazine, Peterson's Magazine,* the *Scientific American, North American Review, Yale Review, Ohio Farmer, New York Mirror,* and Horace Greeley's *New-Yorker.* In addition, huge quantities of print were, unfortunately, summarily dismissed as "trash," both by Mott and by contemporaneous editors. These "penny" magazines and "family libraries" abounded but were often poorly printed, poorly edited collections of pirated or fourth-rate material; however, their very existence testifies to the omnivorous demands of Americans at all levels of sophistication for periodical reading materials. And this was the age in which these demands were answered. Call it the age of expansion, call it America's awakening, or call it the "golden age of periodicals" as Mott did, this country did not see such a burgeoning of print again until after 1900.

The pre-Civil War decade saw the establishment of other familiar names: *Harper's Monthly* (1850), *Country Gentleman* (1853), various regional *Christian Advocates* (1850), *Atlantic Monthly* (1857), and a spate of short-lived university publications. By this time, magazines had progressed in form and appearance far beyond their earlier resemblance to newspapers and had blossomed into hand-colored and embellished, highly illustrated offerings whose engravings were often scissored to grace parlor walls. Although more advertising was being accepted, it was carefully segregated from the editorial and textual materials, and small wonder, for much of it ballyhooed the virtues of everything from laxatives and trusses to cures for baldness, cancer, and impotence (all in the same bottle). The lack of regulation for advertising, either by the magazines themselves or by any publishers' or advertisers' associations, resulted in ads with little or no regard for truth or good taste.

The Civil War interrupted this expansion of magazines, but during the last forty years of the century magazine offerings increased in scope and variety.

Popular and enduring titles, such as the *Nation, Harper's Bazaar, Scribner's,* and the *American Magazine,* began in the 1860s and 1870s. And the breadth of magazine coverage is only hinted at in these titles: *U.S. Law Review, Instructor, Locomotive, American Brewer, Coal Trade Journal, Popular Science,* and *American Naturalist.* The brief life of *Keepapichinin* (1870-71) indicates its subscribers didn't, but the popular humor of *Puck* and *Judge* kept Americans laughing right up to and through the turn of the century. It was in this period as well that the print media's own magazine, *Publishers Weekly,* began its observations of this dynamic industry.

Only technological barriers prevented magazines from becoming the mass circulation giants of the twentieth century. Throughout most of the nineteenth century, magazines were printed on flat bed presses from handset type on single pieces of paper, which were hand-fed into the presses. Rarely could a magazine print more than 10,000 impressions, not only because of the time and labor consumed by the process, but because type and engravings wore down after repeated prints. Development in the 1890s of rotary presses, which were capable of printing ten thousand copies an hour on a continuous "web" roll of paper, the development of a cheap wood pulp paper strong enough for this type of printing press, and the use of speedy typesetting machinery removed the barriers to mass production and opened the way for circulations to reach the "magic million."

Not surprisingly, access to such numbers of potential customers drew the attention of industry, and advertising content and revenue grew. The influx of advertising dollars soon matched, then passed, sales input. Beginning with almost equal advertising and circulation income in the 1890s, according to U.S. Bureau of the Census manufacturing data, by the late 1920s advertising revenue was three times greater than subscription and sales income.

The shift of emphasis from magazines as the individual voices of single editors or publishers to their use as the major national advertising medium carried both positive and negative results. Magazines became colorful showcases for U.S. technology and progress, with expensive color advertisements brightening their pages and thickening their issues. Through the first three-quarters of the twentieth century, advertising has become almost as interesting to magazine readers as editorial content, and rightfully so, for it is through such advertising that most Americans become informed about new products, instructed in their uses, and encouraged to purchase everything from toothpaste to Toronados in an economy increasingly dependent on consumerism.

Despite this bounty, realistic appraisal of magazine content suggests that with economic dependence came loss of editorial freedom and that some of the free-swinging, fresh-air aggressiveness of earlier editors has been compromised by magazines' presence at the table of business and industry. This attitude was angrily espoused by Upton Sinclair in *The Brass Check: A Study of American Journalism* in which he called the Curtis publications basically an advertising medium using reading material only to fill the empty spaces between ads. More recently, Herbert Schiller in *The Mind Managers* suggested that one influence of the advertising dollar is to make magazine editors more conservative and less likely to broach topics that are controversial enough to offend either readers or advertisers.

Fortunately magazines have not been muzzled entirely, and their investigative reporting has led to exposés and crusades against giant industries such as drug manufacturers, food processors, auto makers, big labor, big government, big business, and even big medicine. However, because more and more magazines—in fact the majority of them—are not independent businesses but owned by corporations or conglomerates with widespread holdings and interests, the range of modern magazines' lances must inevitably be restricted.

Thus magazines in the last quarter of the twentieth century are consumer products which must be sold to two groups: the magazine readers who purchase the magazine and the businesses who buy the advertising space. Because the latter are the more powerful economically, the editor who fails to meet their needs will witness the death of even a magazine with rising subscriptions and circulation. But the editorial genius who finds a formula for a magazine and is able to adapt it to the rapidly changing American society or to an unchanging segment of the society will have a successful, surviving magazine. Examples of this type of editing and management include the *Reader's Digest, Ladies' Home Journal, Atlantic, Harper's, McCall's, Time, National Geographic, Scientific American,* and *Playboy.* The editor whose publication gets out of step with change, or changes too fast, or never develops a distinct identity, though, must preside over its funeral—sometimes twice. Notable examples include *Coronet, Flair, Look, Collier's, Woman's Home Companion, Life, Saturday Evening Post,* and *WomenSports.*

It is this delicate interrelationship of the reader, the word, and the world of economic and political reality which validates the function of magazines as accurate imprints of American culture and necessitates their special study apart from other print media.

REFERENCE WORKS

Research on American magazines in American culture is hampered in several ways. First, despite their long presence as a distinct entity in American publishing, for most of the nineteenth century, indexing and statistics for magazines were included under a blanket designation, "periodicals." Therefore magazine researchers must often categorize and subdivide census data and commentary on historical or economic importance to separate the role of magazines from newspapers. This is not an easy division, for, as noted, some early magazines were almost indistinguishable from papers. However, the three criteria of form, content, and periodicity will usually serve to make the distinction.

In addition to the identity confusion, magazine study has been most often limited either to discussion of their production as a branch of the craft of journalism or to analysis of their content, as historians and literary critics study certain magazines because some event or author achieved prominence. In the first instance, journalism textbooks examine writing, editing, advertising, layout, and design, with peripheral studies in the economics of publishing and mass communication theory. Another source of professional information comes from associations, organizations, and other groups that report circulation and demographic data.

The focus of attention upon magazines from academic disciplines is even more selective. Whereas most histories of the United States mention Thomas Paine's inflammatory prose, the "muckraking" role of magazines in the early part of the twentieth century, and the radical journals of the 1920s and 1930s, scant attention is given to the continuing role of magazines as reflectors and molders of public opinion and political and social attitudes, and literary criticism has almost uniformly paid more homage to the "books" of American authors than it has to the same writers' works in magazines. Although reaching a vaster audience, magazine writing is commonly dismissed as being of lesser consequence. Even more apparent to the magazine researcher in American popular culture is the qualitative judgment exercised by all three of these approaches in devaluing literally hundreds of magazines as "trash" despite their widespread distribution among the reading public.

Apart from this divison of purpose and approach, the sheer monumental bulk of materials confronting the synthesizing scholar has resulted in numerous works examining such small chips off the mountain as individual editors or magazines with brief life spans, but none encompassing the whole. This essay and bibliography attempt to draw together these disparate strands and point to those references, directories, studies, and sources likely to be most useful to the researcher of magazines in American culture.

Access to periodicals themselves is afforded through a number of standard indexes. The *Union List of Serials* provides library locations of magazines in the United States and Canada; it is also helpful for confirming dates of publication and titles and untangling new series/old series confusions. *Ulrich's International Periodicals Directory* is a guide to current domestic and foreign periodicals. Information about early nineteenth-century periodicals is contained in *Poole's Index to Periodical Literature* for the period 1802-1906; although it has only a subject index, an alphabetical title index has been provided in a later *Poole's Index Date and Volume Key.* Other guides include the very timely *Gebbie Press: All-In-One Directory,* which supplies the address, frequency of publication, circulation, and a short identification of audience for current magazines, as does the *Literary Market Place.* These latter two are useful for the magazinist because each magazine's scope and purpose is provided in copy often supplied by the magazine itself. The magazine directory of *The Working Press of the Nation* by Tom Farrell supplies similar information.

Also descriptive in content is *Magazines for Libraries,* compiled by Bill Katz and Berry G. Richards as a guide for librarians and others. Some 6,500 periodicals considered by the editors to be the best of the 65,000 available are described briefly but cogently.

Several other special guides to publications in education, the humanities, social sciences, and other disciplines are available. For the little magazine, the *International Directory of Little Magazines and Small Presses* almost, but not quite, keeps pace with the rapid births and deaths of more than 2,500 of these fragile but fascinating entities. Marion Sader has now edited the eight-volume *Comprehensive Index to English-Language Little Magazines,* an undertaking flawed only by its being organized alphabetically by proper names, of either author or subject, with no topic index.

Another group of magazines overlooked in standard guides is the ethnic press. One attempt to remedy the oversight is the *Encyclopedic Directory of Ethnic Newspapers and Periodicals in the United States,* by Lubomyr Wynar, a fairly comprehensive listing. Of lesser value is Sharon Murphy's *Other Voices: Black, Chicano, and American Indian Press,* which contains more excerpts from periodicals than listings. Additional examples of ethnic directories include Karl J. R. Arndt's *German-American Newspapers and Periodicals 1732-1955,* and another, *A Century of the Swedish-American Press,* by Jonas Oscar Backlund, which reviews the hundred years from 1851 to 1951. *The Black Press, U.S.A.,* by Roland E. Wolseley, covers the remarkably active publishing period just before World War I as well as the more recent expansions. *The 1967 Directory of U.S. Negro Newspapers, Magazines and Periodicals in 42 States: The Negro Press—Past, Present and Future,* edited by Frank B. Sawyer, though dated, gives a more complete listing.

Although cumbersome to search, the *Reader's Guide to Periodical Literature,* both current issues and the *Nineteenth Century Reader's Guide to Periodical Literature: 1890-1899, with Supplementary Indexing, 1900-1922,* may be used to locate articles examining editors and periodicals from the perspectives of contemporaries and peers. Contents of the more scholarly journals may be found through the use of a series of indexes first titled the *International Index,* then the *Social Sciences and Humanities Index,* and currently, the new *Humanities Index,* which surveys 260 magazines, and the even newer (in concept and design) *Social Sciences Index* which lists articles from 263 periodicals. *America: History and Life,* Part D, indexes articles from more than three thousand U.S. and foreign periodicals and journals. Although articles on U.S. magazines are occasionally printed abroad, the difficulties of locating and using the foreign journals usually outweigh their value, since most are rather general in content. Part A of the same publication, which is issued annually, contains abstracts of many of the articles; Part B is a book review index; and Part C contains a bibliography of books, articles, and dissertations on American history.

Several bibliographies are journalism-oriented. *Journalist's Bookshelf,* by Roland E. Wolseley, is well annotated, yet here again the viewpoint is largely that of the professional journalist or journalism educator rather than the cultural historian. The "Biography" and "History" sections provide real assistance in identifying major figures and publications. Another frequently listed bibliography, *A Bibliography for the Study of Magazines,* by John H. Schacht, is disappointingly brief and primarily useful for a fairly comprehensive list of articles on magazines published in the 1950s. Warren C. Price and Calder M. Pickett produced *An Annotated Journalism Bibliography 1958-1968,* which is comprehensive and useful. The annotations are sufficiently complete and accurate to serve the serious researcher, even though the scattered magazine articles must be located through a numerical entry index providing access to the alphabetized entries. Other bibliographies and current indexes may be found in Paul Vesenji's *An Introduction to Periodical Bibliography,* intended primarily as a guide to librarians but useful to magazine scholars as well. Finally, of course, *Dissertation Abstracts International* is the source of the latest scholarly research in the field.

Some of the aforementioned materials are part of computer data banks, but computer-search yields are usually disappointing since *magazine* is infrequently used as a descriptor. A recent comparison of manual search and computer search of *Dissertation Abstracts* produced sixty possible titles using the traditional method, whereas the electronic detective found only six. Until a better system of more accurate descriptors is developed, computer searches are of very limited value.

RESEARCH COLLECTIONS

Almost every public or university library has a periodicals collection, often with extensive bound back issues. But almost no library has all of the known periodicals, not even the redoubtable Library of Congress, although it comes close. Two directories for locating those libraries with special collections or strengths in magazines are Margaret L. Young's *Subject Directory of Special Libraries and Information Centers* based on her similarly titled *Directory of Special Libraries and Information Centers.*

Special collections of interest to magazinists include the collection of nineteenth-century periodicals at the Atheneum of Philadelphia and a similar grouping at the American Antiquarian Society in Massachusetts. Of historical significance is the Edward C. Kimble Collection of Printing and Publishing at the California Historical Society Library in San Francisco. Outstanding collections are found at the Columbia University School of Journalism Library in New York, and the University of Missouri-Columbia Journalism Library has over 3,000 bound periodicals. The University of Minnesota Journalism Library has an extensive pamphlet collection, and the Indiana University Journalism Library has numerous microform and slide holdings. The American Newspaper Publishers Association's library in Washington, D.C., has complete microform files of *Editor & Publisher,* the industry magazine that complements *Publishers Weekly.* Special collections also include the small press offerings found in the Beyond Baroque Foundation Library in Venice, California, and the Marvin Sukon Collection of Little Magazines in the Memorial Library of the University of Wisconsin-Madison. A growing collection is housed in the Popular Culture Library at Bowling Green State University, Ohio, with emphasis on pulp magazines and other popular forms.

HISTORY AND CRITICISM

Magazine history and criticism for the period from 1741 to 1950 can very nearly be summed up by one man's name, Frank Luther Mott, whose five-volume *A History of American Magazines, 1741-1930* is the sole existing attempt of a comprehensive nature. For years it has been the standard source for information on magazines of the past. Unfortunately Mott died before he could personally extend the work past 1930. This has been left for others to do. Mott's method was to present a chronological overview of a period in each volume and then append detailed individual histories of twenty or more magazines. The thoroughness of his scholarship on those periodicals treated is rarely questioned, but his interpretation of the magazines is almost uniformly journalistic, with few attempts to analyze the audiences for those magazines. The most severe limitation for the popular culture historian is that many magazines receive a citation, a paragraph, or a page, but Mott's selection of "certain important magazines which flourished" in any given period totals only 229, and most of these were definitely mid-cult and high-cult periodicals. Nevertheless, Mott's *History* is the chartbook to which the magazine scholar must repeatedly return.

Mott, who was dean of the University of Missouri School of Journalism for a number of years, also wrote *American Journalism: A History, 1690-1960,* recommended for its treatment of the growth of publishing in America. Theodore Peterson was a student and colleague of Mott, and in 1964 he updated, in somewhat different fashion, the history of magazines to that time. His *Magazines in the Twentieth Century* shows a greater awareness of the interaction between the reading public and the magazine publisher but still leaves a sixteen-year period (to the present) untabulated. The historian who has made the most notable American culture approach to magazine history is Roland E. Wolseley, in a small volume called *The Changing Magazine,* published in 1973, in which he states his intention to "go beyond the descriptive volumes about magazines which I and others have produced." (Wolseley's other books, all helpful and substantive, include *Understanding Magazines, The Magazine World,* and *The Black Press, U.S.A.*) In this, his most recent book, Wolseley examines the dynamics of magazines as a cultural force in American life while being at the same time tools of American industrialism. He explores some of the perils of conglomerate ownership of magazines but concludes that magazines do have a future in the present electronic age. The book includes a brief annotated bibliography.

The other full-scale studies of magazines include Algernon Tassin's early *The Magazine in America* (1916), an informal history of the magazine up to the end of the nineteenth century. James Playsted Wood wrote *Magazines in the United States,* and John W. Tebbel contributed *The American Magazine: A Compact History.* Both books are readable and suitable for general readers, but Tebbel's, with a 1969 copyright, is more up-to-date. Tebbel has also begun a project almost of the magnitude of Mott's undertaking, *A History of Book Publishing in the United States.* The three volumes presently completed bring the account to 1940. Of interest to magazinists in this series is the creation of periodicals by book publishers as a way of advertising and promoting their other publications.

Earlier histories of magazines in America that treat beginnings include Lyon N. Richardson's *A History of Early American Magazines: 1741-1789,* first published in 1931 and issued in reprint in 1967, and two nineteenth-century works of limited usefulness. Albert H. Smyth, in *The Philadelphia Magazines and Their Contributors, 1741-1850,* gives anecdotal accounts of periodicals and persons in those years. Printed in 1892, the book has no index—a frustration to the modern researcher. In 1898, William B. Cairns traced the *Development of American Literature: 1815-1833* through periodicals of the time, claiming that American literature developed a distinctive voice and identity through the magazines rather than books. Cairns also identifies 137 periodicals not found in *Poole's Index.* John Bakeless, in *Magazine Making,* another older work, provides valuable descriptions of early printing technology and the developments in the craft that made mass magazines possible.

Checklists of American periodicals of the early republic may be found in two scholarly works by Benjamin M. Lewis: *An Introduction to American Magazines: 1800-1810* and *A Register of Editors, Printers, and Publishers of American Magazines: 1741-1810.* Covering the same period, Neal L.

Edgar's more recent *A History and Bibliography of American Magazines: 1810-1820* picks up on "literary newspapers" which he claims fall between magazines and newspapers. William Beer's *Checklist of American Magazines 1741-1800* is another guide to those early years when publishers themselves often did not clearly define their product. Lastly, Mary Noel's *Villains Galore* examines the popular story weeklies.

Because full-scale histories and interpretations are so limited, specialized studies of segments of the whole become important. One such study, a doctoral dissertation published by the Dutch equivalent of University Microfilms, is an extremely well-researched and documented study of the deaths of the "big four," *Collier's, Look, Saturday Evening Post,* and *Life, The Life Cycle of Magazines,* subtitled *A Historical Study of the Decline and Fall of the General Interest Mass Audience Magazine in the United States during the Period 1946-1972,* in which A. J. van Zuilen, a former director of the New York office of a Dutch publishers' association, uses an integrative, interdisciplinary approach. He includes a lucid explanation of the delicate balances between the public's taste and the advertiser's economic needs that a periodical must maintain to survive. Finally, van Zuilen states that magazines follow cyclical patterns or successions through stages of birth, maturity, decay, and death and that, although individual magazines will continue to follow that cycle, at any given time there will continue to be more magazines born than dying, thus confirming the viability of the medium and the industry as a whole. Van Zuilen's occasional awkwardness of language points to the need for an American edition of the work, but this in no way obscures the authority and insight with which he writes. The book contains the most recent magazine bibliography to 1978 and is especially useful for the connections and comparisons drawn between the health of the magazine industry and the growth of electronic media.

House organs, business and association magazines, and others of that type, though far more numerous than standard mass market magazines, have attracted little attention. James L.C. Ford discusses these magazines and their publishers in *Magazines for Millions.* Usually a subsidiary printing operation of a large publishing house like McGraw-Hill, which publishes thirty or more, or Chilton, which runs between twenty-five and thirty, the editorial content of the magazines is supplied by the given business or industry. Many of the publications are of extremely high quality, underwritten as they are by the firms for whom they are produced. Ford's book is predominantly descriptive and suffers indexing deficiencies, but it is the only one available outside of instructional texts. One example of those is Abigail Fisher Hausdorfer's *House Organ Production,* which includes a bibliography of periodical articles on house organs.

Several collections of essays give overviews of publishing history. James Woodress edited a festschrift, *Essays Mostly on Periodical Publishing in*

America, which offers nine essays on varied topics, including historic and contemporary magazines. *The American Magazine, 1890-1940* was edited by this writer as a companion piece to a Delaware Art Museum exhibition examining the role of magazines in American culture during that fifty-year period. A special focus issue of the *Journal of American Culture* [3:1 (1980)], also edited by this writer, contains more extensive essays covering approximately the same period. Walter Davenport and James C. Derieux present brief sketches on nineteenth-century magazines and their editors in *Ladies, Gentlemen and Editors.* And in *The American Reading Public: What It Reads, Why It Reads*, Roger H. Smith collects a number of essays originally published in *Daedalus* on the state of the print media in the 1960s.

The remainder of magazine histories, for the most part, concentrate on one magazine or magazine group, one editor or publisher, or perhaps one magazine genre. Such works might well be represented by the excellent *The House of Harper* by Henry J. Harper, an important book on nineteenth-century publishing, or by one of the numerous books on the Curtis publishing house, beginning with James Playsted Wood's *The Curtis Magazines,* a compact history of the *Saturday Evening Post* and the other magazines in the group that is so representative of American mass magazines. Joseph Goulden recorded the earlier heydays of the house in *The Curtis Caper*, and one of the best accounts of the failure of that giant is Otto Friedrich's *Decline and Fall. George Horace Lorimer and the Saturday Evening Post* by John W. Tebbel covers the glory years of that publication, whose story would not be complete without the memoirs of its foremost artist, *My Adventures as an Illustrator*, by Norman Rockwell. The women's branch of the Curtis triumvirate of *Saturday Evening Post, Country Gentleman*, and *Ladies' Home Journal* is described by Bruce Gould and Beatrice Gould in their *American Story.* The long reign of an earlier editor of the *Ladies' Home Journal*, Edward Bok, son-in-law of Cyrus Curtis but an editorial genius himself, is recounted in his autobiography, *The Americanization of Edward Bok*, and his subsequent biography of Curtis, *The Man from Maine*. In both books, the curious mixture of altruism and business acumen that is the mark of success in publishing prevails. More recently, Salme Harju Steinberg in *Reformer in the Marketplace* attests to Bok's skill in working for the betterment of society within the exigencies of a business establishment.

Other early editors and publishers have received attention. In *Success Story: The Life and Times of S. S. McClure* by Peter Lyon, that crusading editor, whose magazine earned the epithet *muckraker* from Teddy Roosevelt, is given an absorbing analysis with a historical perspective lacking in McClure's own *My Autobiography*. That era of publishing is perhaps the best covered of all, but one of the better attempts is Harold S. Wilson's recent *McClure's Magazine and the Muckrakers*. The biographies of some of the principals at the time are also informative, especially Lincoln Steffens's *Autobiography* and Ida M. Tarbell's *All in the Day's Work*.

An editor-publisher of the turn of the century, Frank A. Munsey, was easily the most flamboyant and innovative of the dime magazine publishers. He tells his own history in *The Story of the Founding and Development of the Munsey Publishing House* with an effervescent egotism that cannot be wholly discounted. A later work by George Britt, *Forty Years—Forty Millions: The Career of Frank A. Munsey*, affirms the fact of his publishing genius. Street & Smith, also pulp publishers, are featured in a well-illustrated and entertaining book by Quentin Reynolds called *Fiction Factory*. Other pulp history is found in *Pulpwood Editor* by Harold Hersey. Backward glances appear in Frank Gruber's *The Pulp Jungle*, Peter Haining's edition of *The Fantastic Pulps*, and Tony Goodstone's *The Pulps*.

Outstanding among the studies of single magazines or publishing houses in addition to the ones above are the two volumes by Robert T. Elson on the Luce publishing empire: *Time, Inc.: The Intimate History of a Publishing Enterprise, 1923-1941*, and *The World of Time, Inc.: The Intimate History of a Publishing Enterprise, 1941-1960*. Although Elson's works are probably definitive, another writer, W. A. Swanberg, had access to much of the same material when he wrote the Pulitzer Prize-winning biography *Luce and His Empire*. John Kobler's entry in Luce illumination is coyly titled *Luce: His Time, Life and Fortune*. The earlier *Life*, a humor magazine whose name Luce appropriated for his periodical, is treated in *Life, the Gentle Satirist* by John Flautz. But in *That Was the Life*, Dora J. Hamblin takes the reader into the exciting world of photojournalism, a genre also explored in the classic *Words and Pictures* by Wilson Hicks, and in Margaret Bourke-White's own excellent autobiography, *Portrait of Myself*.

Almost every major popular magazine has had at least one article or book published about it. The casualties especially receive attention as people wonder why the magazines didn't survive. Paul C. Smith, a former publishing executive with Crowell-Collier, wrote in *Personal File* of his attempts to save *Look* and *Collier's*, and part of Theodore H. White's *In Search of History: A Personal Adventure* gives another insider's view of that episode.

Some of the more literary and intellectual periodicals have received more than their share of attention, with numerous essays and works on the *Dial*, or *American Mercury*, or *Atlantic* available, despite their limited circulations. But even the diminutive perennial *Reader's Digest*, despite its mid-cult designation, has had at least three books written about it. The earliest is a gossipy account by John Bainbridge, called *Little Wonder, or The Reader's Digest and How It Grew*. Continuing the praises of DeWitt and Lucy Wallace and their one-of-a-kind publication is James Playsted Wood's *Of Lasting Interest: The Story of the Reader's Digest*, and the latest pleasant anecdotal account of the phenomenon of Pleasantville is

Samuel A. Schreiner Jr.'s *The Condensed World of the Reader's Digest.*

Treatment of women's magazines or women editors is not as comprehensive as it should be. An English book, *Women's Magazines, 1693-1968*, by Cynthia L. White, concentrates on British periodicals but contains a good section and useful tables on American women's magazines. In *The Lady Persuaders*, Helen Woodward chastises the hypocrisy of the magazines' claiming to be noble organs of public service while actually being governed strictly by advertising interests and economic concerns. Accounts of early editors include Ruth E. Finley's *The Lady of Godey's: S. J. Hale* and Olive Burt's *First Women's Editor, Sara Josepha Hale*. Hale's long tenure with *Godey's Ladies' Book* set records for quiet crusading and longevity. Margaret Fuller, one-time editor of the *Dial*, is treated by Faith Chippenfield in *In Quest of Love: The Life and Death of Margaret Fuller* in a work as vivid as its subject. Two later editors of competing women's fashion magazines, *Harper's Bazaar* and *Vogue*, tell their experiences in Carmel Snow's *The World of Carmel Snow*, written with Mary Louise Aswell, and Bettina Ballard's *In My Fashion*.

Little magazines have had influence stretching far beyond their circulations. A collection of essays, *The Little Magazine in America: A Modern Documentary History*, edited by Elliott Anderson and Mary Kinze, provides views of a number of "important" little magazines as well as the philosophies of their editors. Reed Whittemore's *Little Magazines* attempts to define them and gives limited examples, whereas Lois Rather gives only a very personal history in *Some "Little" Magazines*. An excellent treatment of a single little magazine is Paul R. Stewart's *The "Prairie Schooner" Story: A Little Magazine's First 25 Years—1927-1951*. One unusual source of small press and little magazine publication is surveyed in Russell N. Baird's *The Penal Press*, which lists the papers and magazines produced inside U.S. prisons.

Another infrequent but entertaining area of information and insight on popular magazines is found in popular fiction. Again, uneven quality plagues the lot, but some do provide more than just a good read. The novel by Theodore H. White, *The View from the Fortieth Floor*, is perhaps as close to experiencing the publishing world as a lay reader may come. Clay Blair's *The Board Room: A Novel* is based on his own participation in the life (and death) of the *Saturday Evening Post.* Earlier novels, though dated in style, reveal inner workings of various periods in publishing history. Ralph Ingersoll satirizes a Luce-like couple in *The Great Ones*. Several novels examine the conflict between personal values and job values, including John Brooks's *The Big Wheel* and Matthew Peters's *The Joys She Chose*. Two other novels deal specifically with women in publishing: *Women, Inc.* by Jane Kesner Morris, and *Manhattan Solo* by Marjorie Worthington.

Georgette Carneal in *The Great Day* wrote an early exposé novel of the sleazy world of tabloids and confession magazines, and the latter-day descendents are treated nonfictionally in *The Pious Pornographer* by William Iverson. Charles Beaumont, a contributing editor to *Playboy*, looks back to the media's past in *Remember? Remember?* Also in the exposé mode is Samm Sinclair Baker's *The Permissible Lie*, which reveals the less-than-truthful tactics of advertisers in the mass media.

An area of magazine research somewhat neglected by previous analysts but essential to the understanding of magazines as a cultural force in American life is sociological and demographic data. Knowledge of audience numbers is essential to the advertiser buying space, and some early publishers were not above inflating their circulation figures to command higher advertising fees. Thus in 1914 the Audit Bureau of Circulation (ABC) was established as an industry self-regulatory agency. Their annual reports contain the sworn circulations of member publications. These figures, and data from other sources, are contained in the *N. W. Ayer Directory of Publications*, an annual publication. Charles O. Bennett tells the story of the establishment of the ABC in *Facts Without Opinion: First Fifty Years of the Audit Bureau of Circulation*, and Ralph M. Hower chronicles its story in the *History of an Advertising Agency: N. W. Ayer and Son at Work, 1869-1949.*

Modern publishers and advertisers need to know more about reader audiences than merely numbers and location, so surveys, opinion polls, and other demographic profiling have become common. At least twelve agencies in addition to the publisher's own survey departments produce such reports, and these are listed in a pamphlet from the Magazine Publishers Association, *Sources of Information About Magazines*. Interesting examples of such reports include the Magazine Advertising Bureau's *Magazines for Advertisers: Their Size, Their Markets, Their Results*; the W. R. Simmons's *A Study of the Retention of Advertising in 5 Magazines;* the Association of National Advertisers' *Magazine Circulation and Rate Trends: 1940-1967*; and the Politz Research studies of readers of *Life, Better Homes and Gardens, American Home*, and others, which detail reader characteristics down to the last pair of shoes purchased. Not surprisingly, the surveys show a close correlation of interests, attitudes, and affluence between audience and magazine, again affirming the value of magazines as mirrors of American society.

Sociologists usually treat magazine reading as one of Americans' many informational and recreational activities, but rarely do they single it out for much emphasis. As a result, no comprehensive study of magazines from that perspective is available, although mention of magazines as a part of the mass media is frequent. There are a number of good articles in journals such as *American Journal of Sociology, Sociological Quarterly,* and *Social Forces*. Of particular interest are those articles which examine the impact of advertising found in popular periodicals. Not infrequently, content analysis of magazine fiction reveals pervasive stereotyping which affects and/or reflects widespread social attitudes.

ANTHOLOGIES AND COLLECTIONS

Anthologies and collections, especially those designed for classroom use in communications, literature, and the study of rhetoric, as well as American history "casebooks," routinely use selections from periodicals. Examples would include such titles as *Our Times: The Best from the "Reporter"* edited by Max Ascoli, Francis William Weeks' *Readings in Communication from "Fortune,"* and *One Hundred Years of the "Nation,"* collected by Henry M. Christman. Some of the anthologies include thematic collections from a number of magazines, festschrift from individual magazines, or anniversary collections. Of myriad editorship and uncertain quality, the collections yet offer easy access to sometimes hard-to-find material. Nevertheless, for the true flavor of the individual magazines, or those of a period, the backfiles of the periodicals themselves are preferred. Some of the better anthologies are William Wasserstrom's *A Dial Miscellany*, William Phillips and Philip Rahv's *Partisan Review Anthology, The Good Housekeeping Treasury* from that magazine's files, *A Cavalcade of Collier's* edited by Kenneth McArdle, and *Great Reading from "Life": A Treasury of the Best Stories and Articles Chosen by the Editors.*

Other collections present a particular point of view or trace a unique influence. The history of women in magazines is found in *Harper's Bazaar: One Hundred Years of the American Female*, edited by Jane Trahey, and in Helen Otis Lamont's *A Diamond of Years: The Best of the "Woman's Home Companion."* Examinations of American culture are offered in collected essays either by a single author or by a group of social critics. Marya Mannes, in her collection of essays from the *Reporter, But Will It Sell?*, criticizes the rampant materialism and consumer mentality in American culture, while in Arthur M. Weinberg's and Lila Weinberg's *The Muckrakers*, the focus is on that era in U.S. history as illustrated in the magazines of the period 1902-12. John K. M. McCaffery assembled material for *The American Dream: A Half-Century View from American Magazine* stressing that periodical's emphasis in both editorial and advertising content: the American "success myth."

Other collections also give overviews of particular periods. Cleveland Amory's and F. Bradlee's *"Vanity Fair": Selections from America's Most Memorable Magazine—A Cavalcade of the 1920s and 1930s,* with text and pictures from those decades, rather immodestly claims to be the voice of the sophisticated world of that time. In *Adventures of the Mind*, Richard Thruelson and John Kobler bring together portraits of the 1950s from the pages of the *Saturday Evening Post*. Another fascinating collection is Ray Brosseau's *Looking Forward: Life in the Twentieth Century as Predicted in the Pages of American Magazines from 1895-1905*, wherein the editor finds within the pages of 1895-1905 magazines predictions about life in the latter twentieth century. The wide-ranging and scattered emphases of other collections and anthologies prohibit the inclusion of them all, but most are readily accessible.

One further publication type should be mentioned. Occasionally facsimile editions of early magazines are printed, and these are of great interest, especially if microforms are the researcher's primary exposure to early periodicals. Handling even a facsimile version reaffirms the appeal of popular magazines as attractive creations of art, design, writing, advertising, and unique insight into the America that is and was.

NOTES

1. James Playsted Wood, *Magazines in the United States*, 3rd ed. (New York: Ronald Press, 1956), pp. 33-34.

2. Frank Luther Mott, *A History of American Magazines*, Vol. 1: *1741-1850*, 5 vols. (Cambridge: Harvard University Press, The Belknap Press, 1957-68), p.124.

BIBLIOGRAPHY

BOOKS

America: History and Life. Santa Barbara, Calif.: ABC-Clio, 1964-. Annual.

Amory, Cleveland, and F. Bradlee, eds. *"Vanity Fair": Selections from America's Most Memorable Magazine: A Cavalcade of the 1920s and 1930s*. New York: Viking, 1960.

Anderson, Elliott, and Mary Kinze, eds. *The Little Magazine in America: A Modern Documentary History*. Yonkers, N.Y.: Pushcart Press, 1979.

Arndt, Karl J. R., ed. *German-American Newspapers and Periodicals 1732-1955*. Heidelberg: Quelle & Meyer, 1961.

Ascoli, Max, ed. *Our Times: The Best from the "Reporter."* New York: Farrar, Strauss, 1960.

Association of National Advertisers. *Magazine Circulation and Rate Trends: 1940-1967*. New York: ANA, 1969.

The Audiences of Five Magazines: Newsweek, Time, U.S. News & World Report, Saturday Evening Post, Life. New York: Newsweek, 1962.

N. W Ayer Directory of Publications. Philadelphia: Ayer, 1905-. Annual.

Backlund, Jonas Oscar. *A Century of the Swedish-American Press*. Chicago: Swedish-American Newspaper, 1952.

Bainbridge, John. *Little Wonder, or the Reader's Digest and How It Grew*. New York: Reynal, 1945.

Baird, Russell N. *The Penal Press*. Evanston, Ill.: Northwestern University Press, 1967.

Bakeless, John. *Magazine Making.* New York: Viking, 1931.

Baker, Samm Sinclair. *The Permissable Lie.* New York: World, 1968.

Ballard, Bettina. *In My Fashion.* New York: McKay, 1960.

Beaumont, Charles. *Remember? Remember?* New York: Macmillan, 1963.

Beer, William. *Checklist of American Magazines 1741-1800.* Worcester, Mass: American Antiquarian Society, 1923.

Bell, Marion V., and Jean C. Bacon. *Poole's Index Date and Volume Key.* Chicago: Association of College and Reference Libraries, 1957.

Bennett, Charles O. *Facts Without Opinion: First Fifty Years of the Audit Bureau of Circulation.* Chicago:ABC, 1965.

Blair, Clay. *The Board Room: A Novel.* New York: Dutton, 1969.

Bok, Edward. *The Americanization of Edward Bok.* New York: Scribner's, 1920.

———. *The Man from Maine.* New York: Scribner's, 1923.

Bourke-White, Margaret. *Portrait of Myself.* New York: Simon & Schuster, 1963.

Boyenton, William H. *Audit Bureau of Circulations.* Chicago: ABC, 1949.

Britt, George. *Forty Years—Forty Millions: The Career of Frank A. Munsey.* New York: Farrar & Rinehart, 1935. Reprint. Port Washington, N.Y.: Kennikat Press, 1972.

Brooks, John. *The Big Wheel.* New York: Harper, 1949.

Brosseau, Ray. *Looking Forward: Life in the Twentieth Century as Predicted in the Pages of American Magazines from 1895-1905.* New York: American Heritage Press, 1970.

Burt, Olive. *First Women's Editor: Sara Josepha Hale.* New York: Messner, 1960.

Cairns, William B. *Development of American Literature: 1815-1833.* Madison: University of Wisconsin Press, 1898.

Carneal, Georgette. *The Great Day.* New York: Liveright, 1932.

Chippenfield, Faith. *In Quest of Love: The Life and Death of Margaret Fuller.* New York: Coward, 1957.

Christman, Henry M., ed. *One Hundred Years of the "Nation."* New York: Macmillan, 1965.

Davenport, Walter, and James C. Derieux. *Ladies, Gentlemen and Editors.* Garden City, N.Y.: Doubleday, 1960.

Dissertation Abstracts International. Ann Arbor, Mich.: University Microfilms, 1970-.

Edgar, Neal L. *A History and Bibliography of American Magazines: 1810-1820.* Metuchen, N.J.: Scarecrow Press, 1975.

Elson, Robert T. *Time, Inc.: The Intimate History of a Publishing Enterprise, 1923-1941.* New York: Atheneum, 1968.

———. *The World of Time, Inc. The Intimate History of a Publishing Enterprise, 1941-1960.* New York: Atheneum, 1973.

Farrell, Tom. *The Working Press of the Nation.* New York: Public Relations Press, Farrell Corporation, 1945-. Annual.

Finley, Ruth E. *The Lady of Godey's: S. J. Hale.* Philadelphia: Lippincott, 1931.

Flautz, John. *Life, The Gentle Satirist.* Bowling Green, Ohio: Bowling Green University Popular Press, 1972.

Ford, James L. C. *Magazines for Millions.* Carbondale: Southern Illinois University Press, 1969.

Friedrich, Otto. *Decline and Fall.* New York: Harper & Row, 1970.

Gebbie Press: All-In-One Directory. New Paltz, N.Y.: Gebbie Press, 1978.
Good Housekeeping. *Good Housekeeping Treasury.* New York: Simon & Schuster, 1960.
Goodstone, Tony. *The Pulps.* New York: Chelsea House, 1976.
Gould, Bruce, and Beatrice Gould. *American Story.* New York: Harper, 1968.
Goulden, Joseph. *The Curtis Caper.* New York: Putnam, 1965.
Gruber, Frank. *Pulp Jungle.* Los Angeles: Sherbourne, 1967.
Haining, Peter, ed. *The Fantastic Pulps.* New York: St. Martin's Press, 1975.
Hamblin, Dora J. *That Was the Life.* New York: Norton, 1978.
Harper, Henry J. *The House of Harper.* New York: Harper, 1912.
Harper's Bazaar. *Harper's Bazaar: 100 Years of the American Female.* New York: Random House, 1967.
Hausdorfer, Abigail Fisher. *House Organ Production.* Philadelphia: Temple University Press, 1954.
Hersey, Harold. *Pulpwood Editor.* New York: Stokes, 1938. Reprint. Westport, Conn.: Greenwood Press, 1974.
Hicks, Wilson. *Words and Pictures.* New York: Harper, 1952.
Hower, Ralph M. *The History of an Advertising Agency: N. W. Ayer and Son at Work, 1869-1949.* Cambridge: Harvard University Press, 1949.
Humanities Index. New York: H. W. Wilson, 1974-. Annual.
Ingersoll, Ralph. *The Great Ones.* New York: Harcourt Brace, 1948.
International Directory of Little Magazines and Small Presses. Len Fulton and Ellen Ferber, eds. Paradise, Calif.: Dustbooks, 1970-. Annual.
International Index. New York: H .W. Wilson, 1907-65.
Iverson, William. *The Pious Pornographer.* New York: Morrow, 1963.
Katz, Bill, and Berry G. Richards. *Magazines for Libraries.* 3rd. ed. New York: Bowker, 1978.
Kobler, John. *Luce: His Time, Life and Fortune.* Garden City, N.Y.: Doubleday, 1968.
Lamont, Helen Otis, ed. *A Diamond of Years: The Best of the "Woman's Home Companion."* Garden City, N.Y.: Doubleday, 1961.
Lewis, Benjamin M. *An Introduction to American Magazines: 1800-1810.* Ann Arbor: University of Michigan Press, 1961.
______. *A Register of Editors, Printers, and Publishers of American Magazines: 1741-1810.* New York: New York Public Library, 1957.
Life Magazine. *Great Reading from "Life": A Treasury of the Best Stories and Articles Chosen by the Editors.* New York: Harper, 1960.
Literary Market Place. New York: Bowker, 1940-. Annual.
Lyon, Peter. *Success Story: The Life and Times of S. S. McClure.* New York: Scribner's, 1963.
McArdle, Kenneth, ed. *A Cavalcade of "Collier's."* New York: Barnes, 1959.
McCaffery, John K. M., ed. *The American Dream: A Half-Century View from American Magazine.* Garden City, N.Y.: Doubleday, 1964.
McClure, S. S. *My Autobiography.* New York: Ungar, 1914; 1963.
Magazine Advertising Bureau, Inc. *Magazines for Advertising: Their Size, Their Markets, Their Results.* New York: MAB, 1953.
Magazine Publishers Association. *Sources of Information About Magazines.* New York: MPA, 1973.

Mannes, Marya. *But Will It Sell?* New York: Lippincott, 1964.
Morris, Jane Kesner. *Women, Inc.* New York: Holt, 1946.
Mott, Frank Luther. *American Journalism: A History 1690-1960.* 3rd ed. New York: Macmillan, 1962.
———. *A History of American Magazines, 1741-1930.* 5 vols. Cambridge: Harvard University Press/Belknap Press, 1957-68.
Munsey, Frank A. *The Story of the Founding and Development of the Munsey Publishing House.* New York: Munsey, 1907.
Murphy, Sharon. *Other Voices: Black, Chicano, and American Indian Press.* Dayton, Ohio: Pflaum/Standard, 1974.
National Research Bureau. *Working Press of the Nation. Vol. II. Magazine Directory.* Chicago: NRB, 1979.
Nineteenth Century Reader's Guide to Periodical Literature: 1890-1899, With Supplementary Indexing, 1900-1922. 2 vols. New York: H. W. Wilson, 1944.
Noel, Mary. *Villains Galore.* New York: Macmillan, 1954.
Peters, Matthew. *The Joys She Chose.* New York: Dell, 1954.
Peterson, Theodore, *Magazines in the Twentieth Century.* Urbana: University of Illinois Press, 1964.
Phillips, William, and Philip Rahv, eds. *The Partisan Review Anthology.* New York: Holt, Rinehart and Winston, 1962.
Politz Research, Inc. *An Audience Study of the American Home Magazine.* New York: PRI, 1957.
———. *A Study of the Accumulative Audience of "Life."* New York: Time, 1950.
———. *A 12-Months Study of Better Homes and Gardens Readers.* Des Moines: Meredith, 1956.
Poole's Index to Periodical Literature, 1802-1881. Rev. ed. Boston: Houghton-Mifflin, 1891. Annual supplements, 1882-1906.
Price, Warren C., and Calder M. Pickett. *An Annotated Journalism Bibliography, 1958-1968.* Minneapolis: University of Minnesota Press, 1970.
Rather, Lois. *Some "Little" Magazines.* Oakland, Cal.: Rather Press, 1971.
Reader's Guide to Periodical Literature. New York: H. W. Wilson, 1900-. Annual.
Reynolds, Quentin. *Fiction Factory.* New York: Random House, 1955.
Richardson, Lyon N. *A History of Early American Magazines: 1741-1789.* New York: Nelson, 1931. Reprint ed. Chicago: Octagon, 1967.
Rockwell, Norman. *My Adventures as an Illustrator.* Garden City, N.Y.: Doubleday, 1960.
Sader, Marion, ed. *Comprehensive Index to English-Language Little Magazines, 1890-1970.* 8 vols. Millwood, N.Y.: Kraus-Thomson, 1976.
Sawyer, Frank B., ed. *1967 Directory of U.S. Negro Newspapers and Magazines and Periodicals in 42 States: The Negro Press—Past, Present and Future.* New York: U.S. Negro World, 1968.
Schacht, John H. *A Bibliography for the Study of Magazines.* Urbana: University of Illinois Press, 1966.
Schiller, Herbert. *The Mind Managers.* Boston: Beacon Press, 1973.
Schmidt, Dorey, ed. *The American Magazine, 1890-1940.* Wilmington: Delaware Art Museum, 1979.

Schreiner, Samuel A., Jr. *The Condensed World of the Reader's Digest.* New York: Stein and Day, 1977.

W. R. Simmons & Associates Research, Inc. *A Study of the Retention of Advertising in 5 Magazines.* New York: W. R. Simmons, 1965.

Sinclair, Upton. *The Brass Check: A Study of American Journalism.* Pasadena, Calif: Upton Sinclair, 1920.

Smith, Paul C. *Personal File.* New York: Appleton, 1964.

Smith, Roger H., ed. *The American Reading Public: What It Reads, Why It Reads.* New York: Bowker, 1963.

Smyth, Albert H. *The Philadelphia Magazines and Their Contributors, 1741-1850.* Philadelphia: R.M. Lindsay, 1892. Reprint. Detroit: Gale, 1970.

Snow, Carmel, with Mary Louise Aswell. *The World of Carmel Snow.* New York: McGraw-Hill, 1962.

Social Sciences and Humanities Index. Vols. 19-61. New York: H. W. Wilson. 1965-74. Annual.

Social Sciences Index. New York: H. W. Wilson, 1974-. Annual.

Steffens, Lincoln. *Autobiography.* New York: Harcourt, Brace, 1968.

Steinberg, Salme Harju. *Reformer in the Marketplace.* Baton Rouge: Louisiana State University Press, 1979.

Stewart, Paul R. *The "Prairie Schooner" Story: A Little Magazine's First 25 Years—1927-1951.* Lincoln: University of Nebraska Press, 1955.

Swanberg, W. A. *Luce and His Empire.* New York: Scribner's, 1972.

Tarbell, Ida M. *All in the Day's Work.* New York: Macmillan, 1939.

Tassin, Algernon. *The Magazine in America.* New York: Dodd, Mead, 1916.

Tebbel, John W. *The American Magazine: A Compact History.* New York: Hawthorn Books, 1969.

———. *George Horace Lorimer and the Saturday Evening Post.* Garden City, N.Y.: Doubleday, 1948.

———. *A History of Book Publishing in the United States.* 3 vols. New York: Bowker, 1975-78.

Thruelson, Richard, and John Kobler, eds. *Adventures of the Mind.* New York: Knopf, 1959.

Trahey, Jane. *Harper's Bazaar: One Hundred Years of the American Female.* New York: Random House, 1967.

Ulrich's International Periodicals Directory. New York: Bowker, 1932-. Annual.

Union List of Serials in Libraries of the United States and Canada. 3rd ed. New York: H. W. Wilson, 1966.

U.S. Department of Commerce. *Historical Statistics: Colonial Times to 1970.* Part 2. Washington, D.C.: U. S. Department of Commerce, Bureau of the Census, 1975.

Vesenji, Paul. *An Introduction to Periodical Bibliography.* Ann Arbor, Mich.: Pierian Press, 1974.

Wasserstrom, William, ed. *A Dial Miscellany.* Syracuse, N.Y.: Syracuse University Press, 1963.

Weeks, Francis William, ed. *Readings in Communication from "Fortune".* New York: Holt, 1961.

Weinberg, Arthur M., and Lila Weinberg, eds. *The Muckrakers: The Era in Journalism that Moved America to Reform—The Most Significant Magazine Articles of 1902-1912.* New York: Simon & Schuster, 1961.
White, Cynthia L. *Women's Magazines 1693-1968.* London: Michael Joseph, 1970.
White, Theodore H. *In Search of History: A Personal Adventure.* New York: Harper & Row, 1978.
———. *The Changing Magazine.* New York: Hastings House, 1973.
Whittemore, Reed. *Little Magazines.* Minneapolis: University of Minnesota Press, 1963.
Wilson, Harold S. *McClure's Magazine and the Muckrakers.* Princeton: Princeton University Press, 1970.
Wolseley, Roland E. *The Black Press, U.S.A..* Ames: Iowa State University Press, 1971.
———. *The Changing Magazine.* New York: Hastings House, 1973.
———. *Journalist's Bookshelf.* 7th ed. Philadelphia: Chilton, 1961.
———. *The Magazine World.* New York: Prentice-Hall, 1951.
———. *Understanding Magazines.* 2nd ed. Ames: Iowa State University Press, 1969.
Wood, James Playsted. *The Curtis Magazines.* New York: Ronald Press, 1971.
———. *Magazines in the United States.* 3rd ed. New York: Ronald Press, 1956.
———. *Of Lasting Interest: The Story of the Reader's Digest.* Garden City, N.Y.: Doubleday, 1958. Reprint ed. Westport, Conn.: Greenwood Press, 1975.
Woodress, James. *Essays Mostly on Periodical Publishing in America.* Durham, N.C.: Duke University Press, 1973.
Woodward, Helen. *The Lady Persuaders.* New York: Obolensky, 1960.
Worthington, Marjorie. *Manhattan Solo.* New York: Knopf, 1937.
Wynar, Lubomyr. *Encyclopedic Directory of Ethnic Newspapers and Periodicals in the United States.* Littleton, Colo: Libraries Unlimited, 1972.
Young, Margaret L., et al., eds. *Directory of Special Libraries and Information Centers.* 5th ed. Detroit: Gale Research, 1977.
———. *Subject Directory of Special Libraries and Information Centers.* 4th ed. Detroit: Gale Research, 1976.
Zuilen, Antoon J. van. *The Life Cycle of Magazines: A Historical Study of the Decline and Fall of the General Interest Mass Audience Magazine in the United States during the Period 1946-1972.* Uithoorn, Netherlands: Graduate Press, 1977.

PERIODICALS

American Brewer. New York, 1868-.
American Journal of Sociology. Chicago, 1895-.
American Magazine. New York (Webster, ed.), 1787-88.
The American Magazine. New York (Leslie's), 1876-1956.
American Magazine, or *A Monthly View of the Political State of the British Colonies.* Philadelphia, January-March 1741.
The American Magazine and Historical Chronicle. Boston, September 1743-December 1746.

American Magazine and Monthly Chronicle. Philadelphia, October 1757-October 1758.
American Mercury. New York, January 1924-.
American Naturalist. Boston, 1867- (Philadelphia, 1878-98.)
Analog. New York, 1963-.
Atlantic Monthly. Boston, November 1857-.
Better Homes & Gardens. Des Moines, July 1922-.
Christian Advocate. New York, 1826-.
Christian Advocate. Philadelphia, January 1823-December 1834.
Coal Trade Journal. New York, 1869-.
Collier's. New York, April 28, 1888-January 4, 1957.
Coronet. Chicago, 1936-61.
Country Gentleman. Philadelphia, January 6, 1853-1955.
The Dial. Chicago and New York, May 1880-July 1929.
Editor & Publisher. New York, June 29, 1901-.
The Family Handyman. St. Paul, 1950-.
Flair. New York, February 1950-January 1951.
Fortune. New York, 1930-.
General Magazine, and *Historical Chronicle, For All the British Plantations in America.* Philadelphia, January-June 1741.
Gentleman's Magazine. (Cave's) London, 1731-1907.
Gentlemen and Lady's Town and Country Magazine. Boston, May-December 1784.
Godey's Lady Book. Philadelphia, July 1830-August 1898.
Graham's Magazine. Philadelphia, January 1826-December 1858.
Harper's Bazaar. New York, 1867-.
Harper's Monthly. New York, June 1850-.
The Instructor. Dansville, New York, 1891-.
Journal of American Culture. Bowling Green, Ohio, 1978-.
Judge. New York, October 29, 1881-January 1939.
Keepapichinin. New York, 1870-71.
Ladies' Home Journal. Philadelphia, December 1883-.
Life. New York, 1936-.
The Literary Magazine, and American Register. Philadelphia, October 1803-December 1807.
Locomotive. Hartford, 1867-.
Look. Des Moines, Iowa, 1937-.
McCall's Magazine. Dayton, Ohio, September 1873-.
Monthly Magazine and American Review. New York, April 1799-December 1800.
The Nation. New York, July 6, 1865-.
National Geographic. Washington, D.C., October 1888-.
New American Magazine. Woodbridge, N.J., 1757-60.
New York Mirror. New York, August 2, 1823-1857(?).
New Yorker. New York, 1925-.
New-Yorker. New York (Greeley, ed.), March 22, 1834-1841.
North American Review. Boston, May 1815-.
Ohio Farmer. Cleveland, 1852-.

Ohio Farmer. Cleveland, 1852-.
Pennsylvania Magazine. Philadelphia, 1775-76.
Peterson's Magazine. Philadelphia, January 1842-April 1898.
Playboy. Chicago, 1953-.
Popular Science Monthly. New York, May 1872-.
The Port Folio. Philadelphia, January 1801-December 1827.
Publishers Weekly. New York, January 18, 1872-.
Puck. New York, March 1877-September 1918.
Reader's Digest. Pleasantville, New York, 1922-.
The Review. London (Defoe, ed.), February 1704-July 1712.
Rolling Stone. San Francisco, 1967-.
Royal American Magazine. Boston, January 1774-March 1775.
Saturday Evening Post. Philadelphia, August 4, 1821-.
Scientific American. New York, August 1845-.
Scribner's. New York, January 1887-May 1939.
Sesame Street Magazine. New York, 1970-.
Social Forces. Chapel Hill, North Carolina, 1922-.
Sociological Quarterly. Carbondale, Illinois, 1960-.
The Spectator. London, March 1711-December 1714.
The Tatler. London, April 1709-January 1711.
Time. New York, March 3, 1923-.
TV Guide. Philadelphia, 1953-.
United States Law Review. St. Louis, New York, 1866-.
United States Magazine. Philadelphia, January-December 1779.
Vogue. New York, December 17, 1892-.
Woman's Home Companion. Cleveland, New York, January (?) 1874- January 1957.
WomenSports. San Mateo, Cal., 1974-79.
Yale Review. New Haven, May 1892-.

CHAPTER 7 Magic and Magicians

Earle J. Coleman

As the nineteenth-century French prestidigitator Robert-Houdin observed, the theatrical magician can be defined as an actor who is playing the role of a conjurer, that is, a being whose supernatural powers enable him to accomplish what is naturally impossible.[1] Magic, like the closely related performing art of pantomime, is basically grounded upon the production of illusions. In fact, every feat of magic depends upon presenting the spectator with a forgery or counterfeit of some object, action, or state of affairs. But whereas the pantomimist presents an intelligible illusion, the magician exhibits an unintelligible illusion; in the case of the former, one understands how it is effected (through skillful body control developed from a host of ballet-like exercises); in the latter, attributing skill to the performer hardly qualifies as an explanation of how the effect is produced.

Magic and magicians are as at home in American popular culture as the long-running comic strip *Mandrake the Magician* by Lee Falk. Indeed, magic or magical themes have figured prominently in American versions of such diverse forms of entertainment as the impromptu street performance, stage show, circus, dime museum, carnival, nightclub, novel, drama, short story, film, radio, and television. Occasionally, a term used by magicians has found its way into wider circulation in American society. The word *gimmick*, for instance, by which magicians describe a concealed device needed as the means for some magical effect, was eventually adopted by the advertising industry to designate anything that attracts attention by injecting an element of novelty. By definition, popular arts are widely enjoyed, but magic is more than popular; it is actually universal in its appeal. A native of China and a citizen of Italy may have real difficulty in grasping, much less appreciating, the dance, music, literature, painting, or architecture of each other's culture, but both individuals are readily entertained by the magician, for in causing a coin to vanish or levitating a woman the conjurer violates the laws of nature under which all human beings live and with which their experience vividly familiarizes them.

One problem may be unique to the student of magic as a performing art. Because the effectiveness of magic is utterly dependent upon the concealment of its secrets, a good deal of the best magic literature is circulated on a very limited basis. Hence, specialized research collections, which include some of the more closely guarded writings of small trade publishers, are crucial to the serious student. Such essential collections will be discussed later in this essay. European magicians and magic books will be cited when they have significantly shaped the development of magic in America.

HISTORIC OUTLINE

That sleight of hand was practiced in ancient Egypt is shown by a wall painting from a Beni Hasan tomb (ca. 2500 B.C.) depicting a performer presenting the classic "cups and balls mystery." Moving from magic in antiquity to the beginnings of American magic and magicians, one discovers that the Colonial climate was decidedly inhospitable to conjurers, actors, and other entertainers; in fact, all such performers were banned from Jamestown, Virginia, in 1612. Perhaps frivolous entertainment was simply deemed incompatible with the sternness that the struggle for survival demanded of the early colonists. While Virginia still outlawed public magic performances in 1740, a member of the state council, William Byrd II, is reported to have enjoyed a private magic show in June of that year; and, by June of 1769, Virginia no longer forbade magicians, for George Washington wrote in his diary entry of September 19, 1769: "went to see slight (sic) of hand performed"; this presentation took place in Alexandria, Virginia. Washington was also present when Peter Gardiner, a magician-puppeteer, presented his act on November 17, 1772, in Williamsburg, Virginia. In the same year, Jacob Meyer, the first American magician to appear in Europe, was entertaining Catherine II in Focsani, Romania. Meyer favored the stage name "Philadelphia," which he borrowed from his native city and found had a sufficiently exotic ring to European ears. Just over a decade later, in 1783, the famous Philadelphian Benjamin Franklin was solidly defeated in a chess game by a chess-playing automaton, which was the brainchild of a Baron Wolfgang von Kempelen. The match took place in Versailles while Franklin was serving as the U.S. ambassador to France. As we shall see, it remained for another celebrated American to argue that the automaton was actually a magic stunt operated by a concealed, chess-playing assistant in the body of the mannequin figure. The year 1783 is also significant because it marks the birth of Richard Potter in Boston (date of death unknown), the first American to succeed as a magician in his own country. Featuring effects such as the standard "cups and balls," Potter attracted appreciative crowds in Canada as well as the United States. As the dark-skinned son of a British tax collector and his black slave, he has the dubious distinction of being the first American magician to experience racial prejudice during a twelve-day engagement in Mobile, Alabama.

On seeing the automaton chess player in Richmond, Virginia, the still largely unknown American writer and poet, Edgar Allan Poe, offered his theory of the phenomenon in the *Southern Literary Messenger* of April 1836. Later history revealed that Poe had been partially correct in his analysis of the talented machine. As he suspected there actually was a concealed chess player, but this person was not located in the body of the automaton itself as Poe believed; rather, the unseen player was hidden in the desk upon which the mannequin rested. A quarter of a century later, John Henry Anderson, a European who advertised himself as "The Great Wizard of the North," was vividly confronted with the fermenting slavery issue in the United States. Irate citizens of Richmond, Virginia, destroyed the advance publicity posters of this charlatan from the North who dared to trespass upon Southern soil! Explaining that Anderson was from northern Scotland was to no avail.

In 1861, the outstanding German conjurer, Carl Hermann, brought his magic to the White House where he performed for President Lincoln. A contemporary, but native American magician, John Wyman, went further by performing for Presidents Van Buren and Fillmore, as well as entertaining Lincoln four times. It was Wyman who pioneered in the exposing of fraudulent spirit mediums who bilked the public, a crusade which obsessed Harry Houdini in his final years. But it was undoubtedly Senior Blitz of London who performed the most memorable magic for Lincoln. In July of 1863, at an outdoor gathering, Blitz produced a pigeon from Lincoln's hat. Attached to the bird's wing was a slip of paper with the message, "Victory, General Grant." The reference, of course, was to the intense battle then being waged at Gettysburg.

By 1884 Harry Kellar, the first native American magician to achieve international fame, had begun his longest run, 267 performances at the Egyptian Hall in Philadelphia. During this engagement, members of the audience included two of his friends, the noted actor Edwin Booth and the equally prominent writer Mark Twain. Born in Erie, Pennsylvania, on July 11, 1849, Kellar performed on five continents before being recognized as a monarch of American magic. His stylishly mounted levitation of a woman illusion was justifiably the centerpiece of his full-evening show.

Although an often neglected topic, American Indian conjuring is the subject of an entire chapter in Melbourn Christopher's excellent *The Illustrated History of Magic.* Perhaps it should not be surprising that Indian magicians favored producing snakes from bags over extracting rabbits from hats. At the Louisiana Exposition of 1904, Shungopavi, an Indian who billed himself as a medicine man, employed an eagle feather for flourishes in place of the traditional magic wand.

Harry Kellar passed his mantle to Howard Thurston, an American born in

Columbus, Ohio, on July 20, 1869. Thurston, who specialized in large-scale illusions, presented his own version of the famous Indian rope trick in which a rope tossed upward remains in mid-air, a boy climbs the rope, and he eventually vanishes. It is worth mentioning parenthetically that the original Indian version of the effect, in which the mystery was presented outside in broad daylight, appears to be purely mythical. Thurston and other magicians offered substantial sums of money to buy a single performance of the trick, and in 1934 the *Times* of India offered 10,000 rupees for one performance; there were no takers. During the same year, Thurston brought an elaborate magic show to the White House of President Roosevelt. One year later, while on what he planned as his farewell tour, Thurston died in Charleston, West Virginia. Having held his title as the United States' leading illusionist for nearly three decades, he had surpassed even the expectations of his predecessor, Kellar.

At about the time that Thurston took over the Kellar show, Thomas Nelson Downs was establishing himself as the greatest coin manipulator in the history of magic. Born in Montour, Iowa, on March 26, 1867, Downs's masterful production of an apparently inexhaustible supply of coins from thin air ensured bookings at first-rate theaters in the United States and on the Continent. One of the most tragic episodes in the history of American magic took place in 1918, when a contemporary of Downs, William E. Robinson, was accidentally shot to death during the performance of his sensational bullet-catching effect. Robinson, who used the stage name Chung Ling Soo, through make-up and costuming convinced his audiences that he actually was an Oriental. A somewhat later figure, Theodore Bamberg (1875-1963), also masqueraded as an Oriental and actually managed to fool even his Oriental audiences.

If the first quarter of this century belonged uniquely to any magician, it belonged to the master escape artist Harry Houdini (1874-1926). Born in Budapest, the son of a rabbi, Houdini, whose real name was Ehrich Weiss, insisted in later years that he was American born. He undoubtedly felt like an American, given that he was brought to the United States while still a child. Several of the biographies on Houdini give credence to the cliche that truth can be stranger and more exciting than fiction. Among his effects were: walking through a brick wall, causing an elephant to vanish on the stage of the New York Hippodrome theatre, and escaping from an endless series of restraining devices—including handcuffs from Scotland Yard. Eventually, Houdini's exploits won him a motion picture contract, his first of several films, *The Grim Game,* being shot in 1919. At the height of his success he received $3,700 a week, the largest salary ever paid to a single performer at the Palladium in London. On each anniversary of Houdini's death, members of the Society of American Magicians demonstrate their regard for him by making a pilgrimage to his Long Island tomb.

During the first three decades of this century, American theater was truly enriched by the phenomenon that came to be known as the full-evening magic show. These productions were extravanganzas which sometimes actually lived up to the superlatives in their advertisements. Elephants, lions, tigers, bears, horses, doves, rabbits, ducks, eagles, or camels, dozens of assistants, elaborate backdrops and scenes which changed frequently, and the use of over a hundred costumes for one performance were the kind of ingredients that contributed to these pageants. But the Depression that hit in 1929 delivered a death blow to most of these elaborately framed presentations. In such an economic climate, the production costs of full-evening shows were prohibitive. The advent of "talkies" in motion pictures and the great popularity of radio also increased the economic risks of large-scale magic shows. Therefore, a majority of American magicians shifted to performing smaller nightclub acts. One magical genius of this era was Cardini (1899-1939). Born Richard Valentine Pitchford, in Wales, Cardini achieved international acclaim for his suave nightclub act which featured unexcelled playing card and cigarette manipulations. For many aspiring American magicians, Cardini's routines became the paradigm of perfection. A few figures such as Harry Blackstone, who was born Henri Bouton in Chicago, and Dante, whose real name was Harry Jansen, carried the full-evening show into the 1940s. Fortunately for contemporary lovers of magic, Harry Blackstone, Jr., is now performing some of his father's magical masterpieces in the baroque environment of Las Vegas hotels. Any chronicle of contemporary American magicians would surely include Joseph Dunninger, whose mental magic gained him popularity from the 1930s through to the 1960s. Dunninger's predictions and demonstrations of telepathy made him extremely successful on stage, radio, and television. In fact, he is one of very few performers who has ever had a series on all three television networks.

Magic today is happily enjoying a rebirth as magicians adapt their art of unreality to the realities of the final quarter of this century. Witness, for example, the popular Broadway play, *The Magic Show,* which fuses the color, flash, and mystery of the old full-evening show with rock music. One of the oldest forms of magic, street conjuring, has been revitalized by artists like Jeff Sheridan, who performs in New York's Central Park. The intimacy of the television camera has enormously increased the audience for close-up magic, which would normally be visible to only one or two dozen spectators. A million-dollar contract with a major Las Vegas hotel has recently been signed by the magic team of Sigfried and Roy, making them the most handsomely paid magicians in history. Causing tigers and other big cats to appear, vanish, or become transformed into human beings, Sigfried Fischbacker and Roy Horn have also appeared in their own program on network television. Senior magicians who lecture to magic societies are finding a growing number of members in these organizations. Bars and restaurants that feature magicians are proliferating throughout the country. In numerous schools from the elementary level to the university a number of magicians specialize in entertaining students. A further expanding market for magic acts has been created by the phenomenon of the theme park. Many of these amusement parks feature half-hour, condensed versions of the full-evening show. In fact, there is now a magic franchise; Mark Wilson, once the star of his own television series, trains and choreographs performers for magic shows at the Busch Gardens theme parks. Even the Houdini escape act has been resurrected by magicians such as the great Randi. Kreskin, drawing perhaps too heavily from the mentalist, Dunninger, has made his mental magic pay through numerous television appearances. It is sobering to realize that the magician who makes one network television presentation has a greater audience than Houdini had in a lifetime. Shimada, the Japanese magician, has reintroduced the exquisite beauty of Oriental magic and is in demand at magic conventions throughout the world. A number of contemporary magicians are being lucratively rewarded for their "commercial magic," that is, magic that is employed to sell a product or service at trade shows and conventions. In our post-Watergate era, the magician can be seen as refreshingly honest; he is the one person who openly announces that he will deceive you and then lives up to his word.

REFERENCE WORKS

Perhaps the single most useful of bibliographical tools is Robert Gill's *Magic as a Performing Art: A Bibliography of Conjuring.* This work judiciously surveys magical literature published during the unprecedentedly fertile period between 1935 and 1975; selected earlier classics are also included. Gill, who possesses the unusual qualifications of being a librarian and a magician, has listed over a thousand publications, briefly described them, and frequently provided evaluations. Further enhancing the value of his text, Gill has presented a succinct appraisal of the most significant bibliographical works in the area of conjuring from the earliest to contemporary studies. Scrupulous scholarship has earned Trevor H. Hall's *A Bibliography of Books on Conjuring in English from 1580 to 1850* the status of a standard reference source. The 323 carefully detailed entries of this book may be effectively supplemented by *Conjuring Books, 1580 to 1850* by Edgar Heyl, a writer who maintains the high bibliographical standards of his predecessor. By far the most monumental bibliographical contribution comes in the form of *The Master Index to Magic in Print* by Jack Potter. His nearly thirty years of research have issued in a fourteen-volume opus which indexes some 2,700 books and monographs.

Of all the contenders for the title "encyclopedia of magic," Harlan

Tarbell's *The Tarbell Course in Magic* is the unqualified winner. The seven volumes that comprise this set excel in both the quantity and quality of their contents, which run the full gamut from sleight-of-hand effects to the largest stage illusions. Quite plausibly, it has been suggested that were all other magic books destroyed, the art could endure through Tarbell's writings alone. Among one-volume reference works, John Northern Hilliard's *Greater Magic* has been hailed as the best single book ever written on magic; although card magic is emphasized in this one thousand-page text, the book does manage to cover a considerably wide range. *Cyclopedia of Magic*, by Henry Hay, is a somewhat dated but still valuable survey of the vocabulary of magic together with an exposition of many well-known effects. Recently Martin Gardner edited the *Encyclopedia of Impromptu Magic*, a diverting compilation of games, stunts, and magic effects that one can play or perform spontaneously with everyday objects. Occasionally Gardner's zeal for exhaustiveness leads him to include effects that are so banal as to be humorous. Gardner himself has noted that it remains for others to provide a needed cross-reference index; he, after all, has provided the always entertaining data. William Doerflinger's *The Magic Catalogue* is a delightful hodgepodge featuring a capsule history of magic from antiquity to the present, a fine general bibliography, advertisements for magic books and apparatus, and data on magic museums, societies, conventions, dealers, courses, and periodicals. Representative types of magic from pocket tricks to stage illusions are also explained. Specialized encyclopedias devoted exclusively to, for example, playing cards or coins, will be discussed in the History and Criticism section below.

RESEARCH COLLECTIONS

The Library of Congress, Washington, D.C., like all public libraries, is limited in its holdings on magic, since much magic literature is simply suppressed and reserved for practicing magicians. Researchers will, however, be pleased with the library's McManus-Young and Houdini collections, Rare Books Division. Because most magic literature is distributed by small trade houses or private individuals rather than lay publishers, specialized collections are the main source of material for the serious researcher. Hollywood, California, is the home of two major magic institutions. The Magical Hall of Fame, founded by the Society of American Magicians, includes photographs, a library, a museum of magic, and an auditorium. The Magic Castle is a lavishly decorated Victorian mansion overlooking Hollywood. Here are collected posters, photographs, books, and the paraphernalia of famous magicians. Virtually all contemporary members of the elite of magic have performed here and continue to do so; membership is private and individuals can gain entrance only after having passed a proficiency test. Researchers wishing to use the superb library must apply for permission to the Academy of Magical Arts at the same address. Still another California center for magic is the Magic Cellar, Earthquake McGoon's Saloon, San Francisco, which features a collection of illusions by the famous American magician of the early twentieth century, Carter the Great. Not only are Carter's props displayed, but sometimes his tricks are actually performed here at the Magic Cellar. The John Mulholland Collection, the Players, New York, contains not only rare books but antique pieces of magical apparatus, playbills, and art works devoted to magic by artists such as Hieronymous Bosch. While the Players is a private society, scholars may apply for permission to use the Mulholland Collection by contacting the curator. The Egyptian Hall Museum of Magical History in Brentwood, Tennessee, is among the world's largest museums devoted to the memorabilia of magic and magicians. Egyptian Hall is open without charge to both magicians and other interested persons by appointment. Most recently opened in this country is the American Museum of Magic in Marshall, Michigan, established and maintained by Robert Lund. This excellent collection includes books, newspaper clippings, letters, programs, magic sets, art works, apparatus, magazines, and nearly three thousand posters. In all the museum, which is open to the public, holds over a quarter of a million items. A newsletter detailing additions to the collection is available. Prominent among European institutions is the Musée Robert-Houdin in Blois, France, devoted exclusively to apparatus once owned by the outstanding French magician Jean Eugène Robert-Houdin who inspired his namesake the great Houdini. The library of the Magic Circle and that of the British Ring of the International Brotherhood of Magicians, both in London, afford their members two of the finest collections of magic literature in existence. Nonmembers may, of course, request permission for visiting scholars status. Given that specialized research collections are relatively few in number and may be inconveniently located, the researcher may wish to consult the catalogs of magic dealers, which list and describe most of the publications that are unavailable through public libraries. Two of the largest such dealers are Abbott's Magic Company, Colon, Michigan 49040, and Louis Tannen, 1540 Broadway, New York, New York 10036. Doerflinger's *The Magic Catalogue* contains a representative list of magic dealers arranged geographically.

HISTORY AND CRITICISM

The present critical survey of books and monographs will treat topics in this order: history, the general field, showmanship and presentation, biography and autobiography, gambling tools such as playing cards and dice, sleight of hand and close-up magic, mental magic and mediums, and miscellaneous subjects. This survey will be followed by a discussion of magazines and specialized journals.

By the late nineteenth century, with Thomas Frost's *The Lives of the Conjurors,* a full-fledged chronicle of magic and an invaluable reference work was available to the student of magic history. For those who wish an overview of magic history from antiquity to the close of the eighteenth century, Henry Ridgely Evans's *History of Conjuring and Magic: From the Earliest Times to the End of the Eighteenth Century* is a skillful condensation. *John Mulholland's The Story of Magic* remains of interest to the student of magic history, but it has been superseded by later books. In *The Great Book of Magic,* Wendy Rydell and George Gilbert have presented a pictorial treat; this volume, produced by a highly regarded publisher of art books, features a well-illustrated, selective history of magic together with the secrets for performing 150 time-tested magic effects. Although only a minimum of dexterity is required, some of the effects can have a professional impact. To date, the definitive history of magic is Milbourne Christopher's *The Illustrated History of Magic,* a work of loving scholarship by a dean of American magicians. Illustrations, color plates, and a bibliography complement the excellent text. An illustrated history of the oldest and possibly purest form of magic, street magic or the magic of the marketplace, is set out by Edward Claflin in *Street Magic,* written with Jeff Sheridan. An excellent choice of graphics and a succinct, articulate text make this study a charming, informal history of a little-known variety of magic.

Appearing in 1876, *Modern Magic,* by Professor Hoffmann (Angelo John Lewis), the first of his truly important writings, would alone have sufficed to ensure him a place of prominence among contributors to magic literature. To be specific, Hoffmann's tome of over five hundred pages covered a wider range of magic than any previous book in the English language. *More Magic,* Hoffmann's second major work, was a sequel which concentrated upon simple props rather than elaborate apparatus. In *Blackstone's Secrets of Magic,* by Harry Blackstone, one finds a collection of mainly standard effects, but it is a suitable introduction for the novice. *Professional Magic for Amateurs,* by Walter Brown Gibson, is an excellent book which lives up to its title by explaining high-quality close-up and stage magic suitable for a beginner. The celebrated gambling expert John Scarne has contributed an easy introduction to all phases of magic in *Scarne's Magic Tricks.* Bruce Elliott's *Classic Secrets of Magic* features a host of innovative ideas for presenting standard effects such as the cups and balls mystery. *The Best in Magic,* another fine compilation by Elliott, consists of excellent effects contributed by outstanding magicians from every branch of magic. In *John Mulholland's Book of Magic,* a well-respected figure in the literature of magic offers the novice useful information on the psychology of magic as well as carefully explained close-up and stage effects. Perhaps most general of all the general studies on magic is Dariel Fitzkee's *The Trick Brain,* a famous manual dealing with refining and inventing effects and methods by means of a systematic procedure.

Among the earlier works devoted to showmanship and presentation, *Our Magic,* by Nevil Maskelyne and David Devant, is a foundational treatise treating magic as a legitimate dramatic art form. Valuable insights into the art, theory, and practice of magic sustain the thesis that the magician is a species of actor. Required reading for those interested in the aesthetics of magic, *Our Magic* explicitly advocates an Aristotelian conception of drama. Fitzkee's *Showmanship for Magicians* is one of those rare books that deal with the ways of presenting magic so as to enhance its entertainment value. Such factors as color, movement, and music are analyzed in detail. In a companion volume, *Magic by Misdirection,* Fitzkee attends to the psychology of deception rather than to manual dexterity or magic equipment. These two books and *The Trick Brain* are so indispensable to the serious student of magic that they are often known as the "Fitzkee trilogy." *Neo Magic: The Art of the Conjuror,* by S. H. Sharpe, is another well-regarded text on the aesthetics of magic. *Showmanship and Presentation* is an established book in which Edward Maurice contributes richly to the topics under consideration. A final recommendation on the subject of showmanship would be Henning Nelms's *Magic and Showmanship: A Handbook for Conjurors;* this is one of the clearest works on a topic whose importance is difficult to overestimate, since showmanship is what distinguishes the successful, entertaining magician from the mere deceiver.

Henry Ridgely Evans's *Magic and Its Professors* sets forth an enlightening biographical survey of prominent nineteenth-century magicians together with their specialties in magic. Less than a decade later Harry Houdini authored one of the most controversial biographical statements in the history of magic, *The Unmasking of Robert-Houdin;* what makes the book provocative is that Houdini attacks his own namesake for stealing his predecessors' inventions. Those who are especially interested in the issue may consult Maurice Sardina's *Where Houdini Was Wrong* for a counterargument and defense of Robert-Houdin. Bernard M. L. Ernst and Hereward Carrington offer more Houdini-related material in *Houdini and Conan Doyle: The Story of a Strange Friendship,* in which letters between Houdini and Doyle furnish the substance for a fascinating book. In *White Magic: The Story of the Maskelynes,* rather than offer a single biography, Jasper Maskelyne has carefully traced the careers of all three generations which constituted the British dynasty of magicians. Comprehensive biographical sketches of Carl and Alexander Hermann make H. J. Burlingame's *Magician's Handbook* of great importance to the historian of magic. *Houdini on Magic,* by Walter Brown Gibson and

Morris N. Young, is one of the finest studies of the man and his magic; not only do the authors disclose many of Houdini's secrets, but through aptly chosen anecdotes they also reveal much of Houdini as a person. Surely Scarne's autobiography, *The Amazing World of John Scarne: A Personal History* is among the most exciting records of a sleight-of-hand artist in our time. His expertise in all aspects of gambling has made his consultation services attractive to Las Vegas casinos and the U.S. Army, not to mention members of organized crime. *The Life and Times of Augustus Rapp* is an autobiography which absorbingly records Rapp's travels through the small towns and villages of the United States. Stuart Cramer's *Germain, the Wizard and His Ledgerdemain* is the biographical sequel to Cramer's *Secrets of Karl Germain;* taken together these books offer a thorough record of Germain's life and magic. Robert E. Olson and Edward Dart have combined biography and exposition in their one-volume treatment of another outstanding professional magician, *Carl Rosini—His Life and His Magic.* In the recent *Houdini: The Untold Story,* Melbourne Christopher has provided what is perhaps the authoritative biography of the most colorful magician of the twentieth century. Here, as in his other writings, Christopher combines clarity and precision with an engaging style. Will Dexter's *The Riddle of Chung Ling Soo* is an engrossing biography of William E. Robinson, whose make-up and costumes enabled him to perform as an Oriental magician and whose flair for the spectacular led to his accidental death while performing the famous bullet-catching stunt. In *My Magic Life,* David Devant goes beyond a well-written autobiography to include perceptions of his contemporaries in the field of magic. *The Magic Man* is an autobiography of Herman Hanson, written with the assistance of John U. Zweers; here again, the details of an intriguing life have been supplemented with an explanation of selected magic effects by one of the most warmly regarded figures in the magic fraternity.

Playing cards, possibly because so readily available, portable, or rich in permutations, have become the most popular prop of both the magician and the gambler. *J. N. Hofzinser's Çard Conjuring,* by Ottokar Fischer, a faithful translation of Hofzinser's *Kartenkunststuke,* originally published in 1910, enables the reader of English to benefit from one of the classic treatises on card magic. Glenn G. Gravatt and W. Von Deusen have included a large percentage of all known card tricks that do not require sleight of hand in *Encyclopedia of Self-Working Card Tricks* and its sequel, *Second Encyclopedia of Self-Working Card Tricks.* Jean Hugard and Frederick Braue have coauthored one of the most acclaimed texts for advanced card control in *Expert Card Technique.* These same authors have also written *The Royal Road to Card Magic,* a well-established book which concentrates upon simplified card magic while offering some tips to the more experienced card manipulator. *Scarne on Card Tricks,* by John Scarne, is an excellent collection of "no-skill" card mysteries which has earned the status of a standard work. His *Scarne on Cards* is a comprehensive reference work featuring a clear exposition of the artifices employed by the card cheat. Edward Marlo's *The Cardician* is a set of masterful effects and sleights for the more accomplished card manipulator. This is only one of the dozens of books and monographs from the fertile mind of a man who is one of the most brilliant writers in the history of card magic. His academically precise style is balanced by the creativity of an artist. Marlo's advanced card technique is only for the most seriously committed card specialists. In *Andrus Deals You In,* Jerry Andrus has delivered sophisticated card magic by a genuine innovator. Although Andrus has written other fine books, this remains his major contribution. Paul LePaul's *The Card Magic of LePaul* is a richly photographed masterpiece which offers one stunning card mystery after another. It is unquestionably one of the finest books on sleight of hand with cards that has ever been published, *Steranko on Cards*, by James Steranko, contains novel, demanding card routines well illustrated by the author, who is himself a professional illustrator. Al Leech's *Super Card Man Stuff* is just one of his over half-dozen monographs on card manipulation and other close-up magic. Leech has a fresh, straightforward style, favors quick effects, and offers material ranging from easy to moderately difficult. A basic grasp of card magic is presupposed in Lewis Ganson's *Dai Vernon's Ultimate Card Secrets.* Affectionately known as the "Professor," Vernon is revered by fellow magicians for his consummate skill with cards. Some of the material in the present book has long been carefully guarded by professional gamblers; thus, the reader is, indeed, being offered inner secrets of card manipulation. *The Complete Illustrated Book of Card Magic,* by Walter Brown Gibson, is a well-photographed, comprehensive, discussion of all phases of card magic. In fact, so much has been divulged that some magicians undoubtedly regret the distribution of this valuable work by a lay publisher. In *Reputation Makers,* as in his other books, Harry Lorayne will reward the reader who is not put off by hyperbole or turgid writing, since once again a number of effective card mysteries have been revealed. *Card Cavalcade,* by Jerry Mentzer, is a stimulating introduction to the inventive card manipulation of a leading contemporary magician. Interested parties should contact a magic dealer for a list of further writings by the prolific Mentzer. In *Cy Enfields's Entertaining Card Magic,* Lewis Ganson demonstrates that Enfield's acclaimed magic is a subtle combination of new effects and innovative methods for performing standard effects. Those seeking an exhaustive treatment of cheating with dice are advised to consult John Scarne's *Scarne on Dice,* a book which any dice player must read for self-protection. Eddie McGuire's *The Phantom of the Card Table: The Real Secrets of Walter Scott* is a monograph which circulated as an underground manuscript around 1930; at that time it sold for the handsome price of fifty dollars. Scott's favorite techniques for cheating at cards, especially his second deal, make this must reading for the would-be card expert. In Frank Garcia's *Marked Cards and Loaded Dice,* the announced topics are treated in illuminating detail. Various ways in which the gambling secrets disclosed can be applied to the performance of magic effects will be apparent to the alert magician. *All in a Nutshell,* by Frank Garcia, is a rich treatise on the three-shell game in which a spectator is asked to follow the movements of a pea that has been placed under one of three shells. A leading authority on gambling, Garcia explores basic principles and offers a selective bibliography.

Dai Vernon's *Select Secrets* contains material that previously had been closely guarded by members of the magic world who excel in sleight of hand. Camille Gaultier's *Magic without Apparatus,* a translation of *La Prestidigitation Sans Appareils,* has served and continues to be of service as a beautiful introduction to sleight of hand for readers of English everywhere. In *The Amateur Magician's Handbook,* Henry Hay presents a fine primer on sleight of hand together with a combined biography and bibliography. With the three-volume series, *Routined Manipulation,* Lewis Ganson has given the magic world a meticulously explained and illustrated modern classic on sleight of hand for close-up or stage conditions. Walter Brown Gibson's *What's New in Magic?* delivers creative, experience-tested ideas for all performers of close-up magic. *The Dai Vernon Book of Magic,* by Lewis Ganson, testifies to Vernon's brilliance as a magic innovator and to his supreme manipulative skills. Some of the effects by this expert at close-up are very difficult, but they are nonetheless worthy of the most diligent practice. Bert Allerton's *The Close-Up Magician* reveals the secrets behind the highly commercial brand of magic that brought him fame as a table and bar performer. Numbered among his many patrons were celebrities from the stage, screen, radio, and television. In *The Magic of Slydini,* by Lewis Ganson, the exquisite close-up magic of Tony Slydini is painstakingly demonstrated through some five hundred photographs. Many of the routines depend upon the performer working at a table in order that he can secretly deposit and remove objects from his lap; hence, the book is a mini-course on the often overlooked art of "lapping," an art which is capable of staggering the spectator. *An Evening of Magic with Charlie Miller,* by Robert Parrish, features the witty, unique magic of a performer who is first a fine entertainer and second a skillful magician. Superb material, which lives up to Slydini's reputation for excellence at table magic, is available in *Slydini Encores* by Leon Nathanson. With *Cups and Balls Magic,* Tom Osborne offers both the basic principles of and variations on an effect that can be traced to sleight-of-hand practitioners in ancient Egypt. Tony Slydini's *The Magical World of Slydini* explicates magic of the loftiest quality by a master of sleight of hand whose unsurpassed dexterity has elevated magic to the level of a fine art.

In his crusading work, *A Magician Among the Spirits,* Harry Houdini exposed fraudulent techniques employed by mediums in order to simulate spiritual phenomena. In *The Book Without a Name,* Theodore Annemann emphasizes the subtle mental mysteries and effective card magic that were to characterize his subsequent writings. All of his sixteen monographs are still very much worthy of study and will be found in any well-stocked magic shop. At just over one hundred pages, Robert Alan Nelson's *The Encyclopedia of Mentalism and Allied Arts* hardly qualifies for the category of encyclopedia, but it does include practical, time-tested effects by a noted expert who has established a solid reputation through numerous publications. Tony Corinda's *Thirteen Steps to Mentalism* is a detailed course on the fundamentals of mental magic; in fact, the work could be called encyclopedic in range. Burling Hull has contributed another comprehensive presentation of mental magic in *The Encyclopedic Dictionary of Mentalism.*

J. B. Bobo's *The New Modern Coin Magic* is exhaustive to the point of eclipsing all previous writings on the subject. Whether the reader seeks effects using coins alone, coins with other objects, or specially prepared coins, he will be delighted by the offerings in this unrivaled masterpiece. Nearly thirty years ago, Keith Clark wrote what continues to be the definitive book on the topic of cigarette magic and manipulation, *Encyclopedia of Cigarette Tricks.* Jack Chanin's *Cigar Magic* is perhaps the only work devoted exclusively to the topic, but, of course, much of the material is also applicable to cigarette magic. Harold R. Rice's *The Encyclopedia of Silk Magic* is a virtually all-encompassing labor of love; the magician Francis B. Martineau sketched the nearly six thousand illustrations and hand-lettered the entire text of this mammoth work, which totals 1,542 pages. *The Marian Chavez Encyclopedia of Dove Magic* is the author's revised version of a book that was released originally in 1968. The entire gamut of dove magic is explored, from effects that depend upon skill to those which rely upon self-contained apparatus. Over one thousand pages of valuable ideas make Ian H. Adair's *Encyclopedia of Dove Magic* another leading treatise in the field. *Abbott's Encyclopedia of Rope Tricks,* edited by Stewart James, is a two-volume treatment of rope effects which is rightfully regarded as a definitive text. Harry Houdini's *Handcuff Secrets* was the first valuable study on the art of escaping from handcuffs; and, despite progress in the locksmith's craft, this book remains useful. *Mathematics, Magic, and Mystery,* by Martin Gardner, is a collection of magic tricks based upon concealed mathematical principles. Those who are mathematically inclined will especially enjoy learning his effects, and all readers will be refreshed by Gardner's articulate style. A beautiful exposition of stage magic in the Oriental style by one of the greatest magicians in this generation is to be found in *Okito on Magic,* by Theodore Bamberg (Okito) and Robert Parrish. Representing twenty years of research and occupying six volumes, Francis Ireland Marshall's *Kid Stuff* is the unrivaled bible on the topic of entertaining children with magic. Marshall has supplemented her own insights by drawing upon the experience-tested observations of some exceptional fellow magicians. *Thrilling Magic,* by Leonard A. Miller, explains the secrets of fire eating, sword swallowing, reclining on a bed of nails, and like spectacular feats. *Midway Magic,* by Don Boles, is another study on this much overlooked topic, magic for side shows and circuses. Perhaps a survey of books in the field should conclude with a work devoted to an activity that laymen readily associate with the magician. Jack Chanin's *The Encyclopedia of Sleeving* is a valuable compendium of ways by which to insert and remove undetected a variety of objects from one's sleeves.

A helpful list of periodicals, both American and European, is given in *The Magic Catalogue,* by William Doerflinger. Two of the most widely circulated, general publications are *Genii,* a monthly magazine, P.O. Box 36068, Los Angeles, Cal. 90036, and *The New Tops,* another monthly, Abbott's Magic Co., Colon, Mich. 49040. Two more major publications should be noted. *The Linking Ring* is the official monthly organ of the International Brotherhood of Magicians, 114 North Detroit Street, Kenton, Ohio 43326, and *M.U.M. Monthly* is published by the Society of American Magicians, Lock Drawer 789, Lynn, Mass. 01903. Quite recently a journal with a scholarly turn of mind has appeared, *The Journal of Magic History.* Edited by Steven Tigner, the address is P.O. Box 7149, Toledo, Ohio 43615. This journal "is an interdisciplinary journal devoted to the history of magic as a performing art and to allied aspects of human culture which seek to evoke, to cultivate, or to exploit a sense of wonder."

ANTHOLOGIES AND REPRINTS

Dover Pubications has reprinted a number of classics in the literature of magic and has offered them in well-bound and modestly priced paperback editions. A current Dover catalog should be consulted for a complete list of books that are presently available. One such reprint is Reginald Scot's *The Discovery of Witchcraft,* a reprint of an edition of 1930, which in turn was based upon a 1584 publication. This was a pioneering work in exposing the fact that the performance of the theater magician could be explained in purely natural terms. Sydney W. Clarke's *The Annals of Conjuring from the Earliest Times to the Present,* now recognized as a standard reference work, is a reprint of articles from *The Magic Wand* magazine. In *Magic Tricks and Card Tricks,* two of Wilfred Jonson's books have been combined into a single volume which makes for an excellent introductory manual. As editor, James G. Thompson has assembled a rich collection of innovative ideas by some of the stars of magic in *My Best: A Collection of the Best Originations Conceived by Eminent Creators. Hugard's Magic Monthly* is a nine-volume reprint of material from Jean

Hugard's magazine of the same name; the wide gamut of material covered should suit anyone's taste in magic. *Maskelyne on the Performance of Magic,* by Nevil Maskelyne and David Devant, is a reprint of Part 1 from *Our Magic,* which emphasizes the aesthetics of magic and basic principles of showmanship. *King of Conjurors: Memoirs of Robert-Houdin,* the autobiography of one of the most illustrious performers in the history of magic, is a reprint of the two-volume British edition, which appeared in 1859; the author's colorful career and especially his relationship to Houdini make this required reading for the student of magic history.

S. W. Erdnase's *The Expert at the Card Table* remains for some the uncontested bible for manipulation applicable to cheating at cards as well as entertaining with them. Certain of the more difficult sleights described have been replaced by easier techniques in more recent literature. Three of Jean Hugard's monographs and books dealing with cards have also been reprinted; *Card Manipulations* presents basic sleights with cards as well as practical variations; *More Card Manipulations* explains card mysteries suitable for the more advanced practitioner; and *Encyclopedia of Card Tricks* is a well-known work of nearly five hundred pages. All three works, as well as others by the prolific Hugard, are essential reading for the would-be card expert. Gordon Miller's *Abbott's Anthology of Card Magic* consists of three volumes which contain a collection of fine effects by America's leading card specialists; best of all, most of the material is not especially difficult. W. F. Rufus Steele has rendered his fellow magicians a valuable service by editing and publishing *Paul Rosini's Magical Gems: A Memorial,* an anthology of highly effective close-up magic, with the accent on cards, which exhibits the creativity of Rosini. Bruce Elliott's *Phoenix* is a six-volume reprint of largely close-up magic from the magazine of the same name, which lasted from 1952 to 1954. Because the editor of the magazine had a keen eye for first-rate magic, most of the material is effective to this day. *Stars of Magic,* edited by George Starke, is a reprint of eleven routines by a group of master magicians. Taken together, the excellent photography and lucid text nearly approximate the quality of personal instruction. *Early Vernon: The Magic of Vernon in 1932,* by Dai Vernon, is a reprint of Vernon's early manuscripts, which revolutionized close-up magic and gave rise to his international reputation. For *The Art of Close-Up Magic,* Lewis Ganson has gathered a number of clever effects (none with cards) from a host of famous magicians. James G. Thompson's three-volume *Top Secrets of Magic* features contributions from some of the world's finest exponents of close-up magic. George B. Anderson's *It Must Be Mindreading!* presents outstanding routines for the performer of mental magic and includes a valuable four-page bibliography. *Handkerchief Magic,* by Jean Hugard, is a reprint of *Silken Sorcery;* the text covers the producing, vanishing, and color changing of silks as well as flourishes and knots. *Newspaper Magic,* by Gene Anderson and Frances Marshall, a reprint of a 1968 monograph, contains an excellent group of effects using that readily available and seemingly innocent prop, the newspaper.

NOTE

1. Nevil Maskelyne and David Devant, *Maskelyne on the Performance of Magic* (New York: Dover, 1976), p. 5.

BIBLIOGRAPHY

BOOKS, ANTHOLOGIES, AND REPRINTS

Adair, Ian H. *Encyclopedia of Dove Magic.* 3 vols. Bideford, England: Supreme, 1968-73.

Allerton, Bert. *The Close-Up Magician.* Chicago: Magic, Inc., 1958.

Anderson, Gene, and Frances Marshall. *Newspaper Magic.* Chicago: Magic, Inc., 1974.

Anderson, George B. *It Must Be Mindreading!* Chicago: Magic, Inc., 1963.

Andrus, Jerry. *Andrus Deals You In.* Portland, Me.: Star Magic, 1957.

Annemann, Theodore. *The Book Without a Name.* New York: Max Holden, 1931.

Bamberg, Theodore, with Robert Parrish. *Okito on Magic.* 2nd ed. Chicago: Magic, Inc., 1968.

Blackstone, Harry. *Blackstone's Secrets of Magic.* New York: Garden City, 1958.

Bobo, J. B. *The New Modern Coin Magic.* 2nd ed. Chicago: Magic, Inc., 1966.

Boles, Don. *Midway Magic.* Atlanta, Ga.: Pinchpenny Press, 1964.

Burlingame, H. J. *Magician's Handbook.* Chicago: Wilcox & Follet, 1942.

Chanin, Jack. *Cigar Magic.* Philadelphia: Author, 1937.

______. *The Encyclopedia of Sleeving.* Philadelphia: Author, 1948.

Chavez, Marian. *The Marian Chavez Encyclopedia of Dove Magic.* New York: Louis Tannen, 1979.

Christopher, Melbourne. *Houdini: The Untold Story.* New York: Cassell, 1969.

______. *The Illustrated History of Magic.* New York: Crowell, 1973.

Claflin, Edward, with Jeff Sheridan. *Street Magic.* New York: Doubleday, 1977.

Clark, Keith. *Encyclopedia of Cigarette Tricks.* 2nd rev. ed. New York: Louis Tannen, 1952.

Clarke, Sidney W. *The Annals of Conjuring from the Earliest Times to the Present.* London: Magic Wand, 1929.

Corinda, Tony. *Thirteen Steps to Mentalism.* New York: Louis Tannen, 1968.

Cramer, Stuart. *Germain, the Wizard and His Legerdemain.* Goleta, Calif.: Buffum, 1966.

______. *Secrets of Karl Germain.* Cleveland Heights, Ohio: Merriweather, 1962.

Devant, David. *My Magic Life.* Bideford, England: Supreme, 1971.

Dexter, Will. *The Riddle of Chung Ling Soo.* Bideford, England: Supreme, 1971.

Doerflinger, William. *The Magic Catalogue.* New York: Dutton, 1977.

Elliott, Bruce. *The Best in Magic.* New York: Harper, 1956.
______. *Classic Secrets of Magic.* New York: Harper, 1952.
______, ed. *Phoenix.* 6 vols. New York: Louis Tannen, 1952-54.
Erdnase, S. W. *The Expert at the Card Table.* Chicago: Charles T. Powner, 1953.
Ernst, Bernard M. L., and Hereward Carrington. *Houdini and Conan Doyle: The Story of a Strange Friendship.* London: Hutchinson, 1933.
Evans, Henry Ridgely. *History of Conjuring and Magic: From the Earliest Times to the End of the Eighteenth Century.* Kenton, Ohio: Durbin, 1930.
______. *Magic and Its Professors.* New York: Routledge, 1902.
Fischer, Ottokar. *J. N. Hofzinser's Card Conjuring.* London: Magic Wand, 1931.
Fitzkee, Dariel. *Magic by Misdirection.* San Francisco: St. Raphael House, 1943.
______. *Showmanship for Magicians.* San Francisco: St. Raphael House, 1943.
______. *The Trick Brain.* San Francisco: St. Raphael House, 1944.
Frost, Thomas. *The Lives of the Conjurors.* London: Chatto and Windus, 1876.
Ganson, Lewis. *Routined Manipulation.* 3 vols. London: Unique, 1950-54.
______, ed. *The Art of Close-Up Magic.* 2 vols. Bideford, England: Supreme, 1966.
______. *Cy Enfield's Entertaining Card Magic.* Bideford, England: Supreme, 1974.
______. *The Dai Vernon Book of Magic.* London: Unique, 1957.
______. *Dai Vernon's Ultimate Card Secrets.* London: Unique, 1967.
______. *The Magic of Slydini.* London: Unique, 1960.
Garcia, Frank. *All in a Nutshell.* New York: Million Dollar Productions, 1974.
______. *Marked Cards and Loaded Dice.* Englewood Cliffs, N.J.: Prentice-Hall, 1962.
Gardner, Martin. *Encyclopedia of Impromptu Magic.* Chicago: Magic, Inc., 1978.
______. *Mathematics, Magic, and Mystery.* New York: Dover, 1956.
Gaultier, Camille. *Magic without Apparatus.* Translated by Jean Hugard. Berkeley Heights, N.J.: Fleming, 1945.
Gibson, Walter Brown. *The Complete Illustrated Book of Card Magic.* New York: Kaye and Ward, 1969.
______. *Professional Magic for Amateurs.* Englewood Cliffs, N.J.: Prentice-Hall, 1947.
______. *What's New in Magic?* New York: Hanover House, 1956.
______, and Morris N. Young. *Houdini on Magic.* New York: Dover, 1953.
Gill, Robert. *Magic as a Performing Art: A Bibliography of Conjuring.* London and New York: Bowker, 1976.
Gravatt, Glenn G., and W. Von Deusen. *Encyclopedia of Self-Working Card Tricks.* Los Angeles: Authors, 1936.
______. *Second Encyclopedia of Self-Working Card Tricks.* Los Angeles: Authors, 1936.
Hall, Trevor H. *A Bibliography of Books on Conjuring in English from 1580 to 1850.* Minneapolis: Carl Waring Jones, 1957.
Hanson, Herman, and John U. Zweers. *The Magic Man.* Cincinnati: Haines House of Cards, 1974.
Hay, Henry. *The Amateur Magician's Handbook.* New York: Cromwell, 1950.
______. *Cyclopedia of Magic.* New York: McKay, 1949.
Heyl, Edgar. *Conjuring Books, 1580 to 1850.* Baltimore: Author, 1963.
Hilliard, John Northern. *Greater Magic.* Minneapolis: Carl Waring Jones, 1938.

Hoffmann, Professor (Angelo John Lewis). *Later Magic.* London: Routledge, 1904.
______. *Modern Magic.* London: Routledge, 1876. Reprint. New York: Dover, 1978.
______. *More Magic.* London: Routledge, 1890.
Houdini, Harry. *Handcuff Secrets.* London: Routledge, 1910.
______. *A Magician Among the Spirits.* New York: Harper & Brothers, 1924. Reprint. New York: Arno Press, 1972.
______. *The Unmasking of Robert-Houdin.* London: Routledge, 1909.
Hugard, Jean. *Card Manipulation.* New York: Dover, 1973.
______. *Encyclopedia of Card Tricks.* New York: Dover, 1961.
______. *Handkerchief Magic.* New York: Dover, 1975.
______. *Hugard's Magic Monthly.* 9 vols. New York: Fleming, 1945-53.
______. *More Card Manipulations.* New York: Dover, 1974.
______, and Frederick Braue. *Expert Card Technique.* Brooklyn, N.Y.: Authors, 1944.
______. *The Royal Road to Card Magic.* New York: Faber, 1949.
Hull, Burling. *The Encyclopedic Dictionary of Mentalism.* 3rd rev. ed. Calgary, Canada: Hades, 1973.
James, Stewart, ed. *Abbott's Encyclopedia of Rope Tricks.* 2 vols. Colon, Mich.: Abbott's Magic, 1941-62.
Jonson, Wilfred. *Magic Tricks and Card Tricks.* New York: Dover, 1974.
Leech, Al. *Super Card Man Stuff.* Chicago: Magic, Inc., 1965.
LePaul, Paul. *The Card Magic of LePaul.* New York: Louis Tannen, 1959.
Lorayne, Harry. *Reputation Makers.* New York: Author, 1971.
McGuire, Eddie. *The Phantom of the Card Table: The Real Secrets of Walter Scott.* Reno, Nev.: Gamblers Book Club, 1959.
Marlo, Edward. *The Cardician.* Chicago: Magic, Inc., 1953.
Marshall, Frances Ireland. *Kid Stuff.* 6 vols. Chicago: Magic, Inc.,1954-74.
Maskelyne, Jasper. *White Magic: The Story of the Maskelynes.* London: Stanley Paul, 1936.
Maskelyne, Nevil, and David Devant. *Maskelyne on the Performance of Magic.* New York: Dover, 1976. Reprint of Part 1 of *Our Magic.*
______. *Our Magic.* London: Routledge, 1911.
Maurice, Edward. *Showmanship and Presentation.* London: Goodlife, 1946.
Mentzer, Jerry. *Card Cavalcade.* Parma, Ohio: Author, 1972.
Miller, Gordon, ed. *Abbott's Anthology of Card Magic.* 3 vols. Colon, Mich.: Abbott's Magic, 1968.
Miller, Leonard. *Thrilling Magic.* Colon, Mich.: Abbott's Magic, 1946.
Mulholland, John. *John Mulholland's Book of Magic.* New York: Scribner's, 1963.
______. *John Mulholland's Story of Magic.* New York: Loring and Mussey, 1935.
Nathanson, Leon. *Slydini Encores.* New York: Slydini Studio, 1966.
Nelms, Henning. *Magic and Showmanship: A Handbook for Conjurors.* New York: Dover, 1969.
Nelson, Robert Alan. *The Encyclopedia of Mentalism and Allied Arts.* Calgary, Canada: Hades, 1971.
Olson, Robert E., and Edward Dart. *Carl Rosini—His Life and His Magic.* Chicago: Magic, Inc., 1966.
Osborne, Tom. *Cups and Balls Magic.* Philadelphia: Lee Gray, 1973.

Parrish, Robert. *An Evening with Charlie Miller.* Chicago: Magic, 1961.
Potter, Jack. *The Master Index to Magic in Print.* 14 vols. Calgary, Canada: Hades, 1967-75.
Rapp, Augustus. *The Life and Times of Augustus Rapp.* Chicago: Magic, Inc., 1959.
Rice, Harold R. *The Encyclopedia of Silk Magic.* 3 vols. Cincinnati: Silk King Studios, 1948-62.
Robert-Houdin, Jean Eugene. *King of Conjurors: Memoirs of Robert-Houdin.* New York: Dover, 1973.
Rydell, Wendy, with George Gilbert. *The Great Book of Magic.* New York: Abrams, 1976.
Sardina, Maurice. *Where Houdini Was Wrong.* London: Magic Wand, 1950.
Scarne, John. *The Amazing World of John Scarne: A Personal History.* New York: Crown, 1956.
______. *Scarne's Magic Tricks.* New York: Crown, 1951.
______. *Scarne on Cards.* New York: Crown, 1956.
______. *Scarne on Card Tricks.* New York: Crown, 1950.
______. *Scarne on Dice.* Harrisburg, Pa.: Military Service, 1945.
Scot, Reginald. *The Discovery of Witchcraft.* London: N.p., 1584. Reprint ed. Dover: New York, 1972.
Sharpe, S. H. *Neo Magic: The Art of the Conjuror.* London: Magic Wand, 1932.
Slydini, Tony. *The Magical World of Slydini.* New York: Louis Tannen, 1979.
Starke, George, ed. *Stars of Magic.* New York: Louis Tannen, 1961.
Steele, W. F. Rufus. *Paul Rosini's Magical Gems: A Memorial.* Chicago: Author, 1950.
Steranko, James. *Steranko on Cards.* Chicago: Magic, Inc., 1960.
Tarbell, Harlan. *The Tarbell Course in Magic.* 7 vols. New York: Louis Tannen, 1941-72.
Thompson, James G., ed. *My Best: A Collection of the Best Originations Conceived by Eminent Creators.* Philadelphia: C. H. Hopkins, 1945.
______. *Top Secrets of Magic.* 3 vols. New York: James G. Thompson, n.d.; Reprint. New York: Louis Tannen, Inc., n.d.
Vernon, Dai. *Early Vernon: The Magic of Vernon in 1932.* Chicago: Magic, Inc., 1962.
______. *Select Secrets.* New York: Max Holden, 1941.

PERIODICALS

Genii. Los Angeles, 1937-.
The Journal of Magic History. Toledo, Ohio, 1979-.
The Linking Ring. Kenton, Ohio, 1926-.
M.U.M. Monthly. Lynn, Mass., 1910-.
The New Tops. Colon, Mich., 1936-.

CHAPTER 8 Medicine and the Physician in Popular Culture

Anne Hudson Jones

The aura of power surrounding medicine and its practitioners has made healers and physicians favorite subjects of dramatists, satirists, novelists, and other artists from ancient times to the present. Traditionally physicians have been portrayed as quacks or demigods, reflecting society's ambivalent attitude toward their special status. Although the presentation of medicine and the physician in American popular culture has a rich European heritage, artists have modified and added to that heritage in response both to medicine's extraordinary development in the past century and to America's own changing social concerns.

That popular images of physicians have importance in the real world can be demonstrated by reactions to the "Marcus Welby, M.D." television show. At the height of its popularity, the show elicited approximately five thousand letters a week from people who wrote Welby to ask for his help in dealing with their ills.[1] And not only the lay public responded to the show. Robert Young was invited to address many medical groups, among them the American Academy of Family Physicians and the graduating class of the University of Michigan Medical School. The show received more than thirty awards from medical groups, including one from the American Medical Association (AMA) for special achievement.[2] Such interest by physicians in their public image predates the Welby show, however. In 1955, the AMA set up the Physicians Advisory Committee on Television, Radio and Motion Pictures (PAC) to help maintain medical accuracy in public programming and to protect the image of the practicing physician.[3] In the early 1960s the Joint Committee on Mental Illness and Health recommended that American psychiatrists carefully consider their public image. One result of that recommendation was an article analyzing depictions of psychiatrists in popular fiction and concluding that psychiatrists should indeed be concerned about their unfavorable portrayals.[4]

Despite the acknowledged importance popular beliefs about medicine and popular images of physicians have for both patients and practitioners, there has as yet been little systematic study of medicine and the physician in American popular culture. Few book-length studies exist, but there are several articles in widely scattered journals about one aspect or another of the presentation of medicine and the physician in American literature, cartoons, medicine shows, film, and television. This essay will provide a brief historic summary of those presentations and will survey the scholarly work done to date.

HISTORIC OUTLINE

In Western culture, medicine and the physician have been subjects of literature since ancient times. Early Greek and Roman dramatists, epigrammatists, and satirists frequently aimed barbs at physicians. The first works of prose fiction were popular romances and Milesian tales, which included physicians as minor characters.[5] In later European literature the physician became a stock character, ridiculed or portrayed as a quack. Chaucer's *Canterbury Tales,* Boccaccio's *Decameron,* and the *commedia dell'arte* provide early examples; the famous physicians in Molière's plays follow.[6] The physician as a character taken seriously and portrayed sympathetically, however, did not begin to emerge until the nineteenth century, in the novels of Balzac's *Human Comedy*[7] and in Zola's *Doctor Pascal.* This changed presentation of physicians in fiction seems to have resulted from the advances in scientific knowledge, which gave physicians greater professional stature. European literature is rich in its use of the physician and medical themes and has supplied the material for several book-length studies.[8]

It is easier to trace the history of presentations of medicine and the physician in American literature than it is to decide which of those presentations constitute popular rather than high culture. In nineteenth-century American literature, for example, Nathaniel Hawthorne presents physician-scientists in many of his stories and novels, and Herman Melville satirizes surgeons in several of his works. Later in the century, the physician was portrayed sympathetically in novels of two physician-writers, Oliver Wendell Holmes and S. Weir Mitchell. Fictional women physicians appeared as major characters for the first time in the 1880s, in novels by William Dean Howells, Sarah Orne Jewett, and Elizabeth Stuart Phelps Ward. Certainly the best-known physician-scientist of American literature is Sinclair Lewis's Martin Arrowsmith, who appeared in *Arrowsmith* in 1925. Throughout American literature, physician characters appear frequently and in works of such varied writers as Henry James, Ellen Glasgow, James Gould Cozzens, Robert Penn Warren, John Steinbeck, Katherine Anne Porter, Carson McCullers, William Carlos Williams, and William Faulkner.

Among works of American popular literature dealing with medicine and the physician, none has had more long lasting effects than the Dr. Kildare novels, written between 1940 and 1943 by Frederick Faust, under the pseudonym Max Brand. Several movies, a weekly radio program, and two television series have been based on these books. Frank Slaughter's series of novels, many about physicians and medicine, now number more than fifty and have sold more than fifty million copies worldwide. His *Women in White* was the basis for a four-part television drama in 1979. Richard Hooker's *M*A*S*H* novels came out in the 1960s, and Robin Cook's *The Year of the Intern* and *Coma* were published in the 1970s. A recent smash hit, billed as a medical *Catch-22,* is Samuel Shem's *The House of God,* published in 1978. Two popular genres, detective fiction and science fiction, use physicians in fairly predictable ways. Physicians' training in observation and diagnosis makes them naturals for detective work. Television's "Quincy" is just the latest version of the physician-detective whose line began with Sir Arthur Conan Doyle's Sherlock Holmes, modeled on the surgeon Dr. Joseph Bell, and Dr. Watson. In science fiction, the role of the physician has usually been combined with that of the research scientist, producing almost a stock character, familiar from the time of Mary Shelley's *Frankenstein* in 1816.

With the development of psychiatry and the spread of its influence in American culture, the psychiatrist has become a favorite character in literature and appears with increasing frequency beginning in the 1930s, in works by "standard" authors such as F. Scott Fitzgerald, Eugene O'Neill, Tennessee Williams, and Arthur Miller as well as works by "popular" authors such as Mary Jane Ward, Theodore Isaac Rubin, and Elliott Baker. At least one recognizable subgenre of popular fiction has resulted, derived from a combination of the novel, autobiography, and psychological case history. The outstanding example of this subgenre is Joanne Greenberg's *I Never Promised You a Rose Garden,* published under the pseudonym Hannah Green in 1964. Metaphors of madness and hospital settings, especially mental asylums, abound in modern popular literature. The institutional environment serves as a microcosm of society as a whole, and the insane are often depicted as being more sane than their medical keepers. Ken Kesey's *One Flew Over the Cuckoo's Nest,* published in 1962, is one of the best-known examples.

Recent plays on Broadway reflect a new popular concern with prolonged illness and death and dying. In one year, 1979, Brian Clark's *Whose Life Is It Anyway?,* Bernard Pomerance's *The Elephant Man,* Arthur Kopit's *Wings,* and Steve Carter's *Nevis Mountain Dew* were all playing on Broadway, and Michael Cristofer's *The Shadow Box* was touring the country. Like Sam Shepard's *Inacoma,* based on the Karen Quinlan case, all these plays are responses to possibilities created by sophisticated medical technology.

European medical caricature dates back to the Renaissance, but medical caricature did not develop in the United States until the Civil War period. The first medical cartoon published in this country has been identified as "The Quarantine Question," which appeared in *Harper's Weekly* in 1858. Medical cartoons were published in the 1880s in early American magazines such as *Puck* and *Life,* and gradually they began to appear routinely in most major American newspapers and magazines. The best-known newspaper comic strip featuring a physician as its main character is *Rex Morgan, M.D.* Written by a psychiatrist, Dr. Nicholas Dallis, under the pseudonym Dal Curtis, and drawn by Marvin Bradley and Frank Edgington, *Rex Morgan, M.D.* has run continuously since its first appearance, on May 2, 1948, until the present. Comic books have featured few practicing physicians as heroes, although some use scientist-physicians, such as Dr. Andrew Bryant, Dr. Hugo Strange, and Dr. X.

Medicine shows, which originated as a form of entertainment designed to help quacks and streethawkers sell their patent medicine wares, also have a long European heritage, dating back to medieval times. They flourished in this country from the eighteenth century until they were virtually closed down by legislation in the twentieth century. The real heyday of medical show impresarios such as William Avery Rockefeller, "Nevada Ned" Oliver, John E. Healy, "Texas Charley" Bigelow, and John Austen Hamlin was the nineteenth century, but some, such as Dudley J. LeBlanc, the promoter of Hadacol and the Hadacol Caravans, were well known even as late as the 1950s.

Literally hundreds of physician characters have appeared in American films during this century, but with the exception of the psychiatrists among them they have been little studied. Of major importance is the series of nine Dr. Kildare films, which appeared in the 1930s and 1940s. The first was *Internes Can't Take Money* in 1937, followed in 1938 by *Young Dr. Kildare,* which introduced the famous Lew Ayres (Dr. Kildare) and Lionel Barrymore (Dr. Gillespie) team. In the 1950s a radio show was based on the films, and a television series followed in the 1960s. The movie *M*A*S*H* had equally great success in 1970, inspiring a television series that has lasted longer than any other medical series in the history of television. But by far the most important physician characters in American films are the psychiatrists, who began appearing in minor roles as early as 1906 in the comedy *Dr. Dippy's Sanitarium.* However, only a few films from the early decades of this century depict psychiatric treatment seriously; they include D. W. Griffith's *The Restoration* in 1909; *The Cabinet of Dr. Caligari,* made in Germany in 1919 and distributed in the United States in 1921; and *Private Worlds* in 1935.

By the 1940s, there was a boom in psychological films. *Spellbound* appeared in 1945, *The Dark Mirror* in 1946, *Nightmare Alley* in 1947, and *The Snake Pit* in 1948. Notable psychological films of the 1950s and

1960s include *Harvey* in 1950, *The Cobweb* in 1955, *The Three Faces of Eve* in 1957, both *David and Lisa* and *Freud* in 1962, and *A Fine Madness* in 1966. The indisputable hit of the 1970s crop of psychological films was *One Flew Over the Cuckoo's Nest,* whose anti-psychiatric story found a most receptive audience in 1975.

Radio serials began in the 1920s. Many used physicians as characters, and by the 1930s several were featuring physicians as the main characters of their own series. One of the earliest daytime network serials to do so was "Peggy's Doctor," which began in 1934 and was discontinued in 1935. "Dr. Christian" ran from 1937 until 1953; "Doc Barclay's Daughters" from 1939 to 1940; "The Doctor's Wife" from 1952 through 1956; and "The Affairs of Dr. Gentry" from 1957 through 1959. The longest running was "Young Dr. Malone," which began in 1939 and continued through 1960. At least two of radio's daytime network serials featured women physicians: "Joyce Jordan, Girl Interne" (later "Joyce Jordan, M.D."), which ran from 1938 through 1948 on CBS and was then revived by ABC for the 1951-52 season; and "The Life and Loves of Dr. Susan," which ran only one year, 1939. Others featured nurses: "Woman in White," from 1938 through 1940; "Kate Hopkins, Angel of Mercy," from 1940 through 1942; and "Junior Nurse Corps," about Clara Barton. A spin-off from the earlier Dr. Kildare films was a weekly radio program in the 1950s, "Young Dr. Kildare." As intriguing as these radio programs sound to students of popular culture, very few of them have been preserved in either tape or script form.

The most important medium in American popular culture for the presentation of physicians and medical themes is television. Beginning in the early 1960s, television's daytime network serials picked up where radio left off. Both "General Hospital" and "The Doctors" began in 1963, and "Days of Our Lives" began in 1965. Other 1960s daytime television serials—but not network serials—presenting physicians and medical themes were "Young Dr. Malone," "Dr. Hudson's Secret Journal," and "The Nurses."

Far more impressive than the daytime medical serials have been the prime-time medical shows. From 1952 through 1980 there have been well over thirty of these using physicians as main characters and medical themes as the main subject material. Among the first were "City Hospital" from 1952 to 1953; "Doc Corkle" in 1952; "The Doctor" from 1952 to 1953; and "Medic" from 1954 to 1956. The most successful of the early shows were "Ben Casey" and "Dr. Kildare," both beginning in 1961 and running through 1966. They are the classics of the first-generation doctor shows, and their successful format, an old mentor and a young man, was imitated by many other shows attempting to cash in on their success.

Unlike the movies, which have featured so many psychiatrists, television has favored physicians who are general practitioners or surgeons. But in the early 1960s, there were two television series about psychiatrists: "Breaking

Point," in the 1963-64 season, and "The Eleventh Hour," which lasted two seasons, from 1962 to 1964. By far the most successful of the second-generation medical series, however, was "Marcus Welby, M.D.," which ran from 1969 through 1976 and ranked among the top ten shows in the Nielsen ratings for the first three of those seasons. "Medical Center," which also began in 1969 and ended in 1976, was not far behind "Welby" in the Nielsen ratings for three of its first four seasons. Another successful medical series that began in 1969 was "The New Doctors," one of three segments making up the dramatic series "The Bold Ones."

Ushering in the third generation of doctor shows was the still continuing hit, "M*A*S*H," which premiered in 1972. In its first five seasons, 1973 through 1978, "M*A*S*H" was in the top twenty-five shows on the Nielsen ratings. By now, it is the longest-lived of any prime-time medical series to date. "Emergency!" began the same year as "M*A*S*H" and lasted for six seasons. Of interest because it featured a woman physician, Julie Farr, was "Having Babies," which lasted only five weeks in 1978. Medical series of the 1980s include—along with "M*A*S*H"—"Quincy," "Trapper John, M.D.," and "House Calls."

Factual medical shows providing information about medicine to the general public have not met with much success. Among the best of the attempts have been "Medix," "Today's Health," and "Feeling Good." Another kind of show, factual but with dramatic intent, was "Lifeline," based on activities of real-life physicians involved in life-and-death situations. It premiered in 1978 but did not last a complete season despite the astronomical sums spent filming each episode.

REFERENCE WORKS

There are no reference works or bibliographies specifically designed to bring together information about medicine and the physician in American popular culture. For literature, three bibliographies offer some guidance, although two of them list primary works, not secondary studies. The earliest of these is an article by Evelyn Rivers Wilbanks, "The Physician in the American Novel, 1870-1955," which lists more than four hundred novels with physicians as the main character. The usefulness of the bibliography is limited by Wilbanks's arbitrary, albeit necessary, decision to use only the form and not the quality of the works for her selection. She admits that she has not read all of the books on her list, and she attempts no classification of them as standard literature, popular culture, or trash. Despite its deficiencies, the list is useful simply because it is the only one there is. The other primary bibliography is *Literature and Medicine: Topics, Titles & Notes* by Joanne Trautmann and Carol Pollard. Trautmann's and Pollard's aim was to provide an annotated listing of literary works that could be used by people teaching humanities in a medical school. They use two organizational schemas: a chronological listing, with each entry accompanied by a short plot summary; and a topic list, organizing works under such categories as abortion, alcoholism, doctors, medical ethics, plague, science fiction, surgery, and women as healers and patients. Trautmann and Pollard insist they included only "first-rate" literary works or works of special interest because of their medical topics or themes.

The third bibliography for literature and medicine is a secondary bibliography limited to only one area of medicine: Norman Kiell's *Psychoanalysis, Psychology and Literature: A Bibliography.* Kiell makes no claim to exhaustiveness but has followed a principle of selection that "includes articles, monographs, or books which deal with literary writing from a psychological point of view." Kiell has also edited the only reference work for medical caricatures and cartoons: *Psychiatry and Psychology in the Visual Arts and Aesthetics: A Bibliography,* divided into twenty-one subject categories, of which caricatures and cartoons is one.

There is no reference work for medicine shows or for medicine and the physician in films, radio, or television. However, for films two general reference guides are helpful: *The American Film Institute Catalog of Motion Pictures Produced In The United States: Feature Films 1921-1930,* edited by Kenneth W. Munden, and *The American Film Institute Catalog of Motion Pictures: Feature Films 1961-1970,* edited by Richard P. Krafsur. These two volumes are the first products of the American Film Institute's continuing project to catalog all films produced since the beginning of the motion picture industry. The 1920s and the 1960s catalogs include a volume of entries summarizing each film as well as subject and credit indexes. Because the subject index includes such categories as medicine men, nurses, physicians, psychiatrists, quacks, and surgeons, the catalogs are valuable resources for research on medicine and the physician in American films. For radio, two general guides are of some help: Frank Buxton's and Bill Owen's *The Big Broadcast 1920-1950* (a new edition of their older work, *Radio's Golden Age*) and John Dunning's *Tune In Yesterday: The Ultimate Encyclopedia of Old-Time Radio 1925-1976.* For television, a useful general reference work is Tim Brooks's and Earle Marsh's *The Complete Directory to Prime Time Network TV Shows 1946-present.* This work's limitation is indicated by its title: it covers only prime-time shows. As supplements to it, Vincent Terrace's *The Complete Encyclopedia of Television Programs 1947-1976,* in two volumes, and Les Brown's *The New York Times Encyclopedia of Television* are useful because they give information about daytime programs.

The increased interest in medicine and the physician in popular culture in the past few years may mean that there will eventually be reference tools available, but now it is much easier to point to what is lacking than to what exists.

RESEARCH COLLECTIONS

There are no research collections designed to support scholarly inquiry into medicine and the physician in American popular culture. Although many medical school libraries have collections of prints and caricatures, they include international as well as American items, and few collections are fully cataloged. Even the National Library of Medicine cannot say for certain what percentage of its prints and caricatures is American rather than international. At least four medical school libraries have or had a Weinstein Collection of fiction by and about physicians. These collections have been established by donations from B. Bernard or Eva Evelyn Weinstein. The University of Miami's Weinstein Collection includes approximately six hundred books, but there is no published list of the titles; the University of Mississippi Medical Center's Rowland Medical Library has three hundred titles in its Weinstein Collection, as does the Tulane University Medical Library; the University of North Carolina's Health Affairs Library has dispersed its Weinstein Collection because of space shortage. In addition to the three remaining Weinstein Collections, there are two other small collections of some interest. The first is at the University of Cincinnati where the Health Sciences Library has begun a collection of literary works by or about physicians. The second is at the Medical College of Pennsylvania, where the Archives and Special Collections on Women in Medicine has over five hundred books on women in medicine, including some fiction with women physicians as characters; however, there is no separate listing of the fictional works.

Until there is a cohesive collection of materials on medicine and the physician in popular culture, scholars working in this field will have to use more general research collections, film archives, and popular culture collections.

HISTORY AND CRITICISM

The only book-length studies of images of general physicians in American literature are four unpublished dissertations completed between 1963 and 1976. Of these, the two earlier ones are more interesting. In the first, "The Physician-Scientist as Character in Nineteenth-Century American Literature," Lois Elizabeth DeBakey examines the scientific milieu of the nineteenth century and novels by Nathaniel Hawthorne, Herman Melville, Oliver Wendell Holmes, S. Weir Mitchell, and William Dean Howells and

Sarah Orne Jewett to determine how closely literary depictions of the physician-scientist accord with the historical reality of the medical profession. Her work provides a good, solid introduction to the relationship between literature and medicine in the nineteenth-century United States. The second, Carolyn Brimley Norris's "The Image of the Physician in Modern American Literature," is longer and more complex than DeBakey's. Norris establishes two major categories of physicians—the priest and the Pan—and organizes the works she examines accordingly. Her priest-doctors include characters from F. Scott Fitzgerald, Robert Penn Warren, John Steinbeck, Katherine Anne Porter, Henry James, William Faulkner, and Lloyd C. Douglas. Her Pan-doctors are from Ellen Glasgow and James Gould Cozzens. In addition, Norris devotes one chapter to the black American doctor, one to Sinclair Lewis, and one to the economic doctor; one of her three appendixes is a discussion of priest and Pan physicians on television, Drs. Kildare and Ben Casey, respectively. Norris's categories and discussions are intriguing, and chronologically her study starts where DeBakey's stops. The two later dissertations, Alex John Cameron's "The Image of the Physician in the American Novel 1859 to 1925" and David Edward Stooke's "The Portrait of the Physician in Selected Prose Fiction of Nineteenth-Century American Authors," cover basically the same literature DeBakey does but are shorter and less sophisticated than DeBakey's or Norris's studies.

In addition to the unpublished dissertations, there are several published articles about physicians in American literature. In one entitled "Images of Women Doctors in Popular Fiction: Comparison of the 19th and 20th Centuries," Mary Roth Walsh discusses the three nineteenth-century novels by William Dean Howells, Sarah Orne Jewett, and Elizabeth Stuart Phelps Ward that use women physicians as main characters and compares those early presentations of women physicians with the few that exist in popular twentieth-century fiction. She does not attempt any real literary analysis of the works, however. In "The Doctor as Scapegoat: A Study in Ambivalence," Nancy Y. Hoffman analyzes physician characters of Sherwood Anderson, Sinclair Lewis, John Steinbeck, F. Scott Fitzgerald, Carson McCullers, and Joseph Heller to show how society makes scapegoats of them. "Literature and Medicine," a cover article in *MD Medical Newsmagazine*, offers a brief historical survey of the relationship between the two disciplines from Homer to Gerald Green.

The categories of scientist and physician overlap, and articles about scientists in fiction sometimes include discussion of works whose main character is a physician-scientist. Thomas D. Clareson's "The Scientist as Hero in American Science-Fiction 1880-1920" offers a short discussion of Edward Bellamy's *Dr. Heidenhoff's Process.* In "The Scientist in Contemporary Fiction," Bentley Glass includes discussion of Sinclair Lewis's *Arrowsmith,* as does Jay Tepperman in his article "The Research Scientist in Modern Fiction."

Charles E. Rosenberg's "Martin Arrowsmith: The Scientist as Hero" provides valuable background information about the people and events that influenced Lewis in his creation of the novel.

The psychiatrist in American literature has evoked almost as much critical response as have all the other kinds of physicians combined—and this despite the fact that psychiatry did not emerge as a separate medical specialty until this century. Three unpublished dissertations focus on the psychiatrist in American fiction. The first, Herbert Jordan Guthmann's "The Characterization of the Psychiatrist in American Fiction, 1859-1965," surveys literary depictions of mental healers and psychiatrists from the novels of Oliver Wendell Holmes and S. Weir Mitchell through those of Joseph Heller and Thomas Pynchon. Not surprisingly, Guthmann concludes that in more recent fiction psychiatrists are portrayed far less favorably than they were in earlier works. The second, Philip Henry Bufithis's "The Artist's Fight for Art: The Psychiatrist Figure in the Fiction of Major Contemporary American Novelists," examines the conflict between the psychiatrist and artist figures in works of eight novelists: Vladimir Nabokov, William S. Burroughs, Saul Bellow, J. D. Salinger, Norman Mailer, John Barth, James Purdy, and Ken Kesey. The third, Carol Krusen Scholz's "They Share the Suffering: The Psychoanalyst in American Fiction Between 1920 and 1940," offers biographical criticism of five writers—Ludwig Lewisohn, Conrad Aiken, F. Scott Fitzgerald, Waldo Frank, and Vardis Fisher—who use psychoanalysts as characters in their novels.

Several psychiatrists have themselves published analyses of popular presentations of psychiatrists. In "Saturday's Psychiatrist," Harry A. Wilmer reports on his informal survey of all seventy-plus references made to psychiatry by book and play reviewers in 1953 issues of *Saturday Review.* Another psychiatrist, Robert Plank, published a brief and disappointing article called "Portraits of Fictitious Psychiatrists," in which he discusses psychiatrist characters in several obscure works of science fiction. In contrast, Charles Winick's article, "The Psychiatrist in Fiction," is one of the best available. It is of special interest because it was written as a result of the Joint Committee on Mental Illness and Health's recommendation that American psychiatrists "do something about the public 'image' of the psychiatrist." Winick's concern is not with the literary quality or merit of works but with their popularity, as judged by their sales and their ripple effects in movie, play, and television adaptations. This makes the article an especially important resource for students of popular culture. In a much shorter article, "Psychiatrists Portrayed in Fiction," published just a year after Winick's, another psychiatrist, Marjorie C. Meehan, offers her analyses of fictional psychiatrists as villains, noble characters, magicians, spiritual guides, unfeeling scientists, useless nonentities, and complex individuals. Winick's and Meehan's articles make an interesting pair because in her discussion Meehan disagrees with several of Winick's conclusions.

Three critics argue that the popularity of psychiatric themes in fiction has resulted in new subgenres or formulas for the modern novel. Anthony Hopkins, in his article "Physical Models and Spiritual States: Institutional Environments In Modern Fiction," argues that a sizable group of fictional works has the same pattern, based on use of a limited environment, often a hospital or mental institution, as a sustained symbol for society as a whole. Examples of such fiction are Elliott Baker's *A Fine Madness* and Ken Kesey's *One Flew Over the Cuckoo's Nest,* both published in the early 1960s. More convincing is a fine article by Kary K. and Gary K. Wolfe, "Metaphors of Madness: Popular Psychological Narratives," which traces the development of a new subgenre based on a combination of the novel, memoirs, autobiography, and the psychological case history. The outstanding work of this subgenre is Joanne Greenberg's *I Never Promised You a Rose Garden,* published in 1964 under the pseudonym of Hannah Green. The Wolfes discuss representative movies and television shows as well as fiction.

Images of physicians in American drama have also been studied. Two works, both published in 1955, focus specifically on the image of the psychiatrist. One is W. David Sievers's book, *Freud on Broadway: A History of Psychoanalysis and the American Drama,* which is useful, but limited and by now dated. Sievers explores the backgrounds of psychological drama, discusses the first Freudian plays, and then alternates between chapters dealing with specific decades and chapters dealing with specific playwrights. Eugene O'Neill, Philip Barry, Tennessee Williams, and Arthur Miller get special attention; the chronological coverage ends with "War and Post-War Neurosis." The other 1955 study of images of psychiatrists in drama, Harry A. Wilmer's "Psychiatrist on Broadway," is actually more central for the study of popular culture. Wilmer examines the psychiatrist figures in eighteen dramas that played on Broadway between the 1930s and 1955. All eighteen were popular hits; several won the Pulitzer Prize; several won the New York Drama Critics Circle Award; and three had more than eight hundred performances each. They include, for example, George Axelrod's *The Seven Year Itch* and Tennessee Williams's *A Streetcar Named Desire.*

An older and less ambitious study of the relationship between drama and medicine in general is George W. Corner's "Medicine in the Modern Drama." Many of the plays Corner discusses are British or Scottish, but they became part of American popular culture when they played on the New York stage. And Corner discusses specifically two American plays, Sidney Howard's *Yellow Jack,* about Walter Reed's work against yellow fever, and Sydney Kingsley's *Men in White,* a study of the hospital doctor. A recent article by Mel Gussow, "The Time of the Wounded Hero," provides an interesting historical contrast to Corner's article. Gussow discusses the past season's several successful plays dealing with deformity, disability, serious illness, and prolonged dying. Ironically, the technological progress of medicine has shifted the dramatic focus from the doctor to the patient, who is the new hero.

The best article on the history of American medical caricature is Chauncey D. Leake's "Medical Caricature in the United States." Leake traces the development of medical caricature in this country and speculates about why it was so slow. The article includes reproductions of the first American cartoons about physicians, taken from both private collectors and public sources. A second article, Wolfgang Born's "The Nature and History of Medical Caricature," is of some interest for its discussion of European caricature, but its history of American caricature is largely derivative of Leake's. The most interesting article about medical caricatures is "The Psychiatrist in Caricature: An Analysis of Unconscious Attitudes Toward Psychiatry," by Frederick C. Redlich, himself a psychiatrist. Redlich examined thirty cartoons, representing the work of twenty artists, which were originally published in magazines such as the *New Yorker,* the *Saturday Evening Post,* and *Collier's.* Redlich's analysis is fascinating, and his article has become a classic. The best-known newspaper comic strip featuring a physician, *Rex Morgan, M.D.,* has failed to capture the imagination of critics and commentators the way so many other strips have; there are virtually no critical studies or commentaries about it. One article of historical interest is Melinda Wagner's "Psychiatrist at the Drawing Board." Wagner discusses the origin of the strip, written by Dr. Nicholas Dallis, a psychiatrist, and drawn by Marvin Bradley and Frank Edgington. There is some mention of the kinds of episodes chosen for the strip and of the strip's readership.

The best histories of the patent medicine industry in this country are two books by James Harvey Young, *The Toadstool Millionaires: A Social History of Patent Medicines in America before Federal Regulation* and *The Medical Messiahs: A Social History of Health Quackery in Twentieth-Century America.* The former includes a chapter on the "Medicine Show"; the latter, a chapter called "Medicine Show Impresario," which is about Dudley LeBlanc and the Hadacol craze. In addition, Young has published several other articles about patent medicine and popular culture. One is "The Patent Medicine Boom" in *The History of Popular Culture*, edited by Norman F. Cantor and Michael S. Werthman. There Young correlates the increase in Americans' taste for "bitters" during the second half of the nineteenth century with the rise of the temperance movement. In "From Hooper to Hohensee: Some Highlights of American Patent Medicine Promotion," Young traces the history of patent medicine advertising and reproduces some of the early advertisements. Two articles from the *Journal of Popular Culture* are related to this aspect of medicine and popular culture. One is Jerry C. Brigham's and Karlie K. Kenyon's "HADACOL: The Last Great Medicine Show"; the other is Russell W. Gibbons's "Chiropractic in America: The Historical Conflicts of Cultism and Science." But the outstanding history of medicine shows remains Brooks McNamara's *Step Right Up,* which is discussed in Don B. Wilmeth's section on dime museums and medicine shows in his chapter on "Stage Entertainment," which appeared in the first volume of the *Handbook of American Popular Culture*.

The only work dealing with images of general physicians in American film is Jack Spears's invaluable article, "The Doctor on the Screen," which is included in his 1971 anthology of essays entitled *Hollywood: The Golden Era*. In the article, Spears surveys screen presentations of doctors, nurses, and hospitals, from the peep shows at the turn of the century, such as *The Doctor's Favorite Patient* and *The Downward Path*, to the 1969-70 television series, "Marcus Welby, M.D.," "The Bold Ones," and "Medical Center." Spears does more cataloging than critical reviewing, but the comments he does make are helpful. He organizes his article chronologically by subcategories, such as the country doctor; the comic doctor; the western doctor; the military doctor; the woman doctor; medical students, interns, and residents; medical history; and medical ethics.

All the remaining scholarship has been done on psychiatrists and film. Most articles strike a common theme: Hollywood's disappointing oversimplification and sensationalism of psychiatry. One of the earliest, Franklin Fearing's 1946 article "The Screen Discovers Psychiatry," is a good example. Fearing discusses how and why psychiatry should be used in films and then points out how *Spellbound* and *Love Letters* fall short. The next year another article by Fearing, "Psychology and the Films," was accompanied by Lawrence S. Kubie's "Psychiatry and the Films." A psychiatrist himself, Kubie deplores the infantile level Hollywood has maintained in its depiction of psychiatry in films. He uses *Harvey, Shock, Spellbound*, and *The Seventh Veil* to demonstrate his points, and he concludes with suggestions about ways Hollywood could portray psychiatry responsibly in its films. In the companion article, Fearing begins by surveying the stereotyped psychiatrists of the movies: the all-wise father psychiatrist; the insane psychiatrist; the criminal psychiatrist; the seductive female psychiatrist; and the philsophical-whimsical psychiatrist. Then he comments on Kubie's article and calls for research on the effects of films on their audiences. These three articles give a good sense of how psychiatry and psychology were being used in films of the 1940s and of how such films were popularly received.

Two articles from the 1950s indicate that Fearing's and Kubie's criticisms were little heeded in Hollywood. In "Movie Psychiatrics," Martin S. Dworkin contrasts the use of psychiatry in Hollywood films like *Crossfire* and *Blind Alley* with its use in the documentary film *The Lonely Night*, made by Irving Jacoby of Affiliated Films for the Mental Health Film Board. Dworkin's discussion is instructive. The second article from the 1950s is Norman N. Holland's "Psychiatry in Pselluloid." Humorous in intent, the article nevertheless makes good points about Hollywood's failings with psychiatrists in film.

Leslie Y. Rabkin, a clinical psychologist, has added two very helpful articles to the literature about psychiatrists in film. The first, "The Movies' First

Psychiatrist," is about D. W. Griffith's 1909 film, *The Restoration*, which Rabkin considers the first cinematic presentation of psychiatric treatment. The second, "The Celluloid Couch: Psychiatrists in American Films," is organized chronologically and discusses the changes in film presentations of psychiatrists from decade to decade throughout this century. Rabkin's concluding classification of movie psychiatrists seems oversimplistic—too neatly Freudian—but Rabkin's report of his historical research provides a good basis for further studies. Another interesting article is Irving Schneider's "Images of the Mind: Psychiatry in the Commercial Film." Schneider, a psychiatrist, asserts that the history of film and the history of psychiatry have many parallels, thus producing an almost natural interest of the one field in the other. He then surveys presentations of psychiatry and psychiatrists in American film throughout this century and finally concludes that psychiatry, films, and consumers have grown up together.

Comic relief is provided by Lester S. King's short 1972 article, "New Movie Monsters from the Medical World." King reproduces posters from *MAD*'s investigation of a new supply of horror movies with titles like "The Horrors of the Hospital Diet" and "The Ordeal of the Check-Up."

Little has been written about radio or television medical serials outside the context of more general histories of the serials. Two books, Raymond William Stedman's *The Serials: Suspense and Drama by Installment* and Madeleine Edmondson's and David Rounds's *The Soaps: Daytime Serials of Radio and TV*, offer discussion of both radio and television hospital operas as part of their general history of soap opera serials. The first substantial critical article about medical dramas on television is a chapter entitled "Doctors and Lawyers: Counselors and Confessors" in Horace Newcomb's book *TV: The Most Popular Art*. In his chapter, Newcomb traces the evolution of the doctor and lawyer shows on television and compares the formula of the first-generation shows with that of the second. He uses "Ben Casey" and "Dr. Kildare" as examples of first-generation doctor shows; their formula depends largely on the interaction of an older male mentor with a younger pupil. Newcomb chooses "Marcus Welby, M.D." as the best example of a second-generation doctor show; its formula has changed significantly from that of the earlier shows and depends partially on Robert Young's previous success in "Father Knows Best." Welby ministers to the physical and emotional needs of an extended family that includes his assistants, his patients, and the television public. Newcomb's analysis of the doctor shows is excellent and has been said to have "pioneered the study of the medical and [legal genre] on television."[9] The second substantial critical work is Michael R. Real's chapter "Marcus Welby and the Medical Genre," which is included in his book *Mass-Mediated Culture*. Real spends only the very first part of his chapter on fictional medical dramas; in the rest, he deals with documentary medical shows, commercials and health, television's potential, and the question of priorities. The broader scope of Real's chapter makes it useful in ways Newcomb's was not intended to be. David Thorburn's essay "Television Melodrama," included in Horace Newcomb's anthology *Television: The Critical View*, offers some critical discussion of the hospital opera, and especially of "Medical Center."

Several articles from the 1960s and early 1970s are interesting reflections of the medical community's response to its depiction on television. Thelma Schorr's article on "Nursing's TV Image" lays out the criticisms nurses have of "The Nurses" and discusses the producer's way of responding to those criticisms. In "Advice on Medical Accuracy in the Entertainment Media," Dudley M. Cobb, Jr., explains the formation and function of the AMA's Physicians Committee on Television, Radio and Motion Pictures. In 1965, *Television Quarterly* published an interesting pair of articles about the "Ben Casey" show. The first, "Rx for TV Doctors," is by a physician, Murdock Head, who criticizes television doctor shows not just because of the unrealistic images of physicians they project but also because of their possible effects on millions of viewers. He thinks television medical shows can interfere with the physician-patient relationship in real life. Matthew Rapf and Wilton Schiller, the producers of "Ben Casey," answer Head's criticisms in their article, "Let's Not Offend Anyone." They insist that most charges leveled at "Ben Casey" by medical critics are contradictory. For example, some complain that the show is too grim; others complain that it is not grim enough to be realistic because Casey never loses a patient. They conclude that many medical critics probably do not watch the show regularly. Of most interest are Rapf's and Schiller's statements about how they are mindful of the public good in writing the show. In contrast to medical critics of earlier doctor shows, Michael J. Halberstam has few complaints in his article "An M.D. Reviews Dr. Welby of TV." Clearly the formula for the second-generation doctor shows is more acceptable to medical palates than was the formula for the first.

Although physicians on television are more likely to be general practitioners than psychiatrists, an article by Robert Sklar, "Prime-Time Psychology," offers an analysis of television's general presentation of psychiatry. Sklar says that some viewers enjoy seeing psychiatrists ridiculed in stereotyped images, but many viewers still regard psychiatrists as helpers and healers. He attributes to this second attitude of the viewing public the increase in psychiatrists presented favorably in dramatic specials such as "Sybil" and "A Last Cry for Help."

Although not scholarly, the articles in *TV Guide* nonetheless provide helpful information about medical shows on television, and some *TV Guide* articles even offer serious analyses of shows. An example is Richard Gehman's "Caseyitis," which explains the popular appeal of "Ben Casey" as a result of its "*high-minded* violence." Another, Leslie Raddatz's "Let's Play 'Father

Image'," describes the father image formula that seems an important element in the success of medical shows such as "Ben Casey," "The Eleventh Hour," "Breaking Point," and "Dr. Kildare." A second article by Raddatz, "The Destiny of 'The Bold Ones'," explains how the show uses real physicians and nurses as actors whenever possible. "There's a doctor in the house" outlines the relationship between those who produce the television shows and the AMA's advisory committee. Bill Davidson's "Medical Center" presents four ways the medical show of 1971 is different from the medical show of 1961.

Several other *TV Guide* articles deserve mention. Daniel Yergin's "The Merry Medics of 'Doctor in the House'" is an interesting history of the British comedy medical show that aired in the United States for two seasons. "Through the Years With Dr. Kildare" is an historical retrospective of Dr. Kildare's presence in American popular culture from the 1930s to the 1970s. Otto Wahl's article on "TV Myths About Mental Illness" lists six frequent myths about mental illness that television programs propagate. Although basically a personality profile, Bill Davidson's "Jack Klugman of 'Quincy'" explains how Klugman's personal experience with a physician convinced him that he wanted to play in a doctor show. A useful analysis of factual medical shows such as "House Call," "Health Field," "Feeling Fine," "Ounce of Prevention," and "Today's Health" is provided by Marshall Goldberg's "A Doctor Examines TV's Health Shows." In addition to surveying the shows, Goldberg suggests some of the reasons factual medical shows attract so few viewers compared to those attracted by fictional medical shows. Sally Bedell's "Behind the Scenes at 'Lifeline'" is a fascinating account of the filming of an episode in that short-lived series. And finally, David Johnston's "Teamwork 'M*A*S*H'-Style" mentions some of the important changes that have occurred in that show in its eight years on television. They seem to correspond to changes in the general public's attitudes toward physicians during that period of time.

ANTHOLOGIES AND REPRINTS

To date there are very few anthologies or reprints of popular culture materials about medicine and the physician. The best is William H. Helfand's *Medicine and Pharmacy in American Political Prints (1765-1870),* which reproduces from such publications as *Harper's Weekly, Yankee Doodle,* and the *New York Illustrated News* political caricatures that are based on medical and pharmaceutical images. Organized topically, the book's chapters intersperse commentary among the reprints. The other anthologies of medical cartoons are not scholarly in intent. They include Austin Smith's *Dear Patient: A Collection of Cartoons Concerning Doctors and their Patients; More Cartoon Classics from Medical Economics;* and William N. Jeffers' *Antidepressants: Third in a Series of Cartoon Classics from Medical Economics.*

One anthology of literature is especially important: *Great Science Fiction About Doctors,* edited by Edward Groff Conklin and Noah D. Fabricant. Three other anthologies bring together literary materials with medical themes but are designed as textbooks: Joseph Ceccio, *Medicine in Literature;* Sandra Galdieri Wilcox and Marilyn Sutton, *Understanding Death and Dying: An Interdisciplinary Approach;* and Alan Abraham Stone and Sue Smart Stone, *The Abnormal Personality Through Literature.*

NOTES

1. Michael R. Real, "Marcus Welby and the Medical Genre," in *Mass-Mediated Culture* (Englewood Cliffs, N.J.: Prentice-Hall, 1977), p. 121.
2. Michael J. Halberstam, "An M.D. Reviews Dr. Welby of TV," *New York Times Magazine,* January 16, 1972, p. 35.
3. "There's a doctor in the house," *TV Guide* (April 18, 1970), 41-42.
4. Charles Winick, "The Psychiatrist in Fiction," *Journal of Nervous and Mental Disease,* 136 (1963), 43.
5. Darrell W. Amundsen, "Romanticizing the Ancient Medical Profession: The Characterization of the Physician in the Graeco-Roman Novel," *Bulletin of the History of Medicine,* 48 (Fall 1974), 320-37; and Darrell W. Amundsen, "Images of Physicians in Classical Times," *Journal of Popular Culture,* 11 (Winter 1977), 642-55.
6. John H. Dirckx, "The Quack in Literature," *Pharos,* 31 (January 1976), 2-7.
7. F. N. L. Poynter, "Doctors in *The Human Comedy,*" *Journal of the American Medical Association,* 204 (April 1, 1968), 105-8.
8. Examples are Saul Nathaniel Brody, *The Disease of the Soul: Leprosy in Medieval Literature* (Ithaca, N.Y.: Cornell University Press, 1974); Christine E. Petersen, *The Doctor in French Drama 1770-1775* (New York: AMS Press, 1966); Herbert Silvette, *The Doctor on the Stage: Medicine and Medical Men in Seventeenth-Century England* (Knoxville: University of Tennessee Press, 1967); Gian-Paolo Biasin, *Literary Diseases: Theme and Metaphor in the Italian Novel* (Austin: University of Texas Press), 1975; Susan Sontag, *Illness as Metaphor* (New York: Farrar, Straus & Giroux, 1977); and most recently E. R. Peschel, ed., *Medicine and Literature* (New York: Neale Watson Academic, 1980), which also includes a few essays about American literature.
9. Real, "Marcus Welby and the Medical Genre," p. 121.

BIBLIOGRAPHY

BOOKS AND ARTICLES

Bedell, Sally. "Behind the Scenes at 'Lifeline.'" *TV Guide,* 26 (October 7, 1978), 26-31.

Born, Wolfgang. "The Nature and History of Medical Caricature." *Ciba Symposia,* 6 (November 1944), 1910-24.

Brigham, Jerry C., and Karlie K. Kenyon. "HADACOL: The Last Great Medicine Show." *Journal of Popular Culture,* 10 (Winter 1976), 520-33.

BIBLIOGRAPHY

BOOKS AND ARTICLES

Bedell, Sally. "Behind the Scenes at 'Lifeline.'" *TV Guide,* 26 (October 7, 1978), 26-31.

Born, Wolfgang. "The Nature and History of Medical Caricature." *Ciba Symposia,* 6 (November 1944), 1910-24.

Brigham, Jerry C., and Karlie K. Kenyon. "HADACOL: The Last Great Medicine Show." *Journal of Popular Culture,* 10 (Winter 1976), 520-33.

Brooks, Tim, and Earle Marsh. *The Complete Directory to Prime Time Network TV Shows 1946-present.* New York: Ballantine Books, 1979.

Brown, Les. *The New York Times Encyclopedia of Television.* New York: New York Times Book, 1977.

Bufithis, Philip Henry. "The Artist's Fight for Art: The Psychiatrist Figure in the Fiction of Major Contemporary American Novelists." Ph.D. dissertation, University of Pennsylvania, 1967.

Buxton, Frank, and Bill Owen. *The Big Broadcast 1920-1950.* New York: Viking, 1966.

Cameron, Alex John. "The Image of the Physician in the American Novel 1859 to 1925." *Dissertation Abstracts,* 33/11-A (1973), 6342 (University of Notre Dame).

Ceccio, Joseph. *Medicine in Literature.* New York: Longman, 1978.

Clareson, Thomas D. "The Scientist as Hero in American Science-Fiction, 1880-1920." *Extrapolation,* 7 (1965), 18-28.

Cobb, Jr., Dudley M. "Advice on Medical Accuracy in the Entertainment Media." *Western Medicine,* 7 (November 1966), 313-16.

Conklin, Edward Groff, and Noah D. Fabricant, eds. *Great Science Fiction About Doctors.* New York: Collier Books, 1963.

Corner, George W., 4th. "Medicine in the Modern Drama." *Annals of Medical History,* n.s. 10 (July 1938), 309-17.

Davidson, Bill. "Jack Klugman of '*Quincy*'." *TV Guide,* 25 (March 26, 1977), 29-34.

______. "'Medical Center'." *TV Guide,* 19 (July 17, 1971), 12-16.

DeBakey, Lois Elizabeth. "The Physician-Scientist as Character in Nineteenth-Century American Literature." Ph. D. dissertation, Tulane University, 1963.

Dunning, John. *Tune In Yesterday: The Ultimate Encyclopedia of Old-Time Radio 1925-1976.* Englewood Cliffs, N.J.: Prentice-Hall, 1976.

Dworkin, Martin S. "Movie Psychiatrics." *Antioch Review,* 14 (December 1954), 484-91.

Edmondson, Madeleine, and David Rounds. *The Soaps: Daytime Serials of Radio and TV.* New York: Stein and Day, 1973.

Fearing, Franklin. "Psychology and the Films." *Hollywood Quarterly,* 2 (January 1947), 118-21.

______. "The Screen Discovers Psychiatry." *Hollywood Quarterly,* 1 (January 1946), 154-58.

Gehman, Richard. "Caseyitis." In *TV Guide: The First 25 Years.* Edited by Jay S. Harris. New York: Simon & Schuster, 1978, pp. 63-65.

Gibbons, Russell W. "Chiropractic in America: The Historical Conflicts of Cultism and Science." *Journal of Popular Culture,* 10 (Spring 1977), 720-31.

Glass, Bentley. "The Scientist in Contemporary Fiction." *Scientific Monthly,* 85 (December 1957), 288-93.

Goldberg, Marshall. "A Doctor Examines TV's Health Shows." *TV Guide,* 25 (May 14, 1977), 4-8.

Gussow, Mel. "The Time of the Wounded Hero." *New York Times,* April 15, 1979, sec. 2, pp.1, 30.

Guthmann, Herbert Jordan. "The Characterization of the Psychiatrist in American Fiction, 1859-1965." Ph. D. dissertation, University of Southern California, 1969.

Halberstam, Michael J. "An M. D. Reviews Dr. Welby of TV." *New York Times Magazine,* January 16, 1972, pp. 12-13, 30, 32, 34-35, 37.

Head, Murdock. "Rx for TV Doctors." *Television Quarterly,* 4 (Spring 1965), 28-33.

Helfand, William H. *Medicine and Pharmacy in American Political Prints (1765-1870).* Madison, Wisc.: American Institute of the History of Pharmacy, 1978.

Hoffman, Nancy Y. "The Doctor as Scapegoat: A Study in Ambivalence." *Journal of the American Medical Association,* 220 (April 3, 1972), 58-61.

Holland, Norman N. "Psychiatry in Pselluloid." *Atlantic* 203 (February 1959), 105-7.

Hopkins, Anthony. "Physical Models and Spiritual States: Institutional Environments In Modern Fiction." *Journal of Popular Culture,* 6 (Fall 1972), 383-92.

Jeffers, William N. *Antidepressants: Third in a Series of Cartoon Classics from Medical Economics.* Oradel, N.J.: Medical Economics, 1972.

Johnston, David. "Teamwork 'M*A*S*H'-Style." *TV Guide,* 28 (January 5, 1980), 22-26.

Kiell, Norman, ed. *Psychiatry and Psychology in the Visual Arts and Aesthetics: A Bibliography.* Madison: University of Wisconsin Press, 1965.

______. *Psychoanalysis, Psychology and Literature: A Bibliography.* Madison: University of Wisconsin Press, 1963.

King, Lester S. "New Movie Monsters from the Medical World." *Journal of the American Medical Association,* 220 (April 3, 1972), 90-91.

Krafsur, Richard P., ed. *The American Film Institute Catalog of Motion Pictures: Feature Films 1961-1970.* New York: Bowker, 1976.

Kubie, Lawrence S. "Psychiatry and the Films." *Hollywood Quarterly,* 2 (January 1947), 113-17.

Leake, Chauncey D. "Medical Caricature in the United States." *Bulletin of the Society of Medical History of Chicago,* 4 (April 1928), 1-29.

"Literature and Medicine." *MD Medical Newsmagazine,* 6 (August 1962), 115-19.

McNamara, Brooks. *Step Right Up.* Garden City, N.Y.: Doubleday, 1976.

Meehan, Marjorie C. "Psychiatrists Portrayed in Fiction." *Journal of the American Medical Association,* 188 (April 20, 1964), 255-58.

More Cartoon Classics from Medical Economics. Oradell, N.J.: Medical Economics Book Division, 1966.

Munden, Kenneth W., ed. *The American Film Institute Catalog of Motion Pictures Produced In the United States: Feature Films 1921-1930.* New York: Bowker, 1971.

______. "The Movies' First Psychiatrist." *American Journal of Psychiatry,* 124 (October 1967), 545-47.

Raddatz, Leslie. "Let's Play 'Father Image'." *TV Guide,* 12 (May 23, 1964), 24-27.

______. "The Destiny of 'The Bold Ones.'" *TV Guide,* 17 (October 25, 1969), 40-46.

Rapf, Matthew, and Wilton Schiller. "Let's Not Offend Anyone." *Television Quarterly,* 4 (Spring 1965), 34-37.

Real, Michael R. "Marcus Welby and the Medical Genre." In *Mass-Mediated Culture.* Englewood Cliffs, N.J.: Prentice-Hall, 1977, pp. 118-39.

Redlich, Frederick C. "The Psychiatrist in Caricature: An Analysis of Unconscious Attitudes Toward Psychiatry." *American Journal of Orthopsychiatry,* 20 (July 1950), 560-71.

Rosenberg, Charles E. "Martin Arrowsmith: The Scientist as Hero." *American Quarterly,* 15 (Fall 1963), 447-58.

Schneider, Irving. "Images of the Mind: Psychiatry in the Commercial Film." *American Journal of Psychiatry,* 134 (June 1977), 613-20.

Scholz, Carol Krusen. "They Share the Suffering: The Psychoanalyst in American Fiction Between 1920 and 1940." Ph. D. dissertation, University of Pennsylvania, 1977.

Schorr, Thelma. "Nursing's TV Image." *American Journal of Nursing,* 63 (October 1963), 119-21.

Sievers, W. David. *Freud on Broadway: A History of Psychoanalysis and the American Drama.* New York: Hermitage House, 1955.

Sklar, Robert. "Prime-Time Psychology." *American Film,* 4 (March 1979), 59-63.

Smith, Austin, ed. *Dear Patient: A Collection of Cartoons Concerning Doctors and their Patients.* New York: Physicians Publications, 1957.

Spears, Jack. "The Doctor on the Screen." In *Hollywood: The Golden Era.* New York: Barnes, 1971, pp. 314-32.

Stedman, Raymond William. *The Serials: Suspense and Drama by Installment.* Norman: University of Oklahoma Press, 1971.

Stone, Alan Abraham, and Sue Smart Stone, eds. *The Abnormal Personality Through Literature.* Englewood Cliffs, N.J.: Prentice-Hall, 1966.

Stooke, David Edward. "The Portrait of the Physician in Selected Prose Fiction of Nineteenth-Century American Authors." *Dissertation Abstracts,* 37/08-A (1976), 5130 (George Peabody College for Teachers).

Tepperman, Jay. "The Research Scientist in Modern Fiction." *Perspectives in Biology and Medicine,* 3 (Summer 1960), 547-59.

Terrace, Vincent. *The Complete Encyclopedia of Television Programs 1947-1976.* 2 vols. New York: Barnes, 1976.

"There's a doctor in the house." *TV Guide,* 18 (April 18, 1970), 41-44.

Thorburn, David. "Television Melodrama." In *Television: The Critical View.* Edited by Horace Newcomb. 2nd ed. New York: Oxford University Press, 1979, pp. 536-53.

"Through the Years with Dr. Kildare." *TV Guide,* 21 (January 20, 1973), 15-18.

Trautmann, Joanne, and Carol Pollard. *Literature and Medicine: Topics, Titles & Notes.* Philadelphia: Society for Health and Human Values, 1975.

Wagner, Melinda. "Psychiatrist at the Drawing Board." *Today's Health,* 41 (August 1963), 14-17, 58-60, 63.

Wahl, Otto. "TV Myths About Mental Illness." *TV Guide,* 24 (March 13, 1976), 4-8.

Walsh, Mary Roth. "Images of Women Doctors in Popular Fiction: Comparison of the 19th and 20th Centuries." *Journal of American Culture,* 1 (Summer 1978), 276-84.

Wilbanks, Evelyn Rivers. "The Physician in the American Novel, 1870-1955." *Bulletin of Bibliography,* 22 (September-December 1958), 164-68.

Wilcox, Sandra Galdieri, and Marilyn Sutton. *Understanding Death and Dying: An Interdisciplinary Approach.* Port Washington, N.Y.: Alfred, 1977.

Wilmer, Harry A. "Psychiatrist on Broadway." *American Imago,* 12 (Summer 1955), 157-78.

______. "Saturday's Psychiatrist." *American Imago,* 12 (Summer 1955), 179-86.

Wilmeth, Don B. "Stage Entertainment." In *Handbook of American Popular Culture.* Vol. 1. Edited by M. Thomas Inge. Westport Conn.: Greenwood Press, 1978, pp. 293-322.

Winick, Charles. "The Psychiatrist in Fiction." *Journal of Nervous and Mental Disease,* 136 (1963), 43-57.

Wolfe, Kary K., and Gary K. Wolfe. "Metaphors of Madness: Popular Psychological Narratives." *Journal of Popular Culture,* 9 (Spring 1976), 895-907.

Yergin, Daniel. "The Merry Medics of 'Doctor in the House'." *TV Guide,* 20 (September 30, 1972), 38-40.

Young, James Harvey. "From Hooper to Hohensee: Some Highlights of American Patent Medicine Promotion." *Journal of the American Medical Association,* 204 (April 1, 1968), 100-4.

______. *The Medical Messiahs: A Social History of Health Quackery in Twentieth-Century America.* Princeton: Princeton University Press, 1967.

______. "The Patent Medicine Boom." In *The History of Popular Culture.* Edited by Norman F. Cantor and Michael S. Werthman. New York: Macmillan, 1968, pp. 477-79.

______. *The Toadstool Millionaires: A Social History of Patent Medicines in America before Federal Regulation.* Princeton: Princeton University Press, 1961.

CHAPTER 9 Minorities in Popular Culture

Faye Nell Vowell

Although for years it has been accepted that the United States is a nation of immigrants whose individual backgrounds have contributed to shaping the nation's culture, the relationship of minorities to popular culture has been of only minor interest to scholars. This neglect may be due, partly, to the fact that popular culture is at once so amorphous and all pervasive. There are, however, among the many works in the general field of minority or ethnic studies, a sizable number that can introduce the beginning student to the subject of minorities in popular culture.

The influence of minorities on popular culture has, indeed, been great, and a comparatively short essay such as this could not hope to treat that topic adequately in all its complexity and scope. I have, therefore, chosen to focus on the contributions made by three ethnic minority groups: the Indians, the Chicanos, and the blacks. Not only are these three groups the most visible and politically vocal of all ethnic groups, but scholarship dealing with these groups is also more available currently. They are also more likely to interest a student of popular culture.

I should take the opportunity at the outset to discuss my definition of crucial terms and categories. If popular culture is defined as the culture of the mainstream or mass of Americans, then the impact of minorities on this culture may be seen in a number of ways. First, that mainstream culture will possess some vision, or perhaps stereotype, of those minorities based on its contact with them (or its ignorance of or lack of contact with them). Those minorities will possess a corresponding vision of the dominant culture, and the resultant attitudes of both will become manifest in their respective cultures. In addition to this kind of interaction is the inter-cultural "borrowing" between groups. When performed by the ethnic group, this borrowing is called acculturation or assimilation. But the mainstream culture does much the same thing when it popularizes the music or dances of an ethnic group or when, for example, white entrepreneurs sell ethnic foods in fast food chains. Other less obvious evidences of interaction include popular literature by and about minorities, movies, television, politics, folklore, and superstition.

It is the intent of this essay to point out interesting and useful works pertaining to the areas outlined above. Blacks receive more coverage in the essay because more work has been done regarding them than the Indians or the Chicanos. Yet the books touched on here are only a fraction of the available material, and choices for inclusion are of necessity somewhat idiosyncratic. The historic outline that follows contains a capsule history of the minority within this country, especially its interactions with the mainstream culture. The books listed in the section entitled "History and Criticism" were selected because they address the issues and events discussed in this historic outline.

HISTORIC OUTLINE

Indians have inhabited the land which is now the United States much longer than any other people. Archeologists hypothesize that they migrated across the Bering Strait and followed the game southward to the warmer climates of Central and South America, eventually founding such great civilizations as the Mayan and the Aztec. As early as four to five thousand years ago the Indian was growing corn in what is now New Mexico.

The first known Indian contact with Europeans was with Spanish conquistadors in the sixteenth century. Between the years of 1521 and 1528 Florida was explored by Ponce de León, Vásquez de Ayllon, and Panfilo de Naváez. Francisco Vásquez de Coronado's expedition pushed north from Mexico through southeast Arizona to New Mexico looking for the Seven Cities of Cibola. In a search for the kingdom of Quivira the Spaniard penetrated as far north as Oklahoma and Kansas. Not until 1598 was there a Spanish attempt at colonization.

Contact between Indians and Europeans on the east coast of the United States quickly assumed a typical pattern of initial friendship on the part of the Indian and exploitation and destruction on the part of the Europeans as they sought to push the Indian toward the interior. By June 1637 the New England Puritans had annihilated the Pequots. In 1675 the independent power of New England Indians was broken by their defeat in King Philip's War. The colonists' side of the story is recounted in such captivity narratives as that of Mrs. Mary Rowlandson. What is usually left out of the story is the savagery of the colonists who would not even allow Philip to be buried after he had been killed and his body mutilated: his head was exhibited on a pole, and his hand was cut off and sent to Boston where it was placed on public display.

A similar pattern of European-Indian relationships may be seen in the South. By 1680 the Westo tribe of South Carolina had been destroyed.

In the early 1700s the Yamasee had been forced from their home in South Carolina south to Florida. When in 1817 Spain ceded Florida to the United States, the government was ready to turn its attention to totally removing the Indian threat in the South. Andrew Jackson's administration passed the Indian Removal Act in 1830. In 1838-39 the mass movement of the Cherokees, Chickasaws, Choctaws, Creeks, and Seminoles to lands in Oklahoma began. On this Trail of Tears, one-fourth of the Cherokee nation died.

The subjugation of the Indians of the Southwest began in earnest with the 1848 Treaty of Guadalupe Hidalgo ending the Mexican War. Although troops had to be withdrawn during the Civil War, allowing Apaches led by Cochise and Mangas Coloradas temporarily to regain control of areas of Arizona and New Mexico, the Indians were eventually subdued through the efforts of such men as Generals James H. Carleton and George Crook. After much violence, the Northwest was secured with the surrender of Chief Joseph of the Nez Perce.

The Indians of the northern Great Plains held out against white encroachment the longest. Adapting their culture to fit the horse and the rifle introduced by the Europeans, they used the mobility and firepower gained to retain their freedom for over twenty-five years of continuous warfare. The war years 1866-91 saw such watershed battles as the Sand Creek Massacre by the government of over three hundred Cheyenne and Arapahoe, the defeat of General George A. Custer and nearly three hundred men of the Seventh Cavalry at the Battle of the Little Big Horn, and the slaughter of approximately two hundred men, women, and children by remnants of the Seventh Cavalry at Wounded Knee. The struggle for the continent ended with the defeat of the Sioux at Wounded Knee on December 28, 1890.

For the next fifty years the fortunes of the Indian went steadily downward—confined to reservations, viewed as a ward of the government, controlled by the Bureau of Indian Affairs. However, World War II brought an increased involvement in the affairs of the mainstream. This involvement accelerated with the civil rights movement of the 1960s and 1970s. The National Youth Council was formed in 1960, followed by the more militant American Indian Movement in 1969. The various tribes began to see that red power or Indian power was a possibility and that strength lay in a pan-Indian movement. Evidence of the new militancy followed with the takeover of the island of Alcatraz from November 20, 1969 to June 11, 1971, the "Trail of Broken Treaties" demonstrations just before the 1972 elections, and the occupation of Wounded Knee in 1973.

A generation of articulate Indians such as Vine Deloria, Jr., has arisen to fight the white man again—this time with words and legal maneuvers as well as force. They are battling the old stereotypes: the Puritan's vision of the cruel savage, the beautiful Indian maiden Pocahontas protecting Captain John Smith, the noble savage, and even Jay Silverheels saving the

Lone Ranger. Deloria sees a close relationship among the plights of the Indian, the black, and the Chicano. In *We Talk, You Listen: New Tribes, New Turf* he also attacks "traditional stereotypes [which] pictured the black as a happy watermelon-eating darky whose sole contribution to American society was his indiscriminate substitution of the 'd' sound for 'th'." He further notes that "Mexicans were generally portrayed as shiftless and padded out for siesta, without any redeeming qualities whatsoever."[1] Neither stereotype approaches the reality of the situation.

Mexican-Americans view their claim to land in the Southwest as pre-dating that of colonists from Europe. Their heritage began with the Indian tribes who settled *Aztlan* (the southwest United States) before journeying on south and whose blood became mixed with that of the Spaniards when Hernando Cortés landed near present-day Vera Cruz in 1519. Descendants of those original settlers of mixed Indian-Spanish blood still live in such areas of the Southwest as Tierra Amarillo in New Mexico. Although they have inhabited the area for a much longer time, the history of the Mexican American technically begins with the Treaty of Guadalupe Hidalgo which ended the Mexican-American War on February 2, 1848.

By the terms of this treaty, the United States paid Mexico $15 million as an indemnity and acquired over a million miles of territory—an area encompassed by the states of Arizona, California, Nevada, New Mexico, part of Colorado, and Texas. If Mexican citizens elected to stay on their land, they were to be granted citizenship and their property rights were guaranteed. Actual treatment of those Mexicans who elected to remain fell far short of the ideal. They were soon faced with an onslaught of Anglos speaking a different language and living by a different code of laws. In actual practice, most Mexican Americans lost their land. Anglos had gained dominance in California by the 1870s. In New Mexico, the Mexican Americans retained control longer because of the alliance of the *ricos* (upper-class Mexican Americans) and wealthy Anglos. However this alliance did not benefit the small farmer or sheep herder who steadily lost ground. The situation of the Mexican American was probably the worst in Texas. There he faced racial and religious prejudice from Anglo settlers who had come primarily from the fundamentalist-Protestant South and despised the Mexican Americans for their dark skins and their Catholicism. The original Mexican Americans thus came to find themselves in a situation analogous to that of the Indian: they were a conquered people possessing a culture which they had to struggle to retain.

Although the border between the two countries presented no barrier, immigration from Mexico to the United States was minimal until the Mexican Revolution of 1910. Between 1910 and 1920 civil disruption caused some one million Mexicans to flee their homes. Most did not plan to stay in the United States and did not become citizens. They found work in the newly irrigated fields of Arizona, Texas, and California as well as with the railroads and steel companies. During this time they replaced cheap labor from Asia and Europe cut off by the exclusion acts and the Immigration Act of 1924.

But this time of relative prosperity ceased with the Depression of 1929. To reduce welfare rolls, the government began a massive repatriation program. Often there was no discrimination between the Mexican and the Mexican American as they were loaded onto the train that left Los Angeles for Mexico once a month from 1931 to 1933. Mexican Americans met further discrimination during World War II. Two famous incidents are the Zoot Suit Riots, when sailors cruised the streets of Los Angeles assaulting *pachucos,* and the Sleepy Lagoon murder case. In spite of this prejudice, Mexican Americans served the United States well during World War II.

After the war, many took advantage of G.I. benefits to better their education. They also began to demand more equal treatment forming such organizations as the G.I. Forum and the Mexican American Political Organization to assert their civil rights. Their situation was complicated by the continual influx of immigrants from Mexico. *Mojados* (wetbacks), *braceros* (temporary workers brought over under contract), and later "blue carders" and "green carders" continued to come to the United States for economic reasons, thus depressing working conditions. In 1954, the U.S. government initiated "Operation Wetback" to alleviate the labor situation, but indiscriminate deportation of "Mexicans" only resulted in more alienation and mistrust.

Thus in the 1960s Mexican Americans were ready to join the Indians and blacks in a more militant effort to gain their civil rights. The Chicano movement was especially influential among young students who formed such organizations as Mexican American Youth Organization (MAYO) and Movimiento Estudiantil Chicano de Aztlan (MECHA). This movement exalted the Indian side of the Mexican-American heritage and glorified such concepts as *Aztlan* and *La Raza.*

The movement gained support from other areas also. Four charismatic leaders have come to the forefront. In New Mexico, Reies Lopez Tijerina formed the Alianza Federal de Pueblos Libres in 1963. Its purpose was to regain original land grants. The Alianza made headlines in 1967, when members raided the courthouse at Tierra Amarilla, New Mexico. In Texas in 1970, José Angel Gutierrez led La Raza Unida party to political victory in the twenty south Texas counties where Chicanos constitute a majority of the population. The party has since won school board and city council elections in Crystal City, Texas, and city council elections in Carrizo Springs and Cotulla.

In Denver in 1965, Rudolfo "Corky" Gonzalez founded a civil rights organizaton, the Crusade for Justice. The organization sponsored the Chicano Youth Liberation Conference, where *El Plan Espiritual de Aztlan* was articulated in 1969. Gonzalez is also the author of an influential epic poem, "I Am Joaquin" (1967). From California has come the best-known Chicano leader, Cesar Chavez, founder of the United Farm Workers Organizing Committee (UFWOC). In 1965 Chavez initiated a five-year strike, *la huelga,* against California grape growers. Chavez's policy of nonviolence has earned him widespread respect, and he remains a unifying force among Chicanos. *La huelga* was influential in shaping a sense of identity among Mexican-Americans.

A revolutionary peoples' theater developed out of the strike. *Actos* such as *Los Vendidos* by Luis Valdez use the stereotypes Anglos have created of the Chicano and eventually turn them against their creator. Today's Chicano is politically aware and rapidly outpacing the stereotypes of Speedy Gonzales or the Mexican peon taking his siesta under a cactus.

Blacks, the largest ethnic minority in the United States, have also come a long way in destroying the traditional stereotypes possessed by mainstream culture. They share a sense of identity and commonality of problems with the Indians and Chicanos. The epic story of the black man in America also begins with the earliest explorers. Blacks came to America with Hernando de Alarćon and Franciso Vásquez de Coronado, Panfilo de Naváez and Cabeza de Vaca. A black named Esteban himself led the expedition from Mexico into Arizona and New Mexico in 1538. As settlers they came not long after. In 1619 twenty blacks landed at Jamestown, Virginia—the first of a long line of Africans to be brought to America against their will. These first Africans were treated as indentured servants, but by 1661 Virginia had made statutory recognition of slavery, preceded only by Massachusetts in 1641 and Connecticut in 1650. Maryland followed in 1663, New York and New Jersey in 1664, South Carolina in 1682, Rhode Island and Pennsylvania in 1700, North Carolina in 1715, and Georgia in 1750.

From the beginning, blacks resisted. As early as 1658, a group of blacks and Indians rebelled in Hartford, Connecticut; in 1712 blacks revolted in New York, burning a building and shooting nine white men before the uprising was put down and twenty-one of the blacks executed; in the same city in 1741 fears of a slave uprising led to the execution of thirty-one more—eighteen hanged and thirteen burned alive. For both humanitarian and economic reasons slavery diminished in the North. In the South it flourished as plantation owners looked for cheap labor to grow their money crop: cotton. By 1830 there were more than two million slaves.

Life for black Americans within the system of slavery was based on the premise that they were not people but property. They had no legal rights. They could not engage in commerce. They could not socialize with whites or freed blacks. They could not assemble unless supervised by a white person. They could not defend themselves against whites. They could not leave the plantation without the owner's approval. They could not possess firearms. In short, they had no rights at all—except the right to work in a system in which they accrued no money and made no gains.

Just as they had during Colonial times, blacks resisted. In 1822 Denmark Vesey organized a revolt in and around Charleston, South Carolina, that included thousands of blacks. Perhaps the most famous resistance movement of this time took place in 1831, when Nat Turner and his followers killed more than sixty whites in Southampton County, Virginia, before being defeated by state and federal troops.

Despite such acts of rebellion, black Americans stood little chance in their armed confrontations with whites; inevitably, they were simply outgunned. But if active, armed battles were doomed to failure, other measures were open to them—notably, escape through the Underground Railroad. Fostered by the Abolitionist Movement, which grew steadily after 1815, a network of sympathetic "operators" sprang up to aid those blacks who fled organized slavery. Levi Coffin and John Fairfield stand out among the white "conductors"; Jane Lewis, Elijah Anderson, John Mason, and Harriet Tubman among the blacks. It is conjectured that Tubman, perhaps the most famous of all, accounted for approximately three hundred escapes. Although accurate counts are difficult to come by, it has been estimated that more than 100,000 slaves migrated north along the clandestine route of the Underground Railroad during the years between 1810 and 1850.

The decade of the 1850s, filled with increasing tension between North and South and with patchwork attempts at compromise, ended with two events that indicated the inevitability of war: John Brown's raid in 1859 and the election of Abraham Lincoln in 1860. When it came the war left the South devastated both physically and culturally. In the aftermath of the devastation, another war was fought—the war for political and economic control of the area.

Blacks lost ground rapidly in the South after the war. As early as 1866 groups of Southern whites harassed both blacks and Northern whites by forming vigilante groups. In the late 1860s and 1870s they were joined by groups such as the Knights of the White Camellia, the White Brotherhood, the White League of Louisiana, and the Knights of the Ku Klux Klan.

In 1890 a Mississippi convention passed a suffrage amendment that effectively disenfranchised blacks in that state; in 1895 South Carolina accomplished the same; and in 1898 Louisiana introduced the "grandfather clause." Shortly thereafter, all other Southern states would follow in the pattern; and, by 1910, for all intents and purposes, the blacks had lost the right to vote throughout the South. In 1875 the first "Jim Crow" law appeared in Tennessee; soon, the statutes were laden with such laws. When the Supreme Court outlawed the 1875 Civil Rights Act in 1883, blacks in the South found themselves legally separated from whites in almost all areas of their lives, and whites enforced such segregation in the courts by law and in the streets and countryside by violence and terror. In the first two years of the twentieth century there were over two hundred lynchings in the South; by the beginning of World War I over eleven hundred had occurred.

In the face of such organized prejudice and such brutal tactics, black Americans looked for options. Booker T. Washington offered advice that now seems naively tailor-made to the era of the rise of the industrial giants. He urged his fellow blacks to learn agricultural and industrial skills and to emulate the Puritan habits of thrift, good moral behavior, and perseverance; in his view, blacks had to develop a base of skilled craftsmen in a complicated agrarian and industrial nation before they could aspire to more lucrative goals, and he dedicated the Tuskegee Institute to that end. During the years 1895 to 1915, Washington became the most powerful and influential black in the United States, and, when he spoke, both Northern and Southern whites felt that he spoke for all black Americans.

But the lure of the city, particularly in terms of the freedom and economic opportunities to be sought in the Northern city, drew blacks away from farmlands in increasing numbers. In both the North and South, awareness increased among blacks that they needed to organize in order to battle for their rights. In 1909 the nucleus of the Niagara Movement begun by W. E. B. Du Bois and William Monroe Trotter joined with other blacks and whites in the formation of the National Association for the Advancement of Colored People, an organization which has remained important to the black community to the present time.

The NAACP, frequently criticized by militant blacks in the 1960s as too conservative, hardly seemed so at the time of its founding. With Du Bois as its director of publicity and research, the organization quickly launched a campaign against lynching and brutality, called for protection within the law for Southern blacks, and sought to broaden economic opportunities for blacks across the country. As the means to communicate its message, the NAACP launched a magazine, *The Crisis*, edited by Du Bois, which became the first important national publication to provide a voice for black Americans. In addition, in 1911, the National Urban League was formed, its primary mission being to help blacks in their adjustment to life in the nation's cities.

During World War I, black soldiers performed well, many of them experiencing freedoms in Europe that they had never previously enjoyed. They returned to a United States that to most of them must have seemed symbolized by the resurgence of the Ku Klux Klan, which, within a year of the war's end, had grown from a relatively sparse movement to a membership of over 100,000 hooded white men. In the South they persecuted blacks; in the West, the Japanese.

During the decade following World War I, increasing numbers of blacks migrated to Northern industrial centers where they frequently found jobs in the growing automobile industry, paper and bag companies, the food and clothing industries, and transportation and communication. The American Negro Labor Conference, meeting in Chicago in 1925, sought to organize the efforts of black farmers and industrial workers in the hope of bringing more and more blacks into organized labor. During the same year, A. Philip Randolph organized the Brotherhood of Sleeping Car Porters and Maids; although the industry's full recognition of Randolph's union was delayed until 1937, it marked the beginning of significant black unionizing. The Great Depression of the 1930s eliminated many of the gains for which blacks had worked.

When World War II loomed on the horizon, blacks again played a large and meaningful role in the war effort. However, it was not until after the war in 1948 that President Harry S. Truman, in Executive Order 9981, ordered the desegregation of the armed forces.

In the 1950s the civil rights movement gained momentum. Its most important year was 1955. In that year the Supreme Court ordered school desegregation to move "with all deliberate speed" and banned segregation in public recreational facilities; the Interstate Commerce Commission ordered an end to segregation in buses, waiting rooms, and coaches involved in interstate travel; advances in organized labor were symbolized by the elections of two blacks, A. Philip Randolph and Willard Townsend, as vice presidents in the combined AFL and CIO; and, in Montgomery, Alabama, Martin Luther King, Jr., initiated the famous bus boycott on December 5—an action that has come to symbolize the concentrated effort to bring meaningful change in American social structure through organized passive resistance.

From that time to the present, meaningful actions have occurred every year on the march to black equality. In 1957 the Southern Christian Leadership Conference was organized. Sit-ins, marches, freedom rides, and other means of resistance were used to make educational, political, and economic gains.

Violence, unprecedented in its continuing intensity, was directed toward the movement as black Americans took the initiative across a broad front to gain equality. Black churches were burned; black leaders were attacked and murdered; white civil rights activists, often young people working summers in the South, were harassed, beaten, and sometimes killed; working-class whites in Northern cities resorted to mob violence in their efforts to keep blacks from moving into their neighborhoods.

In the South, state public officials of the highest ranks led a battle against the inevitable workings of the law. In the North the more subtle forms of segregation in employment, education, and housing were more difficult to confront, although the NAACP, the Urban League, and newer and more militant organizations like the Congress of Racial Equality (CORE) and the Student Nonviolent Coordinating Committee (SNCC) fought for improvements in these areas. Perhaps it was the very subtlety of Northern racism that led to the frustration that fostered the explosions of race riots in black ghettos during the summer of 1964 and for several years thereafter. In 1964 the black areas of New York City, particularly Harlem and Bedford-Stuyvesant, exploded, and the conflagration spread to Rochester, Jersey City, Paterson, Elizabeth, Chicago, and Philadelphia. In 1965 a black area of Los Angeles, Watts, became the scene of insurrection as blacks battled white police and National Guardsmen. In the following three years major riots occurred in Chicago, Lansing, Waukegan, Atlanta, Nashville, Tampa, Cincinnati, Buffalo, Durham, Minneapolis, Birmingham, Detroit, Memphis, Milwaukee, Cleveland, Gary, and Miami.

On April 4, 1968, Martin Luther King, Jr., was assassinated in Memphis. His death symbolized an end to one era of the black American struggle for equality. Since 1955, the year in which the bus boycott began in Montgomery, some relatively rapid changes had taken place on the surface of black-white relations in the United States. The issues of public accommodations, educational opportunities, the issue of equal housing, and others had been resolved. What remained to be done involved the gnawing difficulties of removing the subtle obstacles so familiar as to become almost unconscious factors in the mores and the manners of the culture.

Some of the black militants of the late 1960s and the beginning of the 1970s, particularly groups like the Black Panthers, stated loudly that events had swept over Martin Luther King, Jr., his beliefs, and his methods. It is important to remember, however, that at the time of his assassination he was not in Memphis to organize a bus boycott or a voter registration drive or a department store sit-in. Those tasks belonged to an earlier time. He was in Memphis to help organize a movement for higher pay for striking sanitation workers—more specifically an economic rather than a racial commitment. Clearly, at the end of his life, King was shifting his sights to the economic imbalances in the United States, imbalances which adversely affect working-class people both white and black. He knew that the way to equality in the United States was in the way to wealth, that economic power and the distribution of wealth were the issues of the future. One of the followers of Dr. King and a long-time activist in the Southern Christian Leadership Conference, Jesse Jackson, now leads a movement called "Operation Push." Its objectives are economic in nature, and, while based in the black community, Operation Push seeks a more broadly based constituency. Its cry of "green power" may represent the wave of the future.

Blacks have also made inroads politically, electing black mayors such as Maynard Jackson of Atlanta and congressional representatives such as Julian Bond, Barbara Jordan, and Yvonne Braithwaite Burke. Andrew Young's appointment as ambassador to the United Nations further symbolized the success of the black in American society. But such recent developments as the May 1980 riots in Miami signal that a large group of blacks are still dissatisfied with their position in the United States.

REFERENCE WORKS

A standard reference for any work on the Indian, the black, or the Chicano is *A Comprehensive Bibliography for the Study of American Minorities* by Wayne Charles Miller et al. It includes an introductory bibliographical essay on each ethnic group followed by partially annotated bibliographical listings.

INDIANS

For a straightforward, somewhat simplified account of the American Indian in general, John Stoutenburgh's *Dictionary of the American Indian* is a good starting point. Arlene B. Hirschfelder has compiled two excellent bibliographies. *American Indian and Eskimo Authors: A Comprehensive Bibliography* is an updating of her earlier *American Indian Authors,* which itself annotates 157 books by 120 authors from 54 tribes. The Office of Indian Affairs has put together a *Biographical and Historical Index of American Indians and Persons Involved in Indian Affairs.* Charles Haywood's *Bibliography of North American Folklore and Folksong* contains over 10,000 entries on the American Indian north of Mexico. It is categorized by geographical areas and further divided into such sections as folklore, music, and individual tribes.

CHICANOS

The field of Chicano studies has developed substantially in the last ten years. A good starting point is Arnulfo D. Trejo's *Bibliografia Chicana: A Guide to Information Sources,* which contains a section on folklore and popular customs as well as a profile of Chicano newspapers and periodicals and a directory of newspapers, periodicals, and publishers. Ernestina Eger's annual bibliography in *Carta Abierta* is the best source to go to for Chicano literature as a supplement to the Miller bibliography. *Chicano Scholars and*

Writers: A Bio-Bibliographical Dictionary by Julio A. Martinez lists information about Chicano writers and scholars and gives information on how to contact them.

BLACKS

A useful resource in the area of black language is Robert W. Glenn's *Black Rhetoric: A Guide to Afro-American Communication.* The book lists anthologies, bibliographies, and speeches as well as essays arranged alphabetically by author; its goal is to provide a guide to available sources about the content of speeches and essays by black Americans. *The Negro Almanac: A Reference Work on the Afro American* by Harry A. Ploski and Warren Marr provides a number of special sections of interest to a student of popular culture: "The Black Entertainer in the Performing Arts," "The Black in Films," "The Black Press and Broadcast Media," and "The Black Woman."

Black personalities—successful business people, politicians, entertainers—are introduced in a three-volume work by the editors of *Ebony* entitled *The Ebony Success Library.* Volume 1 is *1,000 Successful Blacks* from Hank Aaron to the Reverend Rufus Young, Sr.; volume 2, *Famous Blacks Give Secrets of Success,* contains advice from people as diverse as Charley Pride, Diana Ross, and Flip Wilson to Gwendolyn Brooks, Shirley Chisholm, and Jesse Jackson; and volume 3 is a *Career Guide.*

In a similar vein, reference books about black authors abound. James A. Page's *Selected Black American Authors: An Illustrated Bio-Bibliography* lists 453 authors. Ann Allen Shockley and Sue P. Chandler's *Living Black American Authors* includes a list of black publishers as well as a title index. A companion reference work is Robert L. Southgate's *Black Plots and Black Characters: A Handbook for Afro-American Literature,* containing plot summaries of important works of fiction.

Two reference works about blacks in film and television with which to begin are Phyllis Rauch Klotman's *Frame by Frame: A Black Filmography,* which indexes black performers, authors, screen-play writers, producers, and directors, and Anne Powers's *Blacks in American Movies: A Selected Bibliography,* which includes periodical citations on such subjects as "History of Blacks in Films," "Film and Black Athletes," and "The Black Image."

HISTORY AND CRITICISM

INDIANS

The works in this section will aid the beginning researcher or reader in discovering the aspects of Indian, Chicano, and black experience that are of value in assessing their impact on mainstream culture and the view the larger society has of them. Virginia Irving Armstrong's and Frederick

W. Turner, III's *I Have Spoken: American History Through the Voices of the Indians* is an interesting perspective with which to begin, as is Joseph H. Cash's and Herbert T. Hoover's *To Be an Indian: An Oral History.* Ralph W. Andrews's *Indian Leaders Who Helped Shape America, 1620-1900* is a pictorial history beginning with Pocahontas and ending with Quanah Parker.

For an early account the reader should see *Letters and Notes on the Manners, Customs, and Condition of the North American Indians* printed by the author, George Catlin, in London in 1841. A contemporary nineteenth-century view of the Indian-white relationship is General George A. Custer's *My Life on the Plains, or Personal Experiences with the Indians.* The book is a compilation of a series of magazine articles written by Custer for *Galaxy;* they were collected and published in book form in 1874.

A more objective look at Indian history focusing on the four centuries of nearly continuous warfare between Indian and European is John Tebbel's and Keith Jennison's *The American Indian Wars.* Another view of the Indian's struggle is Alvin M. Josephy's *Red Power: The American Indians' Fight for Freedom,* a documentary history of American Indian militancy from its emergence in the 1960s. *Alcatraz Is Not an Island,* edited by Peter Blue Cloud, describes the Indian occupation of Alcatraz from November 1969 to June 1971 using pictures, poetry, and prose from Indians of all tribes.

Vine Deloria, Jr., a Standing Rock Sioux who holds degrees in law and theology, has written a number of books commenting on his view of the Indian situation. His books include *Custer Died for Your Sins: An Indian Manifesto; We Talk, You Listen: New Tribes, New Turf; Of Utmost Good Faith; God Is Red;* and *Behind the Trail of Broken Treaties.* Dee Brown's *Bury My Heart at Wounded Knee: An Indian History of the American West* is probably the best-known treatment of history from an Indian perspective.

For a look at the figure of the Indian in literature, the reader could begin with Albert Keiser's *The Indian in American Literature.* A number of authors have written novels sympathetic to the Indian cause. They include Oliver LaFarge's *Laughing Boy* which won a Pulitzer Prize in 1929; Frank Waters's *The Man Who Killed the Deer* and *People of the Valley;* and Thomas Berger's *Little Big Man* which was made into a motion picture. Novels by Indians about the Indian experience include *Tsali,* an historical novel about the Cherokee Indian removal in 1838, written by Denton R. Bedford, a Minsee Indian; and *House Made of Dawn* by N. Scott Momaday. *Winter in the Blood* by James Welch and *Ceremony* by Leslie Marmon Silko are also important.

Collections of Indian myths, tales, and poetry abound. Among the most useful and accessible are Stith Thompson's *Tales of the North American Indians,* a collection of ninety-six tales popular among many tribes; Jerome

Rothenberg's *Shaking the Pumpkin: Traditional Poetry of the Indian North Americas* which strives to give the reader a sense of the accompanying dances and movements, and John Bierhorst's *The Red Swan: Myths and Tales of the American Indians.*

Alice C. Fletcher's *Indian Story and Song from North America,* originally printed in 1900, is based on Indian performances in sessions of the Congress of Musicians at the Trans-Mississippi Exposition in Omaha in July 1898. It is interesting as an attempt to make Indian music accessible in a popular form for a general audience. Also valuable is a series of pamphlets on Indian music by Frances Densmore published by the Government Printing Office. For a complete listing of Densmore's work see Wayne Miller's *A Comprehensive Bibliography for the Study of American Minorities.*

An introduction to art by and about Indians is available to the reader in Frederick J. Dockstader's *Indian Art in America: The Arts and Crafts of the North American Indian* and *Weaving Arts of the North American Indian. The Image of the Indian and the Black Man in American Art, 1500-1900* by Elwood Parry begins with engravings from Theodore DeBry's "America" and ends with photography by Benjamin Johnston entitled "Class in American History" taken at Hampton Institute, Hampton, Virginia, a coeducational school for blacks and Indians.

Another area of topical interest is folk medicine. Michael Weiner's *Earth Medicine— Earth Foods: Plant Remedies, Drugs and Natural Foods of the North American Indians* is an illustrated alphabetical treatment of the various physical disorders and their natural cures.

A final topic not to be omitted is in the area of women's studies. Interested researchers should go to Jane B. Katz's *I Am the Fire of Time: The Voices of Native American Women* and Dexter Fisher's *The Third Woman: Minority Women Writers of the United States.* Fisher's book contains selections from nineteen American Indian women writers.

CHICANOS

A standard beginning text for the reader interested in the Mexican American or Chicano is *The Mexican American People: The Nation's Second Largest Minority* by Leo Grebler, Joan W. Moore, and Ralph C. Guzman. Equally influential is a book of forty-seven essays on the Chicano of yesterday, today, and tommorrow entitled *Introduction to Chicano Studies: A Reader,* edited by Livie Duran and H. Russell Bernard. Jack D. Forbes's *Aztecas del Norte: The Chicanos of Aztlan* is a general history focusing on the Indian aspect of the Chicano heritage. It also contians "El Plan Espiritual de Aztlan."

The Chicano movement has elicited a number of books explaining its purpose and genesis. Both Armando B. Rendon's *Chicano Manifesto* and

Rudolph Acuna's *Occupied America: The Chicano's Struggle Toward Liberation* are necessary reading on the topic. The Mexican philosopher Octavio Paz has also exerted a great influence on the movement; his book *The Labyrinth of Solitude: Life and Thought in Mexico* is required reading in many Chicano studies programs.

The activities of the Alianza in New Mexico led by Reies Lopez Tijerina are covered in *The Spanish Land Grant Question Examined,* published by the Alianza Federal, and Patricia Bell Blawis's *Tijerina and the Land Grants: Mexican Americans in Struggle for Their Heritage* which follows Tijerina's career up to 1971. *Tijerina and the Courthouse Raid* is a first-hand journalistic account by Peter Nabokov of the events leading to the attack on the Rio Arriba courthouse in 1967.

John Staples Shockley's *Chicano Revolt in a Texas Town* discusses the political affairs of Crystal City, Texas, where Mexican-American citizens twice wrested control of local government from Anglos, once in 1963 and again in 1969. The California grape strike led by Cesar Chavez occasioned a number of books. Mark Day's *Forty Acres: Cesar Chavez and the Farm Workers* is a popular account written by an advocate. Eugene Nelson's *Huelga: The First Hundred Days of the Great Delano Grape Strike* is a day-to-day chronicle of strikers' activities, and *Don Sotaco* by Andy Zermeno is a cartoon treatment of the strike. George Ballis's *Basta!* presents the situation in photographs.

Anglo prejudice against the Chicano has been a fact of life since the cultures first met in Texas. Charles C. Alexander's *The Ku Klux Klan in the Southwest* is one treatment of Anglo prejudice. Walter Prescott Webb's *The Texas Rangers* is yet another to reveal prejudice against the Chicano while elevating the ranger to the status of hero. *Gunpowder Justice: A Reassessment of the Texas Rangers* by Julian Samora examines the situation from the Chicano viewpoint. Theodore Lothrup Stoddard's *The Rising Tide of Color,* a chauvinistic and bigoted response to the Mexican immigrant, is balanced by Julian Samora's *Los Mojados: The Wetback Story,* an objective overview of the situation of the illegal immigrant.

Stereotypes of the Mexican American in literature are examined in Edward Simmen's *The Chicano: From Caricature to Self-Portrait,* an anthology which deals with early caricatures, realistic profiles, and self-portraits of an awakening minority. Cecil Robinson's *Mexico and the Hispanic Southwest in American Literature,* although disputed, is worth reading.

The popular form of the border ballad, or *corrido,* is discussed in Américo Paredes' *"With His Pistol in His Hand"—A Border Ballad and Its Hero,* the history of Gregorio Cortez as well as the *corrido* and variations on it. Mody C. Boatright treats a wider range of material in *Mexican Border Ballads and Other Lore.*

Collections of folklore and folktales about the Mexican-American abound.

Among the best are J. Frank Dobie's *Southwestern Lore,* which includes legends, songs, superstitions, and tales of Mexican and Anglo cowboys, and his *Puro Mexico,* containing legends, animal lore, and ballads dramatizing the Mexican immigrant experience in the United States. *Treasure of the Sangre de Cristos: Tales and Traditions of the Spanish Southwest* by Arthur L. Campa is a collection of tales from the Spanish exploration to the twentieth century.

Mexican American folk songs are presented by Mary R. Van Stone in her *Spanish Folk Songs of the Southwest.* Folk art in New Mexico is treated in Jose E. Espinosa's *Saints in the Valleys: Christian Sacred Images in the History, Life, and Folk Art of Spanish New Mexico* and Robert L. Shalkop's *Wooden Saints: The Santos of New Mexico.* Folk medicine of the Chicano is discussed in Ari Kiev's *Curanderismo: Mexican-American Folk Psychiatry.* A less empirical approach is taken by Wilson M. Hudson's *The Healer of Los Olmos and Other Mexican Lore.*

The relationship between the Chicano and media, especially television, is examined in two useful works. Wes Marshall and others have compiled *Fiesta: Minority Television Programming,* a kind of how-to manual. A more scholarly treatment of the impact of the media on the Mexican American is *The Uses of the Media by the Chicano Movement: A Study in Minority Access* by Francisco J. Lewels, Jr.

In the area of women's studies, Chicanas have begun to scrutinize their role as feminists. Martha P. Cotera's *Diosa y Hembra: The History and Heritage of Chicanas in the U.S.* and *The Chicana Feminist,* a series of essays and public presentations prepared for Chicana feminist activities from 1970 to 1977, are important, as is Mirta Vidal's *Chicanas Speak Out. Women: New Voice of La Raza.*

BLACKS

Because so much has been written about the black experience in America, little more than a brief introduction to the material is possible in a short space. I shall try to indicate here some of the standard sources and treatments as well as new directions. John Hope Franklin's *From Slavery to Freedom: A History of Negro Americans* is a good beginning history. The essays *On Being Negro in America* by J. Saunders Redding, an important black writer, gives a distinctive view of the black position, especially when paired with the views of other black spokesmen. Malcolm Little addresses one side of the black power issue in *Malcolm X Speaks: Selected Speeches and Statements;* as does Stokely Carmichael in *Black Power: The Politics of Liberation in America,* written with Charles V. Hamilton; Martin Luther King, Jr. in *Stride Toward Freedom: The Montgomery Story;* and James

Baldwin in his influential essays in *Notes of a Native Son, Nobody Knows My Name,* and *The Fire Next Time.*

For a look at first-hand accounts of life under slavery, the reader should go to the *Narrative of the Life of Frederick Douglass, an American Slave* first printed in 1845. Good collections of slave narratives are Gilbert Osofsky's *Puttin' On Ole Massa* and Arna Bontemps's *Great Slave Narratives,* which includes accounts of the exploits of Gustavus Vassa (Oladah Equiano), James W. C. Pennington, and William and Ellen Craft. For historical background of this period, the reader may consult Benjamin Quarles's *Black Abolitionists.*

Whites stereotypes of blacks have often been based as much on fear as on guilt or ignorance. One example of the extremes of this stereotyping is Thomas Dixon's *The Clansman: An Historical Romance of the Ku Klux Klan,* a novel of the cult of racism which served as the basis for D. W. Griffith's film *Birth of a Nation* in 1916. Harriet Beecher Stowe's *Uncle Tom's Cabin* created stereotypes biased toward the sentimental, whereas John Pendleton Kennedy's *Swallow Barn, or A Sojourn in the Old Dominion,* also sentimental, defends the plantation system rather than attacking it. For a more extensive treatment of this topic, see Seymour L. Gross's and John Edward Hardy's *Images of the Negro in American Literature,* an anthology of essays that illustrate the passage of the black from stereotype in early American literature to archetype in the works of Ralph Ellison, Richard Wright, and James Baldwin.

Several factual studies of the process of stereotyping give useful background to the study of texts such as those above. Roger Abraham's *Positively Black* uses folk evidence to refute stereotypes of blacks held by whites. Dennis Wepman and others examine *The Life, the Lore and Folk Poetry of the Black Hustler* and *Tally's Corner* by Elliot Liebow is, as its subtitle indicates, *A Study of Negro Streetcorner Men.*

While academics have been studying the bases of prejudice and stereotyping, black writers have been reacting against it. A representative black poet of protest would be Don L. Lee in *Black Pride, Don't Cry! Scream!,* and *Think Black,* all published by the black publishing house, Broadside Press. *The Dutchman,* a play by Imamu Amiri Baraka (LeRoi Jones), looks closely at black and white stereotypes and the results of interaction between black and white. Eldridge Cleaver's autobiographical *Soul on Ice* presents a vision of the white and black worlds through the eyes of a young black in prison.

Black folklore has also received quite a bit of attention. Arna Bontemps's and Langston Hughes's *The Book of Negro Folklore* is a valuable introduction and comprehensive collection of the black contribution to American folklore. *American Negro Folklore* by John Mason Brewer samples animal, ghost, cowboy, and religious tales from both the North and the South. Bruce Jackson's more specialized *The Negro and His Folklore in Nineteenth Century Periodicals* is an anthology of articles and letters published between 1883 and 1900, reflecting the points of view of slaveholders as well as abolitionists. Daryl Cumber Dance's *Shuckin' and Jivin': Folklore from Contemporary Black Americans* contains over 550 humorous folktales, anecdotes, songs, toasts, and maxims collected from a wide cross-section of the black community. Finally, a book with no parallel in American folklore compilations is Harry Middleton Hyatt's *Hoodoo, Conjuration, Witchcraft, Rootwork,* a two-volume collection of material on cures, potions, charms, and witchcraft practiced by black doctors.

One of the larger contributions of the black to the shaping of mainstream culture is his music. *The Negro and His Music* by Alain Locke is a classic history of black American music from Colonial times to the 1930s. Hildred Roach's *Black American Music: Past and Present* is a more current treatment of the subject which includes a list of composers and publishers and a list of repositories. *Music: Black, White, and Blue: A Sociological Survey of the Use and Misuse of Afro-American Music* by Ortiz M. Walton not only attempts to place black music within the general framework of American society but also includes an interesting appendix listing black musicians and their white imitators. Imamu Amiri Baraka (LeRoi Jones) discusses the sociological implications of black music within the context of American cultural history in *Blues People: Negro Music in White America.*

For individual books on the various aspects of black music Harold Courlander's *Negro Folk Music, U.S.A.* is a readable overview of African folk elements in black music. Miles M. Fisher's *Negro Slave Songs in the United States* studies the origins of melodies and their meaning to, as well as effect on, the lives of slaves. *The Book of Negro American Spirituals* compiled by James Weldon Johnson and J. Rosamond Johnson is a comprehensive collection of spirituals originally published in two volumes in 1925 but later reissued in one volume. Hans Nathan's *Dan Emmett and the Rise of Early Negro Minstrels* is useful, as is Rudi Blesh's and Harriet Janis's popular history of ragtime and its musicians from 1890 to 1920, *They All Played Ragtime: The True Story of an American Music. The Bluesmen: The Story of the Music and the Men Who Made the Blues* by Samuel B. Charters examines the music originating in the Delta and Texas up to World War II, and *The Story of the Original Dixieland Jazz Band* by Harry O. Brunn discusses the transition from Dixieland to jazz

Jazz is viewed by many critics as the most influential form of black music. Examples of its influence range from Langston Hughes's *Ask Your Mama: 12 Moods for Jazz,* poetry with the patterns of jazz music, to Baraka's *Black Music,* a collection of articles, reviews, and album notes written between 1959 and 1967 on leading jazz artists such as Sonny Rollins, John

Coltrane, and Ornette Coleman, and Frank Kofsky's impassioned discussion of the importance of jazz in *Black Nationalism and the Revolution in Music.* A trio of books on more recent black musical trends are Arnold Shaw's *The World of Soul: The Black Contribution to Pop Music,* Lawrence N. Reed's *Rock Is Rhythm and Blues: The Impact of Mass Media,* and David Morse's *Motown and the Arrival of Black Music.*

For a comprehensive study of black dance forms that traces the origins and describes their social meanings one may consult Lynne Fauley Emery's *Black Dance in the United States from 1619 to 1970.* Marshall Stearns's and Jean Stearns's *Jazz Dance: The Story of American Vernacular Dance* examines more popular dance forms such as the lindy and the jitterbug.

Representations of the black man in art have been created since their arrival on the shores of North America. For early visions see Elwood Parry's *The Image of the Indian and the Black Man in American Art, 1590-1900.* Of perhaps more current interest are the numerous treatments of blacks in films. Edward Mapp's *Blacks in American Films: Today and Yesterday* surveys the portrayal of the Negro as a major character in recent American films ending with *Shaft* (1971). Henry T. Sampson's *Blacks in Black and White: A Source Book on Black Films* contains information on films with an all-black cast independently produced between 1910 and 1950. In addition to an historic overview, synopses of some films and a list of films viewed during the above years are also included. See also Lindsay Patterson's *Black Films and Film-Makers: A Comprehensive Anthology from Stereotype to Superhero,* Donald Bogle's *Toms, Coons, Mulattoes, Mammies and Bucks,* and Gary Null's *Black Hollywood: The Negro in Motion Pictures.*

NOTES

1. Vine Deloria, Jr., *We Talk, You Listen: New Tribes, New Turf* (New York: Macmillan, 1970), p. 33.

BIBLIOGRAPHY

INDIANS

Andrews, Ralph W. *Indian Leaders Who Helped Shape America, 1620-1900.* Seattle, Wash.: Superior, 1970.

Armstrong, Virginia Irving, and Frederick W. Turner, III. *I Have Spoken: American History Through the Voices of the Indians.* Chicago: Sage, 1971, Reprint. New York: Pocket Books, 1972.

Bedford, Denton R. *Tsali.* San Francisco: Indian Historian Press, 1972.

Berger, Thomas. *Little Big Man.* New York: Dial, 1964. Reprint. Geneva: Edito Service, 1974.

Bierhorst, John. *The Red Swan: Myths and Tales of the American Indians.* New York: Farrar, Straus and Giroux, 1976.

Blue Cloud, Peter. *Alcatraz Is Not an Island.* Berkeley, Calif.: Wingbow Press, 1972.
Brown, Dee. *Bury My Heart at Wounded Knee: An Indian History of the American West.* New York: Holt, Rinehart and Winston, 1970.
Cash, Joseph H., and Herbert T. Hoover. *To Be an Indian: An Oral History.* New York: Holt, Rinehart, and Winston, 1971.
Catlin, George. *Letters and Notes on the Manners, Customs, and Condition of the North American Indians.* London: Author, 1841. Reprint. New York: Dover, 1970.
Custer, George A. *My Life on the Plains, or Personal Experiences with the Indians.* New York: Sheldon, 1881. Reprint. Norman: University of Oklahoma Press, 1968.
Deloria, Vine; Jr. *Behind the Trail of Broken Treaties.* New York: Delta, 1974.
______. *Custer Died for Your Sins: An Indian Manifesto.* New York: Macmillan, 1969.
______. *God is Red.* New York: Grosset and Dunlap, 1973.
______. *Of Utmost Good Faith.* San Francisco: Straight Arrow Press, 1971.
______. *We Talk, You Listen: New Tribes, New Turf.* New York: Macmillan, 1970.
Densmore, Frances. *American Indians and Their Music.* New York: Woman's Press, 1926. Reprint. New York: Johnson, 1970.
______. *Chippewa Music.* Washington, D.C.: U.S. Government Printing Office, 1910-1913. Reprint. 2 vols. New York: Plenum, 1971.
______. *Choctaw Music.* Washington, D.C.: U.S. Government Printing Office, 1943. Reprint. New York: Plenum, 1972.
______. *Mandan and Hidatsa Music.* Washington D.C.: U.S. Government Printing Office, 1923. Reprint. New York: Plenum, 1972.
______. *Menominee Music.* Washington, D.C.: U.S. Government Printing Office, 1932. Reprint. New York: Plenum, 1972.
______. *Music of Acoma, Isleta, Cochiti, and Zuni Pueblos.* Washington, D.C.: U.S. Government Printing Office, 1957. Reprint. New York: Plenum, 1972.
______. *Music of the Indians of British Columbia.* Washington, D.C.: U.S. Government Printing Office, 1943. Reprint. New York: Plenum, 1972.
______. *Nootka and Quileute Music.* Washington, D.C.: U.S. Government Printing Office, 1939. Reprint. New York: Plenum, 1972.
______. *Northern Ute Music.* Washington, D.C.: U.S. Government Printing Office, 1922. Reprint. New York: Plenum, 1972.
______. *Papago Music.* Washington, D.C.: U.S. Government Printing Office, 1929. Reprint. New York: Plenum, 1972.
______. *Pawnee Music.* Washington, D.C.: U.S. Government Printing Office, 1929. Reprint. New York: Plenum, 1972.
______. *Seminole Music.* Washington, D.C.: U.S. Government Printing Office, 1956. Reprint. New York: Plenum, 1972.
______. *The Study of Indian Music.* Washington D.C.: Smithsonian Institution, 1941. Reprint. Seattle, Washington: Shorey, 1970.
______. *Teton Sioux Music.* Washington, D.C.: U.S. Government Printing Ofice, 1918. Reprint. New York: Plenum, 1972.
______. *Yuman and Yaqui Music.* Washington, D.C.: U.S. Government Printing Office, 1932. Reprint. New York: Plenum, 1972.
Dockstader, Frederick J. *Indian Art in America: The Arts and Crafts of the North American Indian.* Greenwich, Conn.: New York Graphic Society, 1966.
______. *Weaving Arts of the North American Indian.* New York: Crowell, 1978.

Fisher, Dexter, ed. *The Third Woman: Minority Women Writers of the United States.* Boston: Houghton Mifflin, 1980.

Fletcher, Alice C. *Indian Story and Song from North America.* Boston: Small, Maynard, 1900. Reprint. New York: AMS Press, 1970.

Haywood, Charles. *Bibliography of North American Folklore and Folksong.* New York: Dover, 1961.

Hirschfelder, Arlene B. *American Indian and Eskimo Authors: A Comprehensive Bibliography.* New York: Association on American Indian Affairs, 1973.

———. *American Indian Authors.* New York: Association on American Indian Affairs, 1970.

Josephy, Alvin M. *Red Power: The American Indians' Fight for Freedom.* New York: McGraw-Hill, 1970.

Katz, Jane B., ed. *I Am the Fire of Time: The Voices of Native American Women.* New York: Dutton, 1977.

Keiser, Albert. *The Indian in American Literature.* New York: Oxford University Press, 1933. Reprint. New York: Octagon, 1970.

LaFarge, Oliver. *Laughing Boy.* Boston: Houghton Mifflin, 1929. Reprinted. New York: New American Library, 1971.

Miller, Wayne Charles et al. *A Comprehensive Bibliography for the Study of American Minorities.* 2 vols. New York: New York University Press, 1976.

Momaday, N. Scott. *House Made of Dawn.* New York: Harper & Row, 1969.

Office of Indian Affairs. *Biographical and Historical Index of American Indians and Persons Involved in Indian Affairs.* Boston: Hall, 1965.

Parry, Elwood. *The Image of the Indian and the Black Man in American Art, 1500-1900.* New York: Braziller, 1974.

Rothenberg, Jerome. *Shaking the Pumpkin: Traditional Poetry of the Indian North Americas.* Garden City, N.Y.: Doubleday, 1972.

Silko, Leslie Marmon. *Ceremony.* New York: Viking, 1977.

Stoutenburgh, John. *Dictionary of the American Indian.* New York: Philosophical Library, 1960.

Tebbel, John, and Keith Jennison. *The American Indian Wars.* New York: Harper, 1960.

Thompson, Stith. *Tales of the North American Indians.* Cambridge; Harvard University Press, 1929. Reprinted. Bloomington: Indiana University Press, 1966.

Walters, Frank. *The Man Who Killed the Deer.* New York: Farrar and Rinehart, 1942. Reprinted. Chicago: Swallow, 1969.

———. *People of the Valley.* New York: Farrar and Rinehart, 1941. Reprinted. Chicago: Swallow, 1971.

Weiner, Michael. *Earth Medicine—Earth Foods: Plant Remedies, Drugs and Natural Foods of the North American Indians.* New York: Macmillan, 1972.

Welch, James. *Winter in the Blood.* New York: Harper & Row, 1974.

CHICANOS

Acuña, Rudolph. *Occupied America: The Chicano's Struggle Toward Liberation.* San Francisco: Canfield Press, 1972.

Alexander, Charles C. *The Ku Klux Klan in the Southwest.* Lexington: University of Kentucky Press, 1965.
Alianza Federal. *The Spanish Land Grant Question Examined.* Albuquerque, N.M.: Alianza Federal, 1966. Reprint New York: Arno Press, 1974.
Ballis, George. *Basta!* Delano, Cal.: Farm Workers Press, 1966.
Blawis, Patricia Bell. *Tijerina and the Land Grants: Mexican Americans in Struggle for Their Heritage.* New York: International, 1971.
Boatright, Mody C. *Mexican Border Ballads and Other Lore.* Dallas, Tex.: Southern Methodist University Press, 1967.
Campa, Arthur L. *Treasure of the Sangre de Cristos: Tales and Traditions of the Spanish Southwest.* Norman: University of Oklahoma Press, 1963.
Cotera, Martha P. *The Chicana Feminist.* Austin, Tex.: Information Systems Development, 1977.
———. *Diosa y hembra: The History and Heritage of Chicanas in the U. S.* Austin, Tex.: Information Systems Development, 1976.
Day, Mark. *Forty Acres: Cesar Chavez and the Farm Workers.* New York: Praeger, 1971.
Dobie, J. Frank. *Puro Mexico.* Austin: Texas Folklore Society, 1935.
———. *Southwestern Lore.* Dallas, Tex.: Southern Methodist University Press, 1965.
Duran, Livie, and H. Russell Bernard, eds. *Introduction to Chicano Studies: A Reader.* New York: Macmaillan, 1973.
Eger, Ernestina. "Bibliographical Notes." *Carta Abierta,* No. 10/11 (June 1978), 2-4. A regular column in subsequent issues.
Espinosa, Jose E. *Saints in the Valleys: Christian Sacred Images in the History, Life, and Folk Art of Spanish New Mexico.* Rev. ed. Albuquerque: University of New Mexico Press, 1967.
Forbes, Jack D. *Aztecas del Norte: The Chicanos of Aztlan.* Greenwich, Conn.: Fawcett, 1973.
Gonzalez, Rudolfo. *I Am Joaquin: An Epic Poem.* New York: Bantam Books, 1973.
Grebler, Leo, Joan W. Moore, and Ralph C. Guzman. *The Mexican American People: The Nation's Second Largest Minority.* New York: Free Press, 1970.
Hudson, Wilson M., ed. *The Healer of Los Olmos and Other Mexican Lore.* Dallas, Tex.: Southern Methodist University Press, 1951.
Kiev, Ari. *Curanderismo: Mexican-American Folk Psychiatry.* New York: Free Press, 1968.
Lewels, Francisco J., Jr. *The Uses of the Media by the Chicano Movement: A Study in Minority Access.* New York: Praeger, 1974.
Marshall, Wes, et al. *Fiesta: Minority Television Programming.* Tucson: University of Arizona Press, 1974.
Martinez, Julio A. *Chicano Scholars and Writers: A Bio-Bibliographical Directory.* Metuchen, N.J.: Scarecrow Press, 1979.
Nabokov, Peter. *Tijerina and the Courthouse Raid.* Albuquerque: University of New Mexico Press, 1969.
Nelson, Eugene. *Huelga: The First Hundred Days of the Great Delano Grape Strike.* Delano, Cal.: Farm Workers Press, 1966.
Paredes, Américo. *"With His Pistol in His Hand"—A Border Ballad and Its Hero.* Austin: University of Texas Press, 1958.

Paz, Octavio. *The Labyrinth of Solitude: Life and Thought in Mexico.* Translated by Lysander Kemp. New York: Grove Press, 1961.
Rendon, Armando B. *Chicano Manifesto.* New York: Macmillan, 1971.
Robinson, Cecil. *Mexico and the Hispanic Southwest in American Literature.* Tucson: Univerity of Arizona Press, 1977.
Samora, Julian. *Gunpowder Justice: A Reassessment of the Texas Rangers.* Notre Dame, Ind.: University of Notre Dame Press, 1979.
———. *Los Mojados: The Wetback Story.* Notre Dame, Ind.: University of Notre Dame Press, 1971.
Shalkop, Robert L. *Wooden Saints: The Santos of New Mexico.* Feldafing: Buchaim Verlag, 1967.
Shockley, John Staples. *Chicano Revolt in a Texas Town.* Notre Dame, Ind.: University of Notre Dame Press, 1974.
Simmen, Edward. *The Chicano: From Caricature to Self-Portrait.* New York: New American Library, 1971.
Stoddard, Theodore Lothrup. *The Rising Tide of Color.* New York: Scribner's, 1921.
Trejo, Arnulfo D. *Bibliografia Chicana: A Guide to Information Sources,* Detroit, Mich.: Gale Research, 1975.
Van Stone, Mary R. *Spanish Folk Songs of the Southwest.* Sausalito, Cal.: Academy Guild Press, 1963.
Vidal, Mirta. *Chicanas Speak Out. Women: New Voice of La Raza.* New York: Pathfinder Press, 1971.
Webb, Walter Prescott. *The Texas Rangers.* Austin: University of Texas Press, 1965.
Zermeno, Andy. *Don Sotaco.* Delano, Cal.: Farm Workers Press, 1966.

BLACKS

Abraham, Roger. *Positively Black.* Englewood Cliffs, N.J.: Prentice-Hall, 1970.
Baldwin, James. *The Fire Next Time.* New York: Dial, 1963.
———. *Nobody Knows My Name.* New York: Dial, 1961.
———. *Notes of a Native Son.* Boston: Beacon Press, 1955.
Baraka, Imamu Amiri (LeRoi Jones). *Black Music.* New York: Morrow, 1969.
———. *Blues People: Negro Music in White America.* New York: Morrow, 1963.
———. *The Dutchman.* New York: Morrow, 1964.
Blesh, Rudi, and Harriet Janis. *They All Played Ragtime: The True Story of an American Music.* New York: Knopf, 1950. Reprint. New York: Grove Press, 1959
Bogle, Donald. *Toms, Coons, Mulattoes, Mammies and Bucks.* New York: Bantam, 1974.
Bontemps, Arna. *Great Slave Narratives.* New York: Macmillan, 1969.
———, and Langston Hughes. *The Book of Negro Folklore.* New York: Dodd, Mead, 1958.
Brewer, John Mason. *American Negro Folklore.* Chicago: Quadrangle, 1968.
Brunn, Harry O. *The Story of the Original Dixieland Jazz Band.* Baton Rouge: Louisiana State University Press, 1960.
Carmichael, Stokely, and Charles V. Hamilton. *Black Power: The Politics of Liberation in America.* New York: Random House, 1967

Charters, Samuel B. *The Bluesmen: The Story of the Music and the Men Who Made the Blues.* New York: Oak, 1967.

Cleaver, Eldridge. *Soul on Ice.* New York: McGraw-Hill, 1968.

Courlander, Harold. *Negro Folk Music, U.S.A.* New York: Columbia University Press, 1963.

Dance, Daryl Cumber. *Shuckin' and Jivin': Folklore from Contemporary Black Americans.* Bloomington: Indiana University Press, 1978.

Dixon, Thomas. *The Clansman: An Historical Romance of the Ku Klux Klan.* New York: Grosset and Dunlap, 1905.

Douglass, Frederick. *Narrative of the Life of Frederick Douglass, an American Slave.* Boston: Published at the Anti-slavery office, 1845: Reprint. Cambridge; Harvard University Press, 1960.

Editors of Ebony. *The Ebony Success Library.* 3 vols. Chicago: Johnson, 1973.

Emery, Lynne Fauley. *Black Dance in the United States from 1619 to 1970.* Palo Alto, Calif.: National Press Books, 1972.

Fisher, Miles M. *Negro Slave Songs in the United States.* New York: Citadel, 1963.

Franklin, John Hope. *From Slavery to Freedom: A History of Negro Americans.* New York: Knopf, 1967.

Glenn, Robert W. *Black Rhetoric: A Guide to Afro-American Communication.* Metuchen, N.J.: Scarecrow Press, 1976.

Gross, Seymour L., and John Edward Hardy. *Images of the Negro in American Literature.* Chicago: University of Chicago Press, 1966.

Hughes, Langston. *Ask Your Mama: 12 Moods for Jazz* New York: Knopf, 1961.

Hyatt, Harry Middleton. *Hoodoo, Conjuration, Witchcraft, Rootwork.* Washington, D.C.: American University Press, 1970.

Jackson, Bruce. *The Negro and His Folklore in Nineteenth Century Periodicals.* Austin: University of Texas Press, 1967.

Johnson, James Weldon, and J. Rosamond Johnson. *The Book of Negro American Spirtuals.* New York: Viking, 1925, 1926. Reprint. New York: Viking, 1969.

Kennedy, John Pendleton. *Swallow Barn, or A Sojourn in the Old Dominion.* Philadelphia: Carey & Lea, 1832. Reprint. New York: Hafner, 1971.

King, Martin Luther, Jr. *Stride Toward Freedom: The Montgomery Story.* New York: Harper, 1958.

Klotman, Phyllis Rauch. *Frame by Frame: A Black Filmography.* Bloomington: Indiana University Press, 1979.

Kofsky, Frank. *Black Nationalism and the Revolution in Music.* New York: Pathfinder Press, 1970.

Lee, Don L. *Black Pride.* Detroit, Mich.: Broadside, 1968.

______. *Don't Cry! Scream!* Detroit, Mich.: Broadside, 1969.

______. *Think Black.* Detroit, Mich.: Broadside, 1968.

Liebow, Elliot. *Tally's Corner: A Study of Negro Streetcorner Men.* Boston: Little Brown, 1967.

Little, Malcolm. *Malcolm X Speaks: Selected Speeches and Statements.* New York: Grove Press, 1966.

Locke, Alain. *The Negro and His Music.* Washington, D.C.: Associates in Negro Folk Education, 1936.

Mapp, Edward. *Blacks in American Films: Today and Yesterday.* Metuchen, N.J.: Scarecrow Press, 1972.

Morse, David. *Motown and the Arrival of Black Music.* London: Studio Vista, 1971.

Nathan, Hans. *Dan Emmett and the Rise of Early Negro Minstrels.* Norman: University of Oklahoma Press, 1962.

Null, Gary. *Black Hollywood: The Negro in Motion Pictures.* New York: Citadel Press, 1977.

Osofsky, Gilbert. *Puttin' On Ole Massa.* New York: Harper & Row, 1969.

Page, James A. *Selected Black American Authors: An Illustrated Bio-Bibliography.* Boston: G. K. Hall, 1970.

Parry, Elwood. *The Image of the Indian and the Black Man in American Art, 1590-1900.* New York: Braziller, 1974.

Patterson, Lindsay. *Black Films and Film-Makers: A Comprehensive Anthology from Stereotype to Superhero.* New York: Dodd, 1975.

Ploski, Harry A., and Warren Marr. *The Negro Almanac: A Reference Work on the Afro American.* New York: Bellwether, 1976.

Powers, Anne. *Blacks in American Movies: A Selected Bibliography.* Metuchen, N.J.: Scarecrow Press, 1974.

Quarles, Benjamin. *Black Abolitionists.* New York: Oxford University Press, 1969

Redding, J. Saunders. *On Being Negro in America.* Indianapolis: Bobbs, Merrill, 1951.

Reed, Lawrence N. *Rock Is Rhythm and Blues: The Impact of Mass Media.* East Lansing: Michigan State University Press, 1974.

Roach, Hildred. *Black American Music: Past and Present.* Boston: Crescendo, 1973.

Sampson, Henry T. *Blacks in Black and White: A Source Book on Black Films.* Metuchen, N.J.: Scarecrow Press, 1977.

Shaw, Arnold. *The World of Soul: The Black Contribution to Pop Music.* New York: Cowles, 1970.

Shockley, Ann Allen, and Sue P. Chandler. *Living Black American Authors.* New York: Bowker, 1973.

Southgate, Robert L. *Black Plots and Black Characters: A Handbook for Afro-American Literature.* Syracuse, N.Y.: Gaylord Professional, 1979.

Stearns, Marshall, and Jean Stearns. *Jazz Dance: The Story of American Vernacular Dance.* New York: Macmillan, 1968.

Stowe, Harriet Beecher. *Uncle Tom's Cabin.* Boston: John P. Jewett, 1852.

Walton, Ortiz M. *Music: Black, White and Blue: A Sociological Survey of the Use and Misuse of Afro-American Music.* New York: Morrow, 1972.

Wepman, Dennis, et al. *The Life, the Lore and Folk Poetry of the Black Hustler.* Philadelphia: University of Pennsylvania Press, 1976.

CHAPTER 10 Newspapers

Richard A. Schwarzlose

Few areas of mass communication are as overdue for popular culture study as is its "serious" side—newspapers. Broadcasting and magazines have attracted much examination as cultural media, and some newspaper features—notably advertising, editorial cartoons, comic strips, and photographs, all treated in separate essays in this *Handbook*—are beginning to undergo cultural examination.

But newspapers' historic news and opinion functions continue for the most part to elude popular culture's gaze, both in the United States and abroad. Perhaps newspapers' gray seriousness or their occasional flights into distasteful sensationalism dissuade popular culture students. Or perhaps newspapers' seemingly endless parade of formulaic short paragraphs and standardized simple writing style turn culturists to more lively fare. Whatever the reason, the researcher is too easily averted.

The American newspaper as continuous reporter of fact and thought to a generally receptive reading audience presents over time a diverse panorama of news-gathering, news-writing, and news-packaging styles. On any one day the newspaper is a community's vehicle for talking to itself about its problems and solutions, its momentary fascinations and foibles, its calamities and conquests. An unmatched yardstick of society's preoccupations and perspectives, the American newspaper has been a constant presence in the nation's life since 1704. Growing faster than population throughout the nineteenth century, both total newspapers and dailies peaked in the first decade of this century at about 18,500 and 2,600 respectively.

As a force in society, newspapers have from their Colonial beginnings attracted and reflected America's political and economic elites; and since about 1870 newspapers have made themselves a necessary part of the average citizen's daily life. Even today, when television is the public's most frequent source of news, opinion polls show that the public still regards the newspaper as a reliable source of news.

Metropolitan dailies can acquire the national prestige of influential, well-staffed, aggressive, investigative journals. The hundreds of papers in medium-sized and small communities throughout the nation, meanwhile, serve as powerful local economic forces, records of local happenings, eyes on the outside world, and a community's tangible identity. It is no less true today than it was in 1835, when Alexis de Tocqueville marveled that "in America there is scarcely a hamlet that has not its newspaper."[1] That vital link between newspaper and community, editorialist and local problem, beat reporter and breaking news event, editor and letters-to-the-editor contributor places the newspaper at the heart of society's affairs, both a mirror of events and values and a catalyst for social change. But the newspaper camouflages its cultural message behind layers of crude, blaring headlines and columns of impenetrable gray body type. It will take an extra measure of patience and cleverness to unlock this mass-produced industrial fortress and break the code of "journalese," but the researcher with such stamina will discover a lush virgin territory.

HISTORIC OUTLINE

As in all significant Colonial matters, the development of the American newspaper closely followed the English prototype in form and content. The printing press had been introduced in England in about 1476 by William Caxton, having made its Continental debut roughly two decades earlier. Although the English monarchs encouraged the early growth of the printing trade, printers and their products needed prior royal approval to escape possible prosecution.

Amsterdam printers, therefore, turned out for British importation English-language pamphlets and books that could not be safely printed in England. Thus, the first English-language news sheet, called a coranto or collection of foreign news items, was published in Amsterdam in December 1620. Seven months later, however, corantos of foreign news were issuing from London printing houses with impunity. It took two more decades and the abolition of the Star Chamber, however, for British printers to attempt domestic news reporting. The first diurnal—the domestic version of coranto—appeared in November 1641, carrying parliamentary proceedings. It was shortly followed by a flood of competing diurnals when it became evident that the authorities would not retaliate. The single-sheet coranto of 1621 gave way within a year to news books of from eight to forty pages, a format utilized by corantos and diurnals until England's first full-fledged newspaper in familiar newspaper format, the Oxford/London *Gazette*, appeared as a semi-weekly in 1665. The term *newspaper* was in common use in 1670. By 1682, with Parliament repeatedly ignoring opportunities to regulate printing, twenty newspapers had appeared. England's first daily newspaper, the London *Daily Courant*, made its appearance on March 11, 1702.

The American Colonies' schedule of newspaper development, while emulating England's, ran between forty years and nearly a century behind the mother country's. The first Colonial press arrived in Cambridge, Massachusetts, in 1638, and after 1654 was associated with Harvard College. The next press appeared in Philadelphia in 1685.

The ill-fated *Publick Occurrences Both Foreign and Domestick* was the Colonies' first newspaper, published in Boston on September 25, 1690, by Benjamin Harris, who had fled England after serving a prison term for printing a seditious pamphlet. Slightly smaller than a piece of notebook paper, the three-page *Publick Occurrences* (the fourth page was blank) was suppressed by the colonial governor after one issue.

The first paper of continuous publication was the weekly Boston *News-Letter*, begun in 1704 by Boston's postmaster, John Campbell. Looking much like the London *Gazette*, the *News-Letter* carried the line "Published by Authority" in its nameplate, signifying that the colonial governor had approved its contents. This arrangement, in turn, meant that Campbell enjoyed privileged access to the colonial government and received lucrative governmental printing contracts. Many early British and Colonial American newspapers proudly displayed this label.

James Franklin, with brother Benjamin as an apprentice printer, introduced the weekly *New England Courant* in Boston on August 7, 1721, the first paper to survive without governmental ties. Indeed, the *Courant* somehow survived for six, at times stormy years, despite its occasional attacks upon the religious and political powers of Massachusetts.

In the small community setting of Colonial America the newspaper's news function was overshadowed by other, more effective, communication systems, such as pamphlets, broadsides, gossip, tavern conversation, and church and town meetings. A newspaper's significant contribution, then, was weeks' or even months' old foreign news, a smattering of news from other Colonial communities, and the editor's own essay contributions to the community's political and religious discussions. The casual, almost random, Colonial newspaper format—inconspicuous label headlines, only a few crude illustrations, very small type faces, indiscriminate mixing of stories, essays, poems, and advertisements—reflects an editorial priority based on assembling a record of available intelligence rather than on generating a lively, attractive, aggressive news report. Not a lucrative undertaking for most Colonial printers, newspapers were in most communities a financial stepsister to the much more profitable job printing trade.

Until the Revolutionary War had set the political and economic course of the new nation, no more than forty newspapers—mostly weeklies, none more frequent than triweekly—operated in the Colonies, and their growth barely kept pace with population growth. During the eighteenth century most Colonial presses, type, and even paper were imported from England.

Two hundred impressions per hour (printing on one side at a time) was considered good press work, and circulations, although difficult to verify, appear to have averaged about five hundered in the largest communities, with a few papers at times claiming more than one thousand copies.

Leading examples of pre-Revolutionary American newspapers and their founding years are: Boston *News-Letter,* 1704; Boston *Gazette,* 1719; *American Weekly Mercury,* (Philadelphia), 1719; *New England Courant,* (Boston), 1721; New York *Gazette,* 1725; *New England Weekly Journal,* (Boston), 1727; Benjamin Franklin's *Pennsylvania Gazette,* (Philadelphia), 1728; John Peter Zenger's New York *Journal,* 1733; Boston *Evening Post,* 1735; and Williamsburg *Virginia Gazette,* 1736.

Colonial newspapers are regarded as having profoundly affected and sharpened the issues confronting the Colonies and as having hastened the Revolutionary War. The growing political crisis of the late 1760s and early 1770s transformed the leisurely essaying of isolated editors into camps, in places well organized, of hot-penned propagandists. Tory papers included *Rivington's New York Gazetteer,* Boston *Chronicle,* Boston *News-Letter,* Boston *Post-Boy,* and Philadelphia *Pennsylvania Ledger.* Representative of the middle of the road, or Whigs, were the Philadelphia *Pennsylvania Chronicle,* Philadelphia *Pennsylvania Evening Post,* and Boston *Evening Post.* The Radical cause, assisted by the Committees of Correspondence (which have been called America's first wire service), found expression in Benjamin Edes's and John Gill's Boston *Gazette or Country Journal,* Isaiah Thomas's *Massachusetts Spy* (printed in Boston 1770-75 and in Worcester after 1775), John Holt's New York *Journal,* Hugh Gaine's New York *Gazette and Weekly Mercury,* and John Dunlap's Philadelphia *Pennsylvania Packet.*

The end of the Revolutionary War acted as a starter's pistol for American newspaper publishing. Two years after Yorktown, on May 30, 1783, Benjamin Towne converted his Philadelphia *Pennsylvania Evening Post* to daily publication, the first daily in the country. The *Post* was challenged by conversion to a daily of the Philadelphia *Pennsylvania Packet* on September 21, 1784, and the *Post* succumbed within a month. Meanwhile, newspapers of all frequencies of publication were appearing and surviving throughout the young nation at a rate faster than population growth, a trend which continued throughout the nineteenth century. Between 1780 and 1790 total newspapers jumped from 39 to 92, the latter figure including eight dailies. In 1800 there were 235 newspapers, 24 of which were dailies; in 1850 total newspapers was 2,302, 254 of which were dailies; and in 1900 total newspapers was 18,487, 2,190 of which were dailies.

But while the Revolution's outcome provided a stable institutional setting for newspaper growth, the long-standing war of words between the English Whigs and French democrats over the nation's future course persisted and hardened into party labels. In response, the entire generation of post-

Revolutionary newspapers became known for its own division into political camps.

This party press movement emerged with Washington's first administration; dominated newspapering until the 1830s or 1840s, and remained in evidence until the end of the Civil War. Although frowned upon today as violating a perceived adversarial relationship between press and government, newspaper's ties with government during the party press period then seemed perfectly appropriate, indeed vital to the interests of both fledgling institutions. Throughout the republic stretched a network of newspapers committed to the cause of the Federalists, Whigs, and Republicans, and a counternetwork dedicated to the Anti-Federalists, Democratic-Republicans, and Democrats.

In addition to editorializing and slanting news in favor of the affiliate party, newspapers participated with government in three distinct activities. First, the editor whose man was mayor, governor, or president was that official's mouthpiece, serving in most cases as the public's only avenue to the thinking and policies of that administration. Second, the editor whose party controlled the city council, state legislature, or Congress was likely to be the preferred reporter of legislative proceedings, at times (in the case of Congress, for example) generating through his newspaper's columns the official record of proceedings. Third, select newspapers throughout the nation regularly published laws, orders, and resolutions of Congress. Totaling between forty and eighty, these papers were selected by the State Department, and their selection generally depended on their allegiance to the presidential administration.

John Fenno's *Gazette of the United States* was the first of a series of presidential organs that continued until Abraham Lincoln in 1861 declined to anoint a newspaper editor as his mouthpiece, preferring instead to rely on the Associated Press—which had no apparent political leaning. Administrations and their official organs were as follows: Washington and John Adams, *Gazette of the United States* (which began in New York City and followed the government to Philadelphia in 1790); Jefferson, Madison, and Monroe, *National Intelligencer* (Washington, D.C.); John Quincy Adams, *National Journal* (Washington, D.C.); Jackson, *United States Telegraph* (Washington, D.C.); 1829-31, and Washington, D.C. *Globe,* 1831-37; Van Buren, Washington, D.C. *Globe;* Harrison, *National Intelligencer* (Washington, D.C.); Tyler, *Madisonian* (Washington, D.C.); Polk, Washington, D.C. *Union;* Taylor, Washington, D.C. *Republic;* Fillmore, *National Intelligencer* (Washington, D.C.); Pierce and Buchanan, Washington, D.C. *Union* (which changed its name to *Constitution* on April 13, 1859).

Exuberant and vitriolic, the party press warred ceaselessly with every type of literary artillery against anyone who opposed the home party, the favored policy, or the fair-haired politician. Early examples of the Federalist-Whig brand of newspapers and their founding years are Fenno's *Gazette of the United States* (New York and Philadelphia), 1789; Benjamin Russell's Boston *Massachusetts* (later *Columbian) Centinel,* 1784; Noah Webster's *American Minerva* (New York), 1793; William Cobbett's *Porcupine's Gazette* (Philadelphia), 1797; and the New York *Evening Post* 1801, founded with the assistance of Alexander Hamilton. Those of the Jeffersonian persuasion are Philip Freneau's *National Gazette* (Philadelphia), 1791; Thomas and Abijah Adams' Boston *Independent Chronicle* (a converted pre-Revolutionary paper); Benjamin Franklin Bache's and William Duane's Philadelphia *General Advertiser* (also called the *Aurora),* 1790; and Samuel Harrison Smith's *National Intelligencer* (Washington, D.C.), 1801. A later Whig paper is James Watson Webb's New York *Courier* and *Enquirer,* merged by Webb in 1829, and a later Democratic paper is Francis Blair's Washington, D.C. *Globe* founded in 1830.

Another type of ideological newspaper appearing during the party press period focused on the Southern slavery question and the plight of Northern blacks. The leading abolitionist voice was William Lloyd Garrison's *Liberator* (Boston), published from 1831 to 1865. Significant among the early black-owned or operated papers, and their periods of existence, are John B. Russwurm's and Samuel Cornish's *Freedom's Journal* (New York), the first black paper, 1827-29; *The Colored American* (New York), 1837-41; *The Ram's Horn* (New York), 1847-48; and Frederick Douglass's *The North Star* (Rochester, N.Y.), renamed *Frederick Douglass' Paper* in 1851, 1847-60.

A much smaller group of papers publishing concurrently with the party or ideological press was the mercantile press, found primarily in large cities and dedicated to factual reporting of business, financial, and shipping news of importance to the business community. The New York *Journal of Commerce,* founded in 1827 by Arthur Tappan but made successful by Gerard Hallock and David Hale, is a prime example of the mercantile press.

Until the 1830s and 1840s newspapers were read almost exclusively by the political or economic elites in America. In the absence of public education, a large middle class, and the technology to produce large quantities of newspapers, editors were content to offer a ponderous political or meticulous mercantile newspaper to the upper classes at about six cents per copy, usually sold by long-term subscription.

In contrast, the penny press editor took advantage of steam-driven, type-revolving presses, which dramatically increased daily production of newspapers, and relied on modest increases in public education and the middle class to offer papers of somewhat wider appeal. Benjamin Day's New York *Sun,* founded in 1833, is considered the first successful penny paper and was followed in this genre by James Gordon Bennett's New York *Herald,* 1835; Horace Greeley's New York *Tribune,* 1841; and Henry J. Raymond's New York *Times,* 1851. Sold for one or two cents by street vendors, the penny press featured street and police news, sometimes embellished with sensationalism, and a variety of political, mercantile, feature, and even sporting news. They were an attempt to bridge the gap between their contemporaries' political-mercantile audience and those one step below on the social ladder. Other early penny papers were the Philadelphia *Public Ledger*, 1836, and the Baltimore *Sun*, 1837.

By the Civil War the penny paper had surpassed the party press's influence in party and governmental affairs and had outreached the mercantile press in gathering and factually presenting news. Their coverage of the Civil War was aggressive and vivid.

The middle third of the nineteenth century saw newspapers attain what is probably their most diverse, interesting, and personal news report. In contrast to newspapering's earlier leadership of propagandists, party workers, and made-over printers, some true writers and thinkers and a few sharp-witted newspaper managers began to populate the news room after the 1830s, giving the news report an esprit, a genuine curiosity about ideas and men, a firmness of opinion without dogmatism, and a new zeal to pursue the news. Newspapers were adopting the more common language of the street and home within story structures that closely resembled the natural flow of events. A sense of reality as experienced daily by people in the streets crept into the news columns.

Type faces remained small, and headlines were still likely to be short labels, except when the news was smashing. Pictures were still few, and advertising still occupied much less than half of a newspaper's column space and amounted to brief business cards or announcements.

Early daily newspapers had hit the streets late in the day, but the coming of telegraphic news dispatches in the late 1840s, coupled with keen competition among newspapers, pushed publication times earlier in the day, until by the Civil War most dailies, whether penny, party or mercantile, were on the street when people went to work, using a midday or late afternoon make-over edition for late local and telegraphic news that materialized during the morning.

Before 1860 Sunday publication was commonly frowned upon as violating the sanctity of the Sabbath, but the urgency of Civil War news forced editors into the Sunday field and thus opened a publishing opportunity which in the twentieth century would become increasingly important to papers' balance sheets.

Between 1865 and 1885 newspapers slowly assumed the structure, news report, and financial support familiar to twentieth-century readers. It was a period when the leaders of the old party, mercantile, and penny press movements left the scene. Some of these papers survived either through progressive management or last-ditch salvage efforts. Notable survivers are: the Baltimore *Sun*, Chicago *Tribune*, Cleveland *Plain Dealer*, Des Moines

Register, Detroit *Free Press,* New York *Herald,* New York *Tribune,* New York *Times,* Philadelphia *Bulletin,* and Washington, D.C. *Star.* But a tidal wave of new newspapers rolled over the industry, establishing many of our twentieth-century newspaper leaders. Significant members of this new generation and their founding years are the San Francisco *Chronicle,* 1865; Minneapolis *Tribune,* 1867; Atlanta *Constitution,* 1868; Louisville *Courier-Journal,* merged in 1869; Boston *Globe,* 1872; Detroit *Evening News,* 1873; St. Louis *Globe-Democrat,* merged in 1875; Chicago *Daily News* and Dallas *Times-Herald,* 1876; Washington *Post,* 1877; Cleveland *Press* and Minneapolis *Star,* 1878; St. Louis *Post-Dispatch,* merged in 1878; Kansas City *Star,* 1880; Los Angeles *Times,* 1881; and Milwaukee *Journal,* 1882.

Another wave of new leaders, some of them reflecting a return to elitist journalism, appeared around the turn of the century: *Wall Street Journal,* (New York), 1889; Denver *Post,* 1895; Houston *Chronicle,* 1901; *Christian Science Monitor,* (Boston), 1908; and Miami *Herald,* 1910. Only a few papers that have attained national prominence have appeared in recent decades, notably the New York *Daily News,* 1919; Long Island *Newsday,* 1940; Chicago *Sun-Times,* merged in 1948, and vestiges here and there of the old Scripps-Howard and Hearst newspaper chains, the former emerging in the 1880s and the later taking shape after 1900.

Post-Civil War newspapers gradually became big business, fell in with the chamber of commerce crowd, routinized news gathering, formularized news writing, relied more heavily on advertising revenue, and accommodated greater advertising space on news pages. The period also saw the return to dominance of the evening newspaper, marked increases in circulation totals, and realization of machine typesetting and high-speed rotary presses capable of cutting and folding newspapers and printing in four colors on both sides of a continuous sheet of newsprint.

Much of the innovation in newspapering at this time is labeled by the literature as "new journalism" and attributed to Joseph Pulitzer, his St. Louis *Post-Dispatch* after 1878, and his New York *World* after 1883. In sum, "new journalism" included developing a news staff organization and formal news-gathering procedures, adopting promotional and civic improvement projects, enticing greatly expanded advertising patronage onto newspaper pages, keeping the price per paper to two or three cents, depersonalizing editorial columns and objectifying news columns, becoming preoccupied with large circulations, championing the cause of laboring classes, and making greater use of eye-catching illustrations and headlines.

This was also the period when newspaper chains first appeared and when regional and national news-gathering consortiums developed and began to influence newspapers' views of what was "acceptable" news writing. Generally a writing style developed that summarized the news event's most important features in the first few paragraphs and arranged remaining details in descending order of importance, that is the inverted pyramid story structure.

Departmentalization of the news staff, creation of beats for reporters to cover, and introduction of the telephone and typewriter in news operations began to give the news room an organized, if not assembly line, atmosphere. The news report that most newspapers sported by the turn of the century was "objective," superficially comprehensive, and impersonal—informative, yet inoffensive to readers and advertisers alike.

The industry has permitted modest occasional flexibility in that writing formula during this century, especially in some departments, but the bulk of the news report remains much the same as it was by World War I. Indeed, newspapering fought hard to ignore another "new journalism" movement in the 1960s and 1970s. This movement, led by such feature writers and authors as Tom Wolfe, Gay Talese, Norman Mailer, Joan Didion, Hunter S. Thompson, and Truman Capote, was seen by commercial newspaper people as too subjective or fictionalized to warrant newspaper play. In the same two decades, however, newspapers increasingly engaged in "interpretative" journalism, meant to explain or provide background for straight news events, and "investigative" journalism, aimed at exposing corruption and criminal behavior in high places.

Within the first decade of the twentieth century daily and total newspapers reached their full growth at about 2,600 and 18,500, respectively. Average daily circulation per newspaper in 1914 was 11,784, and total daily circulation was about 32 percent of total U.S. population. (In 1974 average daily circulation per newspaper was 34,880, and total daily circulation was 29 percent of total U.S. population.) Between 1915 and 1955 newspaper totals (in all publishing frequency categories) declined, reaching in the latter year a plateau where they have since stayed, with dailies holding at about 1,760 and total newspapers at about 11,200.

The forty-year decline was caused by newspaper oversaturation at the turn of the century which led to numerous suspensions and mergers, a stagnant typesetting and printing technology that became increasingly expensive to operate and maintain, two world wars with attendant manpower and materials shortages which brought the demise of marginal papers, and the growth of other media of mass communication that detracted from newspapers' news product and diverted some advertising revenue to the other media.

Several other newspaper trends and episodes in the past century are worthy of brief note to round out this historical outline.

Some metropolitan newspapers engaged in brief stints of extreme sensationalism. The first, so-called yellow journalism during the decade following 1896, was prompted by William Randolph Hearst's New York *Journal's* challenge to Pulitzer's New York *World.* There were some signs of yellow journalism elsewhere in the country, but New York City bore the brunt of this escapade. The second outbreak of sensationalism, the so-called jazz journalism of the 1920s and especially of the tabloids, was led by Joseph Patterson's New York *Daily News*, 1919; Hearst's New York *Mirror*, 1924; and Bernarr Macfadden's New York *Daily Graphic*, 1924.

Foreign-language newspapers had been sparsely interwoven in America's journalism fabric since Benjamin Franklin's Philadelphia *Zeitung* appeared in 1732, but the upsurge of immigrants after 1880 led to a peak of about 1,200 foreign-language newspapers (about 160 of them dailies) at the start of World War 1. Comparable foreign-language figures in 1980 are about half those totals.

Black newspapers have continued to lead marginal existences in the United States, owing apparently to insufficient advertising revenue and black readers' unwillingness to abandon white-controlled newspapers in their cities. It is estimated that in 1920 there were 492 black newspapers in the United States (none of them dailies), and that in 1970 that number had declined to 325 (two or three being dailies).

Moreover, there has been a constant din of special interest, political, life-style, and sensational newspapers in the market. Leftist and pacifist weeklies were much in evidence before each world war. Sensational weeklies, such as the *National Enquirer* and Rupert Murdoch's *Star*, seem to have scored with the grocery store crowd. And during the 1960s and early 1970s, at the height of student unrest over Vietnam and amid counter cultural pursuits, underground or alternative newspapers briefly thrived, only a few surviving as commercial or give-away ventures.

At this writing newspaper totals, despite recent well-publicized newspaper deaths, remain at stable, twenty five-year levels. Absolute circulation figures hold steady while advertising linage and revenue climb slowly in the absence of newspaper competition. While happily settling for a one-newspaper-per-community saturation and the security that rapidly expanding newspaper chains bring, the industry has lately been distressed that its circulation totals have not kept pace with population growth. This concern may breed some interesting tinkerings with the news product in the years ahead.

REFERENCE

Researchers approaching newspapers, either as subjects or as sources, encounter a reasonably well-organized and contained literature and a chaotic and changing picture for newspaper files. The literature on newspapers, being relatively small, has been gathered in several well-prepared bibliographies and continues to be classified and thoughtfully appraised in two multitude of strategies in a maze of available storage forms, indexing tools, depository locations, and access policies.

Pivotal to any study of newspapers in history is Warren C. Price's excellent

The Literature of Journalism which contains 3,147 well-annotated entries up to 1958. Price arranged his material under fifty-two subject headings and provided a complete subject and author index. Price was working on a supplement to the above work at the time of his death in 1967. This task was taken over by Calder M. Pickett and completed under the title *An Annotated Journalism Bibliography, 1958-1968,* with Pickett sharing editorship with Price. Although arranged alphabetically by author (rather than subject) and having briefer annotations, this update contains 2,172 titles (some pre-1958) and has an extensive subject index.

The book review section of *Journalism Quarterly* regularly classifies and discusses journalism literature in its broadest dimension, and *Journalism History,* a quarterly, carries a book review section on historical titles in journalism. Together, these journals update Price and Pickett. Additionally, "Articles on Mass Communication in U.S. and Foreign Journals," a regular feature in *Journalism Quarterly,* notes and summarizes articles in all trade and academic periodicals.

Another valuable aid to the researcher is Eleanor Blum's *Basic Books in the Mass Media* which contains 665 entries emphasizing reference pieces, directories, annuals, indexes, and periodicals on journalism subjects. The annotations give detailed descriptions of the entries' contents. The book has both subject and author-title indexes, and the entries are divided into nine broad subject areas.

Thoughtfully selected bibliographies are in our two journalism histories of note—Edwin Emery and Michael Emery, *The Press and America,* and Frank Luther Mott, *American Journalism: A History.* A guide to journalism and communication research programs and sponsors, communication organizations, media action groups, government policy-making agencies, special libraries and resources, periodicals, and bibliographies in the field is the *Aspen Handbook on the Media,* most recently edited by William L. Rivers, Wallace Thompson, and Michael J. Nyhan. Now in its third biennial edition, the handbook appears to be a continuing offering of the Aspen Institute for Humanistic Studies.

Price and Pickett have largely eliminated the need for bibliographies on specialized newspaper topics. Since research on newspapers may include consideration of the press's legal and legislative climate, the researcher may wish to consult Ralph E. McCoy's *Freedom of the Press: An Annotated Bibliography,* which contains extensive annotations for about eight thousand entries, ranging over four centuries of censorship and free expression throughout the English-speaking world but focusing on the United States.

Prior to Price several specialized bibliographies appeared which for their periods may give the researcher some leads: Thomas F. Barnhart's *The Weekly Newspaper: A Bibliography, 1925-1941;* Ralph O. Nafziger's *International News and the Press: Communications, Organization of News Gathering,*

International Affairs and the Foreign Press—an Annotated Bibliography, published in 1940; two volumes by Harold D. Lasswell, Ralph D. Casey, and Bruce Lannes Smith, *Propaganda and Promotional Activities: An Annotated Bibliography,* in 1935, and *Propaganda, Communication, and Public Opinion: A Comprehensive Reference Guide,* in 1946; and Armistead S. Pride's *The Black Press: A Bibliography,* in 1968. A valuable recent bibliography on women in the field is "The Literature of Women in Journalism History," compiled by Marion Marzolf, Ramona R. Rush, and Darlene Stern in *Journalism History.* Marzolf provided a supplement in a later issue of that journal.

Using newspapers as research sources presents a constant challenge. The researcher, depending on the structure of a project, may have to identify newspapers of a particular period or location, locate extant copies of needed newspapers, gain access to the needed files, and/or find specific stories or editorials within those files. There is no automatic way of recording the existence of a publication if an editor does not make it known beyond its small circle of readers. Remnants of short-lived, obscure, or remote newspapers may be carelessly discarded or tucked away in an attic somewhere and long since forgotten. Without those remnants, a newspaper's very existence can be lost. Armistead S. Pride literally explored attics and basements in search of black newspapers that had passed from the scene unrecorded. The existence of our first newspaper, *Publick Occurrences,* published in Boston in 1690, was not known—or at least not rediscovered—until 1845, when the only extant copy was unearthed in the London Public Record Office. No one knows how many papers have slipped from sight, unrecorded.

The researcher approaching newspaper files would do well to glance through two books by Lucy Maynard Salmon, *The Newspaper and the Historian,* a scholarly study of newspapers' advantages and limitations as sources of historical material, and *The Newspaper and Authority,* a study of how externally imposed restrictions affect newspapers' usefulness to historians. William H. Taft has updated Salmon's companion volumes in *Newspapers as Tools For Historians,* in which he gives special attention to the problems faced by journalists conducting their day-to-day reporting and historians using newspapers as sources.

Identifying newspapers publishing in a given period or in a specific town is ordinarily the easiest task. Extensive, almost monumental, effort has gone into compiling information on known newspapers. Clarence S. Brigham, then director of the American Antiquarian Society, which holds the largest collection of early American newspapers, in 1947 completed the two-volume *History and Bibliography of American Newspapers (1690-1820).* This lists essential information on about all newspapers known to exist during this period and includes sketches of the founders, brief summaries of the newspapers' histories, and depositories in which each newspaper will be found.

A recently published companion volume to Brigham is Edward Connery Lathem's *Chronological Tables of American Newspapers, 1690-1820,* a year-by-year tabulation of which papers were publishing, giving papers' dates of founding, resumption, merger, name change, and suspension.

Brigham's time period is followed by *American Newspapers, 1821-1936, A Union List of Files Available in the United States and Canada* completed in 1936 by Winifred Gregory. Although the historical information in Gregory is not as complete as in Brigham, Gregory gives papers' founding and suspension dates, mergers and name changes, and locations of newspaper files.

One must remember that both Brigham and Gregory list files of newsprint, or "hard," copies of newspapers and that these lists are more than thirty years old; in the intervening time many disasters may have befallen those files. A cheap woodpulp newsprint requiring acid treatment became popular late in the nineteenth century in newspaper publishing. As a result fifty- to eighty-year runs of many newspapers are literally eating themselves up with the acid residue still in the newsprint. The paper yellows, dark spots appear, and newspaper pages eventually become too brittle to turn. If the researcher is lucky, the library has captured the decaying newspaper file in microform; if unlucky, the first touch will literally disintegrate a bound volume of newspaper into so much confetti. In some depositories newspaper files are being discarded either because they have deteriorated beyond the point where they can be transferred to microform or because at an earlier time there was not enough money to transfer the files while they still could be reclaimed.

To identify post-1936 newspapers, and for additional information about earlier newspapers, the researcher should turn to one of the annual directories. *Rowell's American Newspaper Directory,* published annually between 1869 and 1908 by George P. Rowell Advertising Agency, was our first comprehensive and continuous annual listing of newspapers and periodicals. Rowell attempted, for the most part unsuccessfully, to get accurate circulation figures from publishers, but nonetheless classified the listings by circulation as well as by specialty.

Rowell's was absorbed in 1908 by the directory of another advertising agency, N. W. Ayer and Son. The *Directory of Newspaper and Periodicals,* a staple in most library reference rooms, began in 1880 and continues to the present. Arranged by state and city, Ayer's is the most complete listing of periodicals for the United States and some foreign countries, giving editors' names, political leanings, publication frequency, circulation, and subscription and advertising rates. Ayer's has separate sections for college, foreign-language, black, religious, labor, and some other specialized publications. It includes all publications, not just newspapers.

The Editor & Publisher *International Year Book,* begun in 1920, emphasizes daily newspapers, giving numerous staff personnel, founding date, circulation, subscription and advertising rates, and news service suppliers. It also contains brief listings of U.S. weeklies and major foreign newspapers, plus U.S. news and feature syndicates and the composition of U.S. daily newspaper chains. The *International Year Book* originally appeared as an expanded regular number of *Editor & Publisher* magazine, the newspaper trade's weekly, either in July or January, until around World War II, when January became the standard publication month. In 1959 publication of the *International Year Book* was separated from the magazine and sold independently.

As this essay is being prepared, a promising new research tool for identifying and locating newspapers is being assembled. The *Historical Guide to American Newspapers,* edited by James Boylan, will contain historical sketches of America's leading past and present newspapers, giving all significant names and dates, content trends, brief bibliographies, and lists of available files for each selected newspaper.

The *Encyclopedic Directory of Ethnic Newspapers and Periodicals in the United States*, edited by Lubomyr R. Wynar and Anna T. Wynar and in its second edition in 1976, lists 913 publications by ethnic group, giving the editor's name, publication frequency, founding date, circulation, subscription rate, and a sentence or two describing the publication's content.

A scattering of checklists and directories have been attempted on the black press, but one cannot be sure how comprehensive these are. The reader, however, is encouraged to consult Carter R. Bryan's *Negro Journalism in America Before Emancipation,* which identifies forty-three black papers founded between 1827 and 1865; Warren Brown's *Check List of Negro Newspapers in the United States, 1827-1946,* which lists over 450 black papers, their dates of existence, and libraries where copies can be found; Armistead S. Pride's "A Register and History of Negro Newspapers in the United States," a doctoral dissertation; Henry G. La Brie, III's *The Black Press in America: A Guide,* an attempt early in the 1970s at a regular listing; and the Black Press Clipping Bureau's *The Black Press Periodical Directory,* a mid-1970s attempt at a regular listing.

Once the researcher has identified the newspapers for study, the task of locating and gaining access to the desired files looms menacingly. Some hard copies are now in microform, and others now do not exist at all. Brigham's lists of hard files are more reliable because the early newspapers used rag paper, but problems of storing bound or loose hard copies may have dictated transferral to microform. Gregory's lists, embracing the period of woodpulp, should be viewed skeptically. Some researchers will want only hard copies, especially for measuring lengths of stories and the like. While conversion formulas may give approximate dimensions of original hard copies on a case-by-case basis, there are no universal standards for reduction to or projection of microform newspaper files.

The 1970s have witnessed a surge in microform reproduction of newspapers by private firms as well as depositories. Readex Microprint has produced the Early American Newspaper series, complete runs of all extant papers published between 1690 and 1820. Bell & Howell and the Microfilming Corporation of America, a New York *Times* subsidiary, continue to generate microfilm of historical or current runs of nationally or regionally significant newspapers.

In addition to Brigham's and Gregory's checklists of hard copies, the researcher is reminded that the target newspaper will probably have its own back files and within reasonable limits will probably permit scholarly use of them. Don't be surprised, however, to be denied access to newspaper morgues, that is, the paper's clipping and reference library. Many morgues are considered the private domain of staffers. The Special Libraries Association, however, has compiled a guide to libraries operated by 295 newspapers that are open at least in part to the public, the *Directory of Newspaper Libraries in the United States and Canada,* edited by Grace D. Parch.

For locating microfilm of newspapers, consult *Newspapers in Microform: 1948-1972,* compiled by the Library of Congress and representing depositories throughout the nation. Despite its title, *Newspapers in Microform* lists microfilm of pre-1948 newspapers. The library continues to receive reports of depositories' microfilm holdings and has annually published additions to *Newspapers in Microform.* A cumulative edition, *Newspapers in Microform, 1973-77* pulled together the first four annuals and should be used as a supplement to, rather than a replacement for, the 1972 volume.

In 1953 Armistead S. Pride compiled *Negro Newspapers on Microfilm: A Selected List,* an eight-page product of the Library of Congress. The 225 U.S. newspapers permanently retained (and the 400 U.S. papers kept for short periods) by the Library of Congress are listed in the library's biennial *Newspapers Received Currently in the Library of Congress.* Meanwhile, the researcher who does some checking will discover a number of checklists and locating guides available for newspapers of various cities, states, regions, and specific depositories.

One benefit of the sharp increase of newspapers in microform is that the researcher probably has more newspaper files in his home depository to work with and has access, through interlibrary loan, to considerably larger stores of files across the country. An interlibrary loan librarian who knows which distant depositories respond quickly with film and which will not loan materials at all is a valuable ally to the researcher given the necessary delays in borrowing from distant points. Days and even weeks can be cut off the wait for film by a person familiar with the policies and practices of other depositories and the idiosyncrasies of the postal service.

For locating specific news stories or coverage of specific events or persons the researcher has several tools. The old standby, the *New York Times*

Index, beginning with the paper's founding in 1851, probably comes to mind first. The reader, however, is cautioned that while the *Times* is regarded as our national newspaper of record, the paper fell on hard times roughly from the mid-1870s to 1900, during which period the researcher would do well to rely on the New York *Tribune,* which fortunately generated an *Index* of its contents from 1875 to 1906, or on the New York *Herald.*

Newspaper Indexes: A Location and Subject Guide for Researchers, edited by Anita Cheek Milner, lists newspapers being indexed and depositories doing or housing the indexes. The researcher should also be aware of the following newspaper indexing efforts: *Index to the Christian Science Monitor,* beginning in 1950; the Wall Street Journal *Index,* beginning in 1955; *Index to St. Louis Newspapers,* begun in 1975 by the St. Louis Public Library; *Index to Cleveland Newspapers,* begun in 1976 by the Cleveland Public Library; and *Index to Black Newspapers,* begun in 1977 by Bell & Howell.

Bell & Howell's *Newspaper Index* is an expanding, continous effort to index regionally significant newspapers as an adjunct to making microfilm of the newspapers available to depositories. At this writing nine papers have been added to the *Newspaper Index:* Washington *Post,* since January 1971; Chicago *Tribune,* Los Angeles *Times* and New Orleans *Times-Picayune,* since January 1972; Detroit *News,* San Francisco *Chronicle* and Milwaukee *Journal,* since January 1976; Houston *Post,* since January 1977; and Chicago *Sun-Times,* since January 1979.

The Williamsburg *Virginia Gazette Index, 1736-1780,* compiled by Lester J. Cappon and Stella F. Duff, offers assistance for the Colonial period. Donald M. Jacobs has compiled *Antebellum Black Newspapers,* a comprehensive subject index of *Freedom's Journal, 1827-29; The Rights of All,* 1829; *The Weekly Advocate,* 1837; and *The Colored American,* 1837-41.

Facts on File, a weekly summary of news events with bound annual volumes and twice monthly name and subject indexes, cumulative throughout the year and compiled as five-year indexes, will help the researcher identify the dates of newspaper coverage of specific persons or events.

Finally, two additional references might assist the researcher who wishes to contact newspaper reporters and editors directly and by name. *The Working Press of the Nation,* published annually in five volumes, gives addresses, phone numbers, and staff members and their specialties in all media. Volume 1 is devoted to newspapers. *Hudson's Washington News Media Contacts Directory* provides similar information about the Washington, D.C., press corps. Editor & Publisher's *International Year Book* will also assist in this type of inquiry.

RESEARCH COLLECTIONS

The American Antiquarian Society in Worcester, Massachusetts, and the Library of Congress are the nation's two largest newspaper libraries. Isaiah Thomas, publisher of the *Massachusetts Spy,* became wealthy as proprietor of one of America's largest job and book publishing houses in the days after the Revolution. He used part of his wealth to assemble as many Colonial and Revolutionary newspapers as he could in preparation for writing our first history of journalism and printing, *History of Printing in America,* which appeared in 1810. Two years later, armed with this enormous newspaper collection and many other early American imprints, Thomas founded the American Antiquarian Society to house his collection. This is where students of eighteenth-century newspapers must begin their work.

From the start, a guiding principle of the Library of Congress was to maintain a substantial collection of newspapers. Through gifts and congessional allocations, the library's collection has become the largest in the nation, representing all periods of our history in most regions. The library's continuing acquisitions, itemized in *Newspapers Received Currently in the Library of Congress,* is the nation's largest effort to assemble and preserve newspapers.

The libraries of several universities that operate strong journalism schools maintain substantial historical and current newspaper files, noteworthy among them being the University of Illinois at Urbana, which houses files of about a thousand newspapers. Large newspaper collections are also at the New York Public Library, University of Chicago Library, Wisconsin State Historical Society, University of Minnesota, and Center for Research Libraries. The Chicago-based center's *Newspapers,* issued in 1972 with a 1978 supplement, lists the more than two thousand newspapers of all types, including some unusual ones, it holds. A dated, but indicative *Checklist of Newspapers and Official Gazettes in the New York Public Library,* compiled by Daniel C. Haskell in 1915, lists that library's holdings by city of publication and by year.

Among several libraries specializing in mass communication and journalism, a few can be recommended for their comprehensiveness or their focus on newspapers: American Newspaper Publishers Association Library, Reston, Virginia; the Milton Caniff Library at Ohio State University, Columbus; the Columbia University Journalism Library, New York City; the University of Illinois Journalism and Communications Library, Urbana; University of Minnesota Journalism Library, Minneapolis; and University of Missouri Journalism Library, Columbia. Illinois's Journalism Library, the largest of its kind, with over 20,000 volumes, 825 bound periodical volumes, subscriptions to 200 journals and periodicals, and current issues of 20 newspapers, has had its 50,000 catalog cards reproduced in the three-volume *Catalog of Communications Library.*

Beyond these special collections, the researcher generally may assume that city libraries will probably have retained the local newspaper(s) and that the state libraries, historical societies, and state universities hold newspaper collections reflective of the state's newspaper history.

Manuscripts and other primary source materials on newspapers and their personnel present a far less encouraging picture for research than do volumes and reels of old newspapers. The few personalities whose papers are on file are for the most part nineteenth-century newspaper "statesmen"—editors and publishers of public acclaim or of political pretensions. Rarely does one encounter the papers of a reporter (unless he later ascended to publisher, columnist, or politician), and almost never are copyeditors, city editors, or managing editors—the all-important "gatekeepers"—represented in manuscripts. Moreover, many newspaper people will not deposit their papers, wishing to protect news sources, confidences, or the newspaper company they worked for. Similarly, as is common with business and industry, corporate newspaper records almost never find their way into libraries or historical societies.

The Wisconsin State Historical Society's Mass Communications History Center at Madison is the one depository in the nation attempting to gather primary source materials on all facets of mass communications. The center will provide a catalog of its holdings in this area. Otherwise, the researcher will find primary source materials on newspapers, such as they are, scattered throughout the country and will have to rely on the U.S. National Historical Publications Committee's *A Guide to Archives and Manuscripts in the United States,* edited by Philip M. Hamer, and the Library of Congress's *National Union Catalog of Manuscript Collections.*

It should be noted, however, that some large or significant manuscript holdings are housed in the New York Public Library, Baker and Houghton libraries of Harvard University, Syracuse University Library, and the Bentley Historical Library at the University of Michigan. In addition to its large newspaper and manuscript holdings, the New York Public Library has some rare or unusual printed materials on journalism. See Carl L. Cannon's *Journalism, A Bibliography,* published in 1924 and reprinted in 1967, for an indication of that library's holdings.

HISTORY AND CRITICISM

The thrust of the historical and critical literature about newspapers has been distinctly noncultural. Reflecting a heavy contribution from those in newspaper work and from journalism educators whose credentials usually include stints in commercial journalism, the literature, cast in Whig or progressive hues, emphasizes great men, great institutions, and the political impact of newspapers.

When Ronald T. Farrar and John D. Stevens compiled a series of essays in 1971 suggesting new directions for historical research in journalism, *Mass Media and the National Experience,* the eleven contributors skirted or ignored the cultural aspects of newspapers and of the media in general. Two years later, however, the first glimmer of cultural recognition was voiced by James W. Carey in a paper presented at the Association for Education in Journalism convention. Later reprinted as "The Problem of Journalism History" in *Journalism History,* Carey's paper asserted that "the absence of any systematic cultural history of journalism [is] the major deficiency in our teaching and research."[2]

A year later, using the theme "Seeking New Paths in Research," *Journalism History* presented several writers' attempts to respond to Carey with research designs that accommodated his challenge. Since that time the debate has broadened, and *Journalism History,* under Tom Reilly's editorship, has been the principal forum for these explorations. But even with this recent surge of interest in cultural, sociological, institutional, philosophical, and interdisciplinary research, newspaper scholars are still only at the talking stage, with results, it is hoped, to follow. In any event, cultural history and the cultural dimension of newspapers hold much promise in comparison with the stuffy, ponderous, approving literature on newspapers to date.

Our earliest history of newspapers is Isaiah Thomas's *History of Printing in America,* published in 1810 and based on his huge newspaper collection and years as a publisher. Detailed and encyclopedic, Thomas remains the most thorough authority on eighteenth-century newspaper history. After thirty years as a staffer for the New York *Herald,* most of them as the paper's managing editor, Frederic Hudson produced *Journalism in the United States, From 1690 to 1872,* complete and insightful, yet favoring the penny press movement of which Hudson had been a part.

James Melvin Lee's *History of American Journalism,* in 1917, although long since superseded, stands as an attempt to deal with early newspaper development in each state. George Henry Payne's *History of Journalism in the United States,* also long outdated, contains some good chapters on eighteenth-century newspapers.

Willard Grosvenor Bleyer's 1927 *Main Currents in the History of American Journalism* was the literature's twentieth-century trendsetter. More than half of this reliable and detailed text emphasizes the post-1830 great men of newspapers, a theme repeated regularly since. Bleyer's chapter on early English journalism remains a classic of clarity and conciseness.

Bleyer's successor was Frank Luther Mott, whose three editions of *American Journalism: A History* added the dimensions of encyclopedic detail and completeness to the Bleyer perspective. Mott's last edition, published in 1962, is still valuable to the researcher searching for names and dates.

The Press and America, Edwin Emery's entry—with two collaborators along the way—first appeared in 1954, and at this writing is our principal history. The first edition, co-authored with Henry Ladd Smith, was hailed for integrating journalism history with American political, economic, and social forces. Subsequent editions have maintained this blend and a reflection of the Mott-Bleyer tradition. The fourth edition is co-authored with his son, Michael Emery. Despite some severe limitations imposed by the publisher and the authors' reliance on traditional historical perspectives, *The Press and America* serves as an excellent, continuing update of all new developments in research and the literature, regardless of perspective or methodology. The book's bibliographic sections are excellent, thoughtful, up-to-date guides to the literature.

One especially useful and interesting effort at newspaper history is Alfred McClung Lee's *The Daily Newspaper in America: the Evolution of a Social Instrument.* Topical in its organization, sporting a sociological perspective and emphasizing economic factors and statistical data on newspaper development, Lee's book provides information not available elsewhere in the literature.

As noted above, *The Historical Guide to American Newspapers,* being prepared at this writing by James Boylan, will provide biographical sketches of America's leading past and present newspapers. Other general histories exist but are less serviceable than these.

In most periods of newspaper development a few literary offerings stand out as providing the researcher an introduction or insight. For the Colonial period one should consult, in addition to Thomas's *History of Printing in America* and Joseph T. Buckingham's *Specimens of Newspaper Literature,* described below, Elizabeth C. Cook's *Literary Influences in Colonial Newspapers,* on press content as popular literature; Clarence S. Brigham's *Journals and Journeymen; A Contribution to the History of Early American Newspapers,* brief, sensitive essays on aspects of Colonial newspapering; and Sidney Kobre's *The Development of the Colonial Newspaper,* on the political, economic, and social forces affecting newspapers. On newspapers in the Revolution see Arthur M. Schlesinger's *Prelude to Independence: The Newspaper War on Britain, 1764 to 1776* and Philip Davidson's *Propaganda and the American Revolution.*

On the party press period and the general topic of press-government relations, the researcher should see Culver H. Smith's *The Press, Politics, and Patronage, The American Government's Use of Newspapers, 1789-1875;* James E. Pollard's *The Presidents and the Press,* printed in 1947 and supplemented in 1964; and F. B. Marbut's *News from the Capital, The Story of Washington Reporting.* Except for a small cluster of biographies, the mercantile press is not specifically treated in the literature.

Among the expanding literature on frontier journalism, one should see

George S. Hage's *Newspapers on the Minnesota Frontier, 1849-1860,* Douglas C. McMurtrie's and Albert H. Allen's *Early Printing in Colorado,* and Robert F. Karolevitz's *Newspapering in the Old West.*

Unfortunately no one has dealt with the penny press movement as an entity. We have only the stories of editors and newspapers to bridge this period. Hudson's *Journalism in the United States* should be looked at, as should the later chapters of Augustus Maverick's *Henry J. Raymond and the New York Press.* For the penny press, also see Frank M. O'Brien's *The Story of the Sun,* Oliver Carlson's *The Man Who Made News* (James Gordon Bennett), Glyndon Garlock Van Deusen's *Horace Greeley: Nineteenth Century Crusader,* Greeley's own *Recollections of a Busy Life,* Elmer Davis's *History of the New York Times, 1851-1921,* and Francis Brown's *Raymond of the Times.*

Civil War news coverage is treated in J. Cutler Andrews' *The North Reports the Civil War* and *The South Reports the Civil War.* Louis M. Starr's *Bohemian Brigade: Civil War Newsmen in Action* and Robert S. Harper's *Lincoln and the Press* offer additional dimensions.

Post-civil War and twentieth-century newspaper history, again, can best be reflected in a selection of biographies and newspaper histories: Allan Nevins's *The Evening Post: A Century of Journalism;* Harry W. Baehr's *The New York Tribune Since the Civil War;* Candace Stone's *Dana and the Sun,* on Charles A. Dana, the "newspaperman's newspaperman"; Henry Watterson's *"Marse Henry": An Autobiography,* editor of the Louisville *Courier-Journal;* Raymond B. Nixon's *Henry W. Grady: Spokesman of the New South,* the post-Civil war managing editor of the Atlanta *Constitution;* Melville E. Stone's *Fifty Years a Journalist,* Chicago *Daily News* founder; W. A. Swanberg's *Pulitzer,* founder of "new journalism," and *Citizen Hearst,* the loved and hated William Randolph Hearst; Oliver H. Knight's *I Protest: Selected Disquisitions of E. W. Scripps,* creator of the Scripps-Howard newspaper chain; James W. Barrett's *The World, the Flesh, and Messrs. Pulitzer,* about the sale of the New York *World;* Allen Churchhill's *Park Row: A Vivid Re-Creation of Turn of the Century Newspaper Days,* in New York City; Charles H. Dennis's *Victor Lawson, His Time and His Work,* Chicago *Daily News* publisher; *The Autobiography of William Allen White,* powerful editor of the Emporia (Kansas) *Gazette;* Lloyd Wendt's *Chicago Tribune;* John Tebbel's *An American Dynasty,* the Joseph Medill-Robert R. McCormick-Joseph Patterson newspaper family; Simon M. Bessie's *Jazz Journalism,* on tabloid sensationalism in the 1920s; George Britt's *Forty Years—Forty Millions: The Career of Frank A. Munsey,* a newspaper owner and "butcher"; John A. Lent's *Newhouse, Newspapers, Nuisances,* the building of a newspaper empire; William T. Moore's *Dateline Chicago,* a reconstruction of Chicago's "Front Page" days; Gay Talese's *The Kingdom and the Power,* a "new journalism" treatment of the New York *Times* and its people; and David Halberstam's *The Powers That Be,* detailed analyses of the Washington *Post,* Los Angeles *Times, Time* Magazine, and CBS.

Newspaper entanglements with the law are described in Clyde A. Duniway's *The Development of Freedom of the Press in Massachusetts,* covering the eighteenth century; Leonard W. Levy's *Legacy of Suppression,* an excellent revisionist view of the Founding Fathers' notions on free expression; and Levy's *Freedom of the Press from Zenger to Jefferson* and Harold L. Nelson's *Freedom of the Press from Hamilton to the Warren Court,* companion volumes of readings.

Among the works on foreign-language journalism, the researcher should see Robert E. Park's *The Immigrant Press and Its Control,* waiting to be updated but still useful, and Carl F. Wittke's *The German-Language Press in America,* representing the largest foreign-language press movement in the nation for several decades.

Two titles worth examining on women in journalism are Ishbel Ross's *Ladies of the Press* and Marion Marzolf's *Up from the Footnote: A History of Women Journalists.*

For information on black journalism see I. Garland Penn's *The Afro-American Press and Its Editors,* selective but detailed up to 1891; Frederick G. Detweiler's *The Negro Press in the United States,* published in 1922 and giving special attention to the World War I radical black press; and Roland E. Wolseley's *The Black Press: U.S.A.,* an overview with emphasis on the twentieth century.

On the underground, radical, or alternative press, see Robert J. Glessing's *The Underground Press in America,* an academic treatment; Laurence Leamer's *The Paper Revolutionaries: The Rise of the Underground Press,* presented somewhat in underground style; Daniel Aaron's *Writers on the Left,* covering 1912 to the 1940s; Joseph R. Conlin's *The American Radical Press 1880-1960;* and Everette E. Dennis's and William L. Rivers's *Other Voices: The New Journalism in America,* which classifies twentieth-century "new journalism" writing.

As a mass-produced commodity that regularly sticks its nose into others' business and "does it in public," the newspaper has constantly received criticism. The bill of particulars is long and gets tiresome and repetitous to those who work for newspapers. Newspaper people don't like criticism and avoid criticizing each other. Editors, for political or professional reasons, criticized each other until about 1900, after which only the most daring or rebellious journalist would attack his own kind.

This century has seen a rising chorus of serious, at times bitter, criticism, most of it originating outside newspapering. The 1920s produced a substantial indictment of newspapers in the form of four volumes. Social critic Upton Sinclair's *The Brass Check* represents the doctrinaire anti-establishment viewpoint so prevalent early in the twentieth century. Sinclair, outraged by newspapers' ties to business and government, likens journalists to prostitutes. Silas Bent's *Ballyhoo: The Voice of the Press* is a reaction to 1920s sensationalism and tabloid journalism and includes criticism of newspaper chains. Walter Lippmann's classic *Public Opinion* systematically analyzes the nature of news and the impact of the news report upon people's perceptions of reality. Oswald Garrison Villard, editor of the *Nation* and the New York *Evening Post,* provides an up-close condemnation of newspaper leaders in his *Some Newspapers and Newspaper-men.*

In the wake of the Great Depression the fires of criticism were rekindled more systematically and with a new urgency, an attack carried by its own momentum into the World War II years. George Seldes's *Freedom of the Press* fired a broadside. Villard updated and expanded his attack on newspapers in *The Disappearing Daily, Chapters in American Newspaper Evolution.* Reflecting a New Deal viewpoint, cabinet member Harold L. Ickes produced a strong condemnation of the press in *America's House of Lords: An Inquiry into the Freedom of the Press.* Morris L. Ernst, a civil liberties lawyer, analyzed the concentration of economic power in newspaper monopolies, ownership, and cross-media ownership in *The First Freedom.* In 1946 A. J. Liebling began writing news media criticism under "The Wayward Press" and "Notes and Comment" headings in the *New Yorker.* The comments were collected in three books: *The Wayward Pressman, Mink and Red Herring,* and *The Press.*

A major post-World War II statement about the press was offered by the Commission on Freedom of the Press, set up by Henry Luce and the Encyclopedia Britannica to study the legal and ethical status of the media. Out of the deliberations of this blue ribbon panel came a significant new philosophical prescription of press performance—the social responsibility theory of the press. Among several books arising from this effort, the Commission's *A Free and Responsible Press* in 1947 contains the theory's essential features. This theme of social responsibility was taken up later by Wilbur Schramm in *Responsibility in Mass Communication,* in which he grapples with the apparent conflict between corporate bigness in the media and the need for ethical standards. Schramm anticipates a major theme inside the media in the 1970s—the problems of ethical performance and professionalism in news operations, perhaps best exemplified by *Ethics and the Press,* a wide-ranging collection of readings edited by John C. Merrill and Ralph D. Barney.

Carl E. Lindstrom's *The Fading American Newspaper* is one of the few public criticisms of newspapers this century by a newspaperman. His main point is that control of newspapers has passed from editors to business managers.

Recent criticism of newspapers is growing and coming from diverse sources. The Warren Commission's findings regarding the assassination of John F. Kennedy has some harsh comments about media coverage of that event, and the National Advisory Commission on Civil Disorders (the Kerner Commission) following racial unrest in U.S. cities during the late 1960s admonished the press to reflect more accurately minorities' roles in the community.

The past two decades produced numerous organizations and journals to review and critique the media. Accuracy in Media in Washington, D.C., is a watch-dog organization that produces *AIM Report*. The National News Council hears complaints about fairness and accuracy in the media. Only a few remain of the twenty or so journalism reviews that sprang up in the 1960s; two current examples are the *Columbia Journalism Review* and the *Washington Journalism Review*.

Finally trade press coverage of newspapers will be found in *Editor & Publisher, Masthead, Publishers' Auxiliary, Quill, presstime,* and the *Guild Reporter,* the organ of the newspaper reporters' union. Academic studies of newspapers are in *Journalism Quarterly, Journalism Monographs, Journalism History,* and the *Journal of Communication,* which brings an interdisciplinary approach to the subject. The problems of newspapers are discussed in *Nieman Reports, Grassroots Editor,* the *Bulletin* of the American Society of Newspaper Editors, the *Red Book* series of the Associated Press Managing Editors Association, and the journalism reviews mentioned above.

ANTHOLOGIES AND REPRINTS

In view of the mountains of copy newspapers have cranked out in the past 290 years, it is surprising that so few anthologies have been produced. Surely amid the constant flood of news reporting a few journalistic nuggets worth preserving have floated past. In large part, however, our collections seek to feature accounts of historically sensational events. One of the challenges facing this generation is to understand news stories as popular literature, dripping with widely shared social images and values.

In the sensational events genre, one encounters at the top of the list Louis L. Snyder's *Masterpieces of War Reporting: The Great Moments of World War II* and Snyder's and Richard B. Morris's *A Treasury of Great Reporting; "Literature under Pressure" from the Sixteenth Century to Our Own Times,* in its second edition in 1962. An earlier similar effort is Laurence Greene's *America Goes to Press,* later retitled *Headlines of the Past.* Greene's selection only comes up to World War I. See also Ward Greene's *Star Reporters and 34 of their Stories,* from the Stanley-Livingston story of 1872 to Dillinger's shooting in 1934.

Of more serious tone Calder M. Pickett's *Voices of the Past, Key Documents in the History of American Journalism,* attempts a representative sampling of reporting from a wide variety of times and media. George Bourne's *The Spirit of the Public Journals: Or, Beauties of the American Newspapers for 1805* is an interesting collection of 121 stories from 96 newspapers during 1805. A fascinating two-volume 1850 set is Joseph T. Buckingham's *Specimens of Newspaper Literature: With Personal Memoirs, Anecdotes, and Reminiscences,* also known as "Buckingham's Reminiscences." Including historical accounts of forty-five early papers, Buckingham adds the dimension of liberally quoting from the newspapers. Bryce W. Rucker's *Twentieth Century Reporting at Its Best* covers six decades.

The top of the specialized anthology list includes: Allan Nevins's *American Press Opinion: Washington to Coolidge,* editorials from 1785 to 1927; Martin E. Dann's *The Black Press: 1827-1890,* a collection of newspaper articles; Duncan Emrich's *Comstock Bonanza,* stories from newspapers and other sources about the silver rush days in Virginia City, Nevada; *The Abolitionists* by Louis Ruchames, a collection which draws from many sources; Dwight L. Dumond's *Southern Editorials on Secession,* 183 editorials from 31 papers; Howard Cecil Perkins's *Northern Editorials on Secession,* 495 editorials from 190 papers; and *The Greatest Sports Stories from the New York Times: Sports Classics of a Century,* mostly post-1920.

Among the many collections drawn from individual newspapers or the works of individual writers a few might be pointed out: Truman Nelson's *Documents of Upheaval: Selections from William Lloyd Garrison's The "Liberator"; A Century of Tribune Editorials,* the Chicago *Tribune's* output to 1947; *Casual Essays of the Sun,* twenty years of New York *Sun* editorials; Arthur Brisbane's *Editorials from the Hearst Newspapers,* a turn-of-the-century selection; Arthur Krock's *The Editorials of Henry Watterson,* covering fifty years by the editor of the Louisville *Courier-Journal;* Helen Ogden Mahin's collection of William Allen White editorials from 1895 to 1924, *The Editor and His People;* and *The Best of the World,* an anthology of the New York *World* edited by John K. Hutchens and George Oppenheimer. Consult Price's *The Literature of Journalism* and the Price-Pickett *Annotated Journalism Bibliography* for anthologies of many writers and columnists.

Journalists adore reproductions of their newspaper pages. They celebrate newspaper anniversaries by reprinting a selection of old front pages; they adorn the pages of their trade press with miniature reproductions of news pages; the New York *Times* has sold reproductions of its pages to the public. Aside from newspaper people's fascination with such reprints, these representations of page makeup suggest an added cultural dimension of the newspaper. Selection and placement of illustrations, the balance between news and advertisements, the use and style of headlines, the general aesthetic design of newspaper pages, the typographical statement made by the type faces—all these are as much a part of the cultural experience of selecting, purchasing, and reading a newspaper as are the stories and their writing style. The only comprehensive effort to reprint newspaper pages is *America's Front Page News, 1690-1970,* edited by Michael C. Emery, R. Smith Schuneman, and Edwin Emery, a large-format compilation of over three hundred newspaper pages.

Michael Wynn Jones has compiled *Deadline Disaster: A Newspaper History,* meant primarily for trade distribution and covering disasters from 1871 to 1976 as reported in English-language newspapers. The New York *Times* has generated several collections of its pages, some intended for subscription promotions, focusing on such themes as major page-one news events, sports, crime, and disasters. Herbert J. Cohen's *125 Years of Famous Pages from the New York Times, 1851-1976* is perhaps the paper's most historically faithful effort along these lines, although the vast majority of the 124 reproduced newspaper pages are from the twentieth century.

NOTES

1. Alexis de Tocqueville, *Democracy in America* (New York: Knopf, 1945), Vol. 1, p. 186.

2. James W. Carey, "The Problem of Journalism History," *Journalism History,* 1 (Spring 1974), 4.

BIBLIOGRAPHY

BOOKS AND ARTICLES

Aaron, Daniel. *Writers on the Left: Episodes in American Literary Communism.* New York: Harcourt Brace Jovanovich, 1961.

Andrews, J. Cutler. *The North Reports the Civil War.* Pittsburgh: University of Pittsburgh Press, 1955.

———. *The South Reports the Civil War.* Princeton: Princeton University Press, 1970.

Associated Press Managing Editors Association. *Red Book.* New York: Associated Press, 1948-. Annual

Ayer, N. W., and Son. *Directory of Newspapers and Periodicals.* Philadelphia: Ayer, 1880-. Annual.

Baehr, Harry W., Jr. *The New York Tribune Since the Civil War.* New York: Dodd, Mead, 1936.

Barnhart, Thomas F. *The Weekly Newspaper: A Bibliography, 1925-1941.* Minneapolis: Burgess, 1941.

Barrett, James W. *The World, the Flesh, and Messrs. Pulitzer.* New York: Vanguard Press, 1931.

Bell & Howell. *Index to Black Newspapers.* Wooster, Ohio: Bell & Howell, 1977-. Annual.

———. *Newspaper Index.* Wooster, Ohio: Bell & Howell, 1971-. Annual.

Bent, Silas. *Ballyhoo: The Voice of the Press.* New York: Boni and Liveright, 1927.

Bessie, Simon M. *Jazz Journalism.* New York: Dutton, 1938.

Black Press Clipping Bureau. *The Black Press Periodical Directory.* Newark: Systems Catalog, 1973. Supplements, 1975, 1976.

Bleyer, Willard Grosvenor. *Main Currents in the History of American Journalism.* Boston: Houghton Mifflin, 1927.

Blum, Eleanor. *Basic Books in the Mass Media.* Urbana: University of Illinois Press, 1972.

Bourne, George, ed. *The Spirit of the Public Journals: Or, Beauties of the American Newspapers for 1805.* Baltimore: George Dobbin and Murphy, 1806.

Boylan, James, ed. *Historical Guide to American Newspapers.* Westport, Conn.: Greenwood Press, forthcoming.

Brigham, Clarence S. *History and Bibliography of American Newspapers (1690-1820).* 2 vols. Worcester, Mass.: American Antiquarian Society, 1947.

______. *Journals and Journeymen: A Contribution to the History of Early American Newspapers.* Philadelphia: University of Pennsylvania Press, 1950.

Brisbane, Arthur, ed. *Editorials from the Hearst Newspapers.* New York: Albertson, 1906.

Britt, George. *Forty Years—Forty Millions: The Career of Frank A. Munsey.* New York: Holt, Rinehart and Winston, 1935.

Brown, Francis. *Raymond of the Times.* New York: Norton, 1951.

Brown, Warren. *Check List of Negro Newspapers in the United States, 1827-1946.* Jefferson City, Mo.: Lincoln University School of Journalism, 1946.

Bryan, Carter R. *Negro Journalism in America Before Emancipation.* Journalism Monographs, no. 12. Lexington, Ky.: Association for Education in Journalism, September 1969.

Buckingham, Joseph T. *Specimens of Newspaper Literature: With Personal Memoirs, Anecdotes, and Reminiscences.* (Also known as "Buckingham's Reminiscences.") Boston: Charles C. Little and James Brown, 1850.

Cannon, Carl L, comp. *Journalism: A Bibliography.* New York: New York Public Library, 1924. Reprint. Detroit: Gale Research, 1967.

Cappon, Lester J., and Stella F. Duff, comps. *Virginia Gazette Index, 1736-1780.* 2 vols. Williamsburg: Va.: Institute of Early American History and Culture, 1950.

Carey, James W. "The Problem of Journalism History." *Journalism History,* 1 (Spring 1974), 3-5.

Carlson, Oliver. *The Man Who Made News.* New York: Duell, Sloan & Pearce, 1942.

Catalog of the Communications Library. 3 vols. Boston: G. K. Hall, 1975.

Center for Research Libraries. *Newspapers.* Chicago: Center for Research Libraries, 1972. Supplement, 1978.

Chicago Tribune. *A Century of Tribune Editorials, 1847-1947.* Chicago: Tribune, 1947.

Christian Science Monitor and Bell & Howell. *Index to the Christian Science Monitor.* Wooster, Ohio: Bell & Howell, 1950-. Annual.

Churchill, Allen. *Park Row: A Vivid Re-Creation of Turn of the Century Newspaper Days.* New York: Rinehart, 1958.

Cohen, Herbert J. *125 Years of Famous Pages from the New York Times, 1851-1976.* New York: Arno Press, 1976.

Commission on Freedom of the Press. *A Free and Responsible Press.* Chicago: University of Chicago Press, 1947.

Conlin, Joseph R., ed. *The American Radical Press 1880-1960.* 2 vols. Westport, Conn.: Greenwood Press, 1974.

Cook, Elizabeth C. *Literary Influences in Colonial Newspapers, 1704-1750.* New York: Columbia University Press, 1912.

Dann, Martin E., ed. *The Black Press: 1827-1890.* New York: Putnam's 1971.

Davidson, Philip. *Propaganda and the American Revolution.* Chapel Hill: University of North Carolina Press, 1941.

Davis, Elmer. *History of the New York Times, 1851-1921.* New York: New York Times, 1921.

Dennis, Charles H. *Victor Lawson, His Time and His Work.* Chicago: University of Chicago Press, 1935.

Dennis, Everette E., and William L. Rivers. *Other Voices: The New Journalism in America.* San Francisco: Canfield Press, 1974.

Detweiler, Frederick G. *The Negro Press in the United States.* Chicago: University of Chicago Press, 1922.

Dumond, Dwight L., ed. *Southern Editorials on Secession.* New York: Century, 1931.

Duniway, Clyde A. *The Development of Freedom of the Press in Massachusetts.* New York: Longmans, Green, 1906.

Editor & Publisher. *International Year Book.* New York: Editor & Publisher,1920-. Annual.

Emery, Edwin. *The Press and America.* Englewood Cliffs, N.J.: Prentice-Hall, 1954 with Henry Ladd Smith; 1962, 1972, 1978 with Michael Emery.

Emery, Michael C., R. Smith Schuneman, and Edwin Emery, eds. *America's Front Page News, 1690-1970.* New York: Doubleday, 1970.

Emrich, Duncan, ed. *Comstock Bonanza.* New York: Vanguard Press, 1950.

Ernst, Morris L. *The First Freedom.* New York: Macmillan, 1946.

Facts on File. New York: Facts on File, 1940-. Weekly.

Farrar, Ronald T., and John D. Stevens, eds. *Mass Media and the National Experience.* New York: Harper & Row, 1971.

Glessing, Robert J. *The Underground Press in America.* Bloomington: Indiana University Press, 1970.

The Greatest Sports Stories from the New York Times: Sports Classics of a Century. New York: Barnes, 1951.

Greeley, Horace. *Recollections of a Busy Life.* New York: J. B. Ford, 1868.

Greene, Laurence, ed. *America Goes to Press.* Indianapolis: Bobbs-Merrill, 1936. Reprint ed. (as *Headlines of the Past).* Garden City, N.Y.: Garden City Publishing, 1938.

Greene, Ward, ed. *Star Reporters and 34 of Their Stories.* New York: Random House, 1948.

Gregory, Winifred, ed. *American Newspapers, 1821-1936: A Union List of Files Available in the United States and Canada.* New York: H. W. Wilson, 1936.

Hage, George S. *Newspapers on the Minnesota Frontier, 1849-1860.* St Paul: Minnesota Historical Society, 1967.

Halberstam, David. *The Powers That Be.* New York: Knopf, 1979.

Harper, Robert S. *Lincoln and the Press.* New York: McGraw-Hill, 1951.

Haskell, Daniel C., comp. *Checklist of Newspapers and Official Gazettes in the New York Public Library.* New York: New York Public Library, 1915.

Hudson, Frederic. *Journalism in the United States, From 1690 to 1872.* New York: Harper & Brothers, 1873.

Hudson's Washington News Media Contacts Directory. Washington, D.C.: Washington Directories, 1968-. Annual.

Hutchens, John K., and George Oppenheimer, eds. *The Best of the World.* New York: Viking Press, 1973.

Ickes, Harold L. *America's House of Lords: An Inquiry into the Freedom of the Press.* New York: Harcourt, Brace, 1939.

Index to Cleveland Newspapers. Cleveland: Cleveland Public Library, 1976-. Annual.

Index to St. Louis Newspapers. St. Louis: St. Louis Public Library, 1975-. Annual.

Jacobs, Donald M., comp. *Antebellum Black Newspapers.* Westport, Conn.: Greenwood Press, 1976.

Jones, Michael Wynn, ed. *Deadline Disaster: A Newspaper History.* Chicago: Henry Regnery, 1976.

Karolevitz, Robert F. *Newspapering in the Old West.* Seattle: Superior, 1965.

Knight, Oliver H., ed. *I Protest: Selected Disquisitions of E.W. Scripps.* Madison: University of Wisconsin Press, 1966.

Kobre, Sidney. *The Development of the Colonial Newspaper.* Pittsburgh: Colonial Press, 1944.

Krock, Arthur, ed. *The Editorials of Henry Watterson.* New York: H. Doran, 1923.

La Brie, Henry G., III. *The Black Press in America: A Guide.* 3rd edition. Kennebunkport, Me.: Mercer House, 1973.

Lasswell, Harold D., Ralph D. Casey, and Bruce Lannes Smith. *Propaganda and Promotional Activities: An Annotated Bibliography.* Minneapolis: University of Minnesota Press, 1935.

Lathem, Edward Connery, comp. *Chronological Tables of American Newspapers, 1690-1820.* Barre, Mass.: American Antiquarian Society and Barre, 1972.

Leamer, Laurence. *The Paper Revolutionaries: The Rise of the Underground Press.* New York: Simon & Schuster, 1972.

Lee, Alfred McClung. *The Daily Newspaper in America: The Evolution of a Social Instrument.* New York: Macmillan, 1937.

Lee, James Melvin. *History of American Journalism.* Boston: Houghton Mifflin, 1917. Reprint ed. Garden City, N.Y.: Garden City Publishing, 1923.

Lent, John A. *Newhouse, Newspapers, Nuisances.* New York: Exposition Press,1966.

Levy, Leonard W., ed. *Freedom of the Press from Zenger to Jefferson.* Indianapolis: Bobbs-Merrill, 1966.

______. *Legacy of Suppression.* Cambridge: Harvard University Press, 1960.

Library of Congress. *National Union Catalog of Manuscript Collections.* 1959-61, Ann Arbor, Mich.: J. W. Edwards, 1962; 1962, Hamden, Conn.: Shoe String Press, 1964; annual or biennial volumes, 1963 to date, Washington, D.C.: Library of Congress, 1965 to date.

Library of Congress. *Newspapers in Microform, 1948-1972.* Washington, D.C.: Library of Congress, 1973. Annual supplements, 1973-. Cumulation, *Newspapers in Microform, 1973-1977.* Washington, D.C.: Library of Congress, 1978.

______. *Newspapers Received Currently in the Library of Congress.* Washington, D.C.: Library of Congress, 1972-. Biennial.

Liebling, A. J. *Mink and Red Herring: The Wayward Pressman's Casebook.* Garden City, N.Y.: Doubleday, 1949.

———. *The Press.* New York: Ballantine, 1961.
———. *The Wayward Pressman.* Garden City, N.Y.: Doubleday, 1948.
Lindstrom, Carl E. *The Fading American Newspaper.* Gloucester, Mass.: Peter Smith, 1964.
Lippmann, Walter. *Public Opinion.* New York: Harcourt, Brace, 1922.
McCoy, Ralph E., ed. *Freedom of the Press: An Annotated Bibliography.* Carbondale: Southern Illinois University Press, 1968.
McMurtrie, Douglas C., and Albert H. Allen. *Early Printing in Colorado.* Denver: Hirschfeld Press, 1935.
Mahin, Helen Ogden, ed. *The Editor and His People.* New York: Macmillan, 1924.
Marbut, F. B. *News from the Capital, The Story of Washington Reporting.* Carbondale: Southern Illinois University Press, 1971.
Marzolf, Marion. *Up from the Footnote: A History of Women Journalists.* New York: Hastings House, 1977.
———. Ramona R. Rush, and Darlene Stern, comps. "The Literature of Women in Journalism History." *Journalism History,* 1 (Winter 1974-75), 117-28; supplement by Marzolf in *Journalism History,* 3 (Winter 1976-77), 116-20.
Maverick, Augustus. *Henry J. Raymond and the New York Press for Thirty Years.* Hartford, Conn.: A. S. Hale, 1870.
Merrill, John C., and Ralph D. Barney, eds. *Ethics and the Press: Readings in Mass Media Morality.* New York: Hastings House, 1975.
Milner, Anita Cheek, ed. *Newspaper Indexes: A Location and Subject Guide for Researchers.* Metuchen, N.J.: Scarecrow Press, 1977.
Moore, William T. *Dateline Chicago: A Veteran Newsman Recalls Its Heyday.* New York: Taplinger, 1973.
Mott, Frank Luther. *American Journalism: A History.* 3rd edition. New York: Macmillan, 1962.
Nafziger, Ralph O. *International News and the Press: Communications, Organization of News Gathering, International Affairs and the Foreign Press—an Annotated Bibliography.* New York: H. W. Wilson, 1940.
National Advisory Commission on Civil Disorders (Kerner Commission). *Report.* New York: Bantam Books, 1968.
Nelson, Harold L., ed. *Freedom of the Press from Hamilton to the Warren Court.* Indianapolis: Bobbs-Merrill, 1967.
Nelson, Truman, ed. *Documents of Upheaval: Selections from William Lloyd Garrison's The "Liberator," 1831-1865.* New York: Hill & Wang, 1966.
Nevins, Allan, ed. *American Press Opinion; Washington to Coolidge.* New York: Heath, 1928.
———. *The Evening Post: A Century of Journalism.* New York: Boni and Liveright, 1922.
New York Sun. *Casual Essays of the Sun: Editorial Articles on Many Subjects, Clothed with the Philosophy of the Bright Side of Things.* New York: Robert Grier Cooke, 1905.
New York Times Index. Early Series. New York: Bowker, 1851-1913. Current Series. New York: New York Times, 1913-. Annual.
New York Tribune Association. *The New York Daily Tribune Index.* New York: New York Tribune, 1875-1906. Annual.

Nixon, Raymond B. *Henry W. Grady: Spokesman of the New South.* New York: Knopf, 1943.

O'Brien, Frank M. *The Story of the Sun:* New York: George H. Doran, 1918. Reprint. New York: Appleton, 1928.

Parch, Grace D., ed. *Directory of Newspaper Libraries in the United States and Canada.* New York: Special Libraries Association, 1976.

Park, Robert E. *The Immigrant Press and Its Control.* New York: Harper & Brothers. 1922.

Payne, George Henry. *History of Journalism in the United States.* New York: Appleton, 1920.

Penn, I. Garland. *The Afro-American Press and Its Editors.* Springfield, Mass.: Wiley, 1891.

Perkins, Howard Cecil, ed. *Northern Editorials on Secession.* 2 vols. New York: Appleton-Century, 1942.

Pickett, Calder M., ed. *Voices of the Past, Key Documents in the History of American Journalism.* Columbus, Ohio: Grid, 1977.

Pollard, James E. *The Presidents and the Press.* New York: Macmillan, 1947.

______. *The Presidents and the Press: Truman to Johnson.* Washington, D.C.: Public Affairs Press 1964.

Price, Warren C. *The Literature of Journalism.* Minneapolis: University of Minnesota Press, 1959.

______, and Calder M. Pickett. *An Annotated Journalism Bibliography, 1958-1968.* Minneapolis: University of Minnesota Press, 1970.

Pride, Armistead S. *The Black Press: A Bibliography.* Jefferson City, Mo.: Lincoln University Department of Journalism, Minneapolis: Association for Education in Journalism, 1968.

______. *Negro Newspapers on Microfilm: A Selected List.* Washington, D.C.: Library of Congress Photo-duplicating Service, 1953.

______. "A Register and History of Negro Newspapers in the United States." Ph. D. dissertation, Northwestern University, 1950.

Rivers, William L., Wallace Thompson, and Michael J. Nyhan, eds. *Aspen Handbook on The Media, 1977-79 Edition.* New York: Praeger, 1977.

Ross, Ishbel. *Ladies of the Press.* New York: Harper & Row, 1936.

Rowell, George P., and Co. *Rowell's American Newspaper Directory.* New York: George P. Rowell, 1869-1908. Annual.

Ruchames, Louis, ed. *The Abolitionists.* New York: Putnam's, 1963.

Rucker, Bryce W., ed. *Twentieth Century Reporting at Its Best.* Ames: Iowa State University Press, 1964.

Salmon, Lucy Maynard. *The Newspaper and Authority.* New York: Oxford University Press, 1923.

______. *The Newspaper and the Historian.* New York: Oxford University Press, 1923.

Schlesinger, Arthur M. *Prelude to Independence: The Newspaper War on Britain, 1764-1776.* New York: Knopf, 1958.

Schramm, Wilbur. *Responsibility in Mass Communication.* New York: Harper & Brothers, 1957.

"Seeking New Paths in Research." Special issue of *Journalism History* for Summer

1975, with articles by Garth S. Jowett, Richard A. Schwarzlose, John Erickson, Marion Marzolf, and David H. Weaver.

Seldes, George. *Freedom of the Press.* Indianapolis: Bobbs-Merrill, 1935.

Sinclair, Upton. *The Brass Check: A Study of American Journalism.* Pasadena, Calif.: Author, 1920.

Smith, Bruce Lannes, Harold D. Lasswell, and Ralph D. Casey. *Propaganda, Communication and Public Opinion: A Comprehensive Reference Guide.* Princeton: Princeton University Press, 1946.

Smith, Culver H. *The Press, Politics, and Patronage, The American Government's Use of Newspapers, 1789-1875.* Athens: University of Georgia Press, 1977.

Snyder, Louis L., ed. *Masterpieces of War Reporting: The Great Moments of World War II.* New York: Julian Messner, 1962.

———, and Richard B. Morris, eds. *A Treasury of Great Reporting: "Literature under Pressure" from the Sixteenth Century to Our Own Times.* 2nd edition. New York: Simon & Schuster, 1962.

Starr, Louis M. *Bohemian Brigade: Civil War Newsmen in Action.* New York: Knopf, 1954.

Stone, Candace. *Dana and the Sun.* New York: Dodd, Mead, 1938.

Stone, Melville E. *Fifty Years a Journalist.* Garden City, N.Y.: Doubleday, 1921.

Swanberg, W. A. *Citizen Hearst.* New York: Scribner's, 1961.

———. *Pulitzer.* New York: Scribner's, 1967.

Taft, William H. *Newspapers as Tools for Historians.* Columbia, Mo.: Lucas Brothers, 1970.

Talese, Gay. *The Kingdom and the Power.* New York: New American Library, 1969.

Tebbel, John. *An American Dynasty.* Garden City, N.Y.: Doubleday, 1947.

Thomas, Isaiah. *History of Printing in America.* 2 vols. Worcester, Mass.: Isaiah Thomas, Jr., 1810; Albany, N.Y.: Joel Munsell, 1874.

U.S. National Historical Publications Committee. *A Guide to Archives and Manuscripts in the United States.* Edited by Philip M. Hamer. New Haven: Yale University Press, 1961.

Van Deusen, Glyndon Garlock. *Horace Greeley: Nineteenth Century Crusader.* Philadelphia: University of Pennsylvania Press, 1953.

Villard, Oswald Garrison. *The Disappearing Daily, Chapters in American Newspaper Evolution.* New York: Knopf, 1944.

———. *Some Newspapers and Newspaper-men.* New York: Knopf, 1923.

Wall Street Journal. *Index.* New York: Dow Jones, 1955-.

Warren Commission. *The Official Warren Commission Report on the Assassination of President John F. Kennedy.* Garden City, N.Y.: Doubleday, 1964.

Watterson, Henry. *"Marse Henry": An Autobiography.* New York: George H. Doran, 1919.

Wendt, Lloyd. *Chicago Tribune, The Rise of a Great American Newspaper.* Chicago: Rand McNally, 1979.

White, William Allen. *The Autobiography of William Allen White.* New York: Macmillan, 1946.

Wittke, Carl F. *The German-Language Press in America.* Lexington: University of Kentucky Press, 1957.

Wolseley, Roland E. *The Black Press: U.S.A.* Ames: Iowa State University Press, 1971.

The Working Press of the Nation. Burlington, Iowa: National Research Bureau, 1945-. Annual.

Wynar, Lubomyr R., and Anna T. Wynar, eds. *Encyclopedic Directory of Ethnic Newspapers and Periodicals in the United States.* 2nd ed. Littleton, Colo.: Libraries Unlimited, 1976.

PERIODICALS

AIM Report. Washington, D.C.: Accuracy in Media, 1969-. Monthly.

The Bulletin. Easton, Penn.: American Society of Newspaper Editors, 1941-. Monthly.

Columbia Journalism Review. New York: Columbia University, Graduate School of Journalism, 1961-. Bimonthly.

Editor & Publisher. New York: Editor & Publisher, 1884-. Weekly.

Grassroots Editor. Carbondale, Ill.: International Conference of Weekly Newspaper Editors, 1960-. Bimonthly.

The Guild Reporter. Washington, D.C.: American Newspaper Guild, 1933-. Semi-monthly.

Journal of Communication. Philadelphia: Annenberg School of Communication and International Communication Association, 1951-. Quarterly.

Journalism History. Northridge: California State University Northridge Foundation, 1974-. Quarterly.

Journalism Monographs. Lexington, Ky.: Association for Education in Journalism, 1966-. Serially.

Journalism Bulletin. See *Journalism Quarterly.*

Journalism Quarterly. Minneapolis: Association for Education in Journalism, 1924-. Quarterly. (Founded as *Journalism Bulletin.*)

The Masthead. Washington, D.C.: National Conference of Editorial Writers, 1947-. Quarterly.

Nieman Reports. Cambridge, Mass.: Nieman Foundation, 1947-. Quarterly.

presstime. Reston, Va.: American Newspaper Publishers Association, 1979-. Monthly.

Publishers' Auxiliary. Chicago: Western Newspaper Union, 1866-. Weekly.

Quill. Chicago: Society of Professional Journalists/SDX, 1912-. Monthly.

Washington Journalism Review. Washington, D.C.: 1977-. Monthly.

CHAPTER 11 Physical Fitness

Claudius W. Griffin

The general topic of physical fitness in the United States has hardly been studied at all. Only a few historical studies exist, most of them unpublished dissertations. But various aspects of fitness have been written about and studied intensively. There are a number of histories of physical eduction in America; thousands of handbooks on various kinds of exercise and fitness; research studies on the relationship between exercise and health and age; and magazines and books on particular topics such as weight lifting, nutrition, and jogging. This essay assembles a selection of materials from these and other areas. It is the beginning of a collection of materials on physical fitness; I hope others will modify and add to it.

HISTORIC OUTLINE

America has been concerned about physical fitness (the older term was physical culture) from the country's beginnings. Benjamin Franklin, himself an avid swimmer, advocated lifting weights, sleeping in cold rooms, and drinking great quantities of water to obtain fitness and health. In a letter to Thomas M. Randolph, Jr., in 1787, Thomas Jefferson said, "The time necessary to secure [health] by active exercises, should be devoted to it in preference to every other pursuit."[1] And Noah Webster, in his *Address to Young Gentlemen* in 1790, said that it should be "the business of young persons to assist nature and strengthen the growing frame by athletic exercises."[2] Also in 1790, Secretary of the Department of War Henry Knox proposed to Congress a plan to use the schools as training areas to improve the physical fitness of youth eighteen to twenty years old.

During the nineteenth century, there were three major periods of interest in physical fitness in the United States: the 1830s, the 1860s, and the 1880s. During the 1830s, four different fitness systems became popular. The first stressed the drill and discipline of military academy. Both Pierre Thomas, a Frenchman who was appointed physical educator at West Point in 1814, and Captain Alden Partridge, who opened his first military school at Norwich, Vermont, in 1819, stressed this form of exercise for their students.

About ten years later, Dr. Charles Beck and Charles Follen, two German reformers who had fled repression in Germany, brought the Jahn system of gymnastics to the United States. For Friedrich Jahn, founder of this system of gymnastics, the purpose of exercise was to help German youth grow and develop so that they could free his country from the domination of the French and unite Germany as a democracy. Thus Jahn's system, which was later to influence the United States more heavily through the Turner movement, grew out of and always stressed democracy and social reform. Follen introduced the system at Harvard in 1826, and established the first outdoor gymnasium, consisting of exercise apparatus such as bars, ladders, and ropes. Beck introduced the same system at the Round Hill School in Northampton, Massachusetts. Following the lead of Follen at Harvard, a few universities, such as Yale, Brown, Amherst, Williams, Charleston, and Bowdoin, organized outdoor gymnasiums and encouraged gymnastic exercises.

A third fitness system, much more natively American, was based on the idea of getting fitness through manual labor. In 1831, leaders of this movement met in New York and organized the Society for Promoting Manual Labor in Literary Institutions. Basing their ideas on the Biblical evidence that God had ordained manual labor, followers of this system advocated the idea that manual labor was the best form of exercise.

A fourth system, also natively American, was the system of calisthenics for girls and women introduced by Catherine E. Beecher in female seminaries in Hartford and Cincinnati. Through simple movements accompanied by music, she aimed to produce grace, good carriage, and sound health.

A second period of emphasis on fitness came in the 1860s, with the introduction of Dr. Dio Lewis's new gymnastics for men, women, and children. Lewis, who attacked the popular notion that great strength was the mark of well-being and that gymnastics was primarily for gymnasts, directed his system to the "fat men, the feeble men, young boys and females of all ages—the classes most needing physical training."[3] His exercises, usually a series of movements performed with handheld implements, were designed to build not strength but flexibility, agility, and general health. Lewis introduced his system in the vicinity of Boston in 1860; it soon became so popular that it was taught in evening classes throughout the area. His book, *The New Gymnastics for Men, Women and Children,* was published in 1862. Feeling that the presence of a teacher was important to fitness development, he began his Normal Institute of Physical Education in Boston in 1861 to train teachers of physical education.

The 1850s and 1860s also saw a resurgence of gym building. In 1853, the University of Virginia constructed a wooden gym; it was followed shortly by the building of brick and stone gyms at Harvard, Yale, and Amherst and later at Princeton and Miami University of Ohio. Thomas Wentworth Higginson, in an article published in the *Atlantic Monthly* for 1861, described public gyms admiringly:

It is one good evidence of the increasing interest in these exercises, that the American gymnasiums built during the past year or two have surpassed all their predecessors in size and completeness, and have probably no superiors in the world. The Seventh Regiment Gymnasium in New York, just opened by Mr. Abner S. Brady, is one hundred and eighty feet by fifty-two, in its main hall, and thirty-five feet in height, with nearly one thousand pupils. The beautiful hall of the Metropolitan Gymnasium, in Chicago, measures one hundred and eight feet by eighty, and is twenty feet high at the sides, with a dome in the centre, forty feet high, and the same in diameter. Next to these probably rank the new gymnasiums at Cincinnati, the Tremont Gymnasium at Boston, and the Bunker Hill Gymnasium at Charleston, all recently opened.[4]

In 1879, the beginning of the third period of interest in fitness, Mr. Augustus Hemenway gave $110,000 for a new gym to be built at Harvard. Dr. Dudley Allen Sargent, a physician and director of a private gym in New York City, was appointed assistant professor of physical training and director of the Hemenway Gymnasium. Sargent's contribution to the development of fitness was to focus on the individual. Because he believed students were different in physical makeup and physical needs, he developed elaborate measurements of the strength of various parts of the body as well as ways to examine the heart and lungs. This data was then compared to a standard for a given age, and an individual set of exercises was prescribed.

The 1880s saw the second great era of gym building. Colleges such as Smith, Lehigh, Cornell, Tufts, and Johns Hopkins all built gyms. By 1909, 114 colleges had gymnasiums. Physical education departments also began at this time. By 1909, 111 colleges had some sort of physical education department that gave regular instruction in gymnastics.

During the 1890s, a number of movements and people stimulated the growth of fitness. Probably the major influence was the Turner movement, which had begun in the 1840s, diminished in the 1860s, and surged again in the late 1880s and 1890s. In 1848, revolutionary movements had swept over Europe; the German government in particular suppressed demands for a liberal government. As a result of this suppression, thousands of liberal Germans migrated to the United States. Soon these immigrants formed German gymnastic societies, called Turnvereins. The two oldest Turnvereins were organized in Cincinnati and New York in 1848. By 1852 twenty-two such societies had been organized throughout the North.

Emmett A. Rice, in *A Brief History of Physical Education*, describes the Turnvereins in this way:

The aims of the Turnvereine were to promote physical education, intellectual enlight-

> enment and sociability among members. The Turnvereine building was always provided with a gymnasium where classes in the German system of exercises were conducted for men, women, and children. The teachers in the early period were men who had had experience in Germany. Outdoor games and gymnastic meets and exhibitions were frequent. Education and enlightenment on social problems, political issues and American life in general was accomplished through the library, through lectures, debates and the schools. An atmosphere of brotherhood and friendship pervaded all the activities of the society.[5]

While interest in the movement had fallen off in the 1860s, it picked up again by the 1880s and 1890s. During the 1880s, the number of Turnvereins increased from 186 to 277, and total membership increased from 13,387 to 35,912. The primary influence of the Turners was on physical education in the schools. When leading cities began to introduce systematic exercise and games into school programs, the Turners contributed their long experience and well-trained leaders. Between 1885 and 1890, Kansas City, Chicago, Davenport, Cleveland, St. Louis, and Sandusky accepted physical education as part of regular school activity. All these programs were led by prominent Turners, graduates of the Turner normal college.

But other movements and systems also influenced the development of physical fitness during this period. The Swedish Movement Cure, a system of medical gymnastics from Sweden, thought to be the remedy for certain afflictions, became popular in the 1880s. In the early 1890s, the Delsarte System of Physical Culture also became popular. The creator of this system, Francois Delsarte, a French vocal and dramatic teacher, had developed certain physical exercises to train his students. Adding their own ideas, American teachers of education developed a system of exercises that claimed to produce poise, grace, beauty of face and figure, and health. The system came to be thought of as psycho-physical culture, unifying the body and the mind.

The YMCA, an organization formed in the 1840s to improve the spiritual condition of young men engaged in the trades, had been influenced by the interest in gymnastics that had swept the country in the 1850s. By 1860 the national convention favored the establishment of gymnasiums as "a safeguard against the allurement of objectionable places of resort, which have proved the ruin of thousands of the youth of our country."[6] Robert J. Roberts, the first important physical director of the YMCA, steered its approach to fitness between the two extremes of an emphasis on strength and endurance through difficult feats and the Dio Lewis system of working with very light apparatus. In 1887 the YMCA added a physical department to its newly opened International Training School in Springfield, Massachusetts, to train physical directors for the organization. Dr. Luther Gulick, made head of the department after Roberts resigned, helped increase the number of physical directors from 50 in 1887 to 244 in 1900. For Dr. Gulick, physical training was a vital part of the association program; it worked not only for the body but for the physical and spiritual development of the whole man.

The playground movement, which began in Boston in 1885, also contributed to the development of physical fitness. The first playgrounds were little more than sand gardens for young children, supervised by kindergarten teachers. But soon schoolyards were being designated as playgrounds. In 1889, Boston established a recreation center at Charles Bank, with outdoor gymnasiums and buildings equipped for men, women, and children. New York began to establish playgrounds in 1888, and Chicago followed in 1896 with an outdoor gymnasium and two swimming pools for Douglass Park. By 1900 Philadelphia, Pittsburgh, Baltimore, Hartford, New Haven, San Francisco, and Albany had begun playgrounds.

To the popular mind, one of the most entertaining chapters in the history of physical fitness was created by the strong men of Europe and America and their favorite activity, weight lifting. Weight lifting began in Germany and other Central European countries in the middle of the nineteenth century. Famous European strong men were such giants as Josef Steinbach, Karl Swoboda, and Herman Goerner; others were Arthur Saxon and George Hackenschmidt. Weight lifting began in athletic clubs and in the back rooms of taverns; the strong men performed prodigious feats of strength for crowds in taverns, gymnasiums, and circuses. They were usually heavy, with enormous girths, which came from drinking quantities of beer and eating starchy food.

In the late nineteenth and early twentieth centuries, European strong men toured the United States, entertaining audiences with their feats. The most famous was Eugene Sandow, a trim, well-proportioned showman managed by Florenz Ziegfeld. Other strong men, like the gigantic Canadian Louis Cyr and Warren Lincoln Davis of the United States, became famous. They stimulated a wave of strength seeking in America. In 1903, Alan Calvert began the mail order strength business by establishing the Milo Barbell company. Later he published his book *Super Strength* and a small magazine *Strength.* Much later, in 1938, Bob Hoffman began publishing his magazine *Strength and Health,* which is still being published today, and in 1936 he established the York Barbell company. His York Barbell Club won U.S. weight lifting championships, and in 1940 his Olympic club team won nearly every class.

Part of the history of weight lifting are the "Mr." contests. The Mr. America contest began in 1939 and was followed by the Mr. World and Mr. Universe contests. After World War II, these contests sprang up everywhere. Every small town or section had its "Mr. Greenville" or "Mr. South Bronx" contest. These contests probably did as much harm to strength building as good, for participants did not focus on total fitness but on developing ("pumping up" it was called) certain muscles.

At the end of the nineteenth century, physical fitness had become a major concern in the United States. It was being developed in the schools, in organizations such as the YMCA and the Boy Scouts, on public playgrounds, in gymnasiums, and even in circuses and on the stage. What stands out in the first twenty years of the twentieth century are not any new movements but one organization and two men. The organization was the American Association for the Advancement of Physical Education, created in 1885 and later called the American Physical Education Association. It appointed a committee to develop a set of body and strength measurements that would describe the ideal man and then to create a program of physical education to achieve this ideal. But realizing that such measurements did not measure the efficiency of the body in motion, Dr. Dudley Sargent, mentioned earlier in connection with the Hemenway Gymnasium at Harvard, tried to identify the basic abilities common to many forms of gymnastics and athletics. In 1902, he published his "Universal Test for Strength, Speed, and Endurance." This change, from a static to a dynamic concept of fitness, shifted the emphasis from gymnastics to athletics as the way to develop fitness. Ever since, U.S. physical education has emphasized sports, dance, and other "natural" activities.

Two individuals stand out in the history of fitness during this period. The first, Bernarr Macfadden, was the principal advocate of physical culture in the United States. Macfadden emphasized not only the development of muscular strength but the "strengthening of the entire assimilative and vital system."[7] Even better known are the contributions of President Theodore Roosevelt to the development of fitness. Everyone knows the story of how, with his father's inspiration, Roosevelt exercised in a gym regularly as a child, overcoming his asthma. In *The Strenuous Life,* he said: "In the last analysis a healthy state can exist only when the men and women who make it up lead clean, vigorous, healthy lives; when the children are so trained that they shall endeavor, not to shirk difficulties, but to overcome them; not to seek ease, but to know how to wrest triumph for toil and risk."[8]

Roosevelt was true to his word. During his second administration he discovered that the officers of the U.S. military were not in good shape. On December 2, 1907, he directed the secretary of war to begin a program of annual physical qualification in the U.S. Army, suggesting it be three consecutive days of forced cavalry marches. During the next year he asked that both the Navy and Marines institute similar programs. On January 13, 1909, to shame the Army for complaining against his order to keep fit, Roosevelt himself rode one hundred miles from Washington, D.C., to Warrenton, Virginia, over rough roads.

The story of fitness during the first half of the twentieth century is predominately an up-down history of a nation becoming intensely concerned about the state of its fitness during wartime and apathetic during peace time. During World War I, so many men were rejected from the armed services (during 1915-16, almost 82 percent) that the nation aroused itself. A number of states passed legislation making physical education mandatory in the schools. Soon fitness was much improved. At the end of the war, George E. Fisher said the men who served in the military were "in better condition than any similar number of men have ever been at one time in the United States."[9]

Unfortunately, with the prosperity of the 1920s, America forgot fitness. During the Depression which followed, rural youth migrated in masses to the cities. But even though recreation facilities for them grew, interest in physical fitness waned. At the beginning of World War II, once again the nation became concerned about its level of fitness and preparedness for war. In 1940, the physical endurance of a number of draftees was tested by the classic Harvard Step Test, and, with the exception of farm boys and ex-athletes, the men performed no better than the women. Once again, the number of draftees failing their physical examination because they were unfit was thought to be inordinately high.

The nation mobilized itself. National meetings were held, presidential orders were issued, national committees on fitness were formed, and even councils combining committees with organizations such as the American Medical Association were formed. Again, the government focused on fitness in the schools. A series of pamphlets, brochures, news articles, and fitness manuals were published.

New tests for fitness were developed, and new programs were tried in all branches of the military. Even industry became concerned. The recreation department of the C.I.O., for example, developed a physical fitness program. In spite of all these efforts, one-third of the nation's draftees were still considered unfit for duty. A Senate subcommittee investigated the problem. At the conclusion of its hearings, Senator Claude Pepper, the chairman, stated: "We have learned a profound lesson about the effects of sickness and physical and mental defects. This lesson has been driven home to us by the alarming fact that more than four million young men have been found ineligible for military service.[10]

Unfortunately, the nation had not seemed to learn its lesson, for interest in fitness waned almost as soon as the war was over. During the Korean War, General Hershey, director of Selective Service, reported that the rejection rate of inductees was 50 percent. Even this figure did not stir the public.

But the public did wake up in 1953 when Dr. Hans Kraus and Dr. Sonja Weber reported the results of years of research. Their minimum muscular fitness tests, which were simple strength and flexibility tests, were given to 4,264 American children and 2,870 children in Austria, Italy, and Switzerland. A shocking 57.9 percent of the American children failed, compared with 8.7 percent of the European children. President Eisenhower had Vice President Nixon convene a Conference on the Fitness of American Youth to deal with the problem. On advice from the conference, the president established the President's Council on Youth Fitness and the President's Citizens Advisory Committee on the Fitness of American Youth on July 16, 1956. Groups such as the American Association of Health, Physical Education, and Recreation, the YMCA, and the NCAA also called national conferences.

The result was a national focus on fitness. More national conferences were called by the president, forums on fitness were held, fitness tests were developed, and research studies of the relationship between exercise and fitness, heart disease and exercise, and fitness and age were begun. Knowledge about fitness and its relation to health expanded dramatically.

Interest in fitness remained high during the first years of the Kennedy administration. While he was still campaigning, Kennedy was asked by *Sports Illustrated* to write an article about the importance of sports and physical fitness in American life. In his article, Kennedy called the state of fitness in the United States "a national problem" that "requires national action."[11] He took such action just a month after coming to office by calling a Conference on Youth Fitness, at which he personally addressed the delegates. In July 1961, the President's Council on Youth Fitness released its *Youth Physical Fitness* booklet, which outlined a program for achieving fitness in the schools.

In the middle and late 1960s, books outlining systematic, step-by-step ways to achieve fitness began to appear. One of the first was the *Royal Canadian Air Force Exercise Plans for Physical Fitness* published in 1962; in 1968 Major Kenneth Cooper published his *Aerobics*, a system that allowed for a variety of ways to achieve and maintain cardiovascular fitness.

Probably it was Cooper's work that stimulated the current interest in running, jogging, and racing, for he felt that jogging was one of the most efficient ways to become fit. Whatever the case, the decade of the 1970s became the decade of the runner. The bookstores are full of new books on running, and there are over fifty magazines and newsletters on the subject.

At last Americans seem to have become aware of the need for fitness. It is not fashionable anymore to have a paunch or to smoke. Suddenly the streets are full of runners, and fitness centers are booming. Perhaps physical fitness has finally come of age in America.

REFERENCE WORKS

Although aspects of physical fitness and physical education have been the subjects of serious research for years, general reference works are just beginning to appear. There are as yet, for example, no dictionaries or encyclopedias on fitness. However, in the past two years, three new bibliographic indexes have begun. The first, *Physical Education Index,* first published in 1978, indexes 177 titles on such subjects as adaptive physical education, biomechanics-kinesiology, the history and philosophy of sports, and measurement and evaluation.

The Physical Education/Sports Index, also begun in 1978, indexes 105 serials in areas similar to those covered in the *Physical Education Index.* It is divided into two sections, the first listing articles pertaining to physical education (administration, instruction, history, philosophy, and so on) and the second listing articles on forty or more separate sports.

There are two more specialized indexes also. *Physical Fitness/Sports Medicine,* published quarterly by the President's Council on Physical Fitness and Sports, is a bibliography of articles selected from over two thousand periodicals and papers presented at congresses on the medical aspects of sports: exercise physiology, sports injuries, physical conditioning, and the medical aspects of exercise. Another such specialized index is *The Runner's Index,* which indexes articles on running, fitness, and sports medicine. It covers forty periodicals, including the *American Journal of Sports Medicine, Jogger, Research Quarterly, Runner, Runner's World,* and *Running Times.* A helpful bibliographic survey of one specialized fitness area is "The Marathon: A History and Review of the Literature" published in *Medicine and Science in Sports.* It surveys the literature on the physiological, biochemical, and psychological effects of running a marathon on competitors.

Researchers interested in materials on physical fitness contained in popular periodicals should check *Poole's Index to Periodical Literature,* the *Nineteenth Century Reader's Guide to Periodical Literature,* and the *Reader's Guide to Periodical Literature.* It pays to check a number of different headings in these indexes, for example, "physical culture" (in the older indexes), and "physical education and training," "exercise," "physical fitness," "military training" (during and near war times), "health," and, in recent years, "jogging" and "running."

There are a number of bibliographies of physical education and fitness published in historical studies. Surprisingly, the most scholarly history, Fred Eugene Leonard and George B. Affleck's *A Guide to the History of Physical Education,* contains neither a bibliography nor very helpful footnotes. Leonard did publish "A Select Bibliography of the History of Physical Training" in the *American Physical Education Review* in 1902. This helpful bibliography has been reprinted in Aileen S. Lockhard and Betty Spears, *Chronicle of American Physical Education, 1855-1930.* Leonard has divided important works on fitness by subject, ranging from general works and works on fitness in Greece to works on fitness in the United States.

Robert Knight Barney, in his "Physical Education and Sport in North America," published in *History of Physical Education and Sport,* also has a helpful general bibliography on physical education and fitness. The supplementary readings lists at the end of each chapter in Emmett A. Rice's *A Brief History of Physical Education* function as short bibliographies. Probably the most comprehensive bibliography on the history of fitness is in Cyril F. Dean's dissertation, "A Historical Study of Physical Fitness in the United States,

1790 through 1961." Finally, a number of handbooks on developing fitness and books on particular subjects such as fitness physiology or fitness evaluation contain bibliographies.

RESEARCH COLLECTIONS

Throughout the country are several general collections of materials pertaining to physical education, training, and fitness. Probably the largest general collection is at the University of Illinois at Urbana/Champaign, in the Applied Life Studies Library. The library tries to have fairly complete coverage of books published on all aspects of physical education as well as general books on sports. It also has complete coverage of health education and recreation. Its holdings are cataloged in the *Dictionary Catalog of the Applied Life Studies Library.*

There are other libraries with general holdings. The library at the University of Oregon has a general and research collection in health, physical education, recreation, and dance serials. It contains also a collection of 3,632 microcards or microfiche of unpublished research of national significance. The Education Library at George Peabody College for Teachers is particularly strong in physical education as well.

A number of repositories have materials of historical importance. The King Library, Department of Special Collections, at the University of Kentucky, has four hundred volumes of early physical education manuals and textbooks dating to 1925, as well as materials on eighteenth and nineteenth-century sports and games. The Francis Harvey Green Library at West Chester State College has a comprehensive (six hundred cataloged volumes) collection of works (dated 1890-1947) about the development of physical education in its Allen-Ehinger Collection. Finally, the Walter Clinton Jackson Library at the University of North Carolina, Greensboro, has two thousand cataloged volumes, including a collection of one thousand pamphlets. Its Homans Collection of historical materials acquired from Wellesley College dates from the sixteenth century to the early 1900s. It is particularly strong in the history of physical education for women and includes works on gymnastics, dance, physical activity, training, and theory.

The archives of the University Libraries of Indiana University-Purdue University at Indianapolis contain a wealth of materials relating to the American Turner Movement and its Normal College, which was located in Indianapolis after 1907 and was merged with Indiana University in 1941. They contain historical works on the Turners by Henry Metzner, Emil Rinsch, and others. There are also fifty-four boxes of North American Turner records dating from the time the Turners were headquartered in Indianapolis at the Athenaeum Turnverein. However, these records are presently unprocessed and not easily accessible.

HISTORY AND CRITICISM

A good deal of material on the history of physical fitness is available, but the researcher must look for it in a number of different places. Because physical fitness has always been so closely tied to physical education in the schools in the United States, much material is in histories of physical education. In fact, the most general and comprehensive histories of physical education are really histories of physical fitness. The terms are almost synonymous. But the researcher must also consult histories of special movements such as the Turner movement, or the YMCA works by prominent historical figures such as Dio Lewis, works about other well-known people in the history of fitness, histories of fitness specialties such as weight lifting, and a variety of journals.

There is no general history of fitness from its beginnings in America to the present. But by combining materials from several histories, the researcher can develop quite an adequate general history of the field. Fred Eugene Leonard's and George B. Affleck's *A Guide to the History of Physical Education,* although it goes only through the early twentieth century, is the definitive history. This work is scholarly and full of details and references to original documents. No researcher in the history of fitness can do without it. Leonard's *Pioneers of Modern Physical Training* is a popular version of the guide, containing biographical sketches of prominent historical figures.

Emmett A. Rice's *A Brief History of Physical Education,* a text designed for use in colleges and by teachers of physical education, is much less detailed than Leonard and Affleck but, because of this, more readable. The book gives the reader a quick overall description of an influence, movement, or development. C. W. Hackensmith's *History of Physical Education* also emphasizes movements, influences, and people rather than primary documents; it, too, brings the history of fitness up to the 1950s.

Earle F. Zeigler's *History of Physical Education and Sport,* containing different chapters by different authors, has a chapter on "Physical Education and Sport in North America" by Robert Knight Barney. The chapter focuses more on sport than fitness, however. Aileene S. Lockhard and Betty Spears have edited the interesting *Chronicle of American Physical Education, Selected Readings, 1855-1930,* which contains selections from original materials. Some of the articles written in the nineteenth century, by Beecher, Dio Lewis, and Luther Gulick, for example, give the reader a first-hand account of aspects of the development of fitness.

The most comprehensive history of physical fitness in America is Cyril F. Dean's doctoral dissertation, "A Historical Study of Physical Fitness in the United States, 1790 through 1961." Using the histories cited earlier plus other materials, Dean has written a comprehensive survey of the development of fitness organized by chronological periods and focusing on important influences, organizations, people, and trends. This is the place for the researcher unfamiliar with the history of physical fitness to begin.

A number of specialized historical studies of different aspects of fitness have been written. Gwendolyn A. Drew's dissertation, "A Historical Study of the Concern of the Federal Government for the Physical Fitness of Non-Age Youth with Reference to the Schools, 1790-1941," is a detailed investigation of the federal government's concern for physical fitness. Her history is based on federal legislative proposals made from 1790 through 1941. It emphasizes the fact that government has almost always played a major role in the development of fitness. Another dissertation, Patrick J. Carolan's "The History, Development, and Evaluation of a Federal Emphasis on Physical Fitness in Civilian Defense, 1940-1945," describes how the federal government attempted to encourage the development of physical fitness during World War II, sets forth its goals, and evaluates the success of its efforts.

Since 1848, the American Turner movement has played an important role in the history of fitness in America. A number of works have studied the Turners. Henry Metzner's *A Brief History of the American Turnerbund* describes the beginnings of the Turner movement in the United States, its influence on the public schools, and the foundation of its Normal College and sketches the biographies of such important people as Friedrich Jahn, Charles Beck, Charles Follen, and Franz Lieber. Fred Eugene Leonard's article in the *American Physical Education Review,* "German-American Gymnastic Societies and the North American Turnerbund," is a quick, helpful survey of the Turners, done with Leonard's usual detailed, statistical treatment. Emil Rinsch's *History of the Normal College of the American Gymnastic Union of Indiana University, 1866-1966,* traces in detail the history of the Normal College from the time it was first located in Indianapolis until it became a part of Indiana University.

The development of physical fitness in the YMCA is discussed briefly in Sherwood Eddy's *A Century with Youth: A History of the YMCA from 1844 to 1944* and in more detail by C. Howard Hopkins in his *History of the Y.M.C.A in North America.* Dio Lewis described his new gymnastics—its development, philosophy, and practice—in a two-part article, "New Gymnastics," written in 1862-63 for the *American Journal of Education.*

Strong men and weight lifters such as Eugene Sandow, Louis Cyr, George Hackenschmidt, and Milo Steinborn make up one of the most interesting chapters in the history of fitness. Their fame helped popularize the idea of fitness in the United States. Unfortunately, there is not much material available on these strong men. One helpful source is the introduction to Jim Murray's and Peter V. Karpovich's *Weight Training in Athletics,* which describes many famous strong men and their feats. Another source is *Strength and Health* magazine; it frequently runs articles on particular strong men.

Some books about fitness have been written by individuals who have played an important part in its history. Theodore Roosevelt's *The Strenuous Life: Essays and Addresses*, and Bernarr Macfadden's *Macfadden's System of Physical Training* are two such books. The historical researcher should also look at periodicals. Popular magazines are especially helpful sources. The nation's concern about the fitness of men to fight in World Wars I and II is documented in many articles in popular magazines, as is the recent wide popular interest in fitness and jogging. Finally, *Research Quarterly,* the official magazine of the American Association of Health, Physical Education, and Recreation, contains a number of articles on different aspects of the history of fitness.

A considerable body of literature has built up on the subject of fitness in the last one hundred years, especially in the last twenty. There are book-length records of proceedings of colloquia on various aspects of fitness; textbooks on exercise physiology; and books on how to get and stay fit, nutrition and fitness, getting fit for particular sports, running and fitness, weight lifting and fitness. Most of these materials are aimed at a technical audience, such as physicians, physical fitness directors, and physical educators interested in such topics as physiology and fitness testing; or at a popular audience more interested in how to get and stay fit, in a particular topic such as jogging, or in the benefits of fitness.

One example of a major study for technical readers is *Exercise and Fitness; A Collection of Papers Presented at the Colloquium on Exercise and Fitness by Seward C. Staley and others,* sponsored by the University of Illinois and held at Allerton Park, Illinois, in December 1959. The purpose of the colloquium was to review the effects of exercise on fitness. The twenty-one papers in this volume deal with medical, physiological, nutritional, psychological, and educational aspects of exercise and fitness. Later, as a result of an invitation by the officials of the Congress of Sports and Sciences, held in Tokyo in 1964 as a part of the Olympic Games program, the International Committee for the Standardization of Physical Fitness Tests was organized. Its purpose was to standardize assessments of work capacity and physical fitness, using resources and research from the disciplines of medicine, physiology, physique and body composition, and human performance. The result was its report, *Fitness, Health and Work Capacity: International Standards for Assessment,* edited by Leonard E. Larson and published in 1974. The committee's guide to exercise for the layman, *International Guide to Fitness and Health,* by Leonard E. Larson and Herbert Michelman, was published in 1973.

Of a more practical nature but still for technical readers are books on physiology and kinesiology. Generally these are texts for advanced college courses in kinesiology and physiology, such as Jerry N. Barnham and William Thomas,

Anatomical Kinesiology, Per-Olaf Astrand and Kaare Rodahl, *Textbook of Work Physiology*, Peter V. Karpovich, *Physiology of Muscular Activity*, Lawrence G. Morehouse and Augustus T. Miller, *Physiology of Exercise*, Roy J. Shephard, *Alive Man: The Physiology of Physical Activity* and *Endurance Fitness*, and H. A. de Vries, *Physiology of Exercise for Physical Education and Athletics.*

There is also a group of less technical books, probably designed for introductory courses in fitness and exercise. These books give simple explanations of the physiological basis for exercise and deal with practical aspects of fitness such as diet, general health, safety principles, and programs and methods. Examples are Robert V. Hockey's *Physical Fitness, the Pathway to Healthful Living*, Donald R. Casady, Donald F. Mapes, and Louis E. Alley's *Handbook of Physical Fitness Activities*, and Perry Johnson and Donald Stolberg's *Conditioning.* A slightly different kind of book is Arthur H. Steinhaus's *Toward an Understanding of Health and Physical Education*, a collection of his short papers on the meaning of physical education, its physiology, motivational techniques, and current practices.

Ever since the Kraus-Weber tests, students of physical fitness have been concerned with ways to measure fitness. Two books on this subject directed to those preparing for a career in physical education or to those already teaching are Donald K. Mathews's *Measurement in Physical Education* and H. Harrison Clarke's *Application of Measurement to Health and Physical Education.* Both offer numerous specific tests of physical fitness—tests of strength, motor ability, skill, and nutrition.

A slightly different class of books deals with the subject of nutrition and fitness. Books such as L. Jean Bogert, George Briggs, and Doris H. Calloway's *Nutrition and Physical Fitness*; Ernst Jokl's *Nutrition, Exercise, and Body Composition*; Jana Parízková's *Body Fat and Physical Fitness*; *Body Composition and Lipid Metabolism in Different Regimes of Physical Activity*, and Jana Parízková's and V. A. Rogozkin's *Nutrition, Physical Fitness and Health* are directed to serious students of the relationship between nutrition and exercise. Frank I. Katch and William D. McArdle's *Nutrition, Weight Control, and Exercise*, on the other hand, is designed for people who exercise as well as for participants in short courses in physical fitness.

Most of the materials directed to popular readers are handbooks or guides to fitness. These have been around for at least a hundred years. J. Madison Watson, for instance, published his *Handbook of Calisthenics and Gymnastics* in 1864; Dio Lewis, his *The New Gymnastics for Men, Women, and Children* in the same year; and William A. Stecher, *Gymnastics: A Textbook of the German-American System of Gymnastics* in 1896. In *A Brief History of Physical Education*, Emmett A. Rice lists some physical culture manuals published between 1850 and 1890. Some of the titles are *The Illustrated Family Museum*, *Manual of Gymnastics Exercises for Schools and Families*,

How to Get Strong and How to Stay So, and *Sound Bodies for Our Boys and Girls.*

Fitness handbooks have been published throughout the whole history of fitness, but a kind of renaissance in handbooks began in 1968 with the publication of Kenneth H. Cooper's *Aerobics.* Probably because it was one of the first fully systematic guides to exercise and gave ways to measure results immediately, Cooper's *Aerobics* became immensely popular. His later *New Aerobics* was also popular, as was *Aerobics for Women* written with Mildred Cooper. But the Royal Canadian Air Force exercise book, published six years earlier, had been used widely also, because it gave the same specific directions on how to exercise and graduated charts setting forth exercise times and number of repetitions for achieving different levels. *The Official Y.M.C.A. Physical Fitness Handbook* by Clayton R. Myers, more recent than Cooper or the Royal Canadian books, also gives exercise levels and particular exercises to achieve fitness.

Besides these, there are any number of other popular guides and handbooks on fitness. Typical is Howard G. Knuttgen and David Shepro, *Complete Conditioning: The No-Nonsense Guide to Fitness and Good Health,* which prescribes methods and exercises to obtain fitness, weight control, and health and also discusses such topics as nutrition, calories, respiration, circulation, and exercise and heart rate. A similar book is Donald K. Mathews's *Beginning Conditioning,* which describes the values and history of conditioning and gives exercises for flexibility, endurance, and strength. Other such handbooks are Charles T. Kuntzleman's *The Exerciser's Handbook: How to Get More out of the Exercises You Are Doing—Jogging, Weight-lifting, Swimming, Tennis, Bicycling, or Any Other Serious Exercise;* Raymond Harris and Lawrence J. Frankel's *Guide to Fitness After Fifty; Physical Fitness: How to Get It and Keep It,* published by *U.S. News and World Report;* and Dan Millman's *Whole Body Fitness: Training Mind, Body and Spirit.*

A number of other handbooks are directed more to the physical educator but are useful for a popular reader. Examples in this category are Jack R. Peebler's *Controlled Exercise for Physical Fitness;* Philip E. Allsen, Joyce M. Harrison, and Barbara Vance, *Fitness for Life: An Individualized Approach;* and Frank Vitale's *Individualized Fitness Programs.*

Other books describe particular ways to gain fitness. An example is Sidney Filson's and Claudia Jessup's *Jump into Shape: The Fast Fun Way to Physical Fitness.* Still others describe how to control weight or slim a figure through exercise. Some examples are Patricia White's *Body Contouring, Fitness, and Poise,* M. G. Sholtis's *Slimnastics Is Fun,* and Blanche J. Drury, *Posture and Figure Control Through Physical Education,* as well as Linda Garrison, Phyllis Leslie, and Deborah Blackmore's *Fitness and Figure Control: The Creation of You,* a book which purports to show how to shape your life as well as your figure.

In an article published in October 1898, Frances Alice Kellor wrote, "If women are to accomplish the same quantity of intellectual work as men, one of the essentials is a more active, variable physical life."[12] A glance at some of the fitness handbooks for women shows that her wish is being fulfilled. There are books like Ellington Darden's *Especially for Women,* which deals with such subjects as strength training, keeping in shape during pregnancy, and diet and nutrition. Kathryn Lance's book *Getting Strong: A Woman's Guide to Realizing Her Potential* focuses on strength and how women can develop it, and *Jane Boutelle's Lifetime Fitness for Women,* written by Boutelle and Samm Sinclair Baker, shows how to develop a lifetime fitness plan.

Nor have children been slighted in the fitness field. There are programs for developing fitness in school-age children. *Children and Fitness, A Program for Elementary Schools, Report,* edited by Sue M. Hall and *Youth and Fitness, A Program for Secondary Schools, Report,* both published by the American Association for Health, Physical Education, and Recreation, are examples. Other books show educators how to develop fitness in children and adolescents: Albert V. Carron's and Donald Bailey's *Strength Development in Boys from 10 to 16 Years* and Earl L. Wallis's and Gene A. Logan's *Exercise for Children* are two.

A number of books deal with fitness and sports. James A. Michener's *Sports in America* has an excellent chapter on "Sports and Health," dealing with the relationship between sports and fitness. His tables and charts describe how sports can lead to particular levels of fitness by showing the demand each makes for oxygen and calories. A new guide to fitness for the athlete is John Unitas and George Dintiman, *Improving Health and Perfection in the Athlete,* which deals in a question-answer format with areas such as athletics and drugs, nutrition, exercise and aging, and training programs. A number of other handbooks deal with how to be fit for sports. Some are general in nature: *Interval Training: Conditioning for Sports and General Fitness* by Edward L. Fox and Donald K. Mathews, *Athletic Training and Physical Fitness: Physiological Principles and Practices of the Conditioning Process* by Jack H. Wilmore, and *Athletic Fitness: The Athlete's Guide to Training and Conditioning* by Dewey Schurman. Others show how to become fit for a particular sport: *Shaping Up to Ship Out: Exercises for Water Sports and General Outdoor Fitness* by James Holechek and *Wrestling Physical Conditioning Encyclopedia* by John Jesse are examples.

The contemporary American who thinks of physical fitness probably thinks of jogging. Jogging is so popular as a way to attain fitness that it has developed its own literature, including a number of books and periodicals. The major book in the field is James F. Fixx's *The Complete Book of Running,* published in 1977, which deals with every aspect of running and jogging—from the effects of running and the right gear to common injuries, training schedules, and racing. Other books in the same category as Fixx's are William

J. Bowerman, W. E. Harris, and James M. Shea's *Jogging, A Physical Fitness Program for All Ages,* a detailed instructional guide to jogging, light running, and walking; *The Complete Runner,* edited by the editors of *Runner's World,* containing short articles on the philosophy, psychology, and physiology of running; George Sheehan's *Dr. Sheehan On Running;* and Arthur Shay with Dr. Noel Nequin, *40 Common Errors in Running and How to Correct Them.*

A number of books on running injuries and their treatment have been published. Steven L. Subojnick's *Cures for Common Running Injuries* explains why runners get hurt and what they can do about it; much like it is Eric C. Golanty's *How to Prevent and Heal Running and Other Sports Injuries.* Similar books are Mirkin and Hoffman, *The Sports Medicine Book* and Richard H. Dominguez, *The Complete Book of Sports Medicine,* which deals in part one with sports, fitness, and health, and in part two with sports injuries and problems.

For many, running seems to be an inner as well as an outer experience. George Sheehan's *Running and Being: The Total Experience* explains the relationship between running and the mind. A more systematic approach to the same subject is Valerie Andrews's *The Psychic Power of Running: How the Body can Illuminate the Mysteries of the Mind,* which discusses how running can reawaken feelings, eliminate depression and anxiety, foster creativity, and unravel the mysteries of the unconscious. In two articles published in *Runner's World* in January and February of 1978, Hal Higdon discusses running as therapy for people with emotional problems. Dr. Thaddeus Kostrubala's *The Joy of Running* describes how running has changed his patients' lives.

Marathon racing has attracted a number of writers. Joel Homer, in his *Marathons: The Ultimate Challenge,* describes the history, running courses, records, and famous people of sixteen marathons. A researcher interested in the marathon phenomenon should study the last ten years' issues of such classic running magazines as *Runner's World* and the *Runner.* The December 1979 issue of the *Runner,* for instance, is devoted wholly to the marathon, as is the February 1978 issue of *Runner's World.* A more general survey of running, swimming, and biking marathons is Gail Campbell's *Marathon: The World of the Long-Distance Athlete,* which surveys the history of these different kinds of marathons and describes some famous courses and people who have completed them. Some books on racing and distance running in general are Joe Henderson, *The Long Run Solution,* a conversational account of the pain of long distance running, its benefits, and how to begin and continue running; Henderson, *Run Farther, Run Faster,* describing training, racing, and improving; Jack Daniels, Robert Fitts, and George Sheehan, *Conditioning for Distance Running;* and Marc Bloom, *Cross Country Running.*

But this discussion still has not exhausted the specialty books on running. There are books written by well-known running personalities such as Marty Liquori's *On the Run* and Steve Heidenreich's *Running Back.* There are even running books for travelers. Marlene D'alton's *The Runner's Guide to the USA* describes running trails in over thirty cities, and *The Travelling Runner's Guide* by R. Penelope Scheerer and John R. Schwanbeck describes where to run in twenty-one cities in the country. Finally, at least one book, Peter Steincrohn's *How to Cure Your Jogger Mania: Enjoy Fitness and Good Health Without Running* even attacks running as the key to fitness and explains how one can be fit without exposing himself to its dangers and pains.

Another genre of fitness books is aimed at those who would prefer to walk their way to fitness. *The Complete Book of Walking* by Charles T. Kuntzleman and the editors of *Consumer Guide* describes the value of walking, tells how to begin a walking for fitness program, and guides the walker as to the proper shoes, walking paths, and exercises. Another all-round book on walking is *The New Complete Walker: The Joys and Techniques of Hiking and Backpacking* by Colin Fletcher, which describes how to walk, what to wear, and how to pack and camp.

Americans have been trying to heft their way to fitness for about as long as they have been thinking about the subject. Late nineteenth- and early twentieth-century strong men stimulated an interest in weight lifting as a way to gain fitness that is still exemplified in a number of books. For body builders there are books like Jim Murray's *Inside Body Building,* Charles Gaines and George Butler's *Pumping Iron: The Art and Sport of Body Building,* Bruce Randall's *The Barbell Way to Physical Fitness,* and Franco Columbo's and Richard Tyler's *Winning: Weight Lifting and Power Lifting.* For beginners there is Edward Franz's and Bruce Melin's *Beginning Weight Training,* which discusses the value of weight training, its history, and proper equipment and technique, and Daniel P. Riley's *Strength Training by the Experts,* a collection of essays on strength training.

The student of popular culture will be interested in the whole question of the value or effect of physical fitness. Just how does a fitness program, be it calisthenics, weight lifting, jogging, or another form of exercise, help us anyway? People have been speculating about this question for as long as they have been talking about fitness. Between 1890 and 1910, for instance, when fitness was becoming popular in the schools, periodicals such as *Education* and *Proceedings of the National Education Association* speculated on the value of fitness programs.

Answers ranged widely. In fact, to hear proponents tell it, there was hardly anything that fitness programs could not do. They could certainly build brain power, for instance, for with the development of motor abilities came the development of brain cells. In the *Proceedings of the National Educational Association,* one writer stated, "I cannot refrain from making a statement here that I have made on two former occasions before this department: that I have never seen, in all my experience and observation, a single case of brain disorderliness, of brain slovenliness, that was not benefited by physical training."[13] Others commented on the power of fitness programs to build will power, self-reliance, confidence, and grace; to build character through strenuous work; to give one the ability to make proper ethical decisions, and to compensate for physical defects and create a harmonious, aesthetic body. Even as early as the second decade of the twentieth century, articles in popular magazines advised businessmen to exercise—it could help them in their careers.

Currently, people seemed convinced of the benefits of fitness programs. At least there is no denying the current surge of interest in them. YMCA memberships are climbing, and people are joining expensive commercial fitness centers and running on high school tracks or almost any available roadway, grass strip, or sidewalk. The student need go no further than current popular magazines to see just how widespread the fitness movement is. This essay probably surveys the first few materials being developed in the field; in ten years the subject may well require an essay twice the length to survey the materials available.

NOTES

1. Julian P. Boyd, ed., *The Papers of Thomas Jefferson,* 18 vols. (Princeton: Princeton University Press, 1955), 11 (January 1 to August 6, 1787), 558.
2. Noah Webster, *Address to Young Gentlemen* (1790), as quoted in Emmett A. Rice, *A Brief History of Physical Education* (New York: Barnes, 1936), pp. 159-60.
3. As quoted in Rice, p. 176.
4. Thomas Wentworth Higginson, "Gymnastics," *Atlantic Monthly,* 7 (March 1861), 283-302, reprinted in *Chronicle of American Physical Education, 1855-1930,* ed. Aileene S. Lockhard and Betty Spears (Dubuque, Iowa: Wm. C. Brown, 1972), pp. 32-33.
5. Rice, p. 162.
6. C. Howard Hopkins, *History of the Y.M.C.A. in North America* (New York: Associated Press, 1951), pp. 33-34.
7. Bernarr Macfadden, *Macfadden's System of Physical Training* (New York: Hulbert, 1895), p. 6, as quoted in Cyril F. Dean, "A Historical Study of Physical Fitness in the United States, 1790 through 1961" (Ph. D. dissertation, George Peabody College for Teachers, 1964), p. 35.
8. Theodore Roosevelt, *The Strenuous Life: Essays and Addresses* (New York: Century, 1899), p. 3.
9. George E. Fisher, "Points of Emphasis in a Post-War Program of Physical Training," *American Physical Education Review,* 24 (1919), 126, as quoted in Dean, p. 35.
10. *New York Times,* July 10, 1944, as quoted in Dean, p. 93.
11. John F. Kennedy, "The Soft American," *Sports Illustrated,* 13 (December 1960), 17.
12. Frances Alice Kellor," A Psychological Basis for Physical Culture," *Education*, 19 (October 1898), 104.
13. William O. Krohn, "Physical Education and Brain Building," *Proceedings of the National Education Association*, 45 (1903), 822.

BIBLIOGRAPHY

BOOKS AND ARTICLES

Allsen, Philip E., Joyce M. Harrison, and Barbara Vance. *Fitness for Life: An Individualized Approach.* Dubuque, Iowa: Wm. C. Brown, 1975.

Andrews, Valerie. *The Psychic Power of Running: How the Body Can Illuminate the Mysteries of the Mind.* New York: Rawson, Wade, 1978.

Astrand, Per-Olaf, and Kaare Rodahl. *Textbook of Work Physiology.* New York: McGraw-Hill, 1970.

Barney, Robert Knight. "Physical Education and Sport in North America." In *History of Physical Education and Sport.* Edited by Earle F. Zeigler. Englewood Cliffs, N.J.: Prentice-Hall, 1979, pp. 171-227.

Barnham, Jerry N., and William Thomas. *Anatomical Kinesiology.* London: Macmillan, 1969.

Bloom, Marc. *Cross Country Running.* Mountain View, Calif.: World, 1978.

Bogert, L. Jean, George Briggs, and Doris H. Calloway. *Nutrition and Physical Fitness.* Philadelphia: Saunders, 1973.

Boutelle, Jane, and Samm Sinclair Baker. *Jane Boutelle's Lifetime Fitness for Women.* New York: Simon & Schuster, 1978.

Bowerman, William J., W. E. Harris, and James M. Shea. *Jogging, A Physical Fitness Program for All Ages.* New York: Grosset & Dunlop, 1967.

Calvert, Alan. *Super Strength.* Philadelphia: Milo, 1924.

Campbell, Gail. *Marathon: The World of the Long-Distance Athlete.* New York: Sterling, 1977.

Carolan, Patrick. "The History, Development, and Evaluation of a Federal Emphasis on Physical Fitness in Civilian Defense, 1940-1945." Ph.D. dissertation, Columbia University, 1952.

Carron, Albert V., and Donald A. Bailey. *Strength Development in Boys from 10 to 16 Years.* Chicago: University of Chicago Press, 1969.

Casady, Donald R., Donald F. Mapes, and Louis E. Alley. *Handbook of Physical Fitness Activities.* New York: Macmillan, 1965.

Clarke, H. Harrison. *Application of Measurement to Health and Physical Education.* Englewood Cliffs, N.J.: Prentice-Hall, 1967.

Columbo, Franco, and Richard Tyler. *Winning: Weight Lifting and Power Lifting.* Chicago: Continental Books, 1979.

Cooper, Kenneth H. *Aerobics.* New York: Evans, 1968.

______. *The New Aerobics.* New York: Evans, 1970.

Cooper, Mildred, and Kenneth H. *Aerobics for Women.* New York: M. Evans, 1972.

D'alton, Marlene. *The Runner's Guide to the USA.* New York: Summit Books, 1978.

Daniels, Jack, Robert Fitts, and George Sheehan. *Conditioning for Distance Running.* New York: Wiley, 1978.

Darden, Ellington. *Especially for Women.* West Point, N.Y.: Leisure Press, 1977.

Dean, Cyril F. "A Historical Study of Physical Fitness in the United States, 1790 through 1961." Ph.D. dissertation, George Peabody College for Teachers, 1964.

de Vries, H. A. *Physiology of Exercise for Physical Education and Athletics.* Dubuque, Iowa: Wm. C. Brown, 1974.

Dictionary Catalog of the Applied Life Sciences Library (Formerly Physical Education

Library), University of Illinois at Urbana-Champaign, Vols. 1-4. Boston: Hall, 1977.

Dominguez, Richard H. *The Complete Book of Sports Medicine.* New York: Scribner's, 1979.

Drew, Gwendolyn A. "A Historical Study of the Concern of the Federal Government for the Physical Fitness of Non-Age Youth with Reference to the Schools, 1790-1941." Ph. D. dissertation, University of Pittsburgh, 1944.

Drury, Blanche J. *Posture and Figure Control Through Physical Education.* Palo Alto, Cal.: National Press, 1961.

Eddy, Sherwood. *A Century with Youth: A History of the Y.M.C.A. from 1844 to 1944.* New York: Associated Press, 1944.

Editors of Runner's World. *The Complete Runner.* Mountain View, Calif.: World, 1974.

Filson, Sidney, and Claudia Jessup. *Jump into Shape: The Fast, Fun Way to Physical Fitness.* New York: F. Watts, 1978.

Fixx, James F. *The Complete Book of Running.* New York: Random House, 1977.

Fletcher, Colin. *The New Complete Walker: The Joys and Techniques of Hiking and Backpacking.* 2nd ed. New York: Knopf, 1974.

Fox, Edward L., and Donald K. Matthews. *Interval Training: Conditioning for Sports and General Fitness.* Philadelphia: Saunders, 1974.

Franz, Edward, and Bruce Melin. *Beginning Weight Training.* Belmont, Calif.: Wadsworth, 1965.

Gaines, Charles, and George Butler. *Pumping Iron: The Art and Sport of Body Building.* New York: Simon & Schuster, 1974.

Garrison, Linda, Phyllis Leslie, and Deborah Blackmore. *Fitness and Figure Control: The Creation of You.* Palo Alto, Calif.: Mayfield, 1974.

Golanty, Eric. *How to Prevent and Heal Running and Other Sports Injuries.* Cranbury, N.J.: Barnes, 1979.

Hackensmith, C. W. *History of Physical Education.* New York: Harper & Row, 1966.

Hall, Sue M., ed. *Children and Fitness, A Program for Elementary Schools, Report.* National Conference on Fitness of Children of Elementary School Age. Washington, D.C.: American Association for Health, Physical Education, and Recreation, 1960.

Harris, Raymond, and Lawrence J. Frankel, eds. *Guide to Fitness After Fifty.* New York: Plenum Press, 1977.

Heidenreich, Steve, and Dave Dorr. *Running Back.* New York: Hawthorn Books, 1979.

Henderson, Joe. *The Long Run Solution.* Mountain View, Calif.: World, 1976.

———. *Run Farther, Run Faster.* Mountain View, Calif.: World, 1979.

Higdon, Hal. "Can Running Cure Mental Illness? Part One: Running and the Mind." *Runner's World,* 13 (January 1978), 36-43.

———. "Can Running Put Mental Patients on Their Feet? Part Two: Running and the Mind." *Runner's World,* 13 (February 1978) 36-43.

Higginson, Thomas Wentworth. "Gymnastics." *Atlantic Monthly,* 7 (March 1861), 283-302.

Hockey, Robert V. *Physical Fitness, the Pathway to Healthful Living.* 3rd ed. St. Louis, Mo.: C. V. Mosby, 1977.

Holechek, James. *Shaping Up to Ship Out: Exercises for Water Sports and General Outdoor Fitness.* Cambridge, Md.: Cornell Maritime Press, 1977.

Homer, Joel. *Marathons: The Ultimate Challenge.* Garden City, N.J.: Dolphin Books/Doubleday, 1979.

Hopkins, C. Howard. *History of the Y.M.C.A. in North America.* New York: Associated Press, 1951.

Jesse, John. *Wrestling Physical Conditioning Encyclopedia.* Pasadena, Calif.: Athletic Press, 1974.

Johnson, Perry, and Donald Stolberg. *Conditioning.* Englewood Cliffs, N.J.: Prentice-Hall, 1971.

Jokl, Ernst. *Nutrition, Exercise, and Body Composition.* Springfield, Ill.: Charles Thomas, 1964.

Karpovich, Peter V. *Physiology of Muscular Activity.* 6th ed. Philadelphia: Saunders, 1965.

Kasch, F. W., and J. L. Boyer. *Adult Fitness.* Palo Alto, Calif.: National Press Books, 1978.

Katch, Frank I., and William D. McArdle. *Nutrition, Weight Control, and Exercise.* Boston: Houghton Mifflin, 1967.

Kennedy, John F. "The Soft American." *Sports Illustrated*, 13 December 1960), 15-17.

Knuttgen, Howard G., and David Shepro. *Complete Conditioning: The No-Nonsense Guide to Fitness and Good Health.* Reading, Mass.: Addison-Wesley, 1976.

Kostrubala, Thaddeus. *The Joy of Running.* Philadelphia: Lippincott, 1976.

Kuntzleman, Charles T. *The Exerciser's Handbook: How to Get More out of the Exercise You are Doing—Jogging, Weight-Lifting, Swimming, Tennis, Bicycling or Any Other Serious Exercise.* New York: McKay, 1978.

———, and the Editors of Consumer Guide. *The Complete Book of Walking.* New York: Simon & Schuster, 1979.

Lance, Kathryn. *Getting Strong: A Woman's Guide to Realizing Her Physical Potential.* Indianapolis: Bantam Books, by arrangement with Bobbs Merrill, 1978.

Larson, Leonard E., ed. *Fitness, Health, and Work Capacity: International Standards for Assessment.* New York: Macmillan, 1974.

———, and Herbert Michelman. *International Guide to Fitness and Health.* New York: Crown, 1973.

Leonard, Fred Eugene. "German-American Gymnastic Societies and the North American Turnerbund." *American Physical Education Review.* 15 (December 1910), 617-28.

———. *Pioneers of Modern Physical Training.* New York: Associated Press, 1915.

———. "A Select Bibliography of the History of Physical Training," *American Physical Education Review*, 7 (March 1902), 39-48.

———, and George B. Affleck. *A Guide to the History of Physical Education.* 3rd ed. Philadelphia: Lea & Febiger, 1947.

Lewis, Dio. "New Gymnastics." *American Journal of Education.* 11 (1862), 531-56; 12 (1863), 665-700.

———. *The New Gymnastics for Men, Women, and Children.* 8th ed. Boston: Ticknor and Fields, 1864.

Liquori, Marty, and Skip Myslenk. *On the Run.* New York: Morrow, 1979.

Lockhard, Aileene S., and Betty Spears, eds. *Chronicle of American Physical*

Education, Selected Readings, 1855-1930. Dubuque, Iowa: Wm. C. Brown, 1972.
Macfadden, Bernarr, *Macfadden's System of Physical Training*, New York: Hulbert, 1895.
"The Marathon." *Runner,* 2 (December 1979), Special issue.
"The Marathon: A Special Report." *Runner's World,* 13 (February 1978), Special issue.
Maron, M. B., and S. M. Horvath. "The Marathon: A History and Review of the Literature." *Medicine and Science in Sports,* 10 (1978), 137-50.
Mathews, Donald K. *Beginning Conditioning.* Belmont, Cal.: Wadsworth, 1965.
______. *Measurement in Physical Education.* 3rd ed. Philadelphia: Saunders, 1968.
Metzner, Henry. *A Brief History of the American Turnerbund.* Translated by Theodore Stempfel. Rev. ed. Pittsburgh: National Executive Committee of the American Turnerbund, 1924.
Michener, James A. *Sports in America.* New York: Random House, 1976.
Millman, Dan. *Whole Body Fitness: Training Mind, Body, and Spirit.* New York: Potter, 1979.
Mirkin, Gabe, and Marshall Hoffman. *The Sports Medicine Book.* Boston: Little, Brown, 1978.
Morehouse, Laurence E., and Augustus T. Miller. *Physiology of Exercise.* 7th ed. St. Louis, Mo.: Mosby, 1976.
Murray, Jim. *Inside Body Building.* Chicago: Continental Books, 1978.
______, and Peter V. Karpovich. *Weight Training in Athletics.* Englewood Cliffs, N.J.: Prentice-Hall, 1956.
Myers, Clayton R. *The Official Y.M.C.A. Physical Fitness Handbook.* New York: Popular Library, 1975.
Parízková, Jana. *Body Fat and Physical Fitness: Body Composition and Lipid Metabolism in Different Regimes of Physical Activity.* The Hague: Nijhoff Medical Division, 1977.
______, and V. A. Rogozkin, eds. *Nutrition, Physical Fitness and Health.* Baltimore: University Park Press, 1978.
Peebler, Jack R. *Controlled Exercise for Physical Fitness.* Springfield, Ill.: Thomas, 1962.
Physical Fitness: How to Get It and Keep It. Washington, D.C.: U. S. News and World Report, 1970.
Pollock, Michael L., Jack H. Wilmore, and Samuel M. Fox. *Health & Fitness Through Physical Activity.* New York: Wiley, 1978.
President's Council on Youth Fitness. *Youth Physical Fitness—Suggested Elements of a School-Centered Program.* Washington D.C.: Government Printing Office, 1961.
Randall, Bruce. *The Barbell Way to Physical Fitness.* Garden City, N.Y.: Doubleday, 1970.
Rice, Emmett A. *A Brief History of Physical Education.* New York: Barnes, 1936.
Riley, Daniel P., ed. *Strength Training by the Experts.* West Point, N.Y.: Leisure Press, 1977.
Rinsch, Emil. *History of the Normal College of the American Gymnastic Union of Indiana University, 1866-1966.* Indianapolis: B & L Composition and Printing, 1966.
Roosevelt, Theodore. *The Strenuous Life: Essays and Addresses.* New York: Century, 1899.

Royal Canadian Air Force Exercise Plans for Physical Fitness. Rev. U.S. ed. New York: Pocket Books, 1962.

Scheerer, R. Penelope, and John R. Schwanbeck. *The Traveling Runner's Guide: Where to Run in 21 Cities and the United States.* New York: Dutton, 1978.

Schurman, Dewey. *Athletic Fitness: The Athlete's Guide to Training and Conditioning.* New York: Atheneum, 1975.

Shay, Arthur, with Dr. Noel Nequin. *40 Common Errors in Running and How to Correct Them.* Chicago: Continental Books, 1979.

Sheehan, George. *Dr. Sheehan on Running.* Mountain View, Cal.: Bantam Books, by arrangement with World, 1975.

______. *Running and Being: The Total Experience.* New York: Simon & Schuster, 1978.

Shephard, Roy J. *Alive Man: The Physiology of Physical Activity.* Springfield, Ill.: Thomas, 1972.

______. *Endurance Fitness.* 2nd ed. Toronto: University of Toronto Press, 1977.

Sholtis, M. G. *Slimnastics Is Fun.* Merrillville, Ind.: Leisure Service, 1976.

Staley, Seward C., et al. *Exercise and Fitness: A Collection of Papers Presented at the Colloquium on Exercise and Fitness.* Monticello, University of Illinois College of Physical Education and The Athletic Institute, 1959.

Stecher, William A. *Gymnastics: A Textbook of the German-American System of Gymnastics.* Boston: Lee and Shepard, 1896.

Steincrohn, Peter. *How to Cure Your Jogger Mania: Enjoy Fitness and Good Health Without Running.* Cranbury, N.J.: Barnes, 1979.

Steinhaus, Arthur H. *Toward an Understanding of Health and Physical Education.* Dubuque, Iowa: Wm. C. Brown, 1963.

Subojnick, Steven L. *Cures for the Common Running Injuries.* Mountain View, Calif.: World, 1979.

Unitas, John, and George Dintiman. *Improving Health and Perfection in the Athlete.* Englewood Cliffs, N.J.: Prentice-Hall, 1979.

Vitale, Frank. *Individualized Fitness Programs.* Englewood Cliffs, N.J.: Prentice-Hall, 1973.

Wallis, Earl L., and Gene A. Logan. *Exercise for Children.* Englewood Cliffs, N.J.: Prentice-Hall, 1966.

Watson, J. Madison. *Handbook of Calisthenics and Gymnastics.* Chicago: Sherwood, 1864.

White, Patricia. *Body Contouring, Fitness, and Poise.* Palo Alto, Calif.: Peek, 1966.

Wilmore, Jack H. *Athletic Training and Physical Fitness: Physiological Principles and Practices of the Conditioning Process.* Boston: Allyn and Bacon, 1977.

Youth and Fitness, A Program for Secondary Schools, Report. National Conference on Fitness of Secondary School Youth. Washington, D.C.: American Association for Health, Physical Education, and Recreation, 1959.

Zeigler, Earle F. *History of Physical Education and Sport.* Englewood Cliffs, N.J.: Prentice-Hall, 1979.

INDEXES

Abstracts of Popular Culture. Bowling Green, Ohio: Bowling Green Popular Press, 1976-.

Nineteenth Century Reader's Guide to Periodical Literature, 1890-1899. New York: H. W. Wilson, 1944.
Physical Education Index. Cape Girardeau, Mo.: Ben Oak, 1978-.
Physical Education/Sports Index. Albany, N.Y.: Marathon Press, 1978-.
Physical Fitness/Sports Medicine. Washington, D.C.: President's Council on Physical Fitness and Sports, 1978-.
Poole's Index to Periodical Literature. Gloucester, Mass.: Peter Smith, 1802-1906.
Reader's Guide to Periodical Literature. Minneapolis: H. W. Wilson, 1900-.
Runner's Index: A Guide to Periodical Information for Runners. Albany, N.Y.: Mancuso, 1978-.

PERIODICALS

American Journal of Sports Medicine. Baltimore, 1972-.
Education. Boston, 1880-.
Jogger. Washington, D.C., 1977-.
Medicine and Science in Sports. Madison, Wisc., 1969-.
Proceedings of the National Education Association. Washington, D.C., 1858-.
Research Quarterly. Ann Arbor, Mich., 1930-. Since March 1980, *Research Quarterly for Exercise and Sport.*
Runner. New York, 1978-.
Runner's World. Mountain View, Calif., 1966-.
Running Times. Washington, D.C., 1977-.
Sports Illustrated. New York, 1954-.
Strength. Philadelphia, 1955-.
Strength and Health. York, Penn., 1932-.

CHAPTER 12 Pornography

Paul P. Somers, Jr.,
and Nancy Pogel

Much has been written about pornography in attempts to define, discredit, or justify it. The term *pornography* is derived from the Greek for "letters of prostitutes." According to Drs. Albert Ellis and Albert Abarbanel, pornography's intention is "to evoke erotic imagery in the reader in order to bring about sexual arousal. In other words, pornographic writings are meant to function as psychological aphrodisiacs and are successful only to the extent that they accomplish this particular purpose."[1] Kenneth Tynan writes even more bluntly about hard-core pornography when he asserts that it is "orgasmic in intent and untouched by the ulterior motives of traditional art. It has a simple and localized purpose: to induce an erection."[2]

Student and creator of pornography Michael Perkins stands on neutral ground as he distinguishes soft-core eroticism "from true erotic writing by its sentimentality and its respect for social conventions. It does not enlighten nor does it threaten the reader."[3] D. H. Lawrence in his classic essay, "Pornography and Obscenity," sees pornography as having both negative and positive potential. He approves of pornography that leads to "life" and to lovemaking and disapproves when it leads to masturbation and "death."[4] Still others, like pornography scholar Gershon Legman, emphasize the social values of erotic literature: "It serves an important need. This need is twofold: the education of the inexperienced young, and the excitation of the impotent or old."[5]

Still more to the point for students of American popular culture and intellectual history are David Meltzer's observations:

> America's secret life is revealed in its wars and religious tracts certainly as well as in its fuckbooks. The so-called fuckbook pop-subculture is nothing more than dreams.
>
> Lovemaking is, after all, more than what a man needs or a woman insists on. It is something confronted every second and something still, as our culture would indicate, unknown and unrealized.[6]

Despite the so-called sexual revolution and a liberalized attitude toward sexual literature and film in recent years, pornography has not yet become socially acceptable. Thus the reader or researcher must familiarize himself or herself with the "adult" underground. The exploration of the subject becomes not only an eye-opening adventure, shattering to easy idealism and candied world views, but a frustrating exercise with uncataloged and uncatalogable items and too much ephemera. Pornographic publishers, those dealers in fantasy, sometimes disappear as soon as their glossy wares hit the marketplace.

Despite these and other pitfalls, however, pornography is an interesting and (should one say?) stimulating field that offers ample research opportunities and significant insights for the reader of popular culture willing to travel to special libraries, frequent adult bookstores, peruse "S and M" books or bedroom curiosities without blushing, and receive through the mails numbers of strange items concealed in plain brown wrappers.

HISTORIC OUTLINE

The student seeking out the beginnings of American pornography will hardly be surprised to learn that, along with introducing to America the volunteer fire department, the lending library, and the editorial cartoon, Benjamin Franklin was the first American to own a copy of John Clelland's *Fanny Hill; Or Memoirs of a Woman of Pleasure* (1747). Further, his "Advice to a Young Man on Choosing a Mistress" (1745) was the first indigenous work circulated as pornography. His burlesque, "A Letter to the Royal Academy at Brussels," purporting to have discovered a scientific way to deodorize farts, was written sometime between 1772 and 1782 and circulated in manuscript, and the "Speech of Polly Baker" was published in London's *Gentleman's Magazine* in 1747.

In 1810, Isaiah Thomas of Worcester, Massachusetts, put out the first American edition of *Fanny Hill,* a limited edition under the faked imprint "G. Fenton, 1747." (Understandably, the faked imprint is a protective artifice employed by writers and sellers of erotica, depending on the legality of the enterprise in their particular time and locale.) Pressure from authorities forced him to destroy the unbound editions in 1814.

In 1846 the Irishman William Haynes began to publish erotic books in New York, and the 1850s saw the rise to prominence of George Thompson. Under pseudonyms, the most famous of which was "Greenhorn," he wrote hundreds of pornographic novels such as *The G'hals of Boston* (1850) and *The Delights of Love; Or, The Lady Liberated* (ca. 1850). *Fanny Greely; Or, The Confessions of a Free-Love Sister Written by Herself* (ca. 1850) exploited the story of John Humphrey Noyes's scandalous Perfectionist sect at Oneida, New York, which had been driven out by its outraged neighbors.

Also in the 1850s, a series of erotic pocket volumes was published in New Orleans.

The Civil War proved a predictable impetus to pornographers. *Cupid's Own Library* offered to soldiers erotic volumes costing twenty-five cents, fifty cents, and one dollar. *The Rakish Rhymer* (date unknown), an erotic songbook, was widely circulated. Graphic pornography will be discussed later, but obscene prints and photographs circulated among Civil War soldiers and officers.

Among print pornography is Samuel Clemens's scatological satire, *1601: A Conversation as It Was at the Social Fireside in the Time of the Tudors.* Clemens wrote it around 1879 and dedicated it to his friend, the Reverend Joseph Twichell. It was first printed in a limited edition of one hundred copies at the U.S. Military Academy at West Point. H. Montgomery Hyde states that over forty U.S. editions had appeared by 1964. Clemens's *Some Thoughts on the Science of Onanism* (1879), from a speech given by Clemens in 1879 before the Stomach Club, while considered stylistically inferior, has also enjoyed considerable notoriety.

Otherwise, late nineteenth-century fanciers of pornography could always turn to *National Police Gazette,* a barbershop favorite featuring lurid stories of sex and seduction. Pornographic daguerrotypes were increasing in vogue when the first motion picture films were made in 1894. As far as is known, the first pornographic films appeared shortly after, in 1896. So significant was this development to the history of American pornography that its chronicling will require a separate section.

Like Samuel Clemens, many other popular authors wrote pornographic works, primarily for circulation in manuscript among their friends. One of these covert classics was Eugene Field's *Only a Boy* (1896), which was distributed clandestinely but enjoyed a notoriety much wider and greater than its author had originally intended. His homoerotic verse "When Willie Wet the Bed" was printed in some medical journals in the 1880s.

A turn-of-the-century work that is often mentioned in surveys of American pornography is the sado-masochistic *The Memoirs of Dolly Morton; the Story of a Woman's Part in the Struggle to Free the Slaves* (1904). According to Hyde, the book was published in Paris by Charles Carrington, the infamous seller and publisher of pornographic books.[7] It was popular in America and Europe and is said to deal more frankly with the psychology of slavery than does *Uncle Tom's Cabin,* which was "also a favourite with devotees of the whip in spite of its high moral tone."

Some idea of the strictness of American censorship during the Victorian period and after may be gained from a look at the legal difficulties of Theodore Dreiser. In 1900 *Sister Carrie* was withdrawn from the bookstores after a public outcry over its "immorality," even though it contained no explicit descriptions of erotic activity. Merely depicting an "immoral" way of life without condemning or punishing its practitioners was enough to get an author in trouble. In 1916 Dreiser's *The Genius* was banned in Cincinnati, and his publisher withdrew the book when threatened with prosecution.

In 1917 Charles Carrington reissued *The Rakish Rhymer* from the Civil War period as *Some Yarns.* The only extant copy is in the Kinsey collection at the Institute for Sex Research. *My Lives and Loves* (1925-29), the erotic autobiography of Frank Harris, has some claim to inclusion in a survey of American pornography, since its first volume was written in America, although it was published in Germany. Volumes 2 through 4 were written and printed in France. U.S. customs officials were ever alert to keep works such as *My Lives and Loves* out of the country. There was considerable pressure to import such works, for erotic literature flourished in France between the years 1926 and 1956. Olympia Press, for example, published numerous titles.

In 1927 the first volume of *Anecdota Americana* appeared with the false imprint "Joseph Fliesler, ed., Boston." According to Legman in *The Horn Book,* it was probably published in New York by Humphrey Adams.[8] The second volume came out in 1934. The 1930s were also marked by several anonymous American supplements to *My Secret Life,* such as *Marital Frolics* (1934), and by the flourishing of the "eight-pagers."

The eight-pagers were a form of pornography that was quite close to folk art. Originating perhaps in the 1920s, they were small, anonymously drawn comic books (their alternate name, "Tijuana Bibles," gives a clue to one source) which depicted popular cartoon characters such as Popeye, Henry, and so forth, engaged in explicitly erotic activity. They were disseminated variously by distributors of erotic films and naughty novelties and by traveling salesmen, truck drivers, carnival people, and other mobile individuals. Their customers were primarily blue collar and lower-level white collar workers, who had neither the money for "dirty movies" (eight-pagers reached their peak during the Depression) nor the education for more literary erotica. Their popularity waned during World War II and revived briefly in the late 1940s. They disappeared in the 1950s.

The 1930s were a decade of legal battles, such as the famous *Ulysses* decision of 1933. Judge John Woolsey of the U.S. District Court for the Southern District of New York ruled that James Joyce's *Ulysses* was not obscene, and the New York Circuit Court of Appeals upheld his decision. In 1950 folklorist Vance Randolph produced his "unprintable" collection, *Pissing in the Snow and Other Ozark Folktales,* which was long available only in the Library of Congress and at the Institute for Sex Research. At the end of the decade, in 1959, Grove Press published the unexpurgated edition of D. H. Lawrence's *Lady Chatterly's Lover.* In between these years, the decade was characterized by soft-core eroticism. In addition to the obligatory sex scenes in works by major authors such as Erskine Caldwell and Norman Mailer, titillating fiction was provided consistently by Pyramid, Beacon, and other paperback publishers.[9] Orrie Hitt and Jack Woodford were two of the writers who supplied this material. Soft-core continued into the 1960s, although the publication of *Fanny Hill* by G. P. Putnam in 1963 extended somewhat the boundaries of what was permissible.

Events in France had had a strong influence on American publishing of erotic materials with at least some pretense to literary merit, for the French government had begun prosecuting Olympia Press in 1956. According to Michael Perkins in *The Secret Record: Modern Erotic Literature,* "by the early sixties Girodias was confronted with an eighty-year ban on his publishing activities, a six-year prison sentence and a sizable fine; every book he published—including *Lolita*—was banned as soon as it appeared."[10] The French crackdown, plus the relaxing of U.S. censorship, led Girodias to move Olympia Press to New York in 1967. He reissued Olympia's classics and also moved to develop a stable of native erotic authors which eventually included writers of erotic satire such as Ed Martin, Jett Sage, and George Kimball; erotic biographers such as Diane di Prima; surrealists such as Lola Seftali, Renee Auden, Barry Malzberg, and Doreen Peckinpah; and employers of a naturalistic narrative form: Marco Vassi, Angelo d'Arcangelo, and Clarence Major.

In the same year (1967) Milton Luros of Parliament News in North Hollywood undertook an erotic publishing venture reportedly as artistically ambitious as Olympia's. Under the editorship of Brian Kirby, the resultant lines, Brandon House (1967) and, especially, Essex House (1968), Parliament News became the West Coast equivalent of Olympia Press, both for the reprinting of erotic classics and the introduction of new authors. What raised the writers of Essex House above the level of ordinary pornographic writers was not only their superior talent (Kirby forbade the use of pseudonyms) and, in many instances, their willingness to experiment with the form of the novel but also, according to Michael Perkins, their incorporation into their novels of the goals of the youth revolution of the 1960s, which they shared with the somewhat more sophisticated writers of the Olympia Press. Notable Essex House writers include poets Charles Bukowski, *Notes of a Dirty Old Man* (1969), David Meltzer, *How Many Blocks in the Pile?* (1968), Hank Stine, *Thrill City* (1969), Charles McNaughton, Jr., *Mindblower* (1969), Richard E. Geis, *Raw-Meat* (1969), Alice Ramirez, *The Geek* (1969), Paul V. Dallas, *Binding with Briars* (1968), P. N. Dedeaux, *Tender Buns* (1969), Barry Luck, *Gropie* (1969), and well-known science fiction writer, Philip José Farmer, *The Image of the Beast* (1968), *Blown* (1969), and *A Feast Unknown* (1969). Concerned as he is with the literary potential of erotic writing, Perkins concludes that, in spite of possible immaturity, the Essex House novels "considered as a body of work... are the fresh, energetic beginnings of a new erotic literature."[11]

If some of the best erotic novels grew out of the political and social rebelliousness of the late 1960s, so did some of the most vigorous American art. Inspired by the eight-pagers of earlier years, Robert Crumb and S. Clay Wilson began in 1968 to draw adult comic books with titles like *Snatch* and *Jiz.* Underground comics such as these reflected the rebellion of that generation by depicting graphically, sometimes realistically and sometimes grotesquely, sex organs and acts. Crumb was probably the most prominent of the underground cartoonists, although, according to Mike Barrier, "Wilson's work has far more to do with real pornography than does Crumb's since it reflects the fear and disgust felt by pornography readers."[12] Such sex hatred and fear is expressed typically by a cartoon from *Death Rattle* No. 1 (1972), which shows a man making love to a vampirish woman who in the final panel chews off his penis.

Women artists among the underground cartoonists reacted against the sexism of their male counterparts. Some of them were Shary Flenniken (presently an editor of *National Lampoon* and creator of "Trots and Bonnie"), Trina Robbins *(It Ain't Me Babe Comix* and *Tales of Sex and Death),* Willy Mendes, and Meredith Kurtzman. As Mark Estren writes, "Underground cartoonists are preoccupied with sex (as is everyone in our culture), and there is sexism—both kinds. Their irreverence will be their biggest contribution, sexually speaking."[13]

The alacrity with which artists adapt each new art form to the purpose of pornography testifies to its eternal vitality: the Institute for Sex Research has pornographic daguerrotypes dating back to 1839. As mentioned above, the artistic medium of film was used to treat sexual themes and subjects almost from its inception in 1894. Sketchy records exist of some early French erotic films, *Le Bain* (1896) and *Le Voyeur* (1907). In the United States, May Irwin and John Rice delighted audiences and dismayed moral guardians in the essentially innocent *The Kiss* (1896). Edison's camera recorded Fatima, the sensation of the 1893 Columbia Exposition, performing the dance that had made her famous. Censors permitted copies to be shown only after obscuring bars had been placed across forbidden portions of the dancer's anatomy on each frame of every film that was circulated. Early nickelodeon fare, such as *The Bridal Chamber,* was often racier than films shown in theaters. The first municipal boards of censorship were established in 1907.

One of the earliest American stag films was *A Free Ride,* alternately titled *A Grass Sandwich.* Made in 1915, the film is on file at the Institute for Sex Research. Copies also exist of *Strictly Union* (1917) and *On the Beach* (1925). A more modern classic, the 1930s *Mexican Dog,* was distributed as late as the mid-1960s under the title *Sportie.* Some mainstream films of the early twentieth century featured nudity: *Daughter of the Gods* (1916), *A Man's World* (1916), *Ben-Hur* (1925), and *The Sign of the Cross* (1933).

A film which has been regarded as pornographic is *Extase* (1933), in which

Hedy Lamarr made her debut at age sixteen. The film won a Golden Lion award at the 1934 Venice Film Festival but was widely banned in the United States.

The Hollywood film industry had its own censor, Will Hayes. In 1934 he cooperated with Catholic decency groups to develop the Motion Picture Production Code, which spelled out in great detail what could *not* be shown on the screen. The Legion of Decency began publishing its list of "condemned" movies in the same year. U.S. Customs also continued to censor incoming films as well as books.

In the gray area of the sexploitation film, Italian immigrant Louis Sonney had founded Sonney Amusements in 1921. Beginning with a "crime doesn't pay" carnival film show, he realized in the 1930s that people were more interested in sex than justice. He therefore turned to the production and exhibition of psuedo-moralistic films such as *Gambling with Souls* and *Forbidden Oats.* In the 1930s and 1940s, distribution of sexploitation films was largely dominated by a group of road show men known as the "Forty Thieves."

Their 1940s successor was Kroger Babb, who produced and marketed "clap operas" such as *Birth of a Baby* (1944). A typical package would include a film, a lecture, and a "nurse" to sell supposedly instructional books. In their excellent book, *Sinema,* Kenneth Turan and Stephen F. Zito interview modern millionaire sexploiter David F. Friedman, who bought out Babb in 1956. Friedman claims Babb as his entrepreneurial idol and says that Babb's *Mom and Dad* grossed $40 million.[14]

From the mid-1950s to the mid-1960s, an increasing number of theaters ventured to show an increasing amount of sex, and later sex and violence, in the form of nudies and roughies to an ever widening audience. The 1955 nudist film *Garden of Eden* was the subject of the Desmond decision, the New York State Court of Appeals' ruling that nudity as such was not indecent. This decision led to a decade of nudie exploitation films like *My Bare Lady* (1962). In 1959 Russ Meyer began his spectacular string of movie successes with *The Immoral Mr. Teas,* a low-budget gag film about a meek man suddenly blessed with x-ray vision. *Mr. Teas* grossed over a million dollars, and Meyer was to make ten more voyeuristic comedies in the next decade. Others followed suit: John McCarthy *(The Ruined Bruin)* and Barry Mahon *(Nude Scrapbook),* to name two.

In 1963 David F. Friedman and Herschell G. Lewis released *Blood Feast,* the first roughie. They also produced such edifying epics as *Color Me Blood Red* (1965). Never one to miss the dollar signs written on the wall, Russ Meyer turned to roughies with *Mud Honey* (1969) and *Faster, Pussycat! Kill! Kill! Kill!* (1966). (Arthur Knight and Hollis Alpert have a classification, called "kinkies," but their boundaries are unclear.)

In 1967 the Supreme Court declined to censor *The Raw Ones'* depiction of frontal nudity. By the mid-1960s, according to Don Druker, some 750 films exploiting sex and violence had been released. Some surpassed the above-mentioned in their violence: George Weiss's and Joseph A. Mawra's *Olga's Girls* (1964) and *White Slaves of Chinatown* (1964). By and large, the censors let the roughies alone.

There were other trends in American erotic films of the 1960s. In the same vein as *Birth of a Baby* and *Mom and Dad,* films like Barry Mahon's *White Slavery* preached against various sex-related evils while depicting them in a most sensational fashion. Toward the end of the decade, even more explicit "educational" films like *Man and Wife* (1969) were being shown.

Also in the 1960s, gay erotic films were made by serious film makers, among them Kenneth Anger *(Scorpio Rising,* 1964), Andy Warhol *(Blow Job,* 1964), and Jack Smith (*Flaming Creatures,* 1963). Los Angeles's Pat Rocco pioneered the gay exploitation film with *Marco of Rio* (1969), *Sex and the Single Gay* (1970), and others.

Foreign films with erotic content hit the United States in two waves: in the late 1950s and early 1960s *La Dolce Vita* (1959), *Monika* (1953), and *Hiroshima, Mon Amour* (1958) were distributed through the exploitation market. Ingenious importers "doctored" some of the films by intercutting sex scenes. A doctored version of *Illicit Interlude* (1952), into which Larry Moyer had introduced a spurious nude bathing scene, was shown and even praised by critics for years. In the late 1960s, even more explicit foreign films such as *I, a Woman* (1965), which grossed $4 million, and *I Am Curious (Yellow)* (1967) were shown in this country.

The year 1967 was a milestone in the history of mass-distributed American erotic films, for that year saw the birth of the "beaver" film in San Francisco. The first gay hard-core loops were made in San Francisco in 1969. More devious efforts were soon necessary when censors forced producers to prove "redeeming social value." According to Kenneth Turan and Stephen F. Zito, the first, best, and most popular of these pseudo-histories was Alex de Renzy's *A History of the Blue Movie* (1970). Bill Osco made *Hollywood Blue Movie* (1971) and *Making the Blue Movie* (1971). *Personals,* directed by Armand Weston and Howard Winters, featured interviews with members of the erotic "scene" intercut with film of their activities.

An oddity of 1970 stands out: Alf Stillman, Jr's. 3-D success, *The Stewardesses.* Although the film showed no explicit sex, the novelty of 3-D and the potency of the stewardess's sexual stereotype made the film a $24 million grosser.

Also in 1970 appeared what was, according to Turan and Zito, the first sixty-minute hard-core 16 mm. film, or at least "the first to be known by name and promoted nationwide." *Mona, the Virgin Nymph* was technically competent and had credible plot and character development.

It was in 1972 that the most spectacularly successful hard-core feature appeared. Made in six days at a cost of $24,000, director Gerard Damiano's

Deep Throat had grossed some $5 million by mid-1973. That same year, Mitchell Brothers, a Los Angeles film group, showed America some hitherto unsuspected attributes of Marilyn Chambers, the Ivory Snow girl, in *Behind the Green Door* (1972). Wakefield Poole's gay hard-core film, *Boys in the Sand* (1971), returned a $400,000 gross on an $8,000 cost.

Although these and other large productions, lavish by the standards of stag films, seemed to signal a new day in slick, even aesthetically pleasing pornographic movies for mass audiences, a 1973 Supreme Court decision put a quick end to such dreams (or nightmares) by making big-budget, X-rated movies impractical due to the legal risks involved.

REFERENCE WORKS

Because of the clandestine nature of the subject, bibliographers of erotic and pornographic literature have always been at a great disadvantage. Indeed, as Ralph Ginzburg says, "Erotic bibliography is generally considered the most heavily obstructed pursuit in the field of library science."[15]

Erotica is often published and distributed under the table; much of it never reaches anyone but small groups of private collectors. To make matters worse, libraries have traditionally refused to collect erotica or have cataloged what little they have collected in confusing or intentionally impeditive ways. Furthermore, authors and their publishers make cataloging difficult to impossible, since they tend to disguise themselves with false names and phony publication dates and places and to hide the contents of their books behind titles veiled in foreign language and euphemism.

The few available bibliographies cannot usually be checked for accuracy because many of the works cited either no longer exist or were originally drawn from private collections rather than public depositories. Although bibliographers may have examined a number of the books listed, others appear in their bibliographies only through hearsay or reputation. Several editions of a single work may also be cited under different titles and authorships so that identification of the original requires careful reading and testing of the texts, which are frequently unavailable for such close comparison.

Social taboos in the United States, especially, put the student or collector of American erotica and pornography at the mercy of restrictions. The reputable reference books that do exist are primarily compilations of European erotica by European bibliographers. Thus the American student of erotica is forced in great part to depend on ingenuity and shrewdness to gain entrance to private collections and libraries and to learn the erotica underground that is accessible to the consumer through the adult bookstore and mail order houses.

The best background and explanations of these difficulties and the best places for students of erotica to start their investigations are probably

Gershon Legman's introductory chapters to *The Horn Book: Studies in Erotic Folklore and Bibliography:* "The Bibliography of Prohibited Books: Pisanus Fraxi" and "*The Horn Book* and Other Bibliographical Problems," as well as Rebecca Dixon's fine chapter in *An Intellectual Freedom Primer,* "Bibliographical Control of Erotica." Although Legman's biases and colorful style may put some readers off, in substance his work is an invaluable and relatively comprehensive scholarly treatment of the subject. Dixon's seventeen-page discussion is also well documented, sensitive to the issues, and particularly helpful because of the suggestions she makes about the contemporary situation. This section of our chapter on American pornography is much indebted to both sources.

Another handy reference, less scholarly, less reliable, and less comprehensive, but readily available in most libraries, is Ralph Ginzburg's *An Unhurried View of Erotica*, a thin 125-page volume that is more history than bibliography but which includes a section of introduction to reference works and a bibliography of one hundred titles. In the course of his discussion Ginzburg deals in an "unhurried" and candid way with a hard core of two thousand titles of classical erotica in the English language.

From these guides the student will be directed to the early European bibliographies for background, to such standard works as Jules Gay's *Bibliographie des ouvrages relatifs à l'amour, aux femmes, au mariage, indiquant les auteurs de ces ouvrages, leurs éditions, leur valeur et les prohibitions ou condamnations dont certains d'entre eux ont été l'objet.* Gay's bibliography, published in 1861 and in three additional editions, is not highly regarded as scholarship, but it is the only nineteenth-century bibliography of French erotica. In the same period (1875) Hugo Nay collected German erotica in a bibliography privately printed in Leipzig, *Bibliotheca Germanorum Erotica.*

The first and still the most respected English bibliographer of erotica is Henry Spencer Ashbee. Ashbee's *Index Librorum Prohibitorum: Being Notes Bio-Biblio-Iconographical and Critical, on Curious and Uncommon Books* was privately printed in London, with an obviously euphemistic and obscure title and under the memorable pseudonym, Pisanus Fraxi. Ashbee published a second volume, *Centuria Librorum Absconditorum* in 1879, and a third, *Catena Librorum Tacendorum* in 1885. His three volumes were reprinted in 1966 as *A Complete Guide to Forbidden Books,* by Brandon House, publishers of popular erotica and sex-oriented literature.

According to most authorities, Ashbee's work is probably the most comprehensive bibliography of erotica available in the English language. Ashbee, a wealthy businessman, world traveler, and collector of erotica, had enough money and prestige to purchase erotica "under the counter" and at the nineteenth century's high market prices. His own collection provides the heart of his reference work. Included is alphabetized erotica in several languages, indexed in each volume and copiously annotated. Ashbee was fond, too, of quoting tempting tidbits (sometimes extensively) from his favorite texts. Scholars and bibliophiles find both the original three volumes and the more recent reprint in one volume among the most useful bibliographies of erotica published up to the turn of the century. Gershon Legman's discussion of Pisanus Fraxi in *The Horn Book* provides additional insights into the man and into the era when Ashbee wrote.

Twentieth-century book-length bibliographies in English are hard to come by. More often than not readers will have to look at short indexes and bibliographies that include history and criticism books and at unpublished bibliographies available from private collectors and libraries. Among the very few available book-length bibliographies of erotica published in the twentieth century is the *Registrum Librorum Eroticorum,* produced privately in London in 1936 by Rolf S. Reade, a pseudonym for Alfred Rose. Reprinted in 1965, it lists over five thousand titles, including some erotica titles not mentioned in Ashbee and some titles from the British Museum collection.

Catalogi Librorum Eroticorum: a Critical Bibliography of Erotic Bibliographies and Book Catalogues is also a major erotica reference tool written in the twentieth century. Published in 1964 in London and compiled by Terence J. Deakin, the book lists seventy-eight bibliographies of erotic literature and their locations. According to Rebecca Dixon, the only bibliography to include contemporary literature, a three-volume work by Al Hull Watson to be called "Bibliographia Sexualis," has not been published to date. Dixon also notes that forty-four of the bibliographies mentioned in the Deakin book may be found in the Institute for Sex Research collection at the University of Indiana rather than the smaller number attributed to that collection by Deakin. Gershon Legman observes with regret that no bibliography has yet been published that is wholly devoted to English-language erotic literature. Although Legman has been collecting materials for twenty-five years, he has not yet been able to find a publisher who will handle so large a work.

In addition, contemporary bibliographical help—but only bits and pieces—may be found in Frank A. Hoffman's *An Analytical Survey of Anglo-American Traditional Erotica,* David Loth's *The Erotic in Literature,* and in popular soft-cover books such as Bernhardt J. Hurwood's *The Golden Age of Erotica,* Paul J. Gillette's *An Uncensored History of Pornography,* which includes a "Chronology of Major Authors of Erotica," and Harford Montgomery Hyde's *A History of Pornography.* Also see Franklin S. Klaf and Bernhardt J. Hurwood, *A Psychiatrist Looks at Erotica.* A reputable short modern bibliography is found, too, in the *Encyclopedia of Sexual Behavior* by Albert Ellis and Albert Abarbanel. Legman also cites several other bibliographies that "touch only slightly on the field," such as Theodore Schroeder's *Free Speech Bibliography* and Roger Goodland's *A Bibliography of Sex Rites and Customs.*

Of minor interest, too, is the running bibliography in Anne Lyon Haight's *Banned Books,* but Haight's book deals primarily with major works that have usually entered the mainstream following legal battles and censorship problems. Students may also wish to look at Robert George Reisner's *Show Me the Good Parts: The Reader's Guide to Sex in Literature,* which catalogs thirty-three categories of sexual activities from "adultery" to "voyeurism" in literature. Similarly, Harry E. Wedeck's *Dictionary of Erotic Literature* lists alphabetically books, authors, and appropriate terms important to the reader of erotic literature and includes a bibliography. Erotica bibliography is also found in *The Report of the Commission on Obscenity and Pornography,* which annotates some entries but like many bibliographies of erotica includes several discrepancies.

Additional short modern bibliographies of pornography or erotica are available to scholars (with appropriate credentials) from the Institute for Sex Research at Indiana University. Joan Scherer Brewer and Rod W. Wright have collected some of these bibliographies in the book-length study *Sex Research: Bibliographies from the Institute for Sex Research;* see especially the brief section on erotica. The Brewer-Wright bibliography includes citations to selected articles as well as books. Other specialized bibliographies compiled from the institute collection are available in xeroxed, typescript form from the institute's information service, 416 Morrison Hall, Indiana University, Bloomington, Indiana 47401. Write for a list of available titles.

A few special interest bibliographies that include some erotica citations have also been published or are available as unpublished papers from collections. Noteworthy are Gene Damon, Jan Watson, and Robin Jordan, *The Lesbian in Literature* as well as William Parker's *Homosexuality: A Selective Bibliography of over 3,000 Items* and its supplement. The brief but well-selected bibliography of "Sex and Cinema" in Brewer's and Wright's compilation is supplemented, too, by thirty-four pages of filmography keyed to pornographic themes in Al Di Lauro's and Gerald Rabkin's *Dirty Movies: An Illustrated History of the Stag Film, 1915-1970.* A short bibliography of Russ Meyer items is Sandra Holtzman's unpublished paper, found at the Institute for Sex Research. A short bibliography of the striptease by M. B. Wallace is in the Kinsey collection as well.

To familiarize themselves with the popular pornography "scene" or the erotica underworld, readers should examine Phyllis Kronhausen and Eberhard Kronhausen, *The Sex People: Erotic Performers and Their Bold New Worlds,* a serious journalistic approach to sex shows and their stars, such as Linda Lovelace, Marilyn Chambers, and Harry Reems. Bob Hoddeson's *The Porn People* is also a series of interviews that forms a strong composite picture of the pornographic underground not often revealed to the public. Included are interviews with *Screw's* Al Goldstein, *Erotic Cinema's* William Rossler, *Box Office International's* Joe Steinman, and actress Marilyn

Chambers as well as articles on massage parlors and nude encounters.

Similarly, Carolyn See's *Blue Money, Pornography and the Pornographers* provides an intimate look at the sex industry. See writes about sex star Linda Lovelace and sex industry "tycoons" Marvin Miller, Matt Cimber, Jim Hollander, and others. Sara Harris's *The Puritan Jungle: America's Sexual Underground* is also compiled from interviews with male and female prostitutes, porno actors and actresses, mate swappers, and other members of the erotica scene forced underground by American censors.

In addition to published and unpublished bibliographies, publishers' and distributors' catalogs are a major source of references for students of erotica. H. Nichols, J. Lemmenyer of Rouen, Isidore Liseuz, George Briffaut, and especially Charles Carrington were important publishers who produced catalogs of the works they printed in the nineteenth and early twentieth centuries. A few of these can be found in some major libraries and collections. Dixon also notes that some of the pseudo-scientific sex studies of the early twentieth century appear in various published library catalogs, such as those of the Library of Congress. Further information about publishers of European erotica may be found in the important *Bilderlexikon der Erotik*, Volume 2, and Paul Englisch's *Geshichte der Erotischen Literatur*, as well as his *Irrgarten der Erotik*.

Brochures and catalogs of erotic titles since the turn of the century are cataloged in some libraries and collections. Major publishers of erotica such as Maurice Girodias's Olympia Press, and lesser lights such as Falstaff Books, Book Awards, Book Gems, Arrowhead Books, and Golden Hind Press are only a few of the significant publishing names of early twentieth-century erotica.

A small portion of contemporary erotica has been taken on by major paperback publishers who distribute through popular channels, who advertise in trade publications, and whose catalogs and book lists are readily available through conventional means; however, the greater number of erotica items, especially fetish literature and hard-core pornography, are available primarily through the so-called secondary or "adult" erotica industry, a large group of mail order houses and distributors to adult bookstores which has begun to prosper, especially in the last fifteen or twenty years. Many of these publications are ephemeral pulp books and periodicals that are not copyrighted or recorded in the Library of Congress. There is no comprehensive list of such publishers, who frequently change their names and addresses. However, Daniel Eisenberg's "Toward a Bibliography of Erotic Pulps Published in the U.S., 1962-1972," an unpublished paper, is available in the Institute for Sex Research collection. Rebecca Dixon notes that the 1973 *Publisher's Trade List Annual* included catalogs from Brandon House, Barclay House, Academy Press, Sexcope Press, and Socio-Library (all subsidiaries of Parliament News in Los Angeles), and Grove

Press and included a few listings for Holloway House; other important erotica mail order publishers, however, such as Surrey House (San Diego), Aquarius 7 (North Hollywood), Orpheus Classics (a subsidiary of Carlyle Communications in New York), Star Distributors (New York), Eros Publishing (Wilmington), Greenleaf Classics (San Diego), and Olympia Press were not included. Still other publishers not noted in Dixon's review in 1974 include Chelsea Library, Press of Manchester Publications (San Diego), Gloucestor Publishing (South Laguna, California), Male Merchandizing Mart (Los Angeles), Stag Books (St. Chatsworth, California), Bob Anthony Studios (New York), Bristol Library Press (San Diego), G/P Sales (Studio City, California), Ram Classics (Van Nuys, California) and Surree Limited (Santee, California). Samples of contemporary mail order publishers who are not listed in the usual bibliographies require a visit to the local adult bookstore or to a major erotica library such as that at the Institute for Sex Research, which has an extensive collection of mail order publications, advertisements, and catalogs not available in most public or institutional libraries in the United States.

RESEARCH COLLECTIONS

Because prominent interpreters disagree about what constitutes "erotica," they also argue over where to find the most significant and the largest collections of it. Ralph Ginzburg in *An Unhurried View* claims that the foremost collection is in the Vatican. Taking issue with what he calls Ginzburg's "priceless allegation," Gershon Legman retorts that in the Vatican there are "no really erotic books and positively no erotic pictures." Yet, according to Ginzburg's estimation, the Library of the Vatican in Rome is the champion of erotica collectors, including as it does 25,000 volumes and some 100,000 prints. Ginzburg is probably on safer ground when he cites the British Museum among the top three erotica collections. The 20,000-plus volumes include the famous Henry Spencer Ashbee library, which was donated to the museum.

For American students of erotica, the most important and accessible collection is held at the Alfred C. Kinsey Institute for Sex Research at Indiana University. In addition to the largest data bank of sexual behavior and attitudes in the world, the unique Kinsey collection boasts 54,000 volumes and reprints, of which a healthy percentage are erotica items. The collection is exceptional, not only for its extensive traditional erotica holdings but because it collects popular, underground, and ephemeral erotica as well. Sexual magazines, pamphlets, clippings, and advertisements seldom collected by libraries are found in the Kinsey library. In addition to volumes and reprints, the Kinsey institute keeps vertical files containing mail order advertisements and pamphlets. These files as well as the extensive periodical collections are an unusual storehouse of up-to-date information about pornography and the underground "adult" industry.

Also in the collection are 25,000 items of flat art, 10,800 slides of flat art, and 1,300 art objects of an erotic nature. The library also has 1,500 reels of film and 200 tapes and records, as well as 50,000 photographs (from art photography to pornography). Many of these are erotica items. The Kinsey film collection has a large sample of commercial pornographic films reflecting changes in attitudes and censorship policies over the years. According to a description of the collection, there is also a small sample of experimental, avant-garde films that met with legal difficulties during public exhibition. The objet d'art collection ranges from high sexual art such as Chinese panels inlaid with ivory to popular sexual joke items such as one can find in local novelty shops. The collection of erotica at the Kinsey is constantly growing. In recent years police departments have sent the library confiscated erotic materials.

Although some of the institute's collections are confidential and restricted, the library is open to serious qualified researchers with "demonstrated research needs." There is a $25 fee per reader, and readers must make application to the Institute for Sex Research, 416 Morrison Hall, Indiana University, Bloomington, Indiana 47405.

Other collections in the United States include the Library of Congress holdings—about five thousand items. Until the middle 1960s, the Library of Congress gathered many of its erotica volumes loosely in the "Delta" collection, but in 1964 that group was dispersed into the general library, many of the volumes going into the rare books collection.

According to Ginzburg, additional collections of note are to be found in some of the Ivy League schools that have received the benefit of private, unpublicized donations of private erotica libraries over the years. The Huntington library in San Marino, California, also holds a collection of erotica, the heart of which was real estate-railroad magnate Henry E. Huntington's private collection.

The only other major public collection in the United States is the Kronhausen collection, which forms the heart of the International Museum of Erotic Art in San Francisco. The collection, valued at $1 million, is housed along with erotic art work by Pablo Picasso, Salvador Dali, Betty Dodson, and John Lennon on five floors. Nine centuries of erotic art are included in the collection once belonging to Drs. Phyllis and Eberhard Kronhausen. The museum is operated by the Genesis Church, a nonprofit California corporation, which also owns the National Sex Forum Education Service, distributors of sex education books. A chapter in Bob Hoddeson's *The Porn People,* "New Museum of Earthy Delights Houses International Collection," describes the museum's holdings in greater detail. The International Museum of Erotic Art is located at 540 Powell Street, San Francisco, California 94108.

HISTORY AND CRITICISM

The works dealing with the history and criticism of pornography that treat the subject in a broad or general manner may be divided into two types: those attempting to provide an historical survey, and those presenting a philosophical, moral, or aesthetic opinion. The distinction is rather arbitrary, of course, since it is difficult to make value judgments on pornography without furnishing specific examples for the reader.

Because there is no systematic history of American pornography, it is necessary to hunt through general works on erotica in hopes of gleaning a few random facts from each source. Gershon Legman's *The Horn Book: Studies in Erotic Folklore and Bibliography* serves as a good general introduction to the history of erotica, its collection, and collectors. Since the work has neither index nor bibliography, the student of American pornography must sift through the book's 565 pages of lively if opinionated dissertation. Also of interest is Legman's *Rationale of the Dirty Joke: An Analysis of Sexual Humor.* Ove Brusendorff's and Paul Henningsen's six-volume *A History of Eroticism* contains many glossy illustrations of paintings, etchings, movie stills, and quotes from erotic literature. Volume 5 discusses eroticism in American art in "Striptease a Barometer" and "The Lolita Problem."

Though British in emphasis, Harford Montgomery Hyde's *A History of Pornography* fills in background and touches upon American pornography. It ranges from *The Decameron* and Boswell's *London Journal* to "The Fanny Hill Case" and Frank Harris's *My Secret Life.* Paul J. Gillette's *An Uncensored History of Pornography* surveys erotic literature from the "preliterate pornography" of the Phoenicians, Armenians, and Babylonians up through the Romans, medieval Christians, Boccaccio, and the Marquis De Sade to Henry Miller. It includes two helpful appendixes, "Chronology of Major Authors of Erotica" and "Chronology of Major Works of Erotica." Guiseppe Lo Duca's *A History of Eroticism* has been translated by Kenneth Anger. *A Psychologist Looks at Erotica* by Franklin S. Klaf and Bernhardt J. Hurwood is a brief, informative paperback with a bibliography but no index.

"The Golden Age of Erotica" described in Bernhardt J. Hurwood's book by the same name is the period from the 1660s to the 1890s, primarily in England and Europe. Hurwood's sixth chapter conveys the flavor of American erotica of the eighteenth and nineteenth centuries.

Of the very few works providing much information on the history of American pornography, Frank A. Hoffman's *An Analytical Survey of Anglo-American Traditional Erotica* is one of the most useful. In addition to the bibliography and filmography mentioned in the reference section of this essay, the book provides the modern folklorists' perspective on the study of erotic material.

A scholarly essay by Leo Hamalian, "Nobody Knows My Names: Samuel

Roth and the Underside of Modern Letters," chronicles the activities of the publisher-pirate-pornographer whose name is immortalized in the 1956 Roth decision.

A recent work, Michael Perkins's *The Secret Record: Modern Erotic Literature,* concentrates, as its subtitle indicates, on mid-twentieth-century works with some literary pretensions. It does, however, provide a brief but helpful background on Dionysian literature, Victorian erotica, and French erotic writing. Perkins emphasizes American writing, beginning with the "new Olympia writers," who wrote for Olympia Press after Maurice Girodias moved it to New York in 1967. He touches briefly on writers like Henry Miller, who have received much attention, and devotes a chapter to the novelists of Milton Luros's Essex House and Brandon House Library Editions, published by Parliament News, North Hollywood, California. (Perkins himself is the author of such Essex House titles as *Whacking Off* and *Queen of Heat.)*

Perhaps the best consideration of the philosophical and aesthetic aspects of pornography is Morse Peckham's *Art and Pornography: an Experiment in Explanation.* Peckham writes: "It is, I think, mere carelessness that leads such writers [literary critics] to say that pornography cannot be literature and also that it cannot be art." Eclectic (the index goes from *addiction* to *Zappa, Frank*), the book is thoughtful and literate.

Similar but livelier is Peter Michelson's *The Aesthetics of Pornography,* which discusses not only the classics from *Fanny Hill* and *Justine* to *The Story of O* and the erotic elements in D. H. Lawrence, James Joyce, and William Faulkner's works, but also *Playboy, Screw,* and *Fuck You, a Magazine of the Arts.* Numerous contemporary essays on pornography may be found in Douglas A. Hughes's *Perspectives on Pornography* and Philip A. Nobile's *The New Eroticism.* A less well-balanced collection of essays, *The Case Against Pornography,* has been edited by David Holbrook. Commentators covered include Rollo May, George Steiner, and Benjamin Spock.

David Loth's *The Erotic in Literature* traces the history of ancient, classical, and European erotic literature and pays some attention to American. The book's titillating subtitle, "A Historical Survey of Pornography as Delightful as It Is Indiscreet," notwithstanding, Loth recommends that obscenity laws be abolished so that community standards of censorship may be adopted.

Some works, such as conservative journalist James Jackson Kilpatrick's *The Smut Peddlers,* are avowedly anti-pornography. In his oft-reprinted essay, "Night Words," George Steiner objects to pornography on comparatively enlightened grounds, condemning it not only for being boring but for "cut[ting] deeply not only into the true liberty of the writer, but into the diminishing reserves of feeling and imaginative response in our society." In a popular essay for the other side, Kenneth Tynan suggests that Steiner bores too easily and goes on to defend not only the right to pornography but also (almost single-handedly among the defenders of pornography) the right to self-abuse. Self-abuse, he maintains, is preferable to the abuse of others.

The April 1980 issue of *Mother Jones,* subtitled "Sex, Porn and Male Rage," features several articles emphasizing the degrading effect of pornography on women. It discusses militant feminists' efforts to eliminate pornography and the pros and cons of their arguments. Other partisan authors include Helen Dudar and Marco Vassi. Dudar's article, "America Discovers Child Pornography," is well summarized by Gloria Steinem's introduction, "Is Child Pornography about Sex?" which asserts that pornography is "not sex, but the obscene use of power by adult males." On the other side, Marco Vassi in *Metasex, Mirth & Madness* has postulated the existence of metasexuality, "a distinct modality of being not to be confused with sex *per se.*"

The financial aspects of pornography have also been studied. As its subtitle indicates, *The Sex Industry,* edited by George Paul Csicsery, is "a sex-posé of happy hookers, massage parlors, skin-flicks—every kick money can buy." James Cook's magazine article, "The X-Rated Economy," examines the business of pornography and also profiles *Hustler* publisher Larry Flynt, vibrator tycoon Ron Braverman, pornographers' lawyer Elliot Abelson, and New York Police Department agent Vic Rice, who once ran an adult bookstore under cover.

Nearly every society has expended considerable energy suppressing pornography, and the resultant controversy has produced a staggering number of books and articles. Many of the books belong more properly to a study of the law than of popular culture. Nevertheless, some provide valuable insight into social attitudes. Eberhard Kronhausen's and Phyllis Kronhausen's *Pornography and the Law* is often mentioned as an indispensable survey. Morris Leopold Ernst's and William Sleagle's 1928 classic, *To the Pure,* examines the history and philosophy of Anglo-American censorship. With Alan U. Schwartz, Ernst is also the co-author of *Censorship: The Search for the Obscene.* A solid English volume is *Obscenity and the Law* by Norman St. John Stevas. Alec Craig's *The Banned Books of England and Other Countries* and the more recent *Suppressed Books* are also standard sources of thoughtful historical analyses of censorship. Gershon Legman's *Love & Death: A Study in Censorship* deals with mainstream literature and popular culture and the overall implications of censorship, rather than with pornography as such.

Strictly legal in emphasis are Harry M. Clor's *Obscenity and Public Morality* and Leon Friedman's *Obscenity: The Complete Oral Arguments Before the Supreme Court in the Major Obscenity Cases.* Donald M. Gillmor's article "The Puzzle of Pornography," considers the philosophical and legal aspects of pornography. Published in 1965 it is necessarily dated, but it nevertheless provides a good capsule history of pornography and censorship.

A more personal approach is taken in *The Smut Rakers: A Report in Depth on Obscenity and the Censors* by Edwin A. Roberts, Jr. The book's chapters deal with the principals in the pornography war and explain the role in censorship played by the FBI, the Post Office, the Citizens for Decent Literature, and others. It also reprints the Supreme Court's Ginzburg decisions and the Motion Picture Production Code. The approach of Louis A. Zurcher, Jr., and R. George Kirkpatrick in *Citizens for Decency: Antipornography Crusades as Status Defense* is social-scientific, as they study antipornography crusades in "Midville" and "Southtown." The authors furnish quantitative tables and a good bibliography.

Other studies with a social-scientific slant include W. Cody Wilson's and Michael J. Goldstein's article, "Experience with and Attitudes Toward Explicit Sexual Materials," which uses 2,486 face-to-face interviews. The essay is but one in a special number of the *Journal of Social Issues* entitled "Pornography: Attitudes, Use and Effects." David A. Karp's "Hiding in Pornographic Bookstores: A Reconsideration of the Nature of Urban Anonymity" uses data gathered from patrons of Times Square adult bookstores to assess the relationship between hiding behavior and the need for anonymity. Gershon Legman's "Homosexuality and Toilet Inscriptions: An Analysis" is apparently available only in typescript at the Institute for Sex Research.

In "The Pornographic Fringeland of the American Newsstand," Herbert A. Otto surveys the inventory of the two largest newsstands in Salt Lake City, Utah, and categorizes types of pornography under three headings: erotic paperback books, men's magazines, and men's physique (homosexual) magazines.

Numerous social-scientific and physiological studies are reprinted in the nine-volume *Technical Report of the Commission on Obscenity and Pornography.* The student desiring to use these essential findings might first consult the annotated bibliography in *The Report of the Commission on Obscenity and Pornography.*

The pornography field doesn't offer as many how-to guides as some others, but there are a few. *The Girl Who Writes Dirty Books* is written by "Linda Du Breuil," "The Super-Star Author of Thirty Far-Out Novels, Bestselling Author of *The Wholesome Hooker.*" The book provides some sex, some how-to (write a dirty book, that is), some philosophical observations on pornography, and some legal advice to the would-be writer.

Several numbers of *Writer's Yearbook* are helpful for their analyses of various genres of commercial erotica. D. R. Butler's "The Joy of Sexy Writing" recounts the author's experiences as a men's magazine editor and freelancer with hundreds of sales to such magazines as *Escapade, Stud, Swank,* and *Climax.* William P. Noble's "Writing for the Sex Market" pays less attention to the economics of writing for such publications and more to matters of plot and audience. Most to the point of this bibliographical essay is "Confessions of a Housewife Porn Writer" by "Joanna Farnsworth," a "choir member and PTA president" who sold seventy pornographic novels in two and a half years. Although somewhat apologetic—both on moral and aesthetic grounds—the author knowledgeably discusses plot formulas and taboos and gives the names and addresses of five "established porn publishers."

Scholars have also shed valuable light on pornography's slightly more respectable cousin, soft-core. Tony Goodstone's *The Pulps* devotes two sections, "Exploiting the Girls/6/Innocence" and "Exploiting the Girls/7/ Straight Out Sex," to describing and analyzing pulps from *Snappy Stories* in 1912 to such under-the-counter 1930s magazines as sado-erotic *Spicy Detective Stories.* Stories reprinted include "Hot Rompers" and "The Dinner Cooked in Hell." In "Soft-Core Stylistics," an unpublished paper on file at the Institute for Sex Research, Richard A. Kallan and Robert D. Brooks analyzed the text surrounding the *Playboy*'s Playmate of the Month from 1953 to 1973, and interpreted the style "as a rhetorical strategy designed to render voyeuristic impulses socially acceptable." Tabulating alleged occupations of photo essay models in "candy sex magazines" such as *Genesis, Oui, Stag,* and *Penthouse,* Mary Reige Laner found fewer than half described as being employed, and most of these were in low-status, non-threatening occupations. Attempting to assess differing responses to pornography in males and females, Louis Gould in "Pornography for Women" quotes some surveys by Kinsey and others, including Masters and Johnson. She asserts that women's sexual orientation is less primarily genital than men's and closes with a wish for "human porn," with more diffused, less genitally focused sex.

With the relaxation of censorship in the late 1960s, aboveground theater became involved in the pornography controversy. Robert Craft comments on nude dancers in Hollywood and on *Oh! Calcutta!* in "Paydirt: Notes on the Sex Explosion." John Elsom's *Erotic Theatre* contrasts social and sexual attitudes of 1890-1910 with those of 1950-72, as manifested in the British theater. The book is of marginal interest for its general insight and treatment of plays like *Oh! Calcutta!* and movies like *The Knack,* which were popular in the United States.

It is in the graphic arts that technology has most drastically influenced pornography. Paul Aratow's *100 Years of Erotica: A Photographic Portfolio of Mainstream American Subculture from 1845-1945* gives a critical history of this clandestine art form along with some one hundred pages of erotic photographs. *America's Erotic Past: 1868-1940* by G. G. Stoctay reproduces numerous photographs and provides a running text which discusses the photographic technique, history and sociology of the photo, and sometimes history of the erotic work from which a particular illustration was taken.

Thomas B. Hess's and Linda Nochlin's *Woman as Sex Object: Studies in Erotic Art, 1730-1970* is only generally relevant to popular culture, but chapter 6 on "Manet, 'Olympia' and Pornography" is interesting for its exploration of the relationship between high art and pornographic photography. Informal but nonetheless informative are the two volumes of *Smut from the Past,* the first edited by Michael Perkins and the second by John Milton. These books trace the development of American erotic photography from "The Beginning," roughly 1890 to 1910, through the 1950s, with a chapter for each decade. The copy is written primarily to entertain, but the pictures are representative.

For the story of the forbidden side of comic art, Mark James Estren's *A History of Underground Comics* is valuable. Chapter 5, "Sex and Sexism," gives the history of the late 1960s' flowering of erotic counter-culture comics, led by Robert Crumb, who found in the old eight-pagers inspiration for his pioneering *Snatch Comics* and others like them. Of some interest is *Erotic Postcards* by William Ouellette and Barbara Jones Ouellette. To find the few American specimens, however, one must leaf through page by page.

On the level of higher culture, Phyllis Kronhausen and Eberhard Kronhausen are the compilers of *Erotic Art: A Survey of Erotic Fact and Fancy in the Fine Arts.* Stemming from the First International Exhibition of Erotic Art in public museums in the cities of Lund, Sweden, and Aarhus, Denmark, the two-volume work contains a section on "Western Artists." The student must check the index for specific artists to find, for example, the three works by Andy Warhol reproduced in the collection. Similarly, Volker Kahmen's *Eroticism in Contemporary Art,* which reproduces 349 illustrations, some in color, gives the place of birth and residence of the represented artists, many of whom, including Andy Warhol, John de Andrea, Tom Wesselmann, and Richard Lindner, are presently in the United States.

There are numerous books about pornographic movies and their soft-core counterparts, some more "serious" than others. Of the substantial works, probably the best is Kenneth Turan's and Stephen F. Zito's *Sinema: American Pornographic Films and the People Who Make Them.* Part 1, "Uncertain Innocence," presents the history of the nudies and the roughies and interviews Russ Meyer and David F. Friedman. Part 2, "Going All the Way," is the detailed story of hard-core pornographic films, from the 8 mm. loops and the first hard-core feature film, *Mona, The Virgin Nymph,* to *Deep Throat* and other members of the class of '72, probably the last of the comparatively big-budget hard-core films. Among the interviews are ones with Mary Rexroth, "Johnny Wadd," Bill Osco, Wakefield Poole, and Marilyn Chambers. The authors provide plot summaries, stills, and an index.

Dirty Movies: An Illustrated History of the Stag Film, 1915-1970 by Al Di Lauro and Gerald Rabkin reprints numerous appropriately blue-toned stills from stags of all eras, often small, film-frame style, occasionally full page, not to mention two more shots from *Mexican Dog* of the 1930s than the disinterested student will care to see. The authors include a good bibliography and a thirty-two page filmography and title index. Richard Wortley's *Erotic Movies* is copiously illustrated and extensively indexed for actors and titles. The descriptive, readable text covers numerous films.

Arthur Knight and Hollis Alpert have written for *Playboy* a lengthy "History of Sex in Cinema." Part 1, "The Original Sin," appeared in April 1965, and subsequent installments traced the course of hard- and soft-core erotica in American and imported films. "Sex in Cinema" has become an annual feature of the magazine. (See Mildred Lynn Miles's *Index to Playboy* for specific bibliographical citations.)

Sexuality in the Movies, edited by Thomas R. Atkins, reprints a number of thoughtful essays by film critics and professors of film. Subdivided into "Social and Cultural Perspective," "Categories and Genres," and "Contemporary Landmarks," the selections deal with films such as *I Am Curious (Yellow), Midnight Cowboy,* and *Carnal Knowledge.* There is no index. Also worthy of mention is William Rotsler's *Contemporary Erotic Cinema,* which features interviews, a useful appendix of pornographic films, and information about them.

Joseph W. Slade's review-essay, "Recent Trends in Pornographic Films," examines the problems contemporary pornographic film makers have in finding new taboos to violate and assesses some recent attempts to break new ground.

Several works confine themselves to soft-core pornography. One of them is Parker Tyler's excellent, thoroughly indexed *Screening the Sexes: Homosexuality in the Movies,* which explores both latent and overt homosexuality. Also worth seeing is his collection of critical essays, *Sex Psyche Etcetera in the Film.* Don Druker's "Sex in Two Dimensions: Erotic Movies" is a chapter in *Our National Passion: 200 Years of Sex in America,* edited by Sally Banes, Sheldon Frank, and Tem Horowitz. Druker traces the history of soft-core eroticism in film, paying particular attention to the nudies and roughies. Of special interest is his thesis linking these sexploitation films with hostility toward women.

Ove Brusendorff and Paul Henningsen's *Erotica for the Millions: Love in the Movies,* concentrates primarily on European films but does have a chapter on American movie sex. There are numerous black-and-white stills, with the stars, studios, and dates generally identified. Paul Alcuin Siebenand's methodology is descriptive in his doctoral thesis, "The Beginnings of Gay Cinema in Los Angeles: The Industry and the Audience." He interviewed reviewers, actors, directors, and others connected with the gay cinema to seek the identity and motivation of those in the industry and their audience. A popularized exploration of attitudes on the viewing of pornographic films is Henrietta Penza's "Women Rate X-Rated Films." From an informal survey she concludes that women respond more to emotional situations than to genital images, saying, generally, "yes" to *Swept Away* but "no" to *Deep Throat.*

Another group of sources is worth mentioning but is probably less helpful than the previous group, oftentimes because the authors make fewer concessions to scholarship. Some are unabashedly commercial in intent.

Marv Strick's and Robert I. Lethe's *The Sexy Cinema,* for example, contains over one hundred photos but no index. The text is chatty, mentioning many films. It deals with the more respectable sexy films as well as the sexploitative ones and the explicit, hard-core hits of the 1970s like *Deep Throat,* covered in "The Seventies: The Era of the Great Gulp." *The Celluloid Love Feast* by Martin A. Grove and William S. Reuben is a semi-scholarly survey of soft-core and sexploitation films with a helpful bibliography but no index.

A book that emphasizes pictures is Richard Arlen's *Sex and Pornography in the Movies,* which does, however, have a general introduction to the profitability of sex films, censorship, and the rating system. Chapters are concerned with nudies and roughies, lesbian themes, *I Am Curious (Yellow),* and "Hard Core." John Morthland's "Porn Films—An In-depth Report" informally traces the history of erotic films, emphasizing the "big four": *Deep Throat, Behind the Green Door, The Devil in Miss Jones,* and *The Resurrection of Eve.* Irreverent and idiosyncratic, if such terms may be applied to pornography studies, the article is informative and provides some statistics in dollars and inches.

Predictably, some books manage to provide a substantial amount of titillation while purporting to study pornography. In the case of *Pornography for Fun and Profit,* the author, James Harvey, manages to provide a sizable sampling of the evils he sets out to expose: "It's about the life that is no bowl of cherries—with the cosmetics removed and the sickness of souls bared." He details the sordidness of underground movies, camera clubs, and mail order sex, among other types of "sickness." *The Erotic Screen: A Probing Study of Sex in the Adult Cinema* probes mainly through the medium of hard-core stills, with minimal text.

The *Porno Movies; a Documentary Study of the Burgeoning Sex-Movie Scene in America Today—Featuring Some of the Most Breathtaking Nude and Love Scenes Ever Filmed* written by "Roger Blake, Ph.D." features thirty-two pages of black-and-white stills, plus juicy plot summaries, salacious Hollywood gossip, and reactions to films by such subjects as "a twenty-seven year old housewife and mother." An outstanding example of unabashed sexploitation literature is the autobiography of Harry Reems, entitled, appropriately enough, *Here Comes Harry Reems.*

An informative how-to book is Steven Ziplow's *The Filmmaker's Guide to Pornography,* which provides practical advice on the technical, financial, legal, advertising, and distributional aspects of making erotic films. Ziplow also includes an interview with Gerard Damiano, director of *Deep Throat* and *The Devil in Miss Jones.*

NOTES

1. Albert Ellis and Albert Abarbanel, *Encyclopedia of Sexual Behavior* (New York: Hawthorn Books, 1967), p. 849.
2. Kenneth Tynan, "Dirty Books Can Stay," in *The New Eroticism,* ed. Philip Nobile (New York: Random House, 1970), p. 134.
3. Michael Perkins, *The Secret Record: Modern Erotic Literature* (New York: Morrow, 1976), p. 92.
4. D. H. Lawrence, "Pornography and Obscenity," in *The Portable D. H. Lawrence,* ed. Diana Trilling (New York: Viking, 1947), pp. 646-71.
5. Gershon Legman, *The Horn Book: Studies in Erotic Folklore and Bibliography* (New Hyde Park, N.Y.: University Books, 1964), p. 71.
6. David Meltzer, *The Agency* (North Hollywood, Calif.: Essex House, 1968), pp. 158-60.
7. Harford Montgomery Hyde, *A History of Pornography* (New York: Farrar, Straus & Giroux, 1965), p. 132.
8. Legman, p. 485.
9. Perkins, p. 91.
10. Perkins, p. 89.
11. Perkins, p. 125.
12. Cited in *A History of Underground Comics,* by Mark James Estren (San Francisco: Straight Arrow, 1974), pp. 117, 119.
13. Estren, pp. 138-39.
14. Don Druker "Sex in Two Dimensions: Erotic Movies," in *Our National Passion: 200 Years of Sex in America,* ed. Sally Banes, Sheldon Frank, and Tem Horowitz (Chicago: Follett, 1976), p. 139.
15. Ralph Ginzburg, *An Unhurried View of Erotica* (New York: Helmsman Press, 1958), p. 91.

BIBLIOGRAPHY

BOOKS AND ARTICLES

Aratow, Paul. *100 Years of Erotica: A Photographic Portfolio of Mainstream American Subculture from 1845-1940.* San Francisco: Straight Arrow, 1973.

Arlen, Richard. *Sex and Pornography in the Movies.* Beverly Hills, Calif.: Valiant Books, 1971.

Ashbee, Henry Spencer. *Catena Librorum Tacendorum: Being Notes Bio-Biblio-Iconographical and Critical on Curious and Uncommon Books.* London: Privately printed, 1885.

———. *Centuria Librorum Absconditorum: Being Notes Bio-Biblio-Iconographical and Critical, on Curious and Uncommon Books.* London: Privately printed, 1879.

———. *A Complete Guide to Forbidden Books.* North Hollywood, Cal.: Brandon House, 1966.

______. *Index Librorum Prohibitorum: Being Notes Bio-Biblio-Iconographical and Critical, on Curious and Uncommon Books.* London: Privately printed, 1877.

"As Slime Goes By: *Screw's* Carnal Chronicle of the Past 11 Years." *Screw,* 12 (November 5, 1979).

Atkins, Thomas R., ed. *Sexuality in the Movies.* Bloomington: Indiana University Press, 1975.

Bilderlexikon der Erotik. Volume 2. Vienna: Verlag für Kulturforschung, 1928-31.

Blake, Roger. *The Porno Movies; a Documentary Study of the Burgeoning Sex-Movie Scene in America Today—Featuring Some of the Most Breathtaking Nude and Love Scenes Ever Filmed.* Cleveland: Century Books, 1970.

Brewer, Joan Scherer, and Rod W. Wright. *Sex Research: Bibliographies from the Institute for Sex Research.* Phoenix, Ariz.: Oryx Press, 1979.

Brusendorff, Ove, and Paul Henningsen. *Erotica for the Millions: Love in the Movies.* London: Rodney Book Service, 1960.

______. *A History of Eroticism.* 6 vols. New York: Lyle Stuart, 1963-66.

Butler, D. R. "The Joy of Sexy Writing." In *1976 Writer's Yearbook.* Cincinnati: Writer's Digest, 1976.

Clor, Harry M. *Obscenity and Public Morality.* Chicago: University of Chicago Press, 1969.

Cook, James. "The X-Rated Economy." *Forbes,* 122 (September 18, 1978), 81-92.

Craft, Robert. "Paydirt: Notes on the Sex Explosion." In *The New Eroticism.* Edited by Philip Nobile. New York: Random House, 1970.

Craig, Alec. *The Banned Books of England and Other Countries.* London: George Allen & Unwin, 1937.

______. *Suppressed Books.* Cleveland: World, 1966.

Csicsery, George Paul, ed. *The Sex Industry: A Sex-Posé of Happy Hookers, Massage Parlors, Skin-flicks—Every Kick Money Can Buy.* New York: New American Library, 1973.

Damon, Gene, Jan Watson, and Robin Jordan. *The Lesbian in Literature.* Reno, Nev.: Ladder, 1975.

Deakin, Terence J. *Catalogi Librorum Eroticorum: A Critical Bibliography of Erotic Bibliographies and Book Catalogues.* London: Cecil & Amelia Woolf, 1964.

Di Lauro, Al, and Gerald Rabkin. *Dirty Movies: An Illustrated History of the Stag Film, 1915-1970.* New York: Chelsea House, 1976.

Dixon, Rebecca. "Bibliographical Control of Erotica." In *An Intellectual Freedom Primer.* Edited by Charles H. Busha. Littleton, Colo.: Libraries Unlimited, 1977.

Druker, Don. "Sex in Two Dimensions: Erotic Movies." In *Our National Passion: 200 Years of Sex in America.* Edited by Sally Banes, Sheldon Frank, and Tem Horowitz. Chicago: Follett, 1976.

Du Breuil, Linda. *The Girl Who Writes Dirty Books.* New York: Norton, 1975.

Dudar, Helen. "America Discovers Child Pornography." *Ms.*, 6 (August 1977), 45-47, 80.

Eisenberg, Daniel. "Towards a Bibliography of Erotic Pulps Published in the U.S., 1962-1972." Unpublished paper, 1972. Available at Institute for Sex Research, Bloomington, Ind.

Ellis, Albert, and Albert Abarbanel. *Encyclopedia of Sexual Behavior.* New York: Hawthorn Books, 1967.

Elsom, John. *Erotic Theatre.* New York: Taplinger, 1973.

Englisch, Paul. *Geschichte der Erotischen Literatur.* 2nd ed. Stuttgart: J. Pittmann, 1932.

———. *Irrgarten der Erotik.* Leipzig: Lykeion, Kulturwissen Schaftliche Verlagsgesellschaft M.B.H., 1931.

Ernst, Morris Leopold, and Alan U. Schwartz. *Censorship: The Search for the Obscene.* New York: Macmillan, 1964.

Ernst, Morris Leopold, and William Sleagle. *To the Pure.* New York: Viking Press, 1928.

The Erotic Screen: A Probing Study of Sex in the Adult Cinema. Los Angeles: Private Collectors, 1969.

Estren, Mark James. *A History of Underground Comics.* San Francisco: Straight Arrow, 1974.

Farnsworth, Joanna. "Confessions of a Housewife Porn Writer." In *1979 Writer's Yearbook.* Cincinnati: Writer's Digest, 1979.

Friedman, Leon, ed. *Obscenity: The Complete Oral Arguments Before the Supreme Court in the Major Obscenity Cases.* New York: Chelsea House, 1970.

Gay, Jules. *Bibliographie des ouvrages relatifs à l'amour, aux femmes, au mariage, indiquant les auteurs de ces ouvrages, leurs éditions, leur valeur et les prohibitions ou condamnations dont certains d'entre eux ont été l'objet.* Paris: Jules Gay, 1861.

Gillette, Paul J. *An Uncensored History of Pornography.* Los Angeles: Holloway House, 1965.

Gillmor, Donald M. "The Puzzle of Pornography." *Journalism Quarterly,* 42 (Summer 1965), 363-72.

Ginzburg, Ralph. *An Unhurried View of Erotica.* New York: Helmsman Press, 1958.

Goodland, Roger. *A Bibliography of Sex Rites and Customs.* London: Routledge, 1931.

Goodstone, Tony. *The Pulps.* New York: Chelsea House, 1970.

Gould, Lois. "Pornography for Women." *New York Times Magazine,* (March 2, 1975), 10-11, 50-51, 54, 57, 60, 62.

Grove, Martin A., and William S. Reuben. *The Celluloid Love Feast.* New York: Lancer Books, 1971.

Grumley, Michael. *Hard Corps: Studies in Leather and Sadomasochism.* New York: Dutton, 1977.

Haight, Anne Lyon. *Banned Books.* New York: Bowker, 1935. Reprint. New York: Bowker, 1955.

Hamalian, Leo. "Nobody Knows My Names: Samuel Roth and the Underside of Modern Letters." *Journal of Modern Literature,* 3 (April 1974), 889-921.

Harris, Sara. *The Puritan Jungle: America's Sexual Underground.* New York: Putnam's, 1969.

Harvey, James. *Pornography for Fun and Profit.* Los Angeles: Edka, 1967.

Hess, Thomas B., and Linda Nochlin. *Woman as Sex Object: Studies in Erotic Art, 1730-1970.* New York: Newsweek, 1972.

Hoddeson, Bob. *The Porn People.* Watertown, Mass.: American, 1974.

Hoffman, Frank A. *An Analytical Survey of Anglo-American Traditional Erotica.* Bowling Green, Ohio: Bowling Green University Popular Press, 1975.

Holbrook, David, ed. *The Case Against Pornography.* LaSalle, Ill.: Open Court, 1972.

Holtzman, Sandra. "A Russ Meyer Bibliography," 1974. Unpublished paper at the Institute for Sex Research, Bloomington, Ind.
Hughes, Douglas A., ed. *Perspectives on Pornography.* New York: St. Martin's Press, 1970.
Hurwood, Bernhardt J. *The Golden Age of Erotica.* Los Angeles: Sherbourne Press, 1965.
Hyde, Harford Montgomery. *A History of Pornography.* New York: Farrar, Straus & Giroux, 1965.
Kahmen, Volker. *Eroticism in Contemporary Art.* London: Studio Vista, 1972.
Kallan, Richard A., and Robert D. Brooks. "Soft-Core Stylistics." Paper presented at the Fourth Annual Meeting of the Popular Culture Association, Milwaukee, May 24, 1974. On file at the Institute for Sex Research, Bloomington, Ind.
Karp, David A. "Hiding in Pornographic Bookstores: A Reconsideration of the Nature of Urban Anonymity." *Urban Life and Culture,* 1 (January 1973), 427-51.
Kilpatrick, James Jackson. *The Smut Peddlers.* Garden City, N.Y.: Doubleday, 1960.
Klaf, Franklin S., and Bernhardt J. Hurwood. *A Psychiatrist Looks at Erotica.* New York: Ace Books, 1964.
Knight, Arthur. *Playboy's Sex in Cinema.* 7 vols. Chicago: Playboy Press, 1971-77. (Vols. 1-3 with Hollis Alpert. Reprints the annual articles published in *Playboy* from 1969 to 1977.)
Kronhausen, Phyllis, and Eberhard Kronhausen. *Erotic Art: A Survey of Erotic Fact and Fancy in the Fine Arts.* 2 vols. New York: Grove Press, 1969-70.
______. *Pornography and the Law.* 2nd ed. New York: Ballantine, 1964.
______. *The Sex People: Erotic Performers and Their Bold New Worlds.* Chicago: Playboy Press, 1975.
Laner, Mary Reige. "Make-believe Mistresses: Photo-essay Models in the Candy Sex Magazine." *Sociological Symposium,* 15 (Spring 1976), 81-98.
Lawrence, D. H. "Pornography and Obscenity." In *The Portable D. H. Lawrence.* Edited by Diana Trilling. New York: Viking, 1947.
Legman, Gershon. "Homosexuality and Toilet Inscriptions: An Analysis." Typescript, Institute for Sex Research, 1940-41.
______. *The Horn Book: Studies in Erotic Folklore and Bibliography.* New Hyde Park, N.Y.: University Books, 1964.
______. *Love & Death: A Study in Censorship.* New York: Breaking Point, 1949.
______. *Rationale of the Dirty Joke: An Analysis of Sexual Humor.* 2 vols. New York: Grove Press, 1968-75.
Lo Duca, Guiseppe. *A History of Eroticism.* Translated by Kenneth Anger. Paris: Jean-Jacques Pauvert, 1961.
Loth, David. *The Erotic in Literature.* New York: Julian Messner, 1961.
Meltzer, David. *The Agency.* North Hollywood, Cal.: Essex House, 1968.
Michelson, Peter. *The Aesthetics of Pornography.* New York: Herder & Herder, 1971.
Miles, Mildred Lynn. *Index to Playboy.* Metuchen, N.J.: Scarecrow Press, 1970.
Milton, John, ed. *Smut from the Past, 2.* New York: Milky Way, 1974.
Morthland, John. "Porn Films—An In-depth Report." *Take One,* 4 (March-April 1973), 11-17.
Nay, Hugo. *Bibliotheca Germanorum Erotica.* Leipzig: Privatdruck, 1875.
Nobile, Philip A. *The New Eroticism.* New York: Random House, 1970.

Noble, William P. "Writing for the Sex Market." In *1978 Writer's Yearbook.* Cincinnati: Writer's Digest, 1978.

Otto, Herbert A. "The Pornographic Fringeland of the American Newsstand." *Journal of Human Relations,* 12 (1964), 375-90.

Ouellette, William, and Barbara Jones Ouellette. *Erotic Postcards.* New York: Excalibur Books, 1977.

Parker, William. *Homosexuality: A Selective Bibliography of Over 3,000 Items.* Metuchen, N.J.: Scarecrow Press, 1971. (Supplement, 1970-75. Scarecrow Press, 1977.)

Peckham, Morse. *Art and Pornography: An Experiment in Explanation.* Institute for Sex Research Studies in Sex and Society, no. 2. New York: Basic Books, 1969.

Penza, Henrietta. "Women Rate X-rated Films." *Forum,* 5 (September 1976), 36-42.

Perkins, Michael. *The Secret Record: Modern Erotic Literature.* New York: Morrow, 1976.

———, ed. *Smut from the Past, 1.* New York: Milky Way, 1974.

Publisher's Trade List Annual. New York: Bowker, 1973.

Randolph, Vance. *Pissing in the Snow and Other Ozark Folktales.* Champaign: University of Illinois Press, 1976.

Reems, Harry. *Here Comes Harry Reems.* New York: Pinnacle, 1975.

Reisner, Robert George. *Show Me the Good Parts: The Reader's Guide to Sex in Literature.* New York: Citadel Press, 1964.

The Report of the Commission on Obscenity and Pornography. Washington, D.C.: U.S. GPO, September 1970. (Available from Superintendent of Documents, Washington, D.C. 20402 Stock #052-056-00001-2.) (Paperback ed. New York: Bantam, 1970.)

Roberts, Edwin A., Jr. *The Smut Rakers: A Report in Depth on Obscenity and the Censors.* Silver Spring, Md.: National Observer, 1966.

Rose, Alfred. (Pseud. Rolf S. Reade.) *Register of Erotic Books (Registrum Librorum Eroticorum).* 2 vols. London: Rolf S. Reade, 1936. Reprint ed. New York: Jack Russell, 1965.

Rotsler, William. *Contemporary Erotic Cinema.* New York: Ballantine, 1973.

St. John Stevas, Norman. *Obscenity and the Law.* London: Secker and Warburg, 1956.

Schroeder, Theodore. *Free Speech Bibliography.* New York: Wilson, 1922.

See, Carolyn. *Blue Money, Pornography and the Pornographers.* New York: McKay, 1974.

"Sex, Porn and Male Rage." *Mother Jones,* 5 (April 1980), special issue.

Siebenand, Paul Alcuin. "The Beginnings of Gay Cinema in Los Angeles: The Industry and the Audience." Ph.D. dissertation, University of Southern California, 1975.

Slade, Joseph W. "Recent Trends in Pornographic Films." *Society,* (September-October 1975), 77-84.

Steinem, Gloria. "Pornography—Not Sex but the Obscene Use of Power." *Ms.,* 6 (August 1977), front cover, 43-44.

Stoctay, G. G. *America's Erotic Past: 1868-1940.* San Diego: Greenleaf Classics, 1973.

Strick, Marv, with Robert I. Lethe. *The Sexy Cinema.* Los Angeles: Sherbourne Press, 1975.

Technical Report of the Commission on Obscenity and Pornography. 9 vols. Washington, D.C.: Government Printing Office, 1971-72. (Available from the Superintendent of Documents, Government Printing Office, Washington D.C. 20402. Stock #5256-0002 through #5256-0010.)

Turan, Kenneth, and Stephen F. Zito. *Sinema: American Pornographic Films and the People Who Make Them.* New York: Praeger, 1974.
Tyler, Parker. *Screening the Sexes: Homosexuality in the Movies.* New York: Holt, Rinehart and Winston, 1972.
———. *Sex Psyche Etcetera in the Film.* New York: Horizon Press, 1969.
Tynan, Kenneth. "Dirty Books Can Stay." In *The New Eroticism.* Edited by Philip Nobile. New York: Random House, 1970.
Vassi, Marco. *Metasex, Mirth & Madness.* New York: Penthouse Press, 1975.
Wallace, M. B. *The Striptease, an Annotated Bibliography.* Unpublished paper, 1973. Available at the Institute for Sex Research Library, Bloomington, Ind.
Wedeck, Harry E. *Dictionary of Erotic Literature.* New York: Philosophical Library, 1962.
Wilson, W. Cody. "American Experience with Pornography." In *Social Change and Human Behavior: Mental Health Challenges of the Seventies.* Edited by George V. Coelho. Rockville, Md.: National Institute of Mental Health, 1972.
Wilson, W. Cody, and Herbert I. Abelson. "Experience with and Attitudes Toward Explicit Sexual Materials." *Journal of Social Issues,* 29 (1973), 19-41.
Wilson, W. Cody, and Michael J. Goldstein, eds. "Pornography: Attitudes, Use, and Effects." *Journal of Social Issues,* 29 (1973), whole issue.
Wortley, Richard. *Erotic Movies.* New York: Crescent, 1975.
Young, Wayland. *Eros Denied.* New York: Grove Press, 1964.
Ziplow, Steven. *The Filmmaker's Guide to Pornography.* New York: Drake, 1977.
Zurcher, Louis A. Jr., and George R. Kirkpatrick. *Citizens for Decency: Antipornography Crusades as Status Defense.* Austin: University of Texas Press, 1976.

PERIODICALS

Hustler. Los Angeles, 1974-.
Oui. Los Angeles, 1972-.
Playboy. Chicago, 1953-.
San Francisco Ball. Burbank, Calif., 1970-.
Screw. New York, 1969-.
TAB Report. Washington, D.C., 1979-.

CHAPTER 13 Propaganda

Richard Alan Nelson

The growth of propaganda in modern life has resulted largely from certain inventive developments in the late nineteenth and early twentieth centuries—(high speed print, telegraphy, films, radio, and more recently television)—which provided governments and private interests with an unprecedented media arsenal useful in times of both war and peace. Despite the continuing role played by commercial advertising and political propaganda in defining our national culture and institutions, Americans by and large bear a traditional antipathy toward the idea (if not the practice) of propaganda. The sobering thought that arises in preparing a topical review such as this is that, notwithstanding an overwhelmingly negative literature condemning propaganda as inimical to freedom (an argument which is itself open to question, but which nevertheless represents a consensus of published opinion), very little has been done to control its spread. That the term continues to hold a strongly pejorative—even sinister—connotation is somewhat surprising since it was Americans who pioneered the implementation of attitudinal methodologies, mass marketing strategies, and media technologies now considered essential to widespread persuasive communication.

Each one of us has been indoctrinated from childhood, and daily we continue to be bombarded with intrusive messages attempting to inform, manipulate, motivate, redirect, and even placate us. An objective observer is forced to conclude that we live at a time when propaganda, far from abating, is becoming an increasingly pervasive force in democratic as well as totalitarian states. Indeed, given the pluralistic nature of contemporary society, some forms of propagandistic social engineering may be necessary if we hope to reach consensus on the vital (but perhaps controversial) issues facing us.

What then constitutes propaganda? Unfortunately, there is no easy answer. Although we have progressed beyond the insular "us versus them" belief that propaganda is something only our enemies engage in (facetiously described as the other side's case put so convincingly as to be annoying!), a definition remains largely a matter of perspective. Writers on the topic regularly devote entire chapters to this one problem due to the imprecision of the term, which has been interpreted variously to include such functions as advertising, public relations, publicity, political communication, special interest lobbying, radical agitation, psychological warfare, and even education. There is, however, general agreement that propaganda is a form of manipulative communication designed to elicit some predetermined response. Not all propaganda is equally embracive, pervasive, or effective in what the persuader asks us to think or do; nevertheless, propaganda is purposive. We can conveniently separate propaganda into those messages which encourage us to buy a commercial product and those which seek to direct our belief structure and personality in a more fundamental way. In many cases, the job of today's propagandist involves not so much changing minds as finding the right audience in order to reinforce and extend existing attitudes. For purposes of this essay, propaganda is defined as the systematic attempt to influence the emotions, attitudes, opinions, and actions of specified target audiences for ideological or political purposes through the controlled transmission of one-sided messages via mass media channels.

Part of the confusion in terminology stems from the interdisciplinary nature and differing emphases of propaganda studies. Some authors argue that all propaganda is corrosive and a menace, whereas a minority state that propaganda is a neutral tool which can be put to either good or bad uses depending on the purpose of the source. A number of books have focused on the use of propaganda by governments in wartime; others choose a broad historical rather than case study approach. Another way of looking at propaganda favored by social scientists and linguists codifies and analyzes in "cookbook" form various motivational devices and techniques used by propagandists (such as the "glittering generality"). A fourth methodology often used by psychologically oriented communications researchers tests various hypotheses about attitude formation and behavioral change. These are loosely grouped under the banner of "persuasion" studies. Because we still lack clear theoretical bases for understanding the persuasive process, these conclusions (particularly those evaluating the effects of propaganda) remain tentative and are not necessarily generalizable to mass groups. Despite scientific trappings, for example, we still cannot predict with absolute certainty that a particular campaign design will lead to the desired results in a target population.

Given these divergent sources, the literature on propaganda is enormous. Relevant references run into the tens of thousands. Obviously, an introductory guide cannot hope to provide more than a representative overview of the more important works and collections. The appended bibliography, however, lists a number of specialized studies cited in the text which are definitive for their topic or offer interesting insights on American propaganda. Included are selected doctoral dissertations, master's theses, government documents, and pertinent journals and magazine articles. Most books involving public opinion have been excluded because they are technical analyses without direct interest to students of popular culture. Similarly, citations in individual media and related topic areas such as advertising are made only if they bear directly on propaganda as defined above. This limitation is made not only in the interest of space but also because the various volumes of this *Handbook* already provide introductions to their basic literature.

HISTORIC OUTLINE

One can trace the origins of propaganda to remote antiquity. Aristotle's *Rhetoric,* for example, remains a valuable guide to propaganda techniques despite the passage of more than two millenia. By the Middle Ages, the introduction of the printing press in Europe and the spread of literacy were encouraging greater use of books and tracts designed to sway opinion. Much of this literature was religious, and the term *propaganda* was first used widely by the Catholic Church in 1622, with the founding of the Congregatio de propaganda fide (Congregation for the Propagation of Faith) during the Counter-Reformation.

Drawing on this European heritage, religionists coming to America during the pre-Revolutionary period became active publishers not only of biblical texts but also of literature extolling the virtues of the new land. In this endeavor they were joined by wealthy Colonial trading companies, which issued a number of misleading promotional advertisements designed to encourage settlement of their commercial plantations. The political foundations for modern propaganda emerged late in the eighteenth century, when the idea of inalienable rights advanced during the Enlightenment found flower in the Colonial republics. The Declaration of Independence penned by Thomas Jefferson was widely distributed and proved itself a masterful propaganda document not only by expressing the philosophy of the Revolution in language that all Colonialists could understand but also by justifying the American cause overseas and presaging the rise in importance of public opinion.

One should remember, however, that the American Revolution was not a spontaneous popular uprising. Contrary to myth, it was in reality the work of a small group of dedicated persuaders who created our first national propaganda and agitation campaign in order to overthrow a monarchical government. Even today the work of James Otis, Samuel Adams, Patrick Henry, Benjamin Franklin, and Thomas Paine (whose circulation of *Common Sense* in 1776 and *The American Crisis* in 1776-83 helped cement opposition to the Crown) continues to be studied by propaganda researchers. Among the techniques these radical pamphleteers inaugurated that are still utilized in contemporary ideological communication are: (1) the realization that propaganda to be effective requires organization (the Sons of Liberty and

Committees of Correspondence acted as conduits for revolutionary propaganda throughout the Colonies); (2) the creation of identifiable emotive symbols (the Liberty Tree) and slogans ("Don't tread on me" and "Taxation without representation is tyranny"), which simplify issues and arouse emotions; (3) the utilization of publicity and staged events (such as the Boston Tea Party) to attract media attention and enlist support of key cooperators (religious leaders whose sermons were widely published and distributed); (4) the exploitation of differences rather than emphasizing similarities in order to create discontent leading to change; and (5) the saturation of specified groups as well as mass audiences with monolithic reportage on a sustained and unrelenting basis through control of key organs of opinion (press, pamphlets, broadsides, even songs). The "patriots" proved expert at publicizing their story first so as to establish the agenda for debate, while simultaneously discrediting their loyalist opponents.

During the period of controversy surrounding adoption of the Federal Constitution after the war, a series of newspaper articles now known collectively as *The Federalist Papers* (1787-88) were anonymously prepared by Alexander Hamilton, James Madison, and John Jay to sell Americans on the new government. These proved an effective instrument of propaganda among opinion leaders as well as a thoughtful political treatise of more lasting interest. The freedoms secured by the Constitution led to the development early in the nineteenth century of clearly defined political parties and special interest organizations which readily adopted propaganda technologies for their own purposes. Leading American propagandists of the early 1800s include Theodore Dwight, an effective spokesman for the Federalist cause, and Amos Kendall, who served as Andrew Jackson's chief advisor and later earned the title of "first presidential public relations man."

Fears of undue foreign influence in the new republic led to a series of "anti" campaigns (anti-Illuminati, anti-Mason, anti-Catholic, anti-Irish, anti-Jewish, and so on), which even today flourish sporadically. Early propaganda books, typified by *Six Months in a Convent* which appeared in the early 1830s, helped to focus hatred and were underwritten by interests anxious to control immigrant blocks politically and keep their wages artificially low. The outstanding propaganda novel of the century was Harriet Beecher Stowe's powerful indictment of slavery, *Uncle Tom's Cabin* (1851), which sold an unprecedented 300,000 copies during its first year of publication and contributed significantly to the abolitionist movement. Pro-slavery forces were also active in the period up through the Civil War, issuing tracts and lobbying for support in Congress. In this they were secretly aided by "manifest destiny" expansionists in the North, who flooded the country with literature designed to raise patriotic fervor for war with Mexico. In a real sense, words as much as bullets helped to "Win the West."

As sectional differences became more pronounced and a war between the states inevitable, both the North and South recognized the importance of propaganda to the struggle. Particularly in the North where the war remained unpopular (there were draft riots in New York in 1863 and the so-called Copperhead movement fielded peace candidates as late as 1864), propaganda was utilized to mobilize public opinion both at home and abroad. Many of the trappings of contemporary journalism such as the press conference and the press pass were instituted by military leaders in order to censor battle reportage unfavorable to the Union, and Lincoln personally dispatched up to one hundred special agents to Britain along with a boatload of foodstuffs for unemployed English cotton textile workers so as to counter propaganda gains made by the Confederacy. In the North, too, the art of pamphleteering was advanced by the unceasing efforts of private organizations such as the Loyal Publication Society and the Union League Board of Publications.

The full impact of industrialism and the importance of public opinion began to be felt by the end of the war. Public opinion, which was at first narrowly defined to include only educated white male landowners, gradually came to be extended to the middle and working classes (and later in the twentieth century to women and minorities, changes themselves brought about in part by propaganda). Growing urbanism was accompanied by sweeping improvements in communication which extended the power of the press as a corridor into the minds of millions. In the era of yellow journalism (1890-1914) much of the news was, as it is today, artificial; that is, created and promoted by the newspapers who reported the stories as bona fide events. Although the impact of the press as a propaganda organ dates back before the Revolution, by this period the chains of publications controlled by press barons such as William Randolph Hearst had unrivaled influence on American thought. His *New York Journal* is largely credited with exciting the United States to challenge Spain over Cuba in 1898. Besides quadrupling Hearst's circulation, the events leading up to the war also marked the first time motion pictures were utilized meaningfully for propagandistic purposes. Highly patriotic short films such as *Tearing Down the Spanish Flag!* (1898) electrified U.S. audiences when the hated emblem was replaced by "Old Glory." The tremendous popular success of this picture (although it was actually shot on a roof in New York) spawned a host of imitators once actual hostilities broke out. Since cameramen were often prohibited from gaining access to authentic battleground footage, much of the "reportage," such as the series released under the title *The Campaign in Cuba* (1898), was surreptitiously filmed in the wilds of New Jersey. Screen propaganda already had shown flagrant disregard for truth, but this proved secondary to audiences who clamored for the lifelike images on the screen. This power of "actuality" and "documentation" freed propagandists for the first time from near complete reliance on the written word.

As the United States emerged to become a more important twentieth-century international political factor, European nations competing for continental leadership soon realized that the United States could play a pivotal role in the next war. As early as 1910, Germany began an active propaganda campaign to counteract pro-British biases in the leading organs of U.S. opinion. With the outbreak of hostilities in Europe, both Irish-American and German-American propagandists such as George Sylvester Viereck sought to combat the much more pervasive pro-intervention views spread by English agents working through a well-organized network of native sympathizers, press contacts, cultural exchanges, and business and banking ties. Overcoming isolationist impulses thanks to American gullibility, the British view prevailed and the country was successfully maneuvered into collective hatred of all things German through widespread dissemination of maliciously false (but effective) "anti-Hun" atrocity stories.

Even though we were the last major power to enter the war, the United States ironically was the first belligerent to establish an open, fully coordinated propaganda unit known as the Committee on Public Information (CPI). Headed by advertising executive George Creel, the CPI was given the commission to "sell the war to America." To do this, the CPI organized a national speakers bureau of "four-minute men," who galvanized audiences with carefully timed short propaganda messages supporting Liberty Bond sales drives. Recognizing the power of the screen, the Creel committee also arranged for cooperation between the private film industry (including the newsreel companies) and the military. The poster also emerged at this time as an effective mass war medium, and individual governments literally flooded their nations with millions of propaganda posters designed to muster public support for total victory. Among the American artists who lent themselves to the war effort were Charles Gibson, creator of the "Gibson Girl," and Norman Rockwell. Under CPI auspices alone, more than 100 million enthusiastically patriotic posters and other publications were distributed.

Although in the end much of the propaganda effort by Creel and his Allied counterparts proved (like Wilson's famous Fourteen Points as the basis for a just peace) more hyperbole than fact, World War I is important historically because it commemorates the inaugural deployment of contemporary mass propaganda. While the history of propaganda is indelibly linked to war, the seemingly interminable stalemate that marked most of the years of fighting propelled propaganda to the forefront as an important tool of government for sustaining homeland morale and maintaining ties of alliance. With the end of the war, however, Americans' desire to return to "normalcy" led to the quick disbanding of the CPI and a limiting of government propaganda efforts. On the other hand, during the 1920s and 1930s privately originated propaganda increased as numerous pressure groups formed in attempts to influence individual thought and actions as well as affect government policies by harnessing mass opinion. When the social upheavals wrought by the Great

Depression led to installation of a Democratic administration promising a "New Deal," official U.S. propaganda took off once more. The introduction of new social security, public works, labor, housing, agricultural, and other policies required unparalleled peacetime publicity, and the government mobilized all its powers to build a shared consensus. Motion picture advertising (which had already been used for partisan political purposes) was extended, and the Roosevelt leadership further commissioned the filming of a number of documentary films with strong social messages. *The Plow that Broke the Plains* (1936) and *The River* (1937), for example, both pointed to the need for government intervention in conserving natural resources, and their success helped establish a federally controlled U.S. Film Service. Perhaps the most controversial of the early New Deal propaganda campaigns involved the National Recovery Administration (NRA). The totalitarian methods favored by NRA administrators, including enforced display of the blue NRA eagle emblem by "cooperating" businesses, were seen by many as a threat to American democratic principles. Partially on the basis of the propagandistic excesses of its supporters, the NRA was declared unconstitutional and nullified by the Supreme Court.

World propaganda had already entered a new phase with the successes of the Communists in Russia and the National Socialists in Germany. Attention to propaganda issues was further exacerbated by the uncertain economic climate of the period and the increases in the West of ideological movements that used propaganda unhesitatingly for both internal and external distribution. As early as 1919-20, the United States had been engulfed in a "Red scare," but despite this temporary setback Marxist propaganda continued to circulate with growing effectiveness among disenchanted American intellectuals and workers. The sheer amount of propaganda issued by the totalitarian states forced the leading democracies (notably Britain and the United States) to respond with a series of investigations and by upgrading their own propaganda apparatuses. Much of this was once again interventionist in nature, particularly after 1939 and the outbreak of World War II in Europe. Until Pearl Harbor, U.S. antiwar sentiment (epitomized by the America First Committee and the radio sermons of firebrand preacher Father Charles Edward Coughlin) openly competed against the line promoted by Anglophile organizations such as the Fight for Freedom Committee. Even as early as 1938, the United States was moving to shore up its position in Latin America by forming a Division of Cultural Relations in the Department of State, which rigorously issued propaganda designed to portray the United States as an altruistic benefactor in a common struggle against possible foreign aggression.

With the coming of World War II, official U.S. propaganda efforts were mostly directed by the Office of War Information (OWI) which was responsible for internal and external information. The Office of Strategic Services (OSS) conducted clandestine anti-Axis psychological warfare or so-called black propaganda. Coordinating the European operations of the OWI and OSS for military needs was the Psychological Warfare Division at Allied Supreme Headquarters. There were marked differences between U.S. propaganda and that of the Axis powers. Much of the enemy effort relied heavily on radio, and the sarcastic broadcasts of "Lord Haw Haw" (William Joyce) and "Axis Sally" from Germany, "Tokyo Rose" from Japan, and American expatriate poet Ezra Pound from Italy were listened to widely. Apart from broadcasting, the Allies utilized other methods, notably air-dropped leaflets. How effective these were in undermining enemy morale is still debated, but there is no doubt that internally the overall U.S. propaganda effort was successful. On the home front, the major media willingly cooperated in the war effort. The Hollywood studios actively collaborated with federal authorities in grinding out hundreds of racist anti-Japanese and anti-German war epics. Numerous government agencies, including the Treasury Department, took to the airwaves with highly propagandistic radio programs such as *Treasury Star Parade* (1943-44) to sell war bonds and maintain enthusiasm for continuing the fight. Newspapers and newsreels, too, carried regular government-inspired reports and voluntarily censored potentially demoralizing news. Gigantic posters dominated factories and military shipyards to spur production, and even comic books and pulp literature were enlisted to put the country on a war footing unenvisioned even in the darkest days of World War I.

With the defeat of Germany and Japan, U.S. propaganda took on a new direction. Largely because of the struggle with the Soviet Union for postwar dominance, much of the official propaganda issued by the United States since the 1940s has been directed at Eastern Europe and the emerging Third World states. The Voice of America, which transmits news, entertainment, and propaganda worldwide in dozens of languages, now is a division of the new International Communication Agency (USICA), which in 1978 incorporated the former U.S. Information Agency (USIA). The USICA continues to maintain information offices and libraries in sixty countries as well as operate an extensive press and broadcast assistance service. Secret operations are the function of the Central Intelligence Agency (CIA), which for years helped to support the ostensibly private anticommunist Radio Free Europe and Radio Liberty broadcasts. Today the federal government, rather than any Madison Avenue firm or corporate entity, constitutes the single greatest "propaganda machine" in this country. Specialists in forty-seven different federal agencies currently spend over $2.5 billion each year attempting to influence the way Americans think. The government, for example, is the nation's leading publisher and film producer, releasing thousands of magazines and books, hundreds of motion pictures, and countless press releases annually.

For private groups operating nationally, the battle of propaganda is as much as anything else a fight for access to the channels of mass dissemination. Political Action Committees, trade and educational groups, foundations, and other organizations that must compete and lobby for support are often forced to rely on the techniques of propaganda if they are successfully to reach their own institutional goals. Increased use of direct mail and technological breakthroughs may open new doors and opportunities for ideational propagandists as well as those more interested in purely commercial advertising and public relations marketing efforts.

Intervention by the Federal Trade Commission and the Federal Communications Commission in the broadcast advertising marketplace has also helped spur the development of so-called public service announcements (PSAs) that ask us to support approved causes ranging from the United Nations to anti-drug legislation. At the same time, the questionable impact of the FCC-authored "fairness" and "personal attack" doctrines has been to restrict discussions of major issues and limit the content of serious radio and television advertising (advertorials). Other attempts to regulate propaganda have been largely ineffective. The naive assumption voiced by some critics that somehow "rational education" would neutralize "irrational propaganda" has not been borne out by experience.

REFERENCE WORKS

Despite propaganda's long history, serious study of the phenomenon has largely been limited to the last sixty years. Most pre-World I references (including the venerable *Encyclopaedia Britannica*) do not even mention the topic. However, the widespread utilization of propaganda in World War I and the extension of radical ideology in the 1920s led a number of thoughtful writers to reflect on the problems as well as promise of propaganda. Among the first to catalog the growing literature systematically were Kimball Young and Raymond D. Lawrence, whose annotated *Bibliography on Censorship and Propaganda* issued serially in 1928 is still useful for early newspaper and magazine citations dating from the nineteenth century not usually found in later compendiums.

Expanding upon this pioneering work were Harold D. Lasswell, Ralph D. Casey, and Bruce L. Smith, whose *Propaganda and Promotional Activities: An Annotated Bibliography* quickly became a standard reference upon publication in 1935 and remains an indispensable guide to the seminal literature. A 1969 reissue includes a new introduction by Lasswell summarizing his thoughts after nearly forty years of propaganda study. Lasswell (whose communication formula "who says what, in which channel, to whom, with what effect?" remains the basic starting point for most empirical studies) notes that despite scientific advances we are still without a comprehensive theory that can explain as well as analyze human behavior—including the use of propaganda. Originally prepared for the Social Science Research Council, the bibliography has seven divisions. Theories of propaganda management are discussed in a thirty-five-page section, which is followed by references to the propagandas of governments, international agencies, political parties, and other organizations classified by type (business, labor, professional, and so on). Later sections classify propaganda according to the response sought, the symbols manipulated, and the channels used. Also listed are early measurement studies and references that describe the impact of propaganda and censorship on modern society. An author-subject index is appended, helping to compensate for the somewhat loose topical categorization.

The same authors (but with Bruce L. Smith listed first) updated this in 1946 with *Propaganda, Communication, and Public Opinion: A Comprehensive Reference Guide,* which includes four essays on the science of mass communication and within a similar organizational framework provides an excellent selectively annotated bibliography of 2,558 books and articles published for the most part between 1934 and 1943. Bruce L. Smith has additionally co-authored with Chitra M. Smith the supplemental *International Communication and Political Opinion: A Guide to the Literature.* This features another 2,500 entries (among them government documents and unpublished studies) released between 1943 and 1955. Stress is placed on the international and promotional aspects of propaganda. Both of the above works include author and subject indexes.

Reference should also be made to Harwood L. Childs, *A Reference Guide to the Study of Public Opinion,* which is organized topically and continues to hold interest despite the lack of annotations, and to the brief *List of Bibliographies on Propaganda* prepared for publication by the U.S. Library of Congress in 1940. Warren C. Price's *The Literature of Journalism: An Annotated Bibliography* includes a short section devoted specifically to selected books and articles on "public opinion, propaganda, and public relations" (177 citations). Again, a subject-author index provides cross-references. Price supplements this volume with *An Annotated Journalism Bibliography: 1958-1968,* co-authored with Calder M. Pickett. This work has 2,172 listings (most not related specifically to propaganda) organized alphabetically by author rather than subject. To compensate for this stylistic change, the index has been expanded to fifty pages.

Of more direct relevance are Scott M. Cutlip's *A Public Relations Bibliography to 1965* with six thousand entries organized topically; Robert L. Bishop's *Public Relations: A Comprehensive Bibliography—Articles and Books on Public Relations, Communication Theory, Public Opinion, and Propaganda, 1964-1972* which follows Cutlip with another 4,500 subject-divided citations; and the subsequent annual updates by Bishop and Albert Walker which appear in *Public Relations Review.* Even though more than three hundred periodical and other sources were searched in compiling the Cutlip-Bishop-Walker bibliographies, there are unfortunately still omissions.

The more recent Walker-prepared guides, for example, appear less comprehensive, particularly in the area of government and think-tank reports. Each follows a similar format indexing author names and government agencies as well as listing occasional names of companies and countries.

Researchers interested in government publications on the topic of propaganda should not overlook George D. Brightbill's *Communications and the United States Congress: A Selectively Annotated Bibliography of Committee Hearings, 1870-1976,* which provides chronologically arranged guidance to some 1,100 titles issued by the House and Senate. Material on censorship is included, although publishing references are not. This work is further limited because documents, reports, and committee prints are also excluded (a situation perhaps to be rectified by a companion volume). William W. Buchanan and Edna A. Kanely, *Cumulative Subject Index to the Monthly Catalog of United States Government Publications 1900-1971,* published by the Carrollton Press, is invaluable for wading through the wealth of available material. Neglected by many researchers has been another Carrollton service called the "Declassified Documents Reference System." The basic collection includes sixteen thousand official documents made available through the Freedom of Information Act. These are summarized, indexed, photoduplicated on microfilm, and supplied to subscribing research libraries with annual updates (1976 to the present). The importance of this system is that it includes sensitive material previously unavailable to the public taken directly from the files of the CIA, the FBI, and other federal agencies.

A very different orientation is found in *Marxism and the Mass Media: Towards a Basic Bibliography,* issued intermittently by the International Mass Media Research Center (1972 to the present) as part of an ongoing periodical series whose purpose is to compile a global, multilingual, annotated bibliography of left studies on all aspects of communication (including propaganda). As a result this reference journal covers ground often overlooked. Also of considerable reference value is Thomas F. Gordon's and Mary Ellen Verna's *Mass Communication Effects and Processes: A Comprehensive Bibliography, 1950-1975.* The bibliography, although not annotated, has a useful narrative introduction to the literature and features over 2,700 citations arranged alphabetically by author. The subject index is detailed, and there is an unusual index of secondary authors which allows the user to find specific citations.

On political propaganda, see *Political Campaign Communications: A Bibliography and Guide to the Literature* (1974) by Lynda Lee Kaid, Keith R. Sanders, and Robert O. Hirsch, the first comprehensive guide to this specialized area. Included is an annotated introduction to the fifty most important reference books plus an unannotated supplemental listing of hundreds of relevant periodical citations. Dan Nimmo (whose earlier *The Political Persuaders: The Techniques of Modern Election Campaigns* is still required reading for understanding the importance of image over issue in determining electoral outcomes) has more recently published a helpful analysis of *Political Communication and Public Opinion in America*, a useful summary of available knowledge which comments on the general area of political communication as well as the roles played by expert communicators, the language and symbols manipulated, persuasion (including propaganda, advertising, and rhetoric), media channels, and other contemporary pragmatic approaches to influencing voter behavior. In *Information Sources in Advertising History* (1979), edited by Richard W. Pollay, four essays assess the literature and discuss sources, but the book's centerpiece is an annotated bibliography of 1,600 titles arranged by subject, with strength in literature prior to 1940. Although propaganda as such is not one of the topics, related areas such as the psychology and sociology of advertising, marketing, public relations, and broadcasting are covered. Two directories list professional associations and describe special collections and archival holdings.

General overviews of the history and literature of propaganda (often prepared by leading authorities) can be found in most encyclopedias. Among the more complete and analytical are those by Harwood L. Childs in *Collier's Encyclopedia*, W. E. Barber in *Dictionary of American History*, Jackson Giddens in *Encyclopedia Americana*, Harold D. Lasswell in *Encyclopaedia Britannica* and the first edition of the *Encyclopaedia of the Social Sciences*, Bruce L. Smith in *The New Encyclopaedia Britannica* and the *International Encyclopedia of the Social Sciences*, and Horst Reimann in *Marxism, Communism and Western Society: A Comparative Encyclopedia*.

Researchers interested in the more recent serious periodical literature should also consult the basic volume and yearly updates on "Public Opinion, Mass Behavior and Political Psychology" issued as part of the *Political Science, Government, and Public Policy Series* published since 1967. Through use of a computerized key-word system, literally thousands of citations appearing in social and behavioral science literature are cataloged under the heading "Edu/Prop...Education, Propaganda, Persuasion." This is well worth reviewing. Other reference guides and journals regularly summarizing current propaganda writing include *Abstracts of Popular Culture*, *America: History and Life*, *Communication Abstracts*, *Historical Abstracts*, *International Political Science Abstracts*, *Political Communication and Persuasion: An International Journal*, *Sociological Abstracts*, and the review sections of *Journalism Quarterly* and *Mass Media Booknotes*. The latter, published monthly by Temple University communications academic Christopher Sterling, is a particularly useful source; in addition to thoughtful commentary on new publications, it devotes one issue per year to federally issued literature (including reports by propaganda agencies such as the USICA).

Countless articles, monographs, and books have also appeared under the catch-all heading "persuasion research." This, like public opinion, often involves surveys and experimental control studies reported in psychology, sociology, political science, and communications journals. One distinction made is that, although all propaganda attempts to persuade, not all persuasion is propaganda. As a result, much of this material is directed at an empirical audience and is thus far removed from the popular culture literature. (Major exceptions include Vance Packard's *The Hidden Persuaders*, first published in 1957, and Wilson Bryan Key's more recent pseudo-scientific *The Subliminal Seduction: Ad Media's Manipulation of a Not So Innocent America*). The student of propaganda in America, however, should at least be aware that this body of writing exists. Fortunately, there are several excellent guides to help the neophyte. A useful critical introduction is "Persuasion Research: Review and Commentary" by Gerald Miller and Michael Burgoon, which complements "Persuasion, Resistance, and Attitude Change" by William J. McGuire. Among the more important general works, all of which provide an overview of this specialized field, are Erwin P. Bettinghaus, *Persuasive Communication*, Winston Brembeck and William Howell, *Persuasion: A Means of Social Influence*, Gary Cronkhite, *Persuasion: Speech and Behavioral Change*, which has a particularly thoughtful analysis, George N. Gordon, *Persuasion: The Theory and Practice of Manipulative Communication*, Carl Hovland and others, *Communication and Persuasion*, Marvin Karlins and Herbert Abelson, *Persuasion: How Opinions and Attitudes Are Changed*, Charles U. Larson, *Persuasion: Reception and Responsibility*, Wayne Minnick, *The Art of Persuasion*, Michael Roloff and Gerald R. Miller, editors, *Persuasion: New Directions in Theory and Research*, Herbert W. Simons, *Persuasion: Understanding, Practice and Analysis*, Wayne N. Thompson, *The Process of Persuasion: Principles and Readings*, and Philip Zimbardo, Ebbe B. Ebbeson, and Christina Maslach, *Influencing Attitudes and Changing Behavior*. Among the newer persuasion periodicals that should be referenced are *Human Communication Research* and *Social Science Monitor*. The latter, which is aimed at public relations and advertising executives, summarizes findings from behavioral science journals that have implications for the pragmatist interested in "getting the right information into the right minds." Also of relevance is Steuart Henderson Britt's *Psychological Principles of Marketing and Consumer Behavior*, which collates a wealth of data. Now must reading for the contemporary propagandist, his book is organized to describe both what happens in the psyche of a person exposed to directed communication and how the mass of available empirical data can be applied in persuasive campaigns.

RESEARCH COLLECTIONS

Much of the material of the propagandist is ephemeral. Leaflets, broadsides, banners, posters, pamphlets, broadcasts, and even motion pictures are not designed to be long-lasting. The propagandist usually is time-bound and concerned with effecting specific, measurable goals rather than creating permanent monuments to "truth." Therefore, specialized reference and research collections are critical for historical research involving the propaganda activities of particular organizations, agencies, and individuals. Unfortunately, important materials are widely scattered. The difficulty is compounded because reference aids and guides to special collections are inadequately cross-referenced.

With this caveat, the logical place to begin the study of American propaganda is in Washington, D.C. Indispensable in working one's way through the maze of government records is the U.S. National Archives and Records Services's *Guide to the National Archives of the United States* issued in 1974. All photographic and paper holdings in the National Archives are organized by government agency "Record Groups" (RG), now numbering over four hundred. A list of record groups is available on request from the archives; many RGs have printed "preliminary inventories" of real value in tracking down specific documents and manuscripts. Among the more important RGs relating to federal propaganda and informational activities are the following:

RG 44—Office of Government Reports. This office acted as a clearinghouse for government information and helped coordinate homefront aspects of the defense and war effort in World War II until being consolidated with other agencies to form the Office of War Information in 1942. Later, the OGR was briefly reestablished to provide motion picture advertising and liaison services. Within this large collection, for example, are the records of the Office of the Coordinator of Government Films,1941-42; still photos and posters issued by the OWI's Division of Public Inquiries, 1942-45 (14,150 items); and other pertinent propaganda materials from the Division of Press Intelligence, which issued summaries and digests of radio and press comments.

RG 63—Committee on Public Information. More than 110 linear feet of reports, correspondence, posters, bulletins, speeches, films, clippings, and other documents detailing both the domestic and foreign work of the CPI from 1917 to 1919 are housed in this collection. Included are materials describing the anti-Bolshevik propaganda campaign conducted by the United States in Russia following the collapse of the Czarist regime.

RG 111—Office of the Chief Signal Officer. Preserved here are propaganda and informational films and newsreels made by the Signal Corps since World War I, the immense bulk of production files for World War II releases, plus other related post-1945 materials.

RG 131—Office of Alien Property. Minutes, reports, pamphlets, press releases, periodicals, films, and other documents seized from German and Italian organizations operating in the United States (such as the German-American Bund) at the time of our entry into World War II are collected in this Record Group.

RG 200—National Archives Gift Collection. This is a motion picture and newsreel treasure house covering the years from 1919 to 1967. Included in the collection are issues of the *Official War Review*, *March of Time*, *Paramount News*, *Ford Animated Weekly*, and eight commercial films investigated by a Senate subcommittee prior to World War II for their alleged war propaganda.

RG 208—Office of War Information. This is the main source of OWI documentation. Among the holdings are a complete run of *Victory* magazine, 1943-46.

RG 216—Office of Censorship. Established by executive order to coordinate U.S. press censorship in World War II, these records still have restricted entry.

RG 226—Office of Strategic Services. The major archival depository for the OSS. The long-classified U.S. War Department's *War Report of the OSS*, however, has been published recently, and it provides a revealing look at the organization's clandestine psychological operations.

RG 229—Office of Inter-American Coordinator. Records here describe Nelson Rockefeller's work in promoting a favorable U.S. image in Latin America during World War II, particularly through the efforts of Walt Disney.

RG 262—Foreign Broadcast Intelligence Service. Contained are 512 cubic feet of documents dating from the period 1940-47. Included are English translations of monitored foreign broadcasts and actual recordings by U.S. citizens such as Edward Delaney, Douglas Chandler, and Fred Kaltenback aired over German radio. Tokyo Rose broadcasts from Japan and speeches by Allied leaders are also preserved.

RG 306—United States Information Agency. These consist primarily of audio-visual materials, including sound recordings (387 items), issued by the Voice of America from 1950 to 1965. However, unclassified materials relating to USIA's later role in Vietnam are also now available for study.

The National Audio-Visual Center operated by the National Archives and Record Service also rents and/or sells prints of more than nine thousand motion pictures produced by the federal government since the 1930s. Included are many classic propaganda films (for example, all seven releases from the *Why We Fight* series issued in World War II), as well as more recent USIA/USICA productions. The USICA maintains its own library in Washington, D.C., with a large clipping and document collection (much of it devoted to the persuasive efforts of the USICA and its predecessor organizations). Note should also be made of the State Department library, which has tightly restricted entry into its large holdings, including extensive propaganda documentation. The Library of Congress, however, tends to be much more cooperative with independent researchers and offers a wealth of material for the propaganda historian. The Rare Book Division, by way of illustration, has a very large collection of early political broadsides (including over 250 relating to the Continental Congress and the Constitutional Convention of 1787). The Prints and Photographs Division is also rich with posters and political cartoons of all periods, as well as World War II photos issued by the OWI and others. On deposit at the Library of Congress are many important collections of private papers, such as those of CPI director George Creel. The library also houses the records of the National Board for Historical Service (which in World War I conducted an enemy press intelligence service), the Elmer Gertz Papers (with important materials relating to the career of George Viereck), and a series of bound volumes containing pamphlets issued by U.S. radical groups since the early 1900s.

In nearby Lexington, Virginia, the George C. Marshall Research Foundation and Library boasts (in addition to the general's private papers) a small but excellent twentieth-century war poster collection (seven hundred issued in the United States, Germany, and France), over six thousand uncataloged U.S. Signal Corps and OWI photos, and other military propaganda materials. A guide to the poster holdings written by Anthony Crawford was recently published.

Outside the greater Washington area, New York offers perhaps the single greatest concentration of library research materials for the study of American propaganda. The Radio Free Europe/Radio Liberty Reference Library in New York City is open to the public by appointment. Although its holdings largely document current developments in the Soviet Union, there are also runs of RFE/RL publications and other pertinent materials detailing international broadcast propaganda. Anti- and pro-Semitic propaganda from here and abroad are collected at the four major Jewish libraries in New York City: the Jacob Alson Memorial Library of the Anti-Defamation League of B'nai B'rith, the Blaustein Library of the American Jewish Committee, the YIVO Institute for Jewish Research Library and Archives, and the Zionist Archives and Library. The Jewish Division of the New York Public Library also has a large collection of extremist literature. The New York Public Library's American History Division additionally houses a plethora of political propaganda materials, including party pamphlets, presidential campaign buttons, posters, ribbons, coins, and similar material (cataloged on one hundred cards). There are also twenty-nine Civil War enlistment posters and bound photographic volumes of over two thousand World War I posters. Its research libraries also have a strong advertising collection, and regular deposit of newer publications continues from groups such as the Advertising Council (which has had great agenda-setting influence on national "public service" issues). The Bancroft Collection of original manuscripts from the American Revolution at the library includes the papers of the Boston Committee of Correspondence. The New York Public Library also has the papers of Samuel Adams and his grandson, Samuel Adams Wells. While considerable, these personal effects of Adams represent only a small portion of his total correspondence since much of what he wrote suffered from neglect or was destroyed in an effort to protect Adams's reputation. Wells's papers consist of his manuscript notes and partial drafts for an unfinished biography of his grandfather, later utilized by subsequent writers. Other materials at this library of interest to propaganda researchers include wide-ranging anti-slavery materials (including runs of early abolitionist propaganda periodicals such as the *Anti-Slavery Reporter*), over eleven thousand pamphlets from World War I (many of them propagandistic, see also the Socialism Collection), a number of psychological warfare leaflets distributed in Europe and Asia during World War II, and substantial holdings of press releases and other publications issued by various government information services (such as those of the U.S. Central Intelligence Group from the years 1942-47).

Radical literature is also available in abundance in the Tamiment Labor History Collection of New York University's Bobst Library. A free guide can be obtained on request. The New York Historical Society tends to take a longer view and is another source for early Revolutionary and Civil War propaganda broadsides. The society also houses the Landauer Collection of American Advertising—more than one million pictorial items demonstrating the power and art of U.S. business propaganda. Brooklyn College of the City University of New York is the home of the papers of Norman Cousins. These cover the years 1942-58 and include his work with the OWI. The school's Department of Television and Radio also houses an unusual collection of black-and-white TV commercials produced between 1948 and 1958. (Supplementing this is the University of Arizona's Bureau of Audio-Visual Services Archive Collection of Television Commercials, which now includes more than 1,500 spots, predominantly from the 1960s and 1970s. Of related interest is the Broadcast Promotion Association Archive in the Telecommunications Department Library at San Diego State University. This is the world's largest collection of tape, film, and print materials created by radio and television professionals to promote and advertise stations and programs).

Also in New York, the American Institute for Marxist Studies, headed by Herbert Aptheker, has an interesting collection of "progressive" literature and publishes the bi-monthly *AIMS Newsletter* (1964 to the present) describing current activities in the field of Marxist thought, including bibliographical listings of interest to students of Left propaganda. The Museum of Broadcasting, founded in 1976 with seed money from CBS, has already acquired a number of historical materials, including copies of World War II Axis English-language propaganda programs. The Public Relations Society of America operates a Research Information Center from its New York offices. This lending and reference service is primarily for members, but the library and vertical file holdings are open to the public. Although *propaganda* is not a specific subject area, related topics (particularly those of interest to contemporary public relations practitioners) are well covered. The Sarah Lawrence Library in Bronxville also reportedly has propaganda-related materials. The New York State Library in Albany contains extensive propaganda poster holdings from World War I (including the Benjamin Walworth Arnold Collection), World War II (with civilian and war industries issues featured), the United Nations, and a number of other miscellaneous items. Also archived there are records of the now defunct New York State Board of Censors (1910-66) which reviewed all films screened in the state. Scripts were required for purposes of rating and approval, and copies of these (which number over seventy thousand) have been indexed by title and transferred to the jurisdiction of the library's Manuscripts and Special Collections Division. Unfortunately photocopying is restricted, but the collection forms a unique reference for the polemical as well as the purely entertainment film.

The Rockefeller Archive Center in Pocantico Hills contains family and business papers of interest to students of Rockefeller-endowed organizations and people. Among the presidential libraries, the Franklin D. Roosevelt Library in Hyde Park is well organized and has collections and other manuscripts indispensable for research into the 1933-45 period. A useful pamphlet describing historical materials in the library is available on request. Except for the Rutherford B. Hayes Library in Fremont, Ohio, the other presidential collections are administered by the National Archives and continue to receive relevant documents and publications. These include the Herbert Hoover Library in West Branch, Iowa; the Harry S. Truman Library in Independence, Missouri; the Dwight D. Eisenhower Library in Abilene, Kansas; the Lyndon B. Johnson Library in Austin, Texas; the John F. Kennedy Library in Cambridge, Massachusetts; and the recently opened Gerald R. Ford Library in Ann Arbor, Michigan. Unfortunately, in the Johnson and Kennedy complexes a number of propaganda and psychological warfare documents from the Vietnam period remain classified.

Befitting its historic Revolutionary heritage, Pennsylvania boasts several important propaganda collections. The American Philosophical Library in Philadelphia houses the vast Richard Gimbel Collection, formerly at Yale University, of published and unpublished materials by and about Thomas Paine. Other documents have been added to make this the single greatest reference center for the study of Paine's life and work. The Historical Society of Pennsylvania has cataloged the papers of U.S. Senator Jonathan Roberts (1771-1854), which are rich for study of national political history in the post-Revolutionary/pre-Civil War period (particularly the agitation for war with England in 1812 and controversies relating to the charter of the Bank of the United States). The World War II Collection of the library is also strong in broadsides, posters, and other forms of federal publicity and propaganda issued by U.S. government agencies. One of the country's largest collections of war posters and radical-racist literature is found nearby at the Balch Institute in Philadelphia. The Contemporary Culture Center at Temple University has equally impressive holdings of alternative and radical left and right-wing press ephemera and polemical writings. These are supplemented by microfilm documents and taped interviews with neo-Nazi leaders and others. Temple's Rare Books and Manuscripts Room also stores over three thousand U.S. and foreign war posters dating from 1914 through the end of the Vietnam conflict. A card guide exists for World War I issues. See also the Quaker Collection at Haverford College, which includes the records (1821-57) of the Indian Society of Anti-Slavery Friends and the diary of William Charles Allen which discusses at some length the effect of propaganda on American public attitudes in World War I. Swarthmore College, besides material from World War I, also holds propaganda materials issued by the Women's Information League for Peace and Freedom, the League of Nations Association, and the Emergency Peace Campaign of 1937. The Harry S. Baird Papers in the U.S. Army Military History Research Collection at Carlisle Barracks, Pennsylvania, includes a scrapbook of propaganda leaflets dropped over Japan in World War II. For other related materials consult the librarian directly. Another useful source is the Thomas Newcommen Memorial Library and Museum in Exton, Pennsylvania, one of the finest specialized business and industrial history libraries in the world. Since propaganda has depended so closely upon technological advances, this library with its extensive corporate documentation should be canvassed by those interested in business elites' relationship to mass persuasion.

Cambridge and Boston are rightly regarded as among our greatest library centers. In addition to the John F. Kennedy Library, one can consult the Widener Library at Harvard, which has a simply overwhelming collection of Americana primary and secondary materials dating back to the seventeenth century. Researchers working in Cambridge should also visit the Edward L. Bernays Public Relations Library, which features one of the nation's largest propaganda collections. Because of its leadership role in recognizing public relations as a graduate academic discipline, Boston University also has strong propaganda holdings including a substantial number of war posters. Specialized materials on Samuel Adams and other Revolutionary leaders can be reviewed at the Massachusetts Historical Society Research Library in Boston. The papers of Edward R. Murrow and his personal library (with much describing his years as USIA director) are now at the Murrow Center of Public Diplomacy, Fletcher School of Law and Diplomacy, Tufts University in Medford, Massachusetts.

In other New England institutions, the Yale University holdings in New Haven, Connecticut, make it one of the premier library collections in the United States. Besides general references, of interest are the extensive holdings of twentieth-century war posters plus the Ezra Pound Papers (whose propaganda broadcasts from Italy were held by the victorious Allies to be clear proof of his insanity). Rhode Island's history as an anti-slavery capital is reflected in the Harris Collection on the American Civil War and Slavery archived at the Providence Public Library. It includes propaganda pamphlets, books, periodicals, broadsheet music, and other eighteenth and nineteenth-century materials reflecting both sides of the controversy. Archiving more than eighty-five editions of *Uncle Tom's Cabin* in fourteen languages is typical of the thoroughness of the collection. Use is restricted, however, as is photocopying. Large holdings of right-wing political literature, documentation on controversial public relations pioneer Ivy Lee, and propaganda from World War I (including twelve filing drawers of correspondence and business records from the Council on Books in Wartime) are now housed at the Princeton University Library in New Jersey. Nearby, the library at Fairleigh Dickinson University in Madison has been the official depository of the Outdoor Advertising Industry since 1972. Manuscripts, pamphlets, slides, photographs, and even full-sized billboards make up this most unusual collection.

The Midwest is also rich in relevant propaganda research materials. The Center for Research Libraries in Chicago has microfilm copies of Voice of America broadcast scripts in English (1953 to the present), foreign broadcasts monitored by CBS (1939-45), the *Daily Report of Foreign Radio Broadcasts* (1941-) transcribed into English, and other wide-ranging deposits of potential interest. The Newberry Library in Chicago, Northwestern University Library in Evanston, and the Illinois Historical Society Library at the University of Illinois in Urbana all have important holdings dealing with U.S. radicalism and related social, political, and labor struggles. Newberry's is perhaps the strongest for the nineteenth century. The files of the Church League of America in Wheaton, Illinois, offer an unusually detailed clipping collection of materials documenting Communist and leftist propaganda in the United States. Included at this conservative research and lobby organization are complete sets of the hearings and reports issued by the U.S. House and California State Un-American Activities Committees.

The State Historical Society of Wisconsin is yet another surprising source of documents and audio-visual material, particularly in relation to Communist propaganda in the motion picture industry. Papers of Dalton Trumbo, Albert Maltz, Melvyn Douglas, Samuel Ornitz, the Progressive Citizens of America/ Hollywood Democratic Committee, plus Robert Morris and Robert Kenny (lawyers who defended the Hollywood 10) are all available at the Wisconsin Center for Theatre Research, sponsored jointly by the Society and the University of Wisconsin at Madison Department of Communication Arts. Extensive other film and television material is located there, including episodes of the controversial FBI-supported *I Led Three Lives* program aired during the McCarthy era. The papers of Frank Early Mason, also in the society's collections, contain private records of his radio propaganda activities as special assistant to the secretary of the navy in World War II. The university's School of Journalism and Mass Communication additionally operates a reading room with vertical file holdings on propaganda and public opinion. The University of Wisconsin campus at Milwaukee houses in its library an interesting collection of propaganda-related materials documenting third-party movements in U.S. politics.

Other state libraries such as the one at the University of Iowa maintain important reference archives. For example, at Iowa one can consult runs of more than nine hundred propaganda periodicals issued by right-wing groups since the 1920s. The basic collection is now available on microfilm for purchase by other research centers. Iowa also holds the letters, papers (including a confidential psychiatric report), and legal documents of German-American propagandist George Sylvester Viereck. Nearly 1,300 items are included, covering the years 1896-1959, which reflect his long activist career (including representation of the National Socialist government prior to World War II). The American Archives of the Factual Film at Iowa State University now has close to 1,600 "sponsored" films in its collection and is the only major repository of its kind for business, educational, and informational motion pictures prepared for private distribution. The University of Kansas also encompasses strong holdings in radical ephemera from the United States, much of which is cataloged. The Leon Josephson Collection there of pamphlets on modern socialism is particularly definitive with regard to the Communist Party of America. The University of Michigan has an excellent radical literature collection (except for populism) dating from the nineteenth century. These include recordings of rightist figures in addition to limited collections of World War I posters (320 items) and election advertisements dating from the 1950s (500-plus items from the United States, Canada, and Europe). Note should also be made of the Archives of Labor and Urban Affairs in the Walter P. Reuther Library, Wayne State University, Detroit, where the papers of Heber Blankenhorn (a journalist and economist who played an important role in World War II Army psychological warfare efforts) are on deposit.

Benefiting from the trend to microfilm scarce documents has been the Anti-Slavery Collection at Oberlin College in Ohio, now widely available. The American Jewish Archives in Cincinnati is another source worth consulting as it includes the papers of important figures such as Jacob Schiff, Samuel Untermeyer, Felix Warburg, and Isaac Wise. The records of the House Special Committee on Un-American Activities, 1934-39, focusing on Nazi propaganda in the United States have been donated to the AJA by the family of Representative Samuel Dickstein. Similarly, an extensive collection of anti-Jewish propaganda materials issued between 1922 and

1967 is on deposit at the Minnesota Historical Society. The University of Notre Dame Archives contain sixty-nine reels of administrative records for the *Congregatio de propaganda fide* covering Catholic activities in the Americas and Great Britain from 1622 to 1865. A guide to these documents by Finbar Kenneally has been published. Of a more secular nature are the papers of Horace C. Peterson archived in the University of Oklahoma Library, including original papers and references used in writing his book *Propaganda for War: The Campaign Against American Neutrality, 1914-1917* (1939) with subsequent reaction to it. The University of Nebraska at Lincoln is another source for limited circulation materials. The Rare Books and Special Collections Room there has posters, pamphlets, clippings, and other fugitive propaganda issues from World War II numbering over one thousand items.

In the South, the U.S. Army Infantry Museum at Fort Benning (Columbus, Georgia) includes a collection of posters and other militariana from both world wars, and the University of Georgia Library has a noted Confederate Imprint Collection with eighty broadsides and other persuasive documents (official and unofficial) issued between 1861 and 1865. The U.S. Army Institute for Military Assistance Library (formerly the Special Warfare School Library) at Fort Bragg, North Carolina, has more than 45,000 pamphlets and documents related to military strategy and counterintelligence (including propaganda leaflets from World War II and Korea). The University of Louisville's Belknap Campus Library and Allen Hite Art Institute have strong U.S. government-issue poster holdings from both world wars, Red Cross posters from the 1915-21 period, and numerous posters issued by the anti-Vietnam War movement. The Vanderbilt Television News Archive in Nashville is a unique collection of over seven thousand hours of videotaped news and public affairs programs aired since August 1968 (indexed and abstracted since 1972). Disputes over news bias and propaganda in electronic journalism can at last be objectively researched, with individual programs and compilations available at nominal cost. A regional News Archive center also exists at George Washington University in Washington, D.C.

In Texas, several centers other than the Lyndon B. Johnson Presidential Library are of interest. The University of Texas Library at Austin, for example, owns the Frances Harvey Papers, which discuss use of newspaper propaganda in the Southwest following the Civil War. The Edward A. Peden Papers there trace his work distributing U.S. propaganda materials in Germany after World War I. Not affiliated with the university is another Austin institution—the Society of Separationists Library, one of the finer specialized collections of atheist, freethought, and anti-religious propaganda in the country. Unfortunately, the books and other materials are not properly cataloged because of financial constraints and are in rather haphazard condition. (The Library of the American Association for the Advancement of Atheism in San Diego, California, reflects similar interests and encompasses another useful reference center for this topic. Researchers, however, are requested to make prior arrangements before traveling to the library.)

On the West Coast, the Hoover Institution of War, Revolution, and Peace at Stanford University is the largest private repository in the United States. Its library, begun in 1919, alone houses over 1.25 million book volumes dealing with all aspects of modern social, economic, and political change. However, it is for the library's collection of propaganda posters (more than 50,000), letters, leaflets, newspapers, rare photos, diaries, personal records, and limited circulation street propaganda that Hoover Institution is justly famed. Several surveys of holdings and library catalogs have been published, indicating the importance of this research treasure house. Another Northern California resource is the Pacific Studies Center (founded 1969) in Mountain View, which maintains a library with information files covering a wide variety of propaganda-related titles. The center also publishes the bi-monthly *Pacific Research,* a critical journal focusing on U.S. foreign policy and power structure studies concerning the activities of multinational corporations. For the historian, access to scarce left radical propaganda is possible at the Southern California Library for Social Studies and Research in Los Angeles. More than 15,000 volumes on Marxism, a like number of rare pamphlets dating back more than eighty years, over 2,000 tape recordings of contemporary anti-establishment leaders ranging from Angela Davis to Martin Luther King, Jr., plus 150,000 news clips broken down into 800 categories (including propaganda), and selected news films made in the 1930s are arranged for easy use. Also maintained are files documenting hundreds of labor, social, and political campaigns and groups active since before World War I. California State University, Fullerton, has a small but interesting Freedom Center of Political Ephemera which has runs of over eight hundred labor publications dating from the late 1800s, election propaganda and campaign buttons from the twentieth century, and the nearly complete papers of the League of Nations. Yet another archive is found at the University of California at Davis, whose library has a substantial collection of over six thousand pamphlets issued by U.S. radical and social change organizations (1890 to the present), and a more limited number of U.S. and Japanese war posters from the 1940s. An unusually comprehensive resource is the KIRO-CBS Collection of Broadcasts of the World War II Years and After, in the Phonoarchive of the University of Washington, which preserves an inclusive record of one radio network's fare during the early 1940s. A guide to this collection exists, prepared by Milo Ryan. Also of interest in Washington State is the collection of U.S. and French World War I propaganda posters (over 1,000) and pamphlets on file at the Tacoma Public Library. The University of Wyoming similarly has literally thousands of collections of papers, many relating to propaganda (such as those of Lyman Munson, Frank Capra's boss for the *Why We Fight* motion picture series).

This brief overview of available materials gives some idea of the immensity of the topic. Not all sources for the study of American propaganda, however, are to be found within the United States. The Imperial War Museum in London is a major propaganda research center. The museum's library is very strong in twentieth-century pamphlets, film (with over 37 million feet from the two world wars and an increasing collection of post-1945 footage, including Vietnam), art work (the poster collection exceeds 50,000 items, among them significant U.S. issues), photographs, as well as standard book and clipping file materials. Another British contact is the Psywar Society of England, headed by Reginald Auckland in St. Albans, which publishes a fact-filled journal called *The Falling Leaf* and acts as a clearinghouse for pyschological warfare collectors. Auckland, for example, has a personal collection of over nine thousand items (including many rare U.S. Army leaflets). On the continent, the International Mass Media Research Center Library in Bagnolet, France, serves as a documentary archive for those interested in worldwide Marxist studies involving all aspects of communications (including propaganda). The center also publishes useful bibliographical catalogs.

HISTORY AND CRITICISM

The late political scientist Harold D. Lasswell may well be referred to as the father of propaganda study in the United States. His doctoral dissertation published as *Propaganda Technique in the World War* in 1927 (recently reissued as *Propaganda Technique in World War I*) even led one critic to suggest that such "a Machiavellian textbook... should be destroyed." Lasswell's importance stems from the fact that he made a number of contributions toward the development of a comprehensive theoretical basis for analyzing propaganda. This book holds continuing interest because it provides an objective overview of the modern propaganda services organized by the belligerent governments. Lasswell was one of the first to observe that the propagandist usually works within a specific culture in which strategies are circumscribed by the availability of media, the value structures of targeted audiences which limit the variance of messages from current norms, and other pre-existing constraints that are not necessarily international in character. He further notes that war, by extending beyond established frontiers, forces this military propagandist to adapt or fail. The new edition includes a valuable introduction by Lasswell and Jackson A. Giddens summarizing the field after fifty years of subsequent research. Unfortunately the appended bibliography remains unannotated, and the index is inadequate.

Despite these shortcomings, a number of later studies issued during the revisionist period of the 1930s built upon Lasswell without substantively altering his conclusions. Today much of this work appears rather primitive. One glaring weakness of the pioneering propaganda scholars was their cursory treatment of the origin and historical development of propaganda in the United States. Even today, there are relatively few in-depth documentary analyses detailing the historicity of the propaganda phenomenon. Nevertheless, it was only after Lasswell's ground-breaking work that the first serious questions were raised and tentative answers proposed about the nature of attitude change and the general effects of persuasive communications. One useful jumping-off point is the three-volume *Propaganda and Communication in World History* series (1979-80), edited by Lasswell, Daniel Lerner, and Hans Speir. Volume I, subtitled "The Symbolic Instrument in Early Times," covers the period before the emergence of America as a nation. However, Volume II, subtitled "The Emergence of Public Opinion in the West," includes nineteen essays (many original to the work) that begin with the invention of the printing press and trace the development of mass communication and symbol management to the present day. Volume III features fourteen articles on "A Pluralizing World in Formation" and analyzes contemporary marketing, advertising, public relations, and media planning from a social science perspective. Lasswell concludes this last volume with a prophetic look at the future of world communication and propaganda, written shortly before his death in 1978. Each volume has its own introduction, a comprehensive index, and brief biographies of contributors. While virtually a Who's Who of leading political and communication scholars in the field of propaganda, the set suffers from the weakness common to all anthologies by not being a true encyclopedia of propaganda—a work sorely needed. (For other anthologies, see the following section.)

Oliver Thomson's *Mass Persuasion in History: An Historical Analysis of the Development of Propaganda Techniques* is a compact primer valuable for beginning students because of its brevity. After a thoughtful introduction to the problems of historical analysis, Thomson divides propaganda into seven main categories ranked according to the objectives of the propagandist (political, economic, war/military, diplomatic, didactic, ideological, and escapist aimed at achieving social acquiescence). He treats message construction in terms of style, structure, and theme, then follows it with a pragmatic review of propagandistic philosophy and methodologies used for determining effectiveness. Also useful, given the transient nature and unavailability of much propaganda product, is a photographic section, which illustrates appended historical case studies ranging from the Roman Empire through the mobilization propaganda of the Western democracies. The work is faulted, though, by the limited bibliography and index.

Unfortunately the more detailed *3000 Jahre Politische Propaganda* (3000

Years of Political Propaganda) by Alfred Sturminger remains untranslated. Although this profusely illustrated work concentrates on the history of propaganda in Europe, it is useful for the inclusion of such media as postage stamps and cancellations as propaganda tools. Besides art, another interesting section traces pro- and anti-religious propaganda. Standard bibliographic data and indexing facilitates use of the book.

The title of Frederick E. Lumley's *The Propaganda Menace* adequately describes his attitude to the practice. Unlike others who typically lament the barrage of distortion while neglecting historical precedent, Lumley devotes considerable space to the prior development of propaganda. Considering that he wrote nearly fifty years ago, the book holds up well and reflects credibly on his scholarship. One of its valuable attributes is the division into specific topic areas. In addition to the obligatory "Propaganda and War" section, later chapters discuss politics, race, education, and religion as forums for persuasive communication. His fear that then-current trends would make propaganda an increasingly powerful factor in society has been borne out. Lumley's somewhat depressing conclusion that the only antidote for propaganda is the ability to think straight seems as true as ever. One oversight is that no illustrations or photographs are used.

Following closely in Lumley's tradition is Michael Choukas's *Propaganda Comes of Age.* Choukas, who holds a doctoral degree from Columbia University, writes with some authority since he served in the propaganda arm of the OSS during World War II. In tracing the evolution of the vast domestic propaganda network in this country he argues that, because of its deliberately manipulative nature, propaganda is not an informational tool. Rather, says Choukas, propaganda and democracy are at odds, and without strong controls on advertising, lobbying, and so forth the country faces a totalitarian future. Nevertheless, he approves of propaganda directed at foreign audiences in pursuit of governmental policies. The book is enhanced by numerous cartoons, advertisements, leaflets, and so on, but these are not always keyed directly to the text. A serious deficiency is the lack of an index or bibliography.

Despite a rather sensational title, Robert Sobel's *The Manipulators: America in the Media Age* is a serious—if flawed—look at the development of U.S. communications. Writing from a passionate fear that the media are contributing to national instability by the blurring of fact and fiction, Sobel has compiled a big book (458 pages) which documents the emergence of America's newspapers, the role of the university as a training ground for the journalistic elite, the wartime propaganda blitz of the Committee on Public Information, the anti-Axis co-optation of the motion picture industry, and the rise of television and other new technologies as a force in contemporary society. More than simply a history, Sobel raises important questions about the future of our propagandistic culture. The value of this work as a scholarly reference, however, is undermined by inclusion of numerous careless factual errors which work to negate the credibility of Sobel's argumentation.

The Fine Art of Propaganda; a Study of Father Coughlin's Speeches, edited by Alfred McClung Lee and Elizabeth Briant Lee, remains one of the most significant books on propaganda ever published. First issued in 1939 and now available in several reprint editions, the work cuts across several fields. Although only 140 pages, the book's influence stems from its clear organizational analysis of the seven chief devices utilized by professional propagandists (such as "name calling" and "band wagon"). Updating his seminal study, Alfred McClung Lee in 1952 published the probing *How to Understand Propaganda.* Rather than taking a communication-oriented approach, Lee describes how we are all consumers of propaganda. Using numerous illustrations taken from the popular press, he writes that the only way to combat propaganda is to recognize it. Although Lee typically sees propaganda as an often debilitating force assaulting individual free will, he nevertheless points out that propaganda is also used to achieve a variety of desirable socioeconomic and political ends. A similar approach is found in *The Analysis of Propaganda* by William Hummel and Keith Huntress. After offering a general introduction and describing how propaganda can be detected in everyday life, the authors provide a justification for its further study. A rather eclectic reader, ranging from writings by Benjamin Franklin to those of John Steinbeck, is appended. Unfortunately there is no bibliography, and the book is disappointing when contrasted to the Lees' *Fine Art of Propaganda.*

Also of interest is Barry Marks's doctoral dissertation, "The Idea of Propaganda in America" (1957), which traces the origin of the concept of propaganda as a malevolent new social force after World War I, analyzes the "marriage" of propaganda and anti-intellectualism as a challenge to democracy, and treats the influence of propagandistic impact in American progressive education. Marks's study certainly deserves a wider audience.

Another notable contribution to the field is Jacques Ellul's *Propaganda: The Formation of Men's Attitudes.* Challenging many traditional notions (that education is the antidote to propaganda, that there are significant differences between so-called democratic and totalitarian propagandas, that the principal purpose of propaganda is to change belief rather than reinforce existing attitudes or motivate people to action, that small group experiments are necessary if we are to understand the psychology of propaganda, and so on), the brilliant French theorist nevertheless presents a convincing case for the corrosive effect of propaganda. After an introductory review of major trends in propaganda analysis, Ellul describes the primary characteristics and categories of propaganda as he sees them, discusses the underlying conditions that contribute to the widespread existence of propaganda, analyzes the necessity of propaganda for individuals and states, and reviews the results of propaganda. Two appendixes probe the effectiveness and limits of propaganda and dissect the brainwashing techniques of Mao's China. No illustrations and the lack of statistical data are the major weaknesses of the work, but clearly Ellul is obligatory reading. Included is a bibliography and index.

Two books sharing the same title, *Public Opinion and Propaganda*, by Frederick C. Irion and Leonard W. Doob are both geared to the college text market and, given the dramatic changes in media statistics and sociological perspectives, have become somewhat dated. Irion also lacks a bibliography. Each, however, has some historic interest because of the wealth of detail included; thus they are recommended for overviews of the field up till their dates of publication. Doob, particularly, has been an important figure in U.S. propaganda studies since publication of his *Propaganda: Its Psychology and Technique*. Less useful for the specialist is *Propaganda Handbook* by D. Lincoln Harter and John Sullivan. The book reflects the Cold War period in which it appeared and despite the embracive title is rather simplistic. Largely based on secondary sources, its major strength is in synthesis of more original work.

Since numerous studies exist covering specialized topical areas and historical periods, subdivisions have been included in this section to enable readers to identify more easily what is most useful for their particular research interests.

REVOLUTIONARY WAR PERIOD

Philip Davidson's *Propaganda and the American Revolution, 1763-1783* remains the standard history of American propaganda before and during the Revolution. Included are sections on Whig and Patriotic propaganda, as well as the efforts of the Tory-Loyalist counterattack. Although the topical arrangement at times results in some repetition, Davidson's careful scholarship not only forms a solid contribution to the study of the early American experience but also points to the many similarities to be found within all modern revolutionary movements. Challenging many supposed facts about our own history (since much of what we "know" about the Revolution has derived from the propaganda of that era), the author stresses the importance of ideas in deciding the conflict of arms. Perhaps overemphasized is the impact of actions taken in cities such as Boston on the rest of the Colonies, a fault remedied by Robert Smith in his unpublished thesis "What Came After?: News Diffusion and the Significance of the Boston Massacre in Six American Colonies, 1770-1775." Smith traces media coverage of the "Massacre" and concludes that the Patriotic view of the British Army as a major threat to liberty had meaning only for Massachusetts and was relatively unimportant in terms of its propaganda effect outside the Bay Colony. Readers interested in a related aspect of the revolutionary struggle should also refer to "Lafayette as a Tool of American Propaganda," a neglected doctoral study completed by Marguerite Bloxom in 1970.

Useful guides to available propaganda publications of the pre-Constitutional period include Charles F. Heartman, compiler, *The Cradle of the United States, 1765-1789: Five Hundred Contemporary Broadsides, Pamphlets, and a Few Books Pertaining to the History of the Stamp Act, the Boston Massacre and Other Pre-Revolutionary Troubles, the War for Independence and the Adoption of the Federal Constitution;* Ruth Lampham, compiler, *Check List of American Revolutionary War Pamphlets in the Newberry Library;* and the unattributed *Manuscripts of the American Revolution in the Boston Public Library: A Descriptive Catalog.* Heartman had one of the finest collections of its type, alphabetically listing each item "bibliographically, historically and sometimes sentimentally" with an index to materials issued anonymously. Lampham similarly describes 754 tracts issued by American and British sources between 1750 and 1786, including a specific section devoted to Revolutionary propaganda. The Boston collection has the advantage of being larger because of the more recent date of collation but otherwise differs little from its predecessors. Useful insights and references to contemporary materials are also found in Bernard Bailyn's *Ideological Origins of the American Revolution,* which complements his earlier *Pamphlets of the American Revolution, 1750-1776.* The latter reprints original texts selected on the basis of representativeness, contemporary fame, originality of thought, literary distinction, and/or the importance of the author.

Of the American propagandists, Samuel Adams and Thomas Paine have been written about the most. John C. Miller's *Sam Adams: Pioneer in Propaganda* supersedes Ralph Volney Harlow's *Samuel Adams, Promoter of the American Revolution: A Study in Psychology and Politics* as the standard biographical reference for Adams's propagandistic career. Miller draws a picture of the "father of the American Revolution" that is not entirely flattering, but weakening the book is the omission of an introduction (which would have been useful in appraising Adams's significance) and a bibliography. The later edition does add a brief one-page bibliography of books appearing after 1941, but for details one must struggle through the footnotes. While Harlow takes an intriguing Freudian approach in interpreting Adams's motivations and psyche, he tends at times to be inaccurate in detail and biased in his use of supporting evidence. Among early works, *The Life and Public Services of Samuel Adams* by great-grandson William Vincent Wells is of interest. Published in three volumes in 1865, the biography is naturally laudatory but nonetheless demonstrates careful and thorough attention to research as well as a wealth of fascinating minutiae. Of the newer studies, see John R. Galvin, *Three Men of Boston,* which focuses on the interrelationship among Adams, James Otis, and Governor Thomas Hutchinson; Stewart Beach, *Samuel Adams: The Fateful Years, 1764-1776;* and Cass Canfield, *Sam Adams' Revolution (1765-1776),* published in the Bicentennial. While Galvin offers an excellent interpretive account, Canfield unfortunately tells us little we do not already know about Adams. Beach, drawing extensively from Adams's state papers, correspondence, and political essays, believes that he was neither the extremist nor as violent as he is depicted in more conventional biographies. By approaching the Revolution through the eyes of Adams, Beach presents a reappraisal of the whole period which cannot simply be shunted aside. Although lacking footnotes, the book has a particularly useful bibliographic essay which is must reading for anyone interested in Adams and the Revolution. Note also that *The Writings of Samuel Adams 1764-1802* were collected and edited by Harry Alonzo Cushing in four volumes appearing between 1904 and 1908. Only Adams's own surviving writings appear. Letters from others to him, although numerous in the manuscript collections, are not included.

The materials on Paine are if anything more voluminous. The basic biography is the 500-page *Paine,* by David Freeman Hawke, who has written knowledgeably about the Colonial era in numerous other books. Paine, despite an active public career, proves to be a surprisingly introspective and exceedingly private man. Because few of Paine's personal papers survive, the task of the historian is at once complicated and simplified. Complicated, because questions must remain unanswered and details undiscovered; simplified, because most of the remaining Paine materials have been collected under one roof. In readable, even exciting style, Hawke traces Paine's life from his humble origins working as a ladies corsetmaker in Britain to his spectacular rise as a major Revolutionary pamphleteer in America and France, through his later imprisonment and bittersweet return to the United States. The bibliography, albeit extensive, lacks references to publishers and cities of publication for all citations, an unfortunate omission. Other studies of interest include the overly journalistic but still fascinating *Tom Paine: America's Godfather, 1737-1809* by W. E. Woodward (featuring a chapter on "Paine as a Propagandist"); Arnold Kinsey King, "Thomas Paine in America, 1774-1787," an unpublished 1952 dissertation which exhaustively covers Paine's Revolutionary influence; and Alfred Owen Aldridge, *Man of Reason: The Life of Thomas Paine,* which points out that Paine's writings were important not because of his style but because of the substantive appeal and compelling logic they employed. Aldridge includes full chapter notes and fleshes out his narrative with information overlooked by previous researchers. Recent biographies such as Samuel Edwards's *Rebels! A Biography of Tom Paine* and *Thomas Paine* by Jerome D. Wilson and William F. Ricketson are designed more for the popular market. Wilson and Ricketson do, however, include a useful select annotated bibliography; Edwards's book, on the other hand, despite pretentions as an authoritative text, lacks documentation and is rather free in handling sources. Better are Audrey Williamson's *Thomas Paine: His Life, Work and Times* and Eric Foner's *Tom Paine and Revolutionary America.* Williamson includes newly researched details about Paine's life and benefits not only from a rather comprehensive treatment but also the author's British perspective. Foner, rather than pursuing a traditional biography, explores key moments in Paine's career. He suggests that Paine's influence was not merely propagandistic but transcended narrow economic interests when he became an innovative political communicator who really believed in the utopian vision of an egalitarian American society.

No complete collection of Paine's public and private writings is as yet available. *The Writings of Thomas Paine,* collected and edited by Moncure Daniel Conway in four volumes in 1894-96, filled a gap at the time of publication but is now superseded by later works such as the ten-volume large-print *The Life and Works of Thomas Paine* of 1925, edited by William van der Weyde; and Philip S. Foner's *The Complete Writings of Thomas Paine* issued in two volumes in 1945. Unfortunately, all are seriously flawed. Although Foner's is perhaps the most complete, occasional misdating of letters, editorial deletions, a topical organization that makes it difficult to work chronologically, the lack of a comprehensive index, and the failure to include all available Paine material point to the need for a new and truly definitive collation. Numerous student editions of Paine's political writings also exist. Among the best, because of its useful introduction to Paine's career with full explanatory notes, is *Common Sense and Other Political Writings* edited by Nelson F. Adkins in 1953.

PROPAGANDA IN A NEW NATION, 1785-1861

The seventy-five years between the Revolutionary and Civil Wars saw great change, yet they remain among the most neglected in the history of U.S. propaganda. The outstanding document influencing the Constitutional debate is, of course, *The Federalist Papers* by Alexander Hamilton, James Madison, and John Jay. A number of editions of the collected papers exist, but the most used reference text is that edited by Clinton Rossiter based on what is known as the McLean edition of 1788. Included is an informative introduction describing the political and social background, an expanded table of contents with a brief précis for each of the eighty-five essays, an appendix containing the Constitution with cross-references to pertinent sections within the papers, and an index of ideas which helps search out the major political concepts. See also John Heller's unpublished thesis on "The Selling of the Constitution: The Federalist Papers Viewed as an Advertising Campaign." After tracing the historical development of constitutionalism in the United States,

Heller describes the reasons advanced for adopting the Constitution contained within the papers and provides factual data on the authors. Using a content analysis, Heller concludes that the advocacy methodology of the proponents strongly resembles issue-oriented advertising campaigns common today. See also James Constantine's 1953 doctoral dissertation on "The African Slave Trade: A Study of Eighteenth Century Propaganda and Public Controversy," and Powrie Vaux Doctor's "Amos Kendall, Propagandist of Jacksonian Democracy" which thoroughly cover their respective topics.

Most of the other important scholarly materials commenting on U.S. propaganda in this period appear in journals or remain unpublished. Of value in terms of background, however, is Gustavus Myers's monumental *History of Bigotry in the United States,* which gives a very serviceable guide to not only the immediate post-Revolutionary period but more modern eras as well. The footnotes are extensive, although one wishes that they had been organized into a bibliography.

CIVIL WAR

This conflict had the "advantage" of being the first major war fought in the United States when there was general literacy. Given the strong philosophical and ideological differences between Northern and Southern leadership, the increasing presence of large numbers of foreign-born immigrants who needed to be "Americanized," and the lack of enthusiasm for the war among large segments of the non-secessionist population, it is not surprising that the staple of pre-twentieth-century propagandists—pamphlets and broadsides—proliferated in the effort to rally support for what soon was realized as a protracted fight. A basic guide to this material, reprinting fifty-two selected texts, is *Union Pamphlets of the Civil War, 1861-1865,* compiled in two volumes by Frank B. Freidel. Organization here is similar to that employed for the Revolutionary War collection edited by Bailyn. Each pamphlet appears in its entirety, along with appendixes and associated matter (including a fact-filled introduction supplemented by representative illustrations).

The Confederacy also issued literally thousands of imprints. Fortunately, guides and catalogs do exist to assist the researcher in locating pertinent references. Basic works include Marjorie Lyle Crandall, *Confederate Imprints: A Check List Based Principally on the Collection of the Boston Athenaeum* in two volumes, with 5,121 citations; Richard Harwell, *More Confederate Imprints,* two volumes, with 1,773 citations; and Ray O. Hummel, Jr., *Southeastern Broadsides Before 1877: A Bibliography,* with over 5,000 entries. Although not every publication can be classified as propaganda, each guide contains references to official publications by state as well as by topic area for unofficial publications ("Slavery and the Negro," "Religious Tracts," and so on), an author index, and authoritative introductions. Numerous works on the life of Harriet Beecher Stowe are not included here, but of specialized interest is Charles P. Cullop's *Confederate Propaganda in Europe, 1861-1865.* The work is currently unique, features a six-page bibliography, but is only 160 pages long. See also "The Pictorial Reporting and Propaganda of the Civil War" by William F. Thompson, Jr., a fascinating exploration of the role played by wartime illustrators, photographers, cartoonists, and commercial artists in shaping Northern public opinion; and "Generative Forces in Union Propaganda: A Study in Civil War Pressure Groups" by George Winston Smith, written in 1940, another era of crisis.

SPANISH-AMERICAN WAR AND PROGRESSIVISM

Not surprisingly, the flashpoint of propaganda studies in the years between the Civil War and World War I is yet another armed conflict—the Spanish-American War. Two basic references are Marcus M. Wilkerson, *Public Opinion and the Spanish-American War: A Study in War Propaganda* and Joseph E. Wisan, *The Cuban Crisis as Reflected in the New York Press, 1895-1898.* Of the two, Wisan's book is by far the more complete, but each has contrasting insights on the role played by such New York papers as the *Journal* and *World* in whipping up interventionist enthusiasm. Wilkerson is particularly damning in his indictment of the publishers whose primary concern was circulation rather than human rights. Often overlooked, however, is the role played by Cuban nationalists in encouraging U.S. involvement. See, for example, the article by George Auxier on "The Propaganda Activities of the Cuban Junta in Precipitating the Spanish-American War, 1895-1898" appearing in the *Hispanic American Historical Review.*

Readers interested in the propaganda of the populist-progressive movement should consult *Progressivism and Muckraking* by Louis Filler, part of a bibliographic series issued by the R. R. Bowker Company. While the emphasis is on in-print materials, there is much valuable commentary and annotation for the person interested in this traditional undercurrent in U.S. history extending from pre-1898 roots through Watergate. Appended are useful author, subject, and title indexes.

WORLD WAR I

The definitive study of "German Propaganda in the United States, 1914-1917" is the doctoral dissertation completed by David Hirst at Northwestern University in 1962. It identifies the leading propaganda agencies and their leaders and also analyzes pro-German reportage as it appeared in books, films, pamphlets, periodicals, and newspapers (including the New York *Evening Mail* secretly purchased by representatives of the Kaiser in 1915). Another graduate thesis by Elizabeth Gaines presents an independent analysis of "*The Fatherland:* An American Vehicle for German Propaganda, 1914-1917." Gaines's review indicates that the four major propaganda themes stressed by George S. Viereck's publication were maintaining U.S. neutrality, promoting closer U.S.-German political and commercial ties, warning of the dangers of an entangling alliance with Great Britain, and exposing the pro-Ally bias of U.S. news media. Viereck himself later published several works in which he describes his career. See, for example, his *Spreading Germs of Hate* and *My Flesh and Blood: A Lyric Autobiography with Indiscreet Annotations.*

Unlike the Germans, who attempted to keep the United States out of the war, leaders in the United Kingdom sought U.S. intervention. Their ultimate success is chronicled in Horace C. Peterson's *Propaganda for War: The Campaign Against American Neutrality, 1914-1917* cited earlier; James D. Squires's *British Propaganda at Home and in the United States from 1914 to 1917;* and Cate Haste's *Keep the Home Fires Burning: Propaganda in the First World War.* Of the three, Peterson's remains the most definitive and despite the passage of years holds up well in its basic approach. Extensive notes and ten pages of bibliographic references are also useful, although the index is inadequate. Squires's slim book is largely a summary of other works but presents a serviceable and occasionally brilliant outline of the topic. While Haste emphasizes internal propaganda in Britain rather than that designed for overseas consumption, the book benefits from inclusion of thirty-seven illustrations and particularly incisive chapters describing the nature of propaganda in World War I, the impact of prewar images on later propaganda efforts, the organizational machinery used by the British government to mobilize the press and other propaganda cooperators, and the long-term implications that the propaganda onslaught unleashed by England had for postwar stability. This latter theme is treated in greater depth by George C. Bruntz in *Allied Propaganda and the Collapse of the German Empire in 1918,* which despite occasional lapses in the quality of the translation from the original German is objective and well documented. See also the representative studies by Victor S. Mamatey, *The United States and East Central Europe, 1914-1918: A Study in Wilsonian Diplomacy and Propaganda,* which utilizes printed sources, State Department files, plus diaries of key governmental figures and foreign materials to describe the contradictory U.S. policies and propaganda messages that contributed to the break-up of the Hapsburg Empire; Arthur Posonby, *Falsehood in War-time,* which although brief exposes the fabrications, distortions, and official-unofficial lies circulated by the belligerent powers; James Read, *Atrocity Propaganda, 1914-1919,* an excellent, comprehensive summary of the motives, methods, and notorious untruths widely disseminated during the war and after; Albert Buchanan, "European Propaganda and American Public Opinion, 1914-1917," a dissertation; and George T. Blakey, *Historians on the Homefront: American Propagandists for the Great War.*

The American propaganda effort spearheaded by George Creel is well recounted in a number of works. The standard history, *Words that Won the War: The Story of the Committee on Public Information, 1917-1919* by James R. Mock and Cedric Larson is based on the papers of the CPI now in the National Archives. The authors trace the background of American public opinion and the coming of wartime censorship, the committee's use of various media in cooperating with educators, labor organizations, and corporate leaders to create an effective internal propaganda campaign, as well as "the fight for the mind of mankind" overseas. Although there is no bibliography as such, the notes are well organized and supplemented with numerous illustrations. A new scholarly reinterpretation of the CPI is contained in Stephen L. Vaughn's *Holding Fast the Inner Lines: Democracy, Nationalism, and the Committee on Public Information.* This 397-page tome, issued as a supplementary volume to the Papers of Woodrow Wilson series, concentrates on the domestic operations of the CPI. While covering much of the same ground as Mock and Larson, the book is an important addition to the literature of propaganda administration. An extensive bibliography is appended along with an intriguing twenty-page comparative essay on primary and secondary sources. George Creel recounts his experiences in *How We Advertised America: The First Telling of the Amazing Story of the Committee on Public Information that Carried the Gospel of Americanism to Every Corner of the Globe.* Despite Creel's jingoism, evident from the title, this is an important work since Creel reveals the congressional attempt to suppress his public report describing the true nature of the CPI's propaganda activities. Creel himself was proud of his wartime activities and details the history of the CPI's domestic and foreign sections along with an account of the unhappy period of demobilization. A documentary listing of CPI publications along with photographs and an index make this a valuable reference. Creel also later wrote an autobiography, *Rebel at Large: Recollections of Fifty Crowded Years,* in which he reviews his World War I experiences. Also of relevance is "American Foreign Propaganda in World War I," a doctoral study by Jackson Giddens.

FILMS AS PROPAGANDA

During the period of U.S. neutrality, motion pictures were already established as propaganda vehicles attempting to sway public opinion, a trend accelerated by the CPI's wartime involvement and subsequent governmental utilization of Hollywood in World War II and Korea. Current estimates of federal propaganda film work range as high as $500 million a year. (This figure omits commercial, educational, state-financed, and other privately produced "sponsored" motion pictures.) Again the literature is large, and a bibliographic review must be selective. A basic starting point is *Politics and Film,* a collation of available secondary sources with a refreshingly objective perspective by Leif Furhammer and Folke Isaksson, which traces the troubled origins of movie propaganda, details the fervently patriotic efforts of 1914-18 through more current releases, and includes a well-organized analysis of the aesthetics and principles of the genre. Kevin Brownlow's *The War, the West and the Wilderness* is a massive new study of silent films. The largest section of the book, more than two hundred pages, examines the motion picture in the Mexican War and World War I. In addition to published materials, the author conducted interviews with many newsreel and propaganda filmmakers active in the period and had access to previously unpublished letters, diaries, and logbooks. The work is lavishly illustrated, with excellent notes and a detailed index. A thoughtful study of the overuse of war themes by motion picture propaganda, with recommendations on how the screen might have been used for more uplifting purposes, is found in William Marston Seabury's *Motion Picture Problems: The Cinema and the League of Nations*. Also of interest is Winifred Johnston's *Memo on the Movies: War Propaganda, 1914-1939*, a short but nonetheless intriguing polemical study on how "peace-loving people [are] turned to ways of hate" by filmic distortion.

The interrelationship of the "factual" motion picture and propaganda is explored in a number of published studies. These include Erik Barnouw, *Documentary: A History of the Non-Fiction Film;* Richard M. Barsam, *Nonfiction Film: A Critical History;* Thomas Bohn, *An Historical and Descriptive Analysis of the "Why We Fight" Series;* Raymond Fielding, *The American Newsreel: 1911-1967;* Richard Dyer MacCann, *The People's Films: A Political History of U.S. Government Motion Pictures;* Richard A. Maynard, *Propaganda on Film: A Nation at War,* a basic reader comparing U.S., Soviet, and German responses to film propaganda; Tom Perlmutter, *War Movies;* Clyde Jeavons, *A Pictorial History of War Films;* Joe Morella, Edward Z. Epstein, and John Griggs, *The Films of World War II;* Ken Jones and Arthur McClure, *Hollywood at War: The American Motion Picture Industry and World War II,* with a useful introductory essay and filmography of over four hundred releases; and Roger Manvell, *Films and the Second World War,* in which Manvell "offers not only a story of the use of film as propaganda and later as historical interpreter, but...provides a parallel between what actually was happening in the world during the years covered and how that was presented in film." Also promising to be valuable additions to the literature are the forthcoming *Mission to Moscow: The Feature Film as Official Propaganda* by David Culbert, and *Film and Propaganda in America: A Documentary History* also edited by Culbert, with Richard Wood and William Murphy. In the latter, four volumes of new textual analysis and photographs will be supplemented with a "fifth volume" on microfiche to provide a veritable archive of original documents and other materials reproduced in affordable format.

THE INTERWAR PERIOD, 1919-1941

The Bolshevik victory in Russia and other radical uprisings in Europe following World War I caused the United States to be swept by a wave of fear that revolution could similarly happen here. This paranoia was fueled by release of sensational propaganda emanating from supposedly responsible governmental agencies as much as by left- and right-wing extremist groups. The standard account of this phenomenon is Robert Murray's meticulously researched *Red Scare: A Study in National Hysteria, 1919-1920.* Although the federal government conducted several hearings and issued a report on foreign propaganda activities in the United States (see the bibliography for a selective listing of important U.S. documents on Communist and Nazi propaganda), the most complete and detailed published repository of modern radical propaganda literature is found in a four-volume report released in 1920 by a New York State Senate committee chaired by Clayton R. Lusk. The resulting *Revolutionary Radicalism: Its History, Purpose, and Tactics* totals 10,983 pages and is a unique collation of original documents, manifestos, and the like. Care, however, must be maintained in utilizing this collection since the conclusions reached by the committee on the basis of their investigation are open to question.

While much has been written about the growth of the Ku Klux Klan during this period, relatively little has been said about the propaganda methods utilized by its leaders in building their organization. John Shotwell's thesis, "Crystalizing Public Hatred: Ku Klux Klan Public Relations in the Early 1920s," is the first detailed study of the effective, though sometimes nefarious, campaign waged by the Klan to influence key opinion leaders and elites. Also of interest is Ralph Casey's pioneering doctoral study of a propaganda technique in the 1928 election.

"The Propaganda Program of the National Recovery Administration" during the 1930s is the subject of Carol Holgren's unpublished 1962 thesis investigating the NRA as an example of government abuse of its public trust. This is must reading for the topic, particularly for its treatment of the New Deal program as a harbinger of American fascism. Readers interested in the interventionist vs. isolationist controversy might wish to consult Harold Lavine and James Wechsler, *War Propaganda and the United States,* originally prepared for the Institute for Propaganda Analysis in 1940 and subsequently reprinted in several editions; Walter Johnson, *The Battle Against Isolation;* Letty Bergstrom, "The Battle for America: German-English Language Propaganda in the U.S. from 1933 to 1941"; Jane Schwar, "Interventionist Propaganda and Pressure Groups in the United States, 1937-1941," a detailed 1973 doctoral study of prewar organizations actively encouraging U.S. involvement in Europe; David Culbert, *News for Every-*

man: Radio and Foreign Affairs in Thirties America; and Michele Flynn Stenejhem, *An American First: John T. Flynn and the America First Committee.* The latter details the career and philosophy of one of the nation's leading revisionist journalists, concentrating on the 1940-41 period, when Flynn sought to strengthen the U.S. commitment to neutrality. Six appendixes, more than one hundred cited references, and an extensive bibliography help provide access to the majority of other pertinent works.

WORLD WAR II

A number of books have been written about the war years. Two of the more interesting, in that they concentrate on propaganda as a creative cultural phenomenon, are John Morton Blum's *V Was for Victory: Politics and American Culture During World War II*, and Richard R. Lingeman's *Don't You Know There's a War On? The American Home Front, 1941-1945.* The former is an intriguing (if somewhat fawning) look at the legacy of FDR's presidency in shaping American popular culture. The first fifty pages detail the efforts by the Office of War Information to sell the war domestically. Also discussed in this serious account written by a Yale history professor are other official (and unofficial) propaganda activities, including a particularly trenchant review of wartime popular novels. Despite the catchy title of Lingeman's book, his is more than simply a nostalgic overview. Written in an evocative style, *There's a War On* is a solidly researched and richly detailed history of the war years. Included is a discussion of the propagandistic and escapist purposes to which books, motion pictures, comics, and music were put.

Several excellent studies covering visual aspects of the propaganda war have appeared in recent years, among them J. Darracott and B. Loftus, *Second World War Posters*, Denis Judd, *Posters of World War Two*, Anthony Rhodes, *Propaganda—The Art of Persuasion: World War II*, and Zbynek Zeman, *Selling the War: Art and Propaganda in World War II.* Darracott and Loftus concentrate on materials from the Imperial War Museum. Although there are some inaccuracies as well as mediocre integration of text and pictoral matter, Judd does provide a basic introduction to use of posters and offers a lengthy text. Rhodes tends to follow a similar organization to that of Judd (with long sections by country, including the United States), but coverage is broader, with more than 270 color and a like number of black-and-white illustrations superbly reproduced in a lavish oversize 9″ x 12″ volume. Rhodes also gives attention to recordings, radio, and the cinema as propaganda channels, noting how different nations dealt with common themes. Additionally, there is an afterword by Daniel Lerner on the American psychological warfare campaign against Germany, a fifteen-page filmographic essay, as well as a short bibliography and complete index. Zeman, an authority on Nazi propaganda, reprints one hundred of the most effective wartime posters issued by Allied and Axis propagandists (with an emphasis on European rather than American contributions). The strength of the work is in his analysis of what such visual propaganda reveals about the political, military, and moral conditions that lay behind them. The text itself is brief, supplemented with a limited bibliography and index.

Highly critical of U.S. policy is Benjamin Colby's *'Twas a Famous Victory: Deception and Propaganda in the War with Germany.* The author argues in common with several other revisionist historians that Roosevelt deliberately deceived the American people by telling them that American survival—like Britain's—depended on U.S. entry into the war. After reviewing administration cover-ups of Soviet atrocities and distortions of Hitler's true war aims, Colby argues that Roosevelt bears the blame for the needless deaths of thousands of GIs through his propaganda policy designed to cause war. Mobilization of American media (through such institutions as the OWI, the Writers War Board, and the Hollywood studios) again to create hatred of the Germans and enthusiasm for our alliance with the Soviets is also covered. Colby, a former *New York Times* and Associated Press staff journalist, organizes his case well but relies largely on secondary sources for his evidence. That there was a secret conspiracy between Roosevelt and Churchill, however, is now known. The links between the highly clandestine British Security Coordination organization and the U.S. OSS have been recently revealed with the declassification of a number of sensitive wartime documents. For an authoritative account of British intelligence and propaganda activities both before and during World War II, see William Stevenson's *A Man Called Intrepid: The Secret War.*

Four major studies document the history of the OWI: Allan M. Winkler, *The Politics of Propaganda: The Office of War Information, 1942-1945*; Lamar MacKay, "Domestic Operations of the Office of War Information in World War II"; Robert L. Bishop, "The Overseas Branch of the Office of War Information"; and Sydney Weinberg's massive "Wartime Propaganda in a Democracy: America's Twentieth Century Information Agencies." Winkler's text, drawn heavily from original documents in the National Archives, is organized into four chapters describing the OWI's origins, its use of propaganda at home (where the OWI was prohibited from distributing materials directly to the public), political propaganda abroad, and overseas military propaganda. As all four authors make clear, the OWI was limited by its temporary wartime mandate and the fact that it had powerful congressional enemies. Also hampering the agency (which at its height had eleven thousand employees) were the lack of clear-cut U.S. goals other than unconditional victory, the failure to develop long-range policies for the postwar period, personality conflicts within the OWI itself, and continued public distrust of government-issued propaganda. Bishop's study is particularly useful for its discussion of the operations of the Voice of America, directed originally by OWI's Overseas Branch.

In a heavily annotated (and at times repetitious) history with the virtues and weaknesses common to doctoral studies converted to books, Leila J. Rupp's *Mobilizing Women for War: German and American Propaganda, 1939-1945* nevertheless adds an important dimension to our understanding of the effectiveness of mobilization propaganda. Rupp contrasts the image of women carried by popular periodicals and other media with the reality of wartime conditions in both countries. Working from a feminist perspective, she demonstrates that such propaganda was more extensive in the United States and proved critically important in converting women to industrial work so that men could be freed to fight overseas. Scrupulous documentation and a wide-ranging use of sources is confirmed by an extensive fifty-page bibliography.

The U.S. military's postwar de-Nazification efforts at re-educating the German people to support democracy is reported in Albert Norman's *Our German Policy: Propaganda and Culture*. The focus of the book, which relies heavily on primary sources acquired by the author while a member of the occupation government, is a history of the policies and practices applied by U.S. forces in reshaping the media and cultural institutions of a defeated Germany.

PSYCHOLOGICAL WARFARE

Propaganda as a manipulative art naturally has an interest in psychology and human attitudes. An offshoot of World War II, the Korean and Vietnam conflicts, and the establishment of a permanent U.S. governmental propaganda ministry in the USIA/USICA has been increased emphasis on what is known as psychological warfare or psy-war. A basic introduction is Terence H. Qualter's exemplary *Propaganda and Psychological Warfare*, which offers both a philosophical and historical treatment of the subject. Daniel Lerner's *Sykewar: Psychological Warfare Against Germany, D-Day to VE-Day* is the definitive history of Allied wartime efforts in the European theater by an actively involved scholar. Chapters discuss policy, personnel, media, operations, and effectiveness. See also Charles G. Cruickshank's *The Fourth Arm: Psychological Warfare 1938-1945*, written from a British perspective. Writers such as Murray Dyer in *The Weapon on the Wall: Rethinking Psychological Warfare* and Robert T. Holt and Robert W. van de Velde in *Strategic Psychological Operations and American Foreign Policy* have questioned the assumptions underlying American propaganda and psy-war overseas and argued that our naiveté and overreliance on military aspects of political communication undercut the effectiveness of our messages to other peoples. Other basic references include Paul Linebarger's *Psychological Warfare*, a very useful summary of thinking on the topic through the time of publication, and William E. Dougherty's and Morris Janowitz's *A Psychological Warfare Casebook*, which during the Vietnam years served as the chief psy-warrior text. Updating these are Joseph McDonough's "Analysis of Official U.S. Military Psychological Warfare Efforts in the Vietnam Conflict" and Phillip Paul Katz's *A Systematic Approach to Psyop Information*. Less valuable is Charles Roetter's historical *The Art of Psychological Warfare, 1914-1945*, which lacks notes and bibliography and is rather shallow in its coverage.

A review of case studies makes it clear that the "hypodermic theory" model (a blatant campaign organized from the top down in order to inject the populace with information) does not work particularly well and in no way guarantees message reception, understanding , acceptance, or desired action. This points to the central problem facing psychological warfare and propaganda researchers: how does one adequately measure effectiveness? When one wades through the mass of propaganda literature generated since World War I, this area is usually glibly, simplistically, and inadequately addressed. Even in the Korean conflict, very little evaluation was carried out. Since Vietnam, however, the beginnings of a true social science effort to evaluate the output of psychological warfare message systems and activities have been evident. Recommended reading includes Edward Hunter's *Brainwashing: The Story of the Men Who Defied It*, a lucidly reported popular account of the horror techniques used against American POWs in Korea, and Edgar Schein and others, *Coercive Persuasion: A Socio-Psychological Analysis of the "Brainwashing" of American Civilian Prisoners by the Chinese Communists*. Schein notes that the essential prerequisite is to close off the outside environment. Once this condition is met, as in Korea, all kinds of successful manipulations are possible. This is one reason why the United States placed so much reliance on broadcasting in Vietnam in order to break down the local communication structure and replace it with a tightly controlled new one. However, as Thomas William Hoffer points out in his massive two-volume dissertation on "Broadcasting in an Insurgency Environment: USIA in Vietnam, 1965-1970," U.S. advisors underestimated competing propaganda strategies used by the insurgents who acted effectively to limit U.S.-South Vietnam efforts. Adding to the value of Hoffer's analysis are extensive appendixes which reprint a number of rare government reports, memoranda, and other documents. Also recommended is Peter Braestrup's massive two-volume analysis of media performance, *Big Story! How the American Press and Television Reported and Interpreted the Crises of Tet 1968 in Vietnam and Washington*.

UNITED STATES INFORMATION AGENCY

Between 1953 and 1978, when it became the United States International Communication Agency, the USIA issued a series of reports to Congress which contain a wealth of statistical and policy information on operations of the agency, including Voice of America broadcasting. Similar reports exist for the USICA (1979 to the present) and the Board for International Broadcasting (1974 to the present), the latter being responsible for overseeing Radio Free Europe and Radio Liberty. Also of interest are the independent oversight studies prepared by the General Accounting Office for congressional hearings on agency budget requests before the House Committee on Foreign Affairs. Much of the relevant data, along with an expert introduction to working with government documents, has been collected in *The Mass Media: Aspen Institute Guide to Communication Industry Trends* by Christopher H. Sterling and Timothy R. Haight. The USICA also operates an Office of Congressional and Public Liaison (Washington, D.C. 20547), which provides fact sheets and other materials describing current agency activities.

Of the available histories, the most valuable books on the USIA include Robert Elder's *The Information Machine: The United States Information Agency and American Foreign Policy,* John W. Henderson's *The United States Information Agency*, and Leo Bogart's *Premises for Propaganda: The United States Information Agency's Operating Assumptions in the Cold War.* The latter, for example, is based on 142 interviews with key USIA personnel conducted during the 1950s. The book is actually an abridgement of a five-volume report that remained restricted for more than twenty years. Critical studies of the USIA also include George N. Gordon and Irving A. Falk, *The War of Ideas: America's International Identity Crisis*; Eugene W. Castle's polemical *Billions, Blunders and Baloney: The Fantastic Story of How Uncle Sam Is Squandering Your Money Overseas;* and L. Skvortsov, *The Ideology and Tactics of Anti-Communism*, which contains an interesting section on "The Aims and Tactics of Propaganda" written from a pro-Soviet perspective. These supplement personalized subjective accounts by Edward W. Barrett, *Truth Is Our Weapon*, and Thomas C. Sorensen, *The Word War: The Story of American Propaganda.* Recent analyses of U.S. government radio and television propaganda can be consulted in David Abshire, *International Broadcasting: A New Dimension of Western Diplomacy*; Julian Hale, *Radio Power: Propaganda and International Broadcasting*; Maury Lisann, *Broadcasting to the Soviet Union: International Politics and Radio*; and a number of unpublished works.

LOBBYING AND SPECIAL INTEREST PROPAGANDA

Given the growth of the government sector in our society, it is not surprising that special interests attempt to influence the opinions of selected audiences. Joining the traditional corridor lobbyists (an estimated fifteen thousand currently work Capitol Hill pleading causes for their clients) are increasing numbers of Political Action Committees (PACs) which utilize all available channels from personal contact to direct mail and advocacy advertising in order to create support. Corporations are barred by law from making direct political contributions, but following a 1974 ruling of the Federal Election Commission which said there was nothing illegal about businesses soliciting voluntary donations from employees for electoral purposes, the number of business PACs jumped from less than one hundred to over 2,300. *National Trade and Professional Associations of the United States and Canada and Labor Organizations*, edited by Craig Colgate, has annual listings of more than six thousand groups. While PACs are excluded from this work, they do appear in a companion directory issued yearly called *Washington Representatives*. Another useful research reference is *The Encyclopedia of Associations*, edited by Nancy Yakes and Denise Akey, published in three volumes. This is the most complete guide to nonprofit membership organizations with national scope. Listed are the name, location, size, objectives, and other useful data for over 14,000 organizations. All of the above are thoroughly cross-referenced.

The third edition of *The Washington Lobby* published by Congressional Quarterly provides a comprehensive overview of contemporary lobbying tactics in the United States. New introductory material includes a compact history of lobbying in the United States and federal attempts to regulate it. Additional sections describe how the executive branch lobbies in behalf of the White House, trace the development and impact of PACs, profile major business, labor, and public interest lobbies, and analyze the work of foreign lobbyist organizations. There is an index and a detailed bibliography of pertinent books, articles, and documents. All in all, *The Washington Lobby* is mandatory reading for its subject. Also of relevance are *Interest Groups in American Politics*, by L. Harmon Ziegler and Wayne Peak, and *Pressure Groups in American Politics*, by H. R. Mahood.

The links between *Propaganda and Education* have been explored in a report authored by William Wishart Biddle in 1932. This has recently been updated with the issuance of *Hucksters in the Classroom: A Review of Industry Propaganda in Schools* by Sheila Harty. Published by the Ralph Nader-organized Center for the Study of Responsible Law, the book examines four major areas of current controversy (nutrition education, nuclear power advocacy, environmental education, and economics education). A major conclusion is that American school teachers have been largely dependent on business-produced educational materials. Harty is particularly critical of sponsored film distribution by organizations such as the Modern Talking Picture Service. For more on the role of the sponsored film from a less strident perspective, see Jay E. Gordon, *Motion Picture Production for Industry*; and Walter Klein, *The Sponsored Film*. Of related interest are S. Prakash Sethi, *Advocacy Advertising and Large Corporations: Social Conflict, Big Business Image, the News Media, and Public Policy*; and David Paletz, Roberta Pearson, and

Donald Willis, *Politics in Public Service Advertising on Television*. Both note the growing role of and the highly politicized atmosphere surrounding production and airing of corporate "advertorials" and nonprofit PSAs.

Concentrating on organizations as propaganda machines is the highly original *Bureaucratic Propaganda* by David L. Altheide and John M. Johnson. The authors argue that institutions and the people who staff them desire at least the appearance of legitimacy which propaganda helps create. The book is a very innovative guide to the nature, uses, and future trends of bureaucratic propaganda, with additional discussions of its role in television, news reporting, the welfare system, the military, and evangelical crusades.

The interaction of politics, media, and propaganda is well documented in such historical works as the popularized *Political Power and the Press* by CBS Washington Bureau manager William Small; *The Press, Politics and Patronage: The American Government's Use of Newspapers, 1789-1875* by Culver Smith; the early muckraking *Our Press Gang; or, a Complete Exposition of the Corruptions and Crimes of the American Newspapers,* first published in 1859 by Lambert A. Wilmer; the similarly outspoken report on the early twentieth-century press *The Brass Check: A Study in American Journalism* by Upton Sinclair; and the engrossing analysis of the death of truth in wartime by Phillip Knightley entitled *The First Casualty—From the Crimea to Vietnam: The War Correspondent as Hero, Propagandist, and Myth Maker,* which supplements Oscar W. Riegel's gloomily prophetic *Mobilizing for Chaos: The Story of the New Propaganda.* See also George Seldes's angry exposé of corrupt media, *The Facts Are . . . A Guide to Falsehood and Propaganda in the Press and Radio,* and Kent Cooper's *The Right to Know: An Exposition of the Evils of News Suppression and Propaganda.* Less satisfying is David Wise's *The Politics of Lying: Government Deception, Secrecy and Power.* Overly dramatic in tone (befitting Wise's experience as a journalist) and somewhat simplistic in analysis, the book provides a rather vitriolic view of the Nixon administration's attempts to manipulate public opinion ahistorically condemning it as the first to condone habitual lying. Wise's basic problem is that he fails to recognize the failings of the news media themselves and is guilty of many of the same faults he criticizes, such as concealing sources.

Much of the recent criticism has emanated from conservative authors who perceive a deliberate leftist bias in media (particularly broadcasting). Representative publications include *"Distortion by Design"—The Story of America's Liberal Press* by the Reverend Billy James Hargis; *The News Twisters* and *How CBS Tried to Kill a Book,* both by *TV Guide* columnist Edith Efron, which detail controversies in the early 1970s over her findings that there were indeed anti-Nixon media tendencies at the three major networks; Joseph Keeley's somewhat rambling *The Left-Leaning Antenna,* and the work of Accuracy in Media, a Washington-based conservative watchdog organization.

Contrast this with Robert Cirino's mildly left critique, *Don't Blame the People: How the News Media Use Bias, Distortion and Censorship to Manipulate Public Opinion.* See particularly the chapter on "The Importance of Propaganda." Also refer to C. Richard Hofstetter's *Bias in the News: Network Television Coverage of the 1972 Election Campaign,* which argues that McGovern—not Nixon—was the real media victim. A Marxian perspective is provided in James Aronson's now dated *Packaging the News: A Critical Survey of Press, Radio, TV.* For comparison see Dale Minor's *The Information War,* a useful primer on government intervention in the news process. Drawing on his experience as a Pacifica Radio correspondent, Minor traces the cynical cooperation (and occasional confrontation) between government and media gatekeepers in manipulating, censoring, and directing the news for their own corrupt practices. Events in Vietnam form the backdrop for much of Minor's report. Specialized analyses of contemporary U.S. military propaganda activities include former U.S. Senator J. William Fulbright's *The Pentagon Propaganda Machine* and a post-Vietnam update by Juergen Arthur Heise titled *Minimum Disclosure: How the Pentagon Manipulates the News.* This latter work is based on the author's personal encounters with military information officers. Beyond the scope of this chapter are studies attacking American TV exports as a form of "media imperialism." Along with similar analyses decrying Western domination of the major world news agencies, they provide a fascinating perspective on the cultural and propaganda implications of media. Readers interested in exploring the topic further can do so by referring to Jeremy Tunstall's *The Media Are American: Anglo-American Media in the World* and other current international communications literature (particularly recent Unesco reports and the English-language issues of *The Democratic Journalist* published in Czechoslovakia).

ANTHOLOGIES AND REPRINTS

Thirty-one of the most important books issued originally between 1920 and 1962 have now been made available in an International Propaganda and Communications collection by Arno Press. Included are a number of seminal studies already cited above, plus other classics. For further details, request Arno's fully annotated descriptive brochure. Also request the Arno prospectuses for the American Journalists and the History of Broadcasting: Radio to Television series which have several related titles. Greenwood Press, the publisher of this *Handbook,* also has reprinted a variety of Mass Persuasion titles covering the fields of public opinion, advertising, and psychology. A particular service is making Gallup Poll data from 1935 to 1975 conveniently available. In addition, publication has begun of a new one-volume annual, *Index to International Public Opinion,* edited by Elizabeth and Philip Hastings, with comprehensive worldwide coverage of polling data issued by more than fifty leading research organizations.

Despite earlier citations of several excellent reference anthologies, no definitive collation of propaganda essays exists. Given the breadth of the literature, such a work is probably impossible. Among the first to study the relationship of "Pressure Groups and Propaganda" was Harwood Childs, who assembled a series of topical papers by twenty-eight leading authorities and students for a special issue of the *Annals* of the American Academy of Political and Social Sciences in May 1935. Much of this was previously unpublished and, although somewhat dated, continues to have historical and theoretical interest. By the 1950s, as a result of the propaganda onslaught in World War II and the beginning of the Cold War, a number of readers began to appear. These include *Propaganda in War and Crisis: Materials for American Policy*, edited by Daniel Lerner; *America's Weapons of Psychological Warfare*, edited by R. E. Summers; and *Public Opinion and Propaganda: A Book of Readings*, edited for the Society for the Psychological Study of Social Issues by Daniel Katz and other noted researchers. Most such books are geared to the needs of undergraduates, offering a rather eclectic review of public opinion and propaganda as a social science discipline. Updating these with more recent material are massive works such as *Reader in Public Opinion and Communication*, edited by Bernard Berelson and Morris Janowitz; and *Voice of the People: Readings in Public Opinion and Propaganda* by Reo M. Christenson and Robert O. McWilliams. For the less academic, *Language in Uniform: A Reader on Propaganda*, edited by Nick Aaron Ford; and *Propaganda, Polls, and Public Opinion: Are the People Manipulated?*, compiled by Malcolm Mitchell, provide a more directed and simplified introduction. *Teaching About Doublespeak* is a useful primer prepared for classroom use by Daniel Dieterich. Published by the National Council of Teachers of English, this includes a number of readings designed to make students more informed about their daily intake of propaganda (including advertising). A useful sixteen-page bibliography is appended. Note should also be made of the collection of articles "On Propaganda" in the Summer 1979 issue of *ETC.: A Review of General Semantics.* Authors include Jacques Ellul on "The Role of Persuasion in a Technical Society," Thomas Steinfatt on "Evaluating Approaches to Propaganda Analysis," Elizabeth Briant Lee and Alfred McClung Lee on "The Fine Art of Propaganda Analysis—Then and Now," and others. Other journals such as *Public Opinion Quarterly* also occasionally devote entire issues to the subject of propaganda (some earlier *POQ* compilations are included in the Arno Press collection cited above).

What of the future of propaganda in America? As we enter the 1980s, we can expect to see increasing refinements in propaganda technique. Indeed, by the end of the decade the previous work chronicled in this brief bibliographic essay may seem like child's play. New telecommunications technologies, including direct satellite-to-home transmission and extension of two-way cable capacity, promise to redefine our informational environment dramatically. The relatively new concept of "narrowcasting" to highly specialized, homogeneous audiences will allow for cost-effective message placement to specific population subgroups on an unprecedented scale. Much more frightening are the possibilities for genetic alteration and cloning. Combined with the specter of controlled mind-alteration drugs and gases, this may lead some to seek a permanent redirection of society through media-supported biochemical means. As a neutral weaponry system, propaganda can be used either to support or to combat this horrific possibility.

Propaganda is now such an indelible part of our way of life that it may take on a less heinous stature as more individuals come to see that one-sided communication can be an essential component not only of free speech, but of civilization itself. The best antidote to abuse continues to be the absolutely free marketplace of ideas endorsed by America's founding fathers, who more than two centuries ago recognized that the common good is advanced most effectively when private individuals are allowed to pursue their own self-interests. But, like all powerful forces, propaganda must be used wisely and with care if an unintended disastrous backlash is to be avoided. As in Shakespeare's day, we are still players living on a world stage. Unlike his plays, though, our scenario remains unfinished. One certainty is that we have entered an exciting new era for the propagandists but a potentially haunting one for the rest of us.

BIBLIOGRAPHY

BOOKS AND ARTICLES

Abshire, David. *International Broadcasting: A New Dimension of Western Diplomacy.* Beverly Hills, Calif.: Sage, 1976.

Adams, Samuel. *The Writings of Samuel Adams 1764-1802.* 4 vols. Collected and edited by Harry Alonzo Cushing. New York: Putnam's, 1904-8.

Aldridge, Alfred Owen. *Man of Reason: The Life of Thomas Paine.* Philadelphia: Lippincott, 1959.

Altheide, David L., and John M. Johnson. *Bureaucratic Propaganda.* Boston: Allyn and Bacon, 1980.

Archival and Manuscript Materials at the Hoover Institution on War, Revolution and Peace: A Checklist of Major Collections. Special Project. Stanford, Calif.: Hoover Institution Press, 1978.

Aristotle. *Rhetoric.* Translated by Lane Cooper. New York: Appleton Century, 1932.

Aronson, James. *Packaging the News: A Critical Survey of Press, Radio, TV.* New York: International, 1971.

Auxier, George. "The Propaganda Activities of the Cuban Junta in Precipitating the Spanish American War, 1895-1898." *Hispanic American Historical Review,* 19 (August 1939), 286-305.

Bailyn, Bernard. *Ideological Origins of the American Revolution.* Cambridge: Belknap Press of Harvard University Press, 1967.

______, ed. *Pamphlets of the American Revolution, 1750-1776.* Cambridge: Belknap Press of Harvard University Press, 1965.

Barber, W. E. "Propaganda." In *Dictionary of American History.* Rev. ed., Vol. 5. New York: Scribner's, 1976, pp. 41-43.

Barghoorn, Frederick C. *Soviet Foreign Propaganda.* Princeton: Princeton University Press, 1964.

Barnouw, Erik. *Documentary: A History of the Non-Fiction Film.* New York: Oxford University Press, 1974.

Barrett, Edward W. *Truth Is Our Weapon.* New York: Funk & Wagnalls, 1953.

Barsam, Richard M. *Nonfiction Film: A Critical History.* New York: Dutton, 1973.

Bartlett, F. C. *Political Propaganda.* Cambridge: Cambridge University Press, 1940. Reprint. New York: Octagon, 1973.

Beach, Stewart. *Samuel Adams: The Fateful Years, 1764-1776.* New York: Dodd, Mead, 1965.

Berelson, Bernard, and Morris Janowitz. *Reader in Public Opinion and Communication.* 2d. ed. New York: Free Press, 1966.

Bergstrom, Letty. "The Battle for America: German-English Language Propaganda in the U.S. from 1933 to 1941." M.A. thesis, Northwestern University, 1948.

Bettinghaus, Erwin P. *Persuasive Communication.* 3rd. ed. New York: Holt, Rinehart and Winston, 1980.

Biddle, William Wishart. *Propaganda and Education.* New York: Teachers College Press, Columbia University, 1932.

Bishop, Robert L. "The Overseas Branch of the Office of War Information." Ph.D. dissertation, University of Wisconsin at Madison, 1966.

______. *Public Relations: A Comprehensive Bibliography—Articles and Books on Public Relations, Communication Theory, Public Opinion, and Propaganda, 1964-1972.* Ann Arbor: University of Michigan Press, 1974.

______. "Public Relations: A Comprehensive Bibliography of Articles and Books on Public Relations, Communication Theory, Public Opinion, and Propaganda, 1973-1974." *Public Relations Review,* 1 (Winter Supplement 1975-76), 1-200.

______. "Public Relations: A Comprehensive Bibliography of Articles and Books on Public Relations, Communication Theory, Public Opinion, and Propaganda, 1975." *Public Relations Review,* 3 (Summer 1977), 1-145.

Blakey, George T. *Historians on the Homefront: American Propagandists for the Great War.* Lexington: University of Kentucky Press, 1970.

Bloxom, Marguerite. "Lafayette as a Tool of American Propaganda." Ph.D. dissertation, University of Maryland, 1970.

Blum, John Morton. *V Was for Victory: Politics and American Culture During World War II.* New York: Harcourt Brace Jovanovich, 1976.

Bogart, Leo. *Premises for Propaganda: The United States Information Agency's Operating Assumptions in the Cold War.* New York: Free Press, 1976.

Bohn, Thomas. *An Historical and Descriptive Analysis of the "Why We Fight" Series.* New York: Arno Press, 1977.

Braestrup, Peter. *Big Story! How the American Press and Television Reported and Interpreted the Crises of Tet 1968 in Vietnam and Washington.* 2 vols. Boulder, Colo.: Westview Press, 1977.

Brembeck, Winston, and William Howell. *Persuasion: A Means of Social Influence.* 2d ed. Englewood Cliffs, N.J.: Prentice-Hall, 1976.

Brightbill, George D. *Communications and the United States Congress: A Selectively Annotated Bibliography of Committee Hearings, 1870-1976.* Washington, D.C.: Broadcast Education Association, 1978.

Britt, Steuart Henderson. *Psychological Principles of Marketing and Consumer Behavior.* Lexington, Mass.: Lexington Books/Heath, 1978.

Brownlow, Kevin. *The War, the West and the Wilderness.* New York: Knopf, 1979.

Bruntz, George C. *Allied Propaganda and the Collapse of the German Empire in 1918.* Stanford, Cal.: Stanford University Press, 1938.

Buchanan, Albert R. "European Propaganda and American Public Opinion, 1914-1917." Ph.D. dissertation, Stanford University, 1935.

Buchanan, William W., and Edna A. Kanely, comps. *Cumulative Subject Index to the Monthly Catalog of United States Government Publications 1900-1971.* 15 vols. Washington, D.C.: Carrollton Press, 1972-75.

Canfield, Cass. *Sam Adams' Revolution (1765-1776).* New York: Harper & Row, 1976.

Carroll, Wallace. *Persuade or Perish.* Boston: Houghton Mifflin, 1948.

Casey, Ralph Droz. "Propaganda Technique in the 1928 Presidential Campaign." Ph.D. dissertation, University of Wisconsin, 1929.

Castle, Eugene W. *Billions, Blunders and Baloney: The Fantastic Story of How Uncle Sam Is Squandering Your Money Overseas.* New York: Devin-Adair, 1955.

Childs, Harwood L. *An Introduction to Public Opinion.* New York: Wiley, 1940.

———. "Propaganda." In *Collier's Encyclopedia.* Vol. 19. New York: Macmillan, 1979, pp. 410-17.

———. *A Reference Guide to the Study of Public Opinion.* Princeton: Princeton University Press, 1934. Reprint. Ann Arbor, Mich.: Gryphon Books, 1971.

———, ed. "Pressure Groups and Propaganda." *Annals* of the American Academy of Political and Social Sciences, 179 (May 1935). Special issue.

———, and John B. Whitton, eds. *Propaganda by Short Wave* (1942). Bound with C. A. Rigby's *The War on Short Waves* (1943) in a new joint edition as part of the International Propaganda and Communications series. New York: Arno Press, 1972.

Choukas, Michael. *Propaganda Comes of Age.* Washington, D.C.: Public Affairs Press, 1965.

Christenson, Reo M., and Robert O. McWilliams, comps. *Voice of the People: Readings in Public Opinion and Propaganda.* 2d ed. New York: McGraw-Hill, 1967.

Cirino, Robert. *Don't Blame the People: How the News Media Use Bias, Distortion and Censorship to Manipulate Public Opinion.* New York: Vintage/Random House, 1972.

Colby, Benjamin. *'Twas a Famous Victory: Deception and Propaganda in the War with Germany.* New Rochelle, N.Y.: Arlington House, 1974.

Colgate, Craig, Jr., ed. *National Trade and Professional Associations of the United States and Canada and Labor Unions.* 15th. annual ed. Washington, D.C.: Columbia Books, 1980.

Constantine, James. "The African Slave Trade: A Study of Eighteenth Century Propaganda and Public Controversy." Ph.D. dissertation, Indiana University, 1953.

Conway, Moncure D. *The Life of Thomas Paine.* 2 vols. New York: Putnam's, 1892. Reprint. New York: Benjamin Blom, 1969.

Cooper, Kent. *The Right to Know: An Exposition of the Evils of News Suppression and Propaganda.* New York: Farrar, Straus, and Cudahy, 1956.

Crandall, Marjorie Lyle. *Confederate Imprints: A Check List Based Principally on the Collection of the Boston Athenaeum.* 2 vols. Boston: Boston Atheneum, 1955.

Crawford, Anthony. *Posters of World War I and World War II in the George C. Marshall Research Foundation.* Charlottesville: University Press of Virginia, 1979.

Creel, George. *How We Advertised America: The First Telling of the Amazing Story of the Committee on Public Information that Carried the Gospel of Americanism to Every Corner of the Globe.* New York: Harper & Brothers, 1920. Reprint. New York: Arno Press, 1972.

______. *Rebel at Large: Recollections of Fifty Crowded Years.* New York: Putnam's, 1947.

Cronkhite, Gary. *Persuasion: Speech and Behavioral Change.* Indianapolis, Ind.: Bobbs-Merrill, 1969.

Cruickshank, Charles G. *The Fourth Arm: Psychological Warfare 1938-1945.* London: Davis-Poynter, 1977.

Culbert, David, ed. *Mission to Moscow: The Feature Film as Propaganda.* Madison: University of Wisconsin Press, 1980.

______. *News for Everyman: Radio and Foreign Affairs in Thirties America.* Westport, Conn.: Greenwood Press, 1976.

______, Richard Wood, and William Murphy, eds. *Film and Propaganda in America: A Documentary History.* 5 vols. Text and microfiche. Westport, Conn.: Greenwood Press, forthcoming.

Cullop, Charles P. *Confederate Propaganda in Europe, 1861-1865.* Coral Gables, Fla.: University of Miami Press, 1969.

Cutlip, Scott M. *A Public Relations Bibliography to 1965.* 2d ed. Madison: University of Wisconsin Press, 1965.

Darracott, J., and B. Loftus. *Second World War Posters.* London: Imperial War Museum, 1972.

Davidson, Philip. *Propaganda and the American Revolution, 1763-1783.* Chapel Hill: University of North Carolina Press, 1941. Republished as *Propaganda in the American Revolution.* New York: Norton, 1973.

Dieterich, Daniel, ed. *Teaching About Doublespeak.* Urbana, Ill.: National Council of Teachers of English, 1976.

Doctor, Powrie Vaux. "Amos Kendall, Propagandist of Jacksonian Democracy." Ph. D. dissertation, Georgetown University, 1940.

Dobb, Leonard W. *Propaganda: Its Psychology and Technique.* New York: Holt, 1935.

______. *Public Opinion and Propaganda.* 2d ed. Hamden, Conn.: Archon Books, 1966.

Dougherty, William E., and Morris Janowitz. *Psychological Warfare Casebook.* Baltimore: Johns Hopkins University Press, 1958.

Dunham, Donald C. *Kremlin Target: U.S.A.; Conquest by Propaganda.* New York: I. Washburn, 1961.

Dyer, Murray. *The Weapon on the Wall: Rethinking Psychological Warfare.* Baltimore: Johns Hopkins University Press, 1959.

Edwards, Samuel. *Rebel! A Biography of Tom Paine.* New York: Praeger, 1974.

Efron, Edith. *The News Twisters.* Los Angeles: Nash, 1971.

———, and Clytia Chambers. *How CBS Tried to Kill a Book.* Los Angeles: Nash, 1972.

Elder, Robert. *The Information Machine: The United States Information Agency and American Foreign Policy.* Syracuse, N.Y.: Syracuse University Press, 1968.

Ellul, Jacques. *Propaganda: The Formation of Men's Attitudes.* New York: Knopf, 1965.

Evans, Frank Bowen, ed. *Worldwide Communist Propaganda Activities.* New York: Macmillan, 1955.

Fielding, Raymond. *The American Newsreel: 1911-1967.* Norman: University of Oklahoma Press, 1972.

Filler, Louis. *Progressivism and Muckraking.* New York: Bowker, 1976.

Foner, Eric. *Tom Paine and Revolutionary America.* New York: Oxford University Press, 1976.

Ford, Nick Aaron. *Language in Uniform: A Reader on Propaganda.* New York: Odyssey Press, 1967.

Fraser, Lindley. *Propaganda.* New York: Oxford University Press, 1957.

Freidel, Frank B., comp. *Union Pamphlets of the Civil War, 1861-1865.* Cambridge: Belknap Press of Harvard University Press, 1967.

Fulbright, J. William. *The Pentagon Propaganda Machine.* New York: Liveright, 1970.

Furhammer, Leif, and Folke Isaksson. *Politics and Film.* New York: Praeger, 1971.

Gaines, Elizabeth. "*The Fatherland:* An American Vehicle for German Propaganda, 1914-1917." M.A. thesis, Indiana University, 1971.

Galvin, John R. *Three Men of Boston.* New York: Crowell, 1976.

Giddens, Jackson. "American Foreign Propaganda in World War I." Ph. D. dissertation, Fletcher School of Law and Diplomacy, Tufts University, 1967.

———. "Propaganda." In *The Encyclopedia Americana.* International ed. Vol. 22. Danbury, Conn.: Americana, 1979, pp. 656-60.

Gimbel, Richard. *Thomas Paine: A Bibliographical Check List of Common Sense, with an Account of Its Publication.* New Haven: Yale University Press, 1956.

Gipson, Henry Clay. *Films in Business and Industry.* New York: McGraw-Hill, 1947.

Glazier, Kenneth M., and James R. Hobson. *International and English-Language Collections: A Survey of the Holdings at the Hoover Institution on War, Revolution and Peace.* Stanford, Cal.: Hoover Institution Press, 1971.

Gordon, George N. *Persuasion: The Theory and Practice of Manipulative Communication.* New York: Hastings House, 1971.

———, and Irving A. Falk. *The War of Ideas: America's International Identity Crisis.* New York: Hastings House, 1973.

———, and William Hodapp. *The Idea Invaders.* New York: Hastings House, 1963.

Gordon, Jay E. *Motion Picture Production for Industry.* New York: Macmillan, 1961.

Gordon, Thomas F., and Mary Ellen Verna. *Mass Communication Effects and Processes: A Comprehensive Bibliography, 1950-1975.* Beverly Hills, Cal.: Sage, 1978.

Gould, Frederick James. *Thomas Paine (1737-1809).* Boston: Small, Maynard, 1925.

Greenstadt, Melvin. "A Critical Survey of United States Government Films in World War I." M.A. thesis, University of Southern California, 1949.

Hale, Julian. *Radio Power: Propaganda and International Broadcasting.* Philadelphia: Temple University Press, 1975.

Hamilton, Alexander, James Madison, and John Jay. *The Federalist Papers.* Introduction by Clinton Rossiter. New York: New American Library/Mentor Books, 1961.

Hapgood, Norman, ed. *Professional Patriots: An Exposure of the Personalities, Methods and Objectives Involved in the Organized Effort to Exploit Patriotic Impulses in These United States During and After the Late War.* New York: Boni, 1927.

Hargis, Billy James. *Distortion by Design: The Story of America's Liberal Press.* Tulsa, Okla.: Christian Crusade, 1965.

Harlow, Ralph Volney. *Samuel Adams, Promoter of the American Revolution: A Study in Psychology and Politics.* New York: Holt, 1923.

Harter, D. Lincoln, and John Sullivan. *Propaganda Handbook.* Philadelphia: 20th Century, 1953.

Harty, Sheila. *Hucksters in the Classroom: A Review of Industry Propaganda in Schools.* Washington, D.C.: Center for the Study of Responsive Law, 1980.

Harwell, Richard. *More Confederate Imprints.* 2 vols. Richmond: Virginia State Library, 1957.

Haste, Cate. *Keep the Home Fires Burning: Propaganda in the First World War.* London: Allen Lane/Penguin Books, 1977.

Hastings, Elizabeth, and Philip K. Hastings, eds. *Index to International Public Opinion, 1978-1979.* Westport, Conn.: Greenwood Press, 1980. Annual.

Hawke, David Freeman. *Paine.* New York: Harper & Row, 1974.

Heartman, Charles F., comp. *The Cradle of the United States, 1765-1789: Five Hundred Contemporary Broadsides, Pamphlets, and a Few Books Pertaining to the History of the Stamp Act, the Boston Massacre and Other Pre-Revolutionary Troubles, the War for Independence and the Adoption of the Federal Constitution.* Perth Amboy, N.J.: Author, 1922.

Heise, Juergen Arthur. *Minimum Disclosure: How the Pentagon Manipulates the News.* New York: Norton, 1979.

Heller, John. "The Selling of the Constitution: The Federalist Papers Viewed as an Advertising Campaign." M.A.J.C. thesis, University of Florida, 1974.

Henderson, John W. *The United States Information Agency.* New York: Praeger, 1969.

Hirst, David. "German Propaganda in the United States, 1914-1917." Ph.D dissertation, Northwestern University, 1962.

Hoffer, Thomas William. "Broadcasting in an Insurgency Environment: USIA in Vietnam, 1965-1970." Ph.D. dissertation, University of Wisconsin, 1972.

Hofstetter, C. Richard. *Bias in the News: Network Television Coverage of the 1972 Election Campaign.* Columbus: Ohio State University Press, 1976.

Holgren, Carol Jean. "The Propaganda Program of the National Recovery Administration." M.A. thesis, University of Washington, 1962.

Holt, Robert T., and Robert W. van de Velde. *Strategic Psychological Operations and American Foreign Policy.* Chicago: University of Chicago Press, 1960.

Hosmer, James K. *Samuel Adams.* Boston: Houghton Mifflin, 1917.

Hovland, Carl, et al. *Communication and Persuasion.* New Haven: Yale University Press, 1953.

Howe, Quincy. *England Expects Every American to Do His Duty.* New York: Simon & Schuster, 1937.
Howe, Russell Warren, and Sarah Hays Trott. *The Power Peddlers: How Lobbyists Mold America's Foreign Policy.* Garden City, N.Y.: Doubleday, 1977.
Hummel, Ray O., Jr. *Southeastern Broadsides Before 1877: A Bibliography.* Richmond: Virginia State Library, 1971.
Hummel, William, and Keith Huntress. *The Analysis of Propaganda.* New York: William Sloane, 1949.
Hunter, Edward. *Brainwashing: The Story of the Men Who Defied It.* New York: Farrar, Straus and Cudahy, 1956.
International Propaganda/Communications: Selections from the Public Opinion Quarterly. New York: Arno Press, 1972.
Irion, Frederick C. *Public Opinion and Propaganda.* New York: Crowell, 1950.
Irwin, Will. *Propaganda and the News; or, What Makes You Think So?* New York: McGraw-Hill, 1936. Reprint. Westport, Conn.: Greenwood Press, 1970.
Jeavons, Clyde. *A Pictorial History of War Films.* Secaucus, N.J.: Citadel Press 1974.
Johnson, Walter. *The Battle Against Isolation.* Chicago: University of Chicago Press, 1944.
Johnston, Winifred. *Memo on the Movies: War Propaganda, 1914-1939.* Norman, Okla.: Cooperative Books, 1939.
Jones, Ken, and Arthur McClure. *Hollywood at War: The American Motion Picture Industry and World War II.* New York: Castle Books, 1973.
Judd, Denis. *Posters of World War Two.* New York: St. Martins Press, 1973.
Kaid, Lynda Lee, Keith R. Sanders, and Robert O. Hirsch. *Political Campaign Communications: A Bibliography and Guide to the Literature.* Metuchen, N.J.: Scarecrow Press, 1974.
Karlins, Marvin, and Herbert Abelson. *Persuasion: How Opinions and Attitudes Are Changed.* 2d ed. New York: Springer, 1970.
Katz, Daniel, et al. *Public Opinion and Propaganda: A Book of Readings.* New York: Dryden, 1954.
Katz, Phillip Paul. *A Systematic Approach to Psyop Information.* Washington, D.C.: Center for Research in Social Systems, 1970.
Keeley, Joseph. *The Left-Leaning Antenna.* New Rochelle, N.Y.: Arlington House, 1971.
Kenneally, Finbar. *United States Documents in the Propaganda File Archives: A Calendar.* 7 vols. Washington, D.C.: Academy of American Franciscan History, 1966-71.
Key, Wilson Bryan. *The Subliminal Seduction: Ad Media's Manipulation of a Not So Innocent America.* Englewood Cliffs, N.J.: Prentice-Hall, 1973.
King, Arnold Kinsey. "Thomas Paine in America, 1774-1787." Ph.D. dissertation, University of Chicago, 1952.
Klein, Walter. *The Sponsored Film.* New York: Hastings House, 1976.
Knightley, Phillip. *The First Casualty—From the Crimea to Vietnam: The War Correspondent as Hero, Propagandist, and Myth Maker.* New York: Harcourt Brace Jovanovich, 1975.

Lampham, Ruth, comp. *Check List of American Revolutionary War Pamphlets in the Newberry Library.* Chicago: Newberry Library, 1922.

Larson, Charles U. *Persuasion: Reception and Responsibility.* Belmont, Calif.: Wadsworth, 1979.

Lasswell, Harold D. "Propaganda." In *Encyclopaedia Britannica.* Vol. 18. Chicago: Encyclopaedia Britannica, 1973, pp. 624-39.

———. "Propaganda." In *Encyclopaedia of the Social Sciences.* Vol 12. New York: Macmillan, 1933, pp. 521-28.

———. *Propaganda Technique in the World War.* London: Kegan Paul, Trench, Trubner, 1927. Reprinted as *Propaganda Technique in World War I.* Cambridge, Mass.: MIT Press, 1971.

Lasswell, Harold D., Ralph D. Casey, and Bruce L. Smith. *Propaganda and Promotional Activities: An Annotated Bibliography.* Minneapolis: University of Minnesota Press, 1935. Reprint. Chicago: University of Chicago Press, 1969.

Lasswell, Harold D., Daniel Lerner, and Hans Speier, eds. *Propaganda and Communication in World History, Volume 1: The Symbolic Instrument in Early Times.* Honolulu: University Press of Hawaii, 1979.

———. *Propaganda and Communication in World History, Volume II: The Emergence of Public Opinion in the West.* Honolulu: University Press of Hawaii, 1979.

———. *Propaganda and Communication in World History, Volume III: A Pluralizing World in Formation.* Honolulu: University Press of Hawaii, 1980.

Lavine, Harold, and James Wechsler. *War Propaganda and the United States.* New Haven: Yale University Press for the Institute for Propaganda Analysis, 1940. Reprint. New York: Arno Press, 1972.

Lee, Alfred McClung. *How to Understand Propaganda.* New York: Holt, Rinehart, 1952.

———, and Elizabeth Briant Lee. *The Fine Art of Propaganda: A Study of Father Coughlin's Speeches.* New York: Harcourt, Brace, 1939. Reprint. New York: Octagon, 1972; and San Francisco: International Society for General Semantics, 1979.

Lerner, Daniel. "Propaganda." In *Funk & Wagnalls Standard Reference Encyclopedia.* Vol. 20. New York: Standard Reference Works, 1959, pp. 7266-68.

———. *Sykewar: Psychological Warfare Against Germany, D-Day to VE-Day.* New York: George W. Stewart, 1949.

———, ed. *Propaganda in War and Crisis: Materials for American Policy.* New York: George W. Stewart, 1951. Reprint. New York: Arno Press, 1972.

Linebarger, Paul. *Psychological Warfare.* 2d ed. Washington, D.C.: Combat Forces Press, 1954. Reprint. New York: Arno Press, 1972.

Lingeman, Richard R. *Don't You Know There's a War On? The American Home Front, 1941-1945.* New York: Putnam's, 1970.

Lippmann, Walter. *Public Opinion.* New York: Harcourt, Brace, 1922. Rev. ed. New York: Free Press, 1965.

Lisann, Maury. *Broadcasting to the Soviet Union: International Politics and Radio.* New York: Praeger, 1975.

Lowenthal, Leo, and Norbert Guterman. *Prophets of Deceit; a Study of the Techniques of the American Agitator.* 2d ed. Palo Alto, Calif.: Pacific Books, 1970.

Lumley, Frederick E. *The Propaganda Menace.* New York: Century, 1933.
MacCann, Richard Dyer. *The People's Films: A Political History of U.S. Government Motion Pictures.* New York: Hastings House, 1973.
McDonough, Joseph J. "Analysis of Official U.S. Military Psychological Warfare Efforts in the Vietnam Conflict." M.A. thesis, Boston University, 1968.
McGuire, William J. "Persuasion, Resistance, and Attitude Change." In *Handbook of Communication.* Edited by Ithiel de Sola Pool, Wilbur Schramm, et al. Chicago: Rand McNally, 1973, pp.216-52.
MacKay, Lamar. "Domestic Operations of the Office of War Information in World War II." Ph. D. dissertation, University of Wisconsin, 1966.
Mahood, H. R. *Pressure Groups in American Politics.* New York: Scribner's, 1967.
Mamatey, Victor S. *The United States and East Central Europe, 1914-1918: A Study in Wilsonian Diplomacy and Propaganda.* Princeton: Princeton University Press, 1957.
Manuscripts of the American Revolution in the Boston Public Library: A Descriptive Catalog. Boston: Hall, 1968.
Manvell, Roger. *Films and the Second World War.* New York: Dell, 1974.
Marks, Barry. "The Idea of Propaganda in America." Ph.D. dissertation, University of Minnesota, 1957.
Maynard, Richard A. *Propaganda on Film: A Nation at War.* Rochelle Park, N.J.: Hayden Book, 1975.
Miller, Gerald, and Michael Burgoon. "Persuasion Research: Review and Commentary." In *Communication Yearbook 2.* Edited by Brent Ruben. New Brunswick, N.J.: Transaction Books, 1978, pp.29-47.
Miller, John C. *Sam Adams: Pioneer in Propaganda.* Stanford, Calif.: Stanford University Press, 1936.
Minnick, Wayne. *The Art of Persuasion.* 2d. ed. Boston: Houghton Mifflin, 1968.
Minor, Dale. *The Information War.* New York: Hawthorn Books, 1970.
Mitchell, Malcolm. *Propaganda, Polls and Public Opinion: Are the People Manipulated?* Englewood Cliffs, N.J.: Prentice-Hall, 1970.
Mock, James R., and Cedric Larson. *Words that Won the War: The Story of the Committee on Public Information, 1917-1919.* Princeton: Princeton University Press, 1939. Reprint. New York: Russell & Russell, 1968.
Morella, Joe, Edward Z. Epstein, and John Griggs. *The Films of World War II.* New York: Citadel Press, 1973.
Murray, Robert. *Red Scare: A Study in National Hysteria, 1919-1920.* Minneapolis: University of Minnesota Press, 1955. Reprint. New York: McGraw-Hill, 1964.
Murty, B. S. *Propaganda and World Public Order: The Legal Regulation of the Ideological Instrument of Coercion.* New Haven: Yale University Press, 1968.
Myers, Gustavus. *History of Bigotry in the United States.* Rev. ed. New York: Capricorn Books, 1960.
Neilson, Francis. *Escort of Lies: War Propaganda.* Brooklyn, N.Y.: Revisionist Press, 1979.
Nimmo, Dan. *Political Communication and Public Opinion in America.* Santa Monica, Calif.: Goodyear, 1978.
______. *The Political Persuaders: The Techniques of Modern Election Campaigns.* Englewood Cliffs, N.J.: Prentice-Hall, 1970.

Norman, Albert. *Our German Policy: Propaganda and Culture.* New York: Vintage Press, 1951.

"On Propaganda." *Etc.: A Review of General Semantics,* 36 (Summer 1979). Special issue.

Packard, Vance. *The Hidden Persuaders.* New York: McKay, 1957.

Paine, Thomas. *Common Sense and Other Political Writings.* Edited by Nelson F. Adkins. Indianapolis: Bobbs-Merrill, 1953.

———. *The Complete Writings of Thomas Paine.* Edited by Philip S. Foner. 2 vols. New York: Citadel Press, 1945.

———. *The Life and Works of Thomas Paine.* Edited by William van der Weyde. 10 vols. New Rochelle, N.Y.: Thomas Paine National Historical Association, 1925.

———. *The Writings of Thomas Paine.* Edited by Moncure Daniel Conway. 4 vols. New York: Putnam's, 1894-96. Reprint. New York: AMS Press, 1967.

Paletz, David, Roberta Pearson, and Donald Willis. *Politics in Public Service Advertising on Television.* New York: Praeger, 1977.

Perlmutter, Tom. *War Movies.* New York: Castle Books, 1974.

Peterson, Horace C. *Propaganda for War: The Campaign Against American Neutrality, 1914-1917.* Norman: University of Oklahoma Press, 1939. Reprint. Port Washington, N.Y.: Kennikat Press, 1968.

Pirsein, Robert W. *The Voice of America.* New York: Arno Press, 1979.

Pollay, Richard W., ed. *Information Sources in Advertising History.* Westport, Conn.: Greenwood Press, 1979.

Posonby, Arthur. *Falsehood in War-time.* New York: Dutton, 1928.

Price, Warren C. *The Literature of Journalism: An Annotated Bibliography.* Minneapolis: University of Minnesota Press, 1959.

———, and Calder M. Pickett. *An Annotated Journalism Bibliography: 1958-1968.* Minneapolis: University of Minnesota Press, 1970.

Public Opinion, Mass Behavior and Political Psychology. Volume 6 of the Political Science, Government, and Public Policy Series. Princeton, N.J.: Princeton Research/IFI/Plenum Data, 1967. With annual supplements, 1967-.

Qualter, Terence H. *Propaganda and Psychological Warfare.* New York: Random House, 1962.

Read, James M. *Atrocity Propaganda, 1914-1919.* New Haven: Yale University Press, 1941. Reprint. New York: Arno Press, 1972.

Reed, Rebecca Theresa. *Six Months in a Convent.* Boston: N.P., 1835.

Reimann, Horst. "Propaganda" and "Public Opinion." In *Marxism, Communism and Western Society: A Comparative Encyclopedia.* Vol. 7. London: Herder and Herder, 1973, pp. 67-68, 113-23.

Rhodes, Anthony. *Propaganda—The Art of Persuasion: World War II.* New York: Chelsea House, 1976.

Riegel, Oscar W. *Mobilizing for Chaos: The Story of the New Propaganda.* New Haven: Yale University Press, 1934. Reprint. New York: Arno Press, 1972.

Roetter, Charles. *The Art of Psychological Warfare 1914-1945.* New York: Stein & Day, 1974.

Roloff, Michael, and Gerald R. Miller, eds. *Persuasion: New Directions in Theory and Research.* Beverly Hills, Calif.: Sage, 1980.

Rupp, Leila J. *Mobilizing Women for War: German and American Propaganda, 1939-1945.* Princeton: Princeton University Press, 1978.

Ryan, Milo. *History in Sound: A Descriptive Listing of the Kiro-CBS Collection of Broadcasts of the World War II Years and After, in the Phonoarchive of the University of Washington.* Seattle: University of Washington Press, 1963.

Schein, Edgar, et al. *Coercive Persuasion: A Socio-Psychological Analysis of the "Brainwashing" of American Civilian Prisoners by the Chinese Communists.* New York: Norton, 1971.

Schwar, Jane. "Interventionist Propaganda and Pressure Groups in the United States, 1937-1941." Ph.D. dissertation, Ohio State University, 1973.

Seabury, William Marston. *Motion Picture Problems: The Cinema and the League of Nations.* New York: Avondale Press, 1929. Reprint. New York: Arno Press, 1978.

Seldes, George. *The Facts Are...A Guide to Falsehood and Propaganda in the Press and Radio.* New York: In Fact, 1942.

Sethi, S. Prakash. *Advocacy Advertising and Large Corporations: Social Conflict, Big Business Image, the News Media, and Public Policy.* Lexington, Mass.: Lexington Books/Heath, 1977.

Severin, Werner J., and James W. Tankard, Jr. *Communication Theories: Origins—Methods—Uses.* New York: Hastings House, 1979.

Shotwell, John. "Crystalizing Public Hatred: Ku Klux Klan Public Relations in the Early 1920s." M.A. thesis, University of Wisconsin at Madison, 1974.

Simons, Herbert W. *Persuasion: Understanding, Practice and Analysis.* Reading, Mass.: Addison-Wesley, 1976.

Sinclair, Upton. *The Brass Check: A Study of American Journalism.* Pasadena, Calif.: Author, 1919. Reprint. New York: Arno Press, 1974.

Skvortsov, L. *The Ideology and Tactics of Anti-Communism.* Moscow: Progress, 1969.

Small, William. *Political Power and the Press.* New York: Norton, 1972.

Smith, Bruce L. "Propaganda." In *International Encyclopedia of the Social Sciences.* Vol. 12. New York: Macmillan, 1968, pp. 579-89.

______. "Propaganda." In *The New Encyclopaedia Britannica.* Vol. 15, Macropaedia. Chicago: Encyclopaedia Britannica, 1974, pp. 36-45.

Smith, Bruce L., Harold D. Lasswell, and Ralph D. Casey. *Propaganda, Communication, and Public Opinion: A Comprehensive Reference Guide.* Princeton: Princeton University Press, 1946.

Smith, Bruce L., and Chitra M. Smith. *International Communication and Political Opinion: A Guide to the Literature.* Princeton: Princeton University Press, 1956. Reprint. Westport, Conn.: Greenwood Press, 1972.

Smith, Culver. *The Press, Politics, and Patronage: The American Government's Use of Newspapers, 1789-1875.* Athens: University of Georgia Press, 1977.

Smith, George Winston. "Generative Forces in Union Propaganda: A Study in Civil War Pressure Groups." Ph.D. dissertation, University of Wisconsin, 1940.

Smith, Robert W. "What Came After?: News Diffusion and Significance of the Boston Massacre in Six American Colonies, 1770-1775." Ph.D. dissertation, University of Wisconsin at Madison, 1972.

Sobel, Robert. *The Manipulators: America in the Media Age.* Garden City, N.Y.: Doubleday, 1976.

Sorensen, Thomas C. *The Word War: The Story of American Propaganda.* New York: Harper & Row, 1968.

Squires, James D. *British Propaganda at Home and in the United States from 1914 to 1917.* Cambridge: Harvard University Press, 1935.

Stenejhem, Michele Flynn. *An American First: John T. Flynn and the America First Committee.* New Rochelle, N.Y.: Arlington House, 1976.

Sterling, Christopher H., and Timothy R. Haight. *The Mass Media: Aspen Institute Guide to Communication Industry Trends.* New York: Praeger, 1978.

Stevenson, William. *A Man Called Intrepid: The Secret War.* New York: Harcourt Brace Jovanovich, 1976.

Stoetzer, Carlos. *Postage Stamps as Propaganda.* Washington, D.C.: Public Affairs Press, 1953.

Stowe, Harriet Beecher. *The Annotated Uncle Tom's Cabin.* Edited with an introduction by Phillip Van Doren Stern. New York: Eriksson, 1964.

Sturminger, Alfred. *3000 Jahre politische Propaganda.* Vienna: Herold, 1960.

Summers, R. E., ed. *America's Weapons of Psychological Warfare.* New York: H. W. Wilson, 1951.

Thompson, Wayne N. *The Process of Persuasion: Principles and Readings.* New York: Harper & Row, 1975.

Thompson, William F. "The Pictorial Reporting and Propaganda of the Civil War." Ph.D. dissertation, University of Wisconsin, 1959.

Thomson, Charles. *Overseas Information Service of the United States Government.* Washington, D.C.: Brookings Institution, 1948.

Thomson, Oliver. *Mass Persuasion in History: An Historical Analysis of the Development of Propaganda Techniques.* Edinburgh: Paul Harris, 1977.

Tunstall, Jeremy. *The Media are American: Anglo-American Media in the World.* New York: Columbia University Press, 1977.

Vaughn, Stephen L. *Holding Fast the Inner Lines: Democracy, Nationalism, and the Committee on Public Information.* Chapel Hill: University of North Carolina Press, 1980.

Viereck, George S. *My Flesh and Blood: A Lyric Autobiography with Indiscreet Annotations.* New York: Horace Liveright, 1931.

———. *Spreading Germs of Hate.* New York: Horace Liveright, 1930.

Walker, Albert. "Public Relations Bibliography: Sixth Edition, 1976-77." *Public Relations Review,* 4 (Winter 1978), 1-94.

———. "Public Relations Bibliography: Seventh Edition, 1978." *Public Relations Review,* 5 (Winter 1979), 1-114.

The Washington Lobby. 3d ed. Washington, D.C.: Congressional Quarterly, 1979.

Washington Representatives 1980. Washington D.C.: Columbia Books, 1980. Annual.

Weinberg, Sydney. "Wartime Propaganda in a Democracy: America's Twentieth Century Information Agencies." Ph.D. dissertation, Columbia University, 1969.

Wells, William Vincent. *The Life and Public Services of Samuel Adams.* 3 vols. Boston: Little, Brown, 1865.

Wilkerson, Marcus M. *Public Opinion and the Spanish-American War: A Study in War Propaganda.* Baton Rouge: Louisiana State University Press, 1932.

Williamson, Audrey. *Thomas Paine: His Life, Work and Times.* London: Allen & Unwin, 1973.

Wilmer, Lambert A. *Our Press Gang; or, a Complete Exposition of the Corruptions and Crimes of the American Newspapers.* Philadelphia: J. T. Lloyd, 1859. Reprint. New York: Arno Press, 1970.

Wilson, Jerome D., and William F. Ricketson. *Thomas Paine.* Boston: Twayne/Hall, 1978.

Winkler, Allan M. *The Politics of Propaganda: The Office of War Information, 1942-1945.* New Haven: Yale University Press, 1978.

Wisan, Joseph. *The Cuban Crisis as Reflected in the New York Press, 1895-1898.* New York: Columbia University Press, 1934. Reprint. New York: Octagon Books, 1965.

Wise, David. *The Politics of Lying: Government Deception, Secrecy and Power.* New York: Vintage Books, 1973.

Woodward, W. E. *Tom Paine: America's Godfather, 1737-1809.* New York: Dutton, 1945.

Wright, Quincy, ed. *Public Opinion and World-Politics.* Chicago: University of Chicago Press, 1933. Reprint. New York: Arno Press, 1972.

Yakes, Nancy, and Denise Akey, eds. *Encyclopedia of Associations.* 14th ed. 3 vols. Detroit: Gale Research, 1980.

Young, Kimball, and Raymond D. Lawrence. *Bibliography on Censorship and Propaganda.* University of Oregon Journalism Series, no. 1. Eugene: University of Oregon Press, March 1928.

Zeman, Zbynek. *Selling the War: Art and Propaganda in World War II.* London: Orbis, 1978.

Ziegler, L. Harmon, and Wayne C. Peak. *Interest Groups in American Politics.* 2d ed. Englewood Cliffs, N.J.: Prentice-Hall, 1972.

Zimbardo, Philip B., Ebbe B. Ebbesen, and Christina Maslach. *Influencing Attitudes and Changing Behavior.* 2d ed. New York: Addison-Wesley, 1977.

STATE AND FEDERAL GOVERNMENT DOCUMENTS

"Declassified Documents Reference System." Official U.S. documents photoduplicated, summarized, and indexed from Freedom of Information requests. Washington, D.C.: Carrollton Press, 1976-.

New York State Senate. Lusk Committee. *Revolutionary Radicalism: Its History, Purpose and Tactics.* 4 vols. Albany, N.Y.: J. B. Lyon, 1920.

The Psychological Warfare Division, Supreme Headquarters, Allied Expeditionary Force. An Account of its Operations in the Western European Campaign, 1944-45. Bad Homburg, Germany: S.H.A.E.F., 1945.

U.S. Board for International Broadcasting. *Annual Report.* Washington, D.C.: Government Printing Office, 1974-.

U.S. Committee on Public Information. *Complete Report of the Chairman of the Committee on Public Information: 1917, 1918, 1919,* by George Creel ("Creel Report"). Washington, D.C.: Government Printing Office, 1920. Reprint. New York: Da Capo Press, 1972.

U.S. Congress. General Accounting Office. *Suggestions to Improve Management of Radio Free Europe/Radio Liberty.* Report No. ID-76-55. Washington, D.C.: General Accounting Office, June 25, 1976.

______. *Telling America's Story to the World—Problems and Issues.* Report No. B-118654. Washington, D.C.: General Accounting Office, March 25, 1974.

U.S. Congress. House. Committee on Foreign Affairs. *Authorizing Appropriations for Fiscal Years 1980-81 for the Department of State, the International Communication Agency, and the Board for International Broadcasting. Hearings. February 1979.* Washington, D.C.: Government Printing Office, 1979.

______. *Radio Free Europe and Radio Liberty. September 14, 21, 1971.* Washington, D.C.: Government Printing Office, 1972.

______. *USIA: Authorization for Fiscal Year 1973. March, May, 1972.* Washington, D.C.: Government Printing Office, 1972.

______. *U.S. Information Agency Operations.* Parts 1-2. *Part I: Survey of the U.S. Information Service, December 1972; Part II: Hearings on the United States Information Agency, July 1970, September-October 1971.* Washington, D.C.: Government Printing Office, 1973.

______. *Winning the Cold War; the U.S. Ideological Offensive. Hearings Before the Subcommittee on International Organizations and Movements of the Committee on Foreign Affairs.* Parts 1-9. Washington, D.C.: Government Printing Office, 1963-66.

U.S. Congress. House. Committee on Un-American Activities. *Annual Reports.* Washington, D.C.: Government Printing Office, 1946-69.

______. *Cumulative Index to Publications of the Committee on Un-American Activities, 1938-1954.* Washington, D.C.: Government Printing Office, January 20, 1955.

______. *Supplement to Cumulative Index to Publications of the Committee on Un-American Activities, 1950 through 1960.* Washington, D.C.: Government Printing Office, June 1961.

(Note: Between 1945 and 1969, when HUAC became the Internal Security Committee, approximately six hundred publications were issued covering a variety of "un-American" activities. These include transcripts of public hearings, reports, and other documents. Many deal specifically with the effects of subversive propaganda. Rather than list each here, readers are recommended to consult the HUAC indexes, previously cited guides to U.S. government publications, and general studies critically analyzing the work of the committee).

U.S. Congress. House. Special Committee to Investigate Communism in the United States. *Hearings.* 6 parts. Washington, D.C.: Government Printing Office, 1930.

______. *Investigation of Communist Propaganda.* Report No. 2290. Washington, D.C.: Government Printing Office, 1931.

U.S. Congress. House. Special Committee on Un-American Activities. *Appendixes.* 9 parts.Washington, D.C.: Government Printing Office, 1940-44. See particularly Part 3, *Preliminary Report on Totalitarian Propaganda in the United States* (1941); and Part 9, *Communist Front Organizations* (Committee Print, 1944).

______. *Hearings.* 16 vols. Washington, D.C.: Government Printing Office, 1938-43.

______.*Investigation of Nazi and Other Propaganda.* Report No. 153. Washington, D.C.: Government Printing Office, 1935.

______. *Investigation of Nazi Propaganda Activities and Investigation of Certain Other Propaganda Acitivities. Public Hearings.* 6 vols. Washington, D.C.: Government Printing Office, 1934.

______. *Investigation of Un-American Activities and Propaganda.* House Report No. 2. Washington, D.C.: Government Printing Office, January 3, 1939.

______. *Investigation of Un-American Activities and Propaganda.* House Report No. 1476. Washington, D.C.: Government Printing Office, January 3, 1940.

______. *Investigation of Un-American Activities and Propaganda.* House Report No. 1. Washington, D.C.: Government Printing Office, January 3, 1941.

U.S. Congress. Senate. Committee on Foreign Relations. *Foreign Relations Authorization Act, Fiscal Years 1980 and 1981.* Washington, D.C.: Government Printing Office, March 1979.

______. *Foreign Relations Authorization Act: Hearings.* Washington, D.C.: Government Printing Office, April 1977. (Note: Includes Board for International Broadcasting and USIA. See earlier years, as well as following publications as listed below).

______. *Russian Propaganda, Hearings Before a Subcommittee of the Senate Committee on Foreign Relations Pursuant to S. Res. 263.* Washington, D.C: Government Printing Office, 1920.

U.S. Congress. Senate. Committee on Interstate Commerce. *Propaganda in Motion Pictures, Hearings Before a Subcommittee of the Senate Committee on Interstate Commerce Pursuant to S. Res. 152.* Washington, D.C.: Government Printing Office (Committee Print), 1942.

U.S. Congress. Senate. Committee on the Judiciary. *Bolshevik Propaganda, Hearings Before a Subcommittee of the Committee on the Judiciary, Feb. 11, 1919 to Mar. 10, 1919.* Washington, D.C.: Government Printing Office, 1919.

______. *Brewing and Liquor Interests and German and Bolshevik Propaganda. Report, Doc. No. 61.* Washington, D.C.: Government Printing Office, 1919.

______. *The Technique of Soviet Propaganda. A Study Presented by the Subcommittee to Investigate the Administration of the Internal Security Act and Other Internal Security Laws of the Committee on the Judiciary,* by Suzanne Labin. Washington, D.C.: Government Printing Office, 1960.

U.S. Department of State. *Memorandum on the Postwar International Information Program of the United States,* by Arthur W. MacMahon. Publication 2438. Washington, D.C.: Government Printing Office, 1945. Reprint. New York: Arno Press, 1972.

U.S. Department of State. International Information Program. *The Voice of America: 1950-1951.* Washington, D.C.: Department of State, 1951.

______. *Telling America's Story Abroad; the State Department's Information and Educational Exchange Program.* Washington, D.C.: Government Printing Office, 1951.

U.S. Department of State. Library Division. *Psychological Warfare in Support of Military Operations; a Bibliography of Selected Materials with Annotations.* Washington, D.C.: Department of State, Library Division, 1951.

U.S. Foreign Broadcast Intelligence Service. *The Daily Report of Foreign Radio Broadcasts.* Washington, D.C.: Foreign Broadcast Intelligence Service, 1940-47.

U.S. Information Agency. *Propaganda and Information: An Annotated Bibliography.* Washington, D.C.: U.S.I.A. Library, July 1973.

———. *Report to the Congress,* nos. 5, 10-11, 38. Washington, D.C.: Government Printing Office, 1955, 1958, 1972.

———. *Report to the Congress,* nos. 43-46. Washington, D.C.: Government Printing Office, 1974-78.

———. *Review of Operations,* nos. 1-4, 6-9, 12-32, 35. Washington, D.C.: Government Printing Office, 1953-55, 1956-57, 1959-60, 1970.

———. *Semiannual Report to the Congress,* nos. 34, 36-37, 39-42. Washington, D.C.: Government Printing Office, 1970, 1971, 1972-74.

———. *Semiannual Review of Operations* 33. Washington, D.C.: Government Printing Office, 1969.

———. *Soviet Foreign Propaganda: An Annotated Bibliography,* by Anne Boyer. Washington, D.C.: U.S.I.A. Library, 1971.

———. *The United States Information Agency: A Bibliography.* 2d. edition. Washington, D.C.: U.S.I.A. Library, 1976.

U.S. International Communication Agency. Office of Congressional and Public Liaison. *International Communication Agency Fact Sheet.* Washington, D.C.: USICA, October 1979.

———. *Report to Congress 1978-1979.* Washington, D.C.: Government Printing Office, 1980.

U.S. Library of Congress. *A List of Bibliographies on Propaganda,* by Grace Hadley Fuller. Compiled under the direction of Florence S. Hellman. Washington, D.C.: Library of Congress, Division of Bibliography, 1940.

U.S. National Archives and Records Service. *Guide to the National Archives of the United States.* Washington, D.C.: National Archives and Records Service, 1974.

U.S. Office of War Information. *Victory Magazine.* Washington: Office of War Information, 1943-46.

U.S. War Department. *Guide to the Use of Information Materials.* War Department Pamphlet, no. 20-3. Washington, D.C.: Government Printing Office, September 1944.

———. Strategic Services Unit. History Project. Office of the Assistant Secretary of War. *War Report of the O.S.S. (Office of Strategic Services),* Vol. 1; *The Overseas Targets, War Report of the O.S.S. (Office of Strategic Services),* Vol. 2. Previously classified and unavailable. Reprinted with a new introduction by Kermit Roosevelt. New York: Walker, 1976.

JOURNALS

Abstracts of Popular Culture: A Quarterly Publication of International Popular Phenomena. Bowling Green, Ohio, 1976-.

AIMS (American Institute of Marxist Studies) Newsletter. New York, 1964-.

America: History and Life. Santa Barbara, Calif., 1964-.

Annals of the American Academy of Political and Social Sciences. Philadelphia, 1890-.

Anti-Slavery Reporter. New York, 1825-32; 1840-44.

Business and Home TV Screen (formerly *Business Screen*). New York, 1939-.

Communication Abstracts. Beverly Hills, Calif., 1978-.

Communication Monographs (formerly *Speech Monographs).* Falls Church, Va., 1934-.
Communication Research: An International Quarterly. Beverly Hills, Calif., 1974-.
The Democratic Journalist. Prague, Czechoslovakia. 1953-. (In English)
The Falling Leaf. St. Albans, England, 1958-.
Historical Abstracts. Santa Barbara, Calif., 1955-.
Human Communication Research. Austin, Tex., 1974-.
In Fact. New York, 1940-50.
International Political Science Abstracts. Oxford/Paris, 1951-.
Journal of Communication. Philadelphia, 1951-.
Journalism Quarterly. Minneapolis, 1924-.
Marxism and the Mass Media: Towards a Basic Bibliography. Bagnolet, France, 1972-.
Mass Media Booknotes. Philadelphia, 1969-.
Pacific Research. Mountain View, Calif., 1969-.
Political Communication and Persuasion: An International Journal. Washington, D.C., 1980-.
Popular Abstracts. Bowling Green, Ohio, 1978-.
Propaganda Analysis. New York, 1937-41.
Psychological Abstracts. Washington, D.C., 1927-.
Public Opinion Quarterly. Princeton, N.J., 1937-.
Public Relations Review. College Park, Md., 1975-.
Quarterly Journal of Speech. Falls Church, Va., 1915-.
Social Science Monitor. College Park, Md., 1979-.
Sociological Abstracts. New York, 1953-.

CHAPTER 14 Records and the Recording Industry

James Von Schilling

"I was never taken so aback in my life," was Thomas Alva Edison's reaction to the initial sounds coming from the machine he had hastily designed to repeat the spoken word, its first words being Edison's own rendition of "Mary Had a Little Lamb." Amazing as that premiere performance of the first phonograph must have been in 1876, even to its inventor, perhaps much more amazing has been its performance in the hundred-plus years since. The phonograph has survived patent struggles and labor disputes, two world wars and a Great Depression, the break-up of monopolies and the breakdown of distribution systems, the advent of motion pictures, radio, and television, along with the rise and fall of musical tastes, styles, and superstars. At times the industry's sales may have dipped, and there were even moments when the phonograph seemed on its last leg and tipping over, but the general trend for over a century has been continuous growth in product, audience, and profits.

Some have argued that the recent emergence of home videocassettes and videodiscs poses a serious threat to the record industry. After all, why pay to hear a performance you can both see and hear—in the privacy of your own home, at your own convenience? But this argument ignores two of the basic principles that have governed the complex history of recorded music. First, the industry has survived and prospered partly by taking advantage of any new medium that appeared to be its rival, or even conquerer. When radio boomed in the 1920s, for example, it seemed to mark the demise of the record industry. Aided by the onset of the Depression, radio was making the notion of *paying* to hear music at home obsolete, or at least foolish. Within a few years, though, radio had introduced America to "swing" music, a style so popular it triggered as a side-effect a whole new boom in record buying. Similarly, the later notion that television might doom the record industry was disproved in the aftermath of the 1964 appearances of the Beatles on the "Ed Sullivan Show," if not the appearances of Elvis Presley on the same show a decade earlier.

The second principle behind the remarkable growth and survival of the record industry reaches all the way back to Edison's reaction to his "child's" first words. At the very heart of recorded music's relationship to American culture has been its power to take each of us aback, as Edison was, throughout our personal lives. Historians of the phonograph have noted that each new development in recording technology was heralded as introducing the ultimate in life-like sound, only to be rendered hopelessly "tinny" by newer technologies, sometimes just a few years later. This suggests we take such claims (for example, the current publicity about digital recording) with a certain skepticism, but it also illustrates an important point. Despite how inferior the recording techniques and results of the past may seem to us now, they created powerful emotional experiences for the audiences of their time. The essential bond has always been between the listener and the recorded sound, and everything else— the technology, the marketing, the profits— has resulted from that bond and its basic power.

In other words, recorded sound does something of great significance to people, and so it has for over one hundred years of American culture. The variety of styles and performers that have been recorded, as well as the variety of audiences that have been affected by these recordings, makes it difficult to determine exactly what this significance is and where its real power resides. "It's got a good beat and you can dance to it," goes the classic explanation for what makes a rock-and-roll record a memorable experience to its audience, but that hardly works with recordings of other genres: jazz, country, Broadway, opera, and so forth. Regardless of genre, however, all recordings do one thing in common: they capture in time a unique combination of music, performance, and artistry and then enable us to make this "timepiece" part of our personal experience.

When we purchase a record, we generally have little knowledge of the history, technology, or economics behind it. But all that may be incidental; the essence of recorded music may simply be the personal actions of bringing that record home, slitting the cellophane "shrink jacket," placing the disc on the turntable, starting the electricity and machinery, and then experiencing internally the timepiece of music, performance, and artistry awaiting us in the grooves. A nursery rhyme in his own voice took Edison aback; today it may require a multi-tracked, million-dollar electronic production, but the results are the same. We are taken hold, and a truly memorable recording will transcend all the history, technology, and business and not let us back into that other world—at least until the music ends.

HISTORIC OUTLINE

Thomas Edison invented the phonograph the way Columbus discovered America—accidentally, while looking for something else entirely. Edison was actually seeking to improve the newly emerging telephone system by making it more accessible to the middle and lower classes in America. Home telephone equipment was expensive back in 1876; Edison hoped to design a machine for recording messages, with the results capable of being replayed and transmitted at a centrally located telephone. Precisely why anybody would need to record the message beforehand rather than simply speak into the centrally located phone (for instance, today's public telephones) has never been completely established, not that it really mattered. Edison's idea, which was rendered into a working mechanism by an assistant, John Kruesi, in November 1876, quickly took on new applications when introduced to the public the following year. Edison himself soon envisioned a list of ten general uses for his invention, of which only the tenth dealt with telephones. The others included "letter writing and all kinds of dictation," "reproduction of music" (fourth on his list), and "clocks that announce in accurate speech the time for going home, going to meals, etc."[1]

At first the phonograph generated great publicity as Edison's assistants conducted public demonstrations around the country. But by 1880 Edison had rechanneled his energies and redirected his laboratory toward a new idea, the electric lightbulb, and the phonograph slipped into a state of suspended animation for most of the decade. In October 1887, however, Edison switched gears again, "confessing" to America that, despite his apparent fixation on what he called "the electric business.... Nevertheless, the phonograph has been more or less constantly in my mind."[2] Edison's apparent fickleness was, in reality, a shrewd businessman's response to a rapidly changing commercial climate, as his short-lived monopoly over the machine, the industry, and its future was about to end.

Edison's invention was facing a stiff, serious competitor in 1887, the Alexander Graham Bell-sponsored Graphophone; the following year yet a third rival emerged, Emile Berliner's gramophone. The stage was set for the next thirty years of the fledgling industry's history and a series of complex, exhaustive struggles between the pioneering individuals and companies that emerged from these first three rivals. From a technological perspective, the machine that eventually dominated the market after this "Thirty Years War" was a far cry from Edison's mechanism. Instead, it more closely resembled Emile Berliner's gramophone, recording on discs rather than Edison's cylinder products.

From a business viewpoint, two major companies survived out of the dozen or so that played key roles during these early years; although the ranks of "majors" have changed throughout the decades, these two have always made the list. The first company, Victor Talking Machine, came to life in 1901, when Eldridge R. Johnson, who had been Berliner's equipment supplier, staked his own claim in the industry. Twenty-five years later Johnson sold his controlling interest in Victor for $28 million to a firm that soon merged with the Radio Corporation of America (RCA). Columbia Phonograph, the other permanent leg of the record industry, had its origins way back in 1878, as a subsidiary distributor for Bell's Graphophone. Columbia suffered through periods of hard times and one clear case of bankruptcy. Propped up in 1923 by new owners, it survived the Depression and eventually found a safe haven in the early 1930s under the corporate umbrella of RCA's arch-rival, the Columbia Broadcasting System (CBS).

From a musical standpoint, no single style dominated these early years of the record industry as rock music has since the 1950s. Rather, the catalogs of the pioneer companies featured everything from the arias of Enrico Caruso to the popular ditties of George W. Johnson, "The Whistling Coon." Popular music in general, though, clearly dominated the market, no doubt partly because many early phonographs were coin-operated and served as amusements in public locations. But classical performers, particularly opera stars (orchestras fared poorly under the early recording techniques), became crucial weapons in the fierce publicity battles fought between the pioneer companies. Signing a top European tenor or soprano could help establish a company as an industry leader, even though the bulk of that company's sales were likely to fall in the popular market.

Linked so closely to America's popular culture, though, the record industry was subject to the fluctuations of public taste. The medium experienced its first real boom during the Dance Mania of the mid-1910s. Victor scored a coup by signing the period's ballroom royalty, Vernon and Irene Castle, to "supervise" the recording of dance music, while Columbia trumpeted its own expert, G. Hepburn Wilson, who "dances while the band makes the record." Sales of newly designed phonograph consoles, with prices ranging up to $2,000, soared in the United States and Europe and continued strong through the early 1920s, aided by a popular, shocking, and liberating style of music and dance: hot jazz.

But the focus of popular culture shifted unexpectedly in the mid-1920s to a new medium for speech and music—the radio—with one clear technical advantage over the phonograph. The radio was electric: the amplification processes involved in radio transmission produced sounds far superior in quality to the mechanical diaphragm and stylus system that the early phonograph employed. That technological edge gave radio a jump-start and forced the record industry to adapt by adding radio sets to its consoles and developing electrical recording and playback processes itself. But these changes weren't enough to carry the record industry through a second upheaval later that decade, as the Great Depression placed phonograph records on its list of obviously expendable purchases.

Record sales by 1932 had dropped incredibly—to just 6 percent of the 1927 rate—and sales of phonographs sank to similar depths. The industry did climb back, of course, but doing so took the rest of the decade and involved a number of factors, not the least of which was the New Deal's gradual restoration of consumer confidence in general. Within the industry itself, though, several key developments aided the recovery, most notably the sudden leap to sales prominence of Decca Records, founded by an American, Jack Kapp, and financed by a London stockbroker. With the current industry "majors"—Victor, Columbia, and Brunswick—all selling their discs for seventy-five cents apiece, Decca managed to corral some top performers and peddle their records for only thirty-five cents. "Decca Scoops Music World," headlined their ads, and they did indeed scoop up such pop stars as Bing Crosby, the Mills Brothers, and the Dorseys for their roster. RCA-Victor also contributed significantly to the recovery by marketing a popular, budget-priced phonograph called the Duo, Jr., designed to use the home radio for amplification.

Perhaps the biggest boost to the record industry, though, came from America's popular culture, as the "hot jazz" craze of the 1920s settled into a more mainstream, socially acceptable style of entertainment. America thus entered the "Swing" or "Big Band" era, when purchasing the latest tunes by Benny Goodman, Glenn Miller, Harry James, and others became a basic part of life for a whole generation of young Americans. Radio may have popularized the music in the first place, and jukeboxes whetted the public's appetite, but actually owning an "In the Mood" 78 rpm to play in the parlor was the next best thing to jitter-bugging in front of the bandstand. Sales of records picked up slowly at first and then dramatically, reaching a peak of 127 million in 1941—and then the bubble burst again.

At first the problem this time was World War II and the restrictions imposed on the record industry: all manufacturers of electrical equipment were redirected to the war effort, and 70 percent of the nation's shellac resources (from which records were being produced) were devoted to strictly military purposes. But a heavier bomb fell on the homefront in the summer of 1942, when the American Federation of Musicians voted to strike the record industry on the grounds that recorded music was putting the professional musician out of business, or at least severely curtailing the need for live performances. With its sales concentrated solely in the popular market, Decca suffered the most by not being able to record the latest styles and hits (which could still be heard in live performances on the radio) and was forced to capitulate the following year. The terms of the Decca agreement involved the payment of royalties to the AFM, for the support of unemployed musicians, for every record sold. Columbia and RCA held out for a second year but eventually "surrendered" on the same day Germany signed its peace pact with the Allies.

With conflicts both national and international finally settling down, the record industry may have anticipated a relatively calm postwar period. Instead, the following decade featured an upheaval in technology, a disruption of the industry's economic structure, and a shift in American popular culture of earthquake proportions. The revolution in technology surfaced to the public as the "Battle of the Speeds," with the new 33 1/3 rpm album from CBS in one corner and the new 45 rpm "single" from RCA in the other. Actually, a great deal more than different turnable speeds was involved since Peter Goldmark, the CBS engineer who developed the long-playing 33 1/3 album, had virtually reinvented the entire recording and production process along the way. Nothing would ever be the same after Goldmark's album caught on with the public: not the recording studio, with its dramatically improved microphone system; not the records themselves, with their contents expanded up to ten times the two- or three-minute span of the old 78; not even the industry's long-established hierarchy, with Columbia now the leader and RCA playing "catch up." Countering with its own 45, RCA weakly described the little disc's virtues as the ideal form for the popular single. They were in luck, though, as a figure emerged in America's popular culture (conveniently signed to an RCA contract) who would link the 45, with its oversized hole and its undersized playing time, to millions of young people from that point on: the "Hillbilly Cat" from Tupelo, Mississippi—Elvis Presley.

RCA may have reaped the most benefits from the rise of Elvis Presley from "Hillbilly Cat" to superstardom, but the fact is that neither Elvis, Chuck Berry, Little Richard, the Coasters, nor any of the pioneers of rock and roll would have affected our popular culture had it not been for a new force that developed in the postwar record industry: the independent record company, or "indie." These businesses ranked far below the "majors" in total sales, production and promotional budgets, as well as access to distribution (the "majors" at that time being RCA, Columbia, Decca, Capital, Mercury, and MGM). Yet, for several key reasons, such relatively small-scale operations as Chess, Savoy, and Atlantic Records came to assume a position of great importance and, in fact, permanently changed the direction of popular music and the entire record industry. First and perhaps foremost, these independent companies recorded black music performed by black artists in a style that was known as "rhythm and blues" ("R&B") out of which developed rock and roll. With but a few exceptions (for example, Louis Jordan on Decca), the majors either disavowed black music entirely, shunted it onto less-supported subsidiary labels, or recorded black artists like Nat King Cole who were closer to the white mainstream.

In neglecting to record rhythm-and-blues performers, the majors were simply following a pattern that had been established and reestablished throughout the century, in which black artists influenced—and often determined—the course of America's popular music but white artists profited commercially once the new music reached the public. From the industry's viewpoint, the history of recorded music up to that point had clearly shown that any new music emerging from the black subculture could be directed into the mainstream by the majors, with the ensuing profits diverted from the original sources. Such had been the case with hot jazz and swing music; thus, there was every reason to believe that the system would prevail with rhythm and blues, despite the presence of the independent companies. After all, the majors in the early 1950s were holding a tight grip over all possible distribution routes—jukeboxes, radio airplay, record stores, sheet music—or so they thought. At it turned out, the majors failed to assess two additional factors, one sociological, the other commercial, that nearly toppled the whole system.

In sociological terms, the majors failed to adjust to the new realities of America's racial structure, for World War II had brought blacks and whites in much greater proximity. This was clearly the case in America's Northern cities, where thousands of Southern blacks had relocated during the war to seek jobs and had remained afterwards. Segregation and discrimination were still in force, but the music of a people can sometimes penetrate where the people themselves cannot, especially if an ideal commercial means for that penetration exists. In this case, the music—rhythm and blues—found the perfect means in a handful of young and daring radio disc jockeys, such as Alan Freed, Hal Jackson, and Bill Randle, who felt its power and promoted it to anyone who would listen, black or white. Thus, radio undermined the ability of the majors to orchestrate this new popular music, for the one thing RCA, Columbia, and the others couldn't control was the tuning of the American teenager's bedroom or car radio.

Yet, considering all that the majors *could* control, it's a testimony to the power of rhythm and blues that performers such as Chuck Berry, Fats Domino, Ray Charles, the Coasters, Little Richard, Frankie Lymon, and Bo Diddley—all recording for indies—ever managed to gain a white audience. The majors had direct influence, and often outright control, over the entire production, promotion, and distribution stages in the life of most popular tunes up through the 1950s, and they used all their power to fight for the continued success of their performers, many of whom were holdovers from the Big Band era. Their most infamous tactic was the "cover" record: a white version of a black hit, quickly recorded, released, and promoted in the mainstream white markets and on leading white radio stations (for example, Perry Como's cover of "Kokomo," originally recorded by Gene and Eunice). One especially heavy-handed tactic involved public denunciation of the new music by established mainstream figures; Frank Sinatra, for example, used the words "brutal, ugly, desperate, vicious" to describe rock and roll at a 1958 congressional hearing. With less publicity, but perhaps more effectiveness, the industry developed a third key tactic: revamping their commercial operations and strengthening their promotion departments, especially involving radio airplay. The majors now recognized the importance of releasing pop singles quickly, to capitalize on popular trends, and of marketing their releases thoroughly from coast to coast.

In the short run, the majors lost the struggle with the indies. The number of hit singles produced by independent companies at the close of the 1950s was twice that of the majors, a remarkable shift from the immediate postwar years, when only five out of 162 million-sellers belonged to indies. In the long run, though, the majors won the fight, as few of the independent companies survived the 1960s and the industry retrenchment that decade brought. Once again, the forces behind the new shift were numerous and complex. A well-publicized factor was the 1960 congressional investigation into record industry "payola," or the bribing of radio disc jockeys by record personnel to spur airplay for new releases. The big losers in the scandal weren't the major record companies but the free-wheeling rock-and-roll disc jockeys who had played such key roles in the rise of the new music, especially Alan Freed, whose career and personal life crumbled after the hearings. The indies themselves suffered, too, losing whatever respectability they might have gained during the 1950s. Also, any curtailment of payola activities would hurt the indies more than the majors, who could still rely on their own extensive distribution systems and, in the case of RCA and Columbia, their own nationwide home record clubs.

In addition, the style of popular music had by then progressed from the early years of rock and roll and in a direction that benefited the mainstream industry. With a surprising number of rock pioneers removed from the scene for various reasons (Elvis Presley drafted, Chuck Berry jailed), the sound was decidedly less black "R&B" and more white "pop." Top hits, for example, were recorded by numerous television situation-comedy stars, ranging from Shelley Fabares to Walter Brennan. Another portion of the market belonged to the young performers who recorded for the Philadelphia-centered labels associated with Dick Clark's "American Bandstand" television show. Few members of either group remained successful through the mid-1960s, however their brief tenure at the top clearly presaged two trends that have characterized the record industry ever since. First, the record industry had developed economically to the point where cross-ownership and conglomeration were influencing the musical results, that is, television's non-singers owed their recording careers to the tangled webs being weaved during the 1960s among the various entertainment industries. Second, the record industry was now profiting heavily from the "cult of personality" approach to producing and marketing performers. Whether it was the pompadoured teenage idol or the cashmere-sweatered girl-next-door, the *image* of the performing artist was selling records, perhaps more than the music or performance itself.

Neither trend was exactly new to the record industry. After all, RCA and

CBS had been media conglomerates for decades, and numerous recording stars had developed careers in other entertainment fields or had public images that boosted their sales. But it was during the 1960s that the record industry's corporate structure and its promotional apparatus became as important, if not more so, than the recording technology or the music itself. Under such conditions, the companies that did the best weren't necessarily the most inventive or even the most talented, but rather the ones with the strongest economic bases and skills of promotion.

A company whose rise to major status typified the changes in the industry was Warner Records, an independent purchased in the 1960s by Kinney Services, a New York-based conglomerate. With a stock of reasonably talented young performers (based largely in southern California), but with lots of promotional campaigning and enough capital to support its own operations and also acquire Atlantic and Elektra Records, Warner spent the 1960s climbing toward the top of the industry in sales. Warner is often cited as the company best illustrating how the "baby boom" generation and their fixation on popular music brought enormous growth and success to the record industry during the 1960s. Although this sociological approach has obvious validity, it misses the equally obvious point that neither Warner nor the other 1960s majors could have capitalized on the boom and the fixation without their corporate structures and promotional efforts.

Even the Beatles, when viewed in retrospect, were not as spontaneously welcomed by American youth as our popular myths would have us believe. In 1963, the year before "Beatlemania" struck our shores, several Beatles singles were released in the United States on independent labels and caused little reaction. It wasn't until a major company, Capital, bought the distribution rights and launched one of the most extensive promotional campaigns in the history of recorded music that the Beatles attracted their massive following. In other words, "Beatlemania"—along with the other waves of popular music intensity during the last two decades—developed from a combination of factors all present in contemporary America: an unusually large population of young people; the close links that have existed between popular music and the social and emotional lives of young Americans, at least since the mid-1950s and the advent of rock music, although probably extending back through the "swing" and "hot jazz" years; and the existence of well-financed, promotion-oriented record companies to feed huge amounts of product to the vast young audience.

With a large collection of albums and an expensive stereo now important status symbols among American youth, with records now sold everywhere from local supermarkets to coast-to-coast chain stores, and with top performers now rating "cover story" prominence in our national news magazines, it's no surprise that the record industry has climbed past both the radio and the motion picture industry in total annual income. Whether the products on which that climb has been based—the recorded music of the 1960s and 1970s—truly deserve so much promotion, sales, and recognition is subject to debate. Some would draw an imaginary line in the early 1970s to separate, chronologically, the "good" (1960s rock) from the "bad" (1970s disco). Some would draw the line a few years earlier or later, and others would make a distinction throughout both decades between "genuine" popular music expression and "hyped" record industry product.

Still others would argue that all such lines and distinctions are more a reflection of social- and peer-group attitudes than of the relative quality of any of the music. According to this line of thinking, most recorded music since 1960, when the majors began operating on a grander economic scale, has been fashioned with the same basic principles in mind. The ever-present goal has been to maximize profits, as the media conglomerates to which all leading record companies now belong attempt to support current and future acquisitions with all the money generated by all the music. Thus, every trend—even the hint of a trend—is picked up by the industry, worked into salable products, heavily promoted, and eventually dropped by the wayside when a new trend emerges. In the 1970s trends that followed this pattern included country-rock, punk rock, and disco—with "new wave" music perhaps being the first trend to test the pattern's endurance into the 1980s.

The medium of recorded music today is in many ways vastly different from even just one generation past. It now encompasses such new territory as the auto accessory industry, with the advent of cassette and cartridge systems, as well as the fields of demographics and behavior research, with the testing methods now practiced by some companies in their quest for hit records. Today's top albums earn "gold" and "platinum" status not after weeks of high sales but often right at the point of release; some albums cost over $1 million to produce, sell over 10 million units, and bring in over $100 million in gross profits. Today's top recording stars influence fashions, hair styles, sexual mores, drug usage, even social and political decision making. And today's industry scandals are less likely to involve small sums of money paid to free-wheeling disc jockeys than millions of dollars raked in by well-organized "pirates" of illegally copied records and tapes.

In other ways, though, the more things have changed, the more they've remained the same. It took Thomas Edison only months to begin speculating how his new invention, originally a telephone accessory, might expand into new fields and directions: the expansion continues. The industry's early years featured intensely fought struggles between competing companies: the struggles continue with all their intensity. Those first recordings were a mixed lot, mostly based on popular tastes and often disdained by cultural critics: the mixture continues, along with the popular emphasis and critical disdain. And from "Mary Had a Little Lamb" up through "Y.M.C.A.," the sounds of music and voice on record have continued to hold a power all their own, transcending changes in technology and styles of performance. For the future, we can expect both technology and styles to continue changing, with the power remaining strong. It's been over a century now since America played its first record; right now, despite all that's happened to the culture and the industry during those hundred years, there's no sign that the music is about to end.

REFERENCE WORKS

The subject of reference works in the field of records and the recording industry is in itself a revealing topic. For example, there are numerous books that list records falling within certain styles of music, such as rock or jazz, but no book that attempts to bring together all styles. Many books are intended as reference sources for information about performers, but no one has yet published a reference book about record companies. And, although two authors have put together guides to that most elaborate of phonographs, the juke box, no such work exists for the study of the phonograph in general.

The most common reference work on recorded music is the discography, which comes in all styles, years, and sizes. Some discographies might more accurately be labeled "cylinderographies," for they deal solely with the early years of the record industry and the wax cylinders produced for Edison's machines: Brian Rust's *Discography of Historical Records on Cylinders and 78s,* and Allen Koenigsberg's *Edison Cylinder Records: 1889-1912.* Other discographies concentrate on smaller movements within the realm of popular music, such as *Blues and Gospel Records,* by John Godrich and Robert M. W. Dixon, and one book narrows its focus to just one recording group, *All Together Now: The First Complete Beatles Discography; 1961-1975,* by Walter J. Podrazik and Harry Castleman.

A subgenre of the discography is the chronological listing of record releases, usually hit singles and albums. The work of one researcher in this field is particularly noteworthy: Joel Whitburn, who has compiled a series of books listing top pop and rhythm-and-blues records of the last few decades. Less extensive works in this subgenre have also been compiled by Joe Edwards *(Top 10's and Trivia of Rock & Roll and Rhythm & Blues: 1950-1973)* and H. Kandy Rhode *(The Gold of Rock & Roll: 1955-1967).* Another variation on the discography is the guide to record prices, with the leading figure being Steve Propes, author of *Those Oldies But Goodies; A Guide to 50's Record Collecting, Golden Oldies; A Guide to 60's Record Collecting,* and *Golden Goodies*—indispensible works for the pop record collector.

The second leading category of reference works is the so-called encyclopedia, which attempts to catalog information about performers, styles, and other popular-music topics. Roger D. Kinkle's four-volume work, *The Complete Encyclopedia of Popular Music and Jazz,* is perhaps the best example of how extensive and valuable such a work can be. Other outstanding compilations of assorted facts, figures, and anecdotes include Leonard Feather's updated *Encyclopedia of Jazz; The Rolling Stone Illustrated History of Rock 'n' Roll,* edited by Jim Miller; and *Encyclopedia of Country & Western Music,* by L. Brown and G. Fredrich. An interesting variation on the "encyclopedia" theme is the recently published *Rock Almanac,* by Stephen Nugent and Charlie Gillett, which uses a chronological format to present its wealth of material.

The remaining reference works within the field of recorded music fall under a variety of categories. The editors of *Rolling Stone,* for example, have published two critical guides to rock albums based on the reviews from their own publication: *The Rolling Stone Record Book,* edited by Dave Marsh, and *The Rolling Stone Record Review* by the *Rolling Stone* staff. Also dealing with critical reviews is the *Annual Index to Popular Music Record Reviews,* compiled by Andrew D. Armitage and Dean Tudor. Another potentially valuable resource is published by the National Academy of Recording Arts and Sciences, *The Grammy Awards Book,* with lists of current and past award winners in a variety of categories. Finally, as mentioned above, two works have been published as guides to one of the great entertainment bargains left in America, the juke box: Cynthia A. Hoover's *Music Machines—American Style* and J. Krivine's *Juke Box Saturday Night.*

RESEARCH COLLECTIONS

For those to whom popular music is something of a religion, the third floor of the Main Library at Bowling Green State University is nothing short of Mecca, for housed there in the flatlands of Ohio is the best collection of purely popular music in the country. The Audio Center, closely linked to the Center for the Study of Popular Culture, was developed on a shoestring budget by William L. Schurk with the object of collecting an actual copy of every popular record ever made. So far Schurk has put together upwards of a quarter of a million LP albums, singles, old 78s, and Edison cylinders. Other libraries may house more jazz or folk or country records, but no single collection has Bowling Green's range and variety—with the exception of the Library of Congress, which is not a strictly popular archive. Schurk's secret in building such a collection on a limited budget has been to take full advantage of donations, trading opportunities, auctions, and sales. His holdings in rock and roll and obscure, limited issues are particularly noteworthy, as are his extremely rare "soundies," musical motion picture shorts used in a form of early 1940s juke box.

Another strong asset of the Bowling Green collection is its accessability to the public. Although the stacks themselves are closed, with all records handled only by the staff, listening facilities make it possible for the user to hear virtually any request in a matter of minutes. The Audio Center provides taping services for the university community and research opportunities, under certain conditions, for outside groups and individuals. The center also maintains a diverse collection of reference materials, including discographies, industry promotional material, record sleeves, and back issues of most popular music magazines.

The Library of Congress in Washington, D.C., began collecting popular and classical records in 1924, largely through the donations of Victor and the other early major companies. The industry donations continued for decades, while the library's Music Division began developing special collections in folk music and in such government recordings as the World War II "V-discs." In 1972, legislation brought recorded music within the provisions of the copyright law, with one result being that most record companies began automatically submitting most new releases to the library's Recorded Sound Division. Today, the Recorded Sound Division has accumulated the world's largest collection, with over a million recordings and additional tens of thousands acquired each year. An important boost to the library's collection developed recently when a private citizen donated some forty thousand discs and five hundred cylinders of mostly pre-1926 material. According to the library, these new holdings are particularly strong in popular music, especially jazz, humor, minstrel, and vaudeville recordings.

The services provided by the Library of Congress for the recorded music researcher are numerous and include the production of listening tapes, under certain strict conditions, by the division's own recording laboratory. The division is also involved in record production on a small-scale commercial basis, with special anthologies of some of its holdings available to the general public. Limited listening facilities are provided on the premises for researchers and advanced students, who are advised to schedule time well in advance. Also, catalogs of recordings and of printed works on music are distributed twice a year though the library's Descriptive Cataloguing Division, as well as lists of all records received for copyright purposes from 1972 on, the latter service provided by the library's Copyright Office and the U.S. Government Printing Office.

Another major collection of classical and popular recorded music, the Rodgers & Hammerstein Archives of Recorded Sound, is housed at the New York Public Library's Performing Arts Research Center at Lincoln Center. The library itself had been building a collection since the 1930s, but it took a large grant from the Rodgers & Hammerstein Foundation to create the efficient, extensive, multiservice facilities that presently exist. The archives hold well over 300,000 recordings on disc and tape, serving about four thousand users every year. The recordings range from Edison cylinders to commercial classical and popular discs to dramatic and recitative material. A significant percentage of the collection was acquired from WNEW-AM, a top New York popular radio station.

Like Bowling Green's Audio Center, the Rodgers & Hammerstein Archives offer easy public access to their recording collections through the use of headphones and listening carrels, although their taping services have been discontinued due to staffing shortages. Also like the Bowling Green collection, the Lincoln Center facility contains assorted reference material on the record industry, including industry catalogs, clipping files, and scores of related periodicals. In addition, examples of early phonographs and gramophones are displayed throughout the archives.

Other noteworthy collections specialize in certain types of popular music. The John Edwards Memorial Foundation, for example, at UCLA's Folklore and Mythology Center, collects "those forms of American folk music disseminated by commercial media such as print, sound recordings, films, radio and television. These forms include the music referred to as cowboy, western, country & western, old time, hillbilly, bluegrass, mountain, country, cajun, sacred, gospel, race, blues, rhythm and blues, folk and folk rock." The foundation not only collects recordings and various material related to these musical genres, it also reissues "historically significant" out-of-print records as well.

A major collection of jazz records, with some fifty thousand LPs and 78s, is housed at the Institute for Jazz Studies at Rutgers University's Newark campus. The institute, which offers an academic program and publishes the *Journal of Jazz Studies,* also maintains a book collection, clipping files, and back issues of various jazz and jazz-related magazines. Listening facilities are available; in addition, taping services are offered for the researcher (who must supply the blank tape). For the specialist interested in New Orleans jazz, unusually strong collections are maintained at the Archive of New Orleans Jazz at Tulane University (over ten thousand recordings) and at the New Orleans Jazz Museum and Archives (close to five thousand recordings). Finally, a significant new collection is being developed at the New York Public Library's Schomburg Center, which specializes in black culture. The collection so far includes over ten thousand records from a wide range of styles—r&b, jazz, Caribbean, contemporary, classical, and traditional and modern African. Along with listening carrels, the center's new facilities will make available videotaped performances and interviews featuring both past and present black recording artists.

HISTORY AND CRITICISM

The definitive story of the record industry and recorded music has yet to be written. For reasons that perhaps might best be explored by popular culture theorists, this vital and significant medium has spawned countless works of limited scope but none that attempts to deal with the entire picture—historic, economic, social, cultural, and artistic. A leading candidate at this point is Roland Gelatt's *The Fabulous Phonograph—1877-1977,* first written in 1954, amended in 1965, and amended again for the Bicentennial in 1976. As a basic history of the industry's formative years, and especially of the complex machinations that led to the emergence of the disc system and the early major companies, Gelatt's work cannot be faulted. For the popular culturalist, though, the book is flawed by its strong classical-music slant. Gelatt focuses, for example, on the signing of numerous operatic performers and the recording of countless symphonic works, while brushing past the overwhelming majority of recorded performances and record sales, which feature popular styles. The chapters added in the newer versions attempt to cover developments in popular recorded music from Elvis on but without the depth and detailing of Gelatt's earlier sections on the industry's infancy and adolescence.

For an almost exact opposite approach, the popular culture researcher should consider *Rock 'n' Roll Is Here to Pay,* by Steve Chapple and Reebee Garofalo. This 1978 work takes a radical, semi-Marxist look at the record industry, supporting its controversial arguments (for example, that the industry has been and still is racist) with scores of facts, figures, quotations, and anecdotes. As the title indicates, the work focuses on the industry's rock years, with scant treatment of the periods Gelatt covers in great detail. But the title is somewhat deceiving in that Chapple and Garofalo range beyond rock music to study other dimensions of the industry, such as media conglomeration. Its political slant aside, *Rock 'n' Roll Is Here to Pay* is an important, eye-opening study often focusing on significant but usually neglected aspects of the medium and industry.

A third work, combined with those of Gelatt and Chapple and Garofalo, would comprise a fairly good introduction to recorded music and the record industry: R. Serge Denisoff's *Solid Gold.* Professor Denisoff, of the Sociology Department at Bowling Green State University, combines his firsthand experiences within the industry with his discipline's frame of reference to explore the roles and organizational workings of the medium. The focus is on contemporary rock, with the approach objective (as befits a sociologically oriented work) and the range of subjects fairly extensive: for example, industry promotional activities and generational attitudes toward music performers. Perhaps the work's strongest chapters are those delineating the "life" of a record, from concept to recording to marketing to promoting.

Several other books deserve recognition as works that, by themselves, explore a wide range of topics in the field of recorded music. *Billboard,* in honor of both the nation's and the industry's anniversary, published *Music/Records/200* in 1976, featuring a series of informative, well-written essays on various styles and aspects of popular music. Another excellent business-related work is *The Making of Superstars: Artists and Executives of the Rock Music Business,* by Robert Stephen Spitz. The book is basically a collection of narrative essays on the workings of the music industry, based on the words of the industry people themselves. For a more technical perspective tracing the history of records, phonographs, and the recording process, Oliver Read's and Walter L. Welch's *From Tin Foil to Stereo* is the most extensive work currently available.

Two noteworthy books take a more chronological approach and, although their main intent is to present the history of popular music, provide valuable insight into the growth of the record industry and the power of recorded music. Tony Palmer's *All You Need Is Love: The Story of Popular Music* is a colorful, photo-laden work which blends the history of popular music in the United States and Great Britain with the cultural history of both countries. Somewhat similar in approach but with a stronger dose of social history is Ian Whitcomb's *After the Ball: Pop Music from Rag to Rock.* Whitcomb writes from the perspective of a one-shot pop star, having recorded a hit song himself during the 1960s. The chapter on his own career in the record industry provides an interesting conclusion to this intelligent, well-written critical work.

Another category of general introductory works deserves consideration: the collection of essays. The most outstanding examples currently available have one thing in common: they all focus on rock music and the rock record industry. Three of them feature essays culled from the pages of *Rolling Stone,* the leading journal of contemporary music for over a decade: *The Rolling Stone Reader, The Rolling Stone Rock 'n' Roll Reader,* and *What's That Sound?,* the first edited by the Rolling Stone staff and the latter pair edited by Ben Fong-Torres. Two other fine collections of essays, both edited by Jonathan Eisen, can be considered almost "relics," for they were both published before *Rolling Stone* achieved dominance in rock criticism. The books are entitled *The Age of Rock* and *The Age of Rock 2;* published in 1969 and 1970, their titles are (perhaps surprisingly) still appropriate.

Some of the most revealing and readable books about the record industry are those written by "insiders," industry people, usually with the help of professional writers. A perfect example of this genre is *Clive; Inside the Record Business,* by the ex-director of Columbia Records, Clive Davis (with the help of James Willwerth). The career of Clive Davis is fascinating not just because of the performing stars he discovered, nurtured, and/or helped popularize (for example, Janis Joplin, Bob Dylan) but because of what his own quick rise from lawyer to media mogul reveals about the industry's motives and priorities. Davis's even quicker fall from power—he lost his title, job, office, and limousine in less than an hour—makes for an unforgettable and controversial climax to the book, although Davis has since returned to the profession as head of his own successful record company.

Dick Clark's version of his career, *Rock, Roll & Remember,* should be read in conjunction with works more critical of his intentions and accomplishments, such as Chapple's and Garofalo's *Rock 'n' Roll Is Here to Pay.* The balanced picture perhaps best explains how someone can remain both boyish and successful in such a high-pressured, trendy business for a total of four decades—so far. Of particular interest in Clark's work are the chapters concerning his testimony before Congress in the payola scandal. Somehow, Clark managed to confess to building an intricate, self-serving web of holdings in the music industry and at the same time be declared a fine example of American ideals, while others less fortunate saw their careers destroyed.

Another major figure in the record industry with a recently published autobiography is John Hammond, author of *John Hammond on Record.* Hammond's claim to fame as an industry executive has been his uncanny knack for discovering and nurturing, at early stages in their careers, top recording stars and performers, artists ranging from Billie Holiday to Bob Dylan. Hammond's book focuses more on jazz than any other style of music, reflecting the focus of his career as an "a&r" ("artists and repertoire") executive and record producer. Another autobiography that deals mainly with the jazz world is Dave Dexter's *Playback.* Dexter, a prominent figure in the radio industry, relates his colorful, celebrity-studded career as a disc jockey and jazz promoter. One of the more controversial autobiographies published in recent years has been *Nothing Personal: Reliving Rock in the Sixties,* written by Al Kooper and Ben Edmunds. Kooper is best known as a rock "sideman," having backed up performers ranging from Gary Lewis and the Playboys to (once again) Bob Dylan. Kooper, who also helped found the jazz-rock group Blood, Sweat, and Tears, aroused critics and fellow musicians with his autobiography, which is far more candid and less ingratiating than most books of this genre.

Al Kooper's autobiography is also unusual in that, as a contemporary rock performer, he remains one of the few to have already written his memoirs. Perhaps the practice will become widespread within a decade or so, but, in the meantime, the best resource for the researcher interested in the personal reflections of rock artists is a two-volume set of interviews, once again culled by the *Rolling Stone* staff from the pages of the magazine: *The Rolling Stone Interviews,* and *The Rolling Stone Interviews, Vol. 2.*

Related to the "insider" genre of record industry writings is the "inside" book written by an "outsider," a professional author purporting to reveal some aspect of the industry's workings. A number of these books can be considered relatively "light," such as Mike Jahn's *How to Make a Hit Record* and Sharon Lawrence's *So You Want to Be a Rock & Roll Star,* aimed and best suited for the teenage market. But other "inside" works serve as excellent resources—well written, well researched, and usually full of colorful incidents and details. *Making Tracks: Atlantic Records and the Growth of a Multi-Billion Dollar Industry,* by Charlie Gillett, focuses on just one record company, Atlantic (once an independent, now under the Warner corporate umbrella), but that company pioneered rhythm and blues and has always featured trend-setting and colorful performers and other personnel. Two additional recommended works also focus on a single important record company: Colin Escott's and Martin Hawkins's *Catalyst,* an aptly titled study of Sun Records, the small Memphis operation that brought the world Elvis Presley, Carl Perkins, Jerry Lee Lewis, and Johnny Cash, and David Morse's *Motown and the Arrival of Black Music,* exploring America's only black-owned and black-operated record company.

Several important works approach the record industry from the perspective of the performer or group under contract, with a style more new journalistic than biographical. Bob Greene explores the bizarre world of the rock group Alice Cooper in *Billion Dollar Baby,* going so far as actually to participate as a member of the performing stage show (he was assaulted nightly while wearing a Santa Claus costume). David Walley's choice of subject matter is no less bizarre in *No Commercial Potential; The Saga of Frank Zappa and the Mothers of Invention.* In *S.T.P.: A Journey Through America With the Rolling Stones,* Robert Greenfield narrows the focus even further: studying not just a single group but that group on a single tour of U.S. cities.

One of the most interesting works within this genre focuses, unlike the others, on a group that never quite made it to the upper levels of music stardom, Commander Cody & His Lost Planet Airmen, a rock/country/Western-swing band of the 1970s. The book, Geoffrey Stokes's *Starmaking Machinery,* gives a good sense of all the costs, both personal and financial, entailed in the quest for success in the record industry. Two other works that deal with overwhelming personal and financial costs focus on perhaps the most successful recording group of all time, the Beatles: Richard DiLello's *The Longest Cocktail Party* and *Apple to the Core,* by Peter McCabe and D. R. Schonfeld. Both works chronicle the amazing speed and complications involved in the late 1960s' personal breakup and financial collapse of the group that seemed destined to survive at least a whole generation.

The Beatles, as can be expected, have generated a number of works, most of which can be classified as biographies, and some of those relatively superficial. Besides the two mentioned above, other noteworthy Beatles books include the "authorized" biography, Hunter Davies's *The Beatles;* an exhaustive collection of memorabilia entitled *The Beatles Forever,* by Nicholas Schaffner; and a collection of interviews with the group's most outspoken and controversial member, Jann Wenner's *Lennon Remembers,* from the pages of *Rolling Stone.* Perhaps second only to the Beatles in number of biographical studies is Elvis Presley, or, as Paul Lichter describes him in the title of his extensive study, *The Boy Who Dared to Rock: The Definitive Elvis.* Up until his death, the definitive Presley biography was Jerry Hopkins's *Elvis; A Biography,* written earlier in the 1970s. With the seamier sides of his personal life beginning to emerge as the shock of his sudden death wears off, doubtless many new studies will emerge as well, although all will suffer from the same handicap: trying to fathom someone who became so public he felt compelled to make most of his life as private as possible. Thus, unfortunately, we can expect no "Presley Remembers" from this fascinating American who, in "daring to rock," brought recorded music and popular culture in general into a new era.

Several noteworthy biographies have been written about other rock stars who died in the midst of their careers. John Goldrosen has contributed a thoroughly researched study of the life of Buddy Holly, the pioneering rock-and-roll star of the 1950s. The recent film biography of Holly was based ever so loosely on Goldrosen's book, which is entitled *Buddy Holly: His Life and Music.* Chris Welch's *Hendrix: A Biography* deals with the life and career of the late-1960s superstar, guitarist Jimi Hendrix, while *Buried Alive* is Myra Friedman's chronicle of the equally tragic life of rock vocalist Janis Joplin. On the other hand, rock music's most famous producer, Phil Spector, is alive and well and the subject of an excellent biography/"insider" work: *Out of His Head: The Sound of Phil Spector* by Richard Williams.

Ray Charles, the acknowledged "genius" of soul music, is also alive and well and has so far inspired two biographical works, Sharon Bell Mathis's *Ray Charles* and *Brother Ray,* by Ray Charles himself, with the assistance of David Ritz. Both works are a bit better than the average paperback biography, which is often written for the high school market and borders on the edge of public relations material. Also above average is Dave Marsh's recent work on the life and career of one of the recording industry's newest superstars, Bruce Springsteen, a white vocalist in the R&B tradition; the biography is entitled *Born to Run.*

That same black rhythm-and-blues tradition has not only inspired scores of white performing careers, it has also inspired a number of fine critical works. Perhaps the best in the field is Charlie Gillett's *The Sound of the City,* an extensive historical and sociological study of the development, production, and spread of the music that gave us (or perhaps *is*) rock and roll. Even more sociological is Charles Keil's *Urban Blues,* which examines the value systems and cultural practices behind the music, as well as the music itself and some of its leading performers, such as Bobby Bland and B. B. King. A book that deals more with the recordings and performers themselves is Lynn E. McCutcheon's *Rhythm and Blues,* an excellent source of discographical information on this style of music.

One of the most prolific and important writers in the whole field of popular music is Arnold Shaw, whose works manage to bridge the gap between the academic resource text and the mass-market paperback. Two of Shaw's best works deal with black music: *The World of Soul: Black America's Contribution to the Pop Music Scene* and the recently published *Honkers and Shouters: The Golden Years of Rhythm and Blues.* (Shaw has also contributed perhaps the most outstanding study of popular music and the record industry in the 1950s, the decade that became a turning point in the history of recorded music; Shaw's book is entitled *The Rockin' Fifties.*) Another of the best writers in the field, also contributing a major work that focuses on R&B, is rock critic Robert Palmer, a regular contributor to the *New York Times.* Palmer's book, *Baby, That Was Rock & Roll: The Legendary Lieber and Stoller* tells the story of the R&B songwriting and producing duo Jerry Lieber and Mike Stoller, two white men who helped create some of the freshest, most memorable records of the 1950s, including "Yakety Yak" and "Jailhouse Rock." Two other noteworthy books also deal with the lives and careers of white recording artists who chose to follow the black R&B style: Edward K. Engel's *White and Still All Right* and Philip Groia's *They All Sang on the Corner: New York City's Rhythm & Blues Vocal Groups of the 1950's.* Both works focus on the "doo-wop" singers and groups, vocal harmonists whose style took its name from the repeated phrase someone in the background would invariably be singing.

Other styles of recorded music that have inspired numerous critical works include "swing" or "big band" music, with the current leading critical study being Albert McCarthy's *Big Band Jazz,* and country music, which has produced a number of excellent books. The most authoritative study is probably Bill Malone's *Country Music USA,* closely followed by the previous mentioned *Encyclopedia of Country & Western Music* by L. Brown and G. Fredrich and Nick Tosches's *Country: The Biggest Music in America.* Two noteworthy books deal with fascinating subdivisions of the country music industry: Charles R. Townsend's *San Antonio Rose: The Life and Music of Bob Wills,* focusing on "Western swing" (a combination of country and big band music that helped spawn rock and roll), and Michael Bane's *The Outlaws: Revolution in Country Music,* a relatively new book that explores the Waylon Jennings-Willie Nelson world of progressive country.

Although disco music accounted for a large percentage of the record industry's business during the late-1970s, no one has yet contributed a noteworthy study of the disco industry, its recordings, or performers. On the other hand, it took Latin music almost a century of influencing American popular recordings before it managed to inspire a critical study: John Storm Roberts' *The Latin Tinge: The Impact of Latin American Music on the United States,* published in 1979. Roberts is another example of the exceptional writer in this field who has made a point of studying black and black-influenced styles. His new book on Latin music (which gave us the rhumba, samba, tango, mambo, cha-cha, bugaloo, bamba, and even the hustle) will likely remain the definitive work on the subject, but perhaps it won't be another century before the next one is written. And, although it may be far too early to tell, it's likely that Caroline Coon's *1988: The New Wave Punk Rock Explosion* will someday lose its status as the definitive (and lone) work on what may be the emerging style of the 1980s.

Final recognition must be given to a pair of young writers whose works belong to no particular category and, perhaps for that reason, come closest to achieving what the best records themselves do: transcend all the history, technology, and commercialism to reach some powerful, culturally significant emotional level. The writers are Greil Marcus, author of *Mystery Train: Images of America in Rock 'n' Roll Music,* and Michael Lydon, author of *Rock Folk: Portraits from the Rock 'n' Roll Pantheon* and *Boogie Lightning.* Their writings have little in common other than their avoidance of what most authors in this field dwell on and their focus instead on recorded music as both a cultural product and a personal experience. For that reason, and not because their books are excellent sources of information, they've both contributed significantly to our understanding of recorded music. For it may be that, in the long run, those approaches which explore the range of human experiences involved in this medium, from performing to listening, will best explain why recordings have the power to reach so deeply inside us.

NOTES

1. Roland Gelatt, *The Fabulous Phonograph—1877-1977* (New York: Collier, 1977), p. 29.
2. Gelatt, p. 36.

BIBLIOGRAPHY

BOOKS

Albertson, Chris. *Bessie.* New York: Stein & Day, 1972.

Armitage, Andrew D., and Dean Tudor. *Annual Index to Popular Music Record Reviews.* Metuchen, N.J.: Scarecrow Press, 1972-77.

Baggelaar, Kristin, and Donald Milton. *Folk Music: More Than a Song.* New York: Crowell, 1976.

Bane, Michael. *The Outlaws: Revolution in Country Music.* New York: Doubleday/Dolphin, 1978.

Benjaminson, Peter. *The Story of Motown.* New York: Grove Press, 1979.

Berman, Jay. *The Fifties Book.* New York: Berkley Medallion, 1974.

Berry, Peter E. "*...And the Hits Just Keep on Comin'.*" Syracuse, N.Y.: Syracuse University Press, 1977.

Billboard. *Music/Records/200.* New York: Billboard, 1976.
Broadcast Music, Incorporated. *Pop Hits: 1940-1966.* New York: BMI, 1967.
______.*Rhythm and Blues.* New York: BMI, 1969.
Brown, L., and G. Fredrich. *Encyclopedia of Country & Western Music.* New York: Tower Books, 1971.
Carr, Roy. *The Rolling Stones: An Illustrated Record.* New York: Harmony Books, 1976.
Carr, Roy, and Steve Clarke. *Fleetwood Mac: Rumours N'Fax.* New York: Harmony Books, 1978.
Carr, Roy, and Tony Tyler. *The Beatles Illustrated Record.* New York: Harmony Books, 1975.
Cash, Johnny. *Man in Black.* Grand Rapids, Mich.: Londewar, 1975.
Chapple, Steve, and Reebee Garofalo. *Rock 'n' Roll Is Here to Pay.* Chicago: Nelson-Hall, 1978.
Charles, Ray, with David Ritz *Brother Ray.* New York: Dial Press, 1978.
Charters, Samuel. *The Bluesmen.* New York: Oak, 1967.
______. *Robert Johnson.* New York: Oak, 1973.
Christgau, Robert. *Any Old Way You Choose It.* Baltimore: Penguin Books, 1973.
Clark, Dick. *Rock, Roll & Remember.* New York: Crowell, 1976.
Coon, Caroline. *1988: The New Wave Punk Rock Explosion.* New York: Hawthorn Books, 1978.
Cooper, David Edwin. *International Bibliography of Discographies: Classical Music and Jazz & Blues.* Littleton, Colo.: Libraries Unlimited, 1975.
Dalton, David, and Lenny Kaye. *Rock 100.* New York: Grosset & Dunlap, 1977.
Davies, Hunter. *The Beatles.* New York: McGraw-Hill, 1965.
Davis, Clive. *Clive: Inside the Record Business.* New York: Morrow, 1975.
Denisoff, R. Serge. *Solid Gold.* New Brunswick, N.J.: Transaction Books, 1975.
______, and Richard A. Peterson, eds. *The Sounds of Social Change.* Chicago: Rand McNally, 1972.
Dexter, Dave. *The Jazz Story.* Englewood Cliffs, N.J.: Prentice-Hall, 1964.
______. *Playback.* New York: Billboard, 1976.
DiLello, Richard. *The Longest Cocktail Party.* Chicago: Playboy Press, 1972.
Dimmick, Mary Laverne. *The Rolling Stones: An Annotated Bibliography.* Pittsburgh: University of Pittsburgh Press, 1979.
Dixon, Robert M. W., and John Godrich. *Recording the Blues.* New York: Stein & Day, 1970.
Edwards, Joe, *Top 10's and Trivia of Rock & Roll and Rhythm & Blues: 1950-1973.* St. Louis: Blueberry Hill, 1974.
Eisen, Jonathan, ed. *The Age of Rock.* New York: Vintage Books, 1969.
______. *The Age of Rock 2.* New York: Vintage Books, 1970.
Ellington, Edward Kennedy. *Music Is My Mistress.* New York: Doubleday, 1973.
Engel, Edward K. *White and Still All Right.* N.p.: Crackerjack Press, 1977.
Engel, Lyle K. *Popular Record Directory.* New York: Fawcett, 1958.
Epstein, Brian. *A Cellarful of Noise.* New York: Doubleday, 1964.
Escott, Colin, and Martin Hawkins. *Catalyst.* London: Aquarius Books, 1975.
Ewen, David. *History of Popular Music.* New York: Barnes and Noble, 1961.

Feather, Leonard. *Encyclopedia of Jazz* New York: Bonanza Books, 1960.
The Fifty Year Story of RCA Records. New York: Radio Corporation of America, 1953.
Fong-Torres, Ben, ed. *The Rolling Stone Rock 'n' Roll Reader.* New York: Bantam Books, 1974.
______. *What's That Sound?* New York: Anchor Press, 1976.
Friedman, Myra. *Buried Alive.* New York: Bantam, 1974.
Gelatt, Roland. *The Fabulous Phonograph—1877-1977.* New York: Collier, 1977.
Gibb, Barry, Robin Gibb, Maurice Gibb, and David Leaf. *BeeGees: The Authorized Biography.* New York: Dell, 1979.
Gillett, Charlie. *Making Tracks: Atlantic Records and the Growth of a Multi-Billion Dollar Industry.* New York: Dutton, 1974.
______. *The Sound of the City.* New York: Outerbridge and Dientsfrey, 1972.
Godrich, John, and Robert M. W. Dixon. *Blues and Gospel Records.* London: Storyville, 1969.
Goldrosen, John. *Buddy Holly: His Life and Music.* Bowling Green, Ohio: Popular Press, 1975.
Goldstein, Richard. *Goldstein's Greatest Hits.* Englewood Cliffs, N.J.: Prentice-Hall, 1970.
The Grammy Awards Book. Hollywood: National Academy of Recording Arts and Sciences, 1978.
Greene, Bob. *Billion Dollar Baby.* New York: Signet, 1975.
Greenfield, Robert. *S.T.P.: A Journey Through America with the Rolling Stones.* New York: Dutton, 1974.
Grissim, John. *Country Music: White Man's Blues.* New York: Paperback Library, 1970.
Groia, Philip. *They All Sang on the Corner: New York City's Rhythm & Blues Vocal Groups of the 1950's.* New York: Edmund, 1973.
Guralnick, Peter. *Feel Like Going Home.* New York: Dutton, 1971.
Hammond, John. *John Hammond on Record.* New York: Ridge Press, 1977.
Harry, Bill, ed. *Mersey Beat: The Beginning of the Beatles.* London: Omnibus, 1977.
Heckman, Don. "Five Decades of Rhythm and Blues." In *BMI: The Many Worlds of Music.* New York: Broadcast Music, 1969.
Hemphill, Paul. *The Nashville Sound: Bright Lights and Country Music.* New York: Simon & Schuster, 1970.
Hirsch, Paul. *The Structure of the Popular Music Industry.* Ann Arbor: University of Michigan Press, 1969.
Holiday, Billie, and William Duffy. *Lady Sings the Blues.* New York: Doubleday, 1956.
Hoover, Cynthia A. *Music Machines—American Style.* Washington, D.C.: Smithsonian Institution Press, 1975.
Hopkins, Jerry. *Elvis: A Biography.* New York: Simon & Schuster, 1975.
______. *Festival.* New York: Macmillan, 1971.
Horstman, Dorothy. *Sing Your Heart Out, Country Boy.* New York: Dutton, 1975.
Hurst, Walter E. *The Music Industry Book: How to Make Money in the Music Industry.* Hollywood, Calif.: Seven Arts Press, 1963.

Jahn, Mike. *How to Make a Hit Record.* Scarsdale, N.Y.: Bradbury Press, 1976.
———. *Rock: From Elvis Presley to the Rolling Stones.* New York: Quadrangle, 1973.
Jasper, Tony. *Paul McCartney and Wings.* Secaucus, N.J.: Chartwell, 1977.
Jones, LeRoi. *Black Music.* New York: Morrow, 1967.
Karshner, Roger. *The Music Machine.* Los Angeles: Nash, 1971.
Kaufman, Murry. *Murry the K Tells It Like It Is, Baby.* New York: Holt, Rinehart and Winston, 1966.
Keil, Charles. *Urban Blues.* Chicago: University of Chicago Press, 1970.
Kimball, Robert, and William Bolcom. *Reminiscing with Sissle and Blake.* New York: Viking, 1973.
Kinkel, Roger D. *The Complete Encyclopedia of Popular Music and Jazz: 1900-1950.* 4 vols. New Rochelle, N.Y.: Arlington House, 1974.
Koenigsberg, Allen. *Edison Cylinder Records: 1889-1912.* New York: Stellar Productions, 1969.
Kooper, Al, and Ben Edmunds. *Nothing Personal: Reliving Rock in the Sixties.* New York: Stein & Day, 1975.
Krivine, J. *Juke Box Saturday Night.* Secaucus, N.J.: Chartwell, 1977.
Laing, Dave. *The Sound of Our Time.* Chicago: Quadrangle Books, 1969.
Landau, Jon. *It's Too Late to Stop Now: A Rock and Roll Journal.* San Francisco: Straight Arrow Books, 1972.
Lawrence, Sharon. *So You Want to Be a Rock & Roll Star.* New York: Dell, 1976.
Leadbitter, Mike, and Neil Slaven. *Blues Records, 1943-1966.* New York: Oak, 1968.
Leaf, David. *The Beach Boys and the California Myth.* New York: Grosset & Dunlap, 1978.
Leonard, Neil. *Jazz and the White Americans.* Chicago: University of Chicago Press, 1962.
Lichter, Paul. *The Boy Who Dared to Rock: The Definitive Elvis.* Garden City, N.Y.: Doubleday, 1978.
Logan, Nick, and Bob Woffinden. *Illustrated Encyclopedia of Rock.* New York: Harmony, 1977.
Lydon, Michael. *Boogie Lightning.* New York: Dial, 1974.
———. *Rock Folk: Portraits from the Rock 'n' Roll Pantheon.* New York: Dial Press, 1971.
McCabe, Peter, and D. R. Schonfeld. *Apple to the Core.* New York: Pocket Books, 1972.
McCarthy, Albert. *Big Band Jazz.* New York: Berkley, 1977.
McCutcheon, Lynn E. *Rhythm and Blues.* Arlington, Va.: Beatty, 1971.
Malone, Bill. *Country Music USA.* Austin: University of Texas Press, 1974.
Marcus, Greil. *Mystery Train: Images of America in Rock 'n' Roll Music.* New York: Dutton, 1974.
———, ed. *Rock and Roll Will Stand.* Boston: Beacon, 1969.
———. *Stranded: Rock and Roll for a Desert Island.* New York: Knopf, 1979.
Marsh, Dave. *Born to Run.* New York: Hawthorn, 1979.
———, ed. *The Rolling Stone Record Book.* New York: Random House/Rolling Stone Press, 1979.

Mathis, Sharon Bell. *Ray Charles.* New York: Crowell, 1973.

Mattfield, Julius. *Variety Music Cavalcade.* Englewood Cliffs, N.J.: Prentice-Hall, 1964.

Millar, Bill. *The Drifters: The Rise and Fall of the Black Vocal Group.* London: Studio Vista, 1971.

Miller, Jim, ed. *The Rolling Stone Illustrated History of Rock 'n' Roll.* New York: Random House, 1976.

Moore, Jerrold Northrop. *A Matter of Records.* New York: Taplinger, 1976.

Morse, David. *Motown and the Arrival of Black Music.* New York: Macmillan, 1971.

The Music Industry: Markets and Methods for the Seventies. New York: Billboard, 1970.

Nassour, Ellis, and Richard Broderick. *Rock Opera: The Creation of Jesus Christ Superstar from Record Album to Broadway Show to Motion Picture.* New York: Hawthorn Books, 1973.

Nugent, Stephen, and Charlie Gillett. *Rock Almanac.* Garden City, N.Y.: Doubleday, 1978.

Oliver, Paul. *The Story of the Blues.* New York: Chilton Book, 1969.

Orloff, Katherine. *Rock 'n' Roll Lady.* Freeport, N.Y.: Nash, 1974.

Osbourne, Jerry. *Record Album Price Guide.* Phoenix, Ariz.: O'Sullivan, Woodside, 1977.

______. *Record Collector's Price Guide.* Phoenix, Ariz.: O'Sullivan, Woodside, 1976.

Palmer, Robert. *Baby, That Was Rock &Roll: The Legendary Lieber & Stoller.* New York: Harcourt Brace Jovanovich, 1978.

Palmer, Tony. *All You Need Is Love: The Story of Popular Music.* New York: Grossman, 1976.

Passman, Arnold. *The Deejays.* New York: Macmillan, 1971.

Pleasants, Henry. *Serious Music and All That Jazz.* New York: Simon & Schuster, 1969.

Podrazik, Walter J., and Harry Castleman. *All Together Now: The First Complete Beatles Discography: 1961-1975.* Ann Arbor, Mich.: Pierian Press, 1975.

______. *The Beatles Again?* Ann Arbor, Mich.: Pierian Press, 1977.

Propes, Steve. *Golden Goodies.* Radnor, Penn.: Chilton Book, 1975.

______. *Golden Oldies: A Guide to 60's Record Collecting.* Radnor, Penn.: Chilton Book, 1974.

______. *Those Oldies But Goodies: A Guide to 50's Record Collecting.* New York: Collier Books, 1973.

Randle, Bill. *The American Popular Music Discography: 1920-30.* Bowling Green, Ohio: Popular Press, 1974.

Read, Oliver, and Walter L. Welch. *From Tin Foil to Stereo.* New York: Bobbs-Merrill, 1959.

Rhode, H. Kandy. *The Gold of Rock & Roll: 1955-1967.* New York: Arbor House, 1970.

Roberts, John Storm. *The Latin Tinge: The Impact of Latin American Music on the United States.* New York: Oxford University Press, 1979.

Robinson, Richard, ed. *Rock Revolution.* New York: Popular Library, 1976.

Rolling Stone. *The Rolling Stone Interviews.* New York: Paperback Library, 1971.

______. *The Rolling Stone Interviews, Vol. 2.* New York: Paperback Library, 1973.

———. *The Rolling Stone Reader.* New York: Warner Paperback Library, 1974.
———. *The Rolling Stone Record Review.* New York: Pocket Books, 1971.
Rooney, James. *Bossmen: Bill Monroe and Muddy Waters.* New York: Dial, 1971.
Rowe, Mike. *Chicago Breakdown.* New York: Drake, 1975.
Roxon, Lillian, ed. *Lillian Roxon's Rock Encyclopedia.* New York: Grosset & Dunlap, 1969.
Rublowsky, John. *Popular Music.* New York: Basic Books, 1967.
Russcol, Herbert. *The Liberation of Sound.* Englewood, N.J.: Prentice-Hall, 1972.
Rust, Brian. *Discography of Historical Records on Cylinders and 78s.* Westport, Conn: Greenwood Press, 1979.
Scaduto, Tony. *Mick Jagger: Everybody's Lucifer.* New York: Berkley Medallion, 1975.
Schaffner, Nicholas. *The Beatles Forever.* Harrisburg, Penn.: Cameron House, 1977.
Schicke, C.A. *Revolution in Sound: A Biography of the Recording Industry.* Boston: Little, Brown, 1974.
Shapiro, Nat, ed. *Popular Music: An Annotated Index of American Popular Songs.* New York: Adrian Press, 1964.
Shaw, Arnold. *Honkers and Shouters: The Golden Years of Rhythm and Blues.* New York: Macmillan, 1978.
———. *The Rockin' Fifties:* New York: Macmillan, 1974.
———. *Sinatra.* New York: W.H. Allen, 1968.
———. *The World of Soul: Black America's Contribution to the Pop Music Scene.* New York: Cowles Book, 1970.
Shemel, Sidney, and M. William Krasilovsky. *This Business of Music.* New York: Billboard, 1971.
Spitz, Robert Stephen. *The Making of Superstars: Artists and Executives of the Rock Music Business.* Garden City, N.Y.: Anchor Press, 1978.
Stewart-Baxter, Derrick. *Ma Rainey and the Classic Blues Singers.* New York: Stein & Day, 1970.
Stokes, Geoffrey. *Starmaking Machinery.* New York: Vintage Books, 1977.
Taylor, Derek. *As Time Goes By.* San Francisco: Straight Arrow Books, 1973.
Tosches, Nick, *Country: The Biggest Music in America.* New York: Stein & Day, 1977.
Townsend, Charles R. *San Antonio Rose: The Life and Music of Bob Wills.* Urbana: University of Illinois Press, 1976.
Ulanov, Barry. *Handbook of Jazz.* New York: Viking Press, 1960.
Vassal, Jacques. *Electric Children: Roots and Branches of Modern Folkrock.* New York: Taplinger, 1975.
Walley, David. *No Commercial Potential: The Saga of Frank Zappa and the Mothers of Invention.* New York: Outerbridge, 1972.
Welch, Chris. *Hendrix: A Biography.* New York: Flash Books, 1973.
Wenner, Jann. *Lennon Remembers.* San Francisco: Straight Arrow Books, 1971.
Whitburn, Joel. *Top Pop Records: 1940-1955.* Menomee Falls, Wisc.: Record Research, 1973.
———. *Top Pop Records: 1955-1973.* Menomee Falls, Wisc.: Record Research, 1973.

______. *Top Rhythm & Blues Records: 1949-1971.* Menomee Falls, Wisc.: Record Research, 1973.

Whitcomb, Ian. *After the Ball: Pop Music from Rag to Rock.* New York: Simon & Schuster, 1972.

Williams, Allan, and William Marshall. *The Man Who Gave the Beatles Away.* New York: Macmillan, 1975.

Williams, Richard. *Out of His Head: The Sound of Phil Spector.* New York: Outerbridge and Lazard, 1972.

Young, Jean, and Jim Young. *Succeeding in the Big World of Music.* Boston: Little, Brown, 1977.

PERIODICALS

American Record Guide. Melville, N.Y., 1976-.

Billboard. New York, 1894-.

Black Music. London, 1974-.

Bluegrass Unlimited. Broad Run, Va., 1966-.

Blues Unlimited. London, 1963-.

Cadence. Redwood, N.Y., 1976-.

Cashbox. New York, 1942-.

Circus. New York, 1966-.

Coda. Toronto, 1958-.

Country Music. New York, 1972-.

Country Style. Franklin Park, Ill., 1976-.

Creem. Birmingham, Mich., 1969-.

Downbeat. Chicago, 1934-.

High Fidelity. Marion, Ohio, 1951-.

Jazz Forum. New York, 1967-.

Jazz Magazine. Northport, N.Y., 1976-.

John Edwards Memorial Foundation Quarterly. Los Angeles, 1963.

Journal of Country Music. Nashville, Tenn., 1970-.

Journal of Jazz Studies. New Brunswick, N.J., 1973-.

Living Blues. Chicago, 1970-.

Modern Recording. New York, 1973-.

Paul's Record Magazine. Hartford, Conn., 1975-.

Popular Music and Society. Bowling Green, Ohio, 1971-.

Record Exchanger. Anaheim, Calif., 1969-.

Record Research. Brooklyn, N.Y., 1955-.

Record World. New York, 1964-.

Rolling Stone. New York, 1968-.

Storyville. Essex, England, 1965-.

Time Barrier Express. White Plains, N.Y., 1974-.

Variety. New York, 1905-.

Who Put the Bomp. Burbank, Calif., 1974-.

CHAPTER 15 Regionalism in Popular Culture

Anne Rowe

Although regionalism in literature and the arts has long been the subject of numerous studies by scholars and critics, only in the last decade has any attention been given to regionalism as it relates to popular culture. A survey of the handbooks and anthologies of popular culture reveals relatively little material concerned with regionalism. Similarly, papers presented at sections on regionalism at meetings of the Popular Culture Association generally have treated individual writers of a particular region rather than focusing on regionalism as a force. Recently, a number of articles on popular culture and regionalism have appeared, but formal theories concerning regionalism in popular culture have yet to be developed.

The chief thrust of this essay, then, is to survey the studies that have been made of regionalism and to define where these studies have intersected with those of popular culture. A recent work that treats regionalism as it relates to popular culture is Jack Temple Kirby's *Media-Made Dixie; The South in the American Imagination,* an exploration of the image of the South as it has been created and presented in the popular media. Kirby's book points the way to future studies to be undertaken in regionalism in popular culture.

HISTORIC OUTLINE

Although an awareness of regions or sections has existed in America from the Colonial period to the present, regionalism in literature and the arts generally refers to two periods: the local color period of the late-nineteenth century and regionalism of the 1930s and after.

The beginning of the local color movement is usually cited as 1868, when Bret Harte began publishing stories of California mining camps in the *Overland Monthly.* Many provincial sketches and stories appeared in large-circulation magazines during the 1870s, and the local color vogue reached its height during the 1880s and 1890s, tapering off near the end of the century.

Only after the end of the Civil War, when it became clear that the battle for nationalism had been won, was there a dramatic growth of interest in the many sectional differences of the United States. Local color writing, which emphasized the unique setting of a particular region and reproduced the dialect, customs, provincial types, and other qualities of that region, seemed to satisfy the desire of the American people to take a nostalgic look at the good old days of the preindustrialized, prewar period. Thus, much local color writing was rural-based but intended for city consumption. Local color writing grew out of every region, and representative local colorists included Mary E. Wilkins Freeman and Sarah Orne Jewett of New England, Bret Harte of the West, and George Washington Cable and Thomas Nelson Page of the South. After the fall of the Confederacy there was much national interest in and curiosity about the South, and Southern local colorists were heavily represented in nationally circulated magazines.

Local color writing usually appeared as short stories. Plots were highly contrived and characterization was generally superficial, characters usually not transcending the stereotype. Because of these limitations, local color writing of this period is looked upon today as having been more a popular than an artistic success.

In contrast to the term *local color, regionalism* refers to an intellectual movement of the 1930s which posited that each of the regions of the United States is a geographical, cultural, and economic entity. This new concept of regionalism, which was as much sociological as literary, was apparent particularly in the South. The publication of *I'll Take My Stand: The South and the Agrarian Tradition* by Twelve Southerners in 1930 expressed the desire of its authors to resist standardization and to preserve, as far as possible, an agrarian-based culture. Although the Agrarians, as they were called, including John Crowe Ransom, Robert Penn Warren, Donald Davidson, Allen Tate, and others, did not believe that the South could remain an entirely agricultural society, they argued for a set of values that supported a human rather than machine-dominated society.

During the 1930s a number of works appeared which explored the relationship of the regions to the literary and social culture of America. Carey McWilliams, *The New Regionalism in American Literature,* was an early attempt at defining regionalism. *The Attack on Leviathan: Regionalism and Nationalism in the United States* by Donald Davidson posited an agrarian point of view. *American Regionalism: A Cultural-Historical Approach to National Integration* by Howard W. Odum and Harry Estill Moore argued for an integration of cultural, geographical, and historical factors.

One of the most important literary movements related to regionalism in the 1930s was the Southern Renaissance, out of which came the work of William Faulkner, Thomas Wolfe, Robert Penn Warren, and others. In novels, short stories, poetry, and essays, the literary productivity of the South loomed great. Other major writers of the 1930s, Willa Cather and John Steinbeck, for example, also employed a regional base for their works. The important distinction to be made, then, between local color and regionalism is that the latter brought much more breadth and depth to the depiction of a cultural region.

Regionalism as a cultural force has continued to receive attention since the 1930s. For some artists and critics regionalism has a pejorative connotation; it implies limitation. Regionalism, it is argued, must necessarily limit the universal message of the work of art. Proponents of regionalism argue, perhaps more convincingly, that all art must come out of a particular region or culture. That it does so in no way limits its universal statement. For example, although most of Faulkner's work is set in Mississippi, its meaning extends far beyond the boundaries of that state.

Most recently regionalism has aroused the interests of students of popular culture. Although the development of a formal theory concerning regionalism in popular culture is only in the beginning stages, a number of explorations of the relationship between a region and its culture have been undertaken. A challenging aspect of this study is the fact that with the increasing standardization of the media—television shows that are broadcast nationally, top ten radio programming, films that are released simultaneously in all parts of the country—the question of how many regional distinctions will continue to exist during the remaining decades of this century becomes especially important.

REFERENCE WORKS

Although many works provide bibliographical information on regional writings and a number of general guides to popular culture are available, there is very little in the way of reference material devoted specifically to regionalism in popular culture. Standard sources for critical material dealing with earlier regional studies are two volumes compiled by Lewis Leary, *Articles on American Literature, 1900-1950* and *Articles on American Literature, 1950-1967.* Both volumes have special sections on regionalism which provide an invaluable listing of the articles pertaining to regionalism. Another standard research tool is Robert E. Spiller, Willard Thorp, and Thomas H. Johnson, *The Literary History of the United States,* which contains chapters on the various sections of the United States as well as extensive bibliographical material on regionalism, including general studies, New England, New York to Delaware, the South and the Deep South, the Midwest, the Southwest, the Pacific Northwest, and California and the Far West. Other useful bibliographical works on regionalism, although limited to the

South, are Louis D. Rubin, Jr., *A Bibliographical Guide to the Study of Southern Literature* and the volume that updates it, *Southern Literature, 1968-1975: A Checklist of Scholarship,* edited by Jerry T. Williams. *Abstracts of Popular Culture,* which scans over nine hundred magazines, is a major research tool for locating recently published articles on regionalism in popular culture.

RESEARCH COLLECTIONS

The description of research collections that follows must of necessity be eclectic because no comprehensive index to library holdings in popular culture is available. Much of the material cited here includes manuscript holdings of regional materials, only a portion of which pertain to popular culture as such.

Volume 6 of the Popular Culture Association *Newsletter,* edited by Michael T. Marsden, contains a compilation of popular culture holdings of various sizes related to regionalism. A representative listing follows. The Oral History Collection at Brookens Library in Springfield, Illinois, emphasizes regional history of Springfield and Central Illinois. Lees Junior College Library, Jackson, Kentucky, has an Appalachian Oral History Project which includes six hundred taped interviews with mountain residents. Louisiana State University Library, Baton Rouge, has a collection of Acadian folk material and folk music. Northern Arizona University Library, Flagstaff, has a collection of Western pulp novels and Western pulp magazines. Northern Arizona University English Department has original tape recordings of Southwestern folksongs and ballads.

One of the most extensive collections of Western Americana is found in the Bancroft Library of the University of California at Berkeley. The collection includes manuscripts assembled by Hubert Howe Bancroft which center on the history of California and Mexico. Also contained in the Bancroft Library are regional oral history materials including "personal reminiscences of Northern Californians who have made significant contributions to the cultural, economic, intellectual, and social life of the West, particularly the San Francisco Bay region." Norlin Library of the University of Colorado at Boulder has published Ellen Arguimbau's *A Guide to Manuscript Collections: Western Historical Collections,* which describes the 480 individual collections of materials relating to Western culture.

The Subject Directory of Special Libraries and Information Centers, edited by Margaret Labash Young, Harold Chester Young, and Anthony T. Kruzas, provides listings of many collections which relate, in part at least, to regionalism in popular culture. For example, Beik Library, Appalachian State University, Boone, North Carolina, has an Appalachian Regional Collection (music library). The Sam Houston State University Library, Huntsville, Texas, has a collection of ten thousand volumes of Texana and Confederate materials. The Indiana University Lilly Library, Bloomington, contains the Ellison Far West Collection. The Walter Havighurst Special Collections Library at Miami University, Oxford, Ohio, has 4,220 volumes pertaining to Ohio Valley history. Johnson Camden Library at Morehead State University, Morehead, Kentucky, holds a Kentucky Collection of 2,560 volumes. The library of the Pacific-Union Club, San Francisco, has a special collection of two thousand items of Californiana. The Special Collections Department of Rutgers University, New Brunswick, New Jersey, has a special collection of New Jerseyana. The Special Collections Department of the University of Arizona Library, Tuscon, contains collections of Southwest material. The Department of Special Collections in the University of California at Los Angeles Research Library contains a Southern California Regional Oral History Interviews Collection. The Special Collections Library of the University of Idaho, Moscow, has a collection of Pacific Northwest materials. The Kerlan Collection of the University of Minnesota Library, Minneapolis, includes a collection of Minnesota authors and settings. The Special Collections Department/University Archives of University of Nevada's Reno Library has a collection of material on Nevada and the West. The library of the University of Texas at El Paso contains several collections, the most prominent being the Sonnichsen Collection of Southwestern Literature and Fiction (1,200 books and papers), the McNeely Collection of Southwestern and Mexican works, and the Southern Pacific Collection (500 boxes). The Virginia Commonwealth University James Branch Cabell Library, Richmond, has a collection of contemporary Virginia authors. The Pacific Northwest Collection of the University of Washington, Seattle, has materials relating to the anthropology, history, economics, and social conditions of the Pacific Northwest, including Washington, Oregon, Idaho, western Montana, Yukon, British Columbia, and Alaska.

During the 1930s and 1940s, when regional writing was at its peak, Southern writers dominated the market. Listed below are some special collections of Southern regional materials listed in Thomas H. English, *Roads to Research: Distinguished Library Collections of the Southeast.* The Aldermann Library of the University of Virginia, Charlottesville, has a large collection of writings of Southern authors. The George W. Cable Collection of Tulane University includes more than twenty thousand items, among them letters, manuscripts, and typescripts. The Joel Chandler Harris Collection at Emory University is very large and includes an extensive manuscript collection. The Joint University Libraries at Vanderbilt University in Nashville, Tennessee, has a collection of the Fugitive Group. The University of Florida Library has the Marjorie Kinnan Rawlings Collection and a collection of Floridiana. The Southern Historical Collection at the University of North Carolina at Chapel Hill has over 3.6 million items which are private records pertaining to Southern culture and history. The George Washington Flowers Collection of Southern Americana at Duke University has over 2.5 million items covering the entire South for every period of its history. The Georgiana Collection in the University of Georgia Library at Athens provides a record of all phases of history and culture from the Colonial period to the present. In the Department of Archives and Manuscripts at the Louisiana State University Library are nearly 3 million items related to contemporary life in the Lower Mississippi Valley for the past two hundred years. The North Carolina Collection at the University of North Carolina at Chapel Hill has more than 200,000 items relating to every aspect of life in North Carolina. A collection of Tennesseana is held at the Manuscript Division of the Tennessee State Library and Archives.

Special Collections in Libraries of the Southeast, edited by J. B. Howell, cites a collection of five hundred cheap editions of fiction, "displayed for sale in railway bookstalls from the mid-19th century," in the Robert W. Woodruff Library at Emory University. Hutchins Library of Berea College at Berea, Kentucky, has a collection of "8,000 volumes and 250 linear feet of archival and manuscript materials relating to the history and culture of the Southern highlands." The collection includes books, pamphlets, manuscripts, photographs, tapes, and films. Another extensive collection is the Folk-lore, Folk-life and Oral History Archives at the Helm-Cravens Library of Western Kentucky University, Bowling Green. The Mississippi Department of Archives and History, Jackson, has a collection of Mississippiana including the Works Progress Administration Collection of material assembled by WPA workers on the history and culture of Mississippi. At the University of Mississippi Library in University is the Mississippi Collection, consisting of twenty thousand cataloged volumes as well as thousands of uncataloged items pertaining to the culture and history of the state. The Carol Grotnes Belk Library at Appalachian State University, Boone, North Carolina, contains the William Leonard Eury Appalachian Collection comprising over ten thousand volumes, clippings, slides, oral history tapes, original manuscripts, and four extensive collections of ballads. The Library and Media Center of the Country Music Foundation, Nashville, Tennessee, has "70,000 recordings, 2,500 tapes including 150 oral tapes, 2,500 volumes, 2,000 song books, 750 films, 6,000 photographs and extensive files of biographical sketches and newspaper clippings," making this collection "the largest ever assembled in the field of country music."

What is most obvious about the listing above is that it refers to large collections of regional material only a portion of which may constitute popular culture. The task of cataloging popular culture material in these and other collections has yet to be done.

HISTORY AND CRITICISM

The works treated below are arranged chronologically, and the majority of those focusing strictly on popular culture appear among the more recent critical works. The earlier works cited are important to the understanding of the concept of regionalism as it has influenced American life and art.

Provincial Types in American Fiction by Horace Spencer Fiske, published in 1903, is an early work describing various types of American provincial life as treated since the Civil War by writers in New England, the South, the Midwest, and the Far West. Fiske describes provincial types in fiction according to region, and there are separate introductory sections for each of the regions as well as explication and discussion of the stories by these authors.

Another early work, *The New Regionalism in American Literature* by Carey McWilliams, published in 1930, reflects the growing interest in regionalism. McWilliams provides useful discussions of early journals and collections of writings of the various regions. He concludes that regional writers are trying to create a sense of community through their work.

A seminal study of regionalism in many aspects—geographical, political, as well as cultural—is Howard W. Odum and Harry Estell Moore, *American Regionalism: A Cultural-Historical Approach to National Integration.* Odum and Moore find that "the older authentic literary regionalism stands in direct opposition to our premise of regionalism as a constituent part of the whole and as a tool for national integration of all parts of the nation." Part 1 traces the general rise and incidence in American regionalism; part 2 provides a theoretical-historical account from the perspective of the social sciences; and part 3 enumerates and describes each region. Important to our consideration here is the fact that Odum and Moore make a distinction between local color and regionalism. Local color they find to be a pejorative term, whereas regionalism has positive connotations. They also note, "Next to metropolitan regionalism and sectionalism the rise and characterization of American regionalism has perhaps been more often identified with literary regionalism than with anything else."

An important early statement about regionalism from a perspective very different from that of Odum and Moore is made by Donald Davidson in his collection of essays, *The Attack on Leviathan: Regionalism and Nationalism in the United States.* Davidson's premise is that in attacking Leviathan (the monolithic nationalism in writing) artists and others are "seeking...a definition of the terms on which America may have both the diversity and the unity that gives soundness to a tradition." In a chapter entitled "Regionalism in the Arts," Davidson argues that artistic regionalism "is like the regionalism of the social scientists in so far as it is a new attempt to meet an old problem....To one wing of American criticism regionalists seem to subscribe to some narrow and confining principle of art." Some regionalists on the other hand "are too ready to elevate the word *regional*...into a slogan and a panacea." In an essay entitled "Regionalism and Nationalism in American Literature," Davidson concludes, "The national literature is the compound of the regional impulses, not antithetical to them, but embracing them and living in them as the roots, branch, and flower of its being."

The Tennessee Valley Authority: A National Experiment in Regionalism by Clarence Lewis Hodge is a study of the significance of the Tennessee Valley Authority as a new regional unit in the field of government. Hodge's central premise is that "regionalism is a trend the importance of which has been inadequately recognized by students in the field of government." Although this work does not address regionalism in popular culture as such, it is important for stressing the concept of regionalism as a major influence in people's lives.

Regionalism in America, edited by Merrill Jensen, provides important historical information. Part 1 treats the development and use of the concept of regionalism from its beginnings in the eighteenth century until the present. Part 2 offers an account of three historic regions of the United States—the South, Spanish Southwest, and Pacific Northwest. Part 3 surveys regionalism in American culture and includes a survey of literature, architecture, painting, and linguistics. This section of Jensen's book is of special interest because it treats a variety of genres and disciplines in terms of their regional qualities. Part 4 surveys contributions of those who have dealt with regionalism as a practical concept. Part 5, "The Limitations and the Promise of Regionalism," contains essays arguing for the continuation of discrete regions and for regionalism as leading to the integration of regions.

Mass Culture: Popular Arts in America, edited by Bernard Rosenberg and David Manning White, is a reader which deals with the interplay between the mass media and society. Its fifty-one contributors include literary critics, social scientists, journalists, and art critics. Although it does not address regionalism specifically, the reader does contain useful essays on mass literature (books, detective fiction, magazines, comic books, and cartoon scripts), motion pictures, television, and radio.

Leo Lowenthal's *Literature, Popular Culture, and Society* provides in its introduction an historical account of popular culture which Lowenthal states is "probably as old as human civilization." Four chapters deal with literature as commodity, and the final chapter treats literature as art. Although not focused on regionalism, the historical account of popular culture is useful.

Regionalism and Beyond: Essays of Randall Stewart, edited by George Core, excludes a consideration of popular literature but does treat American regions extensively, including New England and the Tidewater and Frontier South. Another work appearing in 1968, *Frontiers of American Culture,* edited by Ray B. Browne, Richard H. Crowder, Virgil L. Lokke, and William

T. Stafford, contains an essay by Leslie Fiedler entitled, "The New Western: Or, the Return of the Vanishing American," in which Fiedler posits,

> Geography in the United States is mythological. From the earliest times, at any rate, American writers have tended to define their own country—and, much of our literature has, consequently, tended to define itself—topologically, as it were, in terms of the four cardinal directions: mythicized North, South, East and West.

Another essay in the collection, Richard M. Dorson's, "Folklore in Relation to American Studies," comments on the humor of the Old Southwest and finds that it is "clearly an expression of the popular culture.... One reason... this humorous literature disappeared from sight when its vogue had passed was its lack of recognition or even awareness by highbrow literary critics." Dorson argues that the folklorist can correct the overly exclusive definition of Southwest humor made by literary historians.

Challenges in American Culture, edited by Ray B. Browne, Larry N. Landrum, and William K. Bottorff, is a potpourri of popular culture interests. Related to the study of regionalism in popular culture is an essay by Esther K. Birdsall, "The FWP and the Popular Press." Birdsall gives a brief history of the Federal Writers Project, which "spent 27,189,370 dollars to fill seven twelve feet shelves in the library of the Department of the Interior with publications ranging from the state guides to pamphlets of regional interest" and discusses contemporary reaction to the FWP.

Raymond D. Gastil in *Cultural Regions of the United States* cites the greater interest in regionalism in the 1930s as compared with today. Gastil draws on studies of dialect, house styles and architecture, settlement patterns, regional history, and so forth, to demonstrate "that there is still much more life in American regionalism than many of us believed." Gastil describes cultural regions of the United States and concludes that we have exaggerated the disappearance of regionalism.

Western Popular Theatre, edited by David Mayer and Kenneth Richards, is the proceedings of a symposium sponsored by the Manchester University Department of Drama and contains a paper of interest to students of regionalism in popular culture. "The Wild West Exhibition and the Drama of Civilization" by William Brasmer traces the history of the development of the Wild West exhibit.

Floyd C. Watkins, *In Time and Place: Some Origins of American Fiction,* analyzes eight novels, "each of [which] treats a particular culture or a diversity of cultures and reveals the author's ignorance or knowledge in his use of the ways of the communities." The novels are of the South, the Southwest, the prairies, and one *(The Grapes of Wrath)* begins in Oklahoma and ends in California.

Jeffrey Schrank's *Snap, Crackle, and Popular Taste: The Illusion of Free*

Choice in America contains a chapter, "The Packaged Environment: Illusions of Quality and Culture," which discusses kitsch as "a package of phony culture. Kitsch is something ordinary, cheap or simply mass produced but packaged to appear as culture or art with a capital A." *Snap, Crackle, and Popular Taste* deals not so much with regionalism as with its replacement—a packaged sameness that may be found in every part of the United States.

Marshall W. Fishwick's *Springlore in Virginia* treats a very specific aspect of regionalism in popular culture: the culture that grows up around springs. Fishwick defines springlore as "what we know, think, and say about flowing waters, springs and spas, and the people who gather around them. Springs can and do serve as healing places, stage sets, touchstones, cyphers, icons—even tombstones of a class or culture." Fishwick's book focuses on a close cluster of Virginia springs and discusses the culture of the South as it relates to these springs.

Another recent project that treats regionalism in popular culture is the special issue "In-Depth: Cultural Geography and Popular Culture," edited by Alvar Carlson of the *Journal of Popular Culture.* In an essay entitled "The Contributions of Cultural Geographers to the Study of Popular Culture," Carlson points out that "cultural geographers, knowingly or unknowingly, have long had an interest in some aspects of popular culture, although the discipline of popular culture was formally established only within the last decade." Following Carlson's essay are twelve articles treating topics ranging from a geographical examination of alcoholic drink in the United States to massage parlors in the nation's capital.

Media-Made Dixie: The South in the American Imagination by Jack Temple Kirby is one of the few extended works specifically to evaluate regionalism in popular culture. Kirby states that the main object of his inquiry is the "*popular* historical images of the South since the advent of feature movies and annual best-seller lists." Kirby surveys the images of the South in the mass communication media, including films, bestsellers, popular histories, school texts, television, music, radio, drama, sports, and advertising. *Media-Made Dixie* may well be a precursor to other extended works that view popular culture in a regional perspective.

ANTHOLOGIES AND REPRINTS

Because regionalism in popular culture is such an all-inclusive topic, only a sampling of representative anthologies will be treated. The discussion below is based on a sampling of works which contain local color and regional stories. A full listing, of course, would number in the hundreds. A selective list is included in the checklist at the end of this essay.

Some early regional anthologies include Harry R. Warfel and G. Harrison Orians, editors, *American Local-Color Stories,* which has selections from the works of thirty-eight writers. Kendall B. Taft, editor, *Minor Knickerbockers: Representative Selections, with Introduction, Bibliography, and Notes* contains selections of the work of early New York writers. Robert Penn Warren, editor, *A Southern Harvest: Short Stories by Southern Writers* is a good anthology of Southern writing. Midwest and Western anthologies are represented by Benjamin S. Parker, editor, *Poets and Poetry of Indiana;* Mary H. Marable and Elaine Boylan, editors, *A Handbook of Oklahoma Writers;* Thomas M. Pearce and A. P. Thomason, compilers, *Southwesterners Write;* Stewart Hall Holbrook, editor, *Promised Land: A Collection of Northwest Writing;* and Levette J. Davidson and Prudence Bostwick, compilers, *The Literature of the Rocky Mountain West, 1803-1903.*

The Southwest in Literature: An Anthology for High Schools, edited by Mabel Major and Rebecca W. Smith in 1929, is representative of early anthologies intended for school use. The editors state that the purpose of the anthology "is to inspire in the teachers and pupils who use it a proud recognition of how much really good literature and art have already been produced about the Southwest; and to arouse in them a desire to write and to sing and to paint the beauties and the truths of the land which is their own." The anthology is divided into sections describing early pioneers, cowboys, Indians, inheritors of Old Spain, and includes songs, poems, and short stories.

Tall Tales of the Southwest: An Anthology of Southern and Southwestern Humor, 1830-1860, edited by Franklin J. Meine and published in 1930, collects stories written between 1830 and 1860 and provides brief biographical sketches and bibliographical information for each writer. Meine's introduction gives an historical account of the development of frontier humor. Of special interest is a summary of the range of subjects treated in Southwest humor. A distinction must be made, of course, between humor of the Old Southwest, as treated here, including the old southwest frontier—Alabama, Mississippi, western Georgia—and the modern Southwest.

Claude M. Simpson's *The Local Colorists: American Short Stories, 1857-1900* is a seminal study of the local color period. Representative writers of the Northeast, Midwest, South, and West are included, and Simpson's introduction to the collection provides what has become a standard definition of local color. An historical account of the rise of the local color movement is included as well.

Walter Blair's *Native American Humor,* first published in 1937 and published in a revised edition in 1960, is also a standard work. The first half of the book contains essays dealing with nineteenth-century developments in American humor, which Blair groups as follows: changing attitudes of humorists toward comic native characters, changes in humorous techniques, and changing reader attitudes toward this humor. Representative selections of Down East humor (1830-67), humor of the Old Southwest (1830-67), literary comedians (1855-1900), local colorists (1869-1900), and writings of Mark Twain are included.

E. N. Brandt has edited *The Saturday Evening Post Reader of Western Stories,* published by Doubleday. The collection, published in 1960, contains eighteen short stories and two novelettes. Brandt's preface catalogs the "many Wests—the West of the explorers, the West of the Mountain Men and the Indian Wars, the West of the wagon trains, the gold seekers, the homesteaders, the ranchers, and the cowboys. Each one has had its faithful chroniclers."

Another work published in 1960, *Southern Stories,* edited by Arlin Turner, chronologically presents stories by Southern writers. In his introduction Turner provides a brief historical outline of the development of the short story in Southern writing and says that, for Southerners, "the regional affiliation is conspicuous."

Representative of contemporary editions of the works of a single regional writer is M. Thomas Inge's edition of *Sut Lovingood's Yarns* by George Washington Harris. Inge provides an extensive introduction to Harris's life and gives the publication history of his work. Stating that Harris was probably the foremost writer of the Southwest humor school, Inge includes in his edition, "the best of the Sut Lovingood sketches written by Harris between 1854 and 1869, the year of his death."

A book that is representative of the works published in the past decade that collect popular culture materials is Ray B. Browne, editor, *The Alabama Folk Lyric: A Study in Origins and Media of Dissemination.* Browne provides a working definition for the folk song as "any piece, regardless of authorship or date of origin, which is sung by a member or members of the folk and is not subject to the corrective and stabilizing influences of an art form or any non-folk medium of communication." The songs collected in this work are part of a collection of 2,500 ballads and songs made in the summers of 1951, 1952, and 1953, a collection which Browne describes as "the largest...ever made for Alabama, and, indeed one of the biggest made for any state." The 192 pieces included in this work (328, counting variants) represent all classes and geographical sections of the state.

BIBLIOGRAPHY

BOOKS AND ARTICLES

Arguimbau, Ellen, comp., and John A. Brennan, ed. *A Guide to Manuscript Collections.* Boulder: Western Historical Collections, University of Colorado, 1977.

Bargainnier, Earl F. "The Falconhurst Series: A New Popular Image of the Old South." *Journal of Popular Culture,* 10 (Fall 1976), 298-314.

Bigsby, C. W. E., ed. *Approaches to Popular Culture.* Bowling Green, Ohio: Bowling Green University Popular Press, 1976.

Boney, Nash. "The American South." *Journal of Popular Culture*, 10 (Fall 1976), 290-97.

Browne, Ray B., ed. *Abstracts of Popular Culture: A Quarterly Publication of International Popular Phenomena, I.* Bowling Green, Ohio: Bowling Green University Popular Press, 1976-77.

______. *The Alabama Folk Lyric: A Study in Origins and Media of Dissemination.* Bowling Green, Ohio: Bowling Green University Popular Press, 1979.

Browne, Ray B., Richard H. Crowder, Virgil L. Lokke, and William T. Stafford, eds. *Frontiers of American Culture.* Lafayette, Ind.: Purdue Research Foundation, 1968.

Browne, Ray B., Larry N. Landrum, and William K. Bottorff. *Challenges in American Culture.* Bowling Green, Ohio: Bowling Green University Popular Press, 1970.

Carlson, Alvar W. "Cultural Geography and Popular Culture." *Journal of Popular Culture*, 9 (Fall 1975), 482-83.

______, ed. "In-Depth: Cultural Geography and Popular Culture." *Journal of Popular Culture*, 11 (Spring 1978), 829-997 (12 articles).

Core, George, ed. *Regionalism and Beyond: Essays of Randall Stewart.* Nashville, Tenn.: Vanderbilt University Press, 1968.

Davidson, Donald. *The Attack on Leviathan: Regionalism and Nationalism in the United States.* Chapel Hill: University of North Carolina Press, 1938.

English, Thomas H. *Roads to Research: Distinguished Library Collections of the Southeast.* Athens: University of Georgia Press, 1968.

Fishwick, Marshall W. *Springlore in Virginia.* Bowling Green, Ohio: Bowling Green University Popular Press, 1978.

Fiske, Horace Spencer. *Provincial Types in American Fiction.*. Chautauqua, N.Y.: Chautauqua Press, 1907.

Gastil, Raymond D. *Cultural Regions of the United States.* Seattle: University of Washington Press, 1975.

Hodge, Clarence Lewis. *The Tennessee Valley Authority: A National Experiment in Regionalism.* New York: American University Press, 1938. Reprint. New York: Russell and Russell, 1968.

Howell, J. B., ed. *Special Collections in Libraries of the Southeast.* Jackson, Miss.: Howick House, 1978.

Jensen, Merrill, ed. *Regionalism in America.* Madison: University of Wisconsin Press, 1951.

Kirby, Jack Temple. *Media-Made Dixie: The South in the American Imagination.* Baton Rouge: Louisiana State University Press, 1978.

Leary, Lewis. *Articles on American Literature: 1900-1950.* Durham, N.C.: Duke University Press, 1954.

______. *Articles on American Literature: 1950-1967.* Durham, N.C.: Duke University Press, 1970.

Lowenthal, Leo. *Literature, Popular Culture, and Society.* Englewood Cliffs, N.J.: Prentice-Hall, 1961.

Marsden, Michael T., ed. "National Finding List of Popular Culture Holdings Special Collections." *Popular Culture Association Newsletter*, 6 (March 1977).

Mayer, David, and Kenneth Richards, eds. *Western Popular Theatre.* London: Metheun, 1977.
McWilliams, Carey. *The New Regionalism in American Literature.* Seattle: University of Washington Book Store, 1930. Reprint. Folcroft, Penn.: Folcroft Library Editions, 1974.
Odum, Howard W., and Harry Estill Moore. *American Regionalism: A Cultural-Historical Approach to National Integration.* New York: Holt, 1938.
Rosenberg, Bernard, and David Manning White, eds. *Mass Culture: Popular Arts in America.* Glencoe, Ill.: Free Press, 1957.
Rubin, Louis D., Jr. *A Bibliographical Guide to the Study of Southern Literature.* Baton Rouge: Louisiana State University Press, 1969.
Schrank, Jeffrey. *Snap, Crackle, and Popular Taste: The Illusion of Free Choice in America.* New York: Dell, 1977.
Simpson, Claude M., ed. *The Local Colorists: American Short Stories, 1857-1900.* New York: Harper & Row, 1960.
Spiller, Robert E., Willard Thorp, Thomas H. Johnson, Henry Seidel Canby, and Richard M. Ludwig, eds. *Literary History of the United States.* 2 vols. 3rd rev. ed., New York: Macmillan, 1963.
Twelve Southerners. *I'll Take My Stand: The South and the Agrarian Tradition.* New York: Harper & Brothers, 1930.
Watkins, Floyd C. *In Time and Place: Some Origins of American Fiction.* Athens: University of Georgia Press, 1977.
Williams, Jerry T., ed. *Southern Literature, 1968-1975: A Checklist of Scholarship.* Boston: G. K. Hall, 1978.
Wolfe, Margaret Ripley. "The Southern Lady: Long Suffering Counterpart of the Good Ole' Boy." *Journal of Popular Culture,* 11 (Summer 1977), 18-27.
Young, Margaret Labash, Harold Chester Young, and Anthony T. Kruzas, eds. *Subject Directory of Special Libraries and Information Centers.* Detroit: Gale Research, 1975.

ANTHOLOGIES

Blair, Walter. *Native American Humor.* New York: American Book, 1937. Rev. ed. San Francisco: Chandler, 1960.
Brandt, E. N., ed. *The Saturday Evening Post Reader of Western Stories.* Garden City, N.Y.: Doubleday, 1960.
Davidson, Levette J., and Prudence Bostwick, comps. *The Literature of the Rocky Mountain West, 1803-1903.* Caldwell, Idaho: Caxton Printers, 1939.
Davidson, Levette J., and Forester Blake, comps. *Rocky Mountain Tales.* Norman: University of Oklahoma Press, 1947.
Holbrook, Stewart Hall, ed. *Promised Land: A Collection of Northwest Writing.* New York: McGraw-Hill, 1945.
Inge, M. Thomas, ed. *Sut Lovingood's Yarns,* by George Washington Harris. New Haven, Conn.: College and University Press, 1966.
Major, Mabel, and Rebecca W. Smith, eds. *The Southwest in Literature: An Anthology for High Schools.* New York: Macmillan, 1929.

Marable, Mary H., and Elaine Boylan, eds. *A Handbook of Oklahoma Writers.* Norman: University of Oklahoma Press, 1939.

Meine, Franklin J., ed. *Tall Tales of the Southwest: An Anthology of Southern and Southwestern Humor, 1830-1860.* 3rd ed. New York: Knopf, 1946.

Parker, Benjamin S., ed. *Poets and Poetry of Indiana.* New York: Silver, Burdett, 1900.

Pearce, Thomas M., and A. P. Thomason, comps. *Southwesterners Write.* Albuquerque: University of New Mexico Press, 1947.

Taft, Kendall B., ed. *Minor Knickerbockers: Representative Selections, with Introduction, Bibliography, and Notes.* New York: American Book, 1947.

Turner, Arlin, ed. *Southern Stories.* 2d ed. New York: Holt, Rinehart and Winston, 1965.

Warfel, Harry R., and G. Harrison Orians, eds. *American Local-Color Stories.* New York: American Book, 1941. Reprint. New York: Cooper Square, 1970.

Warren, Robert Penn, ed. *A Southern Harvest: Short Stories by Southern Writers.* Boston: Houghton Mifflin, 1937.

CHAPTER 16 Science in Popular Culture

Annette M. Woodlief

One of the strongest influences on the development of American popular and intellectual culture has been the physical sciences, as they have been understood—and sometimes misunderstood—by Americans. However, since the establishment of academic science in the mid-nineteenth century, so-called popular science has not been very popular with scientists, who disdain the necessary oversimplification, though it has been appreciated by the general public. Also the effects of science and especially its product, technology, have become so profound that they are virtually impossible to discuss simply and rationally, even by historians of American culture, who hesitate before the complexities posed by scientific thought. As a result, the scientific component of popular culture has been neglected much more than it deserves.

This chapter is an attempt to make some order out of a chaos spawned by a general failure to realize that the subject of science in American popular culture exists. There are some excellent books— or, more frequently, portions of books—and articles in this area, but they have never been listed or studied as a group. Recognized academic areas such as history of science or science and society are already well covered by scholars, so I have avoided those except to pull out materials particularly relevant to this essay. Also, science education as taught in the schools and universities is better examined elsewhere. It is, however, quite difficult and not very productive to separate completely education and entertainment when considering popular concepts of science, and efforts to do so often result in lopsided studies which accent either positive or negative responses.

The focus of this essay, then, is on works of or about the physical sciences that are read voluntarily by a general audience (including science professionals primarily if out of their fields), whether they explicitly convey scientific knowledge or indirectly express attitudes about science. Since the American public has typically associated science with its practical applications, technology will be considered when necessary. The limitations of the essay preclude detailed treatment of the cultural impact of specialized sciences, though clearly botany, ornithology, oceanography, geology, and astronomy, for example, have long appealed to Americans and are discussed in many of the general science works listed here.

HISTORIC OUTLINE

Science has been too much honored and too little appreciated by the American public, according to Morris Cohen.[1] To that I would add that most Americans throughout history have seen science alternately as creator and destroyer of their more cherished ideals and material progress, but they have rarely tried seriously to understand the goals and methods of pure science, an ignorance fostered by the isolation imposed by increasing specialization.

Science has had an impact, though it has not always been great, on American intellectual and popular culture from our Colonial beginnings. The impetus to study science in the Colonies was threefold: to demonstrate the divine origin and workings of the universe; to keep up with British scientific societies; and especially to exploit the utilitarian benefits of science. Interest in such areas as astronomy, weather, agriculture, botany, and inventions was widespread but rarely organized and generally served the practical concerns involved in establishing a new country.

The Colonial period marked the heyday of the amateur gentleman scientist in America. European science was eagerly followed, especially Newton's ideas, and twenty-five Colonials were elected fellows of the Royal Society of London, including the three John Winthrops, Cotton Mather, and William Bryd. However, there was little effort to establish similar professional endeavors in this country. More typical was the recording of natural observations, written and read by educated Americans, such as the nature accounts of John and William Bartram, notes on Virginia's geology by Thomas Jefferson, Jonathan Edwards's childhood essays on flying spiders and rainbows, and Benjamin Franklin's descriptions of his experiments and inventions. Theoretical science was represented in almanacs, which sometimes added to weather and agricultural advice brief explanations of Newton's ideas and the new astronomy. Such discussions appeared as early as 1659 in Zechariah Brigden's almanac summary of Copernican astronomy and continued in Franklin's *Poor Richard* and in Nathaniel Ames's almanac. These popularized expositions, appearing also in pamphlet form, were read widely, especially by ministers who shared the ideas with their flocks for what they revealed of design in the universe.

The mid-eighteenth century saw the growth of science primarily in the Philadelphia area, encouraged by the efforts of men like Ebenezer Kinnersley, a Baptist preacher who lectured frequently on Franklin's electrical experiments. Louis Wright asserts that lectures such as these on popular science aroused as much interest as political controversies during the 1760s and 1770s.[2] More serious explorations in science were going on, with encouragement and library support from James Logan and Franklin, by John Bartram (botany), Thomas Godfrey (inventor of the mariner's quadrant), and David Rittenhouse (astronomer and mathematician). New Yorker Cadwallader Colden and Virginians John Banister, John Clayton, and Dr. John Mitchell were other active gentleman scientists, although they were more interested in communicating with the Royal society than with the general public.

A few societies devoted to natural history (minerology, botany, zoology, ornithology) were formed during the eighteenth century so that their amateur membership could share observations. The first society was the Junto, formed by Franklin in 1727 for discussion of intellectual and scientific subjects. In 1744 he founded the American Philosophical Society, which became more vigorous when it merged with the Junto in 1769 to become the American Philosophical Society Held at Philadelphia for Promoting Useful Knowledge.

By the end of the century, magazines took over from newspapers the publication of essays on scientific theories and discoveries. The most notable, although short-lived, magazines were *American Magazine* (1769), *Pennsylvania Magazine* (1775-76), *Universal Asylum and Columbian Magazine* (1786-89), *American Magazine* (1787-88), *Worcester Magazine* (1786-88), *Massachusetts Magazine* (1789-96), and *American Museum* (1787-92).

Science in the Colonial period, then, was open to any interested person who would observe, read, and perhaps tinker a bit. It was extolled, whether by ministers or popular magazines, primarily for its capability of providing useful knowledge and demonstrations of the sublime and divine order of nature. But most people were simply too busy to pay much attention to science for purely intellectual reasons.

Freedom from the most pressing political and physical concerns after Independence brought more time for intellectual study at the same time that it broadened the base of popular interest in scientific subjects. This popular support, though, focused on practical results with little appetite for abstract theory, an attitude which surely encouraged the emergence of professional scientific societies and university curricula. Many scientists in the universities worked hard to acquaint the public with the serious nature of their work, but this proved to be a time-consuming and generally losing battle.

The problem was first highlighted by Alexis de Tocqueville, who noted in 1831 that Americans displayed "a clear, free, original, and inventive power of Mind" for practical science, but few were devoted to "the essentially theoretical and abstract portion of human knowledge." He speculated that scientific genius in a democratic society, then, would have to pursue discoveries leading to physical rather than intellectual gratification.[3] Time has not proved him generally wrong here, although he failed to predict the movement of many serious scientists to their ivory towers and labs to protect their professional integrity against public demands for practical results.

The nineteenth-century public had many scientific enthusiasms not necessarily shared by the increasingly professional and specialized scientists. Applied science was linked with material and spiritual progress in the periodicals, a faith which continued even in religious magazines well after the evolution controversy erupted. For much of this period, science, at least the popular Baconianism, was seen as cooperating with religion, and few were disturbed by conflicts incipient in geology and evolutionary theory. Also, Herbert Spencer's social interpretation of Darwinism pointed the way for human behavior based on scentific models of progress.

Most public interest was in discoveries associated with comets, geology, microscopy, meteorology, physics, and especially curiosities of botany and zoology as reported in newspapers and general magazines. Wide support was given the many scientific expeditions, the developing science and natural history museums, and new technological advances, especially in transportation. Scientific nationalism was quite strong, and the popular press was filled with numerous unsubstantiated boasts about American scientific and technological prowess.

Scientific-appearing evidence began being cited to support many dubious theories, such as phrenology and the undesirability of education and birth control for women. As Charles Rosenberg says, almost every social problem of the time attracted scientific discussion, much of it quite ingenious.[4]

Along with the drift toward scientism and pseudo-science grew serious efforts to popularize science. Most notable and far-reaching was the Lyceum movement, founded in 1828 by Josiah Holbrook to spread his interest in natural science. Lectures on science, particularly biology, chemistry, and astronomy, were well attended in the almost three thousand lyceums. This popularity inspired similar lectures offered by the YMCA and the Chatauqua circuit and library exhibits of geological specimens and Holbrook's scientific apparatus. John Griscom, Louis Agassiz, and Benjamin Silliman were scientists who appeared almost as much before an eager public as before their university students. One of Silliman's chemistry lectures in Boston attracted crowds which filled the hall and the neighboring streets, and the New York *Tribune* immediately sold out the 1872 issues printing John Tyndall's lectures on physics.

A natural outgrowth of the lecture movement were publications that could reach more people and require less personal energy of the scientists. Early in the century, the only general scientific magazine was the *Medical Repository,* which reported on scientific and medical developments. Silliman's

American Journal of Science, which began in 1818, was joined by *Scientific American* in 1845; Edward L. Youmans began *Popular Science Monthly* in 1872 to popularize evolutionary theory. General magazines such as the *Port Folio,* the *Friend,* and *Atlantic Monthly* also found good reception for their sections on science. The American Association for the Advancement of Science (AAAS) was organized in 1848 to promote the popular as well as the professional communication of science. Clearly, the more the pure sciences developed professionally, the greater the need to explain themselves to a public interested but not intellectually engaged, especially since these scientific endeavors did require considerable financial support.

The nineteenth century also saw the blooming of quasi-scientific nature essays and the conservation movement. Birdwatching and botanizing were favorite activities in the antebellum South and in the North. For writers like Henry David Thoreau, John Muir, and John Burroughs and their readers, nature provided curious wonders and avenues to spiritual truths.

The wonders were particularly evident in the many natural history and science museums, ranging from the small town hall exhibits to the Smithsonian Institution, founded in 1846. The original motivation for such institutions was primarily theological, to present the order of nature in terms of natural theology, but they continued because of increasing public interest in scientific discoveries. Early museums included the Peabody Museum of Natural History (Yale, 1802), Mineralogical Collection of the University Museum at Harvard (1784), Dartmouth College Museum (1783), and University of Ohio Museum (1823). Influential popular educators were the American Museum of Natural History in New York, the Field Museum of Natural History in Chicago, and the Academy of Natural Science at Philadelphia. Technological aspects of science were the focus of exhibits at the Franklin Institute of Philadelphia, the New York Museum of Science and Industry, and the Museum of Science and Industry in Chicago. Such museums flourish today, promoting natural science and techology through many media: periodicals (most notably the *Smithsonian Magazine* and *Natural History*) and books (such as the "Smithsonian Series"), lectures, films and television, and expeditions. Perhaps less legitimately scientific but decidedly popular are scientific and technological sections of numerous exhibits and World Fairs, beginning with the 1853-54 New York Exhibition. Even Disneyland and Disney World have recognized the entertainment value of such exhibits.

Several societies catering to this popular interest in nature arose in the nineteenth century and began publishing magazines. The National Geographic Society has published its magazine and supported expeditions since 1886; the Audubon Society has promoted popular ornithology in several magazines, beginnning with *Bird Lore.* Other magazines with popular appeal were the *American Naturalist* (now a more specialized biological journal) and *Popular Astronomy,* now *Sky and Telescope.* Although most scientists would question how scientific these museums, exhibitions, and publications were and are, there is no doubt that the general public has long found them educational as well as entertaining.

On the negative side, discoveries in biology and physics in the last part of the nineteenth century initiated a change in public attitude toward science. Science became a clear threat to the idea of divinely instituted progress and was no longer the handmaiden of theology. For educated people like Henry Adams, the thermodynamic concept of entropy suggested that civilization and life itself were running down, not progressing. But the issue affecting most people was that posed by Darwin's theory of evolution, and preachers like Henry Ward Beecher and Lyman Abbott hastened to the aid of scientists Louis Agassiz and John Fiske to demonstrate that evolution could be compatible with Biblical accounts of creation. The debate reached a peak with the John Thomas Scopes trial in 1925, but it continues in fundamentalist Christian circles, as the Smithsonian Museum of Natural History found when it received many letters of protest about its recent exhibit on the "Dynamics of Evolution."

Despite these questions, for much of the public from the Civil War well into the twentieth century, the scientist was the modern hero and science would provide. Surrounded by growing technology making life more comfortable and prosperous, Americans honored scientists as well as engineers and inventors such as Thomas A. Edison. Even the scientific method with its emphasis on objectivity and experiments was extolled, although its practical results were much more appreciated.

Popular fiction of the time reflected this positive image of science. Literary utopias from J. A. Etzler's to Edward Bellamy's were able to erase the problems of leadership (with responsible and rational scientists) and servants (with well-controlled technology) in their perfect worlds. Serious fiction became increasingly realistic, striving for more objective reporting and less sentimentality, led by writers like William Dean Howells, John De Forest, and Mark Twain. As Social Darwinism gained popularity, fiction became more naturalistic, revealing the so-called scientific determinism of social laws, especially for the lower classes. The science romance also reached its peak with the pre-World War I novels centered on scientists who use their vast knowledge to end all war (often by giving their powerful discoveries to the most responsible government, that is, the United States) and in Sinclair Lewis's *Arrowsmith* (1925).

The image of the mad scientist initiated by Mary Shelley's *Frankenstein* (1818) did not develop in this country until progressive optimism began breaking down after World War I, although it had appeared in some of Nathaniel Hawthorne's stories. The film industry, science fiction magazines, and comics seized on this theme, particularly after the debut of the atomic bomb; the white lab coat is still menacing in mass culture media. Actually, the sterotyped scientist is rarely evil, insane, or avaricious, except in B-grade horror films. Like the original Dr. Frankenstein, he's more likely to be idealistic, eccentric, dedicated to his instruments and research, somewhat cold and unfeeling, and not especially interested in long-term practical effects of his discoveries, even if they prove disastrous. He may provide a villain with the means of creating evil or a detective with vital clues, but he is too absorbed in his work to notice. Generally, he is not interesting enough to be the protagonist of a work; the focus is on what he does, not who he is. His quest for order often leads to chaos because of his very human limitations and god-like powers. He may not be mad, but he cannot be trusted, says the popular myth.

The fact that science is complicated and isolated by vocabulary and activities and has access to powerful knowledge not shared by the general public has generated much fear in this century, as is reflected in the news as well as entertainment media. This is not necessarily an unjustified fear. As magazines, newspapers, and books keep reminding the public, there are real and persistent problems created by science and technology; atomic power, chemicals in the environment, and genetic research are among those arousing widespread debate in the past thirty-five years. The promised utopia now looks more like dystopia or even apocalypse for many people.

Science fiction provides a good example of the continuing mixed public response to science. This writing has, as a rule, taken science quite seriously, extrapolating from the known to the possible to create an orderly, logical world. Scientists have been presented as relatively benign, providing the means for plot and characters to operate. Even the pulp science fiction of the 1930s assumed that science, especially the theory of relativity, was useful and valuable, although the stories relied primarily on pseudo-scientific doubletalk. However, science fiction film quickly developed a strong anti-science bias as it exploited superstition, horror, and the fear of the unknown. Necromancy and special effects took precedence over science, even in films adapted from science fiction stories. The favorite line, first used in the 1936 *The Invisible Ray,* has been "There are some things Man is not meant to know," a statement guaranteed to infuriate many science fiction writers. One reason for this split in attitude toward science is not hard to find: the audience. Science fiction—at least that which draws on the physical sciences—has been addressed to readers interested in science and technology, whereas films entertain people who often know nothing about science, and fear can be an exciting common denominator. This deep division in American nonscientific culture between pro- and anti-science concerns can be seen throughout the century in every popular medium.

The vividness of popular anti-science expressions has led many scholars to ignore the fact that science has never been very popular or respected in America, though much of the hero worship has worn off. New discoveries, especially in astronomy, geology, space, and biology are widely heralded by the news media. Interest in scientific biography is indicated by the recent celebration in magazines, on television, and in special exhibits of the Einstein centennial and the good sales of *The Double Helix,* a rather irreverent account of the discovery of the molecular structure of DNA by James D. Watson. Television shows about science, beginning with the long-running Mr. Wizard series in the 1950s and continuing today with shows such as PBS's "NOVA," CBS's "Universe," specials from the National Geographic Society and Jacques Cousteau, and six PBS series on science, including the thirteen-part, $10 million "Cosmos" with Carl Sagan, have become more rather than less popular, although the accent is more on entertainment than education. Science journalism flourishes today in newspapers and magazines, and the many magazines devoted to science are read widely. A recent popular addition is *Omni,* a slick magazine with articles on science and science fiction and *Science 80;* several others are being planned with such titles as *Science Illustrated,* and *Radical Science.* The popularity of science today is further indicated by the fact that the Smithsonian and over four hundred other science-related museums attract millions of visitors each year.

Books on science were particularly big business in the 1970s. Hundreds of books explaining scientific ideas and discoveries, many in paperback or in series, sell substantially, although they might not make the ten best sellers list. Ironically, the books that sell best are often pseudo-science, presenting dubious ideas about UFOs, plants, the Bermuda Triangle, or astrology, wrapped in scientific-appearing evidence. Science fiction continues to be popular, but as the writing has improved the scientific content has decreased and the fantasy element increased. Most significantly, there is a growing yet unnamed genre of books with considerable scientific content and/or viewpoint plus philosophical and poetic musings which are read widely by educated audiences. Some of the most notable include Jacob Bronowski's *The Ascent of Man* (television series and book), Annie Dillard's Pulitzer Prize-winning *Pilgrim at Tinker Creek,* Robert Pirsig's *Zen and the Art of Motorcycle Maintenance,* Fritjov Capra's *The Tao of Physics,* and books by Loren Eiseley, Rachel Carson, Lewis Thomas, and Carl Sagan.

Scientists may decry the diluted and enthusiastic appropriations of their work, especially to support questionable theories, but they also benefit from the accompanying public support and prestige. Even anti-science expressions of fear and distrust indicate popular recognition of the power science holds. For better and for worse, in this century science has become part of the fabric of American popular as well as intellectual culture.

REFERENCE WORKS

Few bibliographies are available for the scholar who wishes to study the impact of science on American popular culture. There are, however, many fine bibliographies on the history and achievements of science or the associated sociology of science, which deals primarily with political or national policy, but they rarely distinguish between academic and popular works. A useful guide to these bibliographies is Ching-Chih Chen's *Scientific and Technical Information Sources,* an annotated listing of guides, bibliographies, encyclopedias, series, directories, and so on. Oriented toward academic science but not annotated are Theodore Besterman's *Physical Sciences* and *Biological Sciences* (both "bibliographies of bibliographies"); Earl James Lasworth's *Reference Sources in Science and Technology,* and Frances B. Jenkins's *Science Reference Sources.* There are also two annotated bibliographies with essays: Denis J. Grogan's *Science and Technology: An Introduction to the Literature* (oriented toward students doing research), and H. Robert Malinowsky, *Science and Engineering Literature: A Guide to Reference Sources.* Additional information on collections can be found in *Scientific Books, Libraries, and Collectors: A Study of Bibliography and the Book Trade in Relation to Science,* by John L. Thornton and R. I. Tully, Jr. Scholars interested in the influence of specific sciences should turn to these bibliographies. My focus here is on reference sources that either present popular forms of general science or discuss its historical impact.

A valuable critical bibliography that lists books and articles on the cultural role of science appears in each issue of *Isis.* Fortunately, the bibliographies from the years 1913-65 have been collected and listed by subject in volume 3 of Magda Whitrow's *Isis Cumulative Bibliography: A Bibliography of the History of Science Formed from Isis Critical Bibliographies 1-90, 1913-1965.* Useful subject headings are popularization of science, general history of science, relations with society and the humanities, and public opinion.

Since the natural history movement has been so important in America, another indispensable bibliography is Max Meisel's three-volume *Bibliography of American Natural History, The Pioneer Century, 1769-1865.* The first volume is an annotated bibliography of publications related to the history, biography, and bibliography of American natural history and its institutions, with a subject and geographic index and a bibliography of biographies. Bibliographies of publications of natural history institutions and appendixes updating the work to 1929 are in the remaining volumes.

Scholars interested in the cultural effects of Colonial science can find much information in the bibliographies appearing in the historical books by Whitfield J. Bell, Jr., Merle Curti, Brooke Hindle, Raymond Stearns, and Louis B. Wright. Bibliographies that also cover the nineteenth century are found in the books by William M. Smallwood and Mabel Smallwood and Sally G. Kohlstedt. Ronald C. Tobey's bibliography covers the relationship between popular and professional science from 1919 to 1930.

Bibliographies in books on popular culture provide little information about science, probably because their focus is on entertainment rather than education. The major exception to this rule is works that focus on science fiction, most notably *Anatomy of Wonder: Science Fiction,* a collection of bibliographical essays edited by Neil Barron. Occasionally, useful entries also appear in other bibliographies listed in the chapters on comic art, film, television, and science fiction in Volume 1 of this *Handbook.*

A number of reference works on science are published for broad educational use by the nonscientific community. Every general encyclopedia has numerous scientific entries, especially the 1972 *Encyclopaedia Britannica,* with *World Book, Encyclopaedia Britannica,* and the *McGraw-Hill Encyclopedia of Science and Technology* issuing yearbooks on science and technology. McGraw-Hill, in fact, specializes in science reference books for the general public. The fourteen-volume *McGraw-Hill Encyclopedia of Science and Technology* has both broad and specific articles with accompanying bibliographies. There are also the *McGraw-Hill Basic Bibliography of Science and Technology,* the two-volume *McGraw-Hill Modern Men of Science,* and the *McGraw-Hill Dictionary of Scientific and Technical Terms,* all of which are reliable with bibliographies and illustrations where necessary.

James R. Newman's *The Harper Encyclopedia of Science,* with four thousand articles in one volume, is directed to both the specialist and the layman. Of particular interest is the bibliography at the end, which provides a graded reading course in science. Less technical and with briefer entries is the one-volume *Cowles Encyclopedia of Science, Industry, and Technology,* whereas the *Van Nostrand's Scientific Encyclopedia* is more technical, without bibliography but with many charts. An unusual and somewhat scholarly reference source is *The Encyclopedia of Ignorance* by Ronald Duncan and Miranda Weston-Smith, which contains articles on what is not known in science yet. Two reference works directed toward younger students and found usually in public libraries are *The New Popular Science, Encyclopedia of the Sciences,* edited by William B. Sill, and the *Pocket Encyclopedia of Physical Science.* Numerous works have been published for young readers more interested in pictures than text, such as the ten-volume *Book of Popular Science,* which is revised annually.

The general public is often more interested in people who make discoveries than the discoveries themselves. There are many biographies, single and collected (as in Bernard Jaffe's *Men of Science in America*) that meet this need; however, brief articles on numerous scientists are offered by several biographical dictionaries and encyclopedias. *American Men and Women of Science,* though in eight volumes, contains rather abbreviated entries in Who's Who style. Clark A. Elliott's *Biographical Dictionary of American Science: The Seventeenth Through the Nineteenth Centuries* gives somewhat longer entries sketching education, career, memberships, scientific contributions, and works. Ironically, more extensive essays, though obviously covering fewer scientists, are to be found in international biographical dictionaries, especially the fourteen-volume *Dictionary of Scientific Biography.* Contemporary scientists appear in the McGraw-Hill *Modern Men of Science,* but no living scientists are in Trevor E. Williams's *A Biographical Dictionary of Scientists,* a one-volume work with short essays and references. For reading rather than research, one should turn to *Asimov's Biographical Encyclopedia of Science and Technology,* which focuses on 1,195 scientists, with biography and scientific contributions in chronological rather than alphabetical order. On the other hand, the *World Who's Who in Science* provides only minimal factual information. Another reference source, probably used only for educational purposes, is the scientific dictionary for the nonscientist. The *McGraw-Hill Dictionary of Scientific and Technical Terms* has more illustrations than *The Penguin Dictionary of Science,* but otherwise the format and information are similar.

Every year hundreds of books are published that explain concepts and discoveries of science to nonprofessional audiences. The American Association for the Advancement of Science publishes several annotated guides to this literature, usually under the editorship of Hilary Deason. The major guide is the *AAAS Science Book List,* which annotates selected books in science and mathematics for nonspecialists. This list was updated in 1978 and is also supplemented by a periodical, *AAAS Science Books,* which has appeared quarterly since 1965 with reviews of science books and which became *Science Books and Films* in 1975. Hilary J. Deason has also edited *A Guide to Science Reading,* which lists and annotates nine hundred paperbound books, and *The Science Book List for Children.* Another valuable reference work is *The Reader's Adviser: A Layman's Guide,* edited by Winifred Courtney. Unfortunately, the eleventh edition (1969) is the last to include an annotated list of good books on science for the intellectual layman, including series such as the popular Time-Life series and numerous field guides; the twelfth edition has dropped the science section completely. One popularizer, Isaac Asimov, keeps writing so much that a special checklist is needed just to keep up with his work, and Marjorie M. Miller has published *Isaac Asimov: A Checklist of Works Published in the United States, March 1939-May 1972.*

RESEARCH COLLECTIONS

As a rule, it is public libraries—local, state, and federal—rather than academic libraries that have the best collections of science for general audiences. However, many libraries, especially in universities, have collections specializing in science or history of science, as listed in Lee Ash's *Subject Collections,* the *Directory of Special Libraries and Information Centers,* and Chen's bibliography. None of these works points out popular science strengths, except for the collection at Buhl Planetarium and the Institute of Popular Science in Pittsburgh. Since there is no real division between academic and popular science before 1900, collections of publications related to Colonial science are relevant; the major collections are found in the Library Company of Philadelphia and the American Philosophical Society in Philadelphia, the Library of Congress, the New York Public Library and the New York Academy of Medicine, and the Harvard College Library. Collections of works in particular sciences and their history are listed by Chin, Thornton and Tully, and Ash under the specialty headings.

Most popular interest has centered on particular scientists, especially the folk heroes, Benjamin Franklin, Thomas Edison, and Albert Einstein, and particular subject areas, such as natural history, geography, and scientific expeditions. The major collections of American scientists' works are in the American Philosophical Library in Philadelphia and the Library of Congress American Manuscript Division in Washington, D.C. Franklin's papers are also to be found at the Yale University Library; Edison's at the U.S. Park Service library at Menlo Park, New Jersey; and Einstein's in New York at the American Institute of Physics and the Albert Einstein Collection of Medicine, Yeshiva University.

Science and natural history museums, including many run by the U.S. Park Service, not only collect popular science materials in their libraries but often create them. The Smithsonian Institution has several libraries, most notably those connected with the Natural History Museum, the Museum of History and Technology, the Air and Space Museum, and the Astrophysical Observatory (in Cambridge, Massachusetts). Since these libraries are open only to qualified scholars, the general public is probably more aware of the numerous Smithsonian Press publications, which are listed in the annual *Smithsonian Year* (1971-). There are two books listing publications currently available from science and natural museums besides the Smithsonian: Paul Wasserman, editor, *Museum Media: A Biennial Directory and Index of Publications and Audio-visuals Available from United States and Canadian Institutions,* and Jane Clapp, editor, *Museum Publications* (volume 2), but neither is annotated. The National Geographic Society is another popular organization that has a library, which specializes in expeditions, natural history, and geography, and many publications and films, as listed in the *National Geographic Index.* The best natural history museum library, especially strong in periodicals and open to the public, is the Academy of Natural Sciences in Philadelphia; Venia T. Phillips and Maurice E. Phillips have compiled a guide to the manuscript collections. Other important natural history museum libraries include the Field Museum of Natural History, the Museum of Science and Industry, and the Newberry Library, all in Chicago, and the Museum of Science and Technology and the Museum of Natural History in New York.

Films are another major medium used to interest the public in science. The *AAAS Science Film Catalog* (which does not list government films) and the *Catalog of Motion Pictures and Filmstrips for Rent and Sale by the National Audiovisual Center* both contain annotated lists which tell where and how the films may be viewed, rented, or bought. Such films would be used primarily for educational purposes.

There are other collections related to subcategories of this very broad topic of science in American popular culture, such as science fiction or related to particular physical sciences, but those listed here are major sources of materials with popular science emphasis.

HISTORY AND CRITICISM

The history of science in American culture has had surprisingly few chroniclers, especially after professionals and amateurs parted company in the mid-nineteenth century. Historical interest has focused on the development of the scientific subculture through learned societies, universities, and scholarly publications on what seems to be the assumption that only academic science counts historically.

One general history to consider the effects of science in American culture is Merle Curti's *The Growth of American Thought.* Although Curti is primarily concerned with the rise of professionalism, he also discusses the intellectual effects of evolutionary thought and the popularization of learning in the nineteenth century. However, aside from noting the controversy over atomic power, he says little about science in the twentieth century, even in the 1964 edition. Scientific nationalism and the "sublime" approach to science were examined by Perry Miller in an uncompleted study of the influence of American science, *The Life of the Mind in America: From the Revolution to the Civil War.* Two sectional summaries on the historical development of science ending with the Civil War are *Yankee Science in the Making* by Dirk J. Struik and *Scientific Interests in the Old South* by Thomas C. Johnson, Jr.

The further back one goes in American history, the more studies on the cultural role of science there are. The best summary of the Colonial period is a chapter on "Scientific Interest and Observation" in Louis B. Wright's *The Cultural Life of the American Colonies: 1607-1763.* A brief survey of Colonial American science prefaces Whitfield J. Bell, Jr.'s *Early American Science: Needs and Opportunities for Study.* Bell mentions the paucity of studies on pseudo-science, popularization, and museums; most of the book is devoted to bibliographical essays on fifty early American scientists. More detailed studies of the eighteenth-century interest in science are Brooke Hindle's *The Pursuit of Science in Revolutionary America, 1735-1789,* and Raymond P. Stearn's *Science in the British Colonies of America,* which pays particular attention to the Royal Society connection and individual scientists.

The major work on science in the nineteenth century is George H. Daniels, *American Science in the Age of Jackson,* but this work is almost entirely concerned with professional scientists in the first half of the century. Primary documents are collected by Nathan Reingold in *Science in Nineteenth-Century America: A Documentary History.* The positive link between science and religion is explored in Theodore D. Bozeman's *Protestants in an Age of Science: The Baconian Ideal and Antebellum American Religious Thought.* Religious hostility and philosophical reaction to science are studied in Morris R. Cohen's *American Thought: A Critical Sketch.*

None of these works addresses itself explicitly to the popular reaction to science as much as several essays from *Isis,* two appearing in Nathan Reingold's *Science in America Since 1820:* Donald Zochert's study of mid-century Milwaukee newspapers and Walter B. Hendrickson's essay on the founding of natural history societies and museums. Also, Brook Hindle's *Early American Science* presents John C. Greene's excellent *Isis* article on "Science and the Public in the Age of Jefferson." *The Idea of Progress in America, 1815-1860* by Arthur A. Ekirch, Jr., analyzes the connection between progress and science made by the popular press. Also relevant is Sally G. Kohlstedt's study on *The Formation of the American Scientific Community: The American Association for the Advancement of Science, 1848-60,* which does discuss amateur scientist members and early demands for popularization, although its subject is the establishment of professional science. Irving H. Bartlett has a short, mostly derivative section on science in *The American Mind in the Mid-Nineteenth Century.* Science in the postwar nineteenth century is examined by George H. Daniels in *Science in American Society; A Social History,* who writes about the rise of charlatans and the faith in progress, and Howard Mumford Jones, who discusses "Landscape and Microscope" in *The Age of Energy: Varieties of American Experience, 1865-1915.*

Most general works, however, fail to be very useful for understanding the popular response to science. The Lyceum movement is described in Struik's book and in more detail in Carl Bode's *The American Lyceum, Town Meeting of the Mind.* Lyceum science lectures can be found occasionally in tract form, such as those published in Boston in the early 1830s. More information on the popularization movement is available in biographies of the busiest popularizers. Benjamin Silliman's contributions, for example, are surveyed in Margaret Rossiter's article and in two biographies, one by George P. Fisher and another by John F. Fulton and Elizabeth H. Thompson. Biologist Louis

Agassiz's popular efforts are described in Edward Lurie's biography. For short biographies of many scientists involved in the nineteenth-century popularization movement there are the collections of Bernard Jaffe and W. J. Youmans.

Several books on scientific fads discuss theories expounded widely in this period, ranging from the belief in the flat earth to phrenology, the best of these being Martin Gardner's *Fads and Fallacies in the Name of Science.* Also useful are Daniel W. Hering, *Foibles and Fallacies of Science;* Curtis MacDougall, *Hoaxes;* Robert Silverberg, *Scientists and Scoundrels: A Book of Hoaxes;* and the more general *The Story of Human Error,* edited by Joseph Jastrow. Phrenology was the most widespread pseudo-science, and it is credited by John D. Davies in *Phrenology, Fad and Science: A Nineteenth-Century Crusade* as being a factor in bringing more legitimate science to public attention. An interesting related book tells of the family who created the commercial phrenological enterprise, *Heads and Headlines: The Phrenological Fowlers* by Madeleine Stern.

Charles E. Rosenberg's thoughtful book, *No Other Gods: On Science and American Social Thought,* finds that Americans used science in the nineteenth century most to support social ideas on heredity and eugenics, women's education, birth control, neurasthenia, agriculture, and public health. As this list shows, much of the popular pseudo-science has been related to health, physical and mental, not so much to the physical sciences. Pseudo-science has not vanished from the American scene today, even though most scientists have realized the futility of fighting scientific misconceptions. There are scattered articles of protest, however, most notably two issues of *The Humanist* on "Antiscience and Pseudoscience" (1976) and "Objections to Astrology" (1975).

The best account of American periodicals before 1850, some of which are science-related, is Frank Luther Mott, *A History of American Magazines, 1741-1850.* Other general sources are listed in the chapter on magazines in this volume. Curti also refers to periodicals in his history, but the definitive study of popular science as represented in magazines has yet to be done, although the *Isis* essays by Zochert, Hendrickson, and Greene cited above are good beginnings in this area.

The natural history movement of the nineteenth century has been studied from several angles. William M. Smallwood's and Mabel Smallwood's book, *Natural History and the American Mind,* collects much information from natural history manuscripts but does little to digest it. Hans Huth's *Nature and the American: Three Centuries of Changing Attitudes* is filled with generalizations about nature in art and literature, but he says little about the popular effect of nature essays. Another approach is through numerous biographies and critiques of the works of major nature enthusiasts, such as *American Naturists* by Henry C. Tracy. Norman Foersters's *Nature in Amer-*

ican Literature: Studies in the Modern View of Nature surveys the literary expressions of the natural history movement.

A major legacy of this movement is the natural history museum, especially the venerable Smithsonian. The most readable history is Paul H. Oehser, *The Smithsonian Institution.* The earliest history was written by George B. Goode in 1897, *The Smithsonian Institution, 1846-1896: The History of Its First Half Century;* a less partisan view is the recent *The Smithsonian: Octopus on the Mall* by Geoffrey Hellman. Books and articles on other natural history museums are listed in Max Meisel's bibliography; museums, publications, and activities of scientific societies are described and listed by Ralph S. Bates in *Scientific Societies in the United States.* T. R. Adam sketched briefly the history of science, technology, and natural history museums in *The Museum and Popular Culture,* but much more needs to be done in this area. Also, there is no study of the image of science conveyed by popular expositions, although there are some descriptions of these fairs, such as *Science and Mechanism, Illustrated by Examples in the New York Exhibition, 1853-54* by Benjamin Silliman, Jr., and C. R. Goodrich.

The relationship between science and religion in the nineteenth-century United States before Darwin is thoroughly explored by Herbert Hovenkamp in *Science and Religion in America, 1800-1860.* Numerous books deal with the intellectual and religious reaction to evolutionary theory, including collections like R. J. Wilson's *Darwinism and the American Intellectual: A Book of Readings,* which present good, short introductory essays to very short excerpts of articles about Darwinism, and George Daniels's collection of twenty articles written between 1859 and 1874 which map out the change of intellectual opinion, *Darwinism Comes to America.* Cynthia E. Russett has analyzed these intellectual reactions in *Darwin in America: The Intellectual Response, 1865-1912.* Two chapters in Thomas F. Glick's *The Comparative Reception of Darwinism* are also quite useful: Edward J. Pfeifer records the history of the controversy after 1879, and Michele L. Aldrich has written a bibliographical essay which pays particular attention to popularizations of the theory. It is virtually impossible to separate the scientific controversy from Social Darwinism, as demonstrated by Richard Hofstadter's *Social Darwinism in American Thought* and Paul Boller, Jr.'s *American Thought in Transition: The Impact of Evolutionary Naturalism, 1865-1900.* There are many records of the theological reaction to evolution, most notably Andrew D. White's ambitious *A History of the Warfare of Science and Theology in Christendom,* Henry Ward Beecher's *Evolution and Religion,* and John Fiske's *Outlines of Cosmic Philosophy* in the nineteenth century. Fundamentalist opposition to evolutionary theory continued in the twentieth century, most notoriously at the Scopes Trial as documented by L. Sprague de Camp's *The Great Monkey Trial,* but still quietly alive, as V. Elving Anderson's essay reveals.

Literary utopias of the nineteenth century, beginning with J. A. Etzler's *The Paradise Within the Reach of All Men, Without Labour, by Powers of Nature and Machinery* in 1836, looked upon science and especially technology quite favorably. Edward Bellamy's *Looking Backward, 2000-1887* was the most popular representative of the utopia-based-on-technology genre, and it inspired a number of less well-written books, which are described and discussed by Kenneth M. Roemer in *The Obsolete Necessity: America in Utopian Writings, 1888-1900.* Robert L. Shurter noted the role of science in these popular books in *The Utopian Novel in America, 1865-1900,* a reprint of his 1936 dissertation. The broader context of literary utopias in America is surveyed by Vernon L. Parrington, Jr., in *American Dreams: A Study of American Utopias,* also originally a dissertation (1942), which describes literary utopias from 1689 to 1963.

The best essays on the positive image of the scientist in the late nineteenth and early twentieth centuries are written by Thomas D. Clareson: "The Scientist as Hero in American Science-Fiction, 1880-1920" and "The Emergence of the Scientific Romance: 1870-1926." Among the more popular romances of this period in which the scientist-hero brought peace are Simon Newcomb's *His Wisdom, the Defender,* Hollis Godfrey's *The Man Who Ended War,* Ray Norton's *The Vanishing Fleets,* J. Stewart Barney's *L.P.M.: The End of the Great War,* and Arthur Train's and William Wood's *The Man Who Rocked the Earth.*

The rise of the literary movements of realism and naturalism owed much to the popular appeal of science. This connection is discussed in Everett Carter's *Howells and the Age of Realism,* but the best history of literary realism is Warner Berthoff's *The Ferment of Realism: American Literature, 1884-1919.* Darwinism has been singled out for its strong influence on the naturalism movement in essays by Malcolm Cowley and Arthur E. Jones, Jr., and in Charles C. Walcutt's *American Literary Naturalism, A Divided Stream.* Science continues to play an ever stronger role in American literature, as the periodic *Isis* bibliographies reflect. Academicians in many fields, especially literature, are beginning to examine this interdisciplinary relationship carefully; the best summary to date is John Woodcock's "Literature and Science Since Huxley."

The modern popular attitude toward science is best discussed in an essay by George Barsalla, "Pop Science: The Depiction of Science in Popular Culture," which asserts that public opinion about science is molded far more by the generally negative images of television, films, and comic strips than by serious science popularizers. Oscar Handlin has also written an essay on the ambivalent response of the general culture to technology and science. The most eloquent yet debatable book on the scientist as creator-destroyer, Prometheus-Epimetheus, is *The New Prometheans: Creative and Destructive Forces in Modern Science,* by Robert S. de Ropp. The impact of technology on the American pastoral ideal is examined by Leo Marx in *The Machine in the Garden: Technology and the Pastoral Ideal in America.* Anti-science attitudes in the 1940s and 1950s are briefly considered in James B. Conant's *Modern Science and Modern Man* and Richard Hofstadter's *Anti-intellectualism in American Life.* Articles by Bentley Glass, Walter Hirsch, and Gerald Holton all discuss the stereotyped images of scientists today, but without the anger of articles like that written by Thomas H. Maugh II, which is representative of many articles protesting the stereotype. Certainly, the popular image of the scientist in literature is not necessarily negative, unless seeing scientists as human is considered derogatory, according to H. J. Medd's article on post-World War II fiction.

Works cited in chapters on the popular media in this *Handbook,* especially the chapters on comic art, films, television, and science fiction in Volume 1, contain further information on the image of the scientist. Particularly useful among these are John Baxter, *Science Fiction in the Cinema,* William K. Everson's chapter on "Mad Doctors and Mad Killers" in *The Bad Guys: A Pictorial History of the Movie Villain,* and Neil Barron's collection of bibliographical esssays in *Anatomy of Wonder: Science Fiction.* In addition, there are several books on science fiction films, although they say little about the image of the scientist as such: Stuart M. Kaminsky's *American Film Genres,* John Brosnan's *Future Tense: The Cinema of Science Fiction,* James R. Parish's and Michael R. Pitts's annotated list, *The Great Science Fiction Pictures,* and a collection of articles on science fiction films edited by William Johnson, *Focus on the Science Fiction Film.* Other approaches to science fiction as a reflection of attitudes toward science include Leonard Isaacs's course outline book, *Darwin to Double Helix: The Biological Theme in Science Fiction* and H. Bruce Franklin's article on "Science Fiction as an Index to Popular Attitudes Toward Science: A Danger, Some Problems, and Two Possible Paths."

It would be impossible to list the many books that deal with science as an environmental threat. Certainly Rachel Carson's *Silent Spring* stands as the most effective in galvanizing public opinion, an impact measured by Frank Graham in *Since Silent Spring.* The recent coincidental juxtaposition of the Three Mile Island nuclear incident and the film, *The China Syndrome,* brought fears of nuclear contamination to the headlines, joining recurrent scares such as the ozone-fluorocarbon controversy. The ethics of scientific decisions are also frequently debated in print, the most recent referring to recombinant DNA and genetic engineering. As with other controversies, this one, which has sometimes centered on the popular notion of cloning, appears widely in American culture, as in the movies *The Boys From Brazil* and Woody Allen's *Sleeper* and the purportedly nonfiction *In His Image: The Cloning of a Man* by David M. Rorvik, as well as academic works such as Clifford Grobstein's *A Double Image of the Double Helix: The Recom-*

binant-DNA Debate or the articles in John Richard's *Recombinant DNA: Science, Ethics, and Politics.*

There have been many efforts to popularize the ideas and image of science, although they have rarely had strong cultural impact. Early popularization work is described by Benjamin C. Gruenberg in *Science and the Public Mind* and Ronald C. Tobey in *The American Ideology of National Science, 1919-1930.* Typical of these popularizations are Edwin E. Slosson's *Chats on Science* and Lancelot T. Hogben's *Science for the Citizen: A Self-Educator Based on the Social Background of Scientific Discovery.* According to James D. Hart's *The Popular Book; A History of America's Literary Taste,* during the 1920s there was a surge of interest in books like J. Arthur Thomson's *Outline of Science* and Albert E. Wiggam's *New Decalogue of Science.* The most tireless popularizer today is Isaac Asimov, who has written numerous books and articles such as *Asimov's Guide to Science* and *New Intelligent Man's Guide to Science.*

The unquestionable and growing popularity of books related to science is probably more a product of increased science education than popularization efforts, judging by the quality of the books. Just the number of paper-bound books is amazing, with over nine hundred titles on general science currently listed in *Paperbound Books in Print.* Some of the best-selling books are the picture science books and field guides, such as the Time-Life series books on space (for example, Willy Ley's *Rockets, Missiles, and Men in Space*) or the fourteen other series listed in Winifred Courtney's *The Reader's Adviser,* and collections of experiments for children.

However, some popular books are for educated readers with some scientific background, such as George Gamov's *One Two Three...Infinity: Facts and Speculations of Science,* Buckminster Fuller's *The Operating Manual for Spaceship Earth,* and cross-disciplinary works like the colorful *Science and Technology in the Arts* by Stewart Kranz. Indeed, every month now, books combining science, philosophy, and often biography are reviewed by popular magazines. Leading recent examples are Carl Sagan's *Broca's Brain; Reflections on the Romance of Science,* Horace F. Judson's *The Eighth Day of Creation: Makers of the Revolution in Biology,* and Freeman Dyson's *Disturbing the Universe;* though technically not best sellers, these books do appeal to a wide adult audience.

Television and films provide other avenues for popularization of science, but there are no studies measuring the impact of these efforts. Of particular interest are the television shows with associated books, such as Don Herbert's "Watch Mr. Wizard," Jacob Bronowski's "The Ascent of Man," the Jacques Cousteau specials, James Burke's "Connections," the NOVA series, and single programs, such as the PBS production of "The Restless Earth," with book by Nigel Calder. The continuing existence of these shows and hundreds of films on science noted in Paul Wasserman's *Museum Media* and in the *Catalog of Motion Pictures and Filmstrips for Rent and Sale by the National Audiovisual Center* indicates a substantial audience, though it may sometimes be captive in classrooms.

Judging from the numerous books, magazines, films, and even television shows, Americans today are more eager than ever to understand science, in spite of the negative image often projected by popular media. Unfortunately, there has been no study of this phenomenon, possibly because of its educational component. Works on American popular culture rarely mention positive responses to science; as Dwight MacDonald did in his essay, they prefer to point to the terror aroused by the scientist's white coat. Also little attention has been paid by either scientists or literature students to the recent excellent works combining science and philosophy, yet many people read them. Clearly, it is time to go beyond popular stereotypes of science and the scientist or AAAS-sponsored glorifications and begin evaluating the full cultural impact of science on the modern mind.

NOTES

1. Morris R. Cohen, *American Thought: A Critical Sketch* (Glencoe, Ill.: Free Press, 1954), p. 85.
2. Louis B. Wright, *The Cultural Life of the American Colonies: 1607-1763* (New York: Harper and Brothers, 1957), p. 236.
3. Alexis de Tocqueville, *Democracy in America,* ed. Henry Reeve, Francis Bowen, and Phillips Bradley, vol. 2 (New York: Knopf, 1966), p. 42.
4. Charles E. Rosenberg, *No Other Gods: On Science and American Social Thought* (Baltimore: Johns Hopkins University Press, 1976), p. 4

BIBLIOGRAPHY

BOOKS AND ARTICLES

AAAS Science Book List: A Selected and Annotated List of Science and Mathematics Books for Secondary School Students, College Undergraduates and Nonspecialists. 3rd ed. Washington, D.C.: AAAS, 1970.

AAAS Science Book List Supplement. Edited by Kathryn Wolf and Jill Story. Washington, D.C.: AAAS, 1978.

AAAS Science Film Catalog. Compiled by Ann Seltz-Petrash and Kathryn Wolff. New York: Bowker and AAAS, 1975.

Adam, T. R. *The Museum and Popular Culture.* New York: American Association for Adult Education, 1939.

Adams, Henry. *The Degradation of the Democratic Dogma.* New York: Macmillan, 1919.

Aldrich, Michele L. "United States: Bibliographical Essay." In *The Comparative Reception of Darwinism.* Edited by Thomas F. Glick. Austin: University of Texas Press, 1972.

American Men and Women of Science. Edited by Jaques Cattell Press. 13th ed., 8 vols. New York: Bowker, 1976.
Anderson, V. Elving. "Evangelicals and Science: Fifty Years After the Scopes Trial (1925-75)." In *The Evangelicals.* Edited by David Wells and John Woodbridge. Nashville, Tenn.: Abingdon Press, 1975.
Ash, Lee. *Subject Collections: A Guide to Special Book Collections and Subject Emphases as Reported by University, College, Public and Special Libraries and Museums in the United States and Canada.* 5th ed. New York: Bowker, 1978.
Asimov, Isaac. *Asimov's Biographical Encyclopedia of Science and Technology.* Rev. ed. Garden City, N.Y.: Doubleday, 1972.
______. *Asimov's Guide to Science.* New York: Basic Books, 1972.
______. *New Intelligent Man's Guide to Science.* New York: Basic Books, 1965.
Barney, J. Stewart. *L.P.M.: The End of the Great War.* New York: Putnam's, 1915.
Barron, Neil, ed. *Anatomy of Wonder: Science Fiction.* New York: Bowker, 1976.
Barsalla, George. "Pop Science: The Depiction of Science in Popular Culture." In *Science and Its Public: The Changing Relationship.* Edited by Gerald Holton and William A. Blanpied. Boston: Reidel, 1976.
Bartlett, Irving H. *The American Mind in the Mid-Nineteenth Century.* New York: Crowell, 1967.
Bates, Ralph S. *Scientific Societies in the United States.* New York: Technology Press, 1958. 3rd ed. Cambridge, Mass.: MIT Press, 1965.
Baxter, John. *Science Fiction in the Cinema.* London: A. Zwemmer; New York: Barnes, 1970.
Beecher, Henry Ward. *Evolution and Religion.* New York: Fords, Howard and Hulbert, 1885.
Bell, Whitfield J., Jr. *Early American Science: Needs and Opportunities for Study.* Williamsburg, Va.: Institute of Early American History and Culture, 1955.
Bellamy, Edward. *Looking Backward, 2000-1887.* Boston: Houghton Mifflin, 1889.
Berthoff, Warner. *The Ferment of Realism: American Literature, 1884-1919.* New York: Free Press, 1965.
Besterman, Theodore. *Biological Sciences: A Bibliography of Bibliographies.* Towata, N.J.: Rowman and Littlefield, 1971.
______. *Physical Sciences: A Bibliography of Bibliographies.* Towata, N.J.: Rowman and Littlefield, 1971.
Bode, Carl. *The American Lyceum, Town Meeting of the Mind.* New York: Oxford University Press, 1956.
Boller, Paul, Jr. *American Thought in Transition: The Impact of Evolutionary Naturalism, 1865-1900.* Chicago: Rand-McNally, 1969.
Book of Popular Science. 10 vols. New York: Grolier, 1970.
Bozeman, Theodore D. *Protestants in an Age of Science: The Baconian Ideal and Antebellum American Religious Thought.* Chapel Hill: University of North Carolina Press, 1977.
Bronowski, Jacob. *The Ascent of Man.* Boston: Little, Brown, 1973.
Brosnan, John. *Future Tense: The Cinema of Science Fiction.* New York: St. Martin's Press, 1978.
Calder, Nigel. *The Restless Earth: A Report on the New Geology.* New York: Viking Press, 1972.

Capra, Fritjov. *The Tao of Physics.* Boulder, Colo.: Shambhala, 1976; New York: Bantam Books, 1977.

Carson, Rachel. *Silent Spring.* Boston: Houghton Mifflin, 1962.

Carter, Everett. *Howells and the Age of Realism.* Hamden, Conn.: Archon Books, 1966.

Catalog of Motion Pictures and Filmstrips for Rent and Sale by the National Audiovisual Center, 1969. Supplements, 1971-. Washington, D.C.: National Audiovisual Center, 1971.

Chen, Ching-Chih. *Scientific and Technical Information Sources.* Cambridge, Mass.: MIT Press, 1977.

Clapp, Jane, ed. *Museum Publications.* 2 vols. Metuchen, N.J.: Scarecrow Press, 1962.

Clareson, Thomas D. "The Emergence of the Scientific Romance: 1870-1926." In *Anatomy of Wonder: Science Fiction.* Edited by Neil Barron. New York: Bowker, 1976.

______. "The Scientist as Hero in American Science-Fiction, 1880-1920." *Extrapolation,* 7 (December 1965), 18-28.

Cohen, Morris R. *American Thought: A Critical Sketch.* Glencoe, Ill.: Free Press, 1954.

Conant, James B. *Modern Science and Modern Man.* New York: Columbia University Press, 1952.

Courtney, Winifred, ed. *The Reader's Adviser; A Layman's Guide.* 11th ed. 2 vols. New York: Bowker, 1969.

Cousteau, Jacques Yves, and James Dugan. *The Living Sea.* New York: Harper & Row, 1963.

Cousteau, Jacques Yves, and Frederic Dumas. *The Silent World.* New York: Harper & Row, 1953.

Cowles Encyclopedia of Science, Industry, and Technology. New York: Cowles Book, 1969.

Cowley, Malcolm. "Naturalism in American Literature." In *Evolutionary Thought in America.* Edited by Stow Persons. New Haven: Yale University Press, 1950.

Curti, Merle. *The Growth of American Thought.* New York: Harper & Row, 1964.

Daniels, George H. *American Science in the Age of Jackson.* New York: Columbia University Press, 1968.

______. *Science in American Society: A Social History.* New York: Knopf, 1971.

______. ed. *Darwinism Comes to America.* Waltham, Mass.: Blaisdell, 1968.

Davies, John D. *Phrenology, Fad and Science: A Nineteenth-Century Crusade.* New Haven: Yale University Press, 1955.

Deason, Hilary J., ed. *A Guide to Science Reading.* New York: New American Library, 1963.

______. *The Science Book List for Children.* Washington, D.C.: AAAS, 1960.

de Camp, L. Sprague. *The Great Monkey Trial.* Garden City, N.Y.: Doubleday, 1968.

de Ropp, Robert S. *The New Prometheans: Creative and Destructive Forces in Modern Science.* New York: Dell, 1973.

de Tocqueville, Alexis. *Democracy in America.* Edited by Henry Reeve, Francis Bowen, and Phillips Bradley. New York: Knopf, 1966.

Dictionary of Scientific Biography. New York: Scribner's, 1976.

Dillard, Annie. *Pilgrim at Tinker's Creek.* New York: Harper's Magazine Press, 1974.

Duncan, Ronald, and Miranda Weston-Smith, eds. *The Encyclopedia of Ignorance.* Oxford and New York: Pergamon Press, 1977.

Dyson, Freeman. *Disturbing the Universe.* New York: Harper & Row, 1979.

Eiseley, Loren. *Darwin's Century: Evolution and the Men Who Discovered It.* Garden City, N.Y.: Doubleday, 1958.

______. *The Firmament of Time.* New York: Atheneum, 1962.

______. *The Immense Journey.* New York: Random House, 1957.

______. *The Unexpected Universe.* New York: Harcourt Brace Jovanovich, 1969.

Ekirch, Arthur A., Jr. *The Idea of Progress in America, 1815-1860.* New York: Columbia University Press, 1951.

Elliott, Clark A. *Biographical Dictionary of American Science: The Seventeenth Through the Nineteenth Centuries.* Westport, Conn.: Greenwood Press, 1979.

Encyclopaedia Britannica. 15th ed. Chicago: Encyclopaedia Britannica, 1972.

Etzler, J. A. *The Paradise Within the Reach of All Men, Without Labour, by Powers of Nature and Machinery.* London: Brooks, 1836.

Everson, William K. *The Bad Guys: A Pictorial History of the Movie Villain.* New York: Citadel Press, 1964.

Fisher, George P. *The Life of Benjamin Silliman.* 2 vols. New York: Scribner, 1866.

Fiske, John. *Outlines of Cosmic Philosophy.* Boston: Houghton Mifflin, 1874.

Foerster, Norman. *Nature in American Literature: Studies in the Modern View of Nature.* New York: Russell and Russell, 1958.

Franklin, H. Bruce. "Science Fiction as an Index to Popular Attitudes Toward Science: A Danger, Some Problems, and Two Possible Paths." *Extrapolation,* 6 (May 1965), 23-31.

Fuller, Buckminster. *Operating Manual for Spaceship Earth.* New York: Dutton, 1969.

Fulton, John F., and Elizabeth H. Thompson. *Benjamin Silliman: Pathfinder in American Science, 1779-1864.* New York: Henry Schuman, 1947.

Gamow, George. *One Two Three...Infinity: Facts and Speculations of Science.* Rev. ed. New York: Viking Press, 1961.

Gardner, Martin. *Fads and Fallacies in the Name of Science.* New York: Dover, 1957.

Glass, Bentley. "The Scientist in Contemporary Fiction." *Scientific Monthly,* 85 (December 1957), 288-93.

Glick, Thomas F., ed. *The Comparative Reception of Darwinism.* Austin: University of Texas Press, 1972.

Godfrey, Hollis. *The Man Who Ended War.* Boston: Little, Brown, 1908.

Goode, George B. *The Smithsonian Institution, 1846-1896: The History of Its First Half Century.* Washington, D.C.: Smithsonian Institution, 1897.

Graham, Frank. *Since Silent Spring.* Boston: Houghton Mifflin, 1970.

Greene, John C. "Science and the Public in the Age of Jefferson." *Isis,* 39 (1958), 13-25. Reprinted in *Early American Science.* Edited by Brooke Hindle. New York: Science History, 1976.

Grobstein, Clifford. *A Double Image of the Double Helix: The Recombinant-DNA Debate.* San Francisco: Freeman, 1979.

Grogan, Denis J. *Science and Technology: An Introduction to the Literature.* Hamden, Conn.: Archon Books, 1970.

Gruenberg, Benjamin C. *Science and the Public Mind.* New York: McGraw-Hill, 1935.

Handlin, Oscar. "Science and Technology in Popular Culture." *Daedalus,* 94 (Winter 1965), 156-70. Reprinted in *Science and Culture.* Edited by Gerald Holton. Boston: Houghton Mifflin, 1965.

Hart, James D. *The Popular Book: A History of America's Literary Taste.* London: Oxford University Press, 1950.

Hellman, Geoffrey. *The Smithsonian: Octopus on the Mall.* Philadelphia: Lippincott, 1967.

Hendrickson, Walter B. "Science and Culture in the American Middle West." In *Science in America Since 1820.* Edited by Nathan Reingold. New York: Science History, 1976.

Herbert, Don. *Mr. Wizard's Science Secrets.* 2nd ed. New York: Hawthorn Books, 1973.

———, and Hy Ruchlis. *Mr. Wizard's Science Activities.* New York: Book-Lab, 1973.

Hering, Daniel W. *Foibles and Fallacies of Science.* New York: Van Nostrand, 1924.

Hindle, Brooke. *The Pursuit of Science in Revolutionary America, 1735-1789.* Chapel Hill: University of North Carolina Press, 1956.

———, ed. *Early American Science.* New York: Science History, 1976.

Hirsch, Walter. "The Image of the Scientist in Science Fiction: A Content Analysis." *American Journal of Sociology,* 63 (March 1958), 506-12.

Hofstadter, Richard. *Anti-intellectualism in American Life.* New York: Knopf, 1963.

———. *Social Darwinism in American Thought.* Rev. ed. Boston: Beacon Press, 1955.

Hogben, Lancelot T. *Science for the Citizen: A Self-Educator Based on the Social Background of Scientific Discovery.* New York: Knopf, 1938.

Holton, George, and William A. Blanpied, eds. *Science and Its Public: The Changing Relationship.* Boston: Reidel, 1976.

Holton, Gerald. "Modern Science and the Intellectual Tradition." *Science,* 131 (1960), 1187-93.

Hovenkamp, Herbert. *Science and Religion in America, 1800-1860.* Philadelphia: University of Pennsylvania Press, 1978.

Huth, Hans. *Nature and the American: Three Centuries of Changing Attitudes.* Berkeley: University of California Press, 1957.

Isaacs, Leonard. *Darwin to Double Helix: The Biological Theme in Science Fiction.* London: Butterworths, 1977.

Jaffe, Bernard. *Men of Science in America.* New York: Simon & Schuster, 1944.

Jastrow, Joseph, ed. *The Story of Human Error.* New York: Appleton-Century, 1936.

Jenkins, Frances B. *Science Reference Sources.* 5th ed. Cambridge, Mass.: MIT Press, 1969.

Johnson, Thomas C., Jr. *Scientific Interests in the Old South.* New York: Appleton-Century, 1936.

Johnson, William, ed. *Focus on the Science Fiction Film.* Englewood Cliffs, N.J.: Prentice-Hall, 1972.

Jones, Arthur E., Jr. "Darwinism and Its Relation to Realism and Naturalism in American Fiction: 1860-1900." *Drew University Bulletin,* 38 (December 1950), 2-31.

Jones, Howard Mumford. *The Age of Energy: Varieties of American Experience, 1865-1915.* New York: Viking Press, 1971.

Judson, Horace F. *The Eighth Day of Creation: Makers of the Revolution in Biology.* New York: Simon & Schuster, 1979.

Kaminsky, Stuart M. *American Film Genres.* New York: Dell, 1974.

Kohlstedt, Sally G. *The Formation of the American Scientific Community: The American Association for the Advancement of Science, 1848-60.* Urbana: University of Illinois Press, 1976.

Kranz, Stewart. *Science and Technology in the Arts.* New York: Van Nostrand Reinhold, 1974.

Lasworth, Earl James. *Reference Sources in Science and Technology.* Metuchen, N.J.: Scarecrow Press, 1972.

Lewis, Sinclair. *Arrowsmith.* New York: Harcourt Brace, 1925.

Ley, Willy. *Rockets, Missiles, and Men in Space.* Rev. ed. New York: Viking Press, 1968.

Lurie, Edward. *Louis Agassiz: A Life in Science.* Chicago: University of Chicago Press, 1960.

MacDonald, Dwight. "A Theory of Mass Culture." *Diogenes,* 3 (Summer 1953), 1-17.

MacDougall, Curtis. *Hoaxes.* 2nd ed. New York: Dover, 1958.

McGraw-Hill Basic Bibliography of Science and Technology. New York: McGraw-Hill, 1966.

McGraw-Hill Dictionary of Scientific and Technical Terms. New York: McGraw-Hill, 1974.

McGraw-Hill Encyclopedia of Science and Technology. 4th ed. 14 vols. New York: McGraw-Hill, 1977.

McGraw-Hill Modern Men of Science. 2 vols. New York: McGraw-Hill, 1966.

Malinowsky, H. Robert. *Science and Engineering Literature: A Guide to Reference Sources.* 2nd ed. Littleton, Colo.: Libraries Unlimited, 1976.

Marx, Leo. *The Machine in the Garden: Technology and the Pastoral Ideal in America.* New York: Oxford University Press, 1967.

Maugh, Thomas H., II. "The Media:The Image of the Scientist Is Bad." *Science,* 200 (April 7, 1978), 37.

Medd, H. J. "The Scientist in Fiction." *Ontario Library Review,* 46 (May 1962), 81-83.

Meisel, Max. *Bibliography of American Natural History, The Pioneer Century, 1769-1865.* 3 vols. Brooklyn: Premier Press, 1929. Reprint ed. New York: Hafner, 1967.

Miller, Marjorie M. *Isaac Asimov: A Checklist of Works Published in the United States, March 1939-May 1972.* Kent, Ohio: Kent State University Press, 1972.

Miller, Perry. *The Life of the Mind in America: From the Revolution to the Civil War.* New York: Harcourt Brace and World, 1965.

Mott, Frank Luther. *A History of American Magazines, 1741-1850.* 4 vols. Cambridge: Harvard University Press, 1938.

National Geographic Index, 1888-1946; 1947-1969. 2 vols. Washington, D.C.: National Geographic Society, 1969.

Newcomb, Simon. *His Wisdom, the Defender.* New York: Harper, 1900.

Newman, James R., ed. *The Harper Encyclopedia of Science.* Rev. ed. New York: Harper & Row, 1967.

Norton, Ray. *The Vanishing Fleets.* New York: Appleton, 1908.

NOVA: Science Adventures on Television. A Series of Reading Lists. Boston: Boston Public Library, 1974.

Oehser, Paul H. *The Smithsonian Institution.* New York: Praeger, 1970.

______. *Sons of Silence: The Story of the Smithsonian Institution and Its Leaders.* New York: Henry Schuman, 1949.

Paperbound Books in Print: Fall, 1978. New York: Bowker, 1978.

Parish, James R., and Michael R. Pitts. *The Great Science Fiction Pictures.* Metuchen, N.J.: Scarecrow Press, 1977.

Parrington, Vernon L., Jr. *American Dreams: A Study of American Utopias.* Rev. ed. New York: Russell and Russell, 1964.

The Penguin Dictionary of Science. New York: Schocken Books, 1972.

Persons, Stow, ed. *Evolutionary Thought in America.* New Haven: Yale University Press, 1950. Reprint. New York: Archon Books, 1968.

Pfeifer, Edward J. "United States." In *The Comparative Reception of Darwinism.* Edited by Thomas F. Glick. Austin: University of Texas Press, 1972.

Phillips, Venia T., and Maurice E. Phillips, comps. *Guide to the Manuscript Collections in the Academy of Natural Sciences of Philadelphia.* Philadelphia: Academy of Natural Sciences, 1963.

Pirsig, Robert M. *Zen and the Art of Motorcycle Maintenance: An Inquiry into Values.* New York: Morrow, 1974.

Pocket Encyclopedia of Physical Science. New York: Golden Press, 1968.

Reingold, Nathan, ed. *Science in America Since 1820.* New York: Science History, 1976.

______. *Science in Nineteenth-Century America: A Documentary History.* New York: Hill and Wang, 1964.

Richards, John, ed. *Recombinant DNA: Science, Ethics, and Politics.* New York: Academic Press, 1978.

Roemer, Kenneth M. *The Obsolete Necessity: America in Utopian Writings, 1888-1900.* Kent, Ohio: Kent State University Press, 1976.

Rorvik, David M. *In His Image: The Cloning of a Man.* Philadelphia: Lippincott, 1978.

Rosenberg, Charles E. *No Other Gods: On Science and American Social Thought.* Baltimore: Johns Hopkins University Press, 1976.

Rossiter, Margaret W. "Benjamin Silliman and the Lowell Institute: The Popularization of Science in Nineteenth-Century America." *New England Quarterly,* 44 (December 1971), 602-26.

Russett, Cynthia E. *Darwin in America: The Intellectual Response, 1865-1912.* San Francisco: Freeman, 1976.

Sagan, Carl. *Broca's Brain: Reflections on the Romance of Science.* New York: Random House, 1979.

Science Year: The World Book Science Annual. Chicago: Field Enterprises Educational, 1965-.

Scientific Tracts and Family Lyceum. Conducted by Jerome V. C. Smith. Boston: Allen and Ticknor, 1830-33, 1834-35.

Scientific Tracts, Designed for Instruction and Entertainment, and Adapted to Schools, Lyceums, and Families. Conducted by Josiah Holbrook and others. 3 vols. Boston: Carter, Hendee, and Babcock, 1831-33.

Shelley, Mary W. G. *Frankenstein or The Modern Prometheus.* London: Lackington, Hughes, Harding, Maver, and Jones, 1818. Reprint. London: Oxford University Press, 1969.

Shurter, Robert L. *The Utopian Novel in America, 1865-1900.* New York: AMS Press, 1973.

Sill, William B., ed. *The New Popular Science Encyclopedia of the Sciences.* Rev. ed. New York: Grosset and Dunlap, 1968.

Silliman, Benjamin, Jr., and C. R. Goodrich. *Science and Mechanism, Illustrated by Examples in the New York Exhibition, 1853-54.* New York: n.p., 1854.

Silverberg, Robert. *Scientists and Scoundrels: A Book of Hoaxes.* New York: Crowell, 1965.

Slosson, Edwin E. *Chats on Science.* New York: Century, 1924.

Smallwood, William M., and Mabel Smallwood. *Natural History and the American Mind.* New York: Columbia University Press, 1941.

Smithsonian Scientific Series. 12 vols. New York: Smithsonian Institution, 1943.

Smithsonian Year: Programs and Activities. Washington, D.C.: Smithsonian Institution Press, 1971-. Annual.

Stearns, Raymond P. *Science in the British Colonies of America.* Urbana: University of Illinois Press, 1970.

Stern, Madeleine. *Heads and Headlines: The Phrenological Fowlers.* Norman: University of Oklahoma Press, 1971.

Struik, Dirk J. *Yankee Science in the Making.* Rev. ed. New York: Collier Books, 1962.

Thomas, Lewis. *The Lives of a Cell: Notes of a Biology Watcher.* New York: Viking Press, 1974.

______. *The Medusa and the Snail: More Notes of a Biology Watcher.* New York: Viking Press, 1979.

Thomson, J. Arthur. *Outline of Science.* New York: Putnam's, 1922.

Thornton, John L., and R. I. Tully, Jr. *Scientific Books, Libraries, and Collectors: A Study of Bibliography and the Book Trade in Relation to Science.* Rev. ed. London: Library Association, 1962.

Tobey, Ronald C. *The American Ideology of National Science, 1919-1930.* Pittsburgh: University of Pittsburgh Press, 1971.

Tracy, Henry C. *American Naturists.* New York: Dutton, 1931.

Train, Arthur, and William Wood. *The Man Who Rocked the Earth.* New York: Doubleday, 1915.

Van Nostrand's Scientific Encyclopedia. 4th ed. New York: Van Nostrand Reinhold, 1976.

Walcutt, Charles C. *American Literary Naturalism, A Divided Stream.* Minneapolis: University of Minnesota Press, 1956.

Wasserman, Paul, ed. *Museum Media: A Biennial Directory and Index of Publications and Audio-visuals Available from United States and Canadian Institutions.* Detroit: Gale Research, 1973.

Watson, James D. *The Double Helix: A Personal Account of the Discovery of the Structure of DNA.* New York: Atheneum, 1968.

White, Andrew D. *A History of the Warfare of Science and Theology in Christendom.* New York: Appleton, 1895.

Whitrow, Magda, ed. *ISIS Cumulative Bibliography: A Bibliography of the History of Science Formed from ISIS Critical Bibliographies 1-90, 1913-1965.* 3 vols. London: Mansell Information, 1976.

Wiggam, Albert E. *New Decalogue of Science.* Indianapolis: Bobbs-Merrill, 1924.

Williams, Trevor E., ed. *A Biographical Dictionary of Scientists.* 2nd ed. New York: Wiley, 1974.

Wilson, R. J., ed. *Darwinism and the American Intellectual: A Book of Readings.* Homewood, Ill.: Dorsey Press, 1967.

Woodcock, John. "Literature and Science Since Huxley." *Interdisciplinary Science Reviews,* 3 (March 1978), 31-45.

World Who's Who in Science. Chicago: Marquis-Who's Who, 1968.

Wright, Louis B. *The Cultural Life of the American Colonies: 1607-1763.* New York: Harper and Brothers, 1957.

Youmans, W. J. *Pioneers of Science in America.* New York: Appleton, 1896.

Young, Margaret L., and Harold C. Young, eds. *Directory of Special Libraries and Information Centers.* 5th ed. 2 vols. Detroit: Gale Research, 1979.

Zochert, Donald. "Science and the Common Man in Ante-Bellum America." In *Science in America Since 1820.* Edited by Nathan Reingold. New York: Science History, 1976.

PERIODICALS

Alaska Geographic. Anchorage, 1972-.

American Birds. New York, 1947-.

The American Journal of Science. New Haven, 1818-.

American Magazine. New York, 1787-88.

American Midland Naturalist. Notre Dame, 1909-.

American Museum. Philadelphia, 1787-92.

American Naturalist. New York, 1867-.

American Progress. New York, 1873-91.

American Scientist. New Haven, 1943-. Formerly *Sigma Xi Quarterly.* New Haven, 1913-42.

Archives of Useful Knowledge. Philadelphia, 1810-13.

Astronomy. Milwaukee, 1972-.

Audubon Magazine. New York, 1899-.

Bulletin of the Atomic Scientists. Chicago, 1945-.

Daedalus. Cambridge, Mass., 1946-.

Discovery. New Haven, 1965-.

The Emporium of Arts and Sciences. Philadelphia, 1812-14.

Environment. St. Louis and Washington, D.C., 1959-.

Explorer. Cleveland. 1938-.
Examples in the New York Exhibition, 1853-54. New York: n.p., 1854.
The Friend. Philadelphia, 1827-.
The Humanist. Buffalo, 1941-.
Illustrated Science News. New York, 1878-81.
Impact of Science on Society. New York, 1950-.
Isis. Philadelphia and Beltsville, Md., 1913-.
Journal of the Franklin Institute. Philadelphia, 1826-.
Journal of Irreproducible Results. Chicago Heights, Ill., 1955-.
Kansas City Review of Science and Industry. Kansas City, 1877-85.
The Literary and Scientific Repository, and Critical Review. New York, 1820-22.
Massachusetts Magazine. Boston, 1789-96.
Mosaic. Washington, D.C., 1970-.
National Geographic. Washington, D.C., 1888-.
Natural History. New York, 1900-.
Naturalist Advertiser. Salem, Mass., 1871-75.
Naturalist and Fancier. Grand Rapids, Mich., 1877-79.
Nature. Hampshire, England, 1869-.
The New Science Review. Philadelphia and New York, 1894-96.
New Scientist. London, 1956-.
Oceans. Menlo Park, California, 1969-.
Omni. New York, 1978-.
Pennsylvania Magazine. Philadelphia, 1775-76.
The Port Folio. Philadelphia, 1801-27.
Popular Astronomy. Northfield, Minn., 1893-1941.
Popular Science. New York, 1872-.
The Popular Science Review. London, 1861-81.
Prairie Naturalist. Grand Falls, N.D., 1968-.
Pursuit. Columbia, N.J., 1969-.
Science. Washington, D.C., 1880-.
Science 80-. Washington, D.C., 1979-.
Science Books and Films. Washington, D.C., 1965-.
Science Digest. New York, 1937-.
Science for the People. Jamaica Plain, Mass., 1969-.
Science Illustrated. Albany, 1946-49.
Science News. Salem, Mass., 1878-79.
Science News. Washington, D.C., 1921-.
The Sciences. New York, 1961-.
STTH (Science/Technology and the Humanities). Melbourne, Fla., 1978-.
Science, Technology, and Human Values. Cambridge, Mass., 1972-.
Science World. New York, 1957-.
Scientific American. New York, 1845-.
The Scientific Journal. New York and Perth Amboy, N.J., 1818-20.
Scientific Man. New York, 1878-82.
Scientific Monthly. Toledo, Ohio, 1875-76.
Scientific Monthly, Washington, D.C., 1915-57.
Scientific Observer. Boston, 1877-87.

Scientific Record. Washington, D.C., 1879-81.
Sci-Quest. Washington, D.C., 1979-.
Search. Seattle, Wash., 1966-.
Sky and Telescope. Cambridge, Mass., 1941-.
Smithsonian. Washington, D.C., 1970/71-.
Space World. Amherst, Wisc., 1960-.
The Universal Asylum and Columbian Magazine. Philadelphia, 1787-92.
West American Scientist. San Diego, 1884-1919.
Worcester Magazine. Worcester, Mass., 1786-88.
Young Scientist. New York, 1878-87.

CHAPTER 17 Stamp and Coin Collecting

John Bryant

In recent decades Americans have turned to leisure activities with an intensity that nearly belies the function of "rest and relaxation." Like sports, hobbies are for millions an outlet or even substitute for passion, controlled forms of mania which allow the participant to escape from or create order in a restless world. The most popular type of hobby is collecting. Our compulsion to collect, notes W. D. Newgold in the *Encyclopaedia Britannica,* probably dates back to those happy, preliterate days when man foraged for nuts and berries.[1] But today's collector does not forage in order to consume; he catalogs and displays his nuts and berries. The modes of collecting are as numerous as the objects that can be collected, and today anything that is abundant enough to be accessible yet scarce enough to be a challenge can become a "collectible." Some collect natural specimens. (We are told that Howard Hughes collected bits of himself.) Some collect rare books or art. Others collect the detritus of our industrial civilization: tinfoil, beer cans, or barbed wire. More collect antiques or dolls. But most people who collect, collect stamps or coins.

The American Philatelic Society reports that its membership now numbers fifty thousand individuals. A likelier estimate of serious stamp collectors is more than double that figure, and the number of "nonprofessional" collectors—the child or adult who keeps a cigar box or tidy album of stamps—undoubtedly swells into the millions. The U.S. Postal Service claims that upward of 20 million Americans use its philatelic windows each year. The American Numismatic Association reports a smaller membership of 34,000, but the recent interest in coin investment is quickly transforming a once elite avocation into a popular hobby.

More impressive than these figures is the remarkable activity that philatelists and numismatists precipitate in both the business and leisure worlds. Many governments maintain philatelic agencies designed to promote collecting and coordinate the year's steady stream of colorful new issues. Coins, too, in recent decades have assumed eye-catching designs. Collectors in both fields belong to local, national, and international associations, nearly all of which hold exhibitions ranging from modest hotel gatherings to major expositions with juried exhibits, lectures, and dealers' tables. Over 130 stamp and 26 coin groups meet regularly to examine special aspects of the hobbies. Each week over one hundred syndicated stamp or coin columns address the general reading public. Also, America's presses generate a bewildering array of books, scholarship, catalogs, and at present well over two hundred specialized stamp or coin periodicals.

To touch the past, to gain mental control over a proliferating world by gathering specimens of it, or simply to research a project—these are human needs that are routinely satisfied by putting a stamp or coin in an album. Determining the social and psychological roots of the collecting phenomenon is challenging; equally fascinating are the cultural implications of the stamps and coins themselves. Overtly, both stamps and coins serve basic economic functions; covertly, they are modes of governmental propaganda. From an aesthetic perspective, they provide unique popular art forms combing miniature and medallic art, engraving, mass production, and, in some cases, the work of premiere American artists and artisans. (At various times, for instance, Americans have been able to purchase an engraved Gilbert Stuart reproduction on a stamp with a coin designed by Augustus St. Gaudens.) Finally, as social icons, stamps and coins reflect shifting American ideologies and may in guarded cases be used as evidence supplementing a scholar's historical or cultural observations.

In the past 150 years, philatelists and numismatists have published a substantial body of literature. Yet the amount of material published by our universities' cultural historians on these subjects is minute. In the process of reporting the scope and nature of philatelic and numismatic literature, assessing the scant number of publications in the area, and suggesting topics for further study, I hope to confront three problems: the phenomenon of collecting, the aesthetic merits of stamps and coins themselves, and the use of stamps and coins as reliable indicators of cultural development.

HISTORIC OUTLINE

Since postal and monetary history are academic fields in their own right and plump bibliographies exist for them elsewhere, I shall not detail the histories of the mails or money except when such details directly influence the development of the two hobbies. Generally speaking, three factors have shaped the growth of philately and numismatics: "democratization," or the spreading of an elite hobby among the masses; "commercialization," or the transformation of the hobby into a business; and "specialization," or the creation within the hobby of special, even scholarly, modes of collecting.

STAMPS

Unlike coins, which are as old as sin, postage stamps are an invention of the industrial age and imperial Britain's need for an efficient communication system. Sir Rowland Hill introduced postal reforms and adhesive postage stamps to the public in 1840. Previously, letters were ink-stamped, and the price of delivery was paid by the receiver to the courier on delivery. Numerous private delivery agencies competed in an open market. Hill instituted a government postal monopoly and essentially inverted the process of mail delivery. Now senders paid for delivery by purchasing one-cent "Penny Black" stamps, which they then affixed to their letters. The result was more revenues going directly into government coffers and broadened mail circulation. Although an American allegedly introduced the idea of prepaid postage stamps to Hill, Americans were slower to adopt the new system. The first official U.S. stamps were not printed until 1847, and the government did not gain a monopoly until 1863.

Serious stamp collecting began some twenty years after Hill's invention. In the 1840s stamps were a fad but not a hobby: a socialite in British Mauritia printed her own "Penny Blacks" to adorn party invitations, and in England something called a "stamp ball" was the rage. The less affluent fancied stamps, too, using them to decorate their walls and lapels. By the 1860s, however, the fad had clearly grown into a hobby. Used stamp transactions were a common sight in the open markets of Europe. London could boast sixty stamp dealers, and French officials, fearing that stamp markets encouraged forgeries and the corruption of youths, closed the Paris markets twice before letting hobbyists be. Philatelic literature ("how-to" books, catalogs, price lists, and even books on counterfeit detecting) appeared as early as 1862. In 1865, British dealer J. W. Scott set up business in New York, and his new company (still a major U.S. stamp firm) stimulated an already growing market in this country.

From the beginning philately shared in the democratic spirit of the age. Although more prominent philatelists have generally been wealthy men (John K. Tiffany, Count Ferarri, King Farouk, Franklin Delano Roosevelt), the hobby has been a relatively cheap, accessible, and convenient pastime shared (as handbook authors like to crow) by "kings and kids" alike. Even the earliest guides to the hobby proclaim philately's universal appeal. Stamps were easily packaged and mailed for trade or purchase; they were generally inexpensive and required no costly paraphernalia (such as the traditional coin cabinet). A working-class child with a few resources could acquire a modest collection through trade and discovery, if not purchase. Moreover, stamp collecting was seen then as now as a form of play providing moral instruction, knowledge, and good preparation for social advancement. The publisher of Henry J. Bellars's *The Standard Guide to Postage Stamp Collect-*

ing, for instance, argues that young collectors "have a more perfect knowledge of their studies, and, above all, obtain a quicker experience of actual life, *and the value of money.*"[2] More than a pastime for the idle rich, philately adhered to the Protestant ethic and gave youngsters a boost up the ladder of success.

To be sure, the major advances and research in the nineteenth century were made by the wealthy. The London (now Royal) Philatelic Society, founded in 1869, was followed in 1886 by the American Philatelic Association (now Society) organized by John Tiffany, a collector since 1859 and a bibliographer of philatelic literature. J. W. Scott presided over the first years of the Collectors Club of New York, founded in 1896, which listed among its members some of the nation's elite. The backbone of American philately, however, was in the middle and working classes; from 1870 to 1890 interest in the hobby was strong enough to sustain some three hundred popular and scholastic periodicals in the United States.

By the turn of the century, major stamp exhibitions in Antwerp (1887) and New York (1889) established philately as an international hobby. In 1890 a third such fair in London celebrated the fiftieth anniversary of Hill's invention and introduced an important decade in the commercialization of the hobby. Until this time governmental postal issues had been predominately portrait stamps. England had Victoria; America had Washington and Franklin. The first major step in the transformation of the hobby into a big government business occurred when authorities reckoned that prettier stamps might attract the eye and pennies of collectors. In the long run they were right, but the idea did not catch on immediately. As early as 1876 the U.S. government had, in fact, issued a series of seven "pictorial" stamps with vignettes of the signing of the Declaration of Independence, the landing of Columbus, and various "icons" such as a locomotive, steamship, and mounted courier; but these stamps did not sell well. A more notorious "experiment" in stamp marketing occurred in 1893, when N. F. Seebeck of the Hamilton Note Company of New York designed and printed a set of colorful stamps for certain Central and South American nations. Called "Seebecks," these stamps were primarily meant to be sold to collectors. The scheme failed, but in 1894 the republic of San Marino set up its philatelic agency to do precisely what Seebeck had hoped to do—create stamps not as postage but as collectors' items.

At first collectors were scandalized by any government's attempt to capitalize on the hobby, but the trend toward special and commemorative stamps was irreversible, and today most government postal services actively promote stamp collecting. The frequency of special issues has grown slowly but distinctly in the United States since the printing in 1893 of our first special issues commemorating Columbus's discovery of America. By the 1920s the United States was printing only about three special issues a year. However,

1932 was a banner year for U.S. commemoratives; nineteen in all were issued. The average number of issues in the 1950s was eleven; but since the Bicentennial the figure has approached thirty a year. Government stamp sales are a significant source of income ranging in the millions of dollars. Some speculate, too, that nearly 40 percent of U.S. stamps each year (almost 1.5 billion stamps in 1974) never circulate; they are collected or bought by dealers to be sold to collectors.

The boom in philately during the 1930s and 1940s deeply penetrated various sectors of American culture. Government, entrepreneurs, educators, churches, radio, and universities promoted the hobby. During his administration Franklin Roosevelt assumed complete control over stamp issues, and his flamboyant Postmaster General James Farley was responsible one year for a $1 million clear profit on the sale of stamps. Also at this time, philately was introduced as a teaching device in public schools. Junior-level history books, for instance, used stamps to "tell the story of America." Church-affiliated stamp clubs sprang up. Bell Telephone encouraged employees to collect, and Ivory Soap sponsored a long-running radio program for collectors. Even the University of Michigan offered a course in philately. Since World War II national and local stamp organizations have strengthened their civic-mindedness. The three major associations, the American Philatelic Society (APS), the Society of Philatelic Americans (SPA), and the American Topical Association (ATA), maintain close ties with civic and educational groups through slide shows, displays, and lecture programs.

For the most part the 1950s and early 1960s brought a continued expansion of philately's democratization and commercialization. More people were adopting the hobby, and the hobby business, in both private and government sectors, was growing. The notion that stamps make good investments has always been an important part of philately's commercial side, but it was not until the early 1950s and the advent of swift inflation that the idea began to sink in. Stamp guides, such as Henry M. Ellis's *Stamps for Fun and Profit,* indicate the trend. Temple University's Business School went so far as to offer a two-year course in philately. Since the Vietnam War, investors have turned more to stamps and coins as hedges against inflation, and Ed Reiter, coin columnist for the *New York Times,* recently reported that in 1980 Adelphi College offered courses in philately and numismatics to educate dealers and investors in the ways of the market.[3] Thus, the history of the commercialization of the postage stamps has moved from fad to hobby to private and government business to speculative finance.

To a certain degree, a history of philately can be keyed to the emergence of new ways to collect or specialize. Just as Jaques discerns seven ages of man, there are roughly the same number of "ages" of specialization for the collector. The first age is the generalist who collects any and all stamps. The first step toward specialization is the focus on the stamps of one nation or a particular historical period. A slightly more refined third "age" is collecting types of stamps (airmail, revenue, postage due) or stamps with peculiar markings or arrangements such as "overprints" and "perfins" (stamps pre-cancelled with perforated initials).

A fourth form of specialization is considered by many to be the height of traditional collecting (and, of course, madness, by the lay person). Here, a philatelist will focus on one particular stamp (usually a regular issue) and collect all of its plate, color, and press variants. Such a mode requires scholastic aptitude since the focal stamp's printing history must be meticulously researched down to the hairline cracks that appear in certain plates. (The process is comparable to literary textual analysis, only more difficult.) Growing out of the need for the analysis of variants and counterfeits was the foundation in 1940 of the Philatelic Research Laboratory of New York, which introduced various technological innovations to the hobby.

Anathema (it seems) to traditional philately is the fifth, upstart age of "topical" collecting. Here philatelists collect internationally but only along the lines of a particular subject matter depicted on the stamp. The American Topical Association, organized in 1940 and now ten thousand strong, recognizes at least seven hundred categories, including John F. Kennedy; space; Americana on American or non-American stamps; journalists, artists, and poets on stamps (JAPOS); women, and so on up to an amazingly self-reflexive topic, stamps with pictures of stamps on them. Topical collecting (or "thematics" as the British call it) has grown in popularity, and some traditional philatelists disparage the mode because it develops an interest in a stamp's message rather than the stamp itself or its history. Government post offices, however, have shaped their special issues to attract the topicalist. In the last two decades the U.S. postal authorities have introduced new printing methods which allow for more color and experimental groupings. (Two or four related stamps, for instance, may be printed together in a strip or block. These are called "*setens*" from the French *se tenant*, and, yes, one can collect only "*setens.*") At the moment, topical collecting is becoming the dominant mode of collecting.

A sixth "age" of philately involves those who collect postal material rather than just stamps. Of recent interest to investors and long-standing interest to postal historians are mailed (or even unused) envelopes or "covers" that bear the intricate markings of the mail service. Cover philatelists may, of course, collect material dating before the invention of the postage stamp, but such items are quite often found in museums. Slightly more accessible modern rarities include air mail covers delivered to Paris by Charles Lindbergh or to the United States via zeppelin. Covers also allow collectors to examine postmarks. Up until the turn of the century, letters were hand-cancelled, and early regional postmasters carved their own cancellation marks. Pumpkins, devils, eagles, and other elaborately designed or "fancy" cancellations can be collected, cataloged, and displayed.

The final age of the philatelist (not to be compared too closely to Jaques's "second childhood") is the most academic: postal history. Today even philatelists do not fully understand the difference between postal history and cover collecting. Since collection categories are interpreted by national and international exhibition judges, we might expect clear distinctions from these authorities, but, as a seminar at a recent southeast Pennsylvania stamp exposition revealed, not all judges agree. Generally speaking, a cover collection is merely a collection of covers, but a postal history collection demonstrates developments in postal history. Thus, as one seminar participant put it, the two types of collections may use precisely the same material but the difference is whether the collection is "written up" to demonstrate history or merely to describe the covers. The philatelist of the future, then, must sharpen his rhetoric.

COINS

Coin collecting presents a significantly different pattern of development. Unlike philately, which began in the industrial age as a fad, spread democratically, yet has become as much an academic pursuit as a hobby, numismatics has been from the beginning and until only recently the concern of the intellectual and social elite. Old coins have always been attractive to the antiquarian; Petrarch, for instance, was one of the first to have collected antique Roman coins. By the eighteenth century no Sun King or even his lesser luminaries could feel properly furnished without a coin cabinet. Men of substance acquired coins as they would art or rare books. Also at this time numismatics entered the university. As early as the Renaissance, gentlemen had written brief treatises on the history of coins, but by the early 1700s in Germany (still the central arena for numismatic research) scholars were beginning to use coins as historical evidence. The compulsion that drove Schliemann a century later to dig at the layered ruins of Troy was in part the same desire that brought early scholars closer to coins. Since then numismatics has been an important handmaiden to the archaeologist and historian as well as the aesthetician.

The nineteenth century brought a number of developments that shaped and redefined numismatics from the study of coins to that of money in general and medals. As Elvira E. Clain-Stefanelli remarks in her monograph (used liberally here), *Numismatics—An Ancient Science: A Survey of Its History,* the Napoleonic wars generated many medals which were in turn studied in weighty French tomes. In the New World, British and American governments struck medals to "honor" American Indian peace alliances. The quickly expanding and contracting economies of the world also generated more varieties of currency: paper money, bank notes, scrip, tokens, and even unofficial yet negotiable coins. The shortage of coins resulting from Andrew Jackson's refusal to recharter the Second Bank of the United States forced banks and merchants to issue fractional currency and "hard times coins" as late as 1844 in order to make change. With more of such items to collect, numismatists began to focus on material of more recent vintage and of the modern nations. By mid-century, museums as well as universities had become the principal lodgings for major collections. More people were able to see the rarities; more people could also afford modest collections of their own. Yet more scholarly research, publication, and cataloging developed during this period. Thus, numismatics was able to broaden its appeal but also rise in academic respectability.

Although American Colonial coinage can be dated back to 1616, we have records of only a few eighteenth-century American coin collectors. American numismatics dates primarily from the mid-nineteenth century. Philadelphia, home of the U.S. Mint, was logically the first center of numismatic interest. As Clain-Stefanelli records, the mint's chief coiner, Adam Eckfeldt, began a collection at the mint that would become one of the United States's and the world's finest. In 1858 several Philadelphians formed the Numismatic and Antiquarian Society. Also founded that year but destined to outlive the Philadelphia organization was the scholarly American Numismatic Society (ANS). This group and the larger, more hobby-oriented American Numismatic Association (ANA), founded in Chicago in 1891, have become the country's principal numismatic organizations. During the latter half of the century, periodicals such as the *American Journal of Numismatics* (no longer in print), *The Numismatist,* and other more ephemeral publications provided amateurs and newcomers with an opportunity to prepare themselves for the rigors of numismatic technique. Landmark works in U.S. numismatic scholarship appeared in these decades. Consonant with international scholarship of that age, American numismatists tended to use currency as clues to economic development rather than as archaeological evidence. It has been only recently that scholars have begun to appreciate the artistic merit of America's coinage.

Although by the turn of the century numismatics was growing, it was still a gentleman-scholar's hobby horse. The democratization of the hobby was impeded by certain obvious physical problems. At the time, cumbersome coins required boxes, drawers, and cabinets for storage. Also, modern collecting was inhibited by the fact that governments (which are still conservative when it comes to coinage) rarely minted commemorative, special, or even new issues. At least three developments served to rectify these problems. First, from 1892 to 1934, the U.S. government experimented with commemorative coins, some of which were issued alongside similar commemorative stamps. Also during this period the mint, in an attempt to generate interest in collecting, made available "proof sets"of each year's new or newly dated coins. Unfortunately, the Depression and World War II slowed down the collection of such items until the 1950s. A third development was the marketing in the late 1930s of "coin books" made of cardboard pages with holes cut to fit individual coins. The convenient device gave the hobby its biggest boost. At the time, traditional numismatists laughed, but hobbyists today continue to search loose change and coin rolls for that elusive 1919 D one-cent to stick in their books.

Although numismatics preceded philately as an intellectual discipline, coin collectors of the 1930s did well by following commercial techniques that had been in vogue among stamp collectors for decades. Chatty but reliable journals such as the *Numismatic Scrapbook Magazine* provided trade and sale information. In 1942 Richard S. Yeoman (who first marketed the coin book) began publishing the *Handbook of United States Coins,* "an objective pricing guide" for dealers, and in 1946 he put out the first edition of the *Guidebook of United States Coins,* now an annual mainstay for collectors.

Since World War II the growth of the hobby can be gauged somewhat by the fact that the mint sold nearly 4 million proof sets in 1964 over the fifty thousand sold in 1950. In recent years private mints have promoted the medallic arts, but the most important force in the hobby today is investment—the hope that coin collecting will somehow keep the wolf of inflation at bay. This, however, may destroy rather than promote the hobby, since the price of gold and silver has recently made even collector's items more valuable if melted down. Ed Reiter reports that more coins are heading toward the furnace. This will reduce the number of collector's items and raise their value but also reduce the number of those who can afford to collect.[4] Thus, this century has seen numismatics develop in ways contrary to philately. Beginning as a highly specialized field, coin collecting has enjoyed an age of democratization which may be cut short by overcommercialization and speculative finance.

REFERENCE WORKS

As already stated, the principal concerns of this essay are the collecting of stamps and coins as both aesthetic objects and social icons and the collecting of stamps and coins as a phenomenon. A remarkably large body of philatelic and numismatic literature exists, but little of it deals with these issues. Most published material addresses specialized audiences for the purposes of identifying, cataloging, and pricing collector's items. Although brief histories of collecting can be found in beginner's guides and some good aesthetic and social interpretations have been published, primarily in philatelic and numismatic periodicals, much remains for the cultural historian to pull together and assess. The following is a selection of the general and more specialized reference works used by philatelists and numismatists in their own fields that are likely to be useful for the student of popular culture or cultural history.

STAMPS

At the moment no complete bibliography of American philatelic literature exists, and, despite valiant efforts among philatelic librarians and bibliographers, no thorough compilation is likely to be published soon. Specialized or incomplete bibliographies do exist; however, they are hard to find. William R. Ricketts's *The Philatelic Literature Bibliography Index* is typical: a privately mimeographed, author-and-subject index of international material from 1863 to 1912, complete only up to the letter K. A more useful resource is Richard H. Rosichan's *Stamps and Coins,* which includes detailed annotations for many of its five hundred philatelic entries. While Rosichan seems to be an astute bibliographer, his selection is limited to works published primarily since 1959. Important early scholastic works are included only if they are still in print. Although international in scope, American works are emphasized, but there are glaring omissions (nothing, for instance, by Max Johl or August Dietz). Lists of current periodicals and libraries are incomplete. Rosichan's book is geared toward the hobbyist, but the scholar beginning to study philately should consult this resource. Found in Rosichan, for instance, are two specialized bibliographic items: Stamps Information Associates, *Collecting: United States* is a list of U.S. stamp catalogs; and James Lowe's *Bibliography of Postcard Literature* should delight all deltiologists.

One man's attempt to give some sense of order to bibliographic problems in philately is John B. Kaiser's "Bibliography: The Basis of Philatelic Research," which lists bibliographies, catalogs, and periodical indexes and is a good starting place for the researcher. Kaiser's "conspectus" of cumulative periodical indexes, for instance, is a simple but useful tool arranging a dozen periodical guides chronologically by coverage dates so that researchers can more readily locate indexes to journals of a particular era.

Published catalogs of philatelic libraries are the best substitutes for bibliographies, but they too are hard to find. John K. Tiffany's *The Philatelical Library: A Catalogue of Stamp Publications* is an excellent reference to nineteenth-century material by one of America's first collectors. The catalog lists 569 books and periodicals, nearly as many price lists and stamp catalogs, and 272 items on collecting and postal history. Supplanting Tiffany is E. D. Bacon's *Catalogue of the Philatelic Library of the Earl of Crawford, K.T.* which is arranged by author and nation. More recent is the Johannesburg

(South Africa) Public Library's *Catalogue of the Philatelic Collection,* also arranged by nation.

Catalogs of significant American collections of philatelic literature include the *Catalogue of the Philatelic Library of the Collectors Club* and *Postage Stamps: A Selective Checklist of Books on Philately in the Library of Congress.* The latter volume includes a prose paean to philately by poet-librarian Archibald MacLeish as well as a fine list of nineteenth-century handbooks, guides, and scholastic works. Lamentably, the Library of Congress has not updated this catalog even though its collection (now located in the Smithsonian) has grown since 1940 to be the best in the nation. On par with the Collectors Club and Smithsonian collections is the American Philatelic Research Library (APRL), which plans to publish by 1982 its catalog of nearly eight thousand books and periodicals. Finally, a convenient and still fairly reliable guide to the location of important bibliographical items can be found in John Freehafer's and Helen K. Zirkle's "A Selective List of Philatelic Handbooks, with a list of Libraries in which they may be found." Not to be dismissed by researchers is the annual *A Master List of Philatelic Literature* put out by the HJMR Publishing Company. It is an exhaustive price list of books and journals arranged by nation and topic.

Over the past two decades, significant bibliographic research has been carried on in the pages of the *Philatelic Literature Review.* As the journal for the American Philatelic Research Library, this quarterly supplements Kaiser's work by publishing indexes to philatelic periodicals. A guide to indexes not found in that journal is James Negus's "A List of Cumulative Indexes to Single Periodicals." The *Philatelic Literature Review* also notices about fifty new philatelic publications per issue. The definitive list of nineteenth- and twentieth-century stamp journals with title, publisher, and dates of publication is Chester Smith's recently published print-out *American Philatelic Periodicals.* A remarkable analysis of philatelic periodical literature in the United States is George T. Turner's "Trends in United States Philatelic Literature." Turner (whose massive philatelic library is now a part of the Smithsonian's collection) provides extensive quantitative analysis of periodical output from 1860 to 1945. The study, of course, needs significant updating, but it should provide a model for similar studies of trends in other forms of philatelic literature such as beginner's guides to the hobby.

A sign of the growing importance of philatelic literature to collectors is that many guides to the hobby include selected bibliographies, some of which can be useful to the researcher if the more complete bibliographies are not available. An exhaustive and convenient guide to the present state of the hobby is *Linn's World Stamp Almanac,* put out yearly by the publishers of America's principal philatelic trade weekly, *Linn's Stamp News.* This fact book's 450-item bibliography is extensive yet went to press without the benefit of the *MLA Style Sheet.* Nevertheless, Linn's list of over two hundred current periodicals is useful. Also in the almanac are the year's philatelic news in review, histories of the U.S. Postal Service and the Bureau of Engraving and Printing, descriptions of important research collections, and various sections on how to get a stamp design accepted by the Citizen's Stamp Advisory Committee and how to start a collection or a stamp club. Here one learns, for instance, that as of 1978 no stamp has been issued on August 8 in any given year. Smaller than Linn's bibliography but covering most major works is the checklist of literature in *Scott's New Handbook for Philatelists,* an adequate introduction to philately which includes a useful list of one hundred designers of U.S. stamps. Other guides elucidate the philatelist's patois. Prominent philatelist Henry M. Konwiser, for instance, provides sometimes quirky but always reliable entries on stamp vocabulary and U.S. postal history in *The American Stamp Collector's Dictionary.* Less ambitious but still useful is R. J. Sutton's and K. W. Anthony's *The Stamp Collector's Encyclopedia.*

The student of stamps and collecting necessarily requires some acquaintance with postal history. Alvin Harlow's *Old Post Bags: The Story of the Sending of a Letter in Ancient and Modern Times* is dated but reliable. More recent is Wayne E. Fuller's *The American Mail: Enlarger of the Common Life,* an excellent history of the people's conception of the post office. The author's bibliographical essay is invaluable. Carl H. Scheele's *A Short History of the Mail Service* is a readable introduction to U.S. postal history in the context of Old World systems. Histories of regional or specialized postal systems are too numerous to mention. Worthy of inclusion, however, are Kay Horowicz's and Robson Lowe's *Colonial Posts in the United States of America, 1606-1783,* August Dietz's *The Postal Service of the Confederate States of America,* and Wayne E. Fuller's *RFD: The Changing Face of Rural America.*

The scholar interested in postage stamps as art objects, social icons, or historical evidence stands before a field virtually untouched by the cultural historian. The few interpretative works on these issues will be treated later. The major concern here is where the researcher can find the stamps or suitable reproductions and basic information on the design, printing, distribution, and popularity of a given stamp. More often than not a pricing catalog is the best available resource.

Given the limited circulation of philatelic literature, most publications are as rare as the stamps they describe. Yet most libraries have at least one of the stamp catalogs put out each year by the publishing firms of Harris, Scott, and Minkus. *Scott's Specialized Catalogue of United States Stamps* is the most extensive. Its numbering systems for stamp types and individual stamps are almost universally accepted. Front matter includes a commemorative stamp index, information for collectors (explaining printing process and postal history), and an "Identifier of Definitive Issues." A black-and-white photo enlargement of each stamp is complemented by details concerning design source, designer, engraver, printer, and date of issue. Useful in gauging the relative popularity of a stamp is the chart of quantities of the commemorative stamps issued. Also included are enlargements of proprietary, local, and Confederate stamps. Although "unofficial" these stamps may, in fact, provide icons more suggestive of American life than official issues.

Several government publications are helpful. *Postage Stamps of the United States* (updated periodically) does not deal with anomalies or variants but does provide good photographs of each stamp type and a verbal description of its dimensions and printing history. End matter includes a table of plates used in printing commemoratives and a table of the quantities of each commemorative issued. Also found are lists of stamp designers and engravers since 1953 and of stamp topics. *The United States Official Postal Guide,* issued annually, is an important storehouse of stamp issues and postal regulations. Finally, since the person responsible for coordinating stamp issues is the third assistant Postmaster General, this official's documents stored in the National Archives constitutes important firsthand information on why a stamp is issued when. See the *Preliminary Inventories of the United States Archives,* nos. 63 (1953), 82 (1955), and 114 (1959) for their location.

Book-length and monographic studies by philatelists fall into four catagories: general histories of the U.S. issue, specialized studies of stamp essays, types, and variants, topical studies, and works on non-stamp philately.

Perhaps the most useful general histories are Lester G. Brookman's two-volume *Nineteenth Century Postage Stamps of the United States* and the five-volume *United States Stamps of the Twentieth Century* by Max Johl and Beverly S. King. Supplementing the latter is Sol Glass's *United States Postage Stamps, 1945-52.* Each work contains illustrations and data on the printing histories of each relevant stamp. Superb printing histories of commemoratives alone are Johl's two-volume *United States Commemoratives of the Twentieth Century* and G. C. Hahn's treatment of an important set of stamps in *United States Famous American Series of 1940.* Other works are Ralph A. Kimble, *Commemorative Postage Stamps of the United States,* and Fred Reinfeld, *Commemorative Stamps of the United States of America.*

To understand the utility of the following specialized studies, the reader may require an explanation of stamp production. The final stamp design of a particular issue is chosen from various engraved trial entries submitted by individual engravers. The rejected samples are called "essays," and in many cases they are completely different in design from the final chosen entry. Thus, fascinating evidence of what officials could have chosen as our postal icons appear in such works as Clarence Brazer's *Essays for United States Adhesive Postage Stamps* and George T. Turner's *Essays and Proofs of United States*

Internal Revenue Stamps. The Smithsonian also possesses in its vault a fine collection of stamp essays. Once a stamp goes to press, various plates, inks, and papers may be used before the run is complete. "Traditional" philatelic research has delineated the types and variants of many definitive U.S. issues. The specificity of this research will not likely aid the cultural historian. However, the art historian may find value in such landmark texts as Stanley B. Ashbrook's *The Types and Plates of the United States One-cent Stamp of 1851-57,* and *The United States Ten-cent Stamp of 1855-57.*

Works on "topicals" dating as far back as 1910 may be most useful to the cultural historian. The American Topical Association's bimonthly *Topical Times* is a good introduction to the various facets of this "sub-hobby." Social, cultural, or popular historians interested in such topics as women, minorities, Americana, art and artists, or such less "traditional" topics as games, toys,and sports might consult the appropriate topic handbooks published each year. APS and ATA study groups also publish their own journals ranging from the *JAPOS Bulletin* to everyone's favorite *Let's Talk Parachutes.* (Do not assume your specialized field has not been made a stamp topic.) Relevant to the nineteenth-century specialists is the *1869 Times* focusing entirely on the important "pictorial" series of 1869. Journals dealing with airmails may provide insights into various conceptions of the history of flight: two such periodicals are the bimonthly *Aero Philatelist Annals* and the monthly *Airpost Journal,* both edited by the American Airmail Society.

Studies of individuals or types of people who appear on stamps are numerous if not scholarly. An excellent guide, however, to all individuals who appear on stamps and which nations have printed their likenesses is Kent B. Stiles's *Postal Saints and Sinners: Who's Who on Stamps.* A general reference to portraiture is Edmund Burke Thompson's *Portraits on Our Postage Stamps.* Two dated works on minorities are Margaret N. McCluer's *Women as Presented on United States Stamps* and H. A. Fischel's provocative article, "Philatelic Portrait of the Modern Jew." This important list reveals that as of 1958 only 3 out of 117 famous Americans on our stamps are Jews. Arieh Lindenbaum's *Great Jews and Stamps* indicates some advancement in that area.

The following works on stamp portraiture are also dated and brief: J. H. van Peursem's *George Washington,* E. M. Allen's "America's Best-selling Portrait: Franklin," Emery Kelen, *Stamps Tell the Story of John F. Kennedy,* and Mary B. Lane and Elliott Perry, *The Harry F. Allen Collection of Black Jacks.* The latter is a catalog of one of America's finest philatelic specimens, the two-cent portrait of Andrew Jackson issued first in 1863. Finally, the Lincoln Society of Philately (Indianapolis) publishes a bimonthly on our sixteenth president predictably styled *The Lincoln Log.*

Non-stamp philatelic material such as illustrated envelopes, postmarks, and cancellation slogans may serve as useful evidence. Envelopes come in various forms, official and unofficial, decorated with elaborate vignettes (called cachets) or not. *Thorp-Bartel's Catalogue of the Stamped Envelopes and Wrappers of the United States,* edited by Prescott H. Thorp, is a thorough analysis and pricing of postal envelopes. The important illustrated catalogs of Civil War postal covers are Robert Laurence's *The George Walcott Collection of Used Civil War Patriotic Covers* and Robert W. Grant's continually updated, loose-leaf *Handbook of Civil War Patriotic Envelopes and Postal History.* An important early study of U.S. postmarks is Delf Norona's recently reprinted *Cyclopedia of United States Postmarks and Postal History.* The subcategory of "fancy" cancellations, or a postmaster's individualized postmark, is treated by Michel Zareski and Herman Herst, Jr., in *Fancy Cancellations on 19th Century United States Postage Stamps.* Lists of postal clichés can be found in Moe Luff's *United States Postal Slogan Cancel Catalog* and in the Smithsonian's Philatelic Collection.

COINS

In recent decades, philatelic scholarship has expanded both in size and scope, but given the age and scholastic roots of numismatics, it is no surprise that the body of numismatic literature is still larger, better indexed, and broader in intellectual range than philatelic literature, as the excellent state of numismatic bibliography indicates. The chief work in the field is Elvira E. Clain-Stefanelli's impressive volume *Select Numismatic Bibliography.* Although not "exhaustive," it is by far the researcher's best starting point. It places "special emphasis" on standard references and other important publications since 1885, as well as "the still used classical works of the past 200 years." Giving particular attention throughout to American references, the author's compilation lists guides, collection and exhibition catalogs, biographies of numismatists, and periodicals. Special sections such as "Art on Coinage" are also useful. Richard H. Rosichan's focus on post-1959 material in *Stamps and Coins* makes his annotated bibliography (discussed earlier in this section) of nearly 1,100 items a good supplement to Clain-Stefanelli. For an important nineteenth-century American bibliography, see Emmanuel J. Attinelli's *Numisgraphics, or a list of catalogues, price lists and various publications of more or less interest to Numismatologists.*

Since 1947, the American Numismatic Society has published *Numismatic Literature,* an excellent annotated listing of numismatic periodical literature appearing in nearly all scholarly journals and many non-numismatic publications. *The Numismatist,* published by the American Numismatic Association, is a felicitous blend of scholarship and trade news. Its author-subject indexes (1939 and 1959) will lead the researcher to important material on iconography, portraiture, coin design, medals, tokens, and the growth of the hobby. The index to the first, but now defunct, coin periodical, *American Journal of Numismatics* (1866-1924), is located in volume 51 (1917).

As with philatelic literature, catalogs of numismatic literature are of vital importance. The American Numismatic Society's seven-volume *Dictionary Catalogue of the Library of the American Numismatic Society* reprints the card catalog for that society's excellent library. Included here are books, all periodicals since 1930, price lists, unpublished manuscripts, and auction catalogs. Also available is the *Library Catalog of the American Numismatic Association.* Of interest to nineteenth-century researchers is the *Catalogue of the Numismatic Books in the Library of the American Numismatic and Archaeological Society.*

A convenient introduction to the hobby and its present state is *Coin World Almanac.* Put out by the people who published *Linn's World Stamp Almanac,* this more elegantly printed tome provides similar articles on the year's numismatic news, numismatic law, and histories of gold, silver, and U.S. coins. Also found here are lists of designers, engravers, and portraits on coins and paper money. (Did you know that Martha Washington graced our one-dollar bill from 1886 to 1891?) Nearly half the book provides facts and analysis of market trends in gold and silver trading. *Cowles' Complete Encyclopedia of United States Coins,* written and illustrated by *Coin World* columnist Mort Reed, is an enjoyable and well-researched introduction to American coins, their iconography, and minting process. A fairly learned, adult-level guidebook to the hobby and science is Philip Grierson's *Numismatics.* Finally, two numismatic word books are Albert Frey's *Dictionary of Numismatic Names* and Mark Salton's *Glossary of Numismatic Terms.* For a survey of monetary history that may be necessary before embarking upon any numismatic study, one can turn to Arthur Nussbaum's *A History of the Dollar,* an authoritative study (with bibliography). For a late nineteenth-century treatment of the same topic see A. Barton Hepburn, *A History of Currency in the United States.* First published in 1903, this work is still consulted today. Specialized studies are not hard to find; two important works are Richard Cecil Todd's definitive *Confederate Finance* (with bibliography) and Irwin Unger's *The Green-back Era: A Social and Political History of American Finance, 1865-1879.*

Standard pricing catalogs are generally the most convenient means a researcher has to view coins. The most widely used is Richard S. Yeoman's *Guidebook of United States Coins.* Referred to as the "Red Book," this annual price list offers a brief introduction to American coinage and suitable photographs of Colonial and official U.S. coin types. Don Taxay's *Comprehensive Catalogue and Encyclopedia of United States Coins* lists proofs and variants as well as their locations in various collections. Abe Kosoff's *An Illustrated History of United States Coins* gives glimpses of proposed coin designs as well as illustrations of definitive issues. Robert Friedberg's *Paper Money of the United States* is a good collector's guide illustrating all U.S. issues. Grover Criswell's and Clarence Criswell's work on *Confederate and Southern States Currency* is the definitive, illustrated catalog in the field of Southern numismatics.

Studies acquainting the researcher with the facts of America's official and unofficial currency are found in general histories of our coinage and works on such specialized topics as commemoratives, essays, paper money, fractional currency, medals, and tokens.

A well-researched assessment of the U.S. Mint and America's definitive issues is Don Taxay's *The United States Mint and Coinage: An Illustrated History from 1776 to the Present.* J. Earl Massey's *America's Money: The Story of Coins and Currency* relates coinage to American history in general. Brief histories by established numismatists can be found in Theodore V. Buttrey, Jr., editor, *Coinage of the Americas,* which includes articles on "Colonial Coinages" by Eric P. Newman and "Coinage of the US" by Walter Breen. An excellent history (with bibliography) is Taxay's *Money of the American Indian and Other Primitive Currencies of the Americas.* Other histories with a narrower focus are Neil Carothers's *Fractional Money: A History of the Small Coins and Fractional Paper Currency of the United States,* William H. Griffiths's *The Story of the American Bank Note Company,* and the U.S. Government Printing Office's *History of the Bureau of Engraving and Printing (1862-1962).*

Studies focusing on the influence of particular individuals on American coinage are the American Numismatic Association's monographs on Benjamin Franklin and Theodore Roosevelt as well as two works by Walter Breen: *The Secret History of the Gobrecht Coinages (1836-1840),* concerning an early chief of the U.S. Mint, and *Brasher and Bailey, Pioneer New York Coiners.* Early histories should not be overlooked. Montroville W. Dikeson's remarkable volume *The American Numismatic Manual* is a thorough and beautifully illustrated study of Indian, Colonial, state, and federal currencies.

General studies of America's commemorative coinage are of particular interest to cultural historians. Don Taxay's *An Illustrated History of United States Commemorative Coins* is the definitive work. Focusing more on topics depicted on coins is Warren A. Ruby's *Commemorative Coins of the United States.* Not to be discounted is Arlie Slaubaugh's *United States Commemorative Coins: The Drama of America as Told by Our Coins.* Despite the didactic subtitle, this study of America's 157 commemorative varieties provides important historical background as well as design and engraving information on each coin.

The numismatic counterpart of the stamp "essay" is the "pattern." Specialized studies of coins in this state are crucial in understanding the evolution of American coin iconography. They are Edgar H. Adams and William H.

Woodin, *United States Patterns, Trial and Experimental Pieces* and J. Hewitt Judd and Walter Breen, *United States Patterns, Experimental, and Trial Pieces,* both of which are fully illustrated. A number of works designed to meet the needs of specialized collectors may also interest the popular art historian. They are Roger S. Cohen and others, *American Half Cents, the "Little Half Sisters": A Reference Book on the United States Half Cent Coined from 1793 to 1857;* William H. Sheldon and others, *Penny Whimsey;* Martin Luther Beistle, *A Register of Half Dollar Varieties and Sub-Varieties;* and Leroy C. Van Allen and A. George Mallis, *Guide to Morgan and Peace Dollars: A Complete Guide and Reference Book on United States Silver Dollars.*

Also of interest to the cultural historian and aesthetician are the icons and designs found on America's "unofficial" currency: bank notes, fractional currency, and scrip. Monographic studies on bank notes by John A. Muscalus provide a wealth of material: *Index of State Bank Notes that Illustrate Characters and Events, Index of State Bank Notes that Illustrate Washington and Franklin, Index of State Bank Notes that Illustrate Presidents, Famous Paintings Reproduced on Paper Money of State Banks, 1800-1866,* and *The Views of Towns, Cities, Falls, and Buildings Illustrated on 1800-1866 Bank Paper Money.* Matt Rothert's *A Guidebook of United States Fractional Currency* is well illustrated and has a good bibliography. For views of what happens to currency when times get tough, see Lyman H. Low's *Hard Times Tokens* and Charles V. Kappen's and Ralph A. Mitchell's *Depression Scrip of the United States.*

Just as philately has expanded to include the collection of non-stamp material, numismatics has, for over a century, embraced the medallic arts. Indeed, the design, iconography, and striking of American medals are as important to the scholar as coins themselves. General surveys of the field include Charles W. Betts, *American Colonial History Illustrated by Contemporary Medals;* Joseph F. Loubat, *The Medallic History of the United States of America, 1776-1876;* Clifford Mishler, *United States and Canadian Commemorative Medals and Tokens;* and Georgia S. Chamberlain's *American Medals and Medalists.* An indispensable resource is Leonard Forrer's *Biographical Dictionary of Medalists.* See also Richard D. Kenney, *Early American Medalists and Die Sinkers.* Studies of special types of medals include Gilbert Grosvenor and others, *Insignia and Decorations of the United States Armed Forces,* Evans E. Kerrigan, *American War Medals and Decorations,* and Jennings Hood's and Charles J. Young's *American Orders and Societies and Their Decorations.* An important branch of American numismatics and one of special interest to American scholars in general are the Indian peace medals. A study of Britain's medals is Melvill Allan Jamieson's *Medals Awarded to North American Indian Chiefs, 1714-1922.* Less tame are the U.S. government medals given to Indians as illustrated in a well-researched volume, Bauman L. Belden's *Indian Peace Medals Issued in the United States, 1789-1889.* Studies of medals struck in honor of individuals or groups include the following: Elston G. Bradfield, "Benjamin Franklin: A Numismatic Summary"; William S. Baker, *Medallic Portraits of Washington;* Robert P. King, "Lincoln in Numismatics: A Descriptive List"; and Edward C. Rochette, *The Medallic Portraits of John F. Kennedy: A Study of Kennediana.*

RESEARCH COLLECTIONS

Generally speaking, it is unlikely that even the best university libraries will have extensive holdings in philatelic or numismatic literature. (In fact, major public libraries generally have better collections.) Even rarer are institutions that can make specimens available to the scholar. Researchers who desire more contact than either Scott's or the Red Book can provide will seek out the libraries and specimens of strong philatelic or numismatic collections. Although the best are located in the East, useful collections can be found in the Midwest and West.

STAMPS

The three best research collections are the National Philatelic Collection, located in the Smithsonian's Museum of History and Technology, Washington, D.C.; the Collectors Club of New York; and the American Philatelic Research Library in State College, Pennsylvania. Once a part of the Library of Congress, the National Philatelic Collection is both library and archive. It maintains an extensive but uncataloged collection of philatelic literature and a massive stamp collection which includes all but one of the American issues and numerous essays. Its photographic collection of over six thousand prints and slides is indispensable. The collection also maintains a postal history clipping file, statistics, paraphernalia, postmaster correspondence on all commemoratives, and a tape and film library. Here you can listen to Tim Healey's radio program, "Ivory Stamp Club of the Air." The collection is open to the public weekdays from ten to five. Nearly three hundred philatelists use the facility each year, so an appointment with the excellent staff is advised.

The Collector's Club of New York maintains a limited membership of about 1,100 people, but its excellent library (only recently surpassed by the Smithsonian) is open by appointment to scholars. Its John N. Luff Reference Collection is extensive, and the J. Bruce Chittenden Memorial Library, with 140,000 items, is particularly strong in pre-twentieth-century material, including postmasters' reports. The American Philatelic Research Library is the research wing of the American Philatelic Society. Its holdings include

7,000 books and monographs, 400 periodicals, and 150 catalogs but no stamp specimens or slides of American stamps. An important aid to scholars is the library's extensive but as yet unpublished index of early philatelic literature. The library is open to the public and material is circulated to non-APS members through interlibrary loan.

Other major collections can be found in the B. K. Miller Collection of the New York Library; the Philatelic Foundation, New York; the George Linn Memorial Research Library, Sidney, Ohio, which holds three thousand volumes and one hundred periodicals; and the Western Philatelic Library of the Sunnyvale (California) Public Library, which maintains a collection of 2,500 books. Futhermore, the public libraries of Chicago, Cleveland, Los Angeles, Milwaukee, Newark (New Jersey), and Pomona (California), and the free libraries of Philadelphia and Baltimore have considerable holdings.

Specialized collections holding philatelic literature and stamps are also attractive to scholars. The Lincoln Shrine in Redlands, California, has philatelic materials relating to Old Abe. Eisenhower's collection can be found in the Cardinal Spellman Philatelic Museum along with the cardinal's personal collection of stamps and eight thousand volumes of philatelic literature. FDR's collection and related materials are located at the FDR Library and Museum in Hyde Park, New York. Finally, the Wiltsee Memorial Collection of Western Stamps in the Wells Fargo Bank History Room, San Francisco, houses stamps of 235 different companies including the Pony Express.

COINS

The two major numismatic organizations maintain fine libraries. The American Numismatic Society, located near Broadway and West 155 Street in New York, has the smaller membership but a larger output of scholastic publication. Its library of fifty thousand items, described earlier, is the nation's best. The American Numismatic Association, located in Colorado Springs, Colorado, has a much smaller library of three thousand volumes, but it is likely to meet the needs of most researchers. Both institutions are open to scholars and lend books through interlibrary loan. As in philately, numismatic libraries can be found in major public libraries. Richard H. Rosichan reports in *Stamps and Coins* that the public libraries of New York and Minneapolis and the Free Library of Philadelphia have good collections. Major university collections of numismatic literature are found at Glassboro (New Jersey) State College, Yale, Washington, and New York universities, and the universities of Chicago and Colorado.

While both ANS and ANA maintain superb numismatic museums, the best specimen collection continues to be the National Numismatic Collection housed in the Smithsonian's Museum of History and Technology, Washington, D.C. The collection began when the U.S. Mint transferred its collection to the Smithsonian in 1923. Since then, and with the help of the ANA and ANS, the collection has grown from about 40,000 to over 150,000 pieces. The Smithsonian as well as the ANA and ANS display many of their specimens, and visitors to all three collections may view vaulted material upon request. An excellent history and description of the National Collection is Vladimir Clain-Stefanelli's monograph *History of the National Numismatic Collections.* The author's appendixes also provide interesting information for those researching the early growth of American numismatics. Some banks such as Detroit National also maintain excellent coin displays.

Like any stamp or coin collection, university coin collections are likely to change hands frequently. Any listing of such collections is bound to be dated. Elvira Clain-Stefanelli reports that major collections can be found at Yale, Dartmouth, Johns Hopkins (although it has just sold its J. W. Garrett Collection), Princeton, Columbia, Vassar, St. Louis, and the universities of Wisconsin, Chicago, and California at Berkeley.

HISTORY AND CRITICISM

To my knowledge, no book-length work of scholarship on the history of stamp collecting or the cultural significance of stamps exists. Some scholarly articles have appeared in the past two decades, but, generally speaking, the ideas and controversies related to philately have been limited to popular magazines and journals. Coins present a slightly different picture. Since numismatics is rooted in traditional scholarship, studies of ancient and some modern coins as cultural artifacts can be found. American coins, however, have only recently received proper attention. To a certain extent, then, what can be said for stamps may apply to coins: much study remains to be done.

STAMPS

Critical works pertaining to philately may be broken down into three groups: those treating the growth of philately as a hobby or business, those exploring the artistic merit of stamps themselves, and those concerning stamps as social icons. It is with the latter issue that I will discuss what I consider to be this essay's major problem: whether the postage stamp can serve as a reliable cultural indicator.

The scores of philatelic guides and memoirs of prominent collectors constitute a major resource of primary material for the student hoping to trace the development of collecting. Frederick Booty's *Stamp Collector's Guide* is probably the first philatelic handbook. Like Bellars's *Standard Guide* already mentioned, it is nothing more than an introduction to the hobby and a price list. Today, the beginner's guide has dispensed with the price list and become a form of "companion literature" which speculates on why people collect;

explains modes of collecting, hobby technique, investment, and clubs; relates hobby lore; and lists philatelic literature and terminology. Philatelic glossaries, which include such locutions as "aerophilately" and "stampic," seem designed to pique the interest of sociolinguists on the trail of the deep structure of hobby language.

Themes in stamp guides often reflect the anxieties of a predominately male leisure class. Early artifacts, for instance, adopt an apologetic tone which strongly argues that the hobby is not idle play but that it engenders care, method, and neatness. As late as the 1930s noted philatelist Ellis P. Butler in *The Young Stamp Collector's Own Book* felt compelled to remind his young, obviously male, readership that collecting is a "form of play" that encompasses adventure, exploration, and hunting and that it is emphatically not a "sissy" pastime. (Evidence that the rank and file of philately are broadening to include more women can be found in Barbara Mueller's *Common Sense Philately,* which points out that as of 1958 women make up about 10 percent of the New York Collectors Club membership, a considerable increase over Butler's era.) The fear that philately is childish or sissified is frequently countered in such guides as *Stamps for Fun and Profit* by Henry M. Ellis and *Everybody's Guide to Stamp Investment* by Joseph E. Granville by the notion that stamps stimulate the manly endeavor of finance.

Popular magazines in nearly every decade have promoted the ideas that stamps are both educational and lucrative. Philately has been seen as an aid to teachers of geography, history, language, and literature. *Parents Magazine* argues that a child's "early collecting instinct should be encouraged."[5] *School Life* states that postage stamps can "stimulate patriotism."[6] The *Journal of Educational Method* instructs us on how to make a "stamp map."[7] Since the 1920s, articles gauging philately's investment potential have appeared in such periodicals as *Business Week,* the *Economist, Nation's Business, Newsweek, Popular Mechanics,* and *Time.* Other nonphilatelic periodicals that have published articles measuring the pulse of the hobby are *Hobbies, Popular Science, Profitable Hobbies, Saint Nicholas,* and *Scientific American.*

Of course, the best resource for recent hobby developments is the trade weekly. *Linn's Stamp News* is probably the largest. *Stamps* (published by Lindquist) and *Mekeel's Weekly Stamp News* are also newspapers of considerable heft. Deeper speculations and more arcane scholarship can be found in the hobby journals. Widely distributed is the *American Philatelist,* the monthly house organ for the American Philatelic Society. Indexed every December, it is an attractive amalgam of trade notes, book reviews, committee reports, news of current stamp issues, specialized departments on taxes, and other collecting problems, and a good deal of scholarship on stamp variants and the cultural history of stamps (international). More modest yet more scholarly is the *SPA Journal* edited by the Society of Philatelic Americans (the number-two national stamp organization). Other specialized journals are the *United States Specialist,* put out by the Bureau Issues Association, which focuses on issues produced by the Bureau of Engraving and Printing, and the *American Revenuer.* These and the *Essay-Proof Journal* are likely to offer the cultural historian important material on U.S. postal history and iconography.

A recurring issue in many hobby publications is the problem of why people collect in the first place. Do we collect in order to touch the past and thereby escape the present, thus making collecting a form of nostalgia? Do we collect in order to classify, to take a slice of a proliferating world, organize it, and create on our own a silent moment of order? Do we collect because we want to know the world, or because we enjoy pretty things? Do we collect, quite simply, because the things, pretty or not, are there in sufficient variety and quantity and are begging to be collected?

What have the psychologists to say of the collecting mania? One philatelist speculates that Freud might categorize the impulse to collect as "repressed imperialism."[8] Lamentably, I have not been able to find any writings by Freud or his immediate brethren substantiating this speculation. Perhaps, psychoanalysts find collecting too healthy to worry about. Recently, however, a group of psychologists led by R. T. Walls studied children's collection preferences and found that, when given a choice of collecting a prescribed set of objects or collecting several copies of one member of that set, children of ages four and ten overwhelmingly prefer to fill out a set. At best, this evidence may explain the popularity of topical over traditional stamp collecting. It may also prove the infantilism of collecting.

Clearly, the psychological aspects of collecting require more systematic study. For the time being the student of the phenomenon must be satisfied with the thin speculations of magazine writers. According to *Literary Digest,* for instance, the parameters of the impulse to collect range "from relaxation to big business."[9] Trimming those limits neatly are F. Neilson who calls for a "cultural avocation" in the nation[10] and A. Repplier who discusses the "pleasure of possession."[11]

Deeper speculations have come from a group of magazine writers in the 1930s who explored what might be called the myth of nostalgia in collecting. For Y.Y. of the *New Statesman and Nation,* philately signaled a return to childhood. In one Wordsworthian recollection, "Grand Passion," he discusses his childhood stamp collection and the loss of innocence inherent in the recent development of philately into a science. Even more sentimental is Guy Boas's belletristic piece "The Mysterious Hobby of Stamp Collecting," which argues that stamps, "like poetry, are a link with salvation."

For every escapist there is a satirist and for every enthusiast a naysayer. Dissenting opinions on the psychic needs and relevance of collecting come from Thomas H. Uzzell, whose "Postage Stamp Psychosis" lightly satirized philatelists. Far from being an escape, stamp collecting, he says, is only a metaphor for the complexity of modern living. Indeed, "the real trouble with this country is its stamp collectors," because, for lack of anything else to do, they have overexamined stamps and found a maddening number of microscopic varieties to collect. Philately does not release us from such modern trends as overspecialization; it adds to them. Philately's biggest naysayer is Harold Nicolson, who in his "Marginal Comments" for *Spectator* issues a scathing denunciation of the hobby. To be a philatelist is "to become excited by objects which are totally unworthy of man's unconquerable mind." Nicolson wants a hobby that will make contributions "to useful knowledge."

Presumably, art is the tacit object most worthy of man's unconquerable mind, and yet, as if to confound Nicolson, some classify the postage stamp as art and worthy of study for its own sake. During the 1950s and 1960s a recurring discussion on the artistic merit of stamps was conducted in the pages of the *New York Times Magazine* (see A. B. Louchheim, "Our Stamps Could Be Artistic, Too," and A. Shuster, "Stamps for Art's Sake"). Sam Iker's "World's Richest Art Competition" reminds us that stamps more than ever are an important arena in the field of art and design. Art historian A. Hyatt Mayor devotes barely a paragraph to the postage stamp in his *Print and People: A Social History of Printed Pictures,* but his characterization of the engraved, mass-produced "miniature print," or stamp, is significant. It "is published in the largest of all editions and exposes a country's taste to global criticism." Notions of taste aside, Mayor clearly sees stamps as a reflection of a nation's culture, and his observation provides us with a simple transition from the problems of the art of collecting and the art of the stamp to a third and yet perhaps most important focus: the problem of the stamp as icon and reliable cultural indicator.

The postage stamp is not only an obvious engine of propaganda but a potential symbol maker. It can sell an idea, and by placing a portrait or object in a perforated frame it can transform that portrait or object into an icon that presumably reflects the sentiments and acceptance of the people. But the critical dilemma is whether these images are forced by the few upon the many or whether the few who issue the stamps are responding genuinely to the pulse of the many. Most likely, postal authorities shape our stamps to what they think is acceptable to the many. Futhermore, any of a number of extraneous factors may enter into the selection of a stamp design. George Washington provides a good example. It is safe to say that the fifty-three stamps that bear the first President's likeness confirm Washington as an American icon, but in fact not every stamp derives from the man's popularity. Four of five essays submitted for one early Washington stamp bore likenesses of Indians; the fifth, accepted essay was simply better executed than the others. Also, the ninety-cent Washington stamp of 1861 was issued simply because the postmaster general wanted the likeness of the president on a stamp of high value. To be sure, these two examples do not undercut the general acceptance of Washington as an icon. But it is clear that with respect to other less-revered figures the cultural historian must not depend too heavily upon the assumption that whatever appears on a stamp is necessarily an icon.

Distribution figures for a stamp may indicate the visibility or familiarity of a stamp, but a widely distributed stamp may not necessarily mean that the stamp is an accepted icon. Only eight stamps (excluding Christmas stamps) have exceeded the billion mark in distribution. To be sure, four of those stamps, depicting Columbus, Harding, and Washington, are likely candidates as stamps with a popular appeal. The remaining four, however, are clearly propagandistic. The National Recovery Act stamp issued during the Depression and the Allied Nations and Four Freedoms stamps issued during World War II promote distinct political ideologies. And, as H. H. Tennant and S. Hershey argue in the *American Mercury,* the 1952 NATO stamp with a distribution of nearly 2.8 billion was issued to help shore up the pact's shaky reputation in its third year. The distribution of a stamp, then, is not necessarily a function of the stamp icon's popularity. An approach to this problem must be ironed out. Two recent articles, W. E. Hensley's "Increasing Response Rate by Choice of Postage Stamp" and Paul Schnitzel's "Note on the Philatelic Demand for Postage Stamps," indicate that the problems are only just beginning to be recognized. Also of help in the area of propaganda may be O. Carlos Stoetzer's *Postage Stamps and Propaganda.*

The only systematic cultural history of stamps in the academic arena is David C. Skagg's essay, "The Postage Stamp as Icon." Inspired by the recent issue of Bicentennial stamps, Professor Skaggs focuses on the one event that is depicted most often in American philately, the Revolution, and compares past and present stamps to determine any trends. His essay is brief but generally accurate as to detail (although he designates Martha Washington as the first woman to appear on an American stamp when in fact Queen Isabella of Spain has that honor.) Skaggs discusses five categories of stamp vignettes (depicting individuals, battle, documents, symbols, and groupings). His general thesis is that although today's stamps reveal a trend toward "democratization" and symbolism (more commoners and liberty bells are featured than statesmen and heroes), the postal service has continued to be fairly "uncontroversial" in its selection of designs. The author looks forward to a time when Americans can recognize that 1776 was as much a civil war as a revolt and will therefore honor on their stamps the defeated and exiled Royalists as much as the standard heroes. "Only time will tell," he concludes, "if iconography can approach reality."

While Skaggs has made some basic observations, his essay is polemical and his methodology lacks rigor. I do not believe that we can be quite as confident as Skaggs is in assuming that the postage stamp "symbolizes the nation's popular self-image." If anything, a stamp is likely to reflect primarily the notions of a select and decidedly unrepresentative group of Americans including federal officials, artists, and artisans, not to mention the members of the Citizens Stamp Advisory Committee, which for decades has approved the nation's stamp topics. Furthermore, Skaggs's article implies that the predominate iconography on stamps stems from the Revolution, when, in fact, a wide range of categories including New World discovery, Western expansion and statehood, the history of flight and technology, and the postal system iself far outweigh the year 1776 and suggest a nation obsessed with growth, progress, and power. By emphasizing the stamp portraits of such revolutionaries as Washington, Franklin, and Jefferson, Skaggs necessarily excludes significant iconography relating to Jackson and Lincoln.

Although Skaggs is correct in stating that the recent Bicentennial issues emphasize the common man rather than the familiar heroes, he overgeneralizes in asserting that these stamps are also more symbolic than early issues. Perhaps a more accurate observation would be that recent stamps are artistically more "stylized" and less allegorical. Finally, Skaggs suggests that the cause for changes in philatelic imagery is our hero-less age, shaped by television's "fuzzy images" of "transitory celebrities." This perfunctory jab at television directs our attention away from more relevant causes. To begin with, today's stamps clearly reflect recent trends in art and design. More importantly, in the past two decades postal authorities have consciously introduced new printing techniques, flashier colors, more varied designs, and innovative stamp arrangements in order to make U.S. stamps more attractive to collectors. It is quite likely that more Bicentennial stamps have been put in albums than on letters. Thus, in dealing with recent stamps as cultural indicators, we must assume that a stamp is as much a reflection of the philatelist's demands as of the people's "self-image."

Despite its methodological shortcomings, Skaggs's article has initiated a legitimate field of study that can yield an abundance of knowledge which, if properly applied, can serve as an intellectual handmaiden to other fields. R. D. Roberts, for instance, in an attempt to derive a fair cross-section of names to determine American surname frequency, compiled a list from the thousands of people who bought stamps from his mail order stamp dealership. The results are questionable since there is no guarantee that certain minorities will be accurately polled; nevertheless, Robert's technique, which yields a wide sampling of middle America, may be of interest to the sociologist. (If anything the list provides an excellent surname profile of the mid-1950s philatelist.)

More intriguing is H. A. Fischel's aforementioned article, "Philatelic Portrait of the Modern Jew," which asserts that the stamp is "a significant medium of recognition in modern society." Unlike Skaggs, who assumes that any portrait or object appearing on a stamp is necessarily an icon,

Fischel uses philately as evidence of the growing acceptance of Jews since World War II. Fischel's main problem is determining who can be classified as a Jew. As of 1958 Marx and Heine were the world's most frequently depicted Jews. Given the growth of the Israeli state, persecution of Soviet Jews, and the loosening of postal restrictions in the United States, we can expect some fascinating modulations in Fischel's findings since 1960. An update of this study is clearly required. Most important, however, is that Fischel's method can serve as a model for similar treatments of the acceptance of other minorities or the evolution of social attitudes.

Scholars can and should turn more frequently to the postage stamp as a useful investigative tool. Handled properly, philatelic material can yield new insights into the myths, symbols, and icons that shape and reflect our lives. Comparative philatelic studies of Washington, Franklin, Jefferson, Jackson, and Lincoln seem to be the most obvious scholastic endeavors. The role of women and minorities in stamps is an equally significant problem. A study of philatelic landscapes might add a chapter to the "pastoral myth." But before we proceed with these projects, it is clear that the cultural historian must examine the work of philatelic researchers, learn the fundamentals of how a stamp is produced, determine the relevance of distribution figures, and distinguish between stamp icons and propaganda. Until a methodology is established, our conclusions will remain shallow and useless.

COINS

Numismatic literature, when it is not overly embroiled in gold and silver market trends, generally achieves a higher degree of scholastic merit than its philatelic counterpart. Numismatists have given us some book length and many monographic studies that approach coins aesthetically and socially, but to my knowledge academic aestheticians and social historians have not examined the topic. Those embarking upon the field of numismatics would do well to seek models in the works of Walter Breen, Elvira and Vladimir Clain-Stefanelli, Don Taxay, and Cornelius Vermeule.

Important material on the nascent age of the coin-collecting hobby can be found in the *Proceedings* of the Numismatic and Antiquarian Society of Philadelphia (1865-67, 1877-1936), the American Numismatic and Archaeological Society (1878-1914), and the American Numismatic Society (1908-). Other important early periodicals are the *American Journal of Numismatics* (1866-1924) and J. W. Scott's *American Journal of Philately and Coin Advertisers* (1879-1886). An interesting nineteenth-century monograph that sheds light on the hobby's early days is Elizabeth B. Johnston's *A Visit to the Cabinet of the United States Mint at Philadelphia.* Since numismatics did not become fully "democratized" until the 1930s, early guidebooks did not, generally speaking, address themselves to juveniles.

Since World War II, however, numismatists have learned a great deal from philatelists on how to "push" their hobby, and the more recent guidebooks may be worth analyzing. Rosichan's section on juvenile literature in *Stamps and Coins* is a suitable starting point in this field. Various popular magazines have, of course, kept abreast of recent events in hobby development. Of interest are Charles French's "Changes in Coin Collecting" and G. Rayner's "History of the Coin Investment Market" both found in *Hobbies.* Ed Reiter's weekly column on numismatics in the *New York Times* provides excellent and readable analysis of the hobby's rapid growth. Hobby magazines and news weeklies are a major resource for hobby trends. *Coin World,* a weekly, and *Coins,* a monthly, are both market-oriented publications. *Calcoin News Quarterly Magazine,* the organ for the California State Numismatic Association, includes articles on coin history and biography. Articles on numismatics as a collecting phenomenon as well as trade news may also be found in the *Numismatist.*

Turning to the cultural analysis of numismatics, the most and best treatments focus on coins as art objects rather than social icons. Traditional numismatic studies of ancient specimens have used coins to clarify or even rectify notions of ancient architecture and portraiture. Aesthetic studies of modern coinage are Carol H. Sutherland's *Art in Coinage: The Aesthetics of Money from Greece to the Present Day* and Thomas W. Becker's *The Coin Makers.* For decades U.S. coins have been derided for their comparative artlessness. Cornelius C. Vermeule's excellent study, *Numismatic Art in America: Aesthetics of the United States Coinage,* sets out to overcome that prejudice by examining coins in the context of American sculpture. Also of interest is Lynn Glaser's series of articles on "Art in American Coinage," in the *Numismatic Scrapbook Magazine.* Vermeule's *Bibliography of Applied Numismatics in the Fields of Greek and Roman Archaeology and Fine Arts,* while not dealing with American art or coinage, will lead the researcher to model works in the field of coin aesthetics.

There is something holy about money that makes coins and paper money better candidates for social icons than stamps. Coins are tokens of social confidence and political power; they last longer and circulate more than stamps. Apparently their influence goes even deeper. According to William H. Desmonde in *Magic, Myth, and Money,* an anthropological study of coins and coin iconography, money is a part of religious ritual. Also of interest here is Giovanni Gorini's article "Coin as Blazon or Talisman: Paramonetary Function of Money." As with stamps, though, the iconic power of coins is necessarily lessened when we realize the propagandistic uses of money designs. F. C. Ross in "Numismatic Thoughts" argues, for instance, that "currencies, from almost the beginning, have been propagandists." Finally, journals that generally publish scholarly works relating to the aesthetics and iconographic aspects of both coins and paper money are the *Numismatist, Paper Money* (quarterly for the Society of Paper

Money Collectors), the *Journal of Numismatic and the Fine Arts,* and the *Essay-Proof Journal.*

NOTES

1. Wilbert D. Newgold, "Hobbies," *Encyclopaedia Britannica: Macropaedia,* 15th ed. (Chicago: Encyclopedia Britannica, 1978), p. 973.

2. Henry John Bellars, *The Standard Guide to Postage Stamp Collecting* (London: John Camden Hotter, 1864), n.p.

3. Ed Reiter, "Numismatics: College Level Training," *New York Times,* December 23, 1979, Sec. D., p. 36.

4. Ed Reiter, "Numismatics: Is the Hobby Suffering from Growing Pains?" *New York Times,* December 30, 1979, Sec. D., p. 36.

5. R. T. Fuller, "Collector's Luck: Early Collecting Instincts Should Be Encouraged," *Parents Magazine,* 10 (June 1935), 19.

6. H. S. New, "Postage Stamp Promotes Popular Education and Stimulates Patriotism," *School Life,* 11 (September 1925), 1.

7. R. M. Adams, "Making a Stamp Map," *Journal of Educational Method,* 4 (October 1924), 63.

8. Mauritze Hallgreen, *All About Stamps: Their History and the Art of Collecting Them* (New York: Knopf, 1940), p. 10.

9. "Collecting: Impulse Ranges from Relaxation to Big Business," *Literary Digest,* 123 (February 27, 1937), 30.

10. F. Neilson, "Need for a Cultural Avocation," *American Journal of Economics,* 16 (January 1957), 145.

11. A. Repplier, "Pleasures of Possession," *Commonweal,* 13 (December 17, 1930), 181.

BIBLIOGRAPHY

BOOKS AND ARTICLES

Stamps

Adams, R. M. "Making a Stamp Map." *Journal of Educational Method,* 4 (October 1924), 63-69.

Allen, E. M. "America's Best-selling Portrait: Franklin." *American Artist,* 20 (April 1956), 70.

Ashbrook, Stanley B. *The Types and Plates of the United States One-cent Stamp of 1851-57.* New York: Lindquist, 1938.

———. *The United States Ten-cent Stamp of 1855-57.* New York: Lindquist, 1936.

Bacon, E. D. *Catalogue of the Philatelic Library of the Earl of Crawford, K.T.* London: Philatelic Literature Society, 1911.

Bellars, Henry J. *The Standard Guide to Postage Stamp Collecting.* London: John Camden Hotter, 1864.

Boas, Guy. "The Mysterious Hobby of Stamp Collecting." *Cornhill,* 160 (July 1939), 46-64.

Booty, Frederick. *Stamp Collector's Guide.* London: Hamilton, Adams, 1862.

Brazer, Clarence. *Essays for United States Adhesive Postage Stamps.* New York: American Philatelic Society, 1941.

Brookman, Lester G. *Nineteenth Century Postage Stamps of the United States.* 2 vols. New York: Lindquist, 1947.

Butler, Ellis P. *The Young Stamp Collector's Own Book.* Indianapolis: Bobbs-Merrill, 1933.

Catalogue of the Philatelic Collection. Johannesburg, South Africa: Johannesburg Public Library, 1960.

Catalogue of the Philatelic Library of the Collectors Club. New York: Collectors Club, 1917.

"Collecting: Impulse Ranges from Relaxation to Big Business." *Literary Digest,* 123 (February 27, 1937), 30-32.

Collecting: United States. Cambridge, Mass.: Stamps Information, 1972.

Dietz, August. *The Postal Service of the Confederate States of America.* Richmond, Va.: Dietz Press, 1929.

Ellis, Henry M. *Stamps for Fun and Profit.* New York: Funk & Wagnalls, 1953.

Fischel, H. A. "Philatelic Portrait of the Modern Jew." *Jewish Social Studies,* 23 (July 1961), 187-208.

Freehafer, John, and Helen K. Zirkle. "A Selective List of Philatelic Handbooks, with a list of libraries in which they may be found." In *The Congress Book 1956.* Philadelphia: American Philatelic Congress, 1956, pp. 93-106.

Fuller, R. T. "Collector's Luck: Early Collecting Instinct Should Be Encouraged." *Parents Magazine,* 10 (June 1935), 19.

Fuller, Wayne E. *The American Mail: Enlarger of the Common Life.* Chicago: University of Chicago Press, 1972.

______. *RFD: The Changing Face of Rural America.* Indianapolis; Indiana University Press, 1964.

Glass, Sol. *United States Postage Stamps, 1945-52.* West Somerville, Mass.: Bureau Issue Association, 1954.

Grant, Robert W. *Handbook of Civil War Patriotic Envelopes and Postal History.* Hanover, Mass.: Robert W. Grant, 1977.

Granville, Joseph E. *Everybody's Guide to Stamp Investment.* New York: Heritage, 1952.

Green, P. D. "Postage Stamp Stampede." *Nation's Business,* 32 (July 1944), 40.

Hahn, G. C. *United States Famous American Series of 1940.* State College, Penn.: American Philatelic Research Library, 1950.

Hallgreen, Mauritze. *All About Stamps: Their History and the Art of Collecting Them.* New York: Knopf, 1940.

Harlow, Alvin. *Old Post Bags: The Story of the Sending of a Letter in Ancient and Modern Times.* New York: Holt, 1928.

Hensley, W. E. "Increasing Response Rate by Choice of Postage Stamp." *Public Opinion Quarterly,* 38 (Summer 1974), 280-83.

Herst, Herman, Jr. "The Mistake of Approaching Your Hobby as Speculative Economic Investments." *Hobbies,* 71 (August 1966), 99.

Horowicz, Kay, and Robson Lowe. *Colonial Posts in the United States of America, 1606-1783.* London: Lowe, 1967.

Iker, Sam. "World's Richest Art Competition." *National Wildlife*, 17 (December 1978), 40-43.

Johl, Max. *United States Commemoratives of the Twentieth Century.* 2 vols. New York: Lindquist, 1947.

———, and Beverly S. King. *United States Stamps of the Twentieth Century.* 5 vols. New York: Lindquist, 1938.

Kaiser, John B. "Bibliography: The Basis of Philatelic Research." In *The Congress Book 1953.* Newark, N.J.: American Philatelic Congress, 1953, pp. 37-54.

Kelen, Emery. *Stamps Tell the Story of John F. Kennedy.* New York: Meredith, 1968.

Kimble, Ralph A. *Commemorative Postage Stamps of the United States.* New York: Grosset and Dunlap, 1936.

Konwiser, Henry M. *The American Stamp Collector's Dictionary.* New York: Minkus, 1949.

Lane, Mary B., and Elliott Perry. *The Harry F. Allen Collection of Black Jacks.* State College, Penn.: American Philatelic Research Library, 1969.

Laurence, Robert. *The George Walcott Collection of Used Civil War Patriotic Covers.* New York: R. Laurence, 1934.

Lindenbaum, Arieh. *Great Jews and Stamps.* New York: Sabra Press, 1970.

Linn's World Stamp Almanac. Sidney, Ohio: Amos Press, 1977.

Louchheim, A. B. "Our Stamps Could Be Artistic, Too." *New York Times Magazine*, May 27, June 10, June 17, 1951.

Lowe, James. *Bibliography of Postcard Literature.* Folsom, Penn.: J. Lowe, 1969.

Luff, Moe. *United States Postal Slogan Catalog.* Spring Valley, N.Y.: M. Luff, 1975.

McCluer, Margaret N. *Women as Presented on United States Stamps.* Kansas City, Mo.: n.p., 1936.

A Master List of Philatelic Literature. North Miami, Fla.: HJMR, 1979.

Mayor, A. Hyatt. *Print and People: A Social History of Printed Pictures.* New York: Metropolitan Museum, 1971.

Mueller, Barbara. *Common Sense Philately.* New York: Van Nostrand, 1956.

Negus, James, "A List of Cumulative Indexes to Single Periodicals." *Philatelic Literature Review*, 23 (June 1974), 100-7.

Neilson, F. "Need for a Cultural Avocation." *American Journal of Economics*, 16 (January 1957), 145-49.

New, H. S. "Postage Stamp Promotes Popular Education and Stimulates Patriotism." *School Life*, 11 (September 1925), 1-4.

Newgold, Wilbert D. "Hobbies." *Encyclopaedia Britannica: Macropaedia.* 15th ed. Chicago: Encyclopaedia Britannica, 1978, VIII, 973-81.

Nicolson, Harold. "Marginal Comments." *Spectator*, 176 (June 21, 1946), 634.

Norona, Delf. *Cyclopedia of United States Postmarks and Postal History.* Lawrence, Mass.: Quarterman, 1975.

"Personal Business: Stamp Collecting." *Business Week* (March 3, 1962), 101-2.

"Philatelic Boom." *Newsweek*, 22 (November 8, 1943), 64.

Philately of Tomorrow. New York: Philatelic Research Laboratory, 1940.

Postage Stamps: A Selective Checklist of Books on Philately in the Library of Congress. Washington, D.C.: Library of Congress, 1940.

Postage Stamps of the United States. Washington, D.C.: Government Printing Office, 1973.

Preliminary Inventories of the United States Archives, nos. 63, 82, 114. Washington, D.C.: Government Printing Office, 1953, 1955, 1959.

Reinfeld, Fred. *Commemorative Stamps of the United States of America.* W. Somerville, Mass.: Bramhall, 1956.

Repplier, A. "Pleasures of Possession." *Commonweal,* 13 (December 17, 1930), 181-33.

Ricketts, William R. *The Philatelic Literature Bibliography Index.* Forty-Fort, Penn.: n.p., 1912.

Roberts, R. D. "Surname Frequency and Stamp Collectors." *Names,* 3 (September 1955), 172-84.

Rosichan, Richard H. *Stamps and Coins.* Littleton, Colo.: Libraries Unlimited, 1974.

Scheele, Carl H. *A Short History of the Mail Service.* Washington, D.C.: Smithsonian, 1970.

Schnitzel, Paul. "Note on the Philatelic Demand for Postage Stamps." *Southern Economics Journal,* 45 (April 1979), 1261-65.

Scott's New Handbook for Philatelists. New York: J.W. Scott, 1967.

Scott's Specialized Catalogue of United States Stamps. New York: J.W. Scott, 1979.

"Search for Freak Stamps Yields Fortune." *Popular Mechanics,* 46 (December 1926), 924-25.

"Selling Coloured Paper." *Economist,* 211 (May 9, 1964), 585.

Shuster, A. "Stamps for Art's Sake." *New York Times Magazine,* September 20, 1961.

Skaggs, David C. "The Postage Stamp as Icon." In *Icons of America.* Edited by Ray B. Browne and Marshall Fishwick. Bowling Green, Ohio: Popular Culture Press, 1978.

Smith, Chester. *American Philatelic Periodicals.* State College, Penn.: American Philatelic Research Library, 1978.

"Stamps: No Gold Mine." *Changing Times,* 17 (February 1963), 19-20.

Stiles, Kent B. *Postal Saints and Sinners: Who's Who on Stamps.* Brooklyn, N.Y.: T. Gaus' Sons, 1964.

Stoetzer, O. Carlos. *Postage Stamps as Propaganda.* Washington, D.C.: Public Affairs Press, 1953.

Sutton, R. J., and K. W. Anthony. *The Stamp Collector's Encyclopedia.* New York: Arco, 1973.

Tennant, H. H., and S. Hershey. "Nearly Everybody Wants to Get in the Stamp Act." *American Mercury,* 76 (February 1953), 79-83.

Thompson, Edmund B. *Portraits on Our Postage Stamps.* Windham, Conn.: E. B. Thompson, 1933.

Thorp, Prescott H., ed. *Thorp-Bartel's Catalogue of the Stamped Envelopes and Wrappers of the United States.* Netcong, N.J.: Thorp, 1954.

Tiffany, John K. *The Philatelical Library: A Catalogue of Stamp Publications.* St. Louis, Mo.: John K. Tiffany, 1874.

Turner, George T. *Essays and Proofs of United States Internal Revenue Stamps.* Arlington, Mass.: Bureau Issues Association, 1974.

______. "Trends in United States Philatelic Literature." In *The Congress Book 1945.* Cleveland, Ohio: American Philatelic Congress, 1945, pp. 145-52.

Uzzell, Thomas H. "Postage Stamp Psychosis." *Scribners Magazine,* 97 (June 1935), 368-70.

van Peursem, J. H. *George Washington.* S'-Gravenhage, Holland: Philatelie en Geschiedenis, 1932.

Walls, R. T., et al. "Collection Preferences of Children." *Child Development,* 46 (September 1975), 783-85.

"Worldwide Market." *Time,* 81 (June 7, 1963), 96.

Y. Y. "Grand Passion." *The New Statesman and Nation,* N.S. 24 (September 26, 1942), 204.

Zareski, Michel, and Herman Herst, Jr. *Fancy Cancellations on 19th Century United States Postage Stamps.* Shrub Oak, N.Y.: Herst, 1963.

Coins

Adams, Edgar H., and William H. Woodin. *United States Patterns, Trial and Experimental Pieces.* New York: American Numismatic Society, 1913.

American Numismatic Society. *Dictionary Catalogue of the Library of the American Numismatic Society.* New York: Hall, 1972.

Attinelli, Emmanuel J. *Numisgraphics, or a list of catalogues, price lists and various publications of more or less interest to Numismatologists.* New York: Attinelli, 1876.

Baker, William S. *Medallic Portraits of Washington.* Iola, Wisc.: Krause, 1965.

Becker, Thomas W. *The Coin Makers.* Garden City, N.Y.: Doubleday, 1969.

Beistle, Martin Luther. *A Register of Half Dollar Varieties and Sub-Varieties.* Omaha, Neb.: Beebe's, 1964.

Belden, Bauman L. *Indian Peace Medals Issued in the United States, 1789-1889.* New Milford, Conn.: N. Flayderman, 1966.

Betts, Charles W. *American Colonial History Illustrated by Contemporary Medals.* Lawrence, Mass.: Quarterman, 1972.

Bradfield, Elston G. "Benjamin Franklin: A Numismatic Summary." *Numismatist,* 69 (1956), 1347-53.

Breen, Walter. *Brasher and Bailey, Pioneer New York Coiners.* New York: American Numismatic Society, 1958.

______. *The Secret History of the Gobrecht Coinages (1836-1840).* Coin Collectors Journal, no. 157. New York: Scott Stamp and Coin, 1954.

Buttrey, Theodore V., Jr., ed. *Coinage of the Americas.* New York: American Numismatic Society, 1973.

Carothers, Neil. *Fractional Money: A History of the Small Coins and Fractional Paper Currency of the United States.* New York: Kelley, 1967.

Catalogue of the Numismatic Books in the Library of the American Numismatic and Archaeological Society. Boston: American Numismatic and Archaeological Society, 1883.

Chamberlain, Georgia S. *American Medals and Medalists.* Annandale, Va.: Turnpike, 1963.

Clain-Stefanelli, Elvira E. *Numismatics—An Ancient Science: A Survey of Its History.* Washington, D.C.: Government Printing Office, 1965.

______. *Select Numismatic Bibliography.* New York: Stacks, 1965.

Clain-Stefanelli, Vladimir. *History of the National Numismatic Collections.* Washington, D.C.: Government Printing Office, 1968.

Cohen, Roger S., et al. *American Half Cents, the "Little Half Sisters": A Reference Book on the United States Half Cent Coined from 1793 to 1857.* Bethesda, Md.: n.p., 1971.

Coin World Alamanac. Sidney, Ohio: Amos Press, 1979.

Criswell, Grover, and Clarence. *Confederate and Southern States Currency.* New York: House of Collectibles, 1961.

Desmonde, William H. *Magic, Myth, and Money.* New York: Free Press, 1962.

Dikeson, Montroville W. *The American Numismatic Manual.* Philadelphia: Lippincott, 1860.

Forrer, Leonard. *Biographical Dictionary of Medalists.* New York: Franklin, 1971.

Franklin and Numismatics. Colorado Springs, Colo.: American Numismatic Association, n.d.

French, Charles. "Changes in Coin Collecting." *Hobbies,* 67 (February 1963), 102.

Frey, Albert. *Dictionary of Numismatic Names.* New York: Barnes and Noble, 1947.

Friedberg, Robert. *Paper Money of the United States.* New York: Coin and Currency Institute, 1972.

Glaser, Lynn. "Art in American Coinage." *Numismatic Scrapbook Magazine* (1962), 2462-79, 2792-800, 3092-101.

Gorini, Giovanni. "Coin as Blazon or Talisman: Paramonetary Function of Money." *Diogenes* (Spring-Summer 1978), 77-88.

Grierson, Philip. *Numismatics.* New York: Oxford University Press, 1975.

Griffiths, William H. *The Story of the American Bank Note Company.* New York: n.p., 1959.

Grosvenor, Gilbert, et al. *Insignia and Decorations of the United States Armed Forces.* Washington, D.C.: National Geographic Society, 1944.

Hepburn, A. Barton. *A History of Currency in the United States.* Clifton, N.J.: Kelley, 1968.

History of the Bureau of Engraving and Printing (1862-1962). Washington, D.C.: Government Printing Office, 1962.

Hood, Jennings, and Charles J. Young. *American Orders and Societies and Their Decorations.* Philadelphia: Bailey, Banks & Biddle, 1917.

Jamieson, Melvill Allan. *Medals Awarded to North American Indian Chiefs, 1714-1922.* London: Spink, 1961.

Johnston, Elizabeth B. *A Visit to the Cabinet of the United States Mint at Philadelphia.* Philadelphia: Lippincott, 1876.

Judd, J. Hewitt, and Walter Breen. *United States Patterns, Experimental and Trial Pieces.* Racine, Wisc.: Whitman, 1962.

Kappen, Charles V., and Ralph A. Mitchell. *Depression Scrip of the United States.* San Jose, Calif.: Globe, 1961.

Kenney, Richard D. *Early American Medalists and Die-Sinkers.* New York: W. Raymond, 1954.

Kerrigan, Evans E. *American War Medals and Decorations.* New York: Viking, 1964.

King, Robert P. "Lincoln in Numismatics: A Descriptive List." *Numismatist,* 37 (1924), 55-74; 40 (1927), 193-204; 46 (1933), 481-97.

Kosoff, Abe. *An Illustrated History of United States Coins: Proposed Designs as well as the Standard Types.* Encino, Calif.: n.p., 1962.

Library Catalogue of the American Numismatic Association. Colorado Springs, Colo.: American Numismatic Association, 1972.

Loubat, Joseph F. *The Medallic History of the United States of America, 1776-1876.* New Milford, Conn.: N. Flayderman, 1967.

Low, Lyman H. *Hard Times Tokens.* San Jose, Calif.: Globe, 1955.

Massey, J. Earl. *America's Money: The Story of Coins and Currency.* New York: Crowell, 1968.

Mishler, Clifford. *United States and Canadian Commemorative Medals and Tokens.* Vandalia, Mich.: Mishler, 1959.

Muscalus, John A. *Famous Paintings Reproduced on Paper Money of State Banks, 1800-1866.* Bridgeport, Conn.: Muscalus, 1938.

———. *Index of State Bank Notes that Illustrate Characters and Events.* Bridgeport, Conn.: Muscalus, 1938.

———. *Index of State Bank Notes that Illustrate Presidents.* Bridgeport, Conn.: Muscalus, 1939.

———. *Index of State Bank Notes that Illustrate Washington and Franklin.* Bridgeport, Conn.: Muscalus, 1939.

———. *The Views of Towns, Cities, Falls, and Buildings Illustrated on 1800-1866 Bank Paper Money.* Bridgeport, Conn.: Muscalus, 1939.

Nussbaum, Arthur. *A History of the Dollar.* New York: Columbia University Press, 1957.

Rayner, G. "History of the Coin Investment Market." *Hobbies,* 82 (October 1977), 131.

Reed, Mort. *Cowles' Complete Encyclopedia of United States Coins.* New York: Cowles', 1969.

Reiter, Ed. "Numismatics," *New York Times,* December 23, 1979, December 30, 1979.

Rochette, Edward C. *The Medallic Portraits of John F. Kennedy: A Study of Kennediana.* Iola, Wisc.: Krause, 1966.

Roosevelt and Numismatics. Colorado Springs, Colo.: American Numismatic Association, n.d.

Ross, F. C. "Numismatic Thoughts." *Hobbies,* 46 (June 1941), 90-92.

Rothert, Matt. *A Guidebook of United States Fractional Currency.* Racine, Wisc.: Whitman, 1963.

Ruby, Warren A. *Commemorative Coins of the United States.* Lake Mills, Iowa: Graphic, 1961.

Salton, Mark. *Glossary of Numismatic Terms.* New York: Barnes and Noble, 1947.

Sheldon, William H., et al. *Penny Whimsy.* New York: Harper, 1958.

Slaubaugh, Arlie, *United States Commemorative Coins: The Drama of America as Told by Our Coins.* Racine, Wisc.: Western, 1975.

Snowden, James Ross. *A Description of Ancient and Modern Coins in the Cabinet Collection at the United States Mint.* Philadelphia: Lippincott, 1860.

Sutherland, Carol H. *Art in Coinage: The Aesthetics of Money from Greece to the Present Day.* New York: Philosophical Library, 1956.

Taxay, Don. *Comprehensive Catalogue and Encyclopedia of United States Coins.* New York: Scott, 1971.

______. *An Illustrated History of United States Commemorative Coins.* New York: Arco, 1967.

______. *Money of the American Indian and Other Primitive Currencies of the Americas.* New York: Nummis, 1970.

______. *The United States Mint and Coinage: An Illustrated History from 1776 to the Present.* New York: Arco, 1966.

Todd, Richard Cecil. *Confederate Finance.* Athens: University of Georgia Press, 1954.

Unger, Irwin. *The Greenback Era: A Social and Political History of American Finance, 1865-1879.* Princeton: Princeton University Press, 1964.

Van Allen, Leroy C., and A. George Mallis. *Guide to Morgan and Peace Dollars: A Complete Guide and Reference Book on United States Silver Dollars.* Silver Springs, Md.: Katen, 1971.

Vermeule, Cornelius C. *Bibliography of Applied Numismatics in the Fields of Greek and Roman Archaeology and Fine Arts.* London: Spink, 1956.

______. *Numismatic Art in America: Aesthetics of the United States Coinage.* Cambridge, Mass.: Harvard University Press, 1971.

Yeoman, Richard S. *Guidebook of United States Coins.* Racine, Wisc.: Western, 1978.

______. *Handbook of United States Coins.* Racine, Wisc.: Western, 1978.

PERIODICALS

Stamps

Aero Philatelist Annals. New York, 1953-71.

Airpost Journal. Albion, Penn., 1929-72.

American Philatelist and Year Book of the American Philatelic Association. Springfield, Mass., 1894-1908.

American Philatelist. State College, Penn., 1909-.

American Revenuer. New York, 1954-.

1869 Times. Memphis, 1975-.

Essay-Proof Journal. Jefferson, Wisc., 1944-.

JAPOS Bulletin. Clinton Corners, N.Y., 1975-.

Let's Talk Parachutes. Fort Worth, Tex., 1976-.

Linn's Weekly Stamp News. Sidney, Ohio, 1928-.

Mekeel's Weekly Stamp News. Portland, Me., 1905-.

Philatelic Literature Review. Conajoharie, N.Y., 1942-.

SPA Journal. Cincinnati, Ohio, 1932-.

Topical Time. Milwaukee, 1949-.

United States Official Postal Guide. Washington, D.C., 1847-.

United States Specialist. West Somerville, Mass., 1930-.

Coins

American Journal of Numismatics, New York, 1866-1924.
Calcoin News Quarterly Magazine. San Jose, Calif., 1947-.
Coin World. Sidney, Ohio 1960-.
Coins. Iola, Wisc., 1962-.
Numismatic Literature. New York, 1947-.
The Numismatist. Monroe, Mich., 1888-.
Paper Money. Jefferson, Wisc., 1962-.
Numismatic Scrapbook Magazine. Chicago, 1935-.
Proceedings of the American Numismatic and Archaeological Society. New York, 1878-1914.
Proceedings of the American Numismatic Society. New York, 1908-.
Proceedings of the Numismatic and Antiquarian Society. Philadelphia, 1865-1936.

Stamps and Coins. (Journals specializing in both fields and popular magazines that often publish articles or columns on either or both.)

American Journal of Philately and Coin Advertisers. New York, 1879-1886.
Essay-Proof Journal. Jefferson, Wisc., 1944-.
Hobbies. Chicago, 1931-.
Popular Science Monthly. New York, 1872-.
Profitable Hobbies. Kansas City, Mo., 1945-.
St. Nicholas. Darien, Conn., 1873-1940.
Scientific American. New York, check files from 1890 to 1930.

CHAPTER 18 Trains and Railroading

Arthur H. Miller, Jr.

For the eminent historian Daniel Boorstin, the "Age of the Railroad is perhaps the most romantic" in the history of American life.[1] This romance is best found in Lucius Beebe's books, which appeared from the 1930s to the 1960s. In introducing his first rail book, *High Iron*, in 1938, Beebe sounded his clarion call: "The most heroic of American legends is the chronicle of railroading."[2] Its epic scale and its relation to the national destiny is further recognized by B. A. Botkin in his introduction to a *Treasury of Railroad Folklore*: "The impact of the railroad on the American imagination has been greater than that of any other industry."[3] In the 1950s Barton K. Davis observed that model railroading alone was the "absorbing interest [of] more than 100,000 Americans."[4] And as the 1980s begin, railroad enthusiasts provide the focus for their own micro-industry: publishers of magazines and books, museums and preserved short lines, memorabilia, modeling, and associations and clubs across the country. Trains and railroading have a long history and vital present and future in American popular culture.

A first step in understanding railroading in the context of popular culture comes in attempting to describe the range of interests of railfans, dedicated railroad hobbyists, in the words of Paul B. Cors, whose 1975 *Railroads* is the standard reference bibliography on the topic. According to Cors, railfans (mostly male) resemble one another little except in their "fascination with and devotion to railroading."[5] Two common characteristics seem to be railfans' tendency to be both photographers and book collectors. Beyond these traits, railfan interests tend to be specialized and partisan. A railroad buff may concentrate on steam or diesel locomotives, on traction (electric railroad and rapid transit) or narrow-gauge railroads, on short lines, on a particular railroad company, on railroad general history and literature, on cars, on stations, on models, on live steam (except scale engines run by real steam and large enough to ride upon), or on collecting toy trains, railroad art, and railroad memorabilia. A list based on recent memorabilia advertisements gives a sense of the range of collectibles: timetables, cap and hat badges, stocks and bonds, passes and tickets, engine plates, calendars, dining car china and silverware, lanterns and lamps, posters and signs, brass whistles, telegraph instruments, depot phones, keys and locks, and pocket watches. In addition, Paul Cors's reference guide lists six pages of publishers who specialize in books for railfans or else cater to them significantly. Pictures, too, are collected, most often of locomotives and in all formats—from postcards and slides to glass negatives, stereopticon views, and steel engravings. Ephemeral material, preferably illustrated, is highly sought: manufacturers' catalogs, travel brochures, and the like. The railfan's most valued pictures or ephemera will record personal experiences, such as snapshots of out-of-the-way and/or endangered lines or handouts from rail museums visited. Enthusiasts endeavor to visit and then ride (or, if too late, walk over) new railroads. These may range from mainline railroads to the most obscure interurban line. In sum, railfan interest is specialized, passionate, cumulative, and oriented toward travel and printed material.

But the railfan phenomenon is only the central core of popular interest in trains and railroading. As the scholar Daniel Boorstin has observed and as the very popular Beebe demonstrated, the romance of railroading appeals to a much wider audience—the general public—which is drawn by nostalgia. An example here is a magnificent coffee table book called *Decade of the Trains: The 1940s*, by Don Ball, Jr. and Rogers E. M. Whitaker ("E. M. Frimbo"). In the preface Ball draws a clear connection between life in the late 1970s and that three decades earlier:

> I hope this book captures the spirit of railroading in the forties and also the unique character... of America during the war and the rest of the decade. During the 1940s, America "worked." It seemed to be an era of good times and almost innocent merriment—even with the dark and terrible war.[6]

According to the jacket, here "the reader becomes an eyewitness. This trip *is* necessary—for everyone who remembers the war years and [of course] for every railroad fan." This nostalgia for a simpler era and for the values of the era—innocence, for example—provides the bridge from railfans' special passions to more general currents of popular interest.

There has been considerable academic and professional interest in the literature of railroading. For the railfan this is delightfully specialized and detailed. Historical material (primary and secondary), company literature, government reports and surveys, technical manuals, and investment information all reach the hobbyist or popular perception at some point.

Important background, too, for viewing America's romance with railroading is the awareness that this is part of an international phenomenon. Particularly in Britain the literature on the subject is well developed and the level of interest intense. Railroads (or railways) began there, first captured the popular imagination there, and first experienced significant abandonment, nostalgia, and comprehensive railfan activity. Thus, British popular interest in railroading has provided a context for the development and continuation of Americans' preoccupation with their rail heritage.

HISTORIC OUTLINE

"Historically," according to Archie Robertson, "the railfan is at least as old as railroads." In his *Slow Train to Yesterday* Robertson provides a charming look at the railfan phenomenon:

> The Charleston & Hamburg..., earliest American railroad, ran its first trains for enthusiasts who just couldn't wait for the public opening. Before the Civil War the B&O ran excursions for camera fans from Washington to Harper's Ferry.... Fan trips were commonplace throughout the nineteenth century although no one called them that.[7]

The history of American railroading cannot, indeed, be separated from the public enthusiasm for rail travel or for the advancement and progress of the railroad industry. In the 1820s the railroad had taken hold in England, and by Christmas 1830 the first scheduled steam-railroad train run in America took place on the Charleston & Hamburg, carrying 141 passengers. The engine, the "Best Friend of Charleston," was the first commercially built U.S. locomotive. The expansion westward from the coast in the early nineteenth century led to rapid deployment of the railroad, at first in what might seem like unusual locations. The new technology captured the imagination and backing first of Southerners, whose seaports were suffering as the water routes further north—particularly the Erie Canal—drew trade to New York and the Northeast. Laying track to the interior offered a new chance for ports such as Charleston and Baltimore to compete. Boston, too, coveted New York's success and in the early 1830s wisely decided to build not more canals but railroads. The nation's first Railway Exhibit was in Boston in 1827, to which enthusiastic crowds paid admission to view the display of English locomotives.

By the 1850s the rail system reached to the Mississippi, as the various coastal establishments tied themselves to western settlements. Already the call for Manifest Destiny was to be heard, to build a railroad to the Pacific. Sectional rivalry, at first, was a stimulus to discussion: should the transcontinental line go across from a more northerly or southerly route, building from slave states or free? In the end the struggle's intensity was so great that it served to delay the transcontinental route until after the Civil War. The North's by then superior rail system contributed significantly to the preservation of the Union, and railroading today forms a key subgrouping of Civil War buff interest. As a result, in the 1950s the "Great Locomotive

Chase" was a popular story and film topic. But before this climactic encounter western cities had hosted railroad conventions to crystallize interest in a line—west from Memphis, St. Louis, or Chicago. As with the earlier Boston exhibition, these special events reflected and served to stimulate popular interest and support. Throughout the century the opening of new lines, anniversaries, and the great fairs of 1876 and 1893 were occasions for celebrating the progress, both geographical and technical, of the railroads.

After the Civil War forces were mobilized quickly, thanks to government incentives, creative management and engineering, and no little corruption, to forge the link to the Pacific. In 1869 the Union Pacific and the Central Pacific met at Promontory Point, Utah, ending the "Great Race." This epic feat was followed in rapid order by the completion of other lines to the north and south. By the end of the century the West was covered by a complete (often redundant) rail network, the Indians had been subdued, and the frontier (according to Frederick Jackson Turner) was closed.

From the end of the war to the closing of the frontier popular interest in the railroads was at a peak. The mighty task of crossing the continent was great by every measure: the profits, the speed at which track could be laid, the iniquity of life on the work gangs ("Hell on Wheels" and boom towns), the tall tales, the personalities (General Dodge, Jack Casement, and Charles Crocker), and the celebrations. In the years that immediately followed, Easterners and travellers from abroad made the trip across the plains and the mountains to San Francisco from Council Bluffs, Iowa, through prairie dog villages, mountain gorges, Indian lands, and deserts. Their accounts and the pictures by the illustrators and photographers who went along were printed and widely distributed, testifying to the railroad's popular appeal.

By the end of this period the railroads had begun to reach beyond opening new possibilities for Americans and immigrants. By the close of the century railroad domination had become a major issue particularly in the trans-Mississippi West. Popular support waned as scandals such as the Credit Mobilier matter, which concerned Union Pacific corruption, reached the public. Land prices, freight rates, and the continuing stock manipulations of the "robber baron" period turned first the Western farmers and later a majority of the public against railroad excesses. The Granger movement reflected the farmers' attempt to organize against the power of the railroads. And train robbers appeared as Robin Hoods in the popular imagination, dime novels, and the mass press. The spectacular exploits of Christopher Evans and John Sontag in the San Joaquin Valley of California are reflected in Frank Norris's more ambitious novel of 1901, *The Octopus.* In general, *The Octopus* best characterizes the popular perception of the Western railroads at the end of the nineteenth century: greed, corruption, impersonality, manipulation, and oppression.

The railfan disappeared after the first blush of transcontinental travel. Archie Robertson reports that his return is first noted some half-century later, by the *Railway Age* in 1927.[8] By the late 1920s automobiles were no longer a novelty, and trains had gained the dignity of age and tradition and, says Robertson, "the sympathy which belongs to the underdog." This respected position has prevailed through much of the last half-century. Cors observes that "in the thirties...the rail hobbyist came into his own," with 1938 being a watershed year: the "first real railfan book," *Along the Iron Trail* by Frederick Richardson and F. Nelson Blount, appeared, along with Lucius Beebe's first rail book, *High Iron. Railroad Magazine* now served the railroad enthusiast as much as the working railroaders. In 1940 Kambach Publishing Company introduced *Trains,* the first "unequivocally" hobbyist periodical.[9] The war brought new reliance on the rail system, but this was short-lived. In the late 1940s further growth in automobile and air travel gave rail travel for passengers permanent underdog status and provided challenges for freight service as well. A new wave of nostalgia boosted modeling and other railfan occupations to record levels in the mid-1950s. The 1960s—with the space program, war, and social change—once again eclipsed railroading in the popular mind. But by the end of the 1970s the railfan had been "born again," as one hobby dealer reported.[10] The reason echoed the heyday of the 1940s: gasoline shortages and a much-heralded return to the rails, nostalgia for a simpler and more personalized era of travel, and a sense of national tradition and destiny. As the 1980s begin, a century and a half of popular fascination with railroading continues.

REFERENCE WORKS

A number of reference and bibliographic tools exist on trains and railroading. For an overview of American railroading—reading beyond the quite useful articles in such encyclopedias or the *Britannica* or the *Americana*—the general reader should turn to two now somewhat venerable titles: Stewart H. Holbrook, *The Story of American Railroads,* and John F. Stover, *American Railroads.* Holbrook provides more business and engineering coverage, while Stover gives more emphasis to social history. A more popular approach is found in Lamont Buchanan's 1955 *Steel Trains and Iron Horses: A Pageant of American Railroads.*

The relation of railroading to culture is explored in *Railroad: Trains and Train People in American Culture,* edited by James Alan McPherson and Miller Williams. This quite recent collection of excerpts and illustrations opens with an essay by McPherson on "Some Observations on the Railroad and American Culture." The excerpts range from scholarly essays and poetry (Emily Dickinson, Karl Shapiro, William Stafford) to early pamphlet material and advertisements for escaped slaves. This attractive, illustrated trade publication missed being reviewed in the academic press, but the hint of regret in the *Library Journal* review is worth noting: "The compilers are, in sum, more successful in raising important questions about political matters, working conditions, and the like than in capturing the romance of steam locomotives, faraway places, and lonely whistles in the night."[11] *Railroad* provides a direct, rich visual and literary experience of the same material covered more formally by Holbrook, Stover, and Buchanan.

Narrower in coverage but providing a firm foundation for academic study are two classic American studies texts: Henry Nash Smith, *The Virgin Land,* and Leo Marx, *The Machine in the Garden.* Smith reviews the popular pressure to build the rail link to the Pacific and the Orient and the subsequent problems of the railroad's domination. The campaigning for a transcontinental route by Thomas Hart Benton, Eli Whitney, and others plays a prominent role, and the sense of the original documents comes through clearly. Marx extends this view of the railroad, relating it more to the literary culture and art.

The literature of railroading is, to repeat, vast; fortunately, two very useful guides are available. Most important for the study of trains and railroading in America is *Railroads* by Paul B. Cors, published by Libraries Unlimited in their series "Spare Time Guides: Information Sources for Hobbies and Recreation." As a guide to railfan literature, Cors's volume begins with an introduction which relates briefly the history and definition of the genre and describes the railfan as well. The railfan has been treated above, but Cors's "identifying characteristics common to most railfan literature" is necessary at this point. Books often are published by small or specialist firms, in small editions that quickly become scarce and highly sought. There is great attention to "precise, technical detail" based on patient research. Emphasis is on equipment and operations rather than corporate and financial matters. Books written for railfans are heavily illustrated: photographs, maps, ephemera, and so forth. More highly priced items contain one or more specially commissioned paintings by one of a group of well-regarded railroad artists.[12] In his guide, Cors goes beyond this body of literature to cover more technical professional material as well as work by scholars. As a handbook to twentieth-century serious popular interest in trains, this guide is indispensable.

Beyond the scope of Cors's interest lies non-North American literature of railroading, as well as writing on modeling. These topics—along with a good selection on U.S. railroads—are covered by the English librarian E. T. Bryant in his *Railways: A Readers Guide.* Introducing his brief American coverage, Bryant points out that "the number of books on American railways probably rivals that on British companies."[13] The publication of books and periodicals outside the United States does center in England, and the resulting body of materials has been made easily accessible in this country. A number of U.S.

and Canadian book dealers regularly channel British titles to railfan collectors, and their catalogs include nearly as many British and foreign titles as American. This literature, then, has provided a foundation for American interest in locomotive and station preservation, short lines, and unusual railroads (or railways, in British parlance), and modeling. Thus, Bryant's guide is essential to gaining an overall sense of railroad literature.

A very useful survey for the researcher is Carl Condit's "The Literature of the Railroad Buff: A Historian's View," which appeared in the Spring 1980 issue of *Railroad History.* Condit's aim is to open the specialized vernacular literature accessible to historians of technology, and he focuses on seventy representative titles: pictorial albums, railroad histories, and motive power catalogs. Noteworthy, too, for the student of popular culture is the suggestive introductory section.

The World of Model Trains, by Guy R. Williams, a 1970 British publication distributed in the United States by Putnam, provides an international perspective on making models, constructing layouts, garden railroads, and so on. American examples are included. The classic work in this country is Louis H. Hertz, *The Complete Book of Model Railroading.* An extensive chapter on "the Model Railroad Hobby" provides a useful and relatively early survey of this aspect of railroad popularity.

These overviews and guides provide, then, a basic reference perspective on the subject. In addition, there are a number of more specialized reference and bibliographic tools on railroading that are useful to the study of railroading in popular culture and give a clue of the range of popular railroad interest. Both Cors and Bryant provide coverage here, but with an emphasis on more recent material. This sketch, therefore, will be highly selective.

The *Railway Directory and Yearbook,* published in London, is a classic reference tool, which can be traced back to 1898, and which provides current international information on rail routes, companies, and personnel. The 1978 volume devotes forty pages to the United States. Even more basic is *Jane's World Railways,* according to Cors "the single most complete source of data."[14] More specialized but a delight to the railfan is the *Car and Locomotive Encyclopedia of American Practice.* The 1970 edition bears a resemblance to earlier volumes dating back to 1879. An extensive "dictionary of car and locomotive terms" is included, along with an exhaustive catalog of current rolling stock.

More specifically designed for the railfan is John Marshall's *Rail Facts and Feats.* Though undocumented and probably requiring verification in more standard or specialized sources, it gives a good sense of the range of superlatives of most interest to railroad enthusiasts. Also, one cannot go far in railroading literature without recourse to a specialized glossary. The language of romantic railroading is made accessible by two guides: *The Language of the Railroader* by Ramon F. Adams and *Rail Talk: A Lexicon of*

Railroad Language, collected and edited by James H. Beck in 1978. Reaching back to the heritage of Casey Jones and Steel Drivin' Men, the language of railroad builders and workers was and is "imaginative, emotional, sensitive, humorous, earthy, literal." Much of it is a permanent, colorful part of our modern speech: "double-leader," "highball," "called on the carpet," "side-tracked," and many more such terms.[15]

A number of guides exist to serve the traveling needs of railfans. An annual (including even discount coupons) is the *Steam Passenger Service Directory Including Electric Lines and Museums,* published since 1966. For the person more interested in "high iron" (a main line), there is *Travel by Train,* by Edward J. Wojtas. Here the emphasis is on major Amtrak routes, but shorter routes—including non-Amtrak lines—earn coverage. Brief mention is made of Canada, Mexico, "auto train," and tourist railroads. The discussion of "America's Trains Today" provides a recent overview designed for a broader general public. For a more specialized group is *Right-of-Way: A Guide to Abandoned Railroads in the United States,* by Waldo Nielsen. Requiring perhaps less hiking are local train watchers' guides. A fine example is *The New Train Watcher's Guide to Chicago,* by John Szwajkart, which is accompanied by a large map. Indicated are what is to be found at a location, the best times to see it, and how to get there. This listing is preceded by capsule descriptions of each line and a discussion of passenger operations in Chicago.

Very briefly, two useful charts deserve mention for the nonspecialist librarian or student of the railfan subculture. The first and most readily available is the table of "Railway Systems of Selected Countries" found under "Railroads and Locomotives" in the *New Encyclopedia Britannica,* 15th edition. Given here is a listing of the gauges for each country, standard or otherwise. At a glance, one can see whether or not a book on the rails of Taiwan would appeal to a narrow-gauge enthusiast. The second aims to aid the reader of literature on locomotives who encounters a series of numbers like the following: 2-4-0 or 2-8-4. These numbers represent the three groupings of locomotive wheels by diameters: the front-end, drivers, and truck wheels. The Whyte Classification is illustrated on a chart by Frederic Shaw in his 1959 *Casey Jones' Locker* (p. 174), along with a brief discussion of the locomotive's evolution.

In addition to the guides by Cors and Bryant, a number of bibliographies are available. To support these guides, reference can be made to the *Railbook Bibliography, 1948-1972: A Comprehensive Guide to the Most Important Railbooks, Publications and Reports,* compiled by F. K. Hudson, which, though unannotated, attempts to list all U.S. and Canadian railroad books and government documents.

For more current information, searches should be made of standard bibliographical and index sources. A good selected list, "Railroads, Interurbans and Highways," appears in *The Frontier and the American West,* compiled by Rodman W. Paul and Richard W. Etulain. In the same series Robert H. Bremner's *American Social History Since 1860* includes a list of works on "Mining, Transportation, and Lumbering" which treats railroading. But more comprehensive is the "Railroads" listings in the *Harvard Guide to American History,* edited by Frank Freidel. *America: History and Life,* a periodical index, provides good ongoing coverage of scholarship. More popular material is available in the *Reader's Guide* (*Poole's Index* for the last century) and the *New York Times Index.*

Some specialized bibliographies are available. By far the most important here is Frank P. Donovan, Jr.'s landmark work, *The Railroad in Literature: Brief Survey of Railroad Fiction, Poetry, Songs, Biography, Essays, Travel and Drama in the English Language and Particularly Emphasizing Its Place in American Literature.* Donovan's "survey" puts a structure on a very substantial body of material and is a highpoint in the bibliographic control of American popular culture. Another listing of importance for earlier material is *A List of References to Literature Relating to the Union Pacific System* from the library of the Bureau of Railway Economics. The coverage is broad, encompassing the debates from the 1830s and 1840s, later travel literature, and government documents; it is a sweeping overview of a central element of the American rail phenomenon. Finally, the rail historian, the railfan, and the student of popular culture all can use *Railroads of the Trans-Mississippi West: A Selected Bibliography,* compiled by Donovan L. Hofsommer. Thorough but selective, three chapters indicate the level of usefulness for social and cultural study: "Regulation and Reaction to Railroad Excesses," "The Captains of Industry/The Robber Barons," and "Railroad Labor/Employees."

RESEARCH COLLECTIONS

In this century libraries and archives have provided much leadership in the serious study of all aspects of railroading. Even more significant than the Bureau of Railway Economics' Union Pacific list of 1922 was its 1912 *Railway Economics: A Collective Catalog of Books in Fourteen American Libraries.* Because few comprehensive studies existed, the bureau's list sought to bring together from several collections the materials needed by the "student of railway transportation."[16] Included are materials from periodicals, collections of miscellaneous essays, and general works, as well as technical information of "historical or economic significance." Most documents and laws, guides, maps and atlases, and timetables are excluded. Still, the listing is massive: a specialized catalog for the bureau plus the Interstate Commerce Commission, the Library of Congress, the New York Public, the Crerar, and collections at Columbia, Stanford, Harvard, Chicago, Illinois, Michigan, Pennsylvania, Wisconsin, and Yale universities. Although the coverage may be more selective in some areas, guides, informal narratives, and maps are presented for many categories.

The best overview of library research collections today is found in Lee Ash's *Subject Collections,* which shows that the great library collectors of the turn of the century have been joined by a number of others. Southern Methodist University reports having one of the world's largest collections of railroad photographs, about 230,000 prints. In addition, there is a 12,000-volume collection of railroadiana. Many local and regional libraries have comprehensive collections, now, relating to more local developments: Bowdoin College, the Maryland and Minnesota historical societies (for example), and the Denver Public Library. Specialized collections can be found at the Connecticut Electric Railway Association, the Baltimore Streetcar Museum, Harvard's Baker Library, and—to savor the very earliest—the American Antiquarian Society. For some of the collections there are special catalogs or guides. In 1935 Columbia's Library published *The William Barclay Parsons Railroad Prints: An Appreciation and Check List.* A popular and important collection is chronicled in the Smithsonian's *The First Quarter Century of Steam Locomotives in North America: Remaining Relics and Operable Replicas with a Catalog of Locomotive Models in the U.S. National Museum,* by Smith Hempstone Oliver. A 1978 Smithsonian publication, *Guide to Manuscript Collections in the National Museum of History and Technology,* records vast holdings of material on railroad companies, individuals, and railroad preservation. Railroad maps have been drawn since the first U.S. tracks were laid in response to Americans' intense interest in routes. The motivating force of popular interest opens the preface to Andrew M. Modelski's *Railroad Maps of the United States: A Selective Annotated Bibliography of Original 19th Century Maps in the Library of Congress.* The thorough scholarly introduction provides a context which is a useful guide to other smaller map collections.

Like the Columbia railroad prints checklist, exhibit catalogs can call attention to promising material. A good example is *From Train to Plane: Travellers in the American West, 1866-1936,* the catalog for a 1979 exhibit at Yale's Beinecke Library. In their preface, Archibald Hanna, Jr., and William S. Reese sound the call:

> The travel literature of the American West in the pre-Civil War era has been more closely examined than any other group of material on the Trans-Mississippi region. The opposite is true of the post-1865 era, when travel opened to the multitude rather than the hardy few. An extensive body of material on later travellers and tourists exists, but it remains largely untapped by researchers.[17]

A particular vision and desire to reach a range of publics is found at the Newberry Library. There, for the serious researcher, are housed the Illinois

Central, Burlington, and Pullman archives, and a printed *Guide to the Illinois Central Archives in the Newberry Library, 1851-1906* by Carolyn Curtis Mohr. But popular interest in railroad history was stimulated by the publication in 1949 of Lloyd Lewis's and Stanley Pargellis's *Granger Country: A Pictorial Social History of the Burlington Railroad.* In a format attractive to general and railfan readers the book calls attention to the collection and makes some of its riches widely accessible. Newberry "marketing" also resulted in serious but accessible scholarship, such as works by historian Richard Overton. Since Pargellis, Newberry librarian Lawrence Towner has added both the Pullman archives (rich in material on the porters) and also collections of railroad lithographs which testify to nineteenth-century popular enthusiasm for the locomotive particularly.

Some libraries have stimulated research and popular appreciation of railroading because their partners and backers have been private collectors. The Newberry, again, provides an example with its Everett D. Graff Collection of Western Americana. Colton Storm's catalog of this originally private library includes a substantial number of materials that either affected or reflected early popular interest in trains: guides to railroad land sales, travel accounts, reminiscences, and other ephemeral material. Similarly, the Thomas Streeter Collection is an important foundation for the American Antiquarian Society's railroad holdings.

Many collections of more recent railroad materials remain in private hands. Some of these are now coming into institutional collections. The Donnelley Library, Lake Forest College, received within the last few years the collection of the late Elliott Donnelley, a serious and wide-ranging railfan and collector. His library, built since 1940, reflects the era of the railfan and encompasses steam, modeling and live steam, short lines, Western railroads, narrow gauge, and railroadiana. The scope is international, as well, with many British imprints especially. These interests are being kept current through special funding for book and periodical purchases. Another collection that followed the Donnelley gift to Lake Forest is that of Munson Paddock. While much of the material is old, this railfan was active in the 1920s and 1930s, and his collection reflects popular interest in the subject during that period. Generally, though, material reflecting popular interest during the last half-century is not yet widely or consistently available in research libraries.

HISTORY AND CRITICISM

Much of the history of trains and railroading in the United States is a blend of hope and enthusiasm with frustration and criticism. Albro Martin's *Enterprise Denied: Origins of the Decline of American Railroads, 1897-1917* exemplifies this situation. In the preface the author speaks of his awareness as a child in the 1930s of the "American Railroad Problem." Martin finds the roots in early twentieth-century government regulation and, in the words of the jacket blurb, the book "chronicles a tragedy for the American people whose hopes for a superb...system...were permanently blighted." The literature on American railroads either centers on epic moments or on blighted hopes and thus reflects a nostalgic tone reminiscent of the ambiance of classic Southern fiction. This special character can be traced from academic to more popular historical writings.

The history and study of railroads began in the last century. The Bureau of Library Economics' catalogue and list on the Union Pacific both testify to this. Early writing reflected the epic quality of railroading. An example is *Memoir of Henry Farnum* by Henry W. Farnum. This key figure in the early trans-Mississippi railway construction, and partner of Thomas C. Durant, is celebrated here by his son. Nevertheless, the material is still useful: Dee Brown drew on it for *Hear That Lonesome Whistle Blow,* an account of the celebration in 1854 at the linking of the Atlantic to the Mississippi at Rock Island, Illinois. Brown drew on many such contemporary and firsthand accounts for his very useful study.

A unique study from early in the century is *North American Railroads: Their Administration and Economic Policy,* by W. Hoff and F. Schwabach. The report of a comprehensive, official German survey of the U.S. rail system, it provides a remarkable view of life behind the railroads' operations. For example: "The principle prevails in general with American business life that the payment of wages for services rendered constitutes the complete settlement between employee and employer."[18] Elsewhere the Germans marvel at companies which deal through ticket "scalpers."[19] Overall, the report gives a view of Americans' railroad expectations through European eyes.

By the 1920s academic studies were more common. One such study is Orville Thrasher Gooden's doctoral dissertation, "The Missouri and North Arkansas Railroad Strike." Gooden deals with the relation of public opinion to one moment of crisis between a railroad and its workers.

Railroad historical scholarship came of age in Richard C. Overton's *Burlington West: A Colonization History of the Burlington Railroad.* In its scope and accomplishment it opened a new era of study and, through its bibliography, pointed to new sources and approaches. An example is the late nineteenth-century popular local history. Overton has continued to set a high standard in *Gulf to Rockies: The Heritage of the Fort Worth and Denver-Colorado and Southern Railways, 1861-1898, Burlington Route: A History of the Burlington Lines,* and many other works. As consulting editor of Macmillan's Railroads of America series, he has overseen the production of works covering the B & O., the Canadian Pacific and National, the Santa Fe, the Illinois Central, and others.

Personalities have been critical in the popular perception of railroads. Thomas C. Cochran, at the beginning of his *Railroad Leaders: 1845-1890,* notes that "our popular heroes have normally been politicians and businessmen."[20] He continues by observing that historians have been too ignorant of the psychology of these figures.

Thus a number of recent biographies have looked anew at how the great railroad moguls were successful. This revision appears graphically in Stanley P. Hirshson's *Grenville M. Dodge: Soldier, Politician, Railroad Pioneer.* Hirshson finds Jacob R. Perkins's 1929 biography of Dodge inadequate because it sought to make his subject a "demi-god" and failed to capture his spirit or his energy, which was the source of his magnetism. Like Richard Overton, Albro Martin went directly to archival material for his *James J. Hill and the Opening of the Northwest.* Among available published material Martin had found relatively little, and what he did find closely fit the robber baron stereotype.

In addition to studies of companies and individuals, modern scholarship has turned its interest to other subgroupings of railroad history. A classic of American sociology is W. Fred Cottrell's *The Railroader,* which gives the railroader's world in a well-defined hierarchy. At higher levels Cottrell found skills to be monopolized, by which he meant that trainmen maintained their superiority over the company, fellow railroaders, and the public. Even by 1940 the demise of this monopoly and, with it, the railroaders' proud community could be seen. The study provides a classic view of "romantic heroes" caught in change and obsolescence.

The field of urban history has also looked in detail at the railroad. Carl W. Condit sees the railroad as center to one developmental phase of the city, prior to the automobile. His *The Railroad and the City* focuses on Cincinnati and shows how fundamental the railroad was to the social organization of urban culture. George W. Hilton and John F. Due describe the important but brief role the interurban railway played in the development of intercity transport in *The Electric Interurban Railways in America.* In spite of the coincident appearance of the automobile, this peculiarly American institution was responsible for greatly increased passenger mobility. One recent dissertation points the way to a link between urban and popular cultural history in this area: David Lynn Snowden's "Rail Passenger Service in the United States Since the Nineteen Thirties: Its Decline, Nostalgia and Esthetics (With Emphasis on Greater St. Louis)."

The notion of taking a more conscious look at rail nostalgia has begun to interest serious students. Rail literature is a primary source for George H. Douglas's article, "Lucius Beebe: Popular Railroad History as Social Nostalgia." Douglas finds that Beebe's books, such as *When Beauty Rode the Rails* or *Hear the Train Blow,* recall that "the railroad in its best days offered the American public an unbeatable combination of eccentric individuality, snob appeal, and high style." The railroad era, as found in Beebe's scores of books and articles, "still evokes fond memories...of an America that once was and doubtless still lies buried just underneath the surface of our consciousness."[21]

As mentioned above, special paintings have accompanied many railfan books. The wide appeal of this specialized kind of art is considered in the introduction to *Great Railroad Paintings,* edited by Robert Goldsborough. Growing out of the pioneer efforts of urban realists such as Reginald Marsh and Edward Hopper, a group of illustrators accepted commissions from railroads for calendars in the 1920s. Out of this development, based in advertising, has come this particular nostalgia and the preservation of a genre, one which was in eclipse in the two decades after 1950. Today, the Santa Fe has commissioned Howard Fogg to paint current scenes, and Amtrak has brought back calendar paintings. Goldsborough's collection reproduces a selection demonstrating the range, from 1923 to the 1970s.

In rounding out this survey of literature relating to railroading in popular culture, a return to the railfan is inevitable. Cors's and Bryant's guides provide a good view, as does Archie Robertson's chapter on the movement in *Slow Train to Yesterday.* This "indefinable affection"[22] which affects so many is discussed, too, by Frederic Shaw in a chapter entitled "Genus Railroadiac" in *Casey Jones' Locker.* Shaw, Robertson, and Cors all examine in detail the various railfan organizations, the vernacular, and the pioneers of the history of trains and railroading. The Railway and Locomotive Historical Society, based at Harvard's Baker Library, is the most scholarly of these organizations, publishing *Railroad History* (Carl Condit is among the contributors), which preserves, documents, and focuses on the industry. Largest is the National Railway Historical Society, which, in conjunction with local chapters, sponsors "fantrips." The oldest group is the Railroad Enthusiasts. Other specialized groups include the Central Electric Railfans' Association, the National Association of Timetable Collectors, the Railroadiana Collectors' Association, and the Railroad Station Historical Society. Perhaps most arcane is the American Vecturists' Association, many of whose members specialize in collecting railroad or streetcar tokens. The variety is endless. In Archie Robertson's words,

> The fan deserves a closer scrutiny than I have given him. He shares many of the surface characteristics of all hobbyists, with one basic difference: he is essentially selfless. He just wants to be around trains and, if possible, to help them out when they get in trouble.[23]

NOTES

1. Daniel J. Boorstin, "Editor's Preface," in *American Railroads,* by John F. Stover (Chicago: University of Chicago Press, 1961), p. v.

2. Lucius Beebe, *High Iron: A Book of Trains* (New York: Appleton-Century, 1938), p. 3.

3. B. A. Botkin, "Introduction," in *A Treasury of Railroad Folklore: The Stories, Tall Tales, Traditions, Ballads and Songs of the American Railroad Man,* ed. B. A. Botkin and Alvin F. Harlow (New York: Bonanza Books, 1953), p. xi.

4. Barton K. Davis, *How to Build Model Railroads and Equipment* (New York: Crown, 1956), p. 4.

5. Paul B. Cors, *Railroads,* Spare Time Guides: Information Sources for Hobbies and Recreation, no. 8 (Littleton, Colo.: Libraries Unlimited, 1975), p. 12.

6. Don Ball, Jr., "Preface," in *Decade of The Trains: The 1940s,* by Don Ball, Jr., and Rogers E. M. Whitaker ("E. M. Frimbo"), (Boston: New York Graphics Society, 1977), p. 11.

7. Archie Robertson, *Slow Train to Yesterday: A Last Glance at the Local* (Boston: Houghton Mifflin, 1945), pp. 151-52.

8. Robertson, p. 152.

9. Cors, pp. 11-12.

10. Charles R. Day, Jr., "All Aboard for a Lifelong Hobby," *Industry Week,* 203 (December 10, 1979), 98.

11. W. C. Robinson, review of *Railroad: Trains and Train People in American Culture,* edited by James Alan McPherson and Miller Williams, in *Library Journal,* 101 (December 15, 1976), 2573.

12. Cors, p. 13.

13. E. T. Bryant, *Railways: A Readers' Guide* (Hamden, Conn.: Archon, 1968), p. 116.

14. Cors, p. 15.

15. See Preface in James H. Beck, ed., *Rail Talk: A Lexicon of Railroad Language* (Gretna, Neb.: James Publications, 1978).

16. Bureau of Railway Economics, *Railway Economics: A Collective Catalogue of Books in Fourteen American Libraries* (Chicago: University of Chicago Press, 1912), p. v.

17. See Preface to *From Train to Plane: Travelers in the American West, 1866-1936* (New Haven: Yale University Library, 1979).

18. W. Hoff and F. Schwabach, *North American Railroads: Their Administration and Economic Policy* (New York: Germania Press, 1906), p. 213.

19. Hoff and Schwabach, pp. 245-50.

20. Thomas C. Cochran, *Railroad Leaders, 1845-1890: The Business Mind in Action* (New York: Russell & Russell, 1965), p. 1.

21. George H. Douglas, "Lucius Beebe: Popular Railroad History as Social Nostalgia," *Journal of Popular Culture,* 4 (Spring 1971), 907.

22. Frederic Shaw, *Casey Jones' Locker: Railroad Historiana* (San Francisco: Hesperian House, 1959), p. 165.

23. Robertson, pp. 162-63.

BIBLIOGRAPHY

BOOKS AND ARTICLES

Adams, Ramon F. *The Language of the Railroader.* Norman: University of Oklahoma Press, 1977.

Ash, Lee, ed. *Subject Collections: A Guide to Special Book Collections and Subject Emphases as Reported by University, College, Public and Special Libraries, and Museums in the United States and Canada.* 5th ed. New York: Bowker, 1978.

Ball, Don, Jr., and Rogers E. M. Whitaker. *Decade of the Trains: The 1940s.* Boston: New York Graphics Society, 1977.

Beck, James H., ed. *Rail Talk: A Lexicon of Railroad Language.* Gretna, Neb.: James Publications, 1978.

Beebe, Lucius. *Hear the Train Blow: A Pictorial Epic of America in the Railroad Age.* New York: Dutton, 1952.

———. *High Iron: A Book of Trains.* New York: Appleton-Century, 1938.

———. *When Beauty Rode the Rails.* Garden City, N.Y.: Doubleday, 1962.

Botkin, B. A., and Alvin F. Harlow, eds. *A Treasury of Railroad Folklore: The Stories, Tall Tales, Traditions, Ballads and Songs of the American Railroad Man.* New York: Bonanza Books, 1953.

Bremner, Robert H. *American Social History Since 1860.* New York: Appleton-Century-Crofts, 1971.

Brown, Dee. *Hear That Lonesome Whistle Blow: Railroads in the West.* New York: Holt, Rinehart and Winston, 1977.

Bryant, E. T. *Railways: A Readers' Guide.* Hamden, Conn.: Archon Books, 1968.

Buchanan, Lamont. *Steel Trains and Iron Horses: A Pageant of American Railroads.* New York: Putnam's, 1955.

Bureau of Railway Economics. *A List of References to Literature Relating to the Union Pacific System.* Newton, Mass.: Crofton, n.d. (reprint of 1922 edition).

———. *Railway Economics: A Collective Catalogue of Books in Fourteen American Libraries.* Chicago: University of Chicago Press, 1912.

Car and Locomotive Cyclopedia. New York: Car and Locomotive Cyclopedia, 1879-. Quadrennial.

Cochran, Thomas C. *Railroad Leaders, 1845-1890: The Business Mind in Action.* New York: Russell & Russell, 1965.

Condit, Carl W. *The Railroad and the City: A Technological and Urbanistic History of Cincinnati.* Columbus: Ohio State University Press, 1977.

———. "The Literature of the Railroad Buff: A Historian's View." *Railroad History,* 142 (Spring 1980), 7-26.

Cors, Paul B. *Railroads.* Spare Times Guides: Information Sources for Hobbies and Recreation, no. 8. Littleton, Col.: Libraries Unlimited, 1975.

Cottrell, W. Fred. *The Railroader.* Stanford, California: Stanford University Press, 1940. Reprint. With an introduction by Scott Greer. Dubuque, Iowa: Brown Reprints, 1971.

Davis, Barton K. *How to Build Model Railroads and Equipment.* New York: Crown, 1956.

Day, Charles R., Jr. "All Aboard for a Lifelong Hobby." *Industry Week*, 203 (December 10, 1979), 98-100.

Donovan, Frank P., Jr. *The Railroad in Literature: Brief Survey of Railroad Fiction, Poetry, Songs, Biography, Essays, Travel and Drama in the English Language and Particularly Emphasizing Its Place in American Literature.* Boston: Railway and Locomotive Historical Society, 1940.

Douglas, George H. "Lucius Beebe: Popular Railroad History as Social Nostalgia." *Journal of Popular Culture*, 4 (Spring 1971), 893-910.

Farnum, Henry W. *Memoir of Henry Farnum.* New Haven: n.p., 1889.

Freidel, Frank, ed. *Harvard Guide to American History.* Rev. ed. 2 vols. Cambridge: Harvard University Press, 1974.

From Train to Plane: Travelers in the American West, 1866-1936. New Haven: Yale University Library, 1979.

Goldsborough, Robert. *Great Railroad Paintings.* New York: Peacock Press/Bantam 1976.

Gooden, Orville Thrasher. "The Missouri and North Arkansas Railroad Strike." Ph.D. dissertation, Columbia University, 1926.

Guide to Manuscript Collections in the National Museum of History and Technology. Washington, D.C.: Smithsonian Institution Press, 1978.

Hertz, Louis H. *The Complete Book of Model Railroading.* New York: Simmons-Boardman, 1951.

Hilton, George W., and John F. Due. *The Electric Interurban Railways in America.* Stanford, Calif.: Stanford University Press, 1960.

Hirshson, Stanley P. *Grenville M. Dodge: Soldier, Politician, Railroad Pioneer.* Bloomington: Indiana University Press, 1967.

Hoff, W., and F. Schwabach. *North American Railroads: Their Administration and Economic Policy.* New York: Germania Press, 1906.

Hofsommer, Donovan L. *Railroads of the Trans-Mississippi West: A Selected Bibliography.* Plainview, Tex.: Wayland College, 1974.

Holbrook, Stewart H. *The Story of American Railroads.* New York: Crown, 1947.

Hudson, F. K., comp. *Railbook Bibliography, 1948-1972: A Comprehensive Guide to the Most Important Railbooks, Publications and Reports.* Ocean, N.J.: Specialty Press, 1972.

Jane's World Railways. London: Macdonald & Jane's, 1966-. Annual.

Lewis, Lloyd, and Stanley Pargellis, eds. *Granger Country: A Pictorial Social History of the Burlington Railroad.* Boston: Little, Brown, 1949.

McPherson, James Alan, and Miller Williams, eds. *Railroad: Trains and Train People in American Culture.* New York: Random House, 1976.

Marshall, John. *Rail Facts and Feats.* New York: Two Continents, 1974.

Martin, Albro. *Enterprise Denied: Origins of the Decline of American Railroads, 1897-1917.* New York: Columbia University Press, 1971.

______. *James J. Hill and the Opening of the Northwest.* New York: Oxford University Press, 1976.

Marx, Leo. *The Machine in the Garden.* New York: Oxford University Press, 1964.

Modelski, Andrew M., comp. *Railroad Maps of the United States: A Selective Annotated Bibliography of Original 19th Century Maps in the Library of Congress.* Washington, D.C.: Library of Congress, 1975.

Mohr, Carolyn Curtis. *Guide to the Illinois Central Archives in the Newberry Library, 1851-1906.* Chicago: Newberry Library, 1951.

New York Times Index. New York: New York Times, 1856-.

Nielsen, Waldo. *Right-Of-Way: A Guide to Abandoned Railroads in the United States.* Bend, Ore.: Old Bottle Magazine, 1972.

Norris, Frank. *The Octopus.* Cambridge, Mass: Robert Bently, 1971.

Oliver, Smith Hempstone. *The First Quarter Century of Steam Locomotives in North America: Remaining Relics and Operable Replicas with a Catalog of Locomotive Models in the U.S. National Museum.* Washington, D.C.: Smithsonian Institution, 1956.

Overton, Richard C. *Burlington Route: A History of the Burlington Lines.* New York: Knopf, 1965.

———. *Burlington West: A Colonization History of the Burlington Railroad.* Cambridge: Harvard University Press, 1941.

———. *Gulf to Rockies: The Heritage of the Fort Worth and Denver-Colorado and Southern Railways, 1861-1898.* Austin: University of Texas Press, 1953.

Paul, Rodman W., and Richard W. Etulain, comps. *The Frontier and the American West.* Arlington Heights, Ill.: AHM, 1977.

Perkins, Jacob R. *Trails, Rails and War: The Life of General G. M. Dodge.* Indianapolis: Bobbs-Merrill, 1929.

"Railroads." In *Encyclopedia Americana.* International ed. Vol. 23. Danbury, Conn.: Americana, 1979, pp. 152-69.

"Railroads and Locomotives." In *New Encyclopedia Britannica.* 15th ed. Vol. 15. Chicago: Encyclopaedia Britannica, 1974, pp. 477-91.

Railway Directory and Yearbook. London, Transport Press, 1898-. Annual.

Readers' Guide to Periodical Literature. New York: Wilson, 1900-. Annual.

Richardson, Frederick H., and F. Nelson Blount. *Along the Iron Trail.* 2nd ed. Rutland, Vt.: Sharp Offset, 1966.

Robertson, Archie. *Slow Train to Yesterday: A Last Glance at the Local.* Boston: Houghton Mifflin, 1945.

Robinson, W. C. Review of *Railroad: Trains and Train People in American Culture,* edited by James Alan McPherson and Miller Williams. *Library Journal,* 101 (December 15, 1976), 2573.

Shaw, Frederic. *Casey Jones' Locker: Railroad Historiana.* San Francisco: Hesperian House, 1959.

Smith, Henry Nash. *The Virgin Land.* Cambridge: Harvard University Press, 1950.

Snowden, David Lynn. "Rail Passenger Service in the United States Since the Nineteen Thirties: Its Decline, Nostalgia and Esthetics (With Emphasis on Greater St. Louis)." Ph.D. dissertation, St. Louis University, 1975.

Steam Passenger Service Directory Including Electric Lines and Museums. New York: Empire State Railway Museum, 1966-. Annual.

Storm, Colton, comp. *A Catalogue of the Everett D. Graff Collection of Western Americana.* Chicago: University of Chicago Press, 1968.

Stover, John F. *American Railroads.* Chicago: University of Chicago Press, 1961.

Szwajkart, John. *The New Train Watcher's Guide to Chicago.* Brookfield, Ill.: John Szwajkart, 1976.

The William Barclay Parsons Railroad Prints: An Appreciation and a Check List. New York: Columbia University Library, 1935.
Williams, Guy R. *The World of Model Trains.* New York: Putnam's, 1970.
Wojtas, Edward J. *Travel by Train.* New York: Rand McNally, 1974.

PERIODICALS

America: History and Life. Santa Barbara, Calif., 1964-.
Railroad History. Westford, Mass., 1921-. (Formerly *Railway and Locomotive Historical Society, Bulletin.*)
Railroad Magazine. New York, 1906-.
Railway Age. Bristol, Conn., 1856-.
Trains: The Magazine of Railroading. Milwaukee, 1940-.

Proper Name Index

Subject Index to Volumes 1-3

About the Contributors

BILL BENNETT has written and edited jazz criticism for the past five years; he is currently production coordinator for the Smithsonian Collection of Recordings, where he produces recordings, both archival and original, of historical interest in the fields of jazz, American musical theater, historic instruments and chamber music, and black American culture.

JAMES J. BEST is associate professor of political science at Kent State University. His research interests in American popular culture deal with American illustration during the period 1885-1915, and he has recently published an article on the impact of the Brandywine School of illustrators in the *Journal of Popular Culture*. In addition to teaching a course on American illustration, he is currently doing research on the relationship between art editors and illustrators at the turn of the century.

JOHN BRYANT was Fulbright lecturer at the universities of Genoa and Turin in 1977-78, and is presently assistant professor of English at Pennsylvania State University, Shenango Valley Campus. He has written essays on pastoralism, American humor, Melville, Poe, and the situation comedy. He is presently researching a history of the latter popular art form in the context of America's social comedy. He also collects stamps.

EARLE J. COLEMAN is an associate professor of philosophy and religious studies at Virginia Commonwealth University. He specializes in philosophy of art, philosophy of religion, and Oriental philosophy. His publications include *Philosophy of Painting by Shih-t'ao,* over a dozen entries for the forthcoming *Abingdon Dictionary of Living Religions,* articles on aesthetics, and book reviews. Professor Coleman has been an active member of the International Brotherhood of Magicians, has published an article on the aesthetics of magic in the *Journal of Magic History,* and has also taught a course on the psychology, aesthetics, and history of American magic and magicians. He is a former student of the internationally known Okito.

ROBERT K. DODGE is associate professor of English at the University of Nevada, Las Vegas. He is co-editor of *Voices from Wah kontah,* an anthology of poetry by contemporary Native Americans. He has published articles on American Indian Literature and on American humor. He is now working on a study of the humor of the early American republic.

CLAUDIUS W. GRIFFIN is associate professor of English and director of the composition and rhetoric program at Virginia Commonwealth University. He has written articles on canoeing, fishing, teaching composition, and transactional analysis and literature. Currently he is working on a writing textbook for people in industry, government, and the academic world.

M. THOMAS INGE, editor of this volume, is professor and head of the Department of English at Clemson University. He has published books on William Faulkner, American humor, Southern literature, and ethnic American writing and is a founding editor of two publications: *Resources for American Literary Study* and *American Humor: An Interdisciplinary Newsletter.* In addition to editing several series of reference guides in popular culture for Greenwood Press, he is engaged in research on the history, development, and appreciation of American comic strips and comic books.

ROBERT H. JANKE is an assistant professor in the Department of Theatre, School of the Arts, Virginia Commonwealth University. Presently he serves as both teacher and director of the school's program in the field of speech communication.

ANNE HUDSON JONES is assistant professor of literature and medicine at the Institute for the Medical Humanities of the University of Texas Medical Branch. She was previously assistant director of the

Center for Programs in the Humanities at Virginia Polytechnic Institute and State University. She has written several articles about literature and medicine and about women in science fiction. She is completing a book on the fiction of Kate Wilhelm.

BERNARD MERGEN is associate professor of American civilization at George Washington University, where he participates in a seminar in material culture offered in cooperation with the Smithsonian Institution. His research interests include the history of labor and leisure, especially the evolution of attitudes toward work and play. He has published articles in *American Quarterly,* the *South Atlantic Quarterly, Industrial and Labor Relations Review, Play: Anthropological Perspectives,* and other books and journals.

ARTHUR H. MILLER, JR., is college librarian at Lake Forest College. He supervises the Elliott Donnelley Railroad Collection in the college's Donnelley Library and, during the spring of 1980, taught an American studies course on the railroad in the American West. He has taught other American studies courses and published articles on library topics.

RICHARD ALAN NELSON is an assistant professor in the School of Communication at the University of Houston Central Campus in Texas. His publications include an essay on the historical precedents of the docudrama and a three-part bibliography on German film for the *Journal of the University Film Association.* He is currently working on a book describing successful corporate advocacy and issue management strategies for the coming decade.

NANCY POGEL is an associate professor of American thought and language and assistant director of student affairs, University College, Michigan State University. Her primary research and teaching interests are American humor and American film. She has delivered papers and published articles on film humor, Jewish humor, Mark Twain and other Midwestern humorists, and Constance Rourke. She is presently an associate textual editor of *Walt Whitman, The Journalism,* volume 2, and she is completing a book-length manuscript on Woody Allen's films.

ANNE ROWE is associate professor of English and director of English studies at Florida State University, Tallahassee. Her research interests are in Southern literature. She is the author of *The Enchanted Country: Northern Writers in the South, 1865-1910,* and is presently at work on a book on images of Florida in American literature.

DOROTHY (DOREY) SCHMIDT is assistant professor of English at Pan American University. A founding and continuing editor of *river-Sedge,* a little magazine of art, poetry, and prose, she is also advisory editor of the *Journal of American Culture* and co-editor of the *Living Author Series.* Her other publications range from poetry to cultural analyses. She is currently preparing a comprehensive bibliographic guide to the magazine in American culture.

RICHARD A. SCHWARZLOSE is associate professor in the Medill School of Journalism, Northwestern University, where he teaches media history, law and ethics, and press-government relations. His articles on these subjects have appeared in several academic and trade publications, and he is currently working on histories of the wire services and of the news report, as well as a Chicago-based oral history project. He spent seven years as a reporter and telegraph editor in daily newspaper journalism.

PAUL P. SOMERS, JR., is associate professor of American thought and language at Michigan State University. His publications include articles in the *French Review,* the *South Atlantic Quarterly,* and *Twentieth Century Literature,* as well as a short story in *Harper's.* He has compiled bibliographies of articles on mass culture for *American Quarterly* and is presently a bibliographer for *Midamerica: The Yearbook for the Society for the Study of Midwestern Literature.*

JAMES VON SCHILLING has taught popular music, mass media, and popular culture at Bowling Green State University's Center for the Study of Popular Culture. A semiprofessional musician on the side, he has written on contemporary music for the *Popular Culture Reader, Creem,* and other publications and is currently producing a series of videotapes on seminal popular musicians of the past.

FAYE NELL VOWELL is an assistant professor of English at Emporia State University. She compiled the section on black Americans for *A Comprehensive Bibliography for the Study of American Minorities* edited by Wayne C. Miller. Her current research interests are the Chicano novel and minorities on the Great Plains. Presently as a part of an NEH grant, she is writing and directing a number of educational television programs about minorities on the Great Plains.

ANNETTE M. WOODLIEF is assistant professor and director of student activities in the English department at Virginia Commonwealth University. She has done research and taught interdisciplinary courses on the relationships between literature and science, women writers, and the American Transcendentalists. Her articles, including annotated checklists on criticism of *Walden* and Emerson's essays, have appeared in *Studies in the American Renaissance, Resources for American Literary Study, Thoreau Journal Quarterly,* and *Southern Humanities Review.*